Spectres of John Ball

Spectres of John Ball
The Peasants' Revolt in English Political History 1381–2020

James Crossley

SHEFFIELD UK   BRISTOL CT

Published by Equinox Publishing Ltd.
UK: Office 415, The Workstation, 15 Paternoster Row, Sheffield, South Yorkshire S1 2BX
USA: ISD, 70 Enterprise Drive, Bristol, CT 06010

www.equinoxpub.com

First published 2022
© James Crossley 2022
All rights reserved. No part of this publication may be reproduced or transmitted in any form or by any means, electronic or mechanical, including photocopying, recording or any information storage or retrieval system, without prior permission in writing from the publishers.

British Library Cataloguing-in-Publication Data
A catalogue record for this book is available from the British Library.

ISBN-13   978 1 80050 135 5   (hardback)
          978 1 80050 136 2   (paperback)
          978 1 80050 137 9   (ePDF)
          978 1 80050 174 4   (ePub)

Library of Congress Cataloging-in-Publication Data

Names: Crossley, James, author.
Title: Spectres of John Ball: The Peasants' Revolt in English Political History, 1381–2020 / James Crossley.
Other titles: Peasants' Revolt in English Political History, 1381–2020
Description: Sheffield, South Yorkshire ; Bristol, CT : Equinox Publishing Ltd, 2022. | Includes bibliographical references and index. | Summary: "This book explains how we get from an apocalyptic priest who promoted a theocracy favouring the lower orders and the decapitation of the leading church and secular authorities to someone who promoted democracy and vague notions about love and tolerance." -- Provided by publisher.
Identifiers: LCCN 2021042470 (print) | LCCN 2021042471 (ebook) |
  ISBN 9781800501355 (hardback) | ISBN 9781800501362 (paperback) |
  ISBN 9781800501379 (pdf) | ISBN 9781800501744 (epub)
Subjects: LCSH: Ball, John, -1381. | Tyler's Insurrection, 1381--Historiography.
Classification: LCC DA235 .C76 2022 (print) | LCC DA235 (ebook) |
  DDC 942.03/8--dc23
LC record available at https://lccn.loc.gov/2021042470
LC ebook record available at https://lccn.loc.gov/2021042471

Typeset by S.J.I. Services, New Delhi, India

Contents

1	Introduction: 1381	1
2	The Quest for the Historical John Ball	13
3	Exit Ball: Late Medieval Receptions	43
4	Ball and the English Reformation	55
5	Ghosts of 1381: Uneasy Heresies, Radicalisms, and Discontents in Late Elizabethan and Early Jacobean England	74
6	The Priest of Baal in Revolutionary England	87
7	Perverted Liberty and the End of Stuart England: Ball among Whigs, Tories, Jacobites, and Other Mobs	104
8	Georgian John: From Mob Rule to Reasonable Demands	130
9	Revolution, Once Again: A Freeborn Englishman in the Late Eighteenth Century	146
10	The Second Coming of John Ball: John Baxter, Robert Southey, and Radicalism of the 1790s	162
11	After Waterloo: The Poet Laureate's John Ball	175
12	'Peaceably If We May, Forcibly If We Must': Ball among the Chartists	199
13	Haranguing after Chartism: The Making of the Victorian Ball	218
14	Class Struggle among the Historians	241
15	William Morris: Delaying Ball's New World	268
16	Still Dreaming of John Ball	298
17	Red John? Ball after the Great War	328

18	Bolshevik Ball	345
19	Cold War Ball	362
20	Rodney Hilton: Ball at the End of Historical Materialism?	386
21	Ball after 1968	402
22	1381/1981	416
23	Twenty-First Century Ball	436
24	Epilogue	459
Bibliography		465
Subject Index		511
Person Index		527

1
Introduction: 1381

Why John Ball?

John Ball was once arguably as famous as the most famous figure to have emerged from the so-called 'Peasants' Revolt' of 1381: Wat Tyler.[1] At times during the long history of his reception, Ball has been just as popular or notorious; other times, less so. Today, it is not unheard of for people to know about some version of the Adam and Eve couplet associated with Ball ('When Adam delved and Eve span, who was then the gentleman?') but his name is barely remembered, despite Ball being taught in schools and featuring in popular historical documentaries about the revolt. While Tyler and the revolt (with some mention of Ball) have been the subject of histories of reception covering the fourteenth century to the present (or some time in between),[2] Ball has not received sustained and detailed treatment. This book is an attempt to fill that gap by tracing the historical figure of Ball

---

1   I have added thanks where appropriate in the notes, but I should add that I am particularly grateful to Christina Petterson who has provided her expert feedback on the manuscript as a whole.
2   E.g., R. B. Dobson, 'Remembering the Peasants' Revolt, 1381–1981', in W. H. Liddell and R. G. Wood (ed.), *Essex and the Great Revolt of 1381* (Essex: Essex Record Office, 1982), 1–20; Brian Bird, *Rebel before His Time: Study of John Ball and the English Peasants' Revolt of 1381* (Worthing: Churchman Publishing, 1987), 132–37; Lister M. Matheson, 'The Peasants' Revolt through Five Centuries of Rumor and Reporting', *Studies in Philology* 95 (1998): 121–52; Alastair Dunn, 'Wat Tyler: The Many Roles of an English Rebel', *History Today* 51 (2001): 28; Alastair Dunn, *The Peasants' Revolt: England's Failed Revolution of 1381* (Stroud: Tempus, 2004), 187–94; Antony Taylor, *London's Burning: Pulp Fiction, the Politics of Terrorism and the Destruction of the Capital in British Popular Culture, 1840–2005* (London: Bloomsbury, 2012), 20–45; Stephen Basdeo, *The Life and Legend of a Rebel Leader: Wat Tyler* (Barnsley: Pen and Sword History, 2018). R. B. Dobson (ed.), *The Peasants' Revolt of 1381* (second edition; New York: Palgrave Macmillan, 1983), also provides some passages (with brief commentary) from the history of the reception of the revolt.

in the fourteenth century through his rises and falls over the centuries and up to the present day.

But why should Ball receive such detailed attention? Beyond the entirely reasonable response that anything is worthy of study no matter how irrelevant others think it to be, the reception of Ball also provides a clear case to those who demand that we study things that 'matter.' For four-hundred years, Ball was variously understood to be a major leader and ideologue of the uprising, a heretic, an exemplar of violent threats to Protestant England, a Cromwellian before his time, a symbol of the constitution gone wrong, a proto-Jacobite, a devilish driver of mob rule in London, a convenient point of reference to dismiss any would-be political reformer, and so on. Ball then went on to become an English revolutionary, a wise teacher of the people, a supporter of working-class political representation, a symbol of the constitution gone right, a Chartist hero, a political reformer, the first English socialist, the first English communist, a Cold War warrior (on both sides), a supporter of equality and diversity, a post-1960s preacher of love and peace, an opponent of Apartheid, a representative of an alternative and inclusive English history, and so on. In other words, the story of Ball and his reception is part of the story of the social and political history of England both from above and from below.

This book started off quite differently. My interests over the past decade have focused on the role of religion and the Bible in modern English political discourse. I wanted to turn to an old academic issue and trace the history of a recurring theme in this discourse: a homegrown radical tradition that was frequently said to have begun in 1381. It seemed reasonable enough that I should start with the example of 1381 and proceed from there to see how, why, and when the idea of this radical tradition emerged. What began as half a chapter on Ball soon became a chapter, then two chapters, and it became clear that there was a vast amount of material on Ball himself which could tell something of this story. While this book is emphatically a history of Ball and his reception, some of my initial interests remain and, as it turned out, were unavoidable anyway. I have also retained my focus on England and English receptions which gives the following history some boundaries, though as expected the material on Ball is overwhelmingly from English contexts, at least geographically speaking. Having said that, I see no need for strict definitions of English and Englishness in my data selection, and material from (for instance) Scotland, Ireland, and America has been used, not least because it is also used in English political, religious, and historical discourses. I have tried to strike some balance between different types of sources where possible (chronicles and histories, theological tracts, plays, novels, political propaganda, newspapers, academic publications, songs, etc.) to try to give a sense of the cultural breadth of the receptions of Ball. I have tried to be relatively comprehensive in chasing references to Ball but to get everything, or even to include everything I found, is simply impossible and the book is long enough as it is. There are other ways Ball has been understood; if every one of them were written down, I suppose that the world itself could not contain the books that would be written (cf. John 21.25).

The 1381 Uprising

One of the recurring features of talking about this research to colleagues is that they have little knowledge of the revolt. It might be helpful to provide a relatively brief summary of what (might have) happened in the summer of 1381 for such readers before we move on to the historical figure of Ball followed by the long history of interpretation.[3] We can start with a brief

---

3   In the following summary, I am, of course, indebted to a huge amount of research and scholarship on the revolt. See (among many others), e.g., Charles Oman, *The Great Revolt of 1381* (Oxford: Clarendon Press, 1906); Andrew Prescott, 'London in the Peasants' Revolt: A Portrait Gallery,' *The London Journal* 7 (1981): 125–43; Andrew Prescott, 'Writing about Rebellion: Using the Records about the Peasants' Revolt of 1381,' *History Workshop Journal* 45 (1998): 1–27; Andrew Prescott, '"The Hand of God": The Suppression of the Peasants' Revolt of 1381,' in Nigel Morgan (ed.), *Prophecy, Apocalypse and the Day of Doom* (Donington: Shaun Tyas, 2004), 317–41; Liddell and Wood (ed.), *Essex and the Great Revolt of 1381*; Dobson (ed.), *Peasants' Revolt of 1381*; Rodney Hilton, *Bond Men Made Free: Medieval Peasant Movements and the English Rising of 1381* (London: Routledge, 1973); Rodney Hilton, *Class Conflict and the Crisis of Feudalism* (revised edition; London: Verso, 1990), e.g., 17–18, 79–91, 143–53; Rodney Hilton and T. H. Aston (eds.), *The English Rising of 1381* (Cambridge: Cambridge University Press, 1984); Nicholas Brooks, 'The Organization and Achievements of the Peasants of Kent and Essex in 1381,' in Henry Mayr-Harting and R. I. Moore (eds.), *Studies in Medieval History Presented to R. H. C. Davis* (London: Hambledon, 1985), 247–70; Caroline M. Barron, *Revolt in London: 11th to 15th June 1381* (London: Museum of London, 1981); Herbert Eiden, 'Joint Action against "Bad" Lordship: The Peasants' Revolt in Essex and Norfolk,' *History* 83 (1998): 5–30; Herbert Eiden, *'In der Knechtschaft werdet ihr verharren...' Ursachen und Verlauf des englischen Bauernaufstandes von 1381* (Trier: Trierer Historische Forschungen, 1995); Herbert Eiden, 'The Social Ideology of the Rebels in Suffolk and Norfolk in 1381,' in Marie-Luise Heckmann and Jens Röhrkasten (eds.), *Von Nowgorod bis London: Studien zu*

note on the main sources for the narrative of the revolt and their use in historical reconstruction. While legal and administrative sources provide important data as we might expect, the main sources for the narrative of the revolt (and the history of reception) are from the chronicles written shortly after. These include: the second of the four volumes of western European history by the Valenciennes-born court historian, Jean Froissart (c. 1337–c. 1405);[4] *Chronica maiora*, from the monk of St Albans, Thomas Walsingham (c. 1340–c. 1422);[5] the *Chronicle* of the Augustinian canon of St Mary de Pratis, Leicester, Henry Knighton (d. 1396);[6] the *Anonimalle*

Handel, Wirtschaft und Gesellschaft im mittelalterlichen Europe. Festschrift für Stuart Jenks zum 60. Geburtstag (Göttingen: V&R Unipress, 2008), 425–40; Herbert Eiden, 'Military Aspects of the Peasants' Revolt of 1381,' in Christopher Thornton, Jennifer Ward, and Neil Wiffen (eds.), *The Fighting Essex Soldier: Recruitment, War and Remembrance in the Fourteenth Century* (Hatfield: University of Hertfordshire Press, 2017), 143–54; Helen Lacey, '"Grace for the Rebels": The Role of the Royal Pardon in the Peasants' Revolt of 1381,' *Journal of Medieval History* 34 (2008): 36–63; Dunn, *Peasants' Revolt*; Juliet Barker, *England, Arise: The People, the King and the Great Revolt of 1381* (London: Little, Brown, 2014); Mark O'Brien, 'Heresy, Rebellion and Utopian Courage: The English Peasant Rising of 1381,' in Michael T. Davis (ed.), *Crowd Actions in Britain and France from the Middle Ages to the Modern World* (New York: Palgrave Macmillan, 2015), 17–30; Andrew Prescott, 'Great and Horrible Rumour: Shaping the English Revolt of 1381,' in Justine Firnhaber-Baker and Dirk Schoenaers (eds.), *The Routledge History Handbook of Medieval Revolt* (London: Routledge, 2016), 76–103. Updates on ongoing research can be found on the website of the project led by Adrian Bell, 'The People of 1381,' https://www.1381.online/.

4   For English translation, I follow Dobson (ed.), *Peasants' Revolt of 1381*, unless otherwise stated. For referencing, I follow Gaston Ray (ed.), *Chroniques de J. Froissart: Tome Dixième 1380–1382* (Paris: Mme. ve. J. Renouard, 1869). I have also consulted Peter Ainsworth and Godfried Croenen (ed.), *The Online Froissart: Version 1.5* (Sheffield: HRIOnline, 2013), http://www.dhi.ac.uk/onlinefroissart.

5   Unless otherwise stated, I use John Taylor, Wendy R. Childs, and Leslie Watkiss (eds.), *The St Albans Chronicle: The* Chronica maiora *of Thomas Walsingham: Volume I 1376–1394* (Oxford: Oxford University Press, 2003). See also H. T. Riley, *Thomae Walsingham, quondam monachi S. Albani, historia Anglicana: Vols. I–II* (London: Longman, Green, Longman, Roberts, and Green, 1863–1864).

6   Unless otherwise stated, I use G. H. Martin (ed.), *Knighton's Chronicle 1337–1396* (Oxford: Clarendon Press, 1995).

Chronicle, associated with St Mary's Abbey, York;[7] and the monkish *Westminster Chronicle*, belonging to the continuation of Ranulf Higden's *Polychronicon*.[8] The chroniclers were predictably hostile towards the rebels. They embellished details, invented confessions, created heroes and martyrs, and sometimes stand in contradiction to one another. Even with some eyewitness testimony, we may not be able to present the details of historical reconstructions with any certainty, but we can talk about the earliest general understandings of the broad gist of what happened in the 1381 uprising. There is also a shared general picture of the uprising in London and the south east which gives us a rough chronology of events.

In June 1381, after the infamous coercive collections of the poll tax in particular, uprisings happened in the south east, London, East Anglia, and well beyond. The target of the insurgents' ire varied from context to context but included lords, justices, government representatives, and royal advisors and leading figures of the realm. At least part of the uprising in the south east appears to have been organised under or in association with Ball, Tyler, and the mysterious Jack Straw, about whom we know little and whose name may even have been a pseudonym. On the ground, the rebellion in the south east was interconnected through rivers, letter-writing, and local administrative networks, as well as through the commercial, legal, and bureaucratic networks in and around London. As we will see in the next chapter, and contrary to what we are told in some of the most influential primary sources, there is the possibility that Ball was not in Kent or London during the events of June 1381. Moreover, Andrew Prescott has provided a corrective to the geographic (and especially London-centric) bias in scholarly (and popular) representations of the revolt.[9] This requires some justification for my primary focus being on the most famous events as they moved from Kent and Essex towards London. There are two main reasons for this. First, whether or not Ball was physically present in London or Kent during the uprising, the influence of ideas associated with Ball on the insurgents as the rebellion moved into London is a prominent emphasis in some of our earliest sources. Froissart put it, 'Of his words and deeds there were much people in London informed, such as had great envy at

7   For English translation, I follow Dobson (ed.), *Peasants' Revolt of 1381*, unless otherwise stated. For referencing, I follow V. H. Galbraith (ed.), *The Anonimalle Chronicle, 1333 to 1381* (Manchester: Manchester University Press, 1970 [1927]).
8   Unless otherwise stated, I use L. C. Hector and Barbara F. Harvey (eds.), *The Westminster Chronicle, 1381–1394* (Oxford: Clarendon Press, 1982).
9   Prescott, 'Great and Horrible Rumour,' in Firnhaber-Baker and Schoenaers (eds.), *Routledge History Handbook of Medieval Revolt*, 76–78.

them that were rich and such as were noble' (*Chroniques* 10.97). Second, the history of the reception of the revolt takes up much of this book and Ball has consistently been associated with events in the south east and London (or thereabout).

As this already suggests, and as has been long noted, the familiar label 'peasants' can be misleading. Sources certainly labelled the rebels *rustici* and it indeed was the case that those associated with working the land were included among insurgent ranks, interests, and demands, not least because late fourteenth-century England was a largely rural society. But there were also a range of occupations represented. There were artisans, servants, brewers, butchers, tailors, local officials, lower clergy, and others, as well as disgruntled and disenfranchised urban dwellers and casual workers in London.[10] On one level, we should be thinking generally (but not exclusively) of the revolt driven by those towards the lower (though often aspirational) ends of urban and rural society, with insurgent demands for 'freedom' involving specific changes in legal and economic status, notably the end of serfdom. The revolt likely also involved the insurgent interest in access to monopolistic economic networks, wider urban rights, and political representation. Among all this, grievances concerning the political disconnect between rural insurgents and governance (national and local) could exist alongside concerns of a range of Londoners and urban dwellers (including connections with the criminal underworld). Similarly, those among the village elites could target and defend their interests from those above them. And, while not necessarily the driving force behind the revolt, we should not underestimate the base opportunities the revolt threw up for settling old scores.

It has long been acknowledged that central to understanding the uprising was the social, economic, and cultural upheaval following the Black Death of 1348/49. The Black Death wiped out perhaps nearly half of the population of England (and Europe). This meant changes in land use and agriculture, tenancy agreements, food supplies and prices, and, crucially,

10 On definitional issues and the range of occupations and interests, as well as the function of labelling the rebels in the chronicles, see, e.g., Hilton, *Bond Men Made Free*, 164, 176–213 (cf. 125–26); Hilton, *Class Conflict*, 17–18, 79, 84–91, 143–53; Prescott, 'London in the Peasants' Revolt'; Christopher Dyer, 'The Social and Economic Background to the Rural Revolt of 1381', in Hilton and Aston (eds.), *The English Rising of 1381*, 9–52; Paul Strohm, *Hochon's Arrow: The Social Imagination of Fourteenth-Century Texts* (Princeton: Princeton University Press, 1992), 36–39; Eiden, 'Joint Action against "Bad" Lordship', 25–27. Dunn, *Peasants' Revolt*, 12–14, 83–85, 143; Ian Cornelius, 'Gower and the Peasants' Revolt', *Representations* 131 (2015): 22–51 (35–39).

labour. Because of a shortage of workers, labour cost more and the already declining institution of serfdom was challenged further as greater opportunities were available to those with some agency who could demand better wages or conditions. In response to the immediate aftermath of the Black Death, Parliament tried to cap wages and restrict mobility (e.g., Statute of Labourers, 1351), as well as attempting to ensure that serfs were tied to the land. But this generated resentment (intensified in places by overzealous implementers), resistance, and tensions in how to deal with the new economic realities.

Other explanatory factors are, of course, important. While assuming a variety of issues specific to locality or region, we might note three overarching ones. First, political crises, power plays, and factionalism involved in the transition from the elderly and ill Edward III to the boy-king Richard II in 1377—including John of Gaunt's influence and his fractious relationship with Londoners—provided a suitable context for various grievances to boil over. Second, costly ongoing wars with France meant more taxation. Despite this, the aristocracy were seen to have failed to provide full protections from coastal raids which in turn did little to quell the longer-term anxieties. Third, between 1377 and 1380, three new and additional taxes were introduced (some of which controversially and provocatively targeted clergy) which exacerbated pre-existing tensions. The third—the poll tax of 1380—appeared to trigger the revolt after evasion of payment and attempted coercion, which Knighton (*Chron.* 210–211) claimed even involved checking girls to see if they had come of age.

London, June 1381

On Thursday 13 June 1381—the feast of Corpus Christi—insurgents arrived in London and joined up with aggrieved Londoners. Rebels, perhaps in their thousands, approached London from the south, via Blackheath, while others came from the north and the west. The rebels from the south managed to enter the city over London Bridge as they endeavoured to get Richard to hear their demands. While there were exceptions, there is (partly against Froissart's emphasis on pillaging) evidence of a degree of discipline and selective targeting of political, economic, legal, and ecclesiastical targets which seems to have been a consistent tendency throughout the attacks on London, and elsewhere (e.g., Cambridge). On arrival at Southwark, rebels attacked the buildings of Marshalsea and released prisoners (as they would at Fleet Prison, Westminster, and Newgate), including prisoners held for debt. At Lambeth Palace, the home of Simon Sudbury (archbishop of Canterbury and chancellor), rebels were said to have revelled in burning books, clothes, and records of registry and taxation, smashing up the kitchens, and draining barrels of wine (*Westminster Chron.* 2–3). At Temple, rebels attacked houses and removed roof tiles and went into the church and took books and documents (including legal ones) to burn in the street. Most spectacularly (at least in popular memory), rebels destroyed an array of expensive fineries and burnt the Savoy Palace of John of Gaunt, who (luckily for him) was away. Elsewhere, other rebels targeted the Hospitalus, St John at Clerkenwell (the Prior was the Treasurer of England, Robert Hales), killing the opposition and burning the building.

There were also xenophobic attacks which may have related to economic grievances, though not reducibly so.[11] Already, on Thursday 13 June, Kentish rebels attacked a brothel near London Bridge 'occupied by Flemish women who had farmed it from the mayor of London' (*Anon. Chron.* 140–141). The infamous attack on Flemish traders (Friday 14 June) picked up on pre-existing resentments among Londoners. One Fleming, Richard Lyons, was beheaded at Cheapside. Lyons had previously been convicted of numerous frauds (as noted in Knighton's account of his death—*Chron.* 217–218) and was allied with John of Gaunt, though Froissart places Lyons's death in the context of Tyler seeking personal revenge for a prior beating (*Chroniques* 10.108).

Chroniclers still reported a concern among the insurgents that it be made clear that they were not simply looting and rioting. Walsingham, for instance, wrote that the rebels told Londoners that they were targeting traitors, that they would pay a fair price and not plunder, and 'if they discovered anyone stealing they executed him, as if those who were thieves were particularly detestable' (*Chronica maiora* 416–417). This line was made especially clear in descriptions of the attack on the Savoy Palace and its spectacular wealth where they 'had it proclaimed, under pain of execution, that no one was to dare to touch anything or to keep for their own use any articles that they found' (*Chronica maiora* 418–419). According to Knighton, the rebels proclaimed that they 'were lovers of truth and justice, not robbers and thieves' after one of their number hid a piece of silver for himself resulting in both him and the silver being thrown into the fire (*Chron.* 214–215). For the *Westminster Chronicle*, the rebels 'did

---

11 Cf. Hilton, *Bond Men Made Free*, 198; Barron, *Revolt in London*, 6; Dunn, *Peasants' Revolt*, 112–13. Steven Justice, *Writing and Rebellion: England in 1381* (Berkeley: University of California Press, 1994), 71–73, also stresses the linguistic markers of difference involved in such incidents.

not dare to purloin any of the valuables, since everybody caught in any act of theft was haled away, without trial or judgement, to death by beheading' (*Westminster Chron.* 4–5). That different chroniclers emphasised this discipline over basic plundering suggests that this was indeed a tendency among the rebels.

Nevertheless, there were further lapses in discipline. While rebels at Lambeth may have drained the barrels of wine, at Fleet Street such newly available wine was seen more as a convenient thirst-quencher for some, even to the point that 'in the evening you could see them lying scattered about on the streets and under the walls, sleeping like slaughtered pigs,' with some taking advantage of their emboldened state to settle personal scores with colleagues (Knighton, *Chron.* 218–219). One lapse in discipline seems to have been an overenthusiastic consumption of good wine which led to a farcical demise: it was said, Knighton claimed, that some of the rebels got into the wine cellar at the Savoy and were satiated to the extent that they got trapped and slowly died (*Chron.* 216–217).

On Thursday 13 June, Richard had sailed from the Tower of London and communicated with rebels at Greenwich from the safety of a barge. The meeting involved the rebels wanting the heads of Richard's close advisors and leading courtiers. Nothing other than delay came of the negotiations and that evening he was said to have seen areas of London in flames (*Anon. Chron.* 142–143). From the Tower, Richard let it be known that he would pardon the rebels if they left but the response was demands for the 'traitors within the Tower' (*Anon. Chron.* 143) to be handed over, along with the end of serfdom and the meeting of other demands. Again, nothing came of it other than further attacks on property and the cry 'around the city that all lawyers, all the men of the Chancery and the Exchequer and everyone who could write a writ or a letter should be beheaded, wherever they could be found' (*Anon. Chron.* 143–144). Richard, perhaps deliberately distancing himself from Sudbury and Hales, left the Tower of London the next morning (Friday 14 June) and met rebels at Mile End to hear their demands, even meeting Tyler according to the *Anonimalle Chronicle* (though notably absent from other chronicles). In addition to handing over 'the traitors,' these demands were 'that henceforward no man should be a serf nor make homage or any type of service to any lord, but should give four pence for an acre of land. They asked also that no one should serve any man except at his own will and by means of regular covenant' (*Anon. Chron.* 144–145). But the same day, the rebels got into the Tower of London and dealt with Sudbury and Hales (among others) by decapitation, with their heads paraded on spikes then displayed at London Bridge. The *Westminster Chronicle* claimed that they put the archbishop's head in a position of prominence and nailed his mitre to the top of his head (*Westminster Chron.* 6–7).

Sudbury had tried to take a boat to escape from the Tower but was prevented by a rebel explicitly gendered in the *Anonimalle Chronicle*: 'a wicked woman (*une malveys femme*) raised a cry against him, and he had to turn back to the Tower, to his own confusion' (*Anon. Chron.* 144). There is some evidence for other women being presented in prominent roles in 1381. In Cambridge (16 June 1381) it was claimed that Margery Starre threw into the air the ashes of university archives, saying, 'away with the learning of clerks, away with it.'[12] Moreover, as Sylvia Federico has shown, judicial records provide further information about the activities of women. Even if we cannot be sure how accurate allegations against women and men were, the fact that cases of women were recorded shows that they could be imagined, and imagine themselves, as active in the revolt.[13] Perhaps the most famous example is Johanna Ferrour. It was reported that, on Thursday 13 June, Ferrour was accused (but not necessarily found guilty) of being involved in the leadership of the Kent rebellion, the attack on the Savoy Palace, and stealing a chest containing £1000, before escaping on a boat and sharing the gold with friends. Ferrour was also said to have led an attack on Sudbury and Hales.[14]

At the meeting with other rebels at Mile End, Richard accepted the demand to end serfdom and pardon criminals and outlaws (Friday 14 June). This was good enough for some rebels who then left. Presumably emboldened by the king's response, some remained, and they were seemingly dominated by the Kentish rebels and apparently included both Ball and Tyler. Tyler gained a meeting at Smithfield the next day (Saturday 15 June) where he was famously said to have met the king. Apparently acting cocky (not taking his hood off, playing with his knife, being overly friendly with

---

12 British Library, Arundel MS 350, fol. 17v. See further, e.g., Edgar Powell, *The Rising in East Anglia in 1381* (Cambridge: Cambridge University Press, 1896), 51–52; Justice, *Writing and Rebellion*, 72; Richard Firth Green, *A Crisis of Truth: Literature and Law in Ricardian England* (Philadelphia: University of Pennsylvania Press, 1999), 52; Sylvia Federico, 'The Imaginary Society: Women in 1381', *Journal of British Studies* 40 (2001): 159–83 (159–60); Barker, *England, Arise*, loc 91, 4811, 5571; 'The City of Cambridge: Medieval History', in J. P. C. Roach (ed.), *A History of the County of Cambridge and the Isle of Ely: Volume 3, The City and University of Cambridge* (London: Oxford University Press, 1959), 2–15, now at *British History Online*, http://www.british-history.ac.uk/vch/cambs/vol3/pp2-15.

13 Federico, 'The Imaginary Society'.

14 Federico, 'The Imaginary Society', 167–68.

the king, loudly drinking water), he rehearsed the list of demands while adding dramatic ones—now including a radical reshaping of the church leadership:

> [Wat Tyler] asked that there should be no law except for the law of Winchester and that henceforward there should be no outlawry in any process of law, and that no lord should have lordship in future, but it should be divided among all men, except for the king's own lordship. He also asked that the goods of Holy Church should not remain in the hands of the religious, nor of parsons and vicars and other churchmen; but that clergy already in possession should have a sufficient sustenance and the rest of their goods should be divided among the people of the parish. And he demanded that there should be only one bishop in England and only one prelate, and all the lands and tenements of the possessioners should be taken from them and divided among the commons, only reserving for them a reasonable sustenance. And he demanded that there should be no more villeins in England, and no serfdom nor villeinage but that all men should be free and of one condition. (*Anon. Chron.* 147; cf. *Westminster Chron.* 10–11)

Richard seemingly agreed and would keep the royal privileges in the carefully worded claim that Tyler could be given everything that Richard 'could fairly grant, reserving only for himself the regality of his crown' (*Anon. Chron.* 147). Amidst the confusion (not least in the sources) and perhaps taking offence at Tyler and his bravado, William Walworth (the Mayor of London) and others (e.g., Ralph Standish) moved against Tyler, stabbing and wounding him fatally. Tyler may also have been seized from hospital and decapitated, with his head placed on a spike for the rebels to see (*Anon. Chron.* 149). Tyler had apparently tried to get his archers to open fire, but Richard rode over to the rebels and said (presumably with no small cunning and ambiguity implied), 'I will be your king, I will be your captain and your leader. Follow me...' (Walsingham, *Chronica maiora* 438–439). The rebels followed the king away from the centre to Clerkenwell fields and the main revolt was effectively over.

Naturally, concessions were repealed, rebels were hunted down, uprisings quelled, and royal authority re-imposed before the end of 1381. The treatment of the leaders was predictably brutal. It was said that Jack Straw was soon captured and made to give a suspiciously elaborate confession, before being executed and his head placed on London Bridge near Tyler's. Ball was captured in Coventry, tried in St Albans in mid-July, and hanged, drawn, and quartered. John Wraw, leader of the Suffolk uprising, remained on the run for a little while longer but he too was captured and allegedly betrayed his colleagues, though he was still drawn and hanged in May 1382. Beyond the leadership and local leaders, there were rebels who were more likely to have the chance of being pardoned and allowed to live, though not all were so lucky. Nevertheless, at Waltham, Richard received messages from Essex rebels about securing their liberty. His response would become (in)famous: 'You have been peasants (*rustici*) and peasants you will continue to be; you will remain in bondage, not as before, but in incomparably worse conditions' (Walsingham, *Chronica maiora* 514–515).

Whatever we might make of the historical accuracy of any of these details amidst the general chaos of June 1381 (and there is plenty up for debate), this summary should provide a gist of the uprising for those unfamiliar and a suitable context in which Ball would be located. However, an understanding of Ball also sheds light on the uprising itself because, through reconstructing the historical figure of Ball, we get some of the most influential (if some of the sources are to be believed) ideological justifications for the insurgents' actions.

2
The Quest for the Historical John Ball

Enter John Ball

Most of what we know about John Ball's ideas comes from what we find in the chroniclers' accounts of the revolt. Even in the case of eyewitness testimony, we may not be able to present historical reconstructions with any certainty, but we can talk about the earliest general perceptions we have of the rebels, including, of course, Ball, who emerges from the sources as an ideologically or theologically coherent figure. Indeed, Walsingham and Knighton even provide us with coded letters from Ball (or people with shared interests) written in English, sometimes pseudonymously, and with allusions to William Langland's contemporary work, *Piers Plowman*. Walsingham (*Chronica maiora* 548–549) claimed to be in possession of a letter written by Ball, discovered in the tunic of a rebel who was to be hanged, and addressed to the commons in Essex. Walsingham further claimed that Ball admitted to writing this and more letters. Crucially, there are five letters, namely those in Knighton (*Chron.* 174–175; 220–225) and the one in Walsingham. Though they may have been independent from one another in Knighton and Walsingham, there are thematic and linguistic similarities between the two. The letters found in Knighton contain two instances of Ball explicitly identified as author plus three with pseudonyms (Iakke Mylner, Iakke Carter, Iakke Trewman).[1] These may be the closest we get to Ball's words, or at least his words transmitted among Ball's sympathisers, assuming they were not fabricated. Prior to 1381, we know little, especially about Ball's place of birth and upbringing. The letters attributed

---

1 For detailed textual analysis, see Richard Firth Green, 'John Ball's Letters: Literary History and Historical Literature,' in Barbara A. Hanawalt (ed.), *Chaucer's England: Literature in Historical Context* (Minneapolis: University of Minnesota Press, 1992), 176–200.

to Ball are of limited help and here we have to turn to alternative records. While legal and ecclesiastical records may have the advantage of helping us piece together Ball's career before 1381, we will soon see that they are not without their difficulties.

We are well enough informed about Ball's last days: it seems he was captured in Coventry then brought before the king, sentenced by Robert Tresilian, and executed in St Albans. His death was delayed through the intervention of the bishop of London, 'who was concerned for the salvation of his soul and obtained this period of time for him to repent,' before his hanging on 15 July. We are even told the fate of parts of his dead body: the four parts were sent to four cities (Walsingham, *Chronica maiora* 548–549; cf. *Westminster Chron.* 14–15), presumably as a threat. Margaret Aston not unreasonably hazarded 'a guess on Canterbury, York, Coventry and Colchester.'[2] Coventry was where Ball was captured and Canterbury lost its archbishop, Simon Sudbury, who seems to have been Ball's bête noire. York and Colchester (and the parts of Essex where the uprising was especially intense)[3] were particularly associated with Ball. From the letters attributed to Ball, we are informed that he was a priest associated with St Mary's, York (typically thought to be St Mary's Abbey or an associate church) but that he had later moved to Essex. According to Walsingham, Ball confessed to writing a letter to the commons under the name 'Iohon Schep, som tyme Seynte Marie prest of York, and nowe of Colchestre' (Knighton also has a letter beginning 'Iohan Balle, Seynte Marye prist'). But what more can we say about Ball beyond this?

Brian Bird and David Stephenson, building on the investigations of Kay Gilmour, noted that the name 'John Ball' turns up earlier in the Colchester Court Rolls, some occurrences of which, we might at least say, are not inconsistent with the described behaviour of the provocative preacher of the 1381 uprisings.[4] There is reference (30 January 1352) to a John Ball, son of Joan Ball and the then deceased William Ball, in Peldon, a village seven miles south of Colchester and close to the Essex coast opposite Mersea Island. This John Ball is said to have come of age and was involved in sorting out a tenancy of a tenement with Joan: 'Grant by John, son and heir of Wm.

---

2   Margaret Aston, 'Corpus Christi and Corpus Regni: Heresy and the Peasants' Revolt,' *Past and Present* 143 (1994): 3–47 (23).
3   Barker, *England, Arise*, loc 2516–2554.
4   Brian Bird and David Stephenson, 'Who Was John Ball?,' *Essex Archaeology and History* 8, third series (1976): 287–88; Brian Bird, *Colchester Rebel: A Short Study of John Ball* (Colchester: John Ball Society, 1981), 7–10; Bird, *Rebel before His Time*, 12–22.

Balle, of Peldon, to Joan, his mother, of a tenement in Colchester, between Eststokwellestr. [East Stockwell Street] and Weststokwellestrat [West Stockwell Street] for her life.'[5] On 23 July of the same year, we are told that this tenement in St Martin's Parish was granted to Thomas de la Neylond.[6] If this was our John Ball, then handing over the tenement (so it was argued) would cohere with a departure to York to train as a priest before his later return to Essex in the 1360s (see below). There are also references to a 'John Ball' who was appointed rector of St James's Church in the 1370s.[7] As rector, this figure was presumably in an ecclesiastical position too high to be our Ball and in any case seems to have died around 1393.[8] However, there is also mention in the Colchester Court Rolls of a chaplain of the same name and at the same church in a position more suited to what we otherwise know about our Ball. The John Ball of the Colchester Court Rolls dated to 11 May 1377 lived with another clergyman, John Proude, in East Street.[9] Ball and Proude claimed that William Crabbe 'entered their house in Est Strat without licence or warrant and, by force took certain goods and vessels away.' Crabbe himself claims he 'took the same for rent due to him and unpaid.' Furthermore, from 9 August 1377, we hear the plea that Andrew and John Danel were acting in self-defence after they were accused of 'assaulting John, clerk of St James.'[10]

Is this, then, a glimpse of the pre-revolt life of *the* John Ball? Such a conclusion is not impossible, but the case remains speculative. While Brian Bird in particular was confident that such evidence pointed to the John Ball of the 1381 uprising, it is not an explanation that has gained much support.[11] One problem is that we do not know for sure if these references were to our Ball. Given that we know that another John Ball was rector of St

---

5   Isaac Herbert Jeayes (ed.), *Court Rolls of the Borough of Colchester, Volume I (1310–1352)* (Colchester: Town Council of the Borough of Colchester, 1921), 229.
6   Jeayes, *Court Rolls of the Borough of Colchester, Volume I*, 238.
7   Isaac Herbert Jeayes (ed.), *Court Rolls of the Borough of Colchester, Volume III (1372–1379)* (Colchester: Town Council of the Borough of Colchester, 1941), 136; cf. W. Gurney Benham (ed.), *The Oath Book or Red Parchment Book of Colchester* (Colchester: Essex County Standard Office, 1907), 73.
8   Richard Newcourt, *Repertorium Ecclesiasticum Parochiale Londinense* (London: Benj. Motte, 1710), 169.
9   Jeayes, *Court Rolls of the Borough of Colchester, Volume III*, 139.
10 Jeayes, *Court Rolls of the Borough of Colchester, Volume III*, 152.
11 Cf. Andrew Prescott, 'Ball, John (d. 1381),' *ODNB* (24 May 2008): 'A suggestion that he was the son of William and Joan Ball of Peldon, a few miles south of Colchester, born c. 1329, appears to be without foundation.'

James's, Colchester, this would already suggest that the insufficiently contextualised occurrences of the name 'John Ball' are not enough to establish whether they refer to our Ball. Another reason to be hesitant is that what we *do* know about the John Ball of the 1381 revolt is that he was known for moving around and being excommunicated, so we should perhaps not expect his name to turn up in this type of record.[12]

What we can say more definitively is that, after coming down from York to Colchester, John Ball acquired a reputation for his notorious activities as an itinerant lower clergyman and, given the timeline involved, was likely over forty years old by 1381. According to one of the letters patent from Edward III (25 February 1364), the king had given the chaplain John Ball special protection after he 'feared bodily injury from some of his enemies in the prosecution of his business.' However, the king claimed that now 'he has learned that John is not prosecuting any business but wanders from country to country preaching articles contrary to the faith of the church to the peril of his soul and the souls of others, especially of laymen, and he has therefore thought fit to revoke such protection.'[13] This important piece of evidence may also suggest, as Andrew Prescott has claimed, that Ball was not quite the marginal figure that he is typically thought to be.[14] There is also the intriguing possibility of viewing this in light of a reference to the activities of a John Ball who was a chaplain of a church in Layer de la Haye, five miles south of Colchester.[15] This John Ball was accused of beating up and breaking the leg of Henry, son of Thomas Waryn, who claimed for compensation. Ball's defence was that the hazing of Henry was necessary for the student's education. Happily for this John Ball, the jury accepted Ball's explanation and he was duly acquitted.[16]

12 So, e.g., Barker, *England, Arise*, loc 6220.
13 *Calendar of the Patent Rolls: Edward III, Vol. XII, 1361–1364* (London: Hereford Times Limited, 1912), 470.
14 Andrew Prescott, 'John Ball Revisited' (unpublished paper, c. 1990s). I am grateful to Andrew Prescott for sharing this paper with me.
15 Barker, *England, Arise*, loc 6220–6239.
16 Robert C. Palmer, *English Law in the Age of the Black Death, 1348–1381: A Transformation of Governance and Law* (Chapel Hill: University of North Carolina Press, 1993), 156–57, which includes the full Latin text. For Barker, this report could be significant because the church at Layer de la Haye belonged to the Augustinian priory of St Botolph, the prior of which led an armed attack on St John's Abbey in 1363 in a dispute that was eventually resolved after papal intervention in 1364. A further reference to a chaplain called John Ball is dated to 1355 and a dispute at a vicarage in Gazeley, Suffolk, which Prescott, 'John Ball Revisited,' sees as a 'hint' of what might have been rather than anything concrete.

It cannot be proven whether this was *the* John Ball and the one involved in the story behind Edward III revoking protection for Ball on discovery of his itinerancy and unorthodox preaching. But we do know that Ball continued to provoke a reaction from 1364 onwards and that he had an especially testy relationship with Sudbury which would ultimately end in both their deaths. Confirmed in a letter dating to 24 October 1364, Sudbury (then bishop of London) had excommunicated Ball whose ongoing activities in the diocese (which included parts of Essex) over time had been noted.[17] On 13 December 1376, reference was made to Ball's excommunication under Sudbury (now archbishop of Canterbury) 'for his manifest contumacy', and Essex clergy were commissioned to take Ball before the sheriff of Essex to answer for his actions against the church.[18]

As late as April 1381, on the eve of the uprisings, Sudbury was condemning Ball as a slippery and evasive character who preached insults against various church authorities.[19] He was, to use Sudbury's specific image, like the fox evading the hunter, which may further reflect a level of local support for Ball given he was able to function in such a manner.[20] Sudbury opened with warnings about false prophets (*pseudoprophetarum*) and their poisoning of the flock before giving the particular example of Ball. Ball's preaching was rejected as being contrary to the apostolic and ecclesiastical tradition with reference to Paul in Romans 10.15: *Quomodo praedicabunt, nisi mittantur?* ('How shall they preach unless they be sent?'). He referred to Ball's earlier career as one of a 'fugitive' or 'vagabond' who had sown errors and schisms (*praedictum vagabundum Johannem Balle, propter errores et schismata per eum seminata*).[21] As we will see, related language of sowing heresy would again be used of Ball's problematic ideas, particularly with reference to the Parable of the Wheat and the Tares (Matthew 13.24–30, 36–43), but it would also be imagery for which Ball would be remembered for throwing back at his ecclesiastical opponents (see below). Sudbury also wrote of Ball's unauthorised and heretical public preaching in or around places such as churches, cemeteries, and public markets,

---

17 Public Record Office, C. 85/121, m. 4; Aston, 'Corpus Christi and Corpus Regni', 21; Barker, *England, Arise*, loc 2516–2526.
18 *Calendar of the Patent Rolls: Edward III, Vol. XVI, 1374–1377* (London: Hereford Times Limited, 1916), 415.
19 David Wilkins, *Concilia Magnae Britanniae et Hiberniae: Volume III* (London, 1737), 152.
20 Wilkins, *Concilia Magnae Britanniae et Hiberniae*, 152; Oman, *Great Revolt of 1381*, 42; Bird and Stephenson, 'Who Was John Ball?', 288; Barker, *England, Arise*, loc 2544.
21 Wilkins, *Concilia Magnae Britanniae et Hiberniae*, 152.

and how he would be the one who would personally decide Ball's fate.[22] This general picture seems to tally with claims in the chroniclers that Ball, who had been in the archbishop of Canterbury's prison three times, had again been imprisoned by the archbishop for 'two or three months to chastise him' for preaching against the lords as people came out of churches (Froissart, *Chroniques* 10.97), and that, after being banned from preaching in churches and parishes, Ball would instead speak in the 'market-squares and streets, or into the fields' (*Chronica maiora* 544–545).

Here, we again run into precise questions of historical accuracy about Ball's last imprisonment before his death. Froissart has Ball associated with Kent, imprisoned by the archbishop of Canterbury, and then out of prison and preaching once more. On 10 June, Ball is said to have been at Canterbury wanting to find Sudbury who was in London at the time before the rebels attacked the cathedral and moved towards London (*Chroniques* 10.95–101). Knighton (and Knighton alone) claimed more precisely that Ball was serving time at the archbishop of Canterbury's pleasure in Maidstone and, early on in the revolt, he was sprung from jail (*Chron.* 210–211). But was he in Maidstone or Kent around this time? As Andrew Prescott showed, the problem here is that a certain John Ball 'the traitor' was a named prisoner sprung by Essex rebels from the jail at Bishop's Stortford on 11 June, which in turn raises further problems about *where* John Ball was active during the uprisings. If this was *the* John Ball, then not only is the accuracy of Ball's alleged activities in Kent during the early parts of the revolt undermined but it even makes it much less likely that he was in London the next day or personally involved with, or witnessed, the beheading of Sudbury (so, e.g., Froissart, *Chroniques* 10.111). It also undermines the likelihood of Ball delivering his famous sermon at Blackheath.[23] With this evidence in mind, it is striking that Walsingham claimed that rebels freed Ball from an unspecified prison and that Ball had 'predicted he would be freed by twenty thousand of his friends. This in fact happened subsequently during the troubles I have described in the kingdom, when the commons broke open all the prisons and made all the prisoners leave' (*Chronica maiora* 544–547). It is possible, then, that the placing of Ball in

---

22 See further, Oman, *Great Revolt of 1381*, 42; F. Donald Logan, *Excommunication and the Secular Arm in Medieval England: A Study in Legal Procedure from the Thirteenth to the Sixteenth Century* (Toronto: Pontifical Institute of Mediaeval Studies, 1968), 63–64; Aston, 'Corpus Christi and Corpus Regni', 21–23.

23 Andrew Prescott, 'Judicial Records of the Rising of 1381' (PhD thesis: University of London, 1984), 303–4. See also Brooks, 'Organization and Achievements', in Mayr-Harting and Moore (ed.), *Studies in Medieval History*, 267 n. 58; Barker, *England, Arise*, loc 3164–3265.

Maidstone by Knighton and in Canterbury by Froissart is the result of confusion arising from Ball's deep and ongoing hostilities with the archbishop of Canterbury or part of an agenda to make Ball a primary malign influence on the revolt. But while we are still left having to speculate about which scenario is the most plausible, the general picture (beneath the exaggerations) is clear enough: Ball was likely sprung from a prison.

If Knighton did make a mistake here then it is perhaps a forgivable one as it is tempting to see the element of longstanding personal hatred between Ball and Sudbury spicing up the ideological differences the two represented as their friction came to a bloody conclusion in the summer of 1381.[24] But, as Sudbury implied, in addition to this seemingly personal feud, other leading ecclesiastical authorities also had problems with Ball. Ball was brought before John Buckingham (bishop of Lincoln) and three of Sudbury's predecessors at Canterbury: William Whittlesey, Simon Langham, and Simon Islip.[25] In 1366, Langham ordered the Dean of Bocking to have Ball brought to Canterbury with a professed concern for the salvation of Ball's soul.[26] It is worth noting that Bocking would later become a central place for the Essex rebels in 1381, including hosting sentiments that chimed with Ball's teachings against the authorities and against villeinage.[27] Whatever the specifics of Ball's activities in the decades leading up to the revolt, they were quite clearly seen as deviant and dangerously popular, and there is no indication that Ball ever intended to change his ways. Or, as Walsingham summarised the situation by the time of the uprising: 'For twenty years or more, John Ball had always preached in various places the things which he knew would please the common people, disparaging men of the Church as well as secular lords, and so won the good will of the commons rather than approval before God' (*Chronica maiora* 544–545).

Ball's Bible

These details of Ball's life are not mere historical trivia because the antagonism between Ball and the church authorities was integral to his preaching

---

24 Or, as Aston ('Corpus Christi and Corpus Regni', 23) put it cautiously in her analysis of Sudbury's denunciations of Ball: 'We might even, without too much imagination, see in it some personal vendetta... Ball undoubtedly had reasons for wanting to get even (or more than even) with Sudbury.'
25 Wilkins, *Concilia Magnae Britanniae et Hiberniae*, 152–53.
26 Wilkins, *Concilia Magnae Britanniae et Hiberniae*, 64–65.
27 Barker, *England, Arise*, loc 2544–2554.

during the revolt. The chroniclers fill out the theological and exegetical teachings of Ball only found in skeletal form in earlier documents. While intellectual justifications for social change would almost inevitably have come from the Bible and Christian tradition, these same sources of authority, of course, supported the status quo. We already saw this in the treatment of Ball by people like Sudbury, and Ball's early interpreters continued to present Ball as behaving heretically and dismissed him as a 'chaplain of evil disposition' (*Anon. Chron.* 137), a 'foolish' priest of Kent (Froissart, *Chroniques* 10.95), and as someone who had (using familiar imagery of heresy—see also below) 'for a long time unprofitably spread the word of the Lord, mixing tares with the wheat' (Knighton, *Chron.* 210–211), despite, or because of, his popularity and designation as a 'prophet' by the commons (*Anon. Chron.* 138). Ball, on the other hand, was presented as using the Bible to attack such elite power. And we can establish some of the key themes in Ball's theology and exegesis—representing at least one strand of ideological justifications for the uprisings—which were developed in the socio-economic context of the revolt and in negotiation with the history of reception of the Bible.[28]

Echoing St Ambrose, the Parable of the Rich Man and Lazarus (Luke 16.18–31), and Jesus's invective against Herod Antipas (Matthew 11.7–8; Luke 7.24–25), as well as a long reception history of such themes, Ball was said to have preached about the lords in fine clothing, dwelling in luxurious houses, and consuming good food and drink while the lower orders were in poor cloth, living off the chaff and water, and working in the fields through wind and rain. By doing this, Ball was said to have argued, the labour of the peasants is appropriated to 'keep and maintain their estates' (Froissart, *Chroniques* 10.96). Prominent, and integral to his preaching against lords, was a certain type of anticlericalism, no doubt aimed at church wealth and landownership. As we saw, Walsingham claimed Ball's popular preaching involved 'disparaging men of the Church as well as secular lords' (*Chronica maiora* 544–545; cf. Knighton, *Chron.* 210–211).

However, Ball went further still in wanting a radical restructuring of the church in England. According to one chronicler, Ball advised the common people 'to get rid of all the lords, archbishops, bishops, abbots and priors, as well as most of the monks and canons so that there should be no bishop in England except for one archbishop, namely himself' (*Anon. Chron.* 137). There was, as we saw, an interest in narrowing down God's representatives

---

28 Cf. Froissart, *Chroniques* 10.97 (*Chronicles* 251): 'Of his words and deeds there were much people in London informed, such as had great envy at them that were rich and such as were noble.'

on earth; it was also claimed by Knighton that the rebels broke him out of Maidstone prison because, inspired by his attacks on church wealth and authority and on the clergy, they wanted to make Ball an archbishop (*Chron.* 210–211). Even if Knighton was mistaken about the location of Ball's imprisonment, it is still an assessment of Ball's future position that was echoed elsewhere. After his preaching during the revolt, it was said elsewhere that the common people 'acclaimed him as the future archbishop and chancellor of the realm. They said he alone was worthy of the honour of the archbishopric, that the archbishop, who was then still alive, had been a traitor to the commons and the realm, and should therefore be executed, wherever in England he could be captured' (*Chronica maiora* 546–549).

Adam, Eve, Bakers, and Shepherds: United Forever in Friendship and Labour

As in related medieval radical traditions, biblical texts and the idea of a purer authoritative past were used to attack almost all holders of established high-political and high-ecclesiastical offices.[29] Through what was presented by Walsingham as a hugely well-attended, tubthumping sermon at Blackheath on 12 June, Ball became particularly associated with the story of Adam and Eve and picking up a traditional theme of reverting back to the beginning of time to critique the present and anticipate a transformed time to come (*Chronica maiora* 546–547). Whether Ball actually delivered this sermon at Blackheath is still up for debate given the possibility he was sprung from Bishop's Stortford jail the previous day, while Froissart's relatively similar sermon attributed to Ball is not identified with Blackheath. Nevertheless, Walsingham's presentation of Ball's teaching coheres with the general portrayal of Ball among the earliest sources and for that reason we should not neglect it in our understanding of Ball's theology, or at least the earliest understandings of Ball's theology.

John Ball's most famous saying was presented here by Walsingham (and tellingly quoted in English) with the opening words for which Ball has been remembered, even though popular sayings or similar sentiments concerning the lives of Adam and Eve at the beginning of human society were certainly known by 1381:[30] 'Whan Adam dalf, and Eve span/Wo was þanne a

29 Hilton, *Bond Men Made Free*, 102–3, 109, 227.
30 Gerald Robert Owst, *Literature and the Pulpit in Medieval England* (revised edition; Oxford: Blackwell, 1966), 291; Hilton, *Bond Men Made Free*, 211–12;

gentilman?' (*Chronica maiora* 546). When associated with Ball, Adam and Eve were thought to point to a time when there was no serfdom and thus serfdom had to be a human invention designed to put people in their place. A typical claim is that the ideas of Ball encapsulated in the Adam and Eve saying represent 'radical egalitarianism.'[31] This is an obviously important emphasis but there should be qualifications because what we also see in the revolt is power connected with alternative, popular hierarchies thought to be more reliable in dispensing justice and fairness. As we have seen, Ball himself was remembered as the person to fill the major ecclesiastical role in the new order. While there is some uncertainty, one clear theme that emerges from the revolt is that of the youthful Richard (potentially?) fitting the role of the just king with some evidence of figures like Wat Tyler taking on some kind of complementary, alternative, and popular leadership or even localised 'kingly' roles (see below).

The assumption of proper representation in this idealised new order is complemented by the assumptions of a broken society and the assumptions of rebel identities united by their labour. The context of Corpus Christi (which, we recall, fell on Thursday 13 June 1381) is significant here, not least because celebration of the Eucharist and the body of Christ had implications for understanding the cohesion (or otherwise) of the social body. As Aston noted, part of the message of the celebrations was about liberation, with Exodus foreshadowing the crucifixion which provided freedom for all. Even if Ball did not pick up on this theme explicitly in his sermon and irrespective of whether he delivered a Corpus Christi sermon at Blackheath or elsewhere, it would not be overly speculative to suggest that, in this context, similar connections could have been made between these themes of sacrifice, community, and freedom, and the ideology and material interests of the uprisings.[32] The allusions to Corpus Christi look clearer in the similar levelling and emancipatory (and ominous) reference in Ball's letter to the Essex commons to 'Iohan þe Mullere haþ ygrounde smal, smal, smal; þe kynges sone of heuene shal pay for al' (Walsingham, *Chronica maiora* 548). Iohan the Mullere (John the Miller) is probably as much a relevant coded or generic name for someone who worked with bread as 'Iohon Schep' (John Shepherd) is for Ball's occupation as a priest in the opening of the letter.

Aston, 'Corpus Christi and Corpus Regni,' 17–18; J. A. Raftis, 'Social Change versus Revolution: New Interpretations of the Peasants' Revolt of 1381,' in Francis X. Newman (ed.), *Social Unrest in the Late Middle Ages* (Binghamton: Center for Medieval and Early Renaissance Studies, 1986), 3–22 (17).

31 So, e.g., Dunn, *Peasants' Revolt*, 78.
32 Aston, 'Corpus Christi and Corpus Regni,' 19–21.

Aston raised the possibility that this passage—tied in as it clearly is with both Christ's death and breadmaking—might include a eucharistic allusion. The language of 'bread of life,' grain, flour, grinding, and milling in relation to Christ and salvation was, she added, seen or heard in sermons, matins, poems, and plays relating to Corpus Christi.[33] We might add that in Ball's letter the emphasis is on the labour involved in the eucharistic bread, and it is the unity of labour that is a unifying feature in Ball's famous sermon and its reference to Adam and Eve's duties.[34] Moreover, elsewhere in Ball's letter, the shared language of labour is used, possibly as a coded call to arms ('biddeth Peres Ploughman go to his werk'). The similar letter attributed to 'Iakke Mylner' (Jack Miller) by Knighton (and possibly written by Ball using another generic pseudonym) is an important parallel in terms of both the bread/eucharist allusions and the unity of labour involved in the production and language of rebellion. Accordingly, the letter opens with 'Iakke Mylner asket help to turne hys mylne aright. He hath gronden smal smal; þe kingus sone of heuen he schal pay for alle.' Furthermore, immediately preceding this, Knighton introduced the letter with reference to a primary role for a 'Baker,' claiming that 'There were reckoned to be 20,000 in that wretched throng...These were their leaders: Thomas Baker, the first mover, although later the principal leader was Iakke Strawe, Iakke Mylner, Iakke Carter, Iakke Trewman. Iakke Mylner addresses his companions thus...'

The King and the Golden Age

As noted, it is likely that this egalitarianism and attacks on the lords did not necessarily mean overthrowing the king who, theoretically, transcended such issues. Froissart claimed that Ball's preaching against serfdom and the lords included the solution (whether with an implied threat or just naivety) of going to the young king to show him such servitude so that Richard would provide freedom (Froissart, *Chroniques* 10.96). On gathering at Dartford, the rebels were said to have claimed that 'they would neither suffer nor allow any king other than King Richard' and in Canterbury they asked the mayor, bailiffs, and the commons 'whether they would swear in good will to be faithful and loyal to King Richard and the loyal commons of England' (*Anon. Chron.* 137). It was even said that the rebels later

---

33 Aston, 'Corpus Christi and Corpus Regni,' 26–33.
34 Cf. Jeffrey H. Aziz, 'Of Grace and Gross Bodies: Falstaff, Oldcastle and the Fires of Reform' (PhD Thesis: University of Pittsburgh, 2007), 9–11.

responded to the king, 'Welcome our Lord King Richard, if it pleases you, and we will not have any other king but you' (*Anon. Chron.* 144). Indeed, one coded message concerned solidarity with King Richard and the true commons. Walsingham claimed that 'John Straw' demanded support for 'King Richard and the commons' (*Chronica maiora* 420–423).[35] Such sentiments chime with the persistent idea among the insurgents about unscrupulous aristocratic advisers misleading the young king. The rebels, of course, lacked parliamentary representation and so the only person who could remedy the situation was the king. Put another way, there was a lingering assumption about the divine legitimacy of kings and the popular (if somewhat vague) myth of the just king.[36]

The ideal of a just king was a centuries old tradition and gained its authority from the Bible. In addition, there were inherited prophecies from Late Antiquity, particularly through the transmission of the *Tiburtine Sibyl* and the *Apocalypse of Pseudo-Methodius*, about the expectation of a final Christian emperor who would vanquish foes and bring justice and prosperity, and which was popular and widespread in medieval eschatological thought.[37] Monarchs played around with related rhetoric to the extent that we might say that sacred kingship, and the idealised expectations of justice, was an embedded and widely accepted tradition. We might also note the common observation that the lofty ideals of Richard II's coronation may have provided the model for the coronation scene in the prologue to *Piers Plowman* (112–145). While Langland's vision or dream poem is a more

35 See also, e.g., Dunn, *Peasants' Revolt*, 12, 82.
36 Cf. Hilton, *Class Conflict and the Crisis of Feudalism*, 91: 'I do not think it will be dangerously teleological to suggest that peasants could not at this stage have provided an alternative ruling class to that of feudal monarchy and its aristocracy…It is also important that the political vision of the rebels' leaders had not developed into a clear picture of an alternative social order. It is true that they had clearly thrown overboard the doctrine of the hierarchy of social orders. They wished to abolish the landed aristocracy, to disendow the Church and to destroy the ecclesiastical hierarchy. But they had not apparently envisaged any role for the towns and could not think of a political regime other than vague schemes for a popular monarchy.' Cf. Hyman Fagan and Rodney H. Hilton, *The English Rising of 1381* (London: Lawrence and Wishart, 1950), 87–88.
37 For a helpful overview of the texts and relevant issues relating to the Last Emperor myth, see, e.g., Stephen J. Shoemaker, 'The *Tiburtine Sibyl*, the Last Emperor, and the Early Byzantine Apocalyptic Tradition,' in Tony Burke (ed.), *Forbidden Texts on the Western Frontier: The Christian Apocrypha from North American Perspectives* (Eugene, OR: Wipf and Stock, 2015), 218–44. This was a key idea for Norman Cohn, *The Pursuit of the Millennium* (revised and expanded edition; Oxford: Oxford University Press, 1970), e.g., 32–35.

reformist, if scathing, take on society around the time of the uprising, its ideas still provided an often-unintentional influence on the insurgents (at least those associated with Ball). In this general sense, we might note the discussion in *Piers Plowman* of a Davidic ruler and a Christian king who would bring peace and just rule, with reference to Isaiah 2.4 and the hope of beating swords into ploughshares (B.3.259–325).[38] Ball's Blackheath sermon, however, looked first to turning ploughshares into swords (so to speak) in the expectation of a more immediate removal of those who would be harmful to the community so that 'they would in the end gain peace themselves and security for the future' and enjoy 'the same nobility, equal dignity, and similar power' (*Chronica maiora* 546–547). While they would have differed over how or even if the transformation would occur and who would be involved, it is likely that Ball and at least some of the rebels shared the general expectation of an ideal Christian king in *Piers Plowman*.

But there is one question relating to the reconstruction of the historical Ball that needs addressing: Did some at the most revolutionary end of the uprising influenced by Ball's style of thinking want to remove the king? Walsingham went further in his suspiciously convenient presentation of a confession from Jack/John Straw before his execution, designed to ease his passage from this life to the next:

> At the time we assembled at Blackheath, when we determined to summon the king, it had been part of our plan to put to death without delay all the knights, esquires, and other gentlemen who had come with him. We had also intended to take the king himself, who appeared amongst us in all his royal splendour, from place to place with us, in order that when everybody saw him, especially the common mob, they would feel obliged to come over to us and join our rebellion more boldly, when they saw that the king himself appeared to be behind our revolt. We brought together a huge throng of the commons from all parts of the country, and immediately killed those lords who could disapprove of us or put up resistance...Finally, we would have killed the king, and have destroyed all men of property in the land, bishops, monks, canons as well as rectors of churches. Only the mendicant orders would have survived in the land... Then when no magnate, no powerful man, and no man of learning was left among us, we would have established laws that suited us under which subjects would have been ruled. We would have appointed Wat Tyler as king in Kent, and separate kings in other counties...Again, on the evening of the day that Wat Tyler was killed, since the common people of London

---

38 Andrew Galloway, *The Penn Commentary on Piers Plowman, Volume 1: C Prologue-Passus 4; B Prologue-Passus 4; A Prologue-Passus 4* (Philadelphia: University of Pennsylvania Press, 2006).

supported us, especially the poorer people, we planned to set the city on fire in four places, quickly burn it down, and divide amongst us as we wished all the valuables which were found. (Walsingham, *Chronica maiora* 498–499)

Whatever we make of the mysterious figure of Jack/John Straw, similar views are attributed to Tyler by Walsingham, who claimed that Tyler was covertly plotting to kill the king, burn down London, and destroy the lawyers and legal system so that 'everything would in future be ordered in accordance with the decrees of the commons' (Walsingham, *Chronica maiora* 435).

But regicidal tendencies as alleged in Walsingham's reports are not found in the other key sources, and there is a constant appeal in and around the revolt to the idea of royal mercy, as Helen Lacey has shown.[39] These points stand even if there is a degree of ambiguity in royalist statements and even if it is possible that capturing the king for propaganda purposes was an aim of certain rebels. Knighton's account of Tyler (here presented as the same person as Jack Straw) has him as a menacing presence in front of the king but this is framed to explain that Walworth thought Richard's life was in danger and so acted to kill the rebel leader. What further counts against Walsingham's assessment of Tyler and Straw is the assumption of (a certain kind of) royalism among the rebels, noted above. Moreover, according to the *Anonimalle Chronicle*, Tyler was present at Mile End and petitioning the king to deal with traitors. Even if Tyler's presence at Mile End is historically debateable (given that this is the only source that mentions it), it is still important that Tyler was remembered as holding the same assumptions of a royal figurehead as those of the rebel group. As they proclaimed, 'Welcome our Lord King Richard, if it pleases you, and we will not have any other king but you' (*Anon. Chron.* 144). In Froissart's account of the events at Smithfield, Tyler plotted to kill all those around the king but was emphatic in his command to 'slay all them except the king; but do the king no hurt, he is young, we shall do with him as we list and shall lead him with us all about England, and so shall we be lords of all the realm without doubt' (*Chroniques* 10.118). Also at Smithfield, Tyler was summoned to meet the king and did so confidently, on a little horse so he could be seen by the commons, and with dagger in hand (playing around with it, according to Knighton) took the king's arm and roughly shook his hand, saying, 'Brother, be of good comfort and joyful, for you shall have, in the fortnight that is to come, forty thousand more commons than you have at present,

---

39 Lacey, "'Grace for the Rebels'".

and we shall be good companions' (*Anon. Chron.* 147). Moreover, in the deal between Tyler and the king, the king was to keep the crown and its privileges. Again, there is no explicit mention of a hidden agenda.

That the *Anonimalle Chronicle* saw no problem presenting Tyler as requiring some sort of royal figurehead may well mean that we should probably be suspicious about suggestions from Walsingham of hard regicidal tendencies among rebel leaders.[40] Indeed, Walsingham agrees that on the fall of Tyler, Richard quelled the commons and proclaimed him to be their king and leader and they duly followed. It may have been the case that Tyler was cocky in front of the king, perhaps even planned to seize him, would not have accepted every royal command, and may even have aggressively bossed around the king's squire. It may have been the case that rebels joked at the expense of Joan of Kent (the king's mother) and her entourage when en route to London (Froissart, *Chroniques* 10.99; cf. *Anon. Chron.* 135; Walsingham *Chronica maiora* 412–413), and later in the Tower of London others may have joked around on the king's bed asking Joan for a kiss (Walsingham, *Chronica maiora* 424–425; Froissart, *Chroniques* 10.112) which, so Froissart claimed, made her faint and need rest and supervision until she was comforted by her son.[41] This episode may represent not only the violation of the private, royal bed but, at least for some, perhaps presents a kind of symbolic rape of Joan as part of the collapse of conventional authority, whether assumed by the chroniclers, the rebels, or both.[42] Nevertheless, the traditions of sacred kingship were, for now, sufficiently embedded that regicide and abolition of the head of the system of medieval power were not prominent options and such claims were more likely specific to Walsingham and designed to discredit Tyler (/Straw). That Ball himself was not accused of regicidal polemics (on the contrary) is similarly telling.[43]

---

40 For a summary of the nuances of Tyler's leadership, see, e.g., Dunn, *Peasants' Revolt*, 75–78.

41 For further discussion, see, e.g., Federico, 'The Imaginary Society', 173–82.

42 E.g., W. Mark Ormrod, 'In Bed with Joan of Kent: The King's Mother and the Peasants' Revolt', in Jocelyn Wogan-Browne, Rosalynn Voaden, Arlyn Diamond, Ann Hutchison, Carol Meale, and Lesley Johnson (eds.), *Medieval Women—Texts and Contexts in Late Medieval Britain: Essays for Felicity Riddy* (Turnhout: Brepols, 2000), 277–92; Federico, 'The Imaginary Society', 189; Hollie L. S. Morgan, *Beds and Chambers in Late Medieval England: Readings, Representations and Realities* (York: York Medieval Press, 2017), 99–100.

43 We might add that the idea of corrupt officials against the just king could be found in stories of outlaws. See, e.g., Fagan and Hilton, *English Rising of 1381*, 87–89; Lacey, '"Grace for the Rebels"', 43.

As the implication that they were in opposition to the king comes from Walsingham's dubious confession of Jack Straw, we should not generalise from this to the rest of the revolt. Indeed, it is possible (and I put it no stronger than that) that regicide may have been an inference drawn by Walsingham from other ideas presented in Walsingham's version of Straw's confession, namely the language of local kings where there is otherwise no obvious indication that leaders were necessarily seen as hostile to *the* king. Elsewhere, the language of royalty did seem to have been mimicked at a lower level of the alternative hierarchy and representation. As Froissart claimed of the rebels gathering at Blackheath, 'they said ever they were the king's men and the noble commons of England' (Froissart, *Chroniques* 10.102) and at Smithfield, Froissart wrote, Tyler plotted to slay all but the young king who they would instead 'lead him with us all about England, and so shall we be lords of all the realm without doubt' (Froissart, *Chroniques* 10.118). Similarly, the dispensing of justice in the beheading of Sudbury and others was presented, Froissart suggested, 'as though they had been traitors to the king and to the realm' (Froissart, *Chroniques* 10.111). The regional 'kings' as presented by Walsingham may point to this sort of mimicry of aristocratic hierarchy—indeed, what other language was available to rebels assuming positions of leadership? Despite all the problems with Walsingham's presentation of Straw's confession, and based on what we know generally from elsewhere, there may be something to the claim attributed to Straw that 'we would have appointed Wat Tyler as king in Kent, and separate kings in other counties,' with the assumption of Tyler as head chief (*Chronica maiora* 498–499). Whatever can and cannot be gleaned about the historical Tyler, he was certainly portrayed as representing an alternative form of leadership and authority, and a point of contact for those from other counties—and conduit to King Richard himself.

Walsingham continued his account by noting that among the rebels of Mildenhall and Bury St Edmunds, Robert Westbrom 'made himself king' with the even more renowned John Wraw as his priest, the latter content to retain his priestly status and not wishing 'to put one crown upon another.' In Norfolk, the dyer Geoffrey Litster (called 'John' by Walsingham and 'William' by Froissart) was said to have 'assumed the royal name and power' and carried both the 'title and the power of a king' (*Chronica maiora* 500–510). Earlier, Walsingham claimed that Litster, the 'King of the Commons' (*regem comunium*), compelled knights to swear to act as his bodyguards and cut up and taste his food before kneeling before their new king when he ate (*Chronica maiora* 490–491). Given that regicide was not an option elsewhere, if such alternative kings were a significant feature of the rebellion, then we should be suspicious about whether they were ever in opposition to the ideal of the overarching monarch. These kings of the commons and counties may have had something of the carnivalesque about them—but such imitation could indeed have been the sincerest form of flattery.

Visual representations of the commons may support this sort of reading. The *Anonimalle Chronicle*, for instance, noted that when the commons of Kent arrived at Blackheath on Wednesday 12 June to await the King, 'they displayed two banners of St George and sixty pennons' (*Anon. Chron.* 139) which would have likely been part of the attempt to connect the rebels' cause with the king.[44] Such representations were, of course, made famous visually in the illuminated Froissart manuscript (c. 1460–1480) of 'Jehan Balle' and the rebels with the banner of St George (British Library MS Royal 18 E. I f.165v).[45] Indeed, we can make a reasonable claim that the networks of these 'true commons' of the king functioned as a presentation of what can be loosely labelled a national English identity from below and an alternative to representations in their recognised official forms. Ball's attack on the lords and the system of exploitation claimed that things were 'not well to pass in England, nor shall do till everything be common' (Froissart, *Chroniques* 10.96). He was pushing for radical political representation, and reflecting what Andrea Ruddick called 'stretch[ing] further' the 'definition of the political public.'[46] In the case of Ball's role, this involved a shared religious identity in England, not only by justifying such claims with reference to Adam and Eve but even providing an implicit bureaucratic structure for

44 Jonathan Bengtson, 'Saint George and the Formation of English Nationalism,' *Journal of Medieval and Early Modern Studies* 27 (1997): 317–40 (325–26); Jonathan Good, *The Cult of St George in Medieval England* (Woodbridge: Boydell Press, 2009), 73–75; Andrea Ruddick, *English Identity and Political Culture in the Fourteenth Century* (Cambridge: Cambridge University Press, 2013), loc 9298. See also the mention of the banner of St George at St Albans (Walsingham, *Chronica maiora* 452–453).

45 Antonia Gransden, *Historical Writing in England II: c. 1307 to the Early Sixteenth Century* (Ithaca, NY: Cornell University Press, 1982), Plate V, between 168 and 169. Colour version available at https://en.wikipedia.org/wiki/John_Ball_(priest)#/media/File:John_Ball_encouraging_Wat_Tyler_rebels_from_ca_1470_MS_of_Froissart_Chronicles_in_BL.jpg.

46 Ruddick, *English Identity*, loc 947, 1141, 1147. Cf. David Aers, '*Vox populi* and the Literature of 1381,' in David Wallace (ed.), *The Cambridge History of Medieval English Literature* (Cambridge: Cambridge University Press, 1999), 432–53; John Watts, 'Public or Plebs: The Changing Meaning of "the Commons", 1381–1549,' in Huw Pryce and John Watts (eds.), *Power and Identity in the Middle Ages: Essays in Memory of Rees Davies* (Oxford: Oxford University Press, 2007), 242–60 (249–50).

the time when there would be 'no bishop in England except for one archbishop, namely himself' (*Anon. Chron.* 137). As Wraw was the priest to Westbrom's regional king, so Ball would be to Richard himself.

'Ball's Bastards'

Such readings of a broken social order in contrast with the rebels' idealised alternative may receive further support from one of the teachings often overlooked in more liberal or romantic portrayals of Ball: 'no one,' Ball was said to have preached, 'was fit for the kingdom of God who had not been born in wedlock' (*Docuit eciam neminem aptum regno Dei, qui non in matrimonio natus fuisset*; Walsingham, *Chronica maiora* 544–545). That Ball might have preached what we could call a certain 'moral conservatism' should not be seen as alien to the history of radical thought, and Ball's letter according to Knighton contains a traditional denunciation of the cardinal sins (though curiously, perhaps conveniently, dropping Wrath).[47] But why was this interest in bastards included in Walsingham's summary of Ball's preaching over the years, which is otherwise presented in terms of conventional socio-economic denunciations and reversals? Of course, something seeming out of place now does not mean it did then. It might, however, only seem out of place when not read in context.

In this spirit, Steven Justice has compellingly argued for 'Ball's bastards' as an application of *Piers Plowman* B, Passus 9, where Wit is encountered in the search for 'Dowel.' In B.9.113–123, there is an attack on wrongdoers and those improperly conceived and born outside marriage as epitomised by Cain (Genesis 4) and including, of course, reference to Eve ('Ac fals folke [and] faithlees theues and lieres / Wastoures and wrecches out of wedloke I trowe / Conceyued ben in yuel [var. cursid] tyme as Caym was on Eue'; B.9.121–123). Part of this logic is that bad parentage produces bad children (hence the need for the Flood) and Wit turns again to those born outside marriage at the end of Passus 9 (195–201). Justice also noted that earlier in Wit's speech there is a description of mutual care and the production and perpetuation of a more just social order with just kings and administrators, though also with a critique of how Christians have failed in acting out such a duty. By contrast, the destructive Cains of this world belong outside this system of obligation and social order. Crucially for understanding Ball, Justice pointed out how bishops are blamed with

---

47 Green, 'John Ball's Letters,' in Hanawalt (ed.), *Chaucer's England*, 182.

the ultimate negative comparison to Judas, who consumes the goods of Christ's poor (B.9.92–94).[48]

The context of Walsingham's summary of Ball's preaching complements what we see in *Piers Plowman*—to some degree. This included a suitably chastened priesthood: tithes will not be paid to a priest who earns more than the giver and who is not living a better moral life than the parishioner. When associated with Ball, the connection between bastardy and a lack of order takes on a deadlier edge. *Piers Plowman* may have seen the solution to the situation involving a refined class of bishop, but Langland may not have been happy with the more direct solution that Ball and his supporters proposed, namely killing Sudbury and putting Ball in a position of ecclesiastical pre-eminence. Justice may have been right in arguing that Wit was speaking 'literally, and only, about those born out of wedlock' but that the reading of 'bastards' invites 'metaphorical annexations like Ball's, which reverse the force of the passage by reversing its social passage.'[49] Nevertheless, some qualifications should be added. This understanding of bastards did not necessarily mean that Ball would have abandoned the literal condemnation of those born out of wedlock if he assumed that disorder came from those who abandoned values—indeed peasant values—associated with family and communal support. Moreover, the potential promotion of Ball and the assumptions of benign kingship show that this did not mean the eradication of hierarchies but a restoration of the true order of the world, with peasantry and the lower orders properly represented and given access to power. In other words, to undo some of the damage done after the days when Adam delved and Eve span.

It might, of course, be the case that Walsingham wanted to discredit Ball here, given that Ball's claim about bastards is followed immediately by Walsingham's denunciation of Ball as a follower of Wycliffe. Ball was accused of preaching 'the perverse doctrines of the perfidious John Wyclif as well as the opinions and false ravings which Wyclif held' (*Chronica maiora* 544–545). This is significant because a similar teaching became associated with the Lollard who had connections to Jan Hus: Richard Wyche. In the eighth of fourteen articles recorded in the *Fasciculi Zizaniorum*,[50] Wyche claimed that those born outside of marriage, including the son of

---

48 Justice, *Writing and Rebellion*, 104–11. On roughly contemporary understandings of Cain, see Margaret Aston, *Faith and Fire: Popular and Unpopular Religion: 1350–1600* (London: Hambledon Press, 1993), 95–132.
49 Justice, *Writing and Rebellion*, 108.
50 Walter Waddington Shirley (ed.), *Fasciculi Zizaniorum magistri Johannis Wyclif cum Tritico* (Rolls Series; London: Longman et al., 1858), 376–77. I owe the Wyche parallel to a discussion with Deane Galbraith.

a priest, cannot be saved (*quod filius sacerdotis nec alicujus extra matrimonium natus potest salvari*), citing Wisdom of Solomon 3.16 and St Paul (1 Corinthians 7.12, 14) in support. Wyche added that bastards are inclined to be disorderly and evildoers, the same kind of argument we saw in *Piers Plowman*. Nevertheless, there is a qualification that the son will not always bear the sins of the parents because of grace, while similar anxieties about salvation, grace, and sins of the parents are also discussed in *Piers Plowman* (B.9.140–201). Wyche cited Jesus's mission to the sinners, his saying about tax collectors and prostitutes entering the kingdom of God (Matthew 21.31), and, from the long ending of Mark's Gospel, the claims about whoever believes and is baptised will be saved but the unbeliever will be condemned (Mark 16.16). We can only speculate whether Ball too took this line.

It is possible that Walsingham wanted to discredit Ball as a Lollard by citing the bastard saying. But the occurrence of closely related themes (bastards, disorder, problematic clergy, grace, etc.) in a different-but-related text like *Piers Plowman* suggests that we should be thinking of Ball's teaching as part of broader disaffections taking place at the end of the fourteenth century and beginning of the fifteenth, coming from a range of interconnected ideological perspectives. We do not have to posit a direct Lollard connection to see that this might be a useful parallel for understanding Ball. As James Gairdner observed over a hundred years ago of Wyche's articles: 'some went beyond Wycliffe himself. The strange article about bastards, for instance, looks very like one of the teachings of John Ball.'[51] Indeed, a direct connection between Ball and Wycliffe is unlikely and it looks as if there was an attempt to discredit both Ball and Wycliffe by associating them with each other, as the *Fasciculi Zizaniorum* would do shortly after by inventing a confession from Ball and claiming he attacked transubstantiation (see the next chapter; strikingly *Fasciculi Zizaniorum* does not include anything on Ball and the bastards). There is no evidence that Ball or the rebels were critiquing (for instance) transubstantiation, and we would surely have such a claim in the chroniclers or from someone like Sudbury if this were the case.

Knighton's attempt to connect Ball and Wycliffe indicates the degree of artificiality in presenting Ball as a perverse precursor. So, just as John the Baptist was the precursor to Christ, so Ball was to Wycliffe and thus he [Ball] 'prepared the way for him [Wycliffe] in people's minds, and it is said that he subverted the beliefs of many with his teaching' (*Chron.*

---

51 James Gairdner, *Lollardy and the Reformation in England: An Historical Survey, Volume 1* (London: Macmillan, 1908), 185.

242–243). Moreover, the 'pestiferous contrivings' of this famed precursor made Ball a 'powerful enemy of the Church's unity, a fomenter of discord between clergy and the laity, a tireless disseminator of illicit beliefs, and a disturber of the church of Christians' (*Chron.* 276–277). There is a long history of associating Ball with Wycliffe and the Lollards, but some additional clarificatory comments should help. We should see this period, and the associated socio-economic turmoil, as one which generated a range of overlapping reactions from reformist views in *Piers Plowman* through to the theological innovations of Lollardy. Somewhere among this was Ball's anticlericalism. Certainly, Ball and the Lollards had shared interests, notably a concern (and perhaps a provocative one) to present their theological ideas and biblical interpretation in the English language rather than Latin.[52] While we should be hesitant in suggesting widespread ideological consistency across the uprisings, there was an idea of the rebel commons as the true representatives of England and English identity. But this does not stop Ball and the rebels identifying themselves (and being identified by others) as theological conservatives (or whatever the appropriate label might be) who would not have accepted key features of Lollardy. Thus, thinking or writing about notions of the commons and English identity was something that likewise concerned *Piers Plowman*. Langland's vision was not a Lollard one, but we can read both as part of the social and ideological turmoil of the late fourteenth century. If we understand the context in such general terms, then the more specific occurrence of shared ideas (e.g., bastardy) and interconnected anxieties, from *Piers Plowman* through Ball to Wyche, is unsurprising.

How to Deal with Poisonous Weeds

Unsurprisingly perhaps, the language of doom, judgement, and/or natural disasters could be used to understand and interpret what had happened in the revolt (cf. John Gower, *Vox Clamantis* I.880–936).[53] From the other

---

52 On English, notions of the vernacular, and uses of literacy in relation to the uprising and identity, see, e.g., Justice, *Writing and Rebellion*, 67–75. Cf. Barker, *England, Arise*, loc 6332, on Ball's letters: 'even more important than any overt or covert radical message he intended to convey, is that he chose to write, as he preached, in English: the language of the people. That in itself was sufficient to condemn him in the eyes of the authorities of Church and state as an agent provocateur.'
53 Hilton, *Class Conflict*, 173–74.

side of the uprising, we should also follow those who categorise some of the ideological underpinnings and Ball's teaching as something like 'millenarian', 'eschatological', or 'apocalyptic',[54] if by those often-nebulous terms we mean the expectation of a dramatic transformation of the socio-political order, and even if not as pronounced in terms of end-time schema (as far as we know), as in various medieval counterparts across Europe. Norman Cohn's argument—that the language of a world cleansed of sin, restoration of love, the liberating of truth, and 'now is the time' in Ball's letters picked up on millennial expectations of a final battle between the poor and their satanic oppressors and the restoration of 'the primal egalitarian State of Nature, a second Golden Age'—may have pushed the rhetoric further than the evidence will allow.[55] Nevertheless, and as we have seen with the references to Adam and Eve, the gist of what we have about Ball does suggest at least a soft form of this expectation, even if lacking the hard millennial

---

54 George Kane, 'Some Fourteenth-Century "Political" Poems', in Gregory Kratzmann and James Simpson (eds.), *Medieval English Religious and Ethical Literature: Essays in Honour of G. H. Russell* (Cambridge, 1986), 82–91; Dobson (ed.), *Peasants' Revolt of 1381*, 19–20 ('the insurrection was accompanied by genuinely irrational elements as well as mild millenarian tendencies—hinted at, rather than expressly stated...opens up an extraordinary and sensational world, for which nothing else in the fourteenth century has quite prepared us'); Hilton, *Bond Men Made Free*, 223 ('millenarian hints have been detected in some of Ball's sayings...Hints of apocalyptic expectations in 1381'); Bird, *Rebel before His Time*, 38 ('Millenarian hopes and aspirations were not altogether lacking in England in 1381, and lower clergy like Ball played a large part in proclaiming that the path lay wide open to egalitarian, even a communistic, millenarianism'); Dunn, *Peasants' Revolt*, 79 ('mix of political anger and quasi-millenarian prophecy that suffused the rebels' ideology'). Norman Cohn saw the revolt as initially 'severely practical' in its demands about serfdom and that, in the Mile End demands, 'there is nothing at all to hint at any impending miraculous restoration of an egalitarian State of Nature' (*Pursuit of the Millennium*, 198–99). However, Cohn also noted that this does not rule out 'such phantasy' among insurgents. Indeed, he located his presentation of Ball in the context of the 'phantasy of the egalitarian State of Nature' rethought as a 'dynamic social myth', eschatological vengeance of the poor, the idea of a divinely inspired prophet, cataclysmic violence, and 'a situation in which it must have been easy enough to proclaim and to believe that the path lay wide open to an egalitarian, even a communistic Millennium' (*Pursuit of the Millennium*, 200–204). Note, however, the important qualifications against an overemphasis on apocalyptic or millenarian thinking in Richard Firth Green's analysis of Ball's letters (Green, 'John Ball's Letters', in Hanawalt (ed.), *Chaucer's England*, 182, 186).
55 Cohn, *Pursuit of the Millennium*, 200–203.

overlay, and this characterises the other presentations of his teaching. The emphasis, at least in the evidence we have, is on human activity in bringing about The Great Change rather than supernatural intervention, though it is still human action based on prophecy, scripture, revelation, and divine authority and even guidance. Put another way, what marks the eschatology of Ball is a focus on now being the time to act out the divine plan.

Echoing Galatians 5.1, Ball's Blackheath sermon carried the claim that God 'had now given them the time during which they could put off their long servitude' (Walsingham, *Chronica maiora* 546–557). This talk of the immediacy of the expected transformation is likewise present in the letters of Ball (and others) reported by Knighton. It looks like imagery of (church) bells could be invoked (as they were literally in the rebellion in Cambridge) to denote that the moment had arrived for the rebels to act: 'Ion Balle gretyþ ȝow wele alle and doþ ȝowe to understande, he haþ rungen oure belle' (Knighton, *Chron.* 222).[56] There is also a stress on the time being now in combination with a stress on truth (e.g., 'Iohan Balle, Seynte Marye prist greteȝ wele alle maner men and byddes hem in þe name of þe trinite, fadur, and sone and holy gost, stonde manlyche to gedyr in trewþe, and helpeȝ trewþe, and trewþe schal helpe ȝowe…God do bote, for nowe is tyme. Amen'; Knighton, *Chron.* 224), which includes the invocation of Mary ('Now is tyme lady helpe to Iesu þi sone…'; Knighton, *Chron.* 222). The close linguistic echoes of Johannine (realised) eschatology (e.g., John 4.23; 5.25; 8.31–32) in the letters further support the idea that we are dealing with a soft eschatological take on social transformation. To give some indication (and this is not to suggest a Lollard connection), we might compare the translation of one such Johannine passage in the Wycliffe New Testament which likewise repeats ideas of truth, time, and God the Father: 'But the tyme is comun, and now it is, whanne trewe worschiperis schulen worschipe the fadir in spirit and treuthe; for also the fadir sekith suche, that worschipen hym' (John 4.23).[57]

Walsingham's presentation of the Blackheath sermon has Ball expressing these eschatological sentiments and using the implicit tension between

---

56 Thomas Pettitt, '"Here Comes I, Jack Straw": English Folk Drama and Social Revolt,' *Folklore* 95 (1984): 3–20 (6–7). Cf. Fagan and Hilton, *English Rising of 1381*, 100–103.

57 Green, 'John Ball's Letters,' in Hanawalt (ed.), *Chaucer's England*, 186–87, notes Ecclesiastes 3.7–8 as the biblical allusion and as a counter to Cohn's obvious overemphasis on millenarianism. That readers or listeners could have picked up on this allusion is, of course, possible, but the combination of 'time' and 'truth' and the immediacy of the moment would suggest the Johannine passages as a more obvious point of reference for what Green called a 'rallying cry.'

(on the one hand) when the hour had come in the dramatic, miraculous emancipatory moment and (on the other), the mundane, disciplined, and patient organisation that would become an ongoing revolutionary theme perhaps even reflected in Ball's letters:[58]

> Continuing the sermon he had begun, he endeavoured, through the words of this saying which he had taken as his text, to introduce and prove the notion that all men were by nature created equal from the beginning, and that servitude had been brought in wrongly by the unjust oppression of human beings, contrary to the will of God; that if God had intended that men should be made serfs, he would certainly have established it at the beginning of the world who was to be a serf, and who a master. Let them therefore realize that God had now given them the time during which they could put off the yoke of their long servitude, if they wished, and rejoice in the liberty they had long desired. He therefore urged them to be men of courage, and out of love for their virtuous fathers who had tilled their land, and pulled up and cut down the noxious weeds which usually choke the crops, to make haste themselves at that present time to do the same (*Quapropter monuit ut essent uiri cordati, et amore boni patrisfamilias excolentis agrum suum, et extirpantis ac resecantis noxia gramina que fruges solent opprimere, et ipsi in presenti facere festinarent*). They must do this first, by killing the most powerful lords of the realm, then by slaying the lawyers, justiciars, and jurors of the land, and finally, by weeding out from their land any that they knew would in the future be harmful to the commonwealth. Thus they would in the end gain peace for themselves and security for the future, if after removing the magnates, there was equal freedom between them, and they each enjoyed the same nobility, equal dignity, and similar power. (*Chronica maiora* 546–547)

Justice notes that this is 'hardly an exceptional simile for a rural audience' and points to the application of similar language in *Piers Plowman*, while Aston looked to a context in Corpus Christi.[59] While not wanting to downplay the importance of such parallels, we should not lose sight of an allusion to the Parable of the Wheat and the Tares in Matthew 13.24–30,

---

58 See, e.g., Green, 'John Ball's Letters,' in Hanawalt (ed.), *Chaucer's England*, 183, 190, for the suggestion that Ball's injunction to 'chastise wel Hobbe þe robbere' (Walsingham) and 'lokke þat Hobbe robbyoure be wele chastysede for lesyng of ȝoure grace' (Iakke Carter in Knighton) might be read in light of the emphasis on discipline among the rebels (e.g., Knighton, *Chron.* 222; Walsingham, *Chronica maiora* 416–419; *Westminster Chron.* 4–5).

59 Justice, *Writing and Rebellion*, 110–11; Aston, 'Corpus Christi and Corpus Regni,' 18–20.

36–43.⁶⁰ The parable talks about an enemy sowing weeds among the good seed and sorting and destroying the good weeds from the bad. The explanation in Matthew is that the Son of Man sows the good seed, and the good seed represents the children of the kingdom. Similarly, the devil sows the bad, and the weeds are the children of the devil. Fittingly, the parable has an eschatological conclusion whereby the harvesting is the end of age and the angels will throw out causes of sin and the evildoers.

The similarities between the parable and the theology attributed to Ball ought to be obvious enough, including some shared language in the Vulgate (e.g., *patris familias* in Matthew 13.27). The idea of tares or bad weeds (*noxia gramina*) in Walsingham's presentation of Ball echoes the language of heresy in late medieval England. Indeed, as Aston noted elsewhere, Cain was associated with the heretical weeds of Matthew 13.⁶¹ It is possible, even likely, that Ball, or at least some from his audience or earliest interpreters, could have connected the weeds with Ball's understandings of bishops as bastards that we saw above likewise connected with Cain. But as we have also seen, the language weeding out heresy was used to attack Ball himself (Knighton, *Chron*. 210–211). We have already seen this in the *Fasciculi Zizaniorum*, the Carmelite collection from the end of the fourteenth and beginning of the fifteenth centuries concerning Wycliffe and Lollardy. As the title implies (and its introduction makes clear), heretical teaching is framed in terms of Matthew 13.24–30, 36–43, but using the distinctive term for poisonous weeds found in the Vulgate and Greek versions of the Matthean parable (*zizania*; ζιζάνια). It also seems that this was the very parable Ball used to attack those harmful to the community with his own socio-economic take on heresy coloured by the ideology that fed into the revolt. It is tempting to see Ball as directly responding to Sudbury's attack on Ball's authority and the allegation that he had 'sown errors and schisms' (see above) but we can at least claim that the language associated with Matthew 13.24–30, 36–43, was a shared one where 'heresy' was a matter of perspective. Ball's concern for weeding was obviously a violent one, probably with eschatological overtones, while claiming divine authority. In one sense, it was a kind of mirror image of, and a challenge to, Sudbury's own claims of divine authority to excommunicate.

60 Cf. Cohn, *Pursuit of the Millennium*, 199, 203–4.
61 Aston, *Faith and Fire*, 96; Aziz, 'Of Grace and Gross Bodies,' 34–36.

All Things in Common

In this presentation of John Ball, egalitarianism—or at least equal access to rank and power—as the goal of this transformation was linked in with an allusion to Acts 2.44–45 and 4.32–35 and ideas about communally shared possessions and distribution according to need in the earliest church. According to Froissart, Ball had preached that things were 'not well to pass in England, nor shall do till everything be common' (*que li bien iront tout de commun*) with no serfdom, no greater lords, and no exploitation of peasant labour because 'all come from one father and one mother, Adam and Eve' (Froissart, *Chroniques* 10.96). There is a hint of such preaching on communal sharing in the *Anonimalle Chronicle*, which claimed that Ball believed that 'no religious house should hold more than two monks or canons, and their possessions should be divided among the laity (*et qe lour possessiones deveroient estre departie entre les laiez gentz*)' (Anon. Chron. 137–138).

Allusions to Acts 2.44–45 and 4.32–35 become clearer when we compare this with the accepted translation of the Bible, the Latin Vulgate. I again give the Wycliffe translation of the Vulgate merely to show how such sentiments might have been consistently expressed (and contextualised) in English:

> 44 Omnes etiam qui credebant erant pariter et habebant omnia communia 45 possessiones et subtantias vendebant et dividebant illa omnibus prout cuique opus erat (Acts 2.44–45, Vulgate)

> 44 And alle that bileueden weren togidre, and hadden alle thingis comyn. 45 Thei selden possessiouns and catel, and departiden tho thingis to alle men, as it was nede to ech. (Acts 2.44–45)

--

> 32 multitudinis autem credentium erat cor et anima una nec quisquam eorum quae possidebant aliquid suum esse dicebat sed erant illis omnia communia 33 et virtute magna reddebant apostoli testimonium resurrectionis Iesu Christi Domini et gratia magna erat in omnibus illis 34 neque enim quisquam egens erat inter illos quotquot enim possessores agrorum aut domorum erant vendentes adferebant pretia eorum quae vendebant 35 et ponebant ante pedes apostolorum dividebantur autem singulis prout cuique opus erat (Acts 4.32–35)

> 32 And of al the multitude of men bileuynge was oon herte and oon wille; nether ony man seide ony thingis of tho thingis that he weldide to be his

owne, but alle thingis weren comyn to hem. 33 And with greet vertu the apostlis yeldiden witnessyng of the ayenrysyng of Jhesu Crist oure Lord, and greet grace was in alle hem. 34 For nether ony nedi man was among hem, for how manye euere weren possessouris of feeldis, ether of housis, thei seelden, and brouyten the pricis of tho thingis that thei seelden, 35 and leiden bifor the feet of the apostlis. And it was departid to ech, as it was nede to ech. (Acts 4.32–35)

Thinking about all things in common—and the kinds of interest groups involved in making such claims and classifications of who gets to share, including and beyond monasticism—was not new. Such ideas were also being discussed in texts more-or-less contemporary with the uprising. *Piers Plowman* presents a concern that friars are said to head to the universities, learn about philosophy, 'And preche men of Plato and preue it by Seneca/ Þat alle þinges vnder heuene ou3te to ben in commune' (B.20.276). Shortly before the revolt, Wycliffe himself, and in dialogue with the philosophical tradition and ideas about the early church and Acts (*De civili dominio* I.14; cf. III.77–81), reflected on such issues and made the theoretical argument that because everyone ought to be in a state of grace and thus be lords over the world, all the goods of God ought to be in common (*omnia bona Dei debent esse communia...deberent habere omnia in communi...omnia debent esse communia*), even if realities were inevitably not like this. We should not make a strict identification of the rebels with Wycliffe and the Lollards in this instance. Wycliffe emphasised that the righteous, in a state of grace, held legitimate authority and, conversely, those in mortal sin had no right to make such claims—and this could include anyone in the clerical hierarchy.[62] This might sound like the concerns of the rebels, but we should recall that Wycliffe was located in high political struggles and was allied with John of Gaunt for whom such anticlerical ideas were found to be useful in countering ecclesiastical power. Another reason for not making a strict connection between the rebels and Wycliffe is because related sentiments (or fears), including myths of peasant freedom lost and a more egalitarian early church, had long been noted, discussed, and disseminated, and could be (re)contextualised accordingly in times of dramatic social

---

62 For summaries of ideas about 'all things in common' in context, see, e.g., Stephen A. Barney, *The Penn Commentary on Piers Plowman, Volume 5: C Passus 20–22; B Passus 18–20* (Philadelphia: University of Pennsylvania Press, 2006), 234–36; Elemér Boreczky, *John Wyclif's Discourse On Dominion in Community* (Leiden: Brill, 2008); Ethan Campbell, *The Gawain-Poet and the Fourteenth-Century English Anticlerical Tradition* (Kalamazoo: Western Michigan University, 2018), 47–50.

upheaval.[63] Norman Cohn's assessment may have been a touch flamboyant but the basic point about how such language can be reapplied according to socio-economic context is well taken: 'when abstracted from their scholastic context and stripped of their qualifying clauses those same comments were barely distinguishable from the mystical anarchism of the Free Spirit' and among those who congregated at Oxford would have been those 'who snatched at such ideas and scattered them abroad, simplified them into propagandist slogans.'[64]

What might it have meant in practice for the insurgents to hold things in common? From what we have already seen, it would obviously have been connected with liberty from serfdom and equality as well as access to resources of the land like a lord, noble, or advisor, even if peasant or certain social hierarchies were to remain and even if rebels were to take on roles of archbishop or even nobles and advisors.[65] In Knighton's account of the meeting between Tyler and Richard at Smithfield, the rebels' petition was that 'all game, whether in waters or in parks and woods should become common to all (*communes fierent omnibus*), so that everywhere in the realm, in rivers and fishponds, and woods and forests, they might take the wild beasts, and hunt the hare in the fields, and do many other

---

63 A. L. Morton, *A People's History of England* (London: Victor Gollancz, 1938), 99; Cohn, *Pursuit of the Millennium*, 200–201; Hilton, *Bond Men Made Free*, xxv–xxvi, 63–134, 211–13, 221–24, 227–29; Rosamond Faith, 'The "Great Rumour" of 1377 and Peasant Ideology', in Rodney Hilton and Trevor H. Aston (ed.), *The English Rising of 1381* (Cambridge: Cambridge University Press, 1984), 43–73; Hilton, *Class Conflict*, 49–65, 79–91, 143–53; Christopher Dyer, 'Memories of Freedom: Attitudes towards Serfdom in England, 1200–1350', in M. L. Bush (ed.), *Serfdom and Slavery: Studies in Legal Bondage* (Abingdon: Taylor & Francis, 1996), 277–95; Aziz, 'Of Grace and Gross Bodies', 20–21. On backgrounds to Ball's letters, see Green, 'John Ball's Letters', in Hanawalt (ed.), *Chaucer's England*. Cohn, *Pursuit of the Millennium*, 200–201.
64 Cohn, *Pursuit of the Millennium*, 201.
65 Claire Valente, *The Theory and Practice of Revolt in Medieval England* (London: Routledge, 2003), 169–70. Cf. Froissart, *Chroniques* 10.118 and *Anon. Chron.* 147–48. Hilton overstated his case, but his general take on Ball's vision of an alternative society remains important: 'In spite of Froissart's version of John Ball's sermon, it is unlikely that it was believed that all things should be held in common. A regime of family ownership of peasant holdings and artisan workshops, with large scale landed property of the church and the aristocracy divided among the peasants, was probably envisaged' (Hilton, *Bond Men Made Free*, 229). Cf. Oman, *Great Revolt*, 52: 'It is notable that Ball is made to preach democracy and not communism—the insurgents wanted to become freeholders, not to form phalansteries and hold all things in common.'

such things without restraint' (*Chron.* 218–219).⁶⁶ Another indication of an immediate understanding of the application of the biblical texts is a type of 'anticlerical' version of distribution according to need in the Acts passages. Ball was said to have instructed people 'that tithes ought not to be paid to an incumbent unless he who should give them were richer than the rector or vicar who was to receive it,' while then adding 'that tithes or oblations should be withdrawn from curates if it was an accepted fact that the subject or the parishioner lived a better life than his priest' (Walsingham, *Chronica maiora* 544–545).

Summarising Ball

Whatever we may or may not think about the possibilities of the historical Ball, what we still have are the earliest portrayals of Ball which would be in place to be taken up, developed, or ignored in the history of reception. Ball was a priest who was in York but became associated with Colchester. He was regularly in trouble with secular and church authorities for his preaching against the lords and church hierarchy, for which he would experience excommunications and imprisonments. He was especially remembered for his ongoing disputes with Simon Sudbury, who would become archbishop of Canterbury and one of the most prominent targets in the 1381 uprising. Ball became a popular wandering priest who preached in streets, markets, cemeteries, and open fields, and whose preaching would be understood (by the chroniclers at least) as part of the ideological underpinnings of the revolt, notably in the south east. During the revolt he claimed that Adam and Eve as workers pointed to a time when there was no serfdom, and that serfdom was implemented as a means of social control. As an alternative to the current hierarchies, Ball pointed to a just and fair social order with himself as the head of the church in England alongside the just king, and with priests in no position to exploit those poorer through tithing. This new order would provide proper representation for those who worked the land and would give access to all the fruits of the land as they would

66 What Christopher Given-Wilson, *Chronicles: The Writing of History in Medieval England* (London: Hambledon, 2004), 197–98, noted of similar demands made at St Albans may apply here, namely that this 'is a very different image of the rebels' motivations from that presented in most of the chronicles, and it is not impossible that it is, for most of those who participated in it, a rather truer picture of the reasons why they did so.'

have all such things in common. To make way for a new order, the current 'bastards' in the church hierarchy and corrupt advisors would have to be weeded out and even killed. Ball stressed the importance of human action in the revolutionary divine plan with 1381 finally the time to act. Little wonder that the chroniclers were hostile towards someone clearly seen as such a seditious and heretical threat. It was not too difficult to make the connection to other figures deemed heretical, most obviously Wycliffe. For those who saw him as a poisonous heretic and dangerous insurgent, Ball epitomised the world gone very wrong.

3
Exit Ball: Late Medieval Receptions

Quite how influential Ball and Ball's letters were on the 1381 uprising is difficult to know partly because of our main sources—the chroniclers wanted to ensure that Ball was to be understood as the driving force behind the revolt and social disharmony. As we saw, Walsingham and Knighton used the revolt to associate Ball with Wycliffe, discredit both, and place both at the ideological heart of the revolt (Walsingham, *Chronica maiora* 544–545; Knighton, *Chron.* 242–243, 276–277). According to Walsingham, Ball's heresy had a wide-ranging influence through his alluring sermons which encouraged evildoing and the delusion that Ball should be archbishop and chancellor while the present archbishop should be beheaded (*Chronica maiora* 546–549). The *Westminster Chronicle* has Ball 'a priest in every respect unworthy of the priestly style,' preaching 'up and down the towns of England doctrines peculiarly designed to incite the masses into joining the conspiracy' (*Westminster Chron.* 14–15; cf. 28–29). For the *Anonimalle Chronicle*, 'Sir John Balle' (*sire Johan Balle*), the 'chaplain of evil disposition,' was similarly the adviser behind the violent actions against the leading lords and clergy and was likewise interested in becoming the sole archbishop (*Anon. Chron.* 137, 140). One of the great twists in the reception history of the celebration of Ball is that some of the teachings attributed to Ball were presumably meant to discredit him. For Froissart, Ball the 'foolish priest' was still the same Ball who believed, ominously, that things will not go well in England until all things are held in common. This Ball was of the same opinion as the common people who held the similarly problematic view that in the beginning of time there were no serfs and therefore none should be bound nor treated like beasts and they should instead be remunerated accordingly for their labour. Indeed, such was Ball's malign influence on the people and his ongoing errors that Froissart concluded that it would have been much better had Ball been 'condemned to perpetual prison or else to have died' (*Chroniques* 10.94–97).[1]

---

1 As Dobson (ed.), *Peasants' Revolt of 1381*, 369, put it, 'the famous sermon which Froissart put into the mouth of John Ball has had an effect on his modern readers quite the opposite of what the author can have intended.'

Nevertheless, that Ball at first provided some inspiration for like-minded rebels also seems clear enough. The 'vagabond' John Shirle of Nottinghamshire was accused of publicly endorsing Ball in a Bridge Street tavern, Cambridge, on the day after his execution. Shirle was alleged to have said,

> that the stewards of the lord the king as well as the justices and many other officers and ministers of the king were more deserving to be drawn and hanged and to suffer other lawful pains and torments than John Balle, chaplain, a traitor and felon lawfully convicted. For Shirle said that he [Ball] had been condemned to death falsely, unjustly and for envy by the said ministers with the king's assent, because he was a true and worthy man, prophesying things useful to the commons of the kingdom and telling of wrongs and oppressions done to the people by the king and aforesaid ministers; and Ball's death would not go unpunished but within a short space of time he would well reward the king and his said ministers and officers.[2]

Shirle was duly hanged. Whatever Shirle did or did not say, Ball's popularity presumably did not entirely vanish overnight. But while there may be hints of familiarity and sympathy with the rebels, and while related sentiments were never likely to disappear entirely, these are not the voices that have any prominence in the early histories.[3] Whatever was happening on the ground, it was the negative portrayal associated first with the chroniclers that became standard for the next four centuries and, whether in agreement or disagreement, the frameworks they provided have been influential right up to the present day.

---

2 Translation from Dobson (ed.), *Peasants' Revolt of 1381*, xxviii–xxix, from JUST 1/103 m. 5. See also Edgar Powell, *The Rising in East Anglia in 1381* (Cambridge: University Press, 1896), 54–55; 'The City of Cambridge: Medieval History,' in Roach (ed.), *A History of the County of Cambridge and the Isle of Ely*, 2–15; Dobson, 'Remembering the Peasants' Revolt,' in Liddell and Wood (eds.), *Essex and the Great Revolt of 1381*, 1–20 (2–4).

3 Dobson (ed.), *Peasants' Revolt of 1381*, 383–85; Dobson, 'Remembering the Peasants' Revolt,' in Liddell and Wood (eds.), *Essex and the Great Revolt of 1381*, 4–7; I. M. W. Harvey, 'Was There Popular Politics in Fifteenth-Century England?,' in Richard H. Britnell and A. J. Pollard (eds.), *The McFarlane Legacy: Studies in Late Medieval Politics and Society* (New York: St Martin's Press, 1995), 155–74 (168).

An Ongoing Problem

That the first chroniclers of the 1381 uprising framed the revolt to suit given agendas and interests is an obvious but nonetheless important point and one that has long been observed. The revolt certainly provided an occasion for such writers to take note of the common people but did so by discrediting and delegitimising the insurgents, whether in popular comparison between them and animals, attributing devilish qualities to them, or portraying them as a wild mob (despite the indications of internal discipline) bent on a perverse reversal of normality. As well as providing explanations for the uprisings familiar to the modern historian (e.g., heavy and heavy-handed taxation, economic changes), explanations associated with divine providence and theological accounts of human behaviour were also given, such as Walsingham's claims involving punishment for sin and a negligent clergy, as well as his penchant for moralising. This was part of an agenda to show that there was a breakdown in social order both from above and below as some social actors did not fulfil their assumed duties.[4]

Other early chroniclers also joined in. The theme of chaos—epitomised by failure of governance combined with the wickedness of Ball—was likewise taken up in a version of events written at the end of the fourteenth century in the *Vita Ricardi*. This retelling mentions heavy and cruel taxation associated with greedy, corrupt, and impious advisors to the king, alongside a crazed and destructive rebellion led by detestable criminals. The slightly confused list of leaders has in its background Ball's letters, including the code name for Ball himself (*Iohon Schep*): 'Jack Shep (*Jak Schep*), John Wraw, Thomas Myllar, Wat Tyler, Hobbe Carter and Jack Straw.' Amidst the chaos was 'a certain chaplain, John Ball, one of Wycliffe's disciples it was said' (*nomine Iohannes Balle, unus, ut dicebatur, de Iohannis Wyclyf discipulus*). Ball is presented in familiar terms as one who preached in many places, was the preferred choice as archbishop of Canterbury, and

---

4 For discussion of these issues, see, e.g., Antonia Gransden, *Historical Writing in England II: c. 1307 to the Early Sixteenth Century* (Ithaca, NY: Cornell University Press, 1982), 130–34, 150–52, 166–71; Derek Pearsall, 'Interpretative Models for the Peasants' Revolt,' in Patrick J. Gallacher and Helen Damico (eds.), *Hermeneutics and Medieval Culture* (Albany: State University Press of New York, 1989), 63–70; Strohm, *Hochon's Arrow*, 33–56; Andrew Prescott, 'Writing about Rebellion: Using the Records about the Peasants' Revolt of 1381,' *History Workshop Journal* 45 (1998), 1–27 (1–6); Christopher Given-Wilson, *Chronicles: The Writing of History in Medieval England* (London: Bloomsbury, 2004), 63, 194–98.

sought no privileges when sentenced to death because he despised the king. Most pertinently, Ball was said to have incited the people to rebel because through this they could gain salvation of their souls.[5]

The idea that Ball was to be associated with Wycliffe was found to be convenient. The short *Kirkstall Abbey Chronicle*, dating from the early fifteenth century, simply claimed that Ball belonged to the Lollards.[6] The connection with sedition likewise continued. In the continuation of the *Polychronicon* of Ranulf Higden (d. 1364) in the Harley MS 2261, we are told about the arrest in Coventry (followed by execution) of 'a preste, Syr lohn Balle, disciple of maister lohn Wyclif,' who had persuaded people to side with 'insurreccions, seyenge that thei scholde rejoice hevyn þerby open in his predicacions.'[7] Most dramatic is Ball's appearance in the *Fasciculi Zizaniorum magistri Johannis Wyclif cum Tritico*.[8] As the title implies (and the introduction makes clear), heretical teaching associated with Wycliffe is framed in terms of the tares in Matthew 13.24–30, 36–43 (Latin: *zizania*; Greek: ζιζάνια), the very parable Ball himself was said to have used to attack those deemed harmful to the community (see Chapter 2). In the *Fasciculi Zizaniorum*, it is claimed that Wycliffe's preaching would provoke another uprising against both the lords and the church, particularly because of a 'beloved follower of Wycliffe, a priest named John Balle' (*Et praecipue cum [esset] dilectus sequax Wycclyff sacerdos dominus Johannes Balle*). The story of Ball's imprisonments for 'heresies that he preached' (*haereses quas praedicavit*), his deliverance from prison, his preaching during the revolt, his incitement to kill Simon Sudbury, assorted turmoil under his leadership, and his trial and death in St Albans are recounted. But an account of Ball's confession adds something doctrinally new to the legend. Here it

---

5   George B. Stow, Jr. (ed.), *Historia Vitae et Regni Ricardi Secundi* (Philadelphia: University of Pennsylvania Press, 1977), 61–72. The English translation is taken from Alison K. McHardy (ed.), *The Reign of Richard II: From Minority to Tyranny 1377–97* (Manchester: Manchester University Press, 2012), 65–71.
6   John Taylor (ed.), *The Kirkstall Abbey Chronicles* (Leeds: Thoresby Society, 1952), 65.
7   Quoted from Joseph Rawson Lumby (ed.), *Polychronicon Ranulphi Higden maonachi Cestrensis: together with the English translations of John Trevisa and of an unknown writer of the fifteenth century, Vol. VIII* (London: Longman & Co, 1882), 459.
8   Shirley (ed.), *Fasciculi Zizaniorum magistri Johannis Wyclif cum Tritico*, 272–74. A translation of the Ball passage is given in Dobson, *Peasants' Revolt of 1381*, 376–78. For further details, see James Crompton, 'Fasciculi Zizaniorum I,' *Journal of Ecclesiastical History* 12 (1961): 35–45, and 'Fasciculi Zizaniorum II,' *Journal of Ecclesiastical History* 12 (1961): 155–66.

is claimed Ball confessed that he had been a disciple of Wycliffe and that he learned from his 'heresies', including openly preaching the 'heresy concerning the sacrament of the altar' (*haeresim de sacramento altaris*), that is, against transubstantiation. Somewhat conveniently, Ball is said to have named Nicholas Hereford, John Aston, and Lawrence Bedenam as part of a select Wycliffite clique who, if they had not encountered resistance, would have destroyed the realm within two years.

Such framings of the revolt went beyond the early chroniclers. John Gower's Ovidian poem/dream vision about the events shortly after the revolt has the rebels portrayed as feral beasts. What is now called *Visio Anglie* was attached to Gower's *Vox Clamantis* and presented the common theme in the early receptions of the revolt: the need to address the failure of governance and morality and the accompanying apocalyptic breakdown of the natural order of the world.[9] What we also get in *Visio* 793–794 is a scathing assessment of an incendiary Ball as the intellectual of the revolt, adding: 'The prophet Ball teaches them: a malicious spirit had previously taught him, and he then constituted their deepest learning' (*Balle propheta docet, quem spiritus ante malignus / Edocuit que sua tunc fuit alta scola*).[10] Such framings of Ball are perhaps no surprise, and similar arguments certainly remained influential in later centuries. But one striking thing happened in a number of prominent fifteenth-century accounts of the revolt: Ball almost vanished before his return to the mainstream in Tudor England. This rest of this chapter will look at why this was and why different emphases concerning Ball could re-emerge in Tudor and Reformation England. But to do this we need to look at the absence of Ball in major histories and the different Ball-free portrayals of the uprisings.

---

9 See, e.g., Cornelius, 'Gower and the Peasants' Revolt', 28, 41–44. On the closeness of Gower to the action, see now Michael Bennett, 'John Gower, Squire of Kent, the Peasants' Revolt, and the *Visio Anglie*', *The Chaucer Review* 53 (2018): 258–82.

10 The prose translation is from Eric W. Stockton (ed.), *The Major Latin Works of John Gower: The Voice of One Crying, and The Tripartite Chronicle* (Seattle: University of Washington Press, 1962), 67. The verse translation by A. G. Rigg in David R. Carlson (ed.), *John Gower: Poems on Contemporary Events: The Visio Anglie (1381) and Cronica tripertita (1400)* (Oxford: Bodleian Library, 2011), 83, reads: 'Ball was the preacher, the prophet and teacher, inspired by a spirit of hell,/And every fool was advanced in his school, to be taught as the devil thought well.'

The Disappearing and Reappearing Ball

The most popular history in the fifteenth century was the influential *Brut* chronicle.[11] The Middle English *Brut* referred to the poll tax as bringing about 'grete myschiff and moche deseȝe to alle communialte of þe Reme' and when the commons rose up, they too 'dede moche harm.'[12] The *Brut* famously referred to the uprising under Jack Straw and Tyler as the 'hurlyng tyme,' a phrase also used by others (e.g., *Short English Chronicle*, Richard Fox, Caxton's *Polychronicon*, Fabyan, Holinshed).[13] As Andrew Prescott argued, this phrase (referring to a rough football game), along with other designations (e.g., the 'rumour,' 'rifling'), recalled the 'carnivalesque revelry' of the revolt and was used to 'denigrate the rebels,' not least for town chroniclers to distance cities like London and Norwich from such memories.[14] The idea of a world turned on its head was presented in different ways in the anonymous *Continuatio Eulogii*, an early fifteenth-century continuation (from 1364 to 1413) of the *Eulogium Historiarum*.[15] Such was the chaos on the ground during the uprising that, even in this relatively tame retelling, there were claims that a respected herald-at-arms said that he had seen a

---

11 On the complex history of the development, languages, translation, and collection of histories making up the *Brut*, as well as the popularity of *Brut* based on its manuscript dissemination, social backgrounds of owners, and dominant use as a source, see Lister M. Matheson, *The Prose* Brut: *The Development of a Middle English Chronicle* (Tempe, AZ: Medieval & Renaissance Texts & Studies, 1998), 56. Matheson added, 'It is clear that it occupied a central position in fifteenth- and sixteenth-century historical writing and was a major influence in shaping national consciousness in medieval and post-medieval England' (9). See also Gransden, *Historical Writing in England II*, 221–27; William Marx, 'Peculiar Versions of the Middle English Prose Brut and Textual Archaeology,' in Jaclyn Rajsic, Erik Kooper, and Dominique Hoche (eds.), *The Prose* Brut *and Other Late Medieval Chronicles: Books Have Their Histories. Essays in Honour of Lister M. Matheson* (Woodbridge: Boydell & Brewer, 2016), 94–104.
12 *Brut* quotations taken from Friedrich W. D. Brie (ed.), *The Brut or The Chronicles of England* (2 vols.; London: Kegan Paul, Trench, Trübner, and Co, 1906–1908).
13 On Fox's text, see Matheson, 'The Peasants' Revolt through Five Centuries of Rumor and Reporting,' 127–28.
14 Prescott, 'Great and Horrible Rumour,' in Firnhaber-Baker and Schoenaers (eds.), *Routledge History Handbook of Medieval Revolt*, 78–79.
15 For a recent discussion of issues relating to provenance, dating, etc., see Christopher Given-Wilson (ed.), *Continuatio Eulogii: The Continuation of the Eulogium Historiarum, 1364–1413* (Clarendon: Oxford, 2019), xi–liii. Quotations are also taken from this critical edition.

hundred thousand men, among them 'several demons' (*plures demones*). A gruesomely comedic element to the subversion of order was added to the death of Tyler, where some people were reported to have declared that he was being knighted (*Continuatio Eulogii*, 37–43).

Though fiercely critical of the young Richard's advisers and what they were able to inflict on the realm because of his tender years, Adam Usk— the Welsh chronicler (among other things) writing in Latin at the beginning of the fifteenth century—could simultaneously talk about how from this occurred that monstrous act (*unde illud accidit monstruosum*) of the commons under the leadership of the wretched Jack Straw (*sub misero duce Jac Straw*). In this example of history-as-moral-teaching, it took the intervention of God and William Walworth to restore order to the realm.[16] Here, as with various retellings of the uprising, Jack Straw took on the role otherwise attributed to Tyler (see also, e.g., *Great Chronicle of London*). Nevertheless, Tyler still received similar treatment in such moralising readings of history. This 'duke' of the commons was a 'proude knaue and malapert' and a 'sedicious man,' according to John Capgrave's *Abbreviation of Chronicles* finished around 1463.[17] Hand-in-hand with the denigration of the rebels like Tyler or Jack Straw was the ongoing praise for Walworth. According to the more popular second version of the rhyming chronicle by John Hardyng (written by the end of 1460; the first version is from 1457):

> Afore Iake Strawe, ye kyng thē stode hodlesse
> Of which Walworth, the Mayre of Londō trewe
> Areasoned hym then, of his greate lewdenesse
> With a dagger, in Smythfelde then hym slewe
> The citezens, with hym then strongly drewe
> And slewe theim downe, and put theim to flight
> And brought the kyng, into the citee right.
>
> The cōmons brent the Sauoye, a place fayre
> For eiuill wyll they had vnto duke Iohn
> Wherfore he fled northwarde in great dispayre

---

16 From Christopher Given-Wilson (ed.), *The Chronicle of Adam Usk 1377–1421* (Oxford: Oxford University Press, 1997). On divine providence, the breakdown of order, morality and example, the rhetorical blaming of the nobles, and the ambiguities of competence involved in Richard's youth, see, e.g., Given-Wilson's 'Introduction,' in *Chronicle of Adam Usk*, xiii–xciii (lxiv–lxxxvi); Steven Justice, *Adam Usk's Secret* (Philadelphia: University of Pennsylvania Press, 2015), 74–75, 80–81.

17 Peter J. Lucas (ed.), *John Capgrave's Abbreuiacion of Cronicles* (Oxford: Oxford University Press, 1983), 185–86.

Into Scotlande, for socoure had he none
In Englande then, to whō he durste make moone
And there abode, tyll commons all were ceased
In England hole, and all the lande well peased.[18]

As with Adam Usk, Hardyng reflected a familiar theme of proper governance. As Sarah Peverley has shown, running throughout Hardyng's work is a theme of how monarchs and advisers provide good and bad examples of kingship and governance—and examples of how to deal with problematic rebellions—for the benefit of future governors. For a reign to work it needed the collective support of the commons and governors, with subjects united behind a common cause but with one eye constantly on what happens in the case of societal breakdown. And, of course, one relevant aspect of this theme is how wise advisors are needed for a young king to succeed.[19] There is something of this theme in Hardyng's framing of the beginning of Richard's reign. In a Latin gloss on the first version of his chronicle (6.2485m) taken from John Gower's *Cronica tripertita*, we read about a declining Fortune when, 'from its source in the king, a transgression of the law arose,' and the people revolted because of his misrule. The king accepted the 'childish and vile counsel of the foolish and decreed that the counsel of the aged was to be rejected.'[20]

---

18 Quoted here from the second version in Henry Ellis's edition of John Hardyng, *The chronicle of Iohn Hardyng: containing an account of public transactions from the earliest period of English history to the beginning of the reign of King Edward the Fourth, together with the continuation by Richard Grafton, to the thirty fourth year of King Henry the Eighth: the former part collated with two manuscripts of the author's own time, the last, with Grafton's duplicate edition: to which are added a biographical and literary preface, and an index by Henry Ellis* (London: F.C. and J. Rivington, 1812). The first version is from British Library MS Lansdowne 204 and is being completed by James Simpson and Sarah Peverley. See James Simpson and Sarah Peverley (eds.), *John Hardyng, Chronicle: Edited from British Library MS Lansdowne 204. Volume 1* (Kalamazoo, MI: Medieval Institute Publications, 2015) and James Simpson and Sarah Peverley (eds.), *John Hardyng, Chronicle: Edited from British Library MS Lansdowne 204. Volume 2* (Kalamazoo, MI: Medieval Institute Publications, forthcoming).

19 Sarah L. Peverley, 'Dynasty and Division: The Depiction of King and Kingdom in John Hardyng's Chronicle,' in Erik Kooper (ed.), *The Medieval Chronicle III: Proceedings of the 3rd International Conference on the Medieval Chronicle (Doorn/Utrecht 12–17 July 2002)* (Amsterdam: Rodopi, 2004), 149–70.

20 Translation is from Simpson and Peverley (eds.), *John Hardyng, Chronicle. Volume 2*. I am grateful to Sarah Peverley for providing me with access to this

With the arrival of movable type in England towards the end of the fifteenth century, there was potential for even greater dissemination and development of chronicles and histories old and new,[21] which included, of course, clichés about the revolt. William Caxton's famous printing press led to a published version of the already popular prose *Brut* (1480, 1482) and the translation of Ranulf Higden's *Polychronicon* (1482), with a continuation including the uprising and familiar accompanying comments (the commons 'dyde moche harme, and it was callyd the hurlyng tyme').[22] The English version in the Harley MS 2261 also contains a list of leaders with names mentioned in Ball's letters, including Ball's pseudonym ('Iak Shepe, Iohn Wrawe, Thomas Mellor, Watte Tyler, Hobbe Carter, and Iacke Strawe'), but with no direct mention of Ball in relation to the list itself, a move that was made elsewhere.[23] The discussion of the 'hurlynge tyme' in Robert Fabyan's chronicle (first published posthumously in 1516, following his death in 1512) includes an assessment of Jack Straw, claiming that after a lack of resistance he 'thought no man his pere' and was 'enflawmyd with presumpcion and pryde.'[24] Similarly, John Rastell, in *The Pastyme of*

---

edition. For further information and translation, see Richard Moll, 'Gower's *Cronica tripertita* and the Latin Glosses to Hardyng's *Chronicle*,' *Journal of the Early Book Society* 7 (2004): 153–58 (154). I am also grateful to Richard Moll for helping me gain access to his article.

21 Daniel R. Woolf, *Reading History in Early Modern England* (Cambridge: Cambridge University Press, 2000), e.g., 11–12.

22 Caxton's continuation of the *Polychronicon* is quoted from Joseph Rawson Lumby (ed.), *Polychronicon Ranulphi Higden maonachi Cestrensis, Vol. VIII* (London: Longman & Co, 1882), 529.

23 *Polychronicon*, 455, though Ball is mentioned at 459. Cf. William Thorne in Roger Twysden (ed.), *Historiae Anglicanae Scriptores X* (London, 1652), 2156: 'habens ductores *Johannem Straw, I. Bank, Iohannem Hales, Thomam Mellere* & alios horum pejores sceleratos' (translation in A. H. Davis [ed.], *William Thorne's Chronicle of Saint Augustine's Abbey, Canterbury* [Oxford: Blackwell, 1934], 614). A similar list of names is also found in a Latin poem, 'On the Slaughter of Archbishop Sudbury,' in Thomas Wright (ed.), *Political Poems and Songs Relating to English History* (Rolls Series; London: Longman, Green, Longman, and Robert, 1859), 227–30: 'Jak Chep, Tronche, Jon Wrau, Thom Myllere, Tyler, Jak Strawe, Erle of the Plo, Rak to, Deer, et Hob Carter, Rakstrawe.' See also, e.g., Thomas Pettitt, '"Here Comes I, Jack Straw": English Folk Drama and Social Revolt,' *Folklore* 95 (1984): 3–20 (9).

24 Quoted here from Henry Ellis (ed.), *The new chronicles of England and France, in two parts by Robert Fabyan. Named by himself The concordance of histories. Reprinted from Pynson's edition of 1516. The first part collated with the editions of 1533, 1542, and 1559; and the second with a manuscript of the author's own*

People, the Chronydes of dyvers Realmys and most specially of the Realme of England (1529), explains how Walworth dealt with Jack Straw's 'pryde and...tyrranye.'²⁵ As ever, we should not forget one of the familiar functions of history writing. For instance, Thomas Cooper (later to be bishop of Lincoln and bishop of Winchester) in the popularising continuation (first published in 1549) of Robert Crowley's *An Epitome of Chronicles* sought to educate advisers to a young ruler on how history can be an example for the good or ill of the realm, as the preface and dedication to Edward VI and the Duke of Somerset made clear. And of the rebels he wrote that, 'They caused muche trouble and businesse in the realme' and 'practised much villanie' but 'rude companye' undone by the 'manhode and wisedome' of Walworth.²⁶

Polydore Vergil: Explaining a Ball-free History

Ball is conspicuous by his absence in these retellings, perhaps tied to the fading threat of Lollardy. One of the major chroniclers of Elizabethan England, Richard Grafton (*Chronicle at large*, 1569), was puzzled by the omission of Ball from his place alongside leaders like Tyler and Jack Straw. Not unreasonably given what earlier chronicles had to say, he pointed out that Ball was integral to the development of the revolt and his role ought

---

time, as well as the subsequent editions: including the different continuations. To which are added a biographical and literary preface, and an index (London: F.C. and J. Rivington, 1811).

25 Quoted here from Thomas Frognall Dibdin's version: John Rastell, *The pastime of people, or the chronicles of divers realms; and most especially of the realm of England* (ed. Thomas Frognall Dibdin; London: F.C. and J. Rivington, 1812).

26 Quoted here from the second edition: Thomas Lanquet, Thomas Cooper, and Robert Crowley, *An epitome of chronicles Conteyninge the whole discourse of the histories as well of this realme of England, as al other cou[n]treys, with the succession of their kinges, the time of their reigne, and what notable actes they did ... gathered out of most probable auctours. Firste by Thomas Lanquet, from the beginning of the worlde to the incarnacion of Christe, secondely to the reigne of our soueraigne lord king Edward the sixt by Thomas Cooper, and thirdly to the reigne of our soueraigne Ladye Quene Elizabeth, by Robert Crowley. Anno. 1559* (Ann Arbor, MI: Text Creation Partnership, 2004). Cf. Chloe Wheatley, *Epic, Epitome, and the Early Modern Historical Imagination* (Farnham: Ashgate, 2011), 13–14.

to be duly noted and explained (see Chapter 4). We might contrast this with the version provided by Polydore Vergil (c. 1470–1555), the humanist from Urbino commissioned to write his *Historia Anglica* by Henry VII, and eventually published in 1534 in Basle and dedicated to Henry VIII, before being revised and expanded for a second edition (1546) and third edition (1555).[27] Despite his own criticisms of pedestrian histories in the dedication ('food without seasoning'), Vergil stood in the tradition of history writing flavoured with providence and morality.[28] More pertinently, Vergil gives us some insight into one reason why Ball—or John Wall (*Ioannem Vallaeum*) as Vergil named him—might have been excluded from earlier chronicles: his presence in the narrative might undermine arguments about the mismanagement of the realm. Thus, Vergil claimed that positing Ball/Wall as the cause of the uprising was contrary to the opinion of the historian who tried to flatter the nobility (*Historia Anglica* 20.3–4).[29]

Despite Vergil downplaying the role of Ball/Wall, he provided some notable points of emphases in his summary of such presentations. Irrespective

---

27 On the distinctive and complex issues of nationalism and internationalism brought about by Vergil's work, see, e.g., Ralf Hertel, 'Nationalising History? Polydore Vergil's Anglica Historia, Shakespeare's Richard III, and the Appropriation of the English Past,' in Barbara Schaff (ed.), *Exiles, Emigrés and Intermediaries: Anglo-Italian Cultural Transactions* (Amsterdam: Rodopi, 2010), 47–70. Denys Hay, *Polydore Vergil: Renaissance Historian and Man of Letters* (Oxford: Clarendon Press, 1952); Gransden, *Historical Writing in England II*, 425, 430–43; William J. Connell, 'Vergil, Polydore [Polidoro Virgili] (c. 1470–1555),' *ODNB* (23 September 2004).

28 So, the Dedication: 'hence, too, there have been men who have not hesitated to seek premature death in order to preserve their nation. But since all these things have partly been erased by the passage of time and partly cast into oblivion by forgetfulness, men next started to celebrate these works and deeds in literature, which confer immortality on them all so that in after time men could observe what good deeds were to be imitated, and what bad ones were to be avoided. For just as history speaks of and proclaims men's praises, so it does not keep silent about their disgraces, nor does it conceal them, and so it passes its judgments about what things are of the greatest use for the conduct of our lives, stimulating some to achieve immortal glory and virtue, and deterring others from vice by fear of infamy.' See also, e.g., Jonathan Arnold, '"Polydorus Italus": Analyzing Authority in Polydore Vergil's *Anglica Historia*,' *Reformation and Renaissance Review* 16 (2014): 122–37 (126–27).

29 Here I use the following Latin text with English translation: *Polydore Vergil, Anglica Historia (1555 version): A hypertext critical edition by Dana F. Sutton* (Birmingham: The Philological Museum, 2010), http://www.philological.bham.ac.uk/polverg/.

of whether those managing the unusual new poll tax were raising funds because it was the right thing to do or for their own greed, their actions nevertheless caused the commons to take up arms against the tax collectors, an issue which may have resonated with Vergil who had been involved in papal tax collection in England. Vergil noted the contrary opinion which cited Ball's/Wall's role at this point in the story:

> a certain priest named John Ball (*Ioannem Vallaeum*), abhorring his own lowly condition as well as that of men like himself, provoked the common people of Kent to take up arms against their noblemen, and the people, eagerly hanging on this man's lips, were moved to snatch up arms in their rashness, and then for the first time to make an outcry because one man possessed more honor than another, just as if the people of England had not previously consisted of Peerage and Commons. (*Historia Anglica* 20.3–4)

Consequently, Vergil's assessment assumes that Ball/Wall was not one of the main leaders of the revolt, who themselves received the kind of assessment we might expect. While there is a degree of sympathy with the plight of the insurgents, their uprising was the 'most horrible thing in human memory' and their leaders, Jack Straw and Tyler, were 'recruited from the dregs of humanity, ready-handed and hot-headed, as their captains.' Note, too, that we lack an overtly 'religious' assessment of Ball/Wall, despite Vergil (who may have remained a Catholic throughout his life) being prepared to critique others who challenged church authority, as well as critiquing church authorities for perceived abuses. But Vergil effectively marked both the end of an era and the beginning of a new one where sedition and religion would dominate as Ball was about to become a useful cipher again in Reformation England.

4
Ball and the English Reformation

Ball could certainly be omitted from retellings of 1381 if need be in Reformation England, such as in William Nelson's pageant for the fishmongers (1590), Richard Johnson's *The Nine Worthies of London* (1592), and the play attributed to Thomas Heywood, *1 Edward IV* (1590s). The reasons for the exclusion of Ball may have been related to those we have already seen but now intensified through the influence of the pageantry of the Elizabethan fishmongers and their promotion of Walworth and his defeat of Tyler.[1] Nevertheless, as we will see, Ball returned to the fore as ideas about rebellion took on new dimensions with England becoming a Protestant state, as well as through the antiquarian interests of Tudor historians. Ball's religious context thus became a feature that needed to be navigated or deliberately ignored because it raised some profoundly problematic and dangerous issues. Was there a connection between religious change and revolt? Was a potentially problematic figure like Ball really a proto-Protestant? And while Polydore Vergil suggested that the idea of Ball as a central figure in the revolt need not be accepted, his summary remained a standard pejorative one for how Ball was generally received and this, as Richard Grafton realised, made him a suitable figure for thinking about sedition and rebellion against the backdrop of the Reformation in England and interrelated European politics.[2]

---

1   Dobson, 'Remembering the Peasants' Revolt', in Liddell and Wood (eds.), *Essex and the Great Revolt of 1381*, 12; Stephen Longstaffe, 'Introduction', in Stephen Longstaffe (ed.), *A Critical Edition of the Life and Death of Jack Straw (1594)* (Lewiston: Edwin Mellen Press, 2002), 1–124 (89).
2   On which see, e.g., Anna Seregina, 'Religious Controversies and History Writing in Sixteenth-Century England', *The Medieval Chronicle* VII (2011): 223–38.

Martyr or Threat to Order?

But this did not necessarily mean Ball was thought to be on the wrong side. With the reclaiming of Wycliffe and the Lollards as precursors to the English Reformation came the issue of how to read their comparison or alleged association with Ball. In his interpretation of the book of Revelation first written in the 1540s in exile from Henry VIII, John Bale's *Image of Both Churches* (here discussing Revelation 11.9–10) put 'Sir' John Ball (the same clerical title is also found in, e.g., *Anon. Chron.* and *Polychronicon* Harley MS 2261) among the list of Lollard martyrs as part of his anti-Catholic propaganda and apocalyptic historiography in order to show the antiquity of what he saw as the true church in England.[3] This was not, however, an endorsement of the revolt; in the preface, Bale made it clear that 'In no wise rebel I here against any princely power or authority given of God'.[4] Elsewhere, Bale defended the importance of antiquarian practice by denouncing the destruction led by Tyler and Jack Straw and paralleled such deeds (as others would) with the radical end of the Reformation in Anabaptism:

> Jack Strawe and watte Tyler, ii, rebellyouse captaynes of the commens in the tyme of Kynge Richard the seconde, brent all the lawers bokes, regesters, and writynges within the cytie of London, as testifyeth Johan Maior and Fabyane in their chronycles.

> The Anabaptystes in our tyme, an vn-quyetouse kynde of men, arrogaunt with-out measure, capcyose and vnlerned, do leaue non olde workes vnbrent, that they maye easely come by, as apered by the lybraryes at Mynster in the lande of Westphaly, whom they most furyously destroyed.[5]

What is striking about this is Bale's reference to the histories of John Major and Robert Fabyan, neither of whom mentioned Ball in their

---

3 Gretchen E. Minton (ed.), *John Bale's 'The Image of Both Churches'* (Dordrecht: Springer, 2013), 186–87.
4 Minton (ed.), *John Bale's 'The Image of Both Churches,'* 47.
5 John Bale, *The laboryouse journey & serche of John Leylande for Englandes antiquitees geven of hym as a Newe Years gyfte to Kynge Henry the VIII in the xxxvii. yeare of his reygne, with declaracyons enlarged: by Johan Bale [1549]* (ed. W. A. Copinger; Priory Press: Manchester 1895), 86–87. For discussion of this passage see, e.g., Thomas Betteridge, *Tudor Histories of the English Reformations, 1530–83* (Aldershot: Ashgate, 1999), 129–31.

accounts of the leaders of the 1381 uprising.[6] Instead, Ball was distanced from the revolt and Ball-the-martyr came (unintentionally) from a different type of hostile source: *Fasciculi Zizaniorum*. We know Bale had a copy of, and knew well, the *Fasciculi Zizaniorum* which has Ball as a Wycliffe follower opposing transubstantiation (see Chapters 2, 3), and this further added legitimacy to Ball-as-Lollard from Bale's perspective.[7]

Bale's younger associate and fellow martyrologist and historian, John Foxe, also had access to the *Fasciculi Zizaniorum* through Bale. The first edition (1563) of Foxe's *Actes and Monuments* includes Ball, though with a cautious use of Polydore Vergil already suggesting just how dangerous Ball's memory could be:

> About the same time or rather somewhat afore. In the yeare of our Lord M.iiiC.lxxxii. [sic] as Polidore witnesseth, there was one Iohn Balle, whome Pollidorus calleth Walle, a priest & a preacher, but only that some men do suspect, he was in the commotion of Kent against kyng Richarde in the yeare of our Lord M. iii C.lxxx. But whether this suspition were true or false, it is vncertaine, albeit Pollidorus dooth not also thinke it to be true, neither doth it seme agreable to truthe, that suche a man as he endowed with suche knowledge and vnderstandinge of the Gospell, would entermedle him selfe in anye matter so farre disagreing with the Gospell. But this surely is worthy to be noted, that when he was deliuered out of prison, afterwarde being apprehended at Couentry by Robert Treuillian, and iudged to be hanged at S. Albons, in the year of our Lord M.iiic.lxxxii. shortly after the sayd Treuillian albeit that he was chief Iustice, suffered the like punishemen, and was hanged at Tiburne, as it is

---

6 Robert Fabyan, *The new chronicles of England and France, in two parts by Robert Fabyan. Named by himself The concordance of histories. Reprinted from Pynson's edition of 1516. The first part collated with the editions of 1533, 1542, and 1559; and the second with a manuscript of the author's own time, as well as the subsequent editions: including the different continuations. To which are added a biographical and literary preface, and an index* (ed. Henry Ellis; London: F.C. and J. Rivington, 1811), 530–31; John Major, *A history of Greater Britain as well England as Scotland* [1521] (ed. Archibald Constable and Aeneas J. G. Mackay; Edinburgh: University Press, 1892), 301–2.

7 On Bale and the *Fasciculi Zizaniorum*, see, e.g., Crompton, 'Fasciculi Zizaniorum I', and 'Fasciculi Zizaniorum II'; Elizabeth Evenden and Thomas S. Freeman, *Religion and the Book in Early Modern England: The Making of John Foxe's 'Book of Martyrs'* (Cambridge: Cambridge University Press, 2011), 39–46.

thought, not without iust cause being requited for the bloud that he had shed. (1563 edition, 2.192)[8]

Ball is not present in the later editions of *Actes and Monuments*. However, Foxe provided a brief but telling treatment of the 1381 revolt where Ball gets omitted precisely where he would have turned up:

> About the same time, also about iij. yeares after, there fell a cruell dissention in England, betwene the commō people and the nobilitie, the which did not a litle disturbe and trouble the common wealth. In this tumulte, Symon of Sudbery Archbiship of Canterbury, was taken by the rusticall and rude people, and was beheaded. In whose place after, succeded William Courtney... (1570 edition, 5.554; cf. 5.702. See also the editions of 1576 [5.453; 5.575], 1583 [5.597])[9]

The text continues with discussion of the persecution of the Lollards and the only mention of the leadership of the revolt is in the marginalia, which in the 1570 edition reads: 'Rebellion in England by Iacke Strawe.' As Susan Royal points out, there are important silences here because the association between the Lollards, the revolt, and Ball is clearly made in earlier accounts, including in Walsingham's which was one of Foxe's sources. The avoidance of such a connection is, then, likely deliberate.[10] Not only did Foxe downplay the connection between proto-Protestantism and revolt, but there is the implication that Ball—with his battles with the church and his accompanying exegesis—could have been more widely read, misread, understood, or misunderstood (depending on your perspective) as a proto-Protestant martyr. This was a problem that Foxe's contemporaries among the Tudor chroniclers tackled in a different way.

---

8   John Foxe, *The Unabridged Acts and Monuments Online or TAMO* (1563 edition) (Sheffield: The Digital Humanities Institute, 2011). Available from: www.dhi.ac.uk/foxe. See also John Foxe, *Commentarii rerum in ecclesia gestarum, maximarumque per totam Europam, persecutionum, a Vuicleui temporibus ad hanc usque aetatem descriptio, Liber primus* (Strasbourg, 1554), 175.
9   John Foxe, *The Unabridged Acts and Monuments Online or TAMO* (1570 edition) (The Digital Humanities Institute, Sheffield, 2011). Available at: www.dhi.ac.uk/foxe.
10 Susan Royal, 'English Catholics and English Heretics: The Lollards and Anti-Heresy Writing in Early Modern England', in James E. Kelly and Susan Royal (eds.), *Early Modern English Catholicism: Identity, Memory and Counter-Reformation* (Leiden: Brill, 2017), 122–41 (132).

Holinshead's Ball

Arguably the most famous Elizabethan chronicler (and well-known historical source for, among others, Shakespeare and Spenser) was Raphael Holinshed and the work that appeared in his name: *Chronicles of England, Scotland, and Ireland*. The first edition of Holinshed's *Chronicles* was published in 1577 and the second posthumously in 1587 under the direction of Abraham Fleming and a team which included another prominent chronicler of the age, John Stow, all of whom inherited or tracked down a range of medieval and sixteenth-century sources.[11] The *Chronicles* also inherited providential and moralising ideas about history, though complicated by the contributors coming from across the range of ideological perspectives—from shades of Protestantism through outward conformity to Catholicism, though Holinshed and Fleming were both Protestants, with Fleming holding the more reformist inclinations.[12] What comes through in the *Chronicles* is a sometimes implicit competition over, and negotiation with, the past but within the constraints of the Elizabethan present.[13] The 1587 edition follows the first edition in the retelling of the revolt, though there are some moralising and evaluative Latin additions and Fleming added a section from Knighton. The account is standard enough concerning the breakdown of the realm and disruption of the ideal social order and roles,[14] including the condemnation of the insurrection (even if not entirely without sympathy): 'To recite what was doone in euerie part of the realme in

---

11 The parallel texts of 1577 and 1587 editions are available at Ian W. Archer, Felicity Heal, Paulina Kewes, and Henry Summerson (eds.), *Holinshed Project*, http://english.nsms.ox.ac.uk/holinshed/. For a summary of the issues, see Ian W. Archer, Felicity Heal, and Paula Kewes, 'Prologue', in Ian W. Archer, Felicity Heal, and Paula Kewes (eds.), *The Oxford Handbook of Holinshed's* Chronicles (Oxford: Oxford University Press, 2013), xxix–xxxvii. On sources, see, in the same volume, Henry Summerson, 'Sources: 1577', 61–76 (67–71), 'Sources: 1587', 77–92, and Ian W. Archer, 'Social Order and Disorder', 389–410 (403–4). An extensive list of Holinshed's sources is also available at http://www.cems.ox.ac.uk/holinshed/chronicles.shtml#two2. Sources for, or references to, the revolt itself included Froissart, Knighton, and Walsingham.

12 Felicity Heal, 'The Holinshed Editors: Religious Attitudes and their Consequences', available at http://www.cems.ox.ac.uk/holinshed/paper2.pdf.

13 On the tensions in Holinshed's *Chronicles* over the representation of religion, see Peter Marshall, 'Religious Ideology', in Archer, Heal, and Kewes (eds.), *The Oxford Handbook of Holinshed's* Chronicles, 411–26.

14 Igor Djordjevic, *Holinshed's Nation: Ideals, Memory and Practical Policy in the 'Chronicles'* (New York: Routledge, 2010), 84–92.

time of those hellish troubles, it is not possible: but this is to be considered, that the rage of the commons was vniuersallie such, as it might séeme they had generallie conspired togither, to doo what mischeefe they could deuise' (1587, III.436; 1577, II. 1032).[15]

After lengthy narration of the uprising, Holinshed provided a distinct section for Ball where he explained his 'disquieting of the realme' in a way familiar from the earlier chroniclers and with no significant changes between the two editions (1577, II.1034–35; 1587, III.437; here I quote from 1587 for convenience), even if the judgement on the revolt itself is intensified and removes potential ambiguities from the earlier version.[16] We are given the details of Ball's capture, trial, and execution, followed by a brief outline and assessment of his career. As per Walsingham, Ball had been a preacher for twenty years and was prohibited from preaching in any church or chapel and so preached in streets and fields before being imprisoned. In prison he 'prophesied' that he would be rescued by twenty-thousand rebels and 'euen so it came to passe in time of the rebellion of the commons'. When prisoners were set free, Ball followed the rebels and at Blackheath ('as some write') he gave his sermon beginning with the Adam and Eve couplet, taking this 'saieng or common prouerbe for his theame'.[17] From this, Ball sought to prove that from the beginning 'all men by nature'

15 Cf. Archer, 'Social Order and Disorder', in Archer, Heal, and Kewes (eds.), *The Oxford Handbook of Holinshed's Chronicles*, 405: 'It is true that the accounts of the rebels are sufficient to engage our sympathies but the chronicles use a variety of devices to condition our responses, and there always remains a crucial distinction between sympathy for the plight of the poor and the justification of rebellion...he [Holinshed] drives home his hostility by diabolizing and dehumanizing them...Holinshed faithfully transmits the vituperative and marginalizing language of the medieval chroniclers.'
16 Djordjevic, *Holinshed's Nation*, 86.
17 As noted in the previous chapter, the Adam and Eve saying now associated with Ball was already known in some form by 1381 and continued to be known independently of him. On the broader popularity of the saying in the sixteenth and seventeenth centuries, see Longstaffe, 'Introduction', in Longstaffe (ed.), *A Critical Edition of the Life and Death of Jack Straw (1594)*, 83–87. Cf. Albert B. Friedman, '"When Adam delved...": Contexts of a Historic Proverb,' in Larry D. Benson (ed.), *The Learned and the Lewed: Studies in Chaucer and Medieval Literature* (Cambridge, MA: Harvard University Press, 1974), 213–30; Christopher Hill, *The English Bible and the Seventeenth-Century Revolution* (London: Penguin, 1993), 202–3. There is an allusion in *Hamlet* (5.1) to the famous rhyme, spoken by one of the Clowns—the Gravedigger—when discussing the nature of Ophelia's death which assumes some knowledge of it among the audience, as does the twist:

were created alike and that 'bondage or seruitude came in by iniust oppression of naughtie men.' He exhorted the great crowd to consider that 'now the time was come appointed to them by God, in which they might (if they would) cast off the yoke of bondage, & recouer libertie.' Similarly, the *Chronicles* included the allusion to Matthew 13.24–30, 36–43 ('after the manner of a good husband that tilleth his ground, and riddeth out thereof such euill wéeds as choke and destroie the good corne') to highlight the point that the rebels 'might destroie first the great lords of the realme, and after the iudges and lawiers, questmoongers, and all other whom they vndertooke to be against the commons' in order to establish peace, equality, liberty, no difference in degrees of nobility, and, with an allusion to Acts 2.44–45 and 4.32–35, 'a like dignitie and equall authoritie in all things brought in among them.' In response, the people affirmed that Ball 'ought to be archbishop and lord chancellour,' with Simon Sudbury worthy of losing his head. Among the many other things reported of Ball (and again following Walsingham) was the letter to chastise Hob the Robber, written as a 'kind of darke riddle' and found in the purse of an executed rebel.

The backdrop of the English Reformation most obviously had an impact on the retelling of the revolt in the *Chronicles* when it came to the handling of Ball's treatment by the church. It is assumed that Ball's prohibition from preaching must have come from the Catholic hierarchy but, with Ball as their opponent, the *Chronicles* keep the specifics suitably vague. Ball was prohibited because 'his doctrine was not according to the religion then by the bishops mainteined.' As Annabel Patterson stressed, it is worth comparing the (presumably) ideological departure in Holinshed's *Chronicles* from the source, Walsingham.[18] Walsingham, as we saw, was far more specific in contextualising Ball alongside 'the perverse doctrines of

---

> *First Clown*: Why, there thou say'st: and the more pity that great folk should have countenance in this world to drown or hang themselves, more than their even Christian. Come, my spade. There is no ancient gentleman but gardeners, ditchers, and grave-makers: they hold up Adam's profession.
> *Second Clown*: Was he a gentleman?
> *First Clown*: He was the first that ever bore arms.
> *Second Clown*: Why, he had none.
> *First Clown*: What, art a heathen? How dost thou understand the Scripture? The Scripture says Adam digged. Could he dig without arms?

As we will see in the next chapter, there is evidence that Shakespeare was aware that this saying could also be associated with Ball.

18 Annabel Patterson, *Reading Holinshed's Chronicles* (Chicago: University of Chicago Press, 1994), 190–95.

the perfidious John Wyclif as well as the opinions and false ravings which Wyclif held' (*Chronica maiora* 544–545). In Holinshed's *Chronicles*, however, Ball's beliefs are constructed as sufficiently different and idiosyncratic and lapped up by an unfortunately gullible audience ('set foorth such kind of doctrine, and other the like fond and foolish toies vnto the people, they extolled him to the starres'). With this sort of vagueness, the emphasis gets placed on Ball as a threat to stability of the realm while diminishing his potential to be read as proto-Protestant.[19] Furthermore, Ball is presented as anything but a martyr. The examples of Bale and Foxe show that it was a live option for Ball to have been understood as a Lollard martyr in Reformation England and one possible interpretation open to Holinshed and Fleming. But Ball's life in Holinshed's *Chronicles* is instead framed at the beginning and end by his death and the death of other rebels who deserved to die for treason. Ball's death for his 'notable treasons' is catalogued briefly with an outline given of the trial, punishment, dates, location, and judge.

This construction of Ball as representing a threat to the realm rather than an overtly 'religious' radical is epitomised by the reference to 'a like dignitie and equall authoritie in all things brought in among them'. This commonality is not presented in Holinshed's *Chronicles* through the lens of the radical Reformation (though this sentiment is elsewhere—see below) but rather it is presented firmly as a threat to the accepted social order and conventional governance. The flipside of Ball's logic of 'a like dignitie and equall authoritie in all things brought in among them' involved 'dispatching out of the waie the great men.' Indeed, this picked up on the earlier episode in Holinshed's account of the rebel demands under Wat Tyler. They were, he claimed, seeking to have 'all law abolished' and to have all legal figures put to death so that 'hauing made all those awaie that vnderstood the lawes all things should then be ordered according to the will and disposition of the common people.' The 1587 edition hit home that this was subversion

---

[19] This reading could counter Igor Djordjevic's admittedly speculative suggestion (*Holinshed's Nation*, 84 n. 105) that Wycliffe's function as 'the unstated causal link…to the event may be another example of Holinshed's oblique manner of proposing a potentially subversive truth to his audience: in this case, that the proto-Protestant martyr idolized by sixteenth-century Reformers and popularized textually by John Foxe's *Book of Martyrs* may have played a part in the popular rebellion against an anointed monarch.' On related tensions at play in Holinshed's *Chronicles* over how to categorise the reception of Lollards such as John Oldfield, see, e.g., Thomas S. Freeman and Susannah Brietz Monta, 'Holinshed and Foxe,' in Archer, Heal, and Kewes (eds.), *The Oxford Handbook of Holinshed's* Chronicles, 217–33. Cf. Summerson, 'Sources: 1587,' in Archer, Heal, and Kewes (eds.), *The Oxford Handbook of Holinshed's* Chronicles, 81–82.

in the extreme as the 'wretches had vtterlie forgotten all law, both diuine and humane', including the Golden Rule itself: 'to doo vnto others as they would be doone vnto, as the verie law of nature (than which there cannot be a better guide) teacheth, Quod tibi vis fieri mihi fac, quod non tibi, noli, Sic potes in terris viuere iure poli' (1587, III.432). It is also worth noting that Fleming's addition of a passage from Knighton includes the rebel demand that 'all warrens, waters, parks and woods should be common' and various other requests which would have been granted 'without contradiction or gainesaieng, and exercise without controlment' (1587, III.433).

While there was an antiquarian interest in collecting and repeating earlier sources, this does not mean, of course, that they had no contemporary resonance among readers and audiences of chronicles—including ideas about the threat of all things in common. Indeed, as Stephen Schillinger notes, relatively radical ideas about commonwealth were of course known from the mid-sixteenth century and he points to Robert Crowley's 1548 petition to Parliament which suggested that the 'whole earth' by right belongs to 'children of men.' But, as Schillinger adds, this was done within the boundaries of official political culture and did not mean getting rid of social hierarchies; it was rather part of a tradition of common responsibility. Moreover, the Crowley petition came with the warning that his words should not be taken to mean 'all things common,' implying, therefore, that people could interpret these sentiments in such a way.[20] Of course, the extremist elements of the revolt itself are presented in Holinshed's *Chronicles* more as attempted usurpation and perversion of the social order than elimination of social hierarchy (Ball was, after all, due a significant promotion). But the worries that the quintessential English uprising could tap into wider anxieties about the radical extent of common responsibility, overthrowing of traditional privileges, and what 'all things in common' might mean in practice, should not be underestimated.[21] Indeed, some readers may have read Holinshed's Ball in the light of the radical

20 Stephen Schillinger, 'Begging at the Gate: "Jack Straw" and the Acting Out of Popular Rebellion,' *Medieval & Renaissance Drama in England* 21 (2008): 87–127 (99, 117 n. 27), citing Crowley from Kate Aughterson, *The English Renaissance: An Anthology and Sources and Documents* (New York: Routledge, 1998), 154–58. For other mid-sixteenth-century examples, see, e.g., Dominique Goy-Blanquet, *Shakespeare's Early History Plays: From Chronicle to Stage* (Oxford: Oxford University Press, 2003), 102.
21 On the interpretations (including subversive ones) of things held in common, see Susan Royal, 'John Foxe's "Acts and Monuments" and the Lollard Legacy in the Long English Reformation' (PhD thesis, Durham University, 2014), 100–102, available at Durham E-Theses Online: http://etheses.dur.ac.uk/10624/.

Reformation and the fate of groups like the Anabaptists or the Family of Love who were judged in Holinshed's *Chronicles* in a vaguely similar way (e.g., 1587, III.1314), irrespective of how radical Fleming's reformist tendencies might have personally been. It should be stressed, though, that the treatment of what was seen as the excessively radical Reformation in Holinshed often foregrounded doctrinal issues (e.g., baptism, sin, nature of Christ, salvation; cf. 1587, III.938, 1261, 1299, 1353, 1354) which were not part of the typical reasons for why the 1381 uprising was thought problematic. Nevertheless, as we will see, it remains possible, if not likely, that some readers might have read the presentation of Ball in light of the more radical end of the Reformation.

Stow's Ball

Holinshed's *Chronicles* may be the most prominent Elizabethan history but worries relating to all things in common, seditious preaching, and concerns about how to map Ball on to the Reformation in England were widespread and found among other prominent histories and historians of the era. One Elizabethan historian of influence in crystallising negative receptions of Ball was Holinshed's contemporary and fellow populariser of English history, John Stow. Indeed, there was a likely two-way influence on their respective writings and rewritings of the revolt, and, as noted, Stow was a contributor to the second edition of Holinshed's *Chronicles*. Though suspected of Catholic sympathies, Stow's ongoing history writing provided an at least outwardly conformist account of the English Reformation. There is minimal detail on the potential precursor Wycliffe (a brief discussion of his view on transubstantiation) who even gets omitted in the abridged versions. Unsurprisingly, then, there is no attempt to make Ball a precursor of the English Reformation or to connect him with Wycliffe, or to even discredit him with the association with the radical Reformation about which Stow could be relatively detached.[22] Stow's handling of Ball instead involved

---

22 On Stow, the Reformation, and Wycliffe—and the extent to which Stow may or may not have been Catholic—see, among others, Barrett L. Beer, 'John Stow and the English Reformation, 1547–1559', *The Sixteenth Century Journal* 16 (1985): 257–71; Barrett L. Beer, *Tudor England Observed: The World of John Stow* (Stroud: Sutton Publishing, 1998), 98–108; Barrett L. Beer, 'English History Abridged: John Stow's Shorter Chronicles and Popular History', *Albion* 36 (2004): 12–27; Patrick Collinson, 'John Stow and Nostalgic Antiquarianism', in

presenting him as a seditious threat, even if his summaries avoid obvious distortion; popular protests and rebellions like that of 1381 went against the inherited ideals of the divinely legitimised and harmonious social order.[23] Building on earlier histories (e.g., Froissart, Hardyng, *Brut*), Stow provided various accounts of the revolt which were modified in different publications.[24] In the 1565 and 1566 editions of *Summarie of Englyshe Chronicles*, which are his earliest accounts of the revolt, Stow, unsure if the name was 'Ball' or 'Wall,' provided little in the way of causes of the rebellion (the commons of Kent and Essex 'sodenly rebelled'). As Vergil might have predicted, this move instead involved separating Ball from the other leaders on the grounds that he provided the ideological motivation for the revolt ('whiche were animated to this rebellion, by one Iohn Wall or Ball'). Stow's negative judgement on Ball involved typical claims that he was a 'very sedicious preacher' (1565), or a 'seditious precher' (1566), while the rebels generally 'caused muche trouble and busines in the Realme, and chiefly about the citie of London, where they practised much vyllanie' (1565).[25]

J. F. Merritt (ed.), *Imagining Early Modern London: Perceptions and Portrayals of the City from Stow to Strype 1598–1720* (Cambridge: Cambridge University Press, 2001), 27–51 (37–47); J. F. Merritt, 'The Reshaping of Stow's Survey: Munday, Strype and the Protestant City,' in Merritt (ed.), *Imagining Early Modern London*, 52–88; Ian W. Archer, 'John Stow, Citizen and Historian,' in Ian Gadd and Alexandra Gillespie (eds.), *John Stow (1525–1605) and the Making of the English Past: Studies in Early Modern Culture and the History of the Book* (London: British Library, 2004), 13–26.

23 On this context for Stow's work, see, e.g., Beer, *Tudor England Observed*, 23–36, 170.
24 Matheson, 'The Peasants' Revolt through Five Centuries of Rumor and Reporting,' 121–33.
25 Quotations taken from John Stow, *A summarie of Englyshe chronicles conteynyng the true accompt of yeres, wherein euery kyng of this realme of England began theyr reigne, howe long they reigned: and what notable thynges hath bene doone durynge theyr reygnes. Wyth also the names and yeares of all the baylyffes, custos, maiors, and sheriffes of the citie of London, sens the Conqueste, dyligentely collected by Iohn Stovv citisen of London, in the yere of our Lorde God 1565. Whervnto is added a table in the end, conteynyng all the principall matters of this booke. Perused and allowed accordyng to the Quenes maiesties iniunctions* (Ann Arbor, MI: Text Creation Partnership, 2003), http://name.umdl.umich.edu/A13030.0001.001; John Stow, *The summarie of English chronicles (lately collected and published) nowe abridged and continued tyl this present moneth of Marche, in the yere of our Lord God. 1566* (Ann Arbor, MI: Text Creation Partnership, 2009), http://name.umdl.umich.edu/A73271.0001.001. See also *The abridgement of the English Chronicle, first collected by M. Iohn*

By the time of the corrected and enlarged edition of 1570, updated after Stow's engagement with Knighton's chronicle,[26] the name 'Ball' is accepted, and added were the letters associated with Ball, Jack Milner, and Jack Trewman, with an additional note mentioning another letter by Jack Carter. In Stow's *The Chronicles of England, from Brute unto this present yeare of Christ 1580,* a marginal note mentioning another letter of Ball was added to Stow's developing history of the revolt following the publication of a new edition of Walsingham, and later published in full in Stow's most voluminous history, *The Annales of England*, which took English history up to 1592.[27] On the letter, Stow has the expected judgement of their perceived hypocrisy: 'Here I thinke good to note some Epistles of Iohn Ball and others, wyth some short notes of their Diuellish demeanor, vnder the colour of zeale and conscience, and so to ende thys matter' (*Chronicles of England*, 1580). After the description of Ball as a seditious and deceitful priest, a summary of his teachings and the Blackheath sermon were added:

> hys sermons vsed to take for his Theame, When Adam dalfe and Eue spanne, who was then a Gentleman. Affirming that al men were made a like by nature, and therefore ought to laye away the yoke of bondage, that they might enioye the wished libertie, too shamefull, sedicious, and damnable to bée taughte, whyche neuerthelesse so pleased the common people, that they cryed hée should be Archbishoppe of Canterburie, and Chauncellour of England.

Ball's capture, trial, and execution were also presented by Stow and cast in blunt, negative terms of someone motivated by hate: 'He woulde not aske the King forgiuenesse, but vtterly despised him' (*Chronicles of England*, 1580). As with Holinshed, it followed naturally in Stow's assumptions that there would be no martyr's death for Ball.

Stow, and after him augmented with very many memorable antiquities, and continued with matters forreine and domesticall, vnto the beginning of the yeare, 1618, by E. H. Gentleman. There is a briefe table at the end of the booke (Ann Arbor, MI: Text Creation Partnership, 2009), http://name.umdl.umich.edu/A13042.0001.001. No page numbers given.

26 Matheson, 'The Peasants' Revolt through Five Centuries', 128–29.

27 John Stow, *The chronicles of England from Brute vnto this present yeare of Christ. 1580. Collected by Iohn Stow citizen of London* (Ann Arbor, MI: Text Creation Partnership, 2009), http://name.umdl.umich.edu/A13043.0001.001; *The Annales of England, faithfully collected out of the most autenticall Authors, Records, and other Monuments of Antiquite, from the first inhabitacion vntill this present yeere 1600 [1592]* (London, 1600 [1592]).

The *Annals of England* became Stow's major historical work, itself going through multiple editions beyond his death. Naturally, the negative assessment of Ball continued. Ball remained a rebellious threat hiding behind the mask of piety, and the inherited tradition made this framing straightforward. 'Sir Iohn Ball' was the chaplain of the commons and a 'wicked Priest' who told them to destroy 'all the Nobility, and Cleargy'.[28] In teaching things to the liking of the commons and slandering 'ecclesiasticall persons' and 'secular Lords,' he sought the 'benevolence of the common people' rather than 'merite towards God'.[29] In line with the *Anonimalle Chronicle*, the *Annals* includes in the summary of Ball: Ball wanting to be archbishop, people regarding him as a prophet, his idea that there be no more than 'two religious persons in one house,' and that their 'possessions should bee deuided among the laye men'.[30] In line with Walsingham, Ball is remembered as a popular figure, as well as for his teachings on tithes and being born in matrimony, and being forced out of (and excommunicated from) the church to preach in the 'streetes and wayes' and in the fields, before he is imprisoned. Ball prophesied that he would be sprung from prison by twenty thousand 'friends' which 'came to passe in the foresaid time of troubles'.[31] The *Annals* incorporates the 'mad deuises' of Ball's Blackheath sermon which wooed the commons, including: the Adam and Eve couplet, all beings made equal from the beginning, how bondage was imposed by 'naughty' men, now being the time given by God to throw aside the yoke of bondage and the enjoyment of 'libertie,' and Matthew 13.24–30, 36–43, being used to justify attacking the various authorities and legal practitioners to achieve their goals. Ball's letter was mentioned in a marginal note to *Chronicles of England* after the publication of a new edition of Walsingham is now included. It is a letter full of riddles and 'darke sentences' and found on the body of a captured rebel. It is now located before the letters associated with Ball, Jacke Miller, and Jacke Trueman which are placed at the end of the account.[32] Perhaps Stow's relatively restrained collecting and rewriting does not tell us too much more than we already know but it served a purpose of perpetuating the assumptions about Ball. Ideology, after all, can be even more effective when it is assumed rather than explained or promoted, and in this sense the antiquarian historian provides a particularly helpful example.

28 Stow, *Annales of England, faithfully collected*, 453.
29 Stow, *Annales of England, faithfully collected*, 468.
30 Stow, *Annales of England, faithfully collected*, 453.
31 Stow, *Annales of England, faithfully collected*, 468.
32 Stow, *Annales of England, faithfully collected*, 469.

Grafton's Ball

Stow's bitter rival was the printer (including a printer of Bibles and chronicles) and King's Printer under Edward VI, Richard Grafton. While imprisoned under Mary I, Grafton developed his own history which was published in 1563 as *An abridgement of the chronicles of England* and dedicated to Robert Dudley. As well as producing new editions, he also published a smaller *Manuell of the Chronicles of Englande* (1565) and an extensive *Chronicle at large and meere Historye of the Affayres of England* (1569), dedicated to William Cecil. *Chronicle at large* also included Thomas Norton's letter which frames the history in terms of divine providence and an emerging Protestant nation.[33] Norton's letter opens with the importance of the ideas of good and evil while praising Grafton as a 'good Englisheman for the profite of the Realme of Englande, and as a good Christian for the furtheraunce of true religion' and for his publishing of the Bible in English, 'that vnvaluable Iewell.'[34] There are warnings against rebellions and praise for stable governance of the sort currently experienced under Elizabeth, though not too far removed from what he saw as an unstable Catholic threat.[35]

In *Chronicle at large*, Grafton referenced his source Froissart at the beginning of his account of the revolt. Part of the usefulness (other than a ready-made narrative) was that Froissart could be used to show how the past was a means to understanding—and thus preventing—rebellion. Grafton started his account of the revolt with the preface that this would be a retelling of when the 'commons of England rebelled, by the which the whole state of the realme was in great perill to be vtterly destroyed and lost: and because ye shall vnderstande the truth thereof, and that the rulers of the realme may preuent and foresee suche lyke mischiefes as maye hereafter ensue, therefore I haue purposed fully to set foorth at length,

---

33 On assumptions of providential history in Elizabethan England at the time of Grafton, cf., e.g., E. J. Devereux, 'Empty Tuns and Unfruitful Grafts: Richard Grafton's Historical Publications,' *Sixteenth Century Journal* 21 (1990): 33–56 (42); Woolf, *Reading History in Early Modern England*, 20–21.
34 *Chronicle at large* quotations are taken from *Grafton's chronicle: or, History of England. To which is added his table of the bailiffs, sherrifs, and mayors, of the city of London. From the year 1189 to 1558, inclusive* (2 vols.; London: J. Johnson et al., 1809).
35 On history as a tool for maintaining the stability of the realm and the avoidance of rebellion for Grafton and his contemporaries, see e.g., Devereux, 'Empty Tuns and Unfruitful Grafts,' 40.

the truth and whole discourse thereof vnto you.' And one such figure who should have been stopped from the start was Ball (Grafton, incidentally, mostly preferred the alias 'John Wall'), whose primacy was unquestionable: Ball was the 'first mouer, and speciall authour, and setter foorth of thys rebellion.'[36] Vergil would, of course, have disliked this shift away from the explanation of bad governance but for Grafton that was half the point in a world that had changed since Vergil.

This was emphatically a rebellion with rebel leaders, including an ideologue. Unlike some earlier writings and rewritings of the revolt, Ball/Wall gets listed among the 'Captaines' of the rebels and rebellious counties (along with Tyler and Jack Straw) in a world turned upside down. Grafton added that Froissart named Ball to be a 'cheife Captaine' (with Tyler the overall leader), even though this designation was lacking in other sources where Jack Straw and Jack Shepherd were more prominent. He then proceeded to talk about how from the beginning of the story this 'simple priest called John Wall' could be understood as the primary instigator of the rebellion and how he sought revenge on the archbishop of Canterbury for imprisoning him for his 'lewde communication that tended to rebellion.' This was expanded earlier in his account (via Froissart) of the leaders entering Canterbury, where Ball/Wall is said to have missed the archbishop who was instead in London with the king. When they were in London, Ball (along with Tyler, Jack Straw, and several hundred rebels) got into the Tower of London and found the archbishop. They beheaded him and others, with their heads paraded on spikes because they were traitors to the realm. Grafton also included the story that 'these wretches' were responsible for terrifying the queen mother in her chamber.[37]

In Grafton's presentation, the teachings of Ball/Wall therefore permeated the rebellion. Following Froissart, we get a general summary of the view of the Kent commons who said:

> in the beginning of the worlde, there were no bond men: neyther ought there to be any nowe, except it were such a one as had committed treason agaynst his Lorde, as Lucifer did to God. But sayde they we can haue no suche battayle, for we are neyther Angelles nor spirites, but men framed and formed to the similitude of our Lordes, and therefore sayde they, why should we then be so kept vnder lyke beastes and slaues? And they playnely sayde they would no longer suffer it, for they would be all one with their Lordes, and if they labored or did anye thing for their Lordes, they woulde haue wages for the same as well as other.

36 Grafton, *Chronicle at large*, 417, 427.
37 Grafton, *Chronicle at large*, 418–19.

These were, of course, known ideas associated with Ball and, as with Froissart, Grafton continued by claiming that 'a foolishe priest in the Countie of Kent called Iohn Wall' was 'of this imagination' and for 'lyke foolishe words' had been imprisoned three times by the archbishop of Canterbury. On Sundays, after the church service, 'this priest' would 'call them back into the Cloyster or Churchyard' and deliver the words now familiar from Froissart that 'matters go not wel to passe in England in these dayes, nor shall not do vntill euery thing be common, and that there be no Villeynes nor gentlemen, but that we be all as one, and that the Lordes be no greater then we be.' There are further summaries of familiar teaching: the attack on servitude defended from the idea of common lineage from 'one father and one mother, Adam and Eue'; attacks on the differences in clothing, food, drink, dwelling, and work between rich and poor, and the lords (sometimes violently) living off the labour of the bondmen; and the idea that the king will be supportive while coupled with the possibility of remedying the situation without him.[38]

Grafton also included (from Froissart) Ball's popularity and influence, claiming that 'many of the meane people loued him: and those that meant no goodnesse, sayde he sayde truth: and so they muttered together one with another in the Fieldes and wayes as they went.' This led to an imprisonment of two or three months by the archbishop of Canterbury with the intention of making Ball see the error of his ways. Because of 'the great mischiefe that did ensue,' however, Grafton (as ever, via Froissart) has the judgement that it would have been better to have imprisoned him for life or for him to have died for, sure enough, upon his release, Ball returned to his old ways. Londoners heard of such words and deeds and began to have 'great enuy at them that were riche.' The rebels said 'the realme of England was euill gouerned,' and that gold and silver were taken from them by those 'by such as were named noble men.' Thus, the revolt began and spread with the knowledge that rebels should come to London to form a united 'Commons of the Citie' who would work with the king to ensure that there would be no bondmen in England.[39] As the narrative follows Froissart, little space is given to the death of Ball, who is simply said to have been betrayed and his head among those replacing the heads of the archbishop and his colleagues. Ball represented rebellion against the realm and social order for Grafton and so, in the same move made by Holinshed and Grafton's great rival Stow, Ball-as-martyr was emphatically not an option that could be entertained. Bale's type of Ball was too dangerous.

38 Grafton, *Chronicle at large*, 417–18.
39 Grafton, *Chronicle at large*, 418.

1381 and the Elizabethan Present

The major Elizabethan historians had re-established Ball as an ideologue central to the revolt, rather than placing the emphasis more exclusively on bad governance and the breakdown of the ideal social order like many of their predecessors. While making connections with broader tendencies and anxieties concerning the Reformation in England involves us reading between the lines of the histories, we also know that in the sixteenth century there were influential readers of the 1381 uprising who could have made connections with the Elizabethan present. Towards the end of his life, Thomas Cooper (now bishop of Winchester) became entangled in the controversies surrounding the puritan Martin Marprelate tracts. He headed an official response in *An Admonition to the People of England* (1589) which challenged radical puritanism from the perspective of the Elizabethan settlement and with the events of 1381 (via Walsingham) seen as a useful point of comparison. *Admonition* refers to 'superstition and idolatrie' while discussing Jeremiah 44 and those who attributed their woes to Jeremiah and other prophets and makes related claims of rebellious subjects ('in common weales, when they seeke to make odious the Princes and gouernours vnder whom they liue, vniustly imputing to them the causes of such things, wherwith they finde themselues grieued'). Thus, the rebels of 1381 reasoned against the king, nobles, lawyers, and other authorities and resolved 'to haue destroyed and ouerthrowen them all, and to haue suffered none other to liue in this Realme with them, but the Gray Friers onely.'[40] As with rebellion against Moses and Aaron, so too did the 'lewde and rebellious subiects' rise against Richard II, determined to 'pull downe the state' and its bureaucracy. They too could cite scripture and here we have obvious echoes of Ball himself:

> At the beginning (say they) when God had first made the worlde, all men were alike, there was no principalitie, there was no bondage, or villenage: that grewe afterwardes by violence and crueltie. Therefore, why should we liue in this miserable slauerie vnder these proud Lords and crafty Lawyers?[41]

---

40 Thomas Cooper, *An Admonition to the People of England* (ed. Edward Arber; Birmingham: The English Scholar's Library, 1589), 84.
41 Cooper, *An Admonition to the People of England*, 118–19.

From the perspective of *Admonition*, such an approach against the establishment hierarchies inevitably leads to disaster and it is one in which puritanism was implicated.

As Stephen Longstaffe put it, 'a preacher leading a commons rising in which an archbishop was killed was a gift to establishment polemicists.'[42] One such example is the 'arch Anti-Puritan,' Richard Bancroft, who would become archbishop of Canterbury in 1604 until his death in 1610.[43] With Bancroft we see further how the connections between the overthrow of the social order and the radical Reformation could be made. In *A suruay of the pretended holy discipline* (1593), Bancroft tackled such issues relating to the puritan and radical Reformation, subversion, and rebellion head on, including direct reference to Ball.[44] Bancroft claimed that even in an anti-bishop position from the radical end of the Reformation there was an acceptance of hierarchies of 'nobleman and gentlemen' as a counter to the more egalitarian claim that people came from one man and one woman, Adam and Eve. A more benign hierarchy (in Bancroft's representation of this position) delivered oppressed people from tyranny and abuse of authority and in return was given the endorsement of the people. For Bancroft there was nothing wrong with turning to the 'first institution' if these words be 'well applied.' However, he argued, 'something was amisse in the Priestes application of his text' and the presence 'amongest a multitude of rebelles' of a related saying which he associated with 'Iohn Wall, or Ball' in his marginal note: 'When Adam digged, and Eue spanne, who was then the Gentleman.' Many sharing 'said Priestes humour' do not think noblemen and gentlemen will 'satisfie their desires' and see the elite as 'an vsurper of such honour, as the people bestowed vpon their auncestors at the first, for defending of them against their gouernours' and now lift themselves above the rest of the children of God. The same levelling attitude applies to 'all true Christians' who are 'fellow heires together of the kingdome of heauen.' But, Bancroft added ominously, 'such and the

---

42 Longstaffe, 'Introduction,' in Longstaffe (ed.), *A Critical Edition of the Life and Death of Jack Straw (1594)*, 74.
43 Patrick Collinson, *Richard Bancroft and Elizabethan Anti-Puritanism* (Cambridge: Cambridge University Press, 2013), 1.
44 Brents Stirling, *The Populace in Shakespeare* (New York: Columbia University Press, 1949), 134–36; Aziz, 'Of Grace and Gross Bodies,' 165–66. Quotations taken from Richard Bancroft, *A suruay of the pretended holy discipline. Contayning the beginninges, successe, parts, proceedings, authority, and doctrine of it: with some of the manifold, and materiall repugnances, varieties and vncertaineties, in that behalfe* (London: Iohn Wolfe, Thomas Scarlet, and Richard Field, 1593; Ann Arbor, MI: Text Creation Partnership, 2003–2009).

like conceits do tend to nothing, but to bloud and confusion' and he was emphatic that the course taken 'in Schwitzerland, and other places in high Almayne (where the people made hauocke both of their noblemen, and gentlemen) shall neuer (whilest I liue) get my approbation.' What we clearly get from Bancroft is a connection between social unrest and the radical end of the Reformation. And in this connection what we also get is blurring of Ball, the 1381 uprising, and Jack Cade's rebellion of 1450, particularly in Bancroft's historically inaccurate accompanying marginal note: 'Iohn Wall, or Ball in the time of Iacke Cades rebellion, in Rich. 2. Daies.'[45]

But this blurring of rebels, rebellions, and Reformation also provided another means for Ball's memory to survive, perhaps even in ways that someone like Bancroft would have found disturbing. Ball in these ideological contexts was being played to wider audiences on the late Elizabethan stage against the backdrop of popular unrest and uncertainty and it is to these broad anxieties we now turn.

---

45 Bancroft, *A suruay of the pretended holy discipline*, 8–10. On the conflation of 1381 and 1450, see Chapter 5 and George Puttenham, *The arte of English poesie* (1589) (ed. Edward Arber; London: Murray & Son, 1869), 267: 'by the comfort of those blind prophecies many insurrections and rebellions haue bene stirred vp in this Realme, as that of *Iacke Straw*, and *Iacke Cade* in *Richard* the seconds time, and in our time by a seditious fellow in Norffolke calling himselfe Captaine Ket and others in other places of the Realme lead altogether by certaine propheticall rymes, which might be constred two or three wayes as well as to that one whereunto the rebelles applied it, our maker shall therefore auoyde all such ambiguous speaches vnlesse it be when he doth it for the nonce and for some purpose.' See also Annabel Patterson, *Shakespeare and the Popular Voice* (Oxford: Blackwell, 1989), 39–40.

5

Ghosts of 1381: Uneasy Heresies, Radicalisms, and Discontents in Late Elizabethan and Early Jacobean England

The very act of transmitting Ball's words and ideas by the chroniclers always provided the potential for more sympathetic (or at least less hostile) interpretations. Moreover, there are hints that popular memories of the 1381 revolt survived beyond the idea of a proto-Protestant martyr associated with Bale and Foxe. I. M. W. Harvey has shown how Jack Straw could remain a point of reference in fifteenth-century popular politics, and further reference to Jack Straw turns up in festive settings, including in the early sixteenth century at Lincoln's Inn where he featured as a kingly figure at Christmas and was consequently banned from future revelries.[1] While Jack Straw has a distinctive reception, there were possibilities for Ball to be perceived differently from the standard histories. In the case of the more public presentations of such voices from below, audiences would have contained divergent interpretations, particularly in the case of more ambiguous presentations. Suspicion of (and lampooning) established hierarchies was nothing new and never went away and so Ball's words, or the sentiments associated with 1381, would not have been self-evidently wrong to everyone. Nevertheless, we should not forget that representations of less official views could also reveal as much about more official anxieties as they do about the ideas from below that they purport to represent.

1   Harvey, 'Was There Popular Politics in Fifteenth-Century England?', in Britnell and Pollard (eds.), *McFarlane Legacy*, 168; Norman Simms, 'Nero and Jack Straw in Chaucer's *Nun's Priest's Tale*', *Parergon* 8 (1974): 2–12 (6); Pettitt, '"Here Comes I, Jack Straw"'; Chris Humphrey, *The Politics of Carnival, Festive Misrule in Medieval England* (Manchester: Manchester University Press, 2001), 49; Dunn, *The Peasants' Revolt*, 190.

And so the revolt was still, at least in public presentations, understood to be a threat to order. Tyler and the rebels provided the model for framing any would-be-rebel leader like the Earl of Essex or to warn against (or of) rebellion more generally.[2] But Ball offered something different. As Ball and his alleged ally Wycliffe were, potentially, associated with wanting all things in common, this brought them into the orbit of the one group especially associated with commonality of goods and uprisings at the radical end of the Reformation: the Anabaptists. Rescuing Wycliffe as a precursor of the English Reformation meant that disentangling him from such problematic associations was a live issue which in turn added another dimension to Ball, who was much more likely to take the blame as the real seditious ideologue. But this was no mere abstract theological theorising. Anxieties about popular uprisings around the turn of the seventeenth century should also be set against the backdrop of rapid population growth in London which quadrupled between 1500 and 1600 and may have doubled from 100,000 to 200,000 between 1580 and 1600,[3] alongside threats of uprisings, war, food shortages, and economic discontents in England of the 1580s and 1590s. Ideas about Ball, the breakdown of an idealised social order, and threats to London and the realm were, then, part of a dense and volatile mix of concerns about radical religion, social discontents, and rebellion in a rapidly changing capital.

John Ball as Jack Cade? Shakespeare's *Henry VI, Part II*

Ideas about revolt, religion and the breakdown of the inherited social order from above and below were mapped out in Shakespeare's *2 Henry VI* and its portrayal of Jack Cade which invites comparisons with Ball. The notoriety of the 1381 revolt meant it was always liable to be a point of comparison with other uprisings, and none more so than Cade's rebellion of 1450 with its generic similarities, such as Kentish rebels, marching on London, and

---

2   Dobson, 'Remembering the Peasants' Revolt', in Liddell and Wood (eds.), *Essex and the Great Revolt of 1381*, 11; Dobson (ed.), *Peasants' Revolt of 1381*, 30; Basdeo, *Life and Legend of a Rebel Leader*, loc 734–806.
3   Ian Munro, *The Figure of the Crowd in Early Modern London: The City and its Double* (New York: Palgrave Macmillan, 2005), 1–5.

the targeting of advisers (see also Chapter 4).⁴ The conflation of 1381 and 1450, then, provided another means for the survival of memories relating to Ball and other rebels from 1381. Used as part of York's ambitious political machinations in *2 Henry VI*, Shakespeare's Cade and followers were presented less by way of the Cade of the chronicles and more by way of Ball and the 1381 revolt instead, possibly with nods to more contemporary moments such as the messianic Hacket insurgency of 1591 and its unlikely threats to depose Elizabeth.⁵

What we have with Cade are further familiar themes associated with 1381, from violent hostility to the judicial system through undermining the very act of writing to a radical reordering of the world. The echoes of Ball

---

4   See, e.g., Annabel Patterson, *Shakespeare and the Popular Voice* (Oxford: Blackwell, 1989), 39–41; Phyllis Rackin, *Stages of History: Shakespeare's English Chronicles* (Ithaca, NY: Cornell University Press, 1990), 204–17; Ellen C. Caldwell, 'Jack Cade and Shakespeare's *Henry VI, Part 2*', *Studies in Philology* 92 (1995): 18–79 (e.g., 69–70); Dunn, *Peasants' Revolt*, 189–90; Longstaffe, 'Introduction', in Longstaffe (ed.), *A Critical Edition of the Life and Death of Jack Straw (1594)*, 70–73; Aziz, 'Of Grace and Gross Bodies', 165–67.

5   For discussion underpinning what follows, see, e.g., among many, Stirling, *The Populace in Shakespeare*, 131–50; Patterson, *Shakespeare and the Popular Voice*, 32–51; Thomas Cartelli, 'Jack Cade in the Garden: Class Consciousness and Class Conflict in *2 Henry VI*', in Richard Burt and John Michael Archer (eds.), *Enclosure Acts: Sexuality, Property, and Culture in Early Modern England* (Ithaca, NY: Cornell University Press, 1994), 48–67; Geraldo U. de Sousa, 'The Peasants' Revolt and the Writing of History in *2 Henry VI*', in David M. Bergeron (ed.), *Reading and Writing in Shakespeare* (Newark: University of Delaware Press, 1996), 178–93; Caldwell, 'Jack Cade and Shakespeare's *Henry VI, Part 2*', 49–51, 57–58, 61–62, 69; Stephen Longstaffe, '"A Short Report and Not Otherwise": Jack Cade in *2 Henry VI*', in Ronald Knowles (ed.), *Shakespeare and Carnival: After Bakhtin* (New York: St Martin's Press, 1998), 13–35; Goy-Blanquet, *Shakespeare's Early History Plays*, 100–106; Chris Fitter, '"Your Captain is Brave and Vows Reformation": Jack Cade, the Hacket Rising, and Shakespeare's Vision of Popular Rebellion in *2 Henry VI*', *Shakespeare Studies* (2004): 173–219 (177–79, 194–95); Roger Chartier, 'Jack Cade, the Skin of a Dead Lamb, and the Hatred for Writing', *Shakespeare Studies* 34 (2006): 77–89 (81–84); Djordjevic, *Holinshed's Nation*, 186–89; Julian Yates, 'Skin Merchants: Jack Cade's Futures and the Figural Politics of Shakespeare's *Henry VI Part II*', in Judith Anderson and Joan Pong Linton (eds.), *Go Figure: Forms, Energy, Matter in Early Modern England* (New York: Fordham University Press, 2011), 149–69 (149–50, 154–55, 158, 161–62); Delphine Lemonnier-Texier, 'Staging Sedition despite Censorship: The Representation of the People on the Shakespearean Stage in *2 Henry VI*', *Revue LISA* 11 (2013), https://journals.openedition.org/lisa/5499?lang=en (e.g., point 2).

include Adam's occupation (as we also see in *Hamlet* 5.1)—in response to the question, 'Villain, thy father was a plasterer; And thou thyself a shearman, art thou not?', Cade says, 'And Adam was a gardener' (*2 Henry VI* 4.2.144–46; cf. 4.2.7–9). Cade's quasi-proverbial use of all things in common in *2 Henry VI* also has obvious echoes of Ball and conflation with the events of June 1381 and the threat from below to the established order and dominant class interests. At Smithfield, Cade proclaims, 'So, sirs: now go some and pull down the Savoy; others to the inns of court; down with them all' and 'Away, burn all the records of the realm: my mouth shall be the parliament of England…And henceforward all things shall be in common' (*2 Henry VI* 4.7.8–9, 15–20). As Phyllis Rackin stressed, all things in common here brought together anxieties relating to loss of property and status with 'fears of unconstrained female sexuality.'[6] Such dramatic changes are, of course, brought into the service of Cade. As he put it:

> The proudest peer in the realm shall not wear a head
> on his shoulders, unless he pay me tribute; there
> shall not a maid be married, but she shall pay to me
> her maidenhead ere they have it: men shall hold of
> me in capite; and we charge and command that their
> wives be as free as heart can wish or tongue can tell. (*2 Henry VI* 4.7.120–25)

Connections between rebels, sexuality, and assumptions about wild, uncontrolled, or threatening rebel masculinity would be something addressed (in different ways) throughout the history of the reception of Ball and the mob (see, e.g., Chapters 6, 8, 19).

Earlier in *2 Henry VI*, we learn more about what all things in common might involve in a world turned upside down where Cade would rule somewhat comically and in place of the received hierarchy and bureaucracy. In this England there will be 'seven halfpenny loaves sold for a penny: the three-hooped pot; shall have ten hoops and I will make it felony to drink small beer: all the realm shall be in common' (*2 Henry VI* 4.2.63–67), which must have had some resonance among the audience against a backdrop of food shortages and a rapidly changing London (cf. *2 Henry VI* 4.2.65–67; 4.6.3–4). Concerns about levelling notions of things shared in common were noted in Chapter 4 and, in Shakespeare's presentation of these anxieties, this future England will be a time when Cade is a king who will ensure that 'there shall be no money' and he will 'apparel them all in one livery, that they may agree like brothers and worship me their lord' (*2 Henry VI*

---

6 Rackin, *Stages of History*, 204.

4.2.72–85). Whatever ambiguous Shakespearean notions of, or sympathies towards, popular concerns might have involved, Cade could no doubt have been viewed as a carnivalesque, if somewhat misguided, leader of this alternative world order. As Chris Fitter has shown in detail, the Shakespearean Cade could have quickly been interpreted by some in light of ideas about excessive and megalomaniacal religion, puritanism, and the more radical Reformation like the messianism of the Hacket insurgency. Thus, we get the punning brag which would not so obviously have had a lower case 'R' (so to speak) when vocalised on stage and would imply religious as well as economic and political change: 'Your captain is brave, and vows reformation' (*2 Henry VI* 4.2.62).[7]

The Life and Death of Jack Straw

The polemical presentations of Ball, and all that his type might threaten, did not entirely drown out the possibilities for more ambiguous portrayals that some have detected in Shakespeare's presentation of Cade, or at least in potential receptions of Cade among audiences. Contemporaneous with *2 Henry VI* is a similar presentation of such worries and discontents, even if the rebels could be assumed (at least in the eyes and ears of the authorities) to be misguided: the anonymous and perhaps carnivalesque *The Life and Death of Jack Straw* (1593/94).[8] The play is a dramatic retelling of the revolt focusing on some of the main characters (Parson Ball, Jack Straw, Wat Tyler, the king, the archbishop, etc.), often based on, for instance, the histories of Grafton, Holinshed, and Stow, though we are also introduced to the fictional rebel Nobs. Though it may have been written some years earlier, the play was printed in 1593/94 by John Danter (which I will use

---

[7] Fitter, 'Your Captain is Brave and Vows Reformation,' 190–92, 194–97, including discussions of the meanings of 'reformation' and 'Reformation' in context. See, e.g., Caldwell, 'Jack Cade,' 51 n. 121, for the 'political' use of 'reformation' in Shakespeare's sources for Cade. See also the discussion of relevant texts linking reform and revolt in Longstaffe, 'Introduction,' in Longstaffe (ed.), *A Critical Edition of the Life and Death of Jack Straw (1594)*, 74–82.

[8] A carnivalesque reading of the play is advocated in Longstaffe, 'Introduction,' in Longstaffe (ed.), *A Critical Edition of the Life and Death of Jack Straw (1594)*, 101–24. Cf. the qualifications made by Schillinger, 'Begging at the Gate,' 95, 114–16. Much of the debate has focused on the extent to which the play upholds or challenges the status quo. For a summary of scholarship, see Maya Mathur, 'Rebellion from Below: Commonwealth and Community in *The Life and Death of Jack Straw*,' *Journal of Medieval and Early Modern Studies* 45 (2015): 343–65 (343–44).

here for convenience) with a second edition in 1604 by Thomas Pavier which may have influenced Rowlands's *Hell's Broke Loose* where 'Parson Ball' is likewise referenced (see below).[9]

There is little remaining of the play's earliest reception, and so speculation and guesswork necessarily dominate questions of authorship and context in this occasionally overlooked work.[10] Given this, it is safest for our purposes to work with useful generalisations to help us understand the ongoing reception of Ball. *The Life and Death of Jack Straw* is a late Elizabethan attempt to navigate live issues of suitable governance, tensions between ruler and commons, rebellion, protest, and riots with, of course, the emphasis on the Elizabethan present as much as the fourteenth century.[11] While in this version of the revolt it is the somewhat tragic and misled figure of Jack Straw who is the leader killed by the lionised William Walworth, it is the 'two arch rebels' Wat Tyler and (especially) Parson Ball who are constructed familiarly by the establishment characters as the most dangerous or least sympathetic of the rebels. Ball is variously referred to by his enemies, including (among others) the king, as 'a naughty and seditious Priest...A person more notorious than the rest,' 'that cursed priest,' 'obstinate,' and an 'accursed and seditious Priest' (4.12.813–15, 820, 835–36, 873). And in doing so, this gave the play official respectability. The Clown, Tom Miller, provides a more comical description of Ball, who shares with the Shakespearean Cade a thirst for a good drink:

> What is he an honest man? the devill he is, he is the Parson of the Towne,
> You thinke ther's no knaverie hid under a black gowne,
> Find him a pulpit but twise in the year,
> And Ile find him fortie times in the ale-house tasting strong beare.
> (1.1.49–54)

9   Irving Ribner, *The English History Play in the Age of Shakespeare* (London: Routledge, [1957] 2005), 71–72. Longstaffe, 'Introduction,' in Longstaffe (ed.), *A Critical Edition of the Life and Death of Jack Straw (1594)*, 1–8 and 78, for possible influence on *Hell's Broke Loose*; Schillinger, 'Begging at the Gate.' For references to the play, I use Longstaffe's *Critical Edition*.

10 On the various suggestions about authorship and contexts see, e.g., Mary Grace Muse Adkins, 'A Theory about *The Life and Death of Jack Straw*,' *The University of Texas Studies in English* XXVIII (1949): 57–82; Ribner, *English History Play*, 71–76; Longstaffe, 'Introduction,' in Longstaffe (ed.), *A Critical Edition of the Life and Death of Jack Straw (1594)*, 1–16; Schillinger, 'Begging at the Gate,' 112, 113–15 n. 5.

11 On the context of discussions about the relationships among the social hierarchy—and different ideas about the correct running of the country from top, bottom, and middle—being played out in *The Life and Death of Jack Straw*, see Mathur, 'Rebellion from Below,' 346–49.

Certainly, the play provides the audience with overt criticisms of Parson Ball who, after all, will fail. In this sense, we have both a conventional presentation of Ball from above and one from below that could certainly be read critically, or at least would not unduly worry a censor.

But, as Stephen Schillinger and Maya Mathur point out in different ways, understanding differing perspectives among the audience and among popular ideas of remedying social ills is important here.[12] In the case of Tom Miller's assessment at least, locating Ball in the tradition of the radicalism of the rural alehouse (and perhaps the comical reputation of the town parson) would have at least made him a familiar figure.[13] Moreover, Parson Ball's extended discussion that follows Tom Miller's assessment could be read as at least a fair airing or representation of Ball's concerns (and Tyler's and Straw's), even if there is an accompanying assumption that they should be rejected. Similarly, Parson Ball and his discussion are presented more sympathetically than the corrosive Nobs and it might be significant that the entirely fictional rebel is also most problematic of them.[14] Indeed, Ball's speech and context provides a more sympathetic portrayal than that found in the chronicles.[15] Shorn of the editorial judgements of the chroniclers, Ball's speech not only reflects the concerns we might expect from someone using chronicles for more antiquarian purposes, but it would have tapped into traditions and concerns of those among the disillusioned lower orders and into contemporary critiques of the states of poverty and neglect in the parishes.[16]

12 Schillinger, 'Begging at the Gate,' 98–99; Mathur, 'Rebellion from Below,' 353–56.
13 Schillinger, 'Begging at the Gate,' 98–99.
14 Schillinger, 'Begging at the Gate,' is a particularly important re-reading of the play in this respect.
15 E.g.: 'It might be remarked parenthetically that since historians report him as a half-mad, renegade priest, he might fitly have been accorded a clownish part. Yet the author uses him for a serious dramatic purpose' (Adkins, 'A Theory about *The Life and Death of Jack Straw*,' 64–65); 'Ball—who in Holinshed is represented as a raving lunatic, wandering the landscape preaching radicalism' (Schillinger, 'Begging at the Gate,' 95). Such assessments are not inaccurate but, beyond the chroniclers' negative judgements, there remains a repeating of inherited sources and a relatively fair-minded presentation of Ball's speeches. For a nuanced take on the complexity of Holinshed's assessment of the rebels, see, e.g., Patterson, *Reading Holinshed's Chronicles*, 19–95.
16 Dobson, *Peasants' Revolt of 1381*, 390, put it this way: 'But much its most interesting feature is the way in which the rebels and their grievances are presented with a considerable degree of sympathy. Like Froissart, and presumably more by accident than design, the author gives the best lines in the play to

Thus, in *The Life and Death of Jack Straw* we still have the Ball who worried about the state of England, who can refer to 'good Scripture' to show that God does not permit such socio-economic exploitation, and who delivered his Adam and Eve saying when 'it were better to have this communitie, Than to have this difference in degrees: The landlord his rent, the lawyer his fees.' This was a time when the 'Rich have all, the poore live in miserie' and, with an allusion to the Parable of the Rich Man and Lazarus, when 'rich men triumph to see the poore beg at their gate' (Luke 16.19–21), and when the widow was not looked after and struggles (cf., e.g., Exodus 22.22; Deuteronomy 24.21; Mark 12.41–44; Luke 21.1–4; Acts 6.1; 1 Timothy 5):

> The Widdow, that hath but a pan of brass,
> And scarse a house to hide her head,
> Sometimes no penny to buy her bread,
> Must pay her Landlord many a groat,
> Or twill be puld out of her throat (1.1.55–89)

But the remedy involved the sort of communal sharing and distribution associated with Acts 2.44–45 and 4.32–35 ('And make division equally/Of each mans goods indifferently,' 1.1.86–87), which was reflective of ongoing anxieties in political discourse concerning commonwealth, as Schillinger has shown with additional reference to the representation of the rebels in the play.[17] Ball and the other rebels know that to achieve this fairer system there needs to be a replacement of the hierarchical system with a new archbishop of Canterbury and chancellor and new lords and masters (I.90–98). Even if elite or other readers saw this as self-serving, it is in line with the earliest portrayals of Ball and not out of place in the history of peasant and

---

John Ball.' Or, as Mary Adkins put it: 'Why, in spite of inartistic mishandling, did he invest the rebels' cause with a considerable sense of right?...the most eloquent spokesman for the rebels is Parson Ball, who talks sententiously but not clownishly' ('A Theory about *The Life and Death of Jack Straw*,' 62, 64; see 67 on critiques about the rich neglecting the 'country poor'). Lister Matheson ('The Peasants' Revolt through Five Centuries,' 143) made a similar assessment: 'the characterization of the rebels is surprisingly dignified and sympathetic.' Cf. Patterson, *Shakespeare and the Popular Voice*, 46–47. For further detailed discussion of the possibilities of sympathetic readings and receptions, including in the second edition, see, e.g., Longstaffe, 'Introduction,' in Longstaffe (ed.), *A Critical Edition of the Life and Death of Jack Straw (1594)*, 89–99; Schillinger, 'Begging at the Gate,' 89–93; Mathur, 'Rebellion from Below,' 359–61.

17 Schillinger, 'Begging at the Gate,' 99. On issues of commonwealth more generally, see Mathur, 'Rebellion from Below.'

rural constructions of an alternative hierarchy, or at least a plea for legitimate access to power.[18] This Ball is accepting (as we might also expect) of necessity of the physical violence required to bring about this change ('And rightly may you follow Armes, To rid you from these civill harmes,' 1.1.88–89), knowing of the consequences of failure, and, in his defiant final words, unrepentant of his ideas and actions (4.12.896–99). Whatever we make of the ideological stance (or stances) of *The Life and Death of Jack Straw*, the play played a role in keeping alive the sort of memory for which Ball would later be partly lauded in the later radical receptions.

Samuel Rowlands's *Hell's Broke Loose*

The same cannot be said for the other reference to Parson Ball from 'The Life and Death of Iohn Leyden' in Samuel Rowlands's verse, *Hell's Broke Loose* (1605).[19] *Hell's Broke Loose* is another example of how the language of 'reformation' (*2 Henry VI* 4.2.62) could be tied in with perceptions of egotism, excessively radical change, and sedition, and the Anabaptists are presented as the example *par excellence*:

> Wee are the men will make our Valours knowne,
> To teach this doting world new reformation:
> New Lawes, and new Religion of our owne.
> To bring our selues in wondrous admiration:
> Let's turne the world cleane vpside downe, (mad slaues)
> So to be talk'd of, when w'are in our Graues. (*Hell's Broke Loose* 17)

What is particularly significant in Rowlands's account is that the theological right-hand-men of the 1520 and 1381 insurgencies from below are intertwined with each other as much as their famous theology is intertwined with sedition:

> Then with my trade, what's hee that hath to doo?
> Old Father *Adam* was a *Taylour* too
> …

---

18 Cf. Longstaffe, 'Introduction,' in Longstaffe (ed.), *A Critical Edition of the Life and Death of Jack Straw (1594)*, 29–30, 93–94; Mathur, 'Rebellion from Below,' 356–59.

19 References to *Hell's Broke Loose* are taken from Edmund Gosse and Sidney J. H. Herrtage (eds.), *The Complete Works of Samuel Rowlands 1598–1628: Vol. 1* (Glasgow: Hunterian Club, 1880), 1–48.

> And let this Title witnes my renowne,
> *IOHN LEYDEN Taylour, King of Munster towne.*
> ...
> *Tom Mynter*, a madd Rogue, our *Parrish Clarke*,
> Whose doctrine wee with diligence did marke.
>
> Hee taught on topp of Mole-hill, Bush, and Tree,
> The Traytors text in *England*; *Parson Ball*
> Affirming wee ought Kings apeece to bee.
> And euery thing be common vnto all:
> For when old *Adam* delu'd, and *Euah* span,
> Where was my silken veluet Gentleman?
>
> Wee *Adams* Sonnes; Hee Monarch of the Earth,
> How can wee chuse but be of Royall blood?
> Beeing all descended from so high a birth?
> Why should not wee share wealth, and worldly good?
> Tush Maisters (quoth *Tom Mynter*) reason binds it,
> Hee that lacks Mony, take it where he finds it. (*Hell's Broke Loose* 14–15)

The typological and theological connections between Ball and 'Tom Mynter' are made explicit in the Prologue by none other than Jack Straw's ghost:

> But that in name, and nature wee agree,
> An *English* Traytor I, *Dutch* Rebell hee.
> In my Consort, I had the Priest *Iohn Ball*;
> *Mynter* the Clarke, unto his share did fall.
> Hee, to haue all things common did intend:
> And my Rebellion, was to such an end. (*Hell's Broke Loose* 9)

Indeed, the very framing of *Hell's Broke Loose* in the preface refers to the 1381 revolt (and the Hacket insurgency) because, like the respective seditious leaders and their theologians, they are comparative types which belong to a wider history and a human (and satanic) phenomenon.

Rowlands's history of prophetic or messianic types, heresy, blasphemy, and sedition stretches back centuries, and examples are given from the first century onward, including Theudas and Judas the Galilean and their promises of Jewish deliverance (Acts 5.35–39; cf. Josephus, *War* 2.118, 433; *Antiquities* 18.23; 20.97–98). But this history is one where religion and political sedition are categories that often go hand-in-hand,[20] even

---

20 Cf. Longstaffe, 'Introduction', in Longstaffe (ed.), *A Critical Edition of the Life and Death of Jack Straw (1594)*, 78: 'the specifically religious element that Ball

though religion is but a pretence. In the case of the Germanic 'Rebels and Heretiques,' they 'would be Reformers of the Church and State; new Doctrine of their owne franticke conceites,' including 'all things should be common.' This is a history that has deluded the people from time-to-time; in addition to the leaders of the Anabaptists, such views were 'imbraced by thousands of the Boores, and vulgar illiterate Clownes' (*Hell's Broke Loose* 6). Thus, the 1381 rebellion, featuring 'Iacke Straw, Watt Tyler, Tom Myller, Iohn Ball &c.' (*Hell's Broke Loose* 7), epitomises this tradition. In one (presumably unintentional) sense, it throws back at Ball the allegation of a disruptive, even devilish lineage (see Chapter 2), for this is a tradition which all of the 'Rebell race' and 'all Traytors' bear witness to a world where God providentially and 'with vengeance rewards all such State-disturbers, and factious Rebels' (*Hell's Broke Loose* 8; cf. Milton, *Paradise Regained* 2.179–81). Different audience members would no doubt have taken a figure like Shakespeare's Cade in different ways, but it is not difficult to see that there was one way they would have been expected to understand a pronouncement of 'reformation' found in Rowlands's history of heresy and sedition.

The Reformation Continues: Robert Persons and Thomas James

Understanding the 1381 uprising in terms of sedition and the threat to the order of things, and its alleged connections with Wycliffe, meant Ball and the insurgents constituted a historical example that had to be handled carefully in Protestant England, as well as (and because of) having potential use for Catholic polemics. Jesuit priest Robert Persons used this history as part of a dispute over the English nature of the Catholic Church.[21] In *The warn-word to Sir Francis Hastinges wast-word* (1602), Persons dealt with Walsingham's potentially problematic presentation of impiety in the pre-Reformation English church by focusing on the example of Wycliffe as

---

signifies is probably the reason for Straw's (as opposed to Cade's or Kett's) presence here.'

21 For context, see, e.g., Francis Edwards, *Robert Persons: The Biography of an Elizabethan Jesuit, 1546–1610* (St Louis, MO: The Institute of Jesuit Sources, 1995); Victor Houliston, 'Persons [Parsons], Robert (1546–1610)', *ODNB* (23 September 2004); Victor Houliston, *Catholic Resistance in Elizabethan England: Robert Persons's Jesuit Polemic, 1580–1610* (Aldershot: Ashgate, 2007), 95–96.

arch-corrupter. Wycliffe's satanic doctrines in turn fuelled the 'most barbarous rebellion of the common people vnder *wat Tyler and Iack straw*,' which paralleled the malign influence of Luther ('as the lyke did in Germany in the yeare 1525. Of Luthers').[22] In response to Persons and in defence of Wycliffe as a good English Protestant, the first librarian of the Bodleian Library and dedicated anti-Catholic, Thomas James, wrote *An apologie for Iohn Wickliffe* (1608).[23] He flatly rejected the claim that Wycliffe's teachings were seditious. James countered Persons's (and Walsingham's) history with reference to Froissart where he read about the 'chiefe cause of that great rebellion of the Commons,' alongside Tyler and Jack Straw: Ball, 'one of Bals Priests...who drew multitudes of people after him.' Ball's 'foule and monstrous heresie' was thus maliciously attributed to Wycliffe. Instead, it was Ball who sought 'to condemne al Laws, despise the Cleargie, and to rebell against there Soveraigne, because there was an equalitie of al men, and communion of al things, which is pure Anabaptisme, or Diabolisme rather.'[24]

We should note here James's reference to Ball as one of Baal's priests which was a label fittingly evoking the ebb and flow of the toleration of idolatry among rulers according to the Old Testament, such as in the story of Elijah challenging the wicked king Ahab, mocking idol worshippers and executing their priests (1 Kings 18–19), and stories of wiping out the house

22 Robert Persons, *The warn-word to Sir Francis Hastinges wast-word conteyning the issue of three former treateses, the Watch-word, the Ward-word and the Wast-word (intituled by Sir Francis, an Apologie or defence of his Watch-word) togeather with certaine admonitions & warnings to thesaid knight and his followers* (Antwerp, 1602), 7–10.

23 For context see, e.g., Richard W. Clement, 'Librarianship and Polemics: The Career of Thomas James (1572–1629),' *Libraries and Culture* 26 (1991): 269–82; R. Julian Roberts, 'James, Thomas (1572/3–1629),' *ODNB* (23 September 2004); Paul Nelles, 'The Uses of Orthodoxy and Jacobean Erudition: Thomas James and the Bodleian Library,' in Mordechai Feingold (ed.), *History of Universities: Volume XXII/1* (Oxford: Oxford University Press, 2007), 21–70; Karen Sawyer Marsalek, 'Staging Allegiance, Re-membering Trials: King Henry VIII and the Blackfriars Theater,' in Kenneth J. E. Graham and Philip D. Collington (ed.), *Shakespeare and Religious Change* (New York: Palgrave Macmillan, 2009), 133–50 (140–42); Alexandra Walsham, 'History, Memory, and the English Reformation,' *The Historical Journal* 55 (2010): 899–938; Royal, 'John Foxe's "Acts and Monuments",' 100–104.

24 Thomas James, *An apologie for Iohn Wickliffe shewing his conformitie with the now Church of England; with answere to such slaunderous obiections, as haue beene lately vrged against him by Father Parsons, the apologists, and others* (Oxford, 1608), 63–66; cf. 37.

of Ahab and Baal worship (2 Kings 9–11; cf. Judges 6.25–32). As we will see in the next chapter, the crude overlapping of Baal/Ball would be taken up in Civil War England and in a polemic against Ball that would make James's look positively tame. For now, we can note that the view complained about by Polydore Vergil—namely, that including Ball as a main cause of the uprising excused the mismanagement of the realm—had become polemically useful and common by the beginning of the seventeenth century. And Ball, or the views associated with him, could even form the same assumptions for Catholic and Protestant alike in constructing the extremities of acceptability by combining sedition with devilish doctrine and the ultimate example of reform in excess: Anabaptism.

The Reformation in England, then, had given the reception of Ball a new lease of life as questions of sedition and religion took on such new meanings. By the early seventeenth century, some of the most prominent publications left behind a Ball who could be understood sometimes contradictorily as a Lollard martyr and precursor to the English Reformation, a radical reformer, an Anabaptist, a heretic, an ideologue, as devilish, a latter-day priest of Baal, a voice of disturbing lower-order discontent, a critic of exploitation, a rabble-rouser, a rebel leader carrying a state-threatening seditious menace, and a more than solid drinker. Whether any of this was a good or bad thing depended on the perspective, though it was typically framed as and assumed to be bad. Certainly, there are contradictory portrayals and there was at least an awareness that Ball gave voice to grievances of the lower orders. But few prominent (Protestant) presentations would publicly agree with Bale's claim in passing that Ball was a precursor to English Protestantism. Rarely presented in heroic terms, Ball was a figure ready for further exploitation in the following centuries where questions of revolution would become more acute.

6
The Priest of Baal in Revolutionary England

The medieval, Tudor, and Jacobean receptions of Ball and 1381 provided a ready-made cipher for the seventeenth-century English revolution where the questions concerning the combined issues of authority, hierarchy, revolt, and religious reform and reformation came to a head. More specifically, the mid-seventeenth century was marked by conflicting public anxieties and concerns about puritanism, religious radicalism, Catholicism, Catholicizing tendencies, Laudianism, Irish Catholic rebels, Scottish Presbyterianism, European wars of religion, religious freedom, received theological ideas, iconoclasm, political representation, democracy, liberty, rights, land ownership, social hierarchies, church hierarchies, anticlericalism, divine authority, parliamentary authority, royal prerogative, the divine right of the monarch, and, of course, regicide. The events of the mid-1640s and 1650s, especially when combined with the 1688 revolution that put William of Orange on the throne, would have a profound influence on the shaping of English political discourse and historiography of the seventeenth and eighteenth centuries and, as we might expect, this had some impact on the history of the interpretation of Ball beyond. But while the pre-existing templates for understanding the revolt could easily be—and emphatically were—reapplied to and updated in light of revolutionary England, it was not automatically apparent on the eve of the Civil War that something even more dramatic than 1381 was about to happen.

John Trussell's Ball and Wall

A case in point is the 1636 continuation of Samuel Daniel's *The collection of the history of England* by the Winchester dignitary, poet, antiquarian, and historian, John Trussell. While not without his idiosyncrasies, Trussell was the type of figure with whom we have become familiar. If he was educated at Westminster School (as is possible though not certain), he would have had an education grounded in the Elizabethan model of the church while later on he certainly engaged in fairly standard anti-puritan polemics. As a younger man it is also possible that he had Catholic sympathies (which may never have quite gone away), though he settled into ecclesiastical and political establishment life—and accompanying understandings of the order of the world—by the time of his *Continuation*.[1]

Trussell's narrative of the 1381 uprising corresponds with what we might now expect. It begins with the poll tax and the problems it caused on both sides ('levying whereof procured much heart-burning, and did much alyen the hearts of the subjects from the King'). But it was 'one *Iohn Balle*' who intensified resentments and worked 'secretly to informe the inferiour sort of people, such as were poore and needy.' Ball was labelled not only 'a factious clergy man' but also a 'scholler of *Wickcliff*,' whose secret teaching was about descent from Adam, the laws of the realm hindering participation in 'Christian liberty,' authority, and land ownership being used to exploit the lower orders. And thus 'amongst Christians there should be an equall share of all things, and that in common.' Through his famous Adam and Eve sermon, Ball traitorously lit the tinderbox of rebellious inclinations in the shires among the 'vulgar...from rusticke to villanie,' and even reached (indeed 'infected') London and the 'poorer sort of mechanicks and handicrafts, desperately inclined to mutinie.'[2]

At this point, we are told not only about the leadership of Wat Tyler but also of others, including a striking use of the alternative spelling, 'Iohn Wall,' who here seems to have been understood as a different person and religious leader who would be associated with Jack Straw in Trussell's narrative.[3] While Ball and Wall seem to be two different characters (partly

1 For details on Trussell's biography and the *Continuation* see, e.g., Adrienne Rosen, 'Trussell, John (bap. 1575, d. 1648),' *ODNB* (3 January 2008); Roxane C. Murph, *Rewriting the Wars of the Roses: The 17th Century Royalist Histories of John Trussell, Sir Francis Biondi and William Habington* (London: McFarland & Company, Inc., 2007); Robert Frederick William Smith, 'John Trussell: A Life (1575–1648)' (PhD Thesis: University of Southampton, 2013).

2 John Trussell, *A Continuation of the Collection of the History of England beginning where Samuel Daniell Esquire ended, with the raigne of Edward the third, and ending where the honourable Vicount Saint Albones began, with the life of Henry the seventh, being a compleat history of the beginning and end of the dissention betwixt the two houses of Yorke and Lancaster. With the matches and issue of all the kings, princes, dukes, marquesses, earles, and vicounts of this nation, deceased, during those times* (London, 1636), 4.

3 '*Wat Tyler* a Taylor who commanded in chiefe, with their grave minister, *Iohn Wall*: *Iacke Straw*, a Thresher, *Iack Sheppard* of the Councell of warre, under

corrected for later editions), Wall is still understood in ways familiar to the history of Ball's reception at this point. During the retelling of the happenings in London, and reinforcing church hierarchies (no doubt with implications for the seventeenth-century present), we are told that the 'Reverend Simon Arch. B. of Canterbury' had previously 'convented their proloquutor *Iohn Wall*, for promulgating his dangerous if not damnable positions.' Wall is similarly given the Ball-esque label, 'that pernitious priest,' with additional hot Protestant qualification in a marginal note, namely a 'Perditus & pernitiosus praesbyter.' It is worth noting that there is close association made here between Wall and 'John Wraw' ('a whelpe of the same litter, a Chaplaine for the Divels good grace'). As the 'tumults' following the attack on Tyler 'were thus in agitation' through Wall, Wrawe was sent to East Anglia, a connection occasionally developed in the history of reception (see, e.g., Paul de Rapin-Thoyras in Chapter 8). In the narration of Ball's activities and capture in Coventry, Ball is said to have 'seconded Wall and Wraw in inciting the multitude to insurrection.'[4]

After the execution of Ball, we are told by Trussell about this 'generall flame of combustion being extinct.'[5] If we (perhaps unfairly) reread this statement in terms of what would happen in the seventeenth century, Trussell could not have been more wrong.

Remembering 1381 in the 1640s

The inherited discourses surrounding 1381 and religious radicalism could be redeployed as England moved towards, into, and beyond civil war and revolution. As John Walter noted, royalist propaganda of spring and summer 1642 connected challenges to royal power with popular uprisings and disorder by invoking comparisons with Tyler, Jack Cade, Robert Kett, and Anabaptism.[6] Indeed, when both houses of Parliament issued the Nineteen

---

the tytle of the Kings men and the servants of the Common-wealth of *England*' (Trussell, *Continuation*, 4).
4 Trussell, *Continuation*, 6–7.
5 Trussell, *Continuation*, 7.
6 John Walter, *Understanding Popular Violence in the English Revolution: The Colchester Plunderers* (Cambridge: Cambridge University Press, 1999), 19. On royalist use of the 1381 revolt, see, e.g., Anthony Fletcher, *The Outbreak of the English Civil War* (London: Edward Arnold, 1981), 296; Michael Braddick, *God's Fury, England's Fire: A New History of the English Civil Wars* (London: Penguin, 2008), 236; Basdeo, *Life and Legend of a Rebel Leader*, loc 772–881. Cf., e.g.,

Propositions concerning checks on royal power, as well as church reform and the suppression of Catholicism, one response in the King's Answer (June 1642) is particularly telling. Encroaching on the traditional balances of power, it was argued, would impact not only the monarchy but also the church and the Lords. With the accompanying popular unrest, the people would,

> set up for themselves, call Parity and Independence, Liberty; devour that Estate which had devoured the rest; Destroy all Rights and Proprieties, all distinctions of Families and Merit; And by this meanes this splendid and excellently distinguished form of Government, end in a dark equall Chaos of Confusion, and the long Line of Our many noble Ancestors in a Jack Cade, or a Wat Tyler.[7]

An extended royalist polemic can be found in the anonymous work *The Iust Reward of Rebels, or the Life and Death of Wat Tyler and Iack Straw* (1642), the main narrative of which did not include Ball despite opportunity to do so (e.g., when the action moves past Maidstone to Blackheath). The story ends with an explicit mention of the reapplication to the Irish rebels as promised on the title page: 'horridnesse of Rebellion; as that of Ireland…whose rebellion and outrages I hope will be considered, and they speedily (by the permission of the Almighty) receive their just rewards.' Ball then gets a mention in the reappearance of Jack Straw's ghost, the same account as found in the preface to 'The Life and Death of Iohn Leyden' in Samuel Rowlands's *Hell's Broke Loose* (1605) (see Chapter 5) but which is now tacked on to the end of *The Iust Reward of Rebels*, presumably by a second hand.[8] But this time there is a marginal note where Irish rebels are mentioned in connection with the claim that 'Traytors are bloudy, and have

---

James F. Larkin (ed.), *Stuart Royal Proclamations 2, Royal Proclamations of King Charles I, 1625–46* (Oxford: Oxford University Press, 1983), 770–75.

7 Charles I, 'XIX Propositions Made by Both Houses of Parliament to the Kings Most Excellent Majestie: With His Majesties Answer Thereunto, York, 1642,' in Joyce Lee Malcolm (ed.), *The Struggle for Sovereignty: Seventeenth-Century English Political Tracts: Volume 1* (Indianapolis: Liberty Fund, 1999), 112–29 (125).

8 Matheson, 'The Peasants' Revolt through Five Centuries of Rumor and Reporting,' 134, suggested a second author responsible, with reference to the appendix contradicting the explanation for the confusion over the deaths of Tyler and Jack Straw. The sudden inclusion of Ball as a central character further strengthens Matheson's claim.

bloudy ends.'[9] If nothing else, the story of 1381 could still be reapplied to whatever rebellions were in mind and this would not be the last time Irish rebels were invoked in the history of Ball's reception.

Perhaps the relative omission of Ball in such polemics should not be surprising with big names like Tyler and Jack Straw always available. But the omission is hardly sustained. The royalist Sir Thomas Aston (1600–1646) of Cheshire was a church moderate and conservative, critical of Laudianism but worried about Presbyterian reform,[10] who used Ball as a point of historical comparison in his polemics. In Aston's *Survey of Presbytery*, Ball turns up in a familiar way in a section on '*The inordinate violence of the Presbyterians*'. In critiquing the idea of a congregation having the keys to the church (rather than pastors or governors), Aston noted the 'seditious argument' that 'wee are all the sons of Adam, borne free, some of them say, the Gospel hath made them free' and that 'Law once subverted' will 'appeare good equitie to such Cancellours, to share the earth equally.' According to the explanatory marginal note, a 'Priest [who] stirred up rebellion' at the time of Richard II was associated with this argument.[11] Presumably some readers would have known just who that priest was and the panic he or his types might create.

Ball's teaching was always more likely to have resonance on the more radical end of the opposing side—as has long been noted, the combination of stories about Adam and Eve and levelling ideas are well attested in radical and apocalyptic texts of the seventeenth century.[12] These did not of course have to include Ball, but some may have implied such a connection. From the letters and papers of the puritan Harley family of Herefordshire, there is an intriguing reference which includes a reference to Ball/Wall:

---

9   Anonymous, *The Iust Reward of Rebels, or The Life and Death of Iack Straw, and Wat Tyler* (London, 1642), no page numbers given.

10 E. C. Vernon, 'Aston, Sir Thomas, first baronet (1600–1646)', *ODNB* (30 May 2013).

11 *Survey of Presbytery* in Thomas Aston, *A Remonstrance, against Presbitery. Exhibited by divers of the nobilitie, gentrie, ministers and inhabitants of the county palatine of Chester with the motives of that remonstrance. Together with a short survey of the Presbyterian discipline* (London, 1641), Sect. 13.

12 For discussion see, e.g., Hill, *English Bible and the Seventeenth-Century Revolution*, 40–41, 127, 132–33, 148, 156, 201–203, 221–22, 371–72, 376, 390; Philip C. Almond, *Adam and Eve in Seventeenth-Century Thought* (Cambridge: Cambridge University Press, 1999), 102–5; Julia Ipgrave, *Adam in Seventeenth Century Political Writing in England and New England* (New York: Routledge, 2017), 120–96.

1642, April 27—Part of a sermon by Dr. Rogers, in which he compares King Charles with David. He refers to the preachers Drew and Wall, one of whom preached on the lines—When Adam delved and Eve span. Who was then the gentleman?[13]

With reference to this text, Christopher Hill claimed that 'in 1642 preachers were quoting "When Adam delved and Eve span, Who was then the gentleman?" So it was only a development, not a daring innovation, when Christopher Feake in 1646 declared that there was an "enmity against Christ" in aristocracy and monarchy.'[14] With reference to Hill, Philip Almond also mentioned Ball's sermon and the Adam and Eve couplet, adding 'It was a text much favoured by preachers in the ferment of the 1640s. To those who asked it, the answer was clear: there were then no gentlemen, for all were of the same level.'[15] But we should be careful about making too much of this meagre evidence when it comes to the case of Ball and anything relating to his personal popularity. As Jacqueline Eales shows, the sermon of the royalist Henry Rogers compared the flight of Charles from London to David's from Jerusalem and attacked Londoners for their insolence and irreverence towards authority and the sovereign. Rogers also presented supporters of Parliament and those responsible for Charles's flight as a lower order rabble featuring Protestant extremists such as Anabaptists. These were part of a historical tradition of heresy which, Rogers noted, had 'sprung up again,' adding, 'and I would there were not some preachers too as John Drew and Wall, one of which chose this text— when Adam delved and Eve span, who was then the gentleman? And so he would have no man about another, but all men alike and to throw down all government, learning and religion.'[16] While levelling ideas understood

13 *The Manuscripts of His Grace the Duke of Portland Preserved at Welbeck Abbey, Vol. III* (London: Eyre and Spottiswoode, 1894), 86. Incidentally, the contemporary name 'John Wall' turns up in relation to a servant in arrears in the previous entry (Nathaniel Tomkins to [Sir Robert Harley], 8 April 1642). On the parliamentarian Harleys, see, e.g., Jacqueline Eales, 'Sir Robert Harley, K.B. (1579–1656) and the "Character" of a Puritan,' *British Library Journal* 15 (1989): 134–57; Jacqueline Eales, *Puritans and Roundheads: The Harleys of Brampton Bryan and the Outbreak of the English Civil War* (Cambridge: Cambridge University Press, 1990); Jacqueline Eales, 'Harley, Sir Robert (bap. 1579, d. 1656),' *ODNB* (17 September 2015).
14 Christopher Hill, *The World Turned Upside Down: Radical Ideas during the English Revolution* (London: Maurice Temple Smith, 1972), 35.
15 Almond, *Adam and Eve*, 102.
16 Rogers's sermon notes (27 April 1642) quoted in Eales, *Puritans and Roundheads*, 140.

with reference to Adam and Eve were no doubt amplified in revolutionary England, and provide an important context for understanding Rogers's sermon, we should probably restrict our reading of Rogers to being another kind of propagandist reference to the events of 1381 being repeated in the present.[17]

Whatever we make of such a passing reference, Ball and the 1381 uprising do not seem to have been a prominent source of authority or a direct reference point for the major mid-seventeenth-century radicals, even if there was the shared resource of the Bible and overlapping ideas that had been developed over the intervening centuries. In the case of the radical democratising ideas of John Lilburne, the 1381 revolt with its emphasis on an alternative ecclesiastical and theocratic order may even have been problematic. Irrespective, Lilburne (8 June 1649), when challenging the Rump Parliament and later at his trial (October 1649), could use the revolt as an assumed point of reference his opponents would understand:

> it is as visible as the Sun when it shines in its glory and splendour, That Corah, Dathan and Abiram of old were never such Rebels against Authoritie as the General and his Councel are, nor the Anabaptists at Munster with John of Leydon and Neperdullion were never more contemners of Authority; nor Jack Straw, nor Wat Tiler, nor all those famous men mentioned with a black pen in our Histories, and called Rebels and Traytors, can never be put in any scale of equall balance, for all manner of Rebellions and Treasons against all sorts and kindes of Magistracy, with the Generall and his Councell.[18]

Among Levellers and soldiers there was further awareness of a live tradition and allegation echoing Ball's views on communality, even if Ball himself is not mentioned. *The English Souldiers Standard* (5 April 1649) noted allegations of associations with 'Jack Cade, and Wat Tiler, and the Anabaptists of Munster' who 'would have all things common, wives and all.' But, the argument goes, 'Your General and Gen. Officers being then Jack Cade and Wat Tiler' who 'would have all things common; who now setting up for themselves, have packt a Parliament and a Councell of State for their

---

17 Worth comparing here is the account by Bulstrode Whitlocke (1605–1675) in *Memorials of the English Affairs, from the suppos'd expedition of Brute to this island, to the end of the reign of King James the first* (London, 1709), 105–7. Here '*John Wall*' stirred up the discontent of the 'Inferior People' after the poll tax with his teaching on descent from Adam and the Adam and Eve couplet.

18 John Lilburne, *The Legall Fundamentall Liberties of the People of England Revived, Asserted, and Vindicated* (London, 8 June 1649), 38.

purpose, must bestow the same language upon them that oppose those, as was bestowed upon themselves.'[19]

Again, this is more of a hint (at most) rather than mention of Ball. But, as the Rogers reference suggests, he would hardly have gone unnoticed given the now weighty history of interpretation accumulated by the seventeenth century. Indeed, in revolutionary England, Ball played a central role in prominent histories of the 1381 revolt as he regularly appeared as one of the great instigators of the uprising which helps us understand more about some of the assumptions behind 1381 as an ongoing point of reference for discussions of betrayal, rebellion, and treason.

Richard Baker's Orator

Towards the end of his life, the devotional writer and MP, Sir Richard Baker (c. 1568–1645), had fallen on hard times. He had lost his wealth by taking on the debts of his father-in-law and consequently spent the rest of his days in Fleet prison, London. During this time, and with sufficient access to books and printing services, he published *A Chronicle of the Kings of England* in 1643. Baker's *Chronicle* was popular enough to be republished several times with revisions and continuations after his death and into the eighteenth century, including a continuation (by John Milton's royalist nephew, Edward Phillips) published in 1660 and a translation into Dutch in 1649.[20] The 1643 edition was dedicated to Prince Charles, son and heir of Charles I, with the conventional advice about a ruler learning and acquiring sounder judgement from understanding the past, though a perspective that was not uncritically accepted by the end of the seventeenth century.[21] But there was also one eye on what was happening in the present. Happy

---

19 *The English Souldiers Standard to repair to, for Wisdom and Understanding in these doleful backsliding times. To be read by every honest Officer to his Souldiers, and by the Souldiers one to another* (London, 5 April 1649). The text is sometimes attributed to William Walwyn.

20 For the details of Baker's life and the publication and reception of *A Chronicle of the Kings of England*, see, e.g., Martine Watson Brownley, 'Sir Richard Baker's "Chronicle" and Later Seventeenth-Century English Historiography', *Huntington Library Quarterly* 52 (1989): 481–500; G. H. Martin, 'Baker, Sir Richard (c. 1568–1645)', *ODNB* (23 September 2004); Ben Dew, *Commerce, Finance and Statecraft: Histories of England, 1600–1780* (Manchester: Manchester University Press, 2018), 74–75.

21 Brownley, 'Sir Richard Baker's "Chronicle"', 489.

though Baker was to have seen the days of Charles I, 'it were not a great unhappines to see them overcast with clouds' for 'when these clouds shal be dispel'd' it might 'make him shine with the greater Splendor.' And so the expected 'joy' of 'glorious times' of Prince Charles's reign would be 'for another Age.'[22]

Ball appears near the beginning of the narrative of the revolt. Ball is tacked on to the famous story (derived from John Stow, even though it has earlier origins)[23] of the sexual assault of *John* Tyler's daughter carried out by the poll-tax collector, after which John Tyler hit the collector so hard that 'his braines flew out.' On hearing of this, Ball ('a factious Clergie-man') took advantage of 'this Misgovernment' and told people 'that this difference of mens Estates, where some are Potentates, and some are Bondmen, was against Christian liberty' and took up the theme of 'When Adam delv'd and Eve span, who was then Gentleman?'[24] Despite the awareness of the claims of some bad governance in the earlier editions ('the rude behaviour of a Collector of the Poll-money'), Ball is still presented as the opportunist primarily responsible for spreading revolt. His preaching incensed the commons and brought them together, beginning in Kent and Essex before spreading throughout various other counties before moving on to Blackheath and London in mass numbers. Notably, this teaching included the idea of loyalty to King Richard and the commons (but not to any king called 'John,' i.e., John of Gaunt).[25] Ball returns in Baker's account after the main actions of the rebels in the retelling of the leaders' executions. The presentation of Ball is in keeping with his malign influence in first spreading the uprising: he is 'their Incendiary.' Baker further added one of Ball's letters (the 'John Sheep' letter, first presented in Walsingham's account) written to 'the Rebell-rabble of Essex' which further shows 'how fit an Oratour he was for such an Auditory, and what strength of perswasion there was in Non-sence.'[26] Ball-the-orator would have a long reception history and in this instance it would not have taken too much imagination for audiences to read into any given religious radical of the mid-seventeenth century.

---

22 Richard Baker, *A chronicle of the Kings of England, from the time of the Romans goverment* [sic] *unto the raigne of our soveraigne lord, King Charles containing all passages of state or church, with all other observations proper for a chronicle* (London, 1643), no page number.
23 Matheson, 'The Peasants' Revolt through Five Centuries,' 133.
24 Baker, *A chronicle of the Kings of England*, 142.
25 Baker, *A chronicle of the Kings of England*, 142.
26 Baker, *A chronicle of the Kings of England*, 143.

John Cleveland's Priest of Baal

No speculation is needed to make such connections in the case of *The Idol of the Clownes, or, Insurrection of Wat the Tyler, with His Priests Baal and Straw* (1654), attributed to the anti-puritan, satirist, and royalist John Cleveland.[27] Where there is some debate over the extent to which some pre-Stuart accounts were polemical towards Ball and the revolt, *Idol of the Clownes* sets the invective loose in its intensification of associating 1381 with disorder, chaos, excessive reform, radical religion, and revolt ('Tyler and his Anabaptists').[28] Cleveland preferred the name 'John Wall.' However, as the title also suggests (and as we saw with Thomas James in Chapter 5), Cleveland made the connection with the priests of Baal and simply calls Wall 'Baal' throughout. As noted in the previous chapter, the stories of Baal worship were about the extent to which idolatry was tolerated, accepted, or rejected among the people and rulers according to the Old Testament (cf. Judges 3.7; 6.25–32; 1 Kings 14.15; 15.13; 18–19; 2 Kings 9–11; 33.4–7) which had ongoing polemical resonance in revolutionary England as a means of labelling a given opponent (and used, not least, among puritans and radicals).[29] Such labelling could, of course, include devilish connotations (cf. Milton, *Paradise Lost* I.419–423) and this is clear enough in *Idol of the Clownes* where 'One Baal the most sottish and most unworthy, but most factious of the Clergy is stirred up by the Devil', the ultimate driver of

---

27 John Cleveland, *The Idol of the Clownes, or, Insurrection of Wat the Tyler with his priests Baal and Straw together with his fellow kings of the commons against the English church, the king, the laws, nobility and royal family and gentry, in the fourth year of K. Richard the 2d, an. 1381* (London, 1654). Later editions can be found under the title *The Rustick Rampant, or Rural Anarchy affronting Monarchy: in the Insurrection of Wat Tyler*, including in *The Works of Mr. John Cleveland* (London, 1687, 1699). For further details of Cleveland's work in context, see, e.g., S. V. Gapp, 'Notes on John Cleveland', *Publications of the Modern Language Association of America* 46 (1931): 1075–86; Lee A. Jacobus, *John Cleveland* (Boston: Twayne Publishers, 1975); A. D. Cousins, 'The Cavalier World and John Cleveland', *Studies in Philology* 78 (1981): 61–86 (79–86). On doubts over the attribution of authorship of *Idol of the Clownes* to Cleveland, see Jacobus, *John Cleveland*, 122. I will continue to refer to Cleveland as author for convenience.

28 Cleveland, *Idol of the Clownes*, 42.

29 Hill, *English Bible and the Seventeenth-Century Revolution*, 212, 253–63, 379–80, 391–93, 419–20. Note also the title of Fiona McCall, *Baal's Priests: The Loyalist Clergy and the English Revolution* (London: Routledge, 2013), and see, e.g., 186.

sedition and rebellion against the divinely ordered world: 'the Devill (who, if rebellion be as the sinne of Witchcraft, is the Father of both) to be the Antichrist of this Reign, to blaspheme and cry down God and Cesar his anoynted, the Rights of God and Cesar.' At this point, it is notable that *Idol of the Clownes* gives us the explicit identification of Wall/Baal, whose behaviour mirrors 'the Devill': '*Of these imaginations…was a foolish Priest in the County* of Kent *called* John Wall (for *Baal*) and to make it plain that he was the Father of the uproare…[continues].'[30]

Any of the meagre inherited sympathy towards the rebels is downgraded further still in *Idol of the Clownes*. While it took until 1730 to remove the story of John Tyler's daughter from Baker's unabridged *Chronicle*, no such act was necessary in the case of Cleveland's *Idol of the Clownes*.[31] The story was removed and the problems (to put it mildly) with Ball are emphasised in an interaction with Polydore Vergil's concerns about the inclusion of Ball as a key causal factor in understanding why the revolt happened. Of Vergil's explanation, which is grounded in the poll tax, Cleveland wrote that it is an example of Vergil defending 'his Priests, who blew the fire, and thrust the silly rout into the midst of it. He [Vergil] takes it ill that *Baal* (*valle* he calls him) should be supposed by I know not what slaterers of the Nobles to have filled these sailes, to have let these windes out of their Caverns.' Nevertheless, as with Baker's *Chronicle*, Baal/Wall of *Idol of the Clownes* remains *the* opportunist who pushes discontents into outright rebellion ('he was the Father of the uproare').[32] The presentation of Ball's letters builds on the standard claim that they were mysterious, 'composed of a jargon,' and 'fuller of Ridles than sense' but adding that they drove on and even duped the rebel army by invoking God's name to, ominously, 'the Cause.'[33]

Cleveland used Froissart, Walsingham, Vergil, and Stow, not only adding occasional corrections but also embellishing standard inherited narratives with much of his own distinctive interpretation and polemic. There may even be an uncommon expansion of 'Ball's bastards' (namely, the argument that Ball was attacking church leaders as being from the destructive line of Cain—see Chapter 2) when *Idol of the Clownes* presents Wall/Baal as asking where 'the word allowes these sweet things called Lords, verily Knaves in Purple, Sons of Caine, of Nimrod, of Esau, of Ishmael, fat by the blood and sweat of the poore innocent Plebeians, honourable in nothing

---

30 Cleveland, *Idol of the Clownes*, 5.
31 Matheson, 'The Peasants' Revolt through Five Centuries,' 134–35.
32 Cleveland, *Idol of the Clownes*, 3–4.
33 Cleveland, *Idol of the Clownes*, 14–15.

but the outside, and noble onely in riots and adulteries, as cruell, as ravenous, as killing (and as barbarously) as the Beares, the Lyons, the Tigers of their escutcheons, the Dragons of their bearing.'[34] Such an embellishment was, needless to say, recorded with one eye on the present. Different sides before, during, and after the civil wars and the Restoration could employ such stories, including using Cain, Nimrod, Esau, and Ishmael as established types of oppression, exploitation, and tyranny which were reapplied accordingly by radical, anti-royalist, and puritan writers in revolutionary England.[35]

Indeed, Cleveland's embellishments primarily served the purpose of paralleling 1381 with the seventeenth-century revolutionary present throughout (Tyler/Idol is an obvious representation of Cromwell), even to the point of Sudbury being, as Alastair Dunn put it, 'more Laudite than Laud…a martyr to Stuart Anglicanism, true to God and King.'[36] Picking up on the earliest understandings of the revolt as regicide-in-the-making, Cleveland claimed that the advice of Baal/Wall 'was to let the King know the resolutions of the new Common-wealthsmen, to tell him where the *Supreme power* lies, whose Trustee he was, that another course must be taken, and if he would not joyne with them, other remedies thought of' while later in the narrative the Idol/Tyler and Baal/Wall decided on a new way of striking at the 'neck of the Nation' by killing the king, 'probably by beheading.'[37] Other instances of contemporary connections are more subtle, though not hugely so. It was fitting, Cleveland argued, that if 'the Church and Government must be blowne up,' then an apostate churchman like Wall would carry it out, being as he was full 'of wonderfull zeale,'[38] a turn of phrase that echoed Cleveland's satirical poem, 'A Dialogue Between Two Zealots concerning the &c in the New Oath' (1640), where he mocked puritan apocalyptic imaginations. And this zeal in the case of Baal/Wall meant that the only thing that was truly sacred was his 'owne ambition, his innovation, and the propagation of his Schisme.'[39]

It would not have been difficult to read seventeenth-century radicals into Cleveland's embellished version of Ball's imprisonment and prediction

---

34 Cleveland, *Idol of the Clownes*, 8.
35 Hill, *English Bible and the Seventeenth-Century Revolution*, 53, 116–18, 125, 155, 163–64, 192–93, 204–22, 239–46, 249, 318, 321, 338, 371, 375–78, 383, 386–89, 410, 415, 420, 438–39.
36 Dunn, 'Wat Tyler', 28.
37 Cleveland, *Idol of the Clownes*, 6, 51.
38 Cleveland, *Idol of the Clownes*, 4.
39 Cleveland, *Idol of the Clownes*, 5.

or prophecy that he would be sprung from jail, especially if we recall the comparatively tame versions of Walsingham and Holinshed:

> he had his Revelations, his Enlightnings, was full of divine raptures, he foretold his deliverance by 20000. men, which happened in the following tumults, when his Disciples made so many Gaole-deliveries. This, knowing what numbers he had seduced and abused, he might presume upon probable conjecture. He was no sooner loose, but he incites and stirs up the unruly Clowns to all the mischiefs possible. He tells them they were pious and necessary excesses, and that the Law of Nature, which allowes all acts for our owne preservation, would justifie them: that a mad Father, who seeks to rob and destroy his off-spring, might be resisted, his thrusts might be put by, the Son might binde his hands, and if there were no other way to escape his furious violence kill him in his owne defence. The safety of the people is the Supreme law. If the Prince persisting (after faire warning) to make himselfe a shield and defence to wicked instruments of mischiefs, Malignants and enemies of the Commons, securing them from the justice of the Commons, endanger himself and his Kingdome, he may thank himselfe; We (sayes he) are willing to hazard our selves (good men) to preserve both; we will never give any impediment, or neglect any proper means of curing the distempers of the Kingdoms, and of closing the dangerous breaches (made by themselves) according to the trust which lies upon us.[40]

Similar contemporary nods are also found in the presentation of the Blackheath sermon. The Adam and Eve couplet in particular 'Was his levelling leud Text,' which may, perhaps, imply its use by his opponents.[41] Indeed, Leveller language was later used, as Nigel Smith put it, 'with ironic effect' by Cleveland: 'the Citizens of London growne wise, and resolute… began now to owne their Prince, their naturall Lord unanimously, and to side with him against all seditious opposers of his Majesty, and the *just rights and liberties* of his people, which they saw like to perish together.'[42] The embellished paralleling with revolutionary England is relentless in *Idol*

40 Cleveland, *Idol of the Clownes*, 6–7.
41 Cf. Hill, *English Bible and the Seventeenth-Century Revolution*, 202.
42 Nigel Smith, *Literature and Revolution in England, 1640–1660* (New Haven: Yale University Press, 1994), 45; Cleveland, *Idol of the Clownes*, 96. Cleveland also mentions the known seventeenth-century radical ideas of delivery from the ongoing Norman Yoke (*Idol of the Clownes*, 52–54, 77–78), on which see, e.g., Christopher Hill, 'The Norman Yoke,' in John Saville (ed.), *Democracy and the Labour Movement: Essays in Honour of Dona Torr* (London: Lawrence and Wishart, 1954), 11–66; Hill, *World Turned Upside Down*, 133–34, 145, 271–72; John Rees, *The Leveller Revolution* (London: Verso, 2016), 41.

of the Clownes and example after example could be given. A few, however, should suffice. Wall/Baal's use of the Parable of the Wheat and the Tares (Matthew 13.24–30, 36–43) is presented eschatologically as it was said to have 'signified *rooting out the wicked, and those who carried the mark of the Beast*,' adding comments (among many) about the 'House of Lords, the Peers...whom he would have *brought to Repentance*,' how 'all the enemies of the commonalty were to be swept from the Earth...lopping off the Heads of those which were too tall, which over-topped too much,' whosoever 'loved not the Cause was a Reprobate, hatefull to God, and damned Body and Soule,' and how for a '*long time there hath beene, and now is, a traiterous plot for the subversion* of us and *the liberty of the Subject.*'[43] It would not take the subtitle of the 1660 edition—*Parallel'd with the late rebellion in 1640, against King Charles I of ever blessed memory*—to suggest that Cleveland harvested his history with the reaper of overstatement.[44]

Robert Howard's Restoration Ball

The Stuart Restoration of 1660 and the return of Charles II provided opportunity to look back at revolutionary England through the prism of 1381—but also to what was unfurling with the impending crisis of James II's reign, the succession, and the 1688 Revolution. For instance, the Protestant politician, playwright, and royalist Sir Robert Howard (1626–1698) wrote (anonymously) *The Life and Reign of King Richard the Second* (London, 1681), with a revised version later incorporated into the work bearing his own name and dedicated to William III: *History of the Reigns of Edward and Richard II* (London, 1690).[45] The preface to the 1690 version discusses issues relating to the divine right of kings, passive obedience, and ideas of Catholic and Protestant succession, with the book itself partly being a cipher for discussing the legitimacy of the claims of James II and William III.[46] Yet such ideas are still implicit (to some extent) in

43 Cleveland, *Idol of the Clownes*, 9–10.
44 Or, more fully, *The rebellion of the rude multitude under Wat Tyler and his priests Baal and Straw, in the dayes of King Richard the IId, Anno. 1381. Parallel'd with the late rebellion in 1640, against King Charles I of ever blessed memory* (London, 1660).
45 For biographical details see, e.g., H. J. Oliver, *Sir Robert Howard, 1626–1698: A Critical Biography* (Durham, NC: Duke University Press, 1963); J. P. Vander Motten, 'Howard, Sir Robert (1626–1698),' *ODNB* (19 May 2011).
46 Oliver, *Sir Robert Howard*, 242–46, 263–73.

the earlier version of *Richard the Second*. Given that Howard would play a role in bringing William of Orange to the throne and supporting the claim that James II had abdicated, then it is perhaps of some significance that Howard had already chosen Richard II as a subject. Indeed, the tensions between king and Parliament in *Richard the Second* involve the claim that the king who did not observe the law could be deposed. As H. J. Oliver put it, 'Howard's political theory here corresponds exactly with his practice in the Revolution of 1688.'[47]

But while ideas about the rights of king and Parliament are in the background, they are not central to the retelling of 1381, which is relatively detached, certainly when compared with Cleveland's account. In the preface to the reader, Howard named Knighton and Walsingham as his key sources, 'their *very words* strictly Translated,' while also including the 'most credible' historians who have written of these times. Matheson suggested that the more recent historians probably included Stow and Holinshed,[48] but some of the emphases overlap with Baker and Cleveland, even if the rhetoric is considerably more restrained than Cleveland's—indeed, Howard included some suggestion of poor planning behind the tax which provoked popular grievances. Though the more recent past would hardly have gone entirely unnoticed in Restoration England, not least in light of Cleveland's account, Howard's more distanced presentation allows readers to fill in the gaps where required, a tendency found elsewhere in *Richard the Second*.[49] The uprising of 1381 might have been 'one of the most formidable and mischievous *Insurrections* that had been heard of almost in any Age,'[50] but no doubt some readers at least would have recalled another. Still, Howard's version of 1381 has much in common with some of the older accounts where events can be described with a relative degree of detachment but constantly accompanied by incredulity at the behaviour of the rebels, the usual prejudices, and various derogatory labels, with an added dash of 'the Providence of God.'[51] In some ways, Howard stands in the tradition of the Elizabethan antiquarian historians and indeed claimed in the preface to the reader to be a mere compiler of history, 'truly to set down naked *Matters of Fact* as he finds them Related by the *best Authors*, without obtruding his own *Fancies or Dreams* under the Notion of *History*.'

---

47 Oliver, *Sir Robert Howard*, 243; cf. 245, 265–68.
48 Matheson, 'The Peasants' Revolt through Five Centuries,' 133.
49 Oliver, *Sir Robert Howard*, 242, 244, 246.
50 Robert Howard, *The Life and Reign of King Richard the Second* (London, 1681), 14–15.
51 Howard, *The Life and Reign of King Richard the Second*, 15.

But recalling the idea that ideology can sometimes be as effective when it is assumed rather than explained (Chapter 4), we can detect some of Howard's Protestant fancies at play, as we can elsewhere in *Richard the Second*. Howard was aware of conflicting accounts of the causes of the uprising but made it clear that Wycliffe and his ideas were not to be blamed. In fact, the reason they were blamed was because of 'some *Monkish Historians* (followed, blindfold by some later Authors) out of hatred to *Wickliffe* and his *Tenets*' who would blame all evils 'concurring with any Attempts of Reformation in Religion' on such things, just as 'the *Heathens* of old imputed all their Calamities to the then new and rising Sect of the *Christians*.'[52] In his discussion of Wycliffe himself, Howard claimed he was treated unreasonably by the church of his day and that '*all Papists* so furiously condemn him to this day as a *wicked Heretick*.' Indeed, for Howard, Wycliffe was now seen as belonging to the Protestant tradition, 'one of the first and most eminent *Authors* of the Reformation in Doctrine, by his painful Writing and Preaching, his Tenets being generally the same with those professed at this day by the *Protestant Churches*.'[53]

Ball, as we might expect, was not to be rescued for the Protestant tradition. Ball and his ideas were instead seen as integral to the uprising and provided Howard with the ideal and immediate contrast to Wycliffe. Ball was 'a factious Clergyman' and an 'Incendiary of that Combustion.'[54] Furthermore, and with some scope for criticism of Richard, the Tyler story (here assumed to be *Wat* Tyler) involving the sexual harassment of the daughter was included by Howard. Nevertheless, the Tyler story comes later in *Richard the Second* and allows the blame to focus on Ball. The Tyler incident provoked rebellion and the crowds to free 'Ball the priest' from his prison in Maidstone. Ball and the crowd then moved on to Blackheath where 'he made a seditious Preachment to them' and took for his theme the 'old Proverb' about Adam and Eve. Howard summarised Ball's preaching in a familiar manner. Howard mentioned descent from Adam, how the laws of the realm were 'injurious to *Christian Liberty*' and 'unjust by making such difference of mens Estates, preferring some to be *Peers* and *Potentates*, with great *Authority* and large *Possessions*, whereby they took advantage of the humble plyable Condition of others.' Howard also mentioned Ball's alternative about 'an equal sharing of all things' to be held in common, a '*Doctrine*' that was 'extreamly pleasing to these *Raggamuffins*' and animated the rebellion, which spread among 'others as mad as themselves in other Counties.'

---

52 Howard, *The Life and Reign of King Richard the Second*, 15.
53 Howard, *The Life and Reign of King Richard the Second*, 35.
54 Howard, *The Life and Reign of King Richard the Second*, 15.

They made strangers swear loyalty to King Richard and the commons and the accompanying disownment of any king called John, and they beheaded 'all *Lawyers* they could catch, saying, Till they were rooted out, the Land would never enjoy free liberty.'[55] After a summary account of the uprisings, Howard included all of Ball's letters which were said to be disseminated among rebels, and, echoing Cleveland, presented them to the reader 'so that he may admire the style of these popular *Orators*, and observe what strength of perswasion there was in Non-sense.' We are further told that 'the *Storm*' was 'happily over-blown,' the rebels were 'suddenly master'd, a competent Force raised to secure the Peace of the Kingdom,' and leaders executed, concluding with Ball being drawn, hanged, and quartered.[56]

Howard's presentation of Richard II's reign may indeed have corresponded with his practice in the Revolution of 1688, as Oliver argued. But histories written in the aftermath of 1688 now had to work their way through ideas for and against the replacement of a monarch and assertion of parliamentary power with the shock of the 1640s and 1650s as a worryingly close analogy. As the reception of Ball moved into the eighteenth century, he could now be found as a negative foil for debates about mixed monarchy, even if he remained at the fringes. Moreover, as such debates were on their way to becoming comparatively settled in the following decades, so too was the related issue of religion when the crisis of James II and a Catholic succession was settled in favour of the ascension of the Protestant William and the Act of Settlement 1701 which formalised Protestant succession. It is to issues and controversies surrounding these debates we now turn but, as we will see, they also (eventually) mark the beginning of the end to Ball being a widely despised figure in political discourse.

---

55 Howard, *The Life and Reign of King Richard the Second*, 16–17.
56 Howard, *The Life and Reign of King Richard the Second*, 24–27, 30.

7
Perverted Liberty and the End of Stuart England: Ball among Whigs, Tories, Jacobites, and Other Mobs

Old debates about religion and politics inherited from medieval, Tudor, and revolutionary England were given new twists among competing high political factions in the aftermath of the constitutional changes surrounding the Stuart line, the Acts of Union (1707) and an officially unified Great Britain, and the accession of the Hanoverians in 1714. Concerns about succession were intertwined with Whig and Tory debates about divine right, absolutism, mixed monarchy, political representation, an English constitution, property rights, rightful resistance, wrongful resistance, and abdication and vacancy, all set against a backdrop of polemics, slurs, and accusations relating to Catholicism and tyranny, radical Protestant subversion, Cromwellian sympathies, anarchy, and loss of liberties. Ball was not only a figure who could be used for thinking about these issues for the sorts of reasons we have already seen; he could also be useful because he spoke about *liberty*, albeit the wrong sort for Whig and Tory alike. As Ball talked about the connections between liberty (and lack of it) in connection with the origins of human society and hierarchy, he was found to be doubly useful as a negative foil as these debates were playing out in competing myths of societal and institutional origins in the light of the new political realities post-1688.

Robert Brady

Understanding the 1381 uprising by way of a dying royalist cause and through criticism of Whig history can be detected in the work of Robert

Perverted Liberty and the End of Stuart England 105

Brady (c. 1627–1700).[1] Brady was a politician, physician, and historian who had been classified as a traitor under the Commonwealth as he briefly went into exile before returning and carrying out some duties as a royalist agent. After the Restoration, he came back into favour and, from the mid-1670s at least, began the process of writing a history of England whilst embroiled in controversies over royal authority and Parliament, very much continuing the royalist cause and Stuart loyalism. Indeed, he had access to records in the Tower of London (which he had to hand over to his rival William Petyt in 1689) and dedicated the first volume of *A Complete History of England* (1685) to James II, claiming, 'of Things done in the Times I Write of, they might have Obteined a right Notion of the Government and State of the Kingdom then, which at this day are much changed from what they were, to the great Ease and Repose of the King, as well as Benefit and Advantage to the People.'[2]

This dedication sets the tone for what is to follow. Brady's particular royalist agenda in *A Complete History of England* (and elsewhere) was up against the influential Whiggish idea (associated with figures like the lawyer Petyt and, as we will soon see, the historian James Tyrrell) of a constitution, representation, and system of law that existed in England from time immemorial and which were not fashioned by monarchs nor should be subject to absolute monarchical power.[3] The historian would in turn trace the ancient history of this principle and show its survival in the face of those who had the temerity to challenge it. Brady provided a high-profile royalist counterargument to this early Whiggish reading of history and did

---

1 On the details of Brady's life and history writing, see, e.g., David C. Douglas, *English Scholars 1600–1730* (revised edition; Eyre & Spottiswoode: London, 1951), 119–38; J. G. A. Pocock, 'Robert Brady, 1627–1700. A Cambridge Historian of the Restoration', *Cambridge Historical Journal* 10 (1951): 186–204; Joseph M. Levine, *The Battle of the Books: History and Literature in the Augustan Age* (Ithaca, NY: Cornell University Press, 1991), 320–23; Philip Hicks, *Neoclassical History and English Culture: From Clarendon to Hume* (Basingstoke: Macmillan, 1996), 82–109; Patrick Wallis, 'Brady, Robert (c. 1627–1700)', *ODNB* (23 September 2004).
2 'To the Most Excellent Majesty of James the Second, King of England, Scotland, France & Ireland, Defender of the Faith, etc.,' in Robert Brady, *The Complete History of England from the First Entrance of the Romans under the Conduct of Julius Caesar unto the End of the Reign of King Henry III* (London, 1685).
3 Pocock, 'Robert Brady'. Cf. J. G. A. Pocock, *The Ancient Constitution and the Feudal Law: A Study of English Historical Thought in the Seventeenth Century, a Reissue with a Retrospect* (Cambridge: Cambridge University Press, [1957] 1987). See the prefaces to Brady, *Complete History of England*.

so by locating the history of England and its laws as products of their time and of changing social systems, including positing the Norman and feudal origins of the medieval system and commons representation in Parliament. Indeed, he further claimed that change could be wilfully imposed from above as well as through gradual and broader historical processes. Despite the historicising agenda, this does not mean that Brady's royalism is undetectable. As J. G. A. Pocock put it, Brady 'was not the man to subject the monarchy to the same scrutiny as parliament and the law, and reduce it to the historical flux with all the other works of men. He was therefore always inclined to treat everything as finite and historical except the crown and, by leaving its historical role unstated and unexamined, to allow his readers to infer its unchanging absolutism.'[4]

The second volume of Brady's history—which covers the 1381 revolt—was published in 1700 (the year Brady died) when his royalist game was up, and lacks the explicit interpretative commentary, leaving effectively only chronicle. But we can, as ever, detect certain tendencies in omissions, inclusions, framing of material, and so on. Even more so than the standard histories we have seen so far, Brady's account of 1381 does not leave much room for sympathising with the plight of the common people. Brady's narrative of the revolt begins with a detailed discussion of taxation, stressing that there was help for those who struggled to pay. It then moves on to the uprisings, which 'The Historians' tell us was due to taxation and the 'Insolence, Incivility, and Rudeness of the *Collectors* to *young Maidens*,' which Brady downplayed by claiming that this 'might at first be the *pretence*.' Nevertheless, this situation effectively gave the leaders of the insurrection the opportunity to exploit the '*Villanes, Natives, Bond-Tenents,* and *Clowns*,' many of whom were said to be in debt and did not know how to satisfy their creditors, and some of whom were said to be criminals fearing severe punishment. Through this widening of the blame (and unlike histories recent to Brady), their situation was not here said to have been exploited by Ball (who is not mentioned at this point), though readers may well have filled in the gaps or heard echoes. Instead, the rebellion was formed under Wat Tyler in Kent and Jack Straw in Essex. The Kentish rebels moved to Blackheath with a telling agenda for a reader with Brady's interests (or knowledge of Brady's interests) in the origins of law and rule and his opposition to the idea of the ongoing survival of a timeless constitution. The rebel agenda featured the ominous implications of such concerns: '*Liberty, changing the Evil Customs of the Nation, and cutting off the Heads of all the Lawyers great and small, and all that had any Offices*

---

4   Pocock, 'Robert Brady,' 199.

in the Law, or Relation to it any way, where-ever they could find them.' And 'until they were killed,' these rebels did not believe that 'the Nation could not enjoy a true Liberty.'⁵ Put differently, is this not where zeal for liberty always leads?

The events in London, the death of Tyler, and uprisings elsewhere are then narrated. Ball appears towards the end of Brady's account as an example of the capture and execution of key rebels where we are then given his backstory familiar from Walsingham, though with some notable omissions, such as the connection with Wycliffe. Ball had been a popular preacher for over twenty years, and more immediately he preached to the crowds at Blackheath using the 'Old Rime' about Adam digging and Eve spinning as his subject. Ball inferred from this that by nature 'all Men' were equal, that servitude was introduced by oppressors against the will of God, that *'then was the time given them by God'* to shake off the yoke of servitude and enjoy their 'long-desired Liberty.' Minus the allusion to the Parable of the Wheat and the Tares, Ball was said to have hastened the rebels to seize the moment by first killing the good and the great of the kingdom, the legal figures, and anyone who might stand in the way of their freedom, liberty, and aspirations. But most tellingly, Ball's Blackheath speech is combined with the confession of 'John Straw' as showing the true designs of the rebels ('This *Speech,* with the *Confession* of *John Straw* at the time of his *death,* discovers the full *Intention* of these *Riots, Rebellions,* and *Tumults*'), a connection made in different ways among other historians in the early eighteenth century as each vied to present their credentials in relation to monarchy and loyalty to the crown. This was the Straw who talked about when the rebels assembled at Blackheath and sent for the king to come to them; they were going to slay the king's entourage, carry the king around with them to generate popular support, and, ultimately, kill the king himself, as well as the landed ecclesiastical figures. Then they would make the laws as they pleased 'by which the People were to be *Governed*' and put county kings in place. They also intended to burn London and divide the riches among themselves.⁶ This emphasis on tying in the pantomime villain Ball with such anti-royalist alternative constitutional sentiments, and perverse and threatening understandings of liberty, may well be one of the final acts of defiance of Brady's own lost royalist cause. Close to the end of Brady's history of England—and effectively the end of his narrative

---

5   Robert Brady, *A Continuation of the Complete History of England Containing the Lives and Reigns of Edward I, II & III and Richard the Second* (London, 1700), 344–45.
6   Brady, *A Continuation of the Complete History of England,* 349–50.

proper—we get the bishop of Carlisle's lengthy defiant speech against the deposition of Richard II which only makes more likely that Brady used Ball to taint opposition to James II's legitimacy.[7]

James Tyrrell

Against Brady stood James Tyrrell (1642–1718), the Whig historian, political theorist, critic of High Church absolutism, and close (though sometimes complicated and estranged) friend of John Locke. Tyrrell was also the grandson of the archbishop of Armagh, James Ussher.[8] As a young man, Tyrrell published Ussher's *The Power Communicated to God by the Prince and Obedience Required of the Subject* (1661, with a dedication to Charles II) but whatever familial loyalties Tyrrell held and lingering influence Ussher may have had, they did not involve an ongoing acceptance of hereditary divine right.[9] In response to Robert Filmer's arguments on divine right, absolutism, and monarchical descent from Adam, Tyrrell published (anonymously) *Patriarcha non Monarcha* (1681). For Tyrrell, Adam did not have absolute power and, rather, parental authority was given to both Adam and Eve, father and mother. This is ultimately a consensual model whereby the patriarch is expected, though may fail, to care for the child until maturity when the offspring will utilise their rational faculties. In this Whig tradition, political systems, governments, ownership, and property should be

---

7   Brady, *A Continuation of the Complete History of England*, 438–51. Cf. While this suggests that Pocock overstated his case, his assessment is still worth noting: 'The only hint of his personal opinion is the bishop of Carlisle's protest against the deposition of Richard II, which, printed in full, closes the narrative part of the volume. This is Brady's rather unheroic last word to rebels and alterers of the succession' (Pocock, 'Robert Brady', 203).
8   For details of biography and Tyrrell's work, see, e.g., J. W. Gough, 'James Tyrrell, Whig Historian and Friend of John Locke', *Historical Journal* 19 (1976): 581–610; Levine, *Battle of the Books*, 322–26; Mark Goldie, 'John Locke's Circle and James II', *Historical Journal* 35 (1992): 557–86; Hicks, *Neoclassical History and English Culture*, 95–98; Melinda S. Zook, *Radical Whigs and Conspiratorial Politics in Late Stuart England* (University Park, PA: Pennsylvania State University Press, 1999), 175–87; Julia Rudolph, *Revolution by Degrees: James Tyrrell and Whig Political Thought in the Late Seventeenth Century* (New York: Palgrave Macmillan, 2002); Mark Goldie, 'Tyrrell, James (1642–1718)', *ODNB* (23 September 2004).
9   Gough, 'James Tyrrell', 582; Zook, *Radical Whigs*, 176.

built on an inherited history of common good and consent between the ruler and the representatives of the people. Whatever opponents may have claimed of this line of thinking, it was not about levelling notions of all things shared in common.[10]

For the Whig Tyrrell, this line of thought against absolutism was connected with the idea of an ancient constitution which took on a new dimension after 1688. He developed and analysed (among other things) such ideas through thirteen then fourteen dialogues in *Bibliotheca Politica* (1692–94, 1702) which opened with praise for the 'wonderful happy Revolution'.[11] This involved the Whiggish downplaying of a Norman conquest and promoting the ideas of consent and the influence of pre-Norman property rights and representation. Legitimate resistance to absolutism could now be constructed in terms of loyalty to and continuation of the ancient constitution. Such ideas about the ancientness of the English constitution were dominant in *The General History of England* (1697–1704) where Brady's different take on English history was duly acknowledged in the preface ('tho I have otherwise a great Value for his Learning, yet…').[12] Three volumes of *The General History of England* were completed reaching the reign of Richard II and thus including the 1381 uprising.

There is a notable contrast with Brady on the causes of, and blame for, the 1381 uprising. Where Brady omitted the connection between Ball and Wycliffe, Tyrrell twice made it clear that this connection was wrong. Indeed, any possibility that the theology of Wycliffe's followers was complicit with the 'several dangerous Rebellions and Insurrections in divers Parts of the Kingdom' is dismissed at the very beginning of Tyrrell's account. He took the conventional route of blaming 'our Monkish Writers' with the additional argument that there is no evidence for such a claim in Wycliffe's ideas. Tyrrell preferred the views of others who 'more truly attribute' the uprisings to the 'severe Collection' of the poll tax.[13] Unlike Brady's defence of tax collection, Tyrrell made the claim that collectors deceitfully carried out their tasks and in doing so 'they committed horrible Oppressions, Exactions, and Insolencies' in different counties. This

---

10 Rudolph, *Revolution by Degrees*, 19–61, which also provides full discussion of these issues in *Patriarcha non Monarcha*. Cf. Gough, 'James Tyrrell,' 586–87.
11 'The Epistle Dedicatory,' in James Tyrrell, *Bibliotheca Politica: Or an Enquiry into the Ancient Constitution of the English Government* (London, 1694), no page number given.
12 James Tyrrell, *The General History of England, as well Ecclesiastical as Civil. Vol. I* (London, 1696), vii.
13 James Tyrrell, *The General History of England, both Ecclesiastical and Civil. Vol. III* (London, 1704), 856–57.

provoked the common people who joined with the bondmen first 'into a Mutiny' and then 'into open Rebellion.' Further discussion of the origins on the revolt in Essex and Kent takes us beyond the limits of acceptable unrest for Tyrrell's Whiggish position. This includes the story of (Wat) Tyler's daughter, where Tyler tried to avoid punishment by drawing together and inciting 'the Rabble' into rebellion.[14] Tyrrell had already used the example of Tyler in *Bibliotheca Politica* in theorising about Whig and Tory ideas concerning illegitimate resistance (and the threat of outlandish and seditious leaders) no matter how understandable grievances may seem, including unfair taxation. The claim made in *Bibliotheca Politica* would doubtlessly have resonated across Whig thought and acted as a counter against anti-Whig critique: 'I do by no means allow the Rabble or Mob of any Nation to take Arms against a Civil Government, but only the whole Community of the People of all Degrees and Orders, commanded by the Nobility and Gentry thereof.'[15]

We get more of a sense of the illegitimacy of this mob uprising when, after introducing Tyler in his *History*, Tyrrell then moved on to the story of the freeing of the 'factious Priest' Ball from Maidstone jail. Ball is described in the marginal note as someone who 'excited' the 'mob' and preached 'against all difference of Quality and Degrees.'[16] In this respect it is also worth noting that after Tyrrell's account of the death of Ball we get Ball's letters, though here associated with 'John Sheep' (from Walsingham) and a 'Lay Leader of that Gang' (Jack Mylner's letter in Knighton), as well as passing mention made of letters from Jack Carter and Jack Trewman (from Knighton). These were letters shared among the shires and leaders. The reason given by Tyrrell for their inclusion is ostensibly due to aesthetics in a way similar to Richard Baker's presentation (see Chapter 6) and which would be taken up positively in centuries to come: 'the Reader's Diversion, that he may admire the Stile of these Popular Orators, and observe what strength of Perswasion there was in Nonsense upon those, who were capable of no better...enough to shew the Stile, and way of Writing, of these illiterate Clowns.'[17]

Even if there is no explicit attribution of the letters to Ball, the warning from history that the figure of Ball gave to Tyrrell and to his assumptions of

14 Tyrrell, *General History of England*, Vol. III, 857.
15 Tyrrell, *Bibliotheca Politica*, 808, cf. 164, 179, 182–83. On Tyrrell and theories of resistance in *Bibliotheca Politica*, see, e.g., Rudolph, *Revolution by Degrees*, 130–47.
16 Tyrrell, *General History of England*, Vol. III, 857.
17 Tyrrell, *General History of England*, Vol. III, 865–66.

right and wrong changes to government is clear enough. After his escape from Maidstone jail, Ball and the growing crowd headed to Blackheath where he made a 'seditious Preachment' to them based on the popular Adam and Eve couplet. Tyrrell provided a brief summary (originally from Walsingham) of Ball's levelling sermon on the proverb which Tyrrell no doubt assumed was incompatible with his own earlier reading of Adam and descent. Ball attempted to prove that, because of descent from Adam, '*all Men were of one Condition*,' servitude was introduced by unjust oppression and contrary to the will of God, and that '*now there was an opportunity offer'd them by GOD*' to '*enjoy their long desired Liberty*,' though, as with Brady, lacking the allusion to the Parable of the Wheat and the Tares found in Walsingham. In terms of how Tyrrell's Ball might have been more popularly understood in distinction from Tyrrell's own take on inheritance from Adam and Filmer's monarchical reading, we might turn to a press report (January 1727) on the aftermath of the 'Terror of the Weavers.' Here there were reflections on some 'odd Heterodox Notions…started by them, like those of Wat Tyler and Jack Straw, of Rebellious memory.' While Ball is unnamed, the reasons given why such rebellions had to be crushed are those elsewhere associated with him: 'That Adam made no Will when he died, and therefore all the Goods he left behind him should be equally distributed among his Children.'[18]

Tyrrell's account of Ball would have provided a similar sort of commentary for prejudicial understandings of people like the Weavers. He claimed that Ball's 'Doctrine' concerning Adam and gaining long-desired liberty was much appreciated by 'the Rabble' who conspired with other rebels 'as Mad as themselves' to take up arms and swear loyalty to Richard and to the commons while opposing the Duke of Lancaster. *The General History of England* narrates the rebels in London, whose 'Pretences were Liberty, and the changing the Evil Laws and Customs of the Nation,' and it is presented in the account as fuelled by Ball. Moreover, it was through 'being excited thereto by *Balle* their Preacher' that the rebels beheaded all the legal figures 'great and small,' an act deemed perversely necessary so that people could 'enjoy true Liberty.'[19] That Tyrrell used almost identical language to Brady's here is telling in that the liberty desired of the rabble was beyond the boundaries of political acceptability—whether Whig or Tory—while implicitly countering polemical claims made of Whigs supposedly accepting levelling and the rule of the mob.

18 *Caledonian Mercury* (23 January 1727).
19 Tyrrell, *General History of England*, Vol. III, 857–58.

112 *Spectres of John Ball*

Tyrrell retold plenty more non-Ball details of the London events, as well as of uprisings in St Albans and East Anglia. The Suffolk uprising was associated with the 'wicked Priest' Jack/John Straw (both 'Jack' and 'John' are used) rather than John Wraw and Ball or Wall as in other accounts (e.g., Trussell, John Hughes, and Paul de Rapin-Thoyras—see below and Chapter 6). After further details on the end of the uprisings, the story of Ball's capture and execution is added to other executions. Still following and summarising the narrative ultimately inherited from Walsingham, we then get more information about Ball's life, to the point of repetition (duly acknowledged by Tyrrell). We are now told that Ball preached doctrines pleasing to the people for twenty years, that he was imprisoned for 'Seditious Sermons' by the time the rebellion happened, and that he spoke to rebels at Blackheath. Specifics of Ball's teachings are spelled out, including those on tithes and priests, and the provocation to kill the great figures of the realm. The comparison with Wycliffe is raised again and dismissed again for the same reasons ('I find no grounds for that in his Writings')—Tyrrell omitted other details from his source, so, if not just fatigued copying of Walsingham, this may have been further emphasis on his part to distance proto-Protestantism from Ball. But at this point in the narrative, Ball is (as in the account of Brady) brought together with the leader of the Suffolk uprising (John Straw) through their final speeches before execution, as evidence of the real intentions of the rebels ('The Speech which *Ball* made at his execution, with the Confession of *John Straw* a little before his Death, plainly discover the Designs of all these Tumults and Rebellions'). This involved the message sent to the king from Blackheath and the plan to kidnap him and carry him with them place-to-place as justification for their cause. Ultimately, of course, the king was to suffer the same fate as the rest of the leading figures of the realms: execution.[20] For Tyrrell, this was obviously a perversion of inherited notions of common good and consent—and an indication of his own understanding of loyalty to the crown.

John Hughes and *A Complete History of England*

White Kennett (1660–1728)—the Whiggish, anti-Catholic, fierce critic of the 1715 Jacobite uprising, ordained Anglican clergyman, and (from 1718)

---

20 Tyrrell, *General History of England, Vol. III*, 864–65.

bishop of Peterborough but with a tolerant view of dissenting Protestants[21]—became associated with the three-volume *A Complete History of England* (1706), though he only wrote the third volume from Charles I to William III. John Hughes (c. 1678–1720)—poet, musician, translator, editor, and Whig from a puritan background—was responsible for the first two volumes which are compilations of previous historians (John Milton, Samuel Daniel, etc.).[22] However, Hughes judged that Trussell's treatment of the reigns of Richard II, Henry IV, V, and VI in Volume 1 was 'so meanly perfom'd' and in a 'Stile so wretch'd' that 'there was a Necessity to have those Reigns new writ, which have therefore been done much larger and more exact, and after Mr. *Daniel*'s Method.'[23]

In Hughes's compilation, the revolt began with the unpopular poll tax which was enforced by 'indiscreet and uncivil Officers'—tied in with the behaviour of the Duke of Lancaster, lawyers, and lords—to bring the people to the brink of rebellion. A longed-for 'Liberty' and deliverance from various burdens in life was sparked by the tax but also by the sermons of Ball, a 'seditious Priest.' Ball preached that 'all Men' were equal as children of Adam and that servitude and laws were therefore imposed unjustly. Ball encouraged them to petition the king and 'require their Liberty' or, if not, 'recover it with their Swords.' The extent to which Ball's sermons provoked the people to rise up is unclear in Hughes's account, though they certainly contributed. The accompanying note explains that Ball was present at Blackheath where he preached on the Adam and Eve couplet and that he was a prisoner in Maidstone freed by 'the Rabble' who were provoked to 'proceed from Riot to Rebellion.'[24] Next, and placed alongside Ball as a potentially alternative origins account, is the story of *Jack* Tyler's daughter as the beginning of the rebellion which spread quickly in Kent and Essex while *Wat* Tyler became head of the rebellion which moved towards London via Blackheath.

---

21 For an overview, see Laird Okie, 'Kennett, White (1660–1728)', *ODNB* (23 September 2004); Laird Okie, *Augustan Historical Writing: Histories of England in the English Enlightenment* (Lanham, MD: University of America Press, 1991), 27–32.

22 See further, Thomas N. McGeary, 'Hughes, John (1678?–1720)', *ODNB* (28 September 2006).

23 'Preface,' in John Hughes (ed.), *A Complete History of England: with the lives of all the kings and queens thereof; from the earliest account of time, to the death of His late Majesty King William III. Containing a faithful relation of all affairs of state, ecclesiastical and civil.* Vol. 1 (London, 1706).

24 Hughes, *A Complete History of England*, 244–45.

After an account of the events in London and Wat Tyler's death, Ball re-emerged and was now associated with John Wraw ('two seditious Priests, who had a special Talent of Haranguing the Rabble into Discontents and Rebellion').[25] They helped spread the rebellion beyond the south east into East Anglia, a move found in Trussell's history and which would soon be developed by Rapin (see Chapters 6, 8). Similarly, after the account of the rebellion in East Anglia (where Wraw was a leader before his capture and execution), we get the quelling of the rebellion and its leaders. Ball's capture in Coventry and trial in St Albans is recounted with the claim that he 'behaved himself with very great Irreverence to the King'; rather than beg for pardon, he 'scorn'd and despis'd his Monitors.'[26] Once the rebels are dealt with in the narrative, we then get a dismissal of the argument concerning Wycliffe's alleged influence and the claim that Ball was a follower. This was, as readers familiar with (for instance) Robert Howard's account of Richard II's reign would have recognised, 'an Aspersion invented by Monkish Historians, to Blacken the Protestant Doctrines' with an explanation that Wycliffe was not present in the south east and that the rebels in fact targeted his patron, John of Gaunt. Moreover, Ball is now identified as suitably *Catholic* (a 'Franciscan friar') rather than someone who was imprisoned for preaching Wycliffe's doctrines—thus blame should instead be put on 'Discontents.' Hughes gave an unambiguous verdict in his Protestant apology: 'neither *Wickcliffe* nor his Doctrines were to blame.'[27] As ever, it is not difficult to map Hughes's emphases on to discussions in post-1688 England—in this case, an updating of the old religious disputes with reference to the crown and the right sort of succession.

Laurence Echard

Nevertheless, it is not always so easy to demarcate what ideas ought to be classified as 'Tory' and 'Whig,' as seen in the first single-authored work of its genre by Laurence Echard (1671–1730) from around the same time as the Hughes/Kennett history: *The History of England from the First Entrance of Julius Caesar and the Romans to the End of the Reign of James I* (1707), with volumes 2 and 3 (1718) dedicated to the first Hanoverian, George I, and continuing up to 1688. A combined edition of all three was published in 1720

---

25 Hughes, *A Complete History of England*, 246.
26 Hughes, *A Complete History of England*, 248.
27 Hughes, *A Complete History of England*, 248.

and Echard's history would become especially remembered for its inclusion of a story about Cromwell's discussion with the devil. As well as being a historian of Rome and England, Echard was an ordained Anglican—he was associated with the diocese of Lincoln and, from 1712 until his death, was the archdeacon of Stowe—and held conventional hostilities towards Catholicism and puritanism. Despite his claims about impartiality, Echard still held to a notion of Providence which, as Ronald T. Ridley put it, always raises issues for historians 'because everyone assumes that Providence is on his or her side. In Echard's case that was the Anglican Church.'[28] One omission in Echard's account of the revolt is worth noting in this respect: there is no mention of Wycliffe's connection with Ball and the uprisings. One function of the lack of connection may have simply been to keep intact the reputation of the heroic harbinger of the English Reformation, who was earlier described by the churchman Echard as 'a Man of an acute Wit, profound Learning, and great Judgment.'[29]

History of England namechecks a range of the most influential historians as sources (Hall, Grafton, Polydore Vergil, Holinshed, Stow, Baker, Howard, Daniel, Brady, Tyrrell, and so on),[30] though quite how we precisely categorise Echard politically is not entirely straightforward. Echard has been remembered as a Tory historian, though some have suggested that he could even have been a Whig, while his history had its fair share of critics from different perspectives.[31] Wherever his political affiliations may have lain, what underlies this debate is that Tory and Whig positions on the hot issues of English history—on the Stuarts, and on the ancient constitution and liberty—could indeed overlap. As Echard put it delicately in the

---

28 Ronald T. Ridley, 'The Forgotten Historian: Laurence Echard and the First History of the Roman Republic,' *Ancient Society* 27 (1996): 277–315 (302). For biographical details and overview, see, e.g., Okie, *Augustan Historical Writing*, 33–40; Hicks, *Neoclassical History and English Culture*, 102–9; R. T. Ridley, 'Echard, Laurence (bap. 1672, d. 1730),' *ODNB* (25 May 2006).

29 Laurence Echard, *The History of England. From the First Entrance of Julius Caesar and the Romans, to the End of the Reign of King James the First. Containing the Space of 1678 Years* (London, 1707), 380.

30 Echard, *From the First Entrance*, 3–4.

31 For discussion, see, e.g., Douglas, *English Scholars 1600–1730*, 134–35; Deborah Stephan, 'Laurence Echard—Whig Historian,' *Historical Journal* 32 (1989): 843–66; Okie, *Augustan Historical Writing*, 33–34; Ridley, 'Forgotten Historian'; Gary Evans, 'Partisan Politics, History and the National Interest (1700–1748),' in David Onnekink and Gijs Rommelse (ed.), *Ideology and Foreign Policy in Early Modern Europe (1650–1750)* (London: Routledge, 2011), 55–92 (71–73).

introduction to the second volume, 'Neither the Prerogative of the King, nor the Liberties of the People, were so fully fix'd and known, nor so effectually examin'd and canvas'd, as they have been in later Times. The ancient Sovereignty of *English* Kings, either by inherent Right, frequent Practice, or meer Accident, was then more unlimited and uncertain; which caus'd the Power of Parliaments to be more precarious and restrain'd.'[32]

Then again, there was the wrong, dangerous sorts of excessive liberty, and, ripe for further emphasis, the 1381 uprising already had a long history of encapsulating such fears about what might happen from below if things got too out-of-hand. In the hands of Echard, the uprising began in unfortunate circumstances, but this was no excuse for what he presented as a combination of the criminal and the seditious, a view which seems to cohere with Echard's broader understanding of mob violence.[33] After money was not duly collected, certain collectors took advantage of the situation to act with a heavier hand, and in line with Tyrrell's account: 'On which Pretence they committed horrible Oppressions, Exactions and Insolencies' which incensed the 'common People' to join with 'Villains or Bondmen,' first to a 'Mutiny' then to an 'open Rebellion.' The 'extraordinary Poll-Tax' was soon, then, 'made use of as a principal Occasion for a very dangerous Insurrection.'[34] Echard continued by retelling the story of (Wat) Tyler's daughter. While sympathy for the plight of those harshly taxed is present in the narrative, there is no forgiveness for Tyler. Tyler was said to have acted 'to avoid Punishment' by drawing together 'the Rabble' and provoking them into 'a most desperate Rebellion.' The story then tells us about how the 'great Multitudes' sprung the 'factious Priest' Ball out of Maidstone prison. Having gained another type of 'Liberty,' Ball joined them and gave his Blackheath sermon on Adam delving and Eve spinning, from which he inferred that 'Inequality of Mankind was contrary to the Will of God.'[35]

Echard not only described Ball's sermon as belonging to the 'usual Topicks of most Rebellions' but also as a 'dangerous Doctrine' which was 'highly applauded by the Vulgar' and provoked them to take up arms, pronouncing fidelity to Richard (and not John of Gaunt) as king. As the rebellious crowds grew—made up mostly of a ragtag of '*Villains*, Bond-Tenants,

32 Laurence Echard, *The History of England. From the Beginning of the Reign of King Charles the First, to the Restoration of King Charles the Second* (London, 1718), 2.
33 Tim Harris, 'Perceptions of the Crowd in Later Stuart London,' in Merritt (ed.), *Imagining Early Modern London*, 253.
34 Echard, *From the First Entrance*, 385.
35 Echard, *From the First Entrance*, 386.

County Clowns, Debtors, and Criminals' led by Tyler—we learn again that their 'Pretences were Liberty,' and the 'Reformation' of laws and customs. Indeed, when decapitating lawyers, they would allege, in that familiar ominous language, *'That the People could never enjoy true Liberty, while they were suffer'd to live in the Nation.'*[36] After the narration of the events in London, the story then moves to events in East Anglia, including the uprising in Suffolk under John Straw (again, 'a wicked Priest'). During the account of the punishment of ringleaders, the 'notorious' priest Ball is (as with the accounts of Brady and Tyrrell) mentioned alongside John Straw and that 'by the Confessions of these two it appear'd what desperate Designs had been laid towards the Ruin and Subversion of the Nation,' notably that the king could have come to them at Blackheath and become their mascot, with the knights and dignitaries slain. Once the king had served his purpose, he too would be killed, along with leading lords and ecclesiastical figures of the realm, and the new order and county kings established.[37] Again, this relatively common claim carried with it an assumption about the right and wrong sorts of loyalty to the crown.

Paul de Rapin-Thoyras

The most popular history in the first half of the eighteenth century was by the French Huguenot exile, Paul de Rapin-Thoyras (1661–1725).[38] Rapin was among William of Orange's troops that had arrived at Torbay in 1688 and his military involvement under William would continue in Ireland (including the Battle of the Boyne), all of which would influence

---

36 Echard, *From the First Entrance*, 386.
37 Echard, *From the First Entrance*, 388.
38 For biographical details and the publication of *Histoire d'Angleterre* and *History of England*, see, e.g., Hugh Trevor-Roper, 'A Huguenot Historian: Paul Rapin,' in Irene Scouloudi (ed.), *Huguenots in Britain and their French Background, 1550–1800* (London: Macmillan, 1987), 3–19, and updated as, 'Our First Whig Historian: Paul de Rapin-Thoyras,' in Hugh Trevor-Roper, *From Counter Reformation to Glorious Revolution* (London: Pimlico, 1993), 249–65; Okie, *Augustan Historical Writing*, 47–73; M. G. Sullivan, 'Rapin, Hume and the Identity of the Historian in Eighteenth-century England,' *History of European Ideas* 28 (2002): 145–62; Michaël Green, 'Early Employment Networks of Paul Rapin-Thoyras: Huguenot Soldier and Tutor (1685–1692),' *Diasporas: Circulations, migrations, histoire* 31 (2018): 101–14; Dew, *Commerce, Finance and Statecraft*, 102–16.

his framing of history. He published *Histoire d'Angleterre* in The Hague between 1723 and 1725 and died shortly after, just when his fame was about to take off through the first English translation by Nicholas Tindal (Matthew Tindal's nephew), *History of England* (London, 1725–1731). As M. G. Sullivan argued, Rapin's history was popular in the sense that it was widely read, regularly republished, translated by different translators, and used in and modified for educational settings throughout the eighteenth century and even into the early nineteenth. But it was also popular in the sense that it did not hold back on the entertainment. If there was proper supportive evidence, 'Rapin included every great story of lust, violence and betrayal from the English annals, however unlikely, lest the interest of the reader wander…Rapin never failed to detail a duplicitous monk, a king who debauched his daughter, or a virgin being burnt to death.'[39]

Rapin's *History of England* also functioned as a justification of the 1688 settlement, its precursors, and the constitutional balancing of the crown and Parliament—in this sense it remained in the tradition of some of the historians and chroniclers discussed in the previous chapter. As it was said to be written for a foreign audience, Rapin was understood in the preface to have been obliged to give a 'particular Account of the *English Constitution*.' As the introductory essay to the *History of England* claimed, this was a system of government that should be traced back to the Saxons and one with 'a *mixt* and *limited* Monarchy…a Power *bounded* by National Laws.' The king always ought to have 'an Eye to the *Publick*, to procure their Good' which in turn benefits the king because he is 'strictly united with his Subjects.' But the various '*Prerogatives of the King*, or *of the Crown*' were kept in check. The monarch could not change laws that had been enacted through the consent of the monarch and the people, nor could monarchs raise taxes as they saw fit. This was connected with the 'numberless Particulars relating to the *Liberty* and *Property* of the Subjects, which the King can't meddle with,' without breaking the distinctively English constitution. 'The Prerogatives of the Crown' and 'the Rights and Privileges of the People' are the groundwork for the laws of the realm which from 'time to time' are generated by the consent of the monarch and the people and should work in harmony with, and respect for, one another. But there were failures to respect the English constitution. There were kings who embraced absolute power, changed laws when they saw fit, and imposed arbitrary taxes on the people which led to '*Confusion* and *Civil Wars*.' The people too did not always accept the limitation of their privileges.[40]

39 Sullivan, 'Rapin, Hume and the Identity of the Historian,' 150–51.
40 Paul de Rapin-Thoyras, *The History of England, as well Ecclesiastical as Civil: Volume I*, translated and edited by N. Tindal (London, 1726), i–iv.

The grand sweep of the history of the nation was about the ups and downs of this supposed harmonious relationship between the crown and people and, of course, the 1381 uprising was an example of the near collapse of this relationship. Parliament imposed the poll tax 'with great Gentleness,' with some collectors excusing people. Nevertheless, there were some—the types who want to enrich themselves 'at the Expence of the Publick'—who wanted to increase the tax and enforce it and persuaded the king and council to do so. Rapin included the story of the daughter of Tyler (this time, Wat) who was under the legal age set down by an Act of Parliament. Ball is not present in the narration at this point and his role in instigating the trouble is downplayed in order to highlight the constitutional breakdown. As with popular discontent in various retellings prior to Rapin's, there was said to be a general underlying 'Spirit of Rebellion' in Kent and Essex which was intensified by the provocative collection. Such discontent was also due to a range of issues, such as French raids, pre-existing hostility towards exploitative legal figures, abuses of the institution of serfdom, and the alleged negligence of the Duke of Lancaster. Such complaints were kept alive by 'seditious Spirits' or ('as some affirm') monks who were also liable to be taxed.[41] Connection with Ball's teaching is implied—the marginal note soon after calls him a priest who 'spirits up the Rebels' while, later in the narrative, he is again labelled a 'seditious' priest and a '*Franciscan Monk*,' a Catholicising label already familiar to eighteenth-century readers of Hughes's narrative.[42]

Nevertheless, in the narrative proper, Ball is not mentioned by name until after a brief description of Tyler's elevation to leader, the march on London, and the freeing of prisoners. Ball also gets a slightly confusing introduction, with echoes of Tressell's confusions about a century earlier (see Chapter 6). He is referred to as a 'Priest of Maidston'—presumably based on the story (ultimately from Knighton) of Ball being sprung from Maidstone prison—and, as Tindal's accompanying note points out, Rapin called him 'John Staw' who had preached the proverbial Adam and Eve saying to the crowds (labelled here an 'Army').[43] At this point in the narrative, Ball's teachings intensified the pre-existing discontent—he may not

---

41 Paul de Rapin-Thoyras, *The History of England, as well Ecclesiastical as Civil: Volume IV*, translated and edited by N. Tindal (London, 1727), 385.
42 Rapin, *History of England, as well Ecclesiastical as Civil: Volume IV*, 391, 393.
43 Rapin, *History of England, as well Ecclesiastical as Civil: Volume IV*, 386; cf. Paul de Rapin-Thoyras, *Histoire D'Angleterre: Tome Troisiéme* (The Hague, 1727), 236. Note that '*Priest of Maidstone*' was taken up elsewhere, e.g., *Gentlemen's Magazine* 6 (1736), 464–65 (which references Rapin's history) and *Caledonian Mercury* (27 March 1769).

have been the fire-starter but he certainly knew how to keep stoking the flames. His 'seditious Sermons raised the Fury of the People to the utmost Height.' Here Ball 'perswaded' the people that because of 'all Men being Sons of Adam,' there ought not to be distinctions among them and therefore he had to reduce 'the World to a perfect Parity.' Following on from this teaching, they carried out their violent attacks on the lords and legal figures, while refusing to acknowledge John of Gaunt as king.[44] After recounting the events in London, Tyler's death, and startled praise for the near miraculous deeds of Walworth and Richard II, Ball reappears in the story, again intensifying the conflicts. In a distinctive move, Rapin's history has Ball active in East Anglia (not just spreading rebellion there as others, e.g., Trussell and Hughes, had previously claimed) alongside the other 'seditious' priest, John Wraw, traditionally known as the priestly leader in the Suffolk uprising. Together they were said to have 'stirred up the Populace of Suffolk' with a 50,000-strong army, committed 'numberless Barbarities,' and were responsible for burning 'all the antient Charters in the Abbey of St. Edmund's-Bury, and in the University of Cambridge.'[45]

After the East Anglian and wider uprisings were quelled and punishments were dished out, Rapin added a curious, perhaps even sympathetic assessment of the claim that the rebels secretly planned to kill the king, establish several kingdoms in England, and make entirely new laws: 'In all likelihood these Projects were framed only in general, and it may be, over a Glass of Wine, whilst they were on their March to *London*.' If this was a gentle raising of the eyebrow to any would-be plotters in Rapin's present (*you've had your fun, now behave yourselves!*), there is still a more deadly warning attached: these things end in 'the Ruin of the Authors.' Indeed, it was said that 1500 'died by the Hangman' and that the judge effectively had free licence to enforce his 'cruel and barbarous Temper in punishing the unfortunate Wretches, to whom he showed no favour.' And to show the contemporary ramifications (without implicating anyone in the post-1688 order), there is an additional warning from recent memory: 'The Cruelties he exercised during his Commission, may well be compared to those which were seen to be practiced of late Years by a Judge of the same Stamp in the Reign of *James* II.'[46]

No doubt, readers could read contemporary rebellions or rebellions-in-the-making into this account, as they could with practically any other preceding account. But Rapin has an emphatic explanation about the alleged

---

44 Rapin, *History of England, as well Ecclesiastical as Civil: Volume IV*, 386.
45 Rapin, *History of England, as well Ecclesiastical as Civil: Volume IV*, 391.
46 Rapin, *History of England, as well Ecclesiastical as Civil: Volume IV*, 392–93.

religious causes of the rebellion. 'It is certain,' he claimed, 'that Religion had no Hand in these Commotions.' In an explanation again familiar in the eighteenth century from Hughes's account, Rapin rejected the claims that the Lollards were to blame, observed that Wycliffe's protector John of Gaunt was in fact a target for the rebels, and noted that Wycliffe was far away from the action and never charged with involvement in the uprising. The only reason why people might think there were religious causes was because of Ball himself who, of course, is given that somewhat suspiciously Catholic label: '*John Ball* a *Franciscan* Monk, one of the Ring-Leaders of the Rebels.' Ball, Rapin added, was indeed thrown into prison by the archbishop of Canterbury for having preached a '*new Doctrine*' but it should not be inferred from this that the 'Insurrection' should be tied in with Wycliffe's followers. In fact, Rapin argued, insurrections are rarely 'caused by a Religious Zeal,' not least ones dealt with in less than a month.[47] It does not take much to read Rapin's own Protestant sympathies and past actions into this explanation.

Rethinking Whiggish History: The Reception of Rapin and Nathan ben Saddi, a Priest of the Jews

Hugh Trevor-Roper argued that Rapin's history—grounded in the myth of the Anglo-Saxon invention of Parliament—was 'sound Whig romance,' adding that the accompanying 'doctrine of the ancient English constitution, with its guarantee of liberty through the separation of powers' meant that 'he produced, just as the Whig Ascendancy was being consolidated in England, the classic exposition of the Whig—the "old whig"—interpretation of history.'[48] Nevertheless, Trevor-Roper also pointed out that the acceptance of Rapin's history spread beyond Whig circles, noting that it was 'accepted as a classic throughout Europe. Catholic and Protestant, English and French, Whig and Tory vied to praise it…it was praised, even by Tories, for its judiciousness.'[49] Rapin's history had the advantage of being

47 Rapin, *History of England, as well Ecclesiastical as Civil: Volume IV*, 393.
48 Trevor-Roper, 'Huguenot Historian,' in Scouloudi (ed.), *Huguenots in Britain and their French Background*, 10, 15. Note, too, the title of the republished version of Trevor-Roper's essay: 'Our first Whig historian: Paul de Rapin-Thoyras.'
49 Trevor-Roper, 'Huguenot Historian,' in Scouloudi (ed.), *Huguenots in Britain and their French Background*, 14.

able to be packaged as being written by an impartial foreigner above party politics ('...there's reason to believe his *Impartiality* was uncommon. For besides his Privilege, as a Foreigner, of speaking the Truth freely, without Fear of offending any Party, he had no Motive or Interest to induce him to be partial for or against *England*').[50] Obviously, this was an ideologically loaded claim concerning someone who landed at Torbay with William and it takes minimal digging to see ideology at work. But the construction of such a persona only meant that Rapin's text was even more easily reapplied to new situations. Indeed, the reception of Rapin's history via Tindall and its Whiggish takes, could be re-read accordingly in light of the vicissitudes of British factional politics. Certainly, a translation (1747) was dedicated to William, Duke of Cumberland, after his crushing of the Jacobite Rising at Culloden in 1745. But a translation (1732) was also dedicated to Cumberland's brother and one-time rival to power, the heir apparent Frederick, Prince of Wales, who had an antagonistic relationship with his father, George II, and became associated with oppositional politics. Indeed, around 1730–1731, Rapin's history even provided some inspiration or justification for the pardoned supporter of the 1715 Jacobite rebellion, Lord Bolingbroke, and his opposition to Walpole's Whig government which effectively turned Whig ideology against itself—Whigs too could now be seen as abusing the limits of power and liberty in terms Rapin would have recognised.[51]

Here we might compare the pseudonymous work of Nathan ben Saddi, a Priest of the Jews, *The Chronicle of the Kings of England Written in the Manner of the Ancient Jewish Historians* (1740), echoing Richard Baker's title from 1643 (see Chapter 6). The mock-history was published elsewhere, including in the edited collection *Trifles* (1745)[52] by Robert Dodsley, the famed bookseller (and poet and dramatist) who is the most likely candidate for the authorship of *Chronicle* and who had very recently been in trouble for publishing Paul Whitehead's controversial satire, *Manners* (1739). *Chronicle* was written in the style of biblical histories (more specifically, of course, the King James Version) partly as a satirical device to rise above factionalism in the present whilst simultaneously not. Nathan ben Saddi is, no

---

50 Nicholas Tindal, 'Preface' to Rapin, *History of England, as well Ecclesiastical as Civil: Volume I*, no page number. On the construction of Rapin's persona, see, e.g., Trevor-Roper, 'Huguenot Historian,' Scouloudi (ed.), *Huguenots in Britain and their French Background*, 14–15; Sullivan, 'Rapin, Hume and the Identity of the Historian,' 147–55.
51 For further discussion of these early receptions of Rapin, see Sullivan, 'Rapin, Hume and the Identity of the Historian,' 152–53.
52 See also, e.g., the appendix to the *Scots Magazine* (3 December 1748).

less, 'a Servant of God, of the House of *Israel*' and the decision to write in the 'Manner of our forefathers, the ancient *Jewish* Historians' was because it was 'most concise' and 'the most venerable Way of Writing,' albeit with a suspicious disclaimer that if 'thou' should be offended at the imitation of 'those sublime Originals' then the reader should not think that this was done in 'Sport' or wantonness of 'Wit.' Instead, this history will provide 'Information and Amusement' as well as 'Instruction.' That the *Chronicle* should have present relevance is clear enough from ben Saddi's comments:

> And it shall come to pass when thou readest of the foolish Kings that have ruled the Land, then shall thy Soul be troubled, and thou shalt say within thyself, how small a Portion of Sense sufficeth to govern a great Kingdom?
>
> But when thou readest of the Kings that were wise and great, then shall thy Heart be glad, and thou shalt compare the passed Times with the present, and rejoice therein, and laugh exceedingly.[53]

As Harry Solomon argued, the satire implicitly ridiculed Walpole and George II to the point where it could easily be taken for an outright antimonarchical piece with monarch after monarch ridiculed.[54] Furthermore, the story of monarchs begins with William the Conqueror as William the Bastard while ending with a list of monarchs in reverse, from George II back to 'the Cousin of *Henry* the First, who was the Brother of *William Rufus* who was the Son of *William* the Conqueror, who was the Son of a Whore. *Thus endeth the Chronicle of the KINGS of ENGLAND,*' which some readers may have noticed as a perverted version of Jesus's genealogy in Luke 3.23–38 (KJV Luke 3.38: 'the sonne of Enos, which was the sonne of Seth, which was the sonne of Adam, which was the sonne of God'; cf. 1 Chronicles 6.31–48).[55]

In this sense, the *Chronicle* complements Bolingbroke's post-Rapin contrasting of the corrupt Whig present with an ancient constitution and Saxon liberty, as well as polemically functioning as a counter to John Hervey's reading of English rulers in support of George II and Walpole in *Ancient and Modern Liberty Stated and Compar'd* (1734).[56] Strikingly, the

---

53 Nathan ben Saddi, a Priest of the Jews, *The Chronicle of the Kings of England Written in the Manner of the Ancient Jewish Historians* (London, 1740), 5–8.
54 Harry M. Solomon, *The Rise of Robert Dodsley: Creating the New Age of Print* (Carbondale: Southern Illinois University Press, 1996), 80–87, which provides a full discussion of the *Chronicle*.
55 ben Saddi, *Chronicle*, 51.
56 Solomon, *The Rise of Robert Dodsley*, 85–86. Cf. ben Saddi, *Chronicle*, 10, and the contrast between Harold and William: 'But the Lord gave up *Harold* into

Chronicle's version of the revolt takes up the story of almost all of the reign of Richard II, 'a wicked Prince' who 'did that which was evil in the Sight of the Lord, oppressing the People, and loading them daily with grievous Impositions.'[57] The story of the oppressive tax collection and Wat Tyler's daughter follows, and the actions are not distanced from the king. In turn, this led to the march on Blackheath and the emergence of Jack Straw and Ball ('Chaplain to the Army'), who spoke his famous Adam and Eve couplet and preached his egalitarian and violent sermon. The rest of the London revolt is narrated and only here do we have explicit critique of the 'Rabble,' notably the arrogance of Tyler. In addition to tying in blame with the king, Richard's downfall is then quickly narrated in pejorative biblical language ('he made unto himself Idols') before placing the crown on Henry IV, who likewise 'did that which was evil in the Sight of the Lord as most of his Fathers had done.'[58] The story of the uprising is standard enough, but it is the connection made with Richard's oppressive behaviour that is the most distinctive feature. In other words, Ball and the rebels are the most convenient foil for ben Saddi to critique monarchs of the past as a means of critiquing the rulers of England in the present.

Thomas Carte

The perspective of an outsider could potentially be a disadvantage. But, equally, such a perspective provided an opportunity for writing a history opposing Rapin, such as Thomas Carte's *A General History of England* (four volumes, published 1747–1755). Carte saw his history as a counter to Rapin's Whiggish, foreign account. Indeed, the claim on the title page— that this history was written by 'Thomas Carte, an Englishman'—was hardly innocent. Not only was Carte a High Church clergyman, he was also a Nonjuror who refused the oath to George I, a Jacobite sympathiser, and

---

the Hands of his Enemies, and he was pierced with an Arrow, and died in the Field of Battle and his Army was routed with exceeding great Slaughter. Then *William* the Bastard took on him the Royal Robes and the Scepter and the Diadem, and was made King of *England*, and was called the Conqueror.'

57 ben Saddi, *Chronicle*, 35.
58 ben Saddi, *Chronicle*, 35–39. Cf. John Hervey, *Ancient and Modern Liberty Stated and Compar'd* (London, 1734), 14, which briefly touches on Richard II and the revolt and vaguely (and perhaps ominously) mentions the 'tumultuous Mob indeed under a rash, intoxicated, ignorant Leader, made a shew of struggling for Liberty.'

a Tory, with an interest in Britishness—albeit a parochial one grounded in the English constitution and the Church of England which, as Paul Monod put it, 'did not leave much room for Roman Catholic or Presbyterian claims.'[59] Nevertheless, his history was funded by Whigs as well as Tories and Jacobites and was meant for a relatively mixed audience, though it was also a history which would receive Whig accusations of Popery and Jacobitism, unsurprisingly so given his background.[60] Indeed, there was an infamous controversy over a footnote in the first volume. Carte mentioned the story of a labourer, Christopher Lovel, who eventually had to go abroad for treatment for scrofula, where he was said to have been healed by the royal touch from none other than 'the eldest lineal descendant of a race of kings,' i.e., the Old Pretender, James II's son and would-be James III, James Francis Edward Stuart.[61] After its completion, Carte's history would not get republished.

Mainly drawing on Froissart, Walsingham, and *Vita Ricardi* for the 1381 uprisings, Carte provided a different take on Ball against the backdrop of concerns about anti-Hanoverian sentiment. The second volume (where we find his account of the 1381 uprising) starts with the preface immediately attacking a 'tribe of scribblers, who, offended at a note upon a point of mere speculation…palmed upon the world their own misrepresentation of the work, and their presumptuous guesses at the secret sentiments of its author.'[62] That the 1381 uprising could be associated with practically any rebellion, including Jacobite ones, meant Carte had extra reason to treat the subject with care. What we get is a standard enough account but one where the 1381 revolt was very much the wrong kind of revolt and against the very order of society itself. This meant hammering home the idea of the rebels as an irrational, wild, destructive mob led by the regicidal Tyler who would far too radically subvert almost anything. The comparison between Ball and Wycliffe does not occur in Carte's narration of the uprising or

---

59 Paul Kléber Monod, 'Thomas Carte, the Druids and British National Identity,' in Paul Monod, Murray Pittock, and Daniel Szechi (eds.), *Loyalty and Identity: Jacobites at Home and Abroad* (New York: Palgrave MacMillan, 2010), 132–48 (143). For Carte's biographical details, in addition to Monod's article, see, e.g., Okie, *Augustan Historical Writing*, 135–54; Hicks, *Neoclassical History and English Culture*, 159–69; Stuart Handley, 'Carte, Thomas (bap. 1686, d. 1754),' *ODNB* (28 May 2015); Dew, *Commerce, Finance and Statecraft*, 134–35.
60 Monod, 'Thomas Carte,' in Monod, Pittock, and Szechi (eds.), *Loyalty and Identity*, 142.
61 Thomas Carte, *A General History of England: Volume I* (London, 1747), 291–92 n. 4.
62 Thomas Carte, *A General History of England: Volume 2* (London, 1750), iii.

its origins, which was presumably one way to avoid any misreading from whatever perspective. Ball himself is presented as a leading agitator among other 'seditious preachers,' encouraging 'insurrections' through preaching the equality of 'all men,' that 'servitude' was contrary to God's will and introduced by oppressors and the wicked, and that people needed to cast off their yoke and 'assert their liberty.'[63]

By whipping up such discontent, the deluded people were already angry by the time the poll tax was introduced, even if collectors 'are said' to have collected the taxes with some brutality. Indeed, there is little sympathy for the peasants despite Carte's awareness of claims that they were treated unfairly. Following Walsingham, Carte claimed the uprising began in Essex, provoked by the spread of false reports (which becomes a telling theme in Carte's account) about the violence of the collection ('There is nothing so absurd, that an English peasant is not capable of believing'). They then rose up, gained numbers through pressing people to join the cause, and promoted an agenda 'asserting their common liberty, for changing the state and evil customs of the kingdom, and for getting rid of all taxes, but the fifteenths.' Indeed, the ranks of the rebels swelled through 'a parcel of needy, debauched rascals, immersed in debts, and criminals of all kinds,' while the leaders such as Thomas Miller, Hob Carter, Jack Straw, and Wat Tyler, took their names from 'their base original and mean employments.'[64] The leaders ultimately got what they deserved for 'their cruel actions, and still more cruel designs' which were grounded in Ball's preaching. And at the fore of Ball's preaching were his exhortations about liberty requiring first the killing of the great and the good.[65] Carte's sympathy towards rebel grievances was certainly in short supply but this was no doubt necessary to try to avoid any more presumptuous guesses about his secret sentiments while not implicating Jacobite interests with the 1381 rebels.

William Guthrie

Scottish threats (real or otherwise) were certainly crucial to eighteenth-century constructions of Ball and the 1381 revolt. But, as we will see further with David Hume (Chapter 8), Scotland would also produce historical writers influential in the history of Ball's reception, as well as

---

63 Carte, *A General History of England: Volume 2*, 558.
64 Carte, *A General History of England: Volume 2*, 558.
65 Carte, *A General History of England: Volume 2*, 562.

in historiography itself, by downplaying, rejecting, or ignoring the role of the divine and Providence in their cultural, social, economic, and political accounts of national histories and the development of liberty.[66] A sometimes overlooked example is the Whiggish political reporter William Guthrie (c. 1708–1770) who was born in Brechin but had long moved to London by the time he wrote his four-volume *General History of England from the Invasion of Julius Caesar to 1688* (1744–1751). Guthrie worked in the tradition of an implicitly Whiggish history, including ideas about the ongoing struggle to restore or later maintain the freedoms associated with Saxon constitutionalism but also coupled with claims about the uneven growth of English prosperity from the Tudors onward. But he also worked in the tradition of claiming to stand beyond partisan politics and religion (though hardly without an anticlerical tendency), while effectively wanting to replace what he saw as Rapin's improperly biased—and foreign—history.[67]

Not unexpectedly, Guthrie's account downplays the influence of religious ideas in influencing the revolt, though Ball remains a standard malign influence. Neither Wycliffe nor his views 'had any effect in spiriting up the people' which was shown, Guthrie argued, by the rebels targeting Wycliffe's patron, John of Gaunt. Major reasons for the revolt were firmly materialistic, including 'the impolitic taxes, and more impolitic method of collecting them' representative of poor governance. Certainly, Ball had long busied himself in 'inculcating into the common people through Essex and Kent, that a state of either villianage or servitude was incompatible with the laws of nature, which means that every person should enjoy an equality of condition with his neighbour.' While the listeners 'greedily drank in this doctrine,' Ball had his limitations as an explanation for the revolt. The demagogical and destructive rebellion that demanded a perverted sort of liberty and a violent abolition of all ranks might not have even happened had the incident involving (Wat) Tyler's daughter not taken place and had Tyler not 'beat the brains out of one of the insolent publicans.' Even so, Guthrie (and here we should, perhaps, recall his anticlericalism) was drawn back to the character of Ball and his excessive religious behaviour—Ball the 'pragmatical priest...incendiary priest...the busy priest' who, on being freed from prison, was 'doubly diligent in stirring his audience up to madness

---

66 Laird Okie, 'William Guthrie, Enlightenment Historian,' *The Historian* 51 (1989): 221–38 (221–23, 235); Okie, *Augustan Historical Writing*, 171–94; Dew, *Commerce, Finance and Statecraft*, 155–56.

67 Okie, 'William Guthrie,' 227–29, 234–35; Dew, *Commerce, Finance and Statecraft*, 157–68; Sullivan, 'Rapin, Hume and the Identity of the Historian,' 158–59, 160.

and fury.' Furthermore, Ball's sermon on the Adam and Eve couplet was dismissed by Guthrie in order to slur both Ball and his audience ('His being void of learning and eloquence gave an advantage to his cause, as he was thereby upon a level with the understandings of his audience').[68]

Nevertheless, 'this mad and ill concerted rebellion' was not presented as completely stupid as it managed a degree of discipline and presentability, no matter how (or because of how) perverse Guthrie thought the reality was. The executions of lawyers and ecclesiastical figures in London were 'barbarously punctual' while the rebels 'affected to preserve an appearance of loyalty and affection' to the king. They 'took care to have very plausible pretences for their rising, and to pay for every thing they had' which helped explain why London could fall so easily—common Londoners found this agreeable and so 'their magistracy there found it would be impossible for them to prevent the rebels from becoming masters of the city.' Yet Guthrie kept returning to the centrality of Ball. Ball knew more about the 'secrets of their designs than any other' and his execution was delayed in order to find out as much information as possible. Echoing Brady, Tyrrell, and Echard, it was Ball's confession which provided the information that the rebels wanted to carry the king around with them for their security, killing him once they had authorised 'their proceedings,' after 'forming a digest of laws of their own, to have elected one of themselves king over each county in England' and permitting only 'the begging friars' to remain in the country. Ball too was a key organiser of the rebellion through his letters (which Guthrie provided) that were 'circulated throughout the kingdom' by the 'chief rebels.' Guthrie even gave the letters a backhanded compliment of sorts ('a very particular rythmical [sic] kind of a dialogue...a wonderful train of an enthusiastic buffoonery'), and seems to have appreciated the antiquarian and cultural value (to a degree) of the letters found in Knighton ('cannot but be agreeable to the reader, who will be thereby enabled to judge the wit and language of the common people in the days of Chaucer').[69] If these were unintentional hints of a rescuing of Ball, then they were just that—unintentional hints. But the heavy emphasis on the wildness of Ball may have had another compensatory function as the cultural logic around the uprising and against the increasingly anachronistic system of serfdom was changing.

---

68 William Guthrie, *A General History of England Beginning with the Reign of Edward the Second and Ending with That of Henry the Eighth*, Vol. II (London, 1747), 309–10.

69 Guthrie, *A General History of England*, 310, 313.

Implicit comparisons between past and present—including concerns about mobs, rebellions, order, and political change—all feature in the most influential eighteenth-century histories of 1381. Whatever their differences, anxieties or assumptions about threats from below to the order of things and stereotypes about mob-driven understandings of liberty continued to unify quite different historians. In the next chapter, we will see further portrayals of just how debauched this liberty from below was understood and how it was propagandistically presented to the public. Nevertheless, the acknowledgement that the mob did have concerns for liberty, in a world where discussions involving the nation, representation, and limitation of monarchical power were taking off across Europe, could easily raise uncomfortable questions from above: What if the mob slogans had a point? This meant that policing the understandings of liberty, and the classes from where such claims came, was a near-inevitable option for the time being, particularly in a century that would become closely associated with the rowdy city mob. And, certainly, eighteenth-century ideas surrounding the mob meant that the old polemics about the deranged rabble of 1381 could be updated and reused accordingly. But serfdom was now an antiquated practice and in the age of Enlightenment, political philosophy, major revolutions in America and France, and demands relating to political representation coupled with a crowd, Ball's ideas of human equality at the beginning of time corrupted by power-hungry feudal lords could not be dismissed so easily. It is for good reason that within a hundred years after the histories of Rapin, Echard, Hughes, Tyrrell, and Brady, and within fifty years of the histories of Carte and Guthrie, Ball's dramatic public transformation would take off.

8
Georgian John: From Mob Rule to Reasonable Demands

'Nothing can be more dangerous than a Mob,' wrote William Prynn in 1736. He was writing in defence of a standing army and the Riot Act and worried about protection of property and popish violence. To illuminate his point about 'Mob Insurrection,' he cited the 'seditious' examples of Wat Tyler and Ball, with particular interest in their attacks from below on nobles and lawyers and the hundred thousand men who 'march'd directly to London' where they unleashed 'their Fury.'[1] That the capital was a place of especial concern is not a surprise, but other details help explain why potential threats caused such anxieties in the eighteenth century. The population of London itself had almost doubled to 900,000 over the course of the century, bringing with it changing social relations and tensions, issues of crowding, and disturbances and riots, including those associated with Sacheverell (1710), Spitalfields weavers (1719, 1760s), St George's Fields (1768), Gordon (1780), and, in its own particular way, the infamous gin craze. As Robert Shoemaker put it, 'This was quintessentially the century of the mob, when, more than before or since, groups of Londoners used the streets on a daily basis to make their views known...this was the most riotous century in London's history.'[2] Throughout the eighteenth century, the unblessed memory of Tyler was widely disseminated, recalling his death and the Walworth/City of London connection and how he posed (and was dealt with as) a deadly or seditious threat tied in with mobs and riots.[3] Such

1 *Gentlemen's Magazine* 6 (1736), 464–65.
2 Robert Shoemaker, *The London Mob: Violence and Disorder in Eighteenth-Century England* (London: Bloomsbury, 2004), 111, and 10 for population figures.
3 See, e.g., *Caledonian Mercury* (17 February 1737); *Ipswich Journal* (29 December 1750); *Scots Magazine* (1 November 1756); *Scots Magazine* (3 November 1760); *Dublin Courier* (25 May 1763); *Scots Magazine* (4 July 1768); *Leeds Intelligencer* (19 July 1768); *Manchester Mercury* (19 July 1768); *Newcastle Chronicle* (23 July 1768); *Derby Mercury* (22 July 1768); *Kentish Gazette* (13 July 1768);

was the menace of 1381 that in December 1743 it was even reported that 'it must be very shocking to hear, that a letter is sent to the Rt. Hon. The Lord Carteret, signed *Wat Tyler*, threatening him with Destruction, if the Hanoverians are employed this year.'[4] While not as prominent in newspapers and journals, Ball himself remained an occasional menacing presence whether in name or allusion.[5]

A Place in Mob History

In fuller accounts of the revolt, Ball retained an important function in the narrative. Ball had taken his place among the most threatening figures of all the mobs and rebellions Britain had seen according to *The History of All the Mobs, Tumults and Insurrections in Great Britain* (1715), begun by the somewhat slippery, opportunist, and conspiratorial Scottish Protestant Robert Ferguson (d. 1714) and 'continued by an Impartial Hand.'[6] The account, which echoes contemporary interest in compiling the lives of infamous criminals,[7] begins by locating the 1381 uprising in 1383 and the story of Tyler's daughter, with Ball (a 'seditious Clergy-man') appearing immediately after Tyler complains to his neighbours about the behaviour of the tax

---

Caledonian Mercury (13 July 1768); *Stamford Mercury* (14 July 1768); *Derby Mercury* (15 July 1768); *Newcastle Chronicle* (16 July 1768); *Bath Chronicle and Weekly Gazette* (19 January 1769); *Kentish Gazette* (21 January 1769); *Leeds Intelligencer* (31 January 1769); *Bath Chronicle and Weekly Gazette* (2 February 1769); *Oxford Journal* (4 February 1769); *Salisbury and Winchester Journal* (6 February 1769); *Leeds Intelligencer* (7 February 1769); *Leeds Intelligencer* (9 April 1771); *Kentish Gazette* (14 June 1780); *Salisbury and Winchester Journal* (19 June 1780); *Caledonian Mercury* (17 July 1780). See also Matheson, 'The Peasants' Revolt through Five Centuries of Rumor and Reporting', 135–36. For similar reasons, an older ballad was collected in Thomas Evans (ed.), *Old Ballads, Historical and Narrative: With Some of Modern Date: Volume the First* (London, 1777), 280–84. See Basdeo, *Life and Legend of a Rebel Leader*, loc 734–772.

4 *Caledonian Mercury* (22 December 1743); *Ipswich Journal* (24 December 1743).

5 E.g., *Caledonian Mercury* (23 January 1727); *The Briton* 16 (11 September 1762), 316–22; *Gentlemen's Magazine* 32 (September 1762), 416–17.

6 Cf. Mike Hill and Warren Montag, *The Other Adam Smith* (Stanford: Stanford University Press, 2015), 156; Melinda Zook, 'Ferguson, Robert (d. 1714)', *ODNB* (14 November 2018).

7 Basdeo, *Life and Legend of a Rebel Leader*, loc 1053–1152.

collectors. Ball stirs up discontent to the point of rebellion with his talk of government mismanagement and infringement of liberties.[8] We then get a standard account of the 'Insurrection which had so nearly effected the perpetual Ruin of the Kingdom, and put an End to all Religion, Law and Liberty.'[9] Among the guilty leaders to be executed was Ball, 'the Priest, first Incendiary,' and his letter to the 'Rabble of Essex' is published (alongside Jack Straw's regicidal confession) so that it may be seen 'how fit an Orator he was for a Mob' and 'what strength of Perswasion there is in Nonscence and Enthusiasm.'[10] One reason for this foregrounding of a figure like Ball is fairly straightforward. *History of All the Mobs, Tumults and Insurrections* was published the same year as the Jacobite uprising and was even prefaced with the addition of the 'Proclamation for the Suppression of Riots and Tumults' which warns of people being stirred up to 'Riots and Tumults' through to 'open Rebellion, a levying of War against his Majesty and his Royal Authority,' and declaring for the Pretender, James Edward Stuart. The Proclamation further stresses the importance of confronting rebels and reflects other concerns for Londoners doing their civil and patriotic duty through the example of 1381 (see below). In this instance, 'Officers Civil and Military' are 'oblig'd' to resist with force to 'supress all such Traitrous Rebellions' and 'all the subjects of this Realm' should likewise aid and assist in the suppression of such rebellions and can act freely in self-defence.[11]

In the eighteenth century, then, the story of the 1381 uprising was one ready-made to be read into and condemn new insurgents—real or otherwise. The publication and republication of an anonymous chapbook, possibly from around 1720, called *The History of Wat Tyler & Jack Straw*, reveals such adaptable concerns combined with an implicit appeal to Londoners to protect the city as they (apparently) did before. As Lister Matheson argued, the likely dates of the editions of *The History of Wat Tyler & Jack Straw* (1720, 1730, 1750, 1776, 1780, 1788, 1790, 1800) roughly correspond with rebellions against Hanoverian authority, including Jacobite risings (1715, 1719, 1745) and the revolt of the American colonies (1776), as well as the French Revolution (1789).[12]

The anonymous retelling of Ball in *The History of Wat Tyler & Jack Straw* is a familiar one. Although the account is dominated by Tyler and Straw

---

8   Robert Ferguson and an Impartial Hand, *The History of All the Mobs, Tumults and Insurrections in Great Britain* (London, 1715), 8.
9   Ferguson and Impartial Hand, *History of All the Mobs*, 11.
10 Ferguson and Impartial Hand, *History of All the Mobs*, 12–13.
11 Ferguson and Impartial Hand, *History of All the Mobs*, no page number given.
12 Matheson, 'Peasants' Revolt through Five Centuries,' 136.

as we might expect, Chapter 1 of *The History of Wat Tyler & Jack Straw* is headed with the claim that the 'great *Rebellion* arose upon *John Wall*, a Priest, Preaching all Men were Lords in *Adam*.'[13] The origins of the uprising are traced to '*John Wall*, a seditious Priest' who took advantage of discontent among the common people about taxation and so 'stir[red] them to Rebellion' through preaching and informing the 'baser sort'. He preached about how all were descended from Adam and so of 'equal Worth', how the laws of the kingdom were unjust, and how differences between lord and beggar were made and perpetuated. Wall was open to persuasion by fair means or, ominously, 'by open Insurrection and Civil War', so that people might acquire 'their own Liberties, and to relieve their own Wants'. Indeed, a presentation of the revolt as a perversion of liberty had a long history and was a concern of historians at the turn of the century (see Chapter 7). Wall's 'treacherous and leud Doctrine' spread among peasants, across shires, and into London among those said to have envied the prosperity of the wealthier Londoners.[14] Much of the account is taken up by a narration of the events in London where Wall gets a brief but significant mention as Simon Sudbury's head is chopped off. The decapitation was said to be at '*Wall*'s Instigation,' because (in line with Froissart) 'when he first began his preaching up Rebellion, he had confined him to a *short*, but easie Imprisonment.'[15] If the ongoing threat of rebellion is one of the reasons for the popularity of *The History of Wat Tyler & Jack Straw*, then there is a specific angle that should be acknowledged here. The contrast between urban and rural, London and the peasantry, may have been playing into a propagandist line that Londoners have a special duty to protect the capital from outside threats from the easily duped or those with more sinister intentions.[16]

As Peter Linebaugh implied, the regular republication of the story in the form of a relatively cheap chapbook over the course of the eighteenth century may also point in the direction of wider, more popular interest in the more ideologically ambiguous tradition of theatrical productions (see further Chapter 5).[17] Linebaugh pointed to the presentation of the 1381 revolt

---

13 Anonymous, *The History of Wat Tyler & Jack Straw, Being a Relation of their Notorious Rebellion* (London, 1720[?]), 2.
14 Anonymous, *The History of Wat Tyler & Jack Straw*, 3.
15 Anonymous, *The History of Wat Tyler & Jack Straw*, 8.
16 Anne Wohlcke, *The 'Perpetual Fair': Gender, Disorder and Urban Amusement in Eighteenth-Century London* (Manchester: Manchester University Press, 2014), 182–84.
17 Peter Linebaugh, *The London Hanged: Crime and Civil Society in the Eighteenth Century* (second edition; London: Verso, 2003), 347.

in the outdoor theatre at Bartholomew Fair (in the vicinity of where Tyler was killed) and here we might note the example of the droll *Wat Tyler and Jack Straw, Or the Mob Reformers* performed at Pinkethman and Giffard's Great Theatrical Booth in 1730. There is further evidence of its popularity. The pro-Walworth droll—which was said to have borrowed the actual dagger used to kill Tyler—was popular enough that it was brought back to replace other performances, printed and sold for 6d, and later performed at the Lord's Mayor's pageant.[18]

Ball is absent from the named *dramatis personae*, but we might note the suspiciously similar (and slightly farcical) character of Zekiel Pease-Stack. The proclaimed king, Tyler, for instance, refers to 'my faithful' Pease-Stack as 'High-Chancellor of *England* (so we call thee from this Time forth).'[19] After tiring somewhat since his 'last Pint of Brandy' (even if a weaker drink than what we might consume, it is still a connection with the tradition of the big-drinking Ball), Tyler asks Pease-Stack to 'Harrangue the Populace.' Pease-Stack explains to the different mobs that what they are about to undertake does not so much require 'the Cloak of Religion, as of Justice,' yet nevertheless immediately says how he has 'turn'd over the Scripture.' He could not find where in the Bible it encourages 'this Rebellion' but he is sure that 'it does not say one Word against it.' He thus assures them that silence is effectively approval using a dark sexualised and gendered analogy: 'Silence in a Maiden is a sure Token of her Consent.' He talks too of a subject's duty to the king but notes that neither 'Richard' nor 'England' are anywhere mentioned in the Bible.[20] Pease-Stack gets approval of the second mob (though the first mob reminds the audience of his consent analogy and that he might be a 'Wag'): 'How like an Angel he argues!— Did you hear that, Neighbours? We have Scripture on our Side as well as Wat Tyler. O, he's a rare man!'[21] The second mob (with agreement from the third) also argues that while there might not be a mention of England in the Bible, it is mentioned 'in the latter End of the first Side of my Bible at home, I read—*London, printed by*—.' An exacerbated Pease-Stack only adds to the farcical nature of the mob but with a notable (ominous?) emphasis on geography: 'Countrymen, are you such Fools, such Asses? Why, I imagin'd

---

18   Sybil Rosenfeld, *The Theatre of the London Fairs in the 18th Century* (Cambridge: Cambridge University Press, 1960), 34.
19   Anonymous, *Wat Tyler and Jack Straw, Or the Mob Reformers. A dramatick entertainment. As it is perform'd at Pinkentham's and Giffard's Great Theatrical Booth in Bartholomew Fair* (London, 1730), 13.
20   Anonymous, *Wat Tyler and Jack Straw, Or the Mob Reformers*, 13–14.
21   Anonymous, *Wat Tyler and Jack Straw, Or the Mob Reformers*, 14.

you were Men of Sense...Cou'd you be so stupid as not to know that it was only Printed here in *London*?'[22]

Nevertheless, Pease-Stack continues his address by more contradictory statements. He says he will come directly to the point but asks baser questions: 'Who is there here that does not love a pretty Wench? Who wou'd refuse a glorious pint of Gin? Or insolently turn his churlish Back on Beef and Pudding?' All the mobs agree with the implied answer. In answer to Pease-Stack's question, 'Does any here love Work and Taxes?', their answer is, of course, neither of them. The reason is that those in disagreement may return to the dunghill and plough while those who agree 'love Liberty and hate Oppression—Liberty, my Boys!' Not only is this the perverse sort of liberty similarly attributed to the rebels in so many of the highbrow histories, but it is, picking up on a tradition going back to the first medieval chroniclers of the revolt, one that involves sexual assault and presumably rape: 'Will it not be delicious, when not a Lad here who likes a Countess, or first Dutchess, but may enjoy her before Night, and she think herself honour'd by the Embrace!' And how do the mobs reply? With cheers for 'Liberty and a Countess!' Pease-Stack even intensifies the crudity by entreating the mobs to throw down 'Nobility and Women at once, and magnanimously lift up Ourselves and Petticoats afterwards.'[23]

Wat Tyler and Jack Straw, Or the Mob Reformers gives us further insight into the concerns about peasant envy of London (or parts of it) as also seen in *The History of Wat Tyler & Jack Straw*. As Anne Wohlcke points out, there is an assumed contrast between the less educated, easily duped, farcical peasant mob and the loyal, knowledgeable Londoner, all set against the backdrop of anxieties about Jacobite rebellions. She adds: 'The underlying message is that Londoners have a unique historical responsibility to stop rebellions and disorderly activities within their city.'[24] Through a figure like Walworth and ideas of loyalty to and of London, the true king and true liberty are pronounced. Indeed, the droll ends with Richard adding the dagger to the City's Coat of Arms and the 'Immortal Deed' is made relevant for 'the happy Years of *George*'s reign' when 'Another Race shall grace our Isle again, Loyal as this, undaunted, and as free, Great, and not proud—yet proud of Liberty.'[25]

Certainly, as Wohlcke stresses, Hanoverian audiences got an effective presentation of their own patriotism and civil loyalties. Yet we should also

---

22 Anonymous, *Wat Tyler and Jack Straw, Or the Mob Reformers*, 15.
23 Anonymous, *Wat Tyler and Jack Straw, Or the Mob Reformers*, 15–16.
24 Wohlcke, *The 'Perpetual Fair*,' 184.
25 Anonymous, *Wat Tyler and Jack Straw, Or the Mob Reformers*, 32.

note further reasons why such presentations might have been felt necessary: the ambiguities involved in the carnivalesque tradition in which *Wat Tyler and Jack Straw, Or the Mob Reformers* and the Lord Mayor's pageant stand and the idea of different audience perceptions of such comedic characters. The drunken Tyler and gin-praising Pease-Stack echo Shakespeare's Cade (/Ball) and Parson Ball in *The Life and Death of Jack Straw* (see Chapter 5). Pease-Stack's promise of drink, food, and sex may likewise have pointed to religious hypocrisy while simultaneously drawing a knowing laugh as a recognisable stereotype. The emphasis on sexual assault of aristocratic women may have played into fears of disorder, violent revenge, and mob rule. But Pease-Stack's encouragement of such acts could have been viewed by some in a Rabelaisian and knowing way as much as a desire for gin, beef, and pudding in a cultural context excited by criminals like Jack Sheppard.[26] In this sense, we might recall Robert Darton's famous analysis of the great cat massacre in a shop in Rue Saint-Séverin in 1730s Paris, where the workers' felinicide tapped into ideas of a symbolic trial, murder, and rape of bourgeois masters in pre-Revolutionary France.[27] Nevertheless, whatever differing audience perceptions might account for the popularity of *Wat Tyler and Jack Straw, Or the Mob Reformers*, its framing of sexual assault is emphatically part of the construction of the deluded perversion of liberty. This is baser and bawdier than most histories and elite presentations of the leaders of 1381, to be sure, but the logic is effectively the same.

Wilkes and Liberty

The language of 'mob reformers,' and the menacing and ambiguous threat of 1381, was also being employed in more highbrow publications and debates about representation and press freedom. According to *The Briton*, a weekly publication run by Tobias Smollett (1721–1771) and supportive of the Earl of Bute's government (1762–1763), Ball and the main figures of the 1381 uprising were found to be the inspiration for alleged anti-royalism, republicanism, and provocations of the extravagant, radical journalist and politician John Wilkes (1725–1797) and his circle. The most notable of the circle was the poet, satirist, and journalist Charles Churchill (1731–1764), a former clergyman who may have been Ball to Wilkes's Jack Straw in the

---

26 Cf. Dunn, 'Wat Tyler: The Many Roles of an English Rebel,' 28.
27 Robert Darnton, *The Great Cat Massacre and Other Episodes in French Cultural History* (New York: Vintage Books, 1984), 75–104.

eyes of *The Briton*.[28] Wilkes ran the provocatively titled *North Briton*—an implicit dig at the Scottish Bute governing in England—and was especially critical of the government's handling of the Seven Years' War, including famously criticising George III's speech in 1763. Wilkes and *North Briton* continued their criticisms of the government post-Bute and the provocative style was popular. Wilkes's imprisonment and legal run-ins with the government over freedom of the press, parliamentary reporting, and thwarted political ambitions led to ongoing street (indeed, 'mob') support, with his name becoming associated with liberty—a recurring point of observation and criticism in the press.[29]

For *The Briton* (September 1762), these emerging reformers were a pale imitation of the 'mob reformers' of yesteryear who at least could claim that they were enslaved rather than freeborn. The medieval mob-reformers included a misnamed 'John Bull,' the 'parson,' 'reverend apostle,' and 'honest priest of those days, who acted as principal incendiary.'[30] Bull/Ball spirited up 'the multitude to mischief and rebellion by inflammatory sermons, quaint rhymes, and treasonable papers, dispersed among the leaders of the people.' 'What a loss it was to mankind,' the article exclaimed, 'and a disgrace to the government of England, that this worthy reformer, in canonicals, should have been hanged as a sower of sedition!' (Hanging—rather than hanged, drawn, and quartered—seems to be one of the more subtle emphases of eighteenth-century retellings.) Where 'Jacky Straw' assures them that 'it is their privilege to be insolent and refractory,' Bull/Ball declares that '*Vox populi est vox Dei*: the voice of the people is the voice of God.'[31]

Smollett's *Complete History of Britain* illuminates his position on Ball/Bull (the misnaming is again present) and its implications for the eighteenth-century present but with a tension important to understanding the reception history of Ball and his public transformation in

28 Tobias Smollett, *Poems, Plays, and 'The Briton'* (ed. Byron Gassman, O. M. Brack, Leslie A. Chilton; Athens: University of Georgia Press, 2014), 484 n. 18, 491 n. 2, 495 n. 10, 497 n. 16, 499 n. 27, 500 n. 11, 518 n. 23. See 221–40 for the story of Smollett and *The Briton*.

29 For further details, see, e.g., John Sainsbury, *John Wilkes: The Lives of a Libertine* (Aldershot: Ashgate, 2006); Arthur Cash, *John Wilkes: The Scandalous Father of Civil Liberty* (New Haven: Yale University Press, 2008); Peter D. G. Thomas, 'Wilkes, John (1725–1797),' *ODNB* (24 May 2008).

30 *The Briton* 16 (11 September 1762), in Smollett, *Poems, Plays, and 'The Briton*,' 316–22 (318–19).

31 *The Briton* 16 (11 September 1762), in Smollett, *Poems, Plays, and 'The Briton*,' 318–19. Cf. *Gentlemen's Magazine* 32 (September 1762), 416–17.

the not-too-distant future. The full account of the uprising shows how much of a threat to order it was but also acknowledged that peasants had reasonable demands. The problem was the turn to extreme violence to achieve these demands and the threat they posed to the very constitution itself, a point which David Hume pushed further still (see below). It was the 'imposition' of the poll tax which 'gave birth to those commotions' that threatened 'to have destroyed the English constitution.' Land tenants had become wealthier and tried to 'recover that freedom to which they thought they had a natural title' and became exempt from 'all manner of servitude.'[32] The meeting at Mile End has Richard agreeing, on condition of an end to the revolt, to ending servitude, 'free liberty' to buy and sell, reduction of land rent for lands under villeinage, and a general pardon which foreshadows some of the reasons for sympathetic establishment readings of the uprising. But this is a notable contrast to when Tyler was later offered these conditions: he instead secretly decided to turn on the king because 'this savage plebeian' was 'intoxicated with power and success, and had now become regicidal, wanting to murder the king and nobles before 'erecting a despotism on the ruins of the constitution.' Incomprehensible in presenting his new, extravagant demands, he was going to plunge his dagger into Richard's heart before being stopped by Walworth. Charters granted to the rebels of Kent and Essex were later revoked because of their 'subsequent rebellion.'[33]

On top of the familiar themes of the causes of the revolt (the infamous poll tax, the oppressive tax collectors, and treatment of Tyler's daughter), Ball played a key role in this turn to mob rule and in sullying the potentially reasonable demands of peasants. Threats of rebellion had prevented such changes but taxes as well as 'seditious preachers' stirred up discontent. Such preachers were clearly Ball-like in their teaching (and turn up in the usual place Ball would) as they asserted that 'by nature all men were equal; that servitude was an unjust oppression, contrary to the will of God; and that it was their duty to shake off the yoke, and maintain their birthright.'[34] After the story of the revolt, Smollett then turned to the 'fanatic priest' Ball/Bull who was deemed to be the 'principal incendiary' who, in words echoing the article in *The Briton*, 'spirited them up to mischief and revolt, by inflammatory sermons and circular letters, couched in quaint

32 Tobias Smollett, *A Complete History of England, from the Descent of Julius Caesar, to the Treaty of Aix la Chapelle, 1748* (third edition; London, 1758), 79–80.
33 Smollett, *A Complete History of England*, 81–83.
34 Smollett, *A Complete History of England*, 79–80.

mysterious rhymes, admirably calculated to work up the minds of ignorant rustics to fury and enthusiasm.' After summarising the Blackheath sermon, Smollett added the claim found among other historians of the age (e.g., Brady, Tyrrell, Echard, Guthrie) that Ball, Straw, and others wanted the king to come to them so that they could eventually kill him and the nobles and make new kings of counties.[35]

With serfdom an institution of the past, even an establishment critique shows how the old framing of the revolt was breaking down and having to be rethought by claiming that the 1381 mob went too far. Read in this light, the voices of Ball/Bull, Straw, and Tyler whispering in the ears of Wilkes and his circles would only distort and pervert liberty for regicidal means and for violent mob rule. And the provocative rhetoric gave way to bloody realities at St George's Field (10 May 1768) when a mass pro-Wilkes protest with open criticisms of the king led to seven deaths, injuries to protesters, and rioting. Tyler, Ball, and 1381 (as well as Cade) were again invoked in the response to popular support for the now outlawed Wilkes and his controversial run for MP in Middlesex.[36] History was seen to provide warnings against over-zealous demands for liberty: 'What terror did that *Idol of Clowns*, Wat. Tyler, attended by the seditious *Priest of Maidstone*, strike in the city of London?' *Idol of Clowns* echoes John Cleveland's polemic (see Chapter 6) while the *Priest of Maidstone* is likely a reference to Ball, a mistaken label found in Rapin's popular history (see Chapter 7) and others who referenced Rapin, such as in the example from Prynn noted above. A certain priestly sympathiser is even called 'the worthy successor of Wat. Tyler's Chaplain.' Such historical precedents, it was claimed in the *Caledonian Mercury* (27 March 1769), were said to be a warning against those with solemn declarations against ill design on the king. These examples show how the 'mob and malcontents of London' then turned on Parliament and ministers to 'redress grievances' which ended in decapitations. But the story also uses the idea of loyal Londoners ultimately preserving peace ('the wiser and most respectable citizens opposed with great firmness and integrity those seditious proceedings'). Wilkes's supporters, the alleged successors to Tyler et al., are (somewhat polemically) encouraged to put faith in the rule of law and parliamentary procedure.

Shortly after, John Sommers took up the pre-existing concerns about Wilkes in the *Scots Magazine* (1 July 1769) through a potted history (via Knighton) of the 'Milendians' of the 1381 revolt and the eventual acts of Londoners in countering the threat. If there was any parallel from former

---

35 Smollett, *A Complete History of England*, 86.
36 *Caledonian Mercury* (27 March 1769).

times, Sommers argued, it was the 'levellers' of Richard II's reign headed by a 'pragmatical priest' and composed of the 'meanest scum of the earth,' though they 'modestly called themselves the people of England.' The sermon of the 'Reverend leader' asserted liberty while killing the leading legal and political figures of the realm. The lesson to be learned from 1381 was to take swift, firm action. Moreover, the implications for reading 1381 into the present is clear. The 'sequel is well known,' Sommers argued, adding that the 'reader will be but too apt of himself to draw a comparison between those and the present times,' even if the modern equivalents have more improved methods. However, Sommers's presentation of the wildness of Ball and the rebels was also a sign that such polemic compensated for a tension in the presentation of the revolt. For all the attacks on Wilkes, by the second half of the eighteenth century there was an accompanying idea that was to assist in the transformation in Ball's reputation, namely that the economic, social, and political world was changing to the extent that the medieval past really was becoming a very different place where they did things differently. No matter how hostile he may have been towards the excesses of Ball (/Bull), Smollett's claim that the rebel demands for freedom were no longer so obviously unreasonable meant that the potential for reclaiming Ball and the 1381 revolt was likewise increasing.

David Hume

It was arguably the Scottish Enlightenment that marked the most significant moment in the beginnings of a shift in high profile understandings of Ball. And the signs of rescuing Ball's memory came from a seemingly unlikely individual source: David Hume (1711–1776), the empiricist whose fame in the eighteenth century was more as a historian than philosopher. Hume had long been interested in the idea of history as popular, engaging, and didactic, and indeed modelled his work more on ancient historians than presenting a detailed and referenced piece of history writing.[37] Indeed, despite some initial problems and controversial reactions, Hume's history

---

37 E.g., David Hume, 'Essay VII. Of the Study of History,' in *Essays, Moral and Political* (Edinburgh, 1741), 69–77, (though withdrawn from a later edition of Hume's essays); David Hume, 'To the Abbé le Blanc (12 September 1754),' in J. Y. T. Greig (ed.), *The Letters of David Hume: Volume I, 1727–1765* (Oxford: Oxford University Press, 1932), 191–94 (193). See Donald T. Stiebert, 'Hume's History of England,' in Paul Russell (ed.), *The Oxford Handbook of Hume*

of England would soon replace Rapin's as the standard work of its type.[38] The controversial first volume—from James I to Charles I—was published as *The History of Great Britain* in 1754. The more agreeable second volume (1757) continued the history to 1688 followed by two volumes on Tudor history (1759) and two volumes from the Romans to the end of the War of the Roses (1761, 1762), the second of which includes the 1381 uprising. A complete history was published in 1761–1762 under a new title (*The History of England from the Invasion of Julius Caesar to the Revolution in 1688*) which shifted from 'Great Britain' to 'England,' a telling indication of where power and interests lay, with further revised editions published soon after (1770, 1773, 1778) and many more editions since.[39]

As we will see, Hume's history represents something distinctive in the history of the interpretation of Ball. But it is worth reminding that his famous irreligiosity marks a notable shift from the dominant history of interpretation that preceded him. Certainly, the miraculous (for instance) was hardly an expected feature in histories of the revolt by Hume's time but ideas of Providence were not confined to the distant past, even if Hume did

---

(Oxford: Oxford University Press, 2016), 546–68 (549–51, 554–57); Sullivan, 'Rapin, Hume and the Identity of the Historian,' 157–58.

38 Obviously, there is a vast bibliography for Hume's life and work, and justice cannot be done to it here. For a recent selection on the issues presented here, including summaries, see, e.g., Okie, *Augustan Historical Writing*, 195–207; Hicks, *Neoclassical History and English Culture*, 170–209; Mark Salber Phillips, '"The Most Illustrious Philosopher and Historian of the Age": Hume's History of England,' in Elizabeth S. Radcliffe (ed.), *A Companion to Hume* (Oxford: Blackwell, 2008), 406–22; David Wootton, 'David Hume: "The Historian,"' in David Fate Norton and Jacqueline Taylor (eds.), *The Cambridge Companion to Hume* (second edition; Cambridge: Cambridge University Press, 2008), 447–79; Sullivan, 'Rapin, Hume and the Identity of the Historian,' 156–62; Timothy M. Costelloe, 'Hume on History,' in Alan Bailey and Dan O'Brien (eds.), *The Bloomsbury Companion to Hume* (London: Bloomsbury, 2012), 364–76; Mark G. Spencer (ed.), *David Hume: Historical Thinker, Historical Writer* (University Park: Pennsylvania State University Press, 2013); Stiebert, 'Hume's History of England,' in Russell (ed.), *Oxford Handbook of Hume*; Jia Wei, *Commerce and Politics in Hume's History of England* (Woodbridge: Boydell & Brewer, 2017); Dew, *Commerce, Finance and Statecraft*, 169–99.

39 On Hume's revisions, see, e.g., Graeme Slater, 'Hume's Revisions of the "History of England,"' *Studies in Bibliography* 45 (1992): 130–57. On Hume's range of English audiences, see, e.g., David Allan, 'Reading Hume's *History of England*: Audience and Authority in Georgian England,' in Spencer (ed.), *David Hume*, 103–20.

not escape analogous categories.[40] He was likewise hostile—in his history, at least[41]—to what he saw as religious zealotry and intolerance in history, from crusaders to puritans. This did not, of course, prevent him from providing his own myth of social origins. Hume was critical of the idea of a social contract from time immemorial, not least on the grounds of a lack of evidence. Instead, he argued, governmental systems evolved over time, first developing family bonds and seeing the advantages brought about through interactions with other family units which in turn required management and sharing of wider resources. While there may be acknowledgement of the benefits that social order can bring, human passions can also mean flouting the rules and, thus, a ruling authority was required. Gradually, governance would develop from this, even accidentally, and with some degree of consent from the people.[42]

With Hume critical of the idea of tracing the English constitution to the distant past, the tension between authority and liberty is perpetual, and striking the right balance was understood to be part of effective governance that would mark 1688 and the British constitution.[43] As a historian, Hume could comparatively downplay Stuart absolutism (hence the controversy provoked by the first volume) while emphasising such tendencies among the Tudors. He could also hold to ideas of Saxon freedom, democracy, and liberty, though not without qualifications. By placing his history in the context of wider cultural, technological, social, economic, and international changes and developments, he could contradict or complement Whig and Tory views on, for instance, absolutism and factionalism. Indeed, he was

40 See Jennifer A. Herdt, 'Artificial Lives, Providential History, and the Apparent Limits of Sympathetic Understanding' and Philip Hicks, '"The Spirit of Liberty": Historical Causation and Political Rhetoric in the Age of Hume,' in Spencer (ed.), *David Hume*, 37–59, 61–79. For a summary see, e.g., Phillips. 'Most Illustrious Philosopher,' in Radcliffe (ed.), *Companion to Hume*, 417–18.
41 Stiebert, 'Hume's History of England,' in Russell (ed.), *Oxford Handbook of Hume*, 558–59.
42 For a fuller overview see Neil McArthur, 'Hume's Political Philosophy,' in Russell (ed.), *The Oxford Handbook of Hume*, 489–504 (esp. 489–90). See also the comments in Andrew Sabl, *Hume's Politics: Coordination and Crisis in the History of England* (Princeton, NJ: Princeton University Press, 2017), 16–17.
43 Jeffrey M. Suderman, 'Medieval Kingship and the Making of Modern Civility: Hume's Assessment of Governance in *The History of England*,' in Spencer (ed.), *David Hume*, 121–42; Stiebert, 'Hume's History of England,' in Russell (ed.), *Oxford Handbook of Hume*, 547; Wei, *Commerce and Politics*, 139–70. Cf. David Hume, 'Part I, Essay V. Of the Origin of Government,' in *Essays Moral, Political, Literary* (ed. Eugene F. Miller; Indianapolis: Liberty Fund 1987), 41–43.

praised for not taking explicit factional sides but while also writing disparagingly about claims he was a Whig, Tory, or whatever else he might have been accused of.[44] But, as ever, aspirations of impartiality have their own ideological function which, in this instance, might be seen as an attempt to present a post-factional justification for the British constitution in the present and a suitable foundation for the Hanoverian political, financial, and commercial interests.[45] Such claims to impartiality also meant that he targeted Rapin. The more he advanced in his work, Hume wrote in a letter to James Oswald, the more he became convinced that 'the History of England has never yet been written, not only for style, which is notorious to all the world; but also for matter; such is the ignorance and partiality of all our historians. Rapin, whom I had an esteem for, is totally despicable.' Hume modestly added that he himself might be liable to 'the reproach of ignorance, but I am certain of escaping that partiality' and that 'the truth is, there is so much reason to blame and praise, alternately, king and parliament.'[46]

In some ways Hume's relatively brief account of the 1381 revolt (with reference to Froissart and Walsingham) is standard enough: the unnecessarily provocative actions of the tax collectors; the rapid spread of the revolt throughout the counties; leadership under the 'feigned names of Wat Tyler, Jack Straw, Hob Carter, and Tom Millar' to denote their 'mean origin'; the gathering at Blackheath (though with no mention of Ball); the assault on the queen mother; Richard journeying on the Thames; the 'most outrageous violences' on the nobility; the destruction in London; decapitations; the story of Sudbury's death; the meeting at Mile End; and Tyler's death and the end of the uprising. Hume also mentioned the story that the rebels' intentions were to seize the king and carry him around as they murdered various elites, though he kept it general and named no specific rebels. Some of Hume's retelling is, however, comparatively unusual in the then history of reception, though explicable in light of Hume's political

---

44 Ernest Campbell Mossner, 'Was Hume a Tory Historian? Facts and Reconsiderations', *Journal of the History of Ideas* 2 (1941): 225–36; Sullivan, 'Rapin, Hume and the Identity of the Historian', 158–60; Stiebert, 'Hume's History of England', in Russell (ed.), *Oxford Handbook of Hume*, 546–49. Cf. David Hume, 'My Own Life', in *The History of England from the Invasion of Julius Caesar to the Revolution in 1688: Volume I* (London, 1770), iii–xiii (viii).

45 Wei, *Commerce and Politics*, 79–106; 171–76; Dew, *Commerce, Finance and Statecraft*, 170; 79–106. Cf. David Hume, 'Part II, Essay XII. Of the Original Contract', in *Essays Moral, Political, Literary*, 253–64.

46 David Hume, 'To James Oswald (28 June 1753)', in Greig (ed.), *The Letters of David Hume: Volume I*, 178–80 (179).

philosophy, increasing chronological and ideological distance from the institution of serfdom, and the emergence of capitalist Britain. As with Smollett, we get a kind of conservative sympathy for rebel demands. The requests for 'a general pardon, the abolition of slavery, freedom of commerce in market-towns without tolls or imposts, and a fixed rent on lands instead of the services due by villenage' were 'extremely reasonable in themselves' but 'the nation was not sufficiently prepared to receive, and which it was dangerous to have extorted by violence, were however complied with.' Indeed, without the support and consent of 'persons of higher quality' such uprisings are doomed to failure, as were attempts at the 'abolition of all rank and distinction.'[47]

Hume focused on Ball and the origins of the revolt to bring out these ideas. Hume contextualised the beginnings of the uprising against the backdrop of the economic cost of warfare requiring Parliament to seek further taxes. The 'new and extraordinary' poll tax 'excited a mutiny, which was very singular in its circumstances,' and Hume added that 'all history abounds with examples, where the great tyrannize over the meaner sort' and here the 'lowest populace rose against their rulers.' The explanation of some sympathy with the plight of the lowest orders was, typically in his account of 1381, qualified by an explanation of their reaction where 'they exercised the most cruel ravages' on their oppressors and 'took vengeance for all their former oppressions.' We also get this tension in the wider contextualisation against the backdrop of European history where the 'faint dawning of the arts and of good government in that age, had excited the minds of the populace, in different states of Europe, to wish for a better condition, and to murmur against those chains, which the laws, enacted by the haughty nobility and gentry, had so long imposed upon them.' This thinking prepared the way for 'insurrection' in England in Hume's narrative with Ball ('a seditious preacher, who affected low popularity') singled out and followed by the story of the assault on the daughter (here of an unnamed blacksmith). Ball went 'about the country' and instilled in his audience 'the principles of the first origin of mankind from one common stock,' their 'equal right to liberty,' the 'tyranny of artificial distinctions,' various abuses, and 'the aggrandizement of a few insolent rulers.' We get a passing allusion to Ball's use of the passages from Acts 2.44–45 and 4.32–35 in the claim that his audience had an equal right 'to all the goods of nature.'[48]

---

47   Hume, *History of England from the Invasion of Julius Caesar to the Accession of Henry VII*, Part II, 245–48.
48   Hume, *History of England from the Invasion of Julius Caesar to the Accession of Henry VII*, Part II, 245.

But here we get a crucial comment, even if made in passing, which went further than Smollett's cautious acknowledgment of peasant grievances. Hume adds, 'these doctrines' were 'agreeable to the populace' and were 'conformable to the ideas of primitive equality,' which 'are engraven in the hearts of all men.' This acknowledgment may have been somewhat backhanded and immediately checked ('greedily received by the multitude; and had scattered the sparks of that sedition, which the present tax raised into a conflagration') but it is a high-profile acknowledgment that still stands out among nearly four centuries of historians and chroniclers. Indeed, in his final corrections published in 1778, Hume added another note of relevance: 'There were two verses at that time in the mouths of all the common people, which, in spite of prejudice, one cannot but regard with some degree of approbation: When Adam delv'd and Eve span, Where was then the gentleman?'[49] The tension is the same: nice sentiment, wrong application. Of course, Hume was never going to side with the rebels or Ball and the reference to 'prejudice' is important. Hume may elsewhere have *speculated* about the possibilities of an ideal commonwealth with power distributed more among (for instance) local authorities, officials, freeholder and householders, without bishops in the House of Lords, and with promotion more on the basis of talent.[50] But this was hardly the utopian vision of Ball. Indeed, though there were extreme exceptions, Hume was typically critical of insurrection and 'violent innovations' in politics—which he believed usually led to a worse situation—and believed that property had to be protected from the worst human passions.[51] Nevertheless, Hume (no doubt unintentionally) represents a moment where Ball was about to make his dramatic comeback.

---

49 Hume, *The History of England from the Invasion of Julius Caesar to the Revolution in 1688: Volume II*, 290.
50 David Hume, 'Part II, Essay XVI. Idea of a Perfect Commonwealth,' in *Essays Moral, Political, Literary*, 279–88.
51 Stiebert, 'Hume's History of England,' in Russell (ed.), *Oxford Handbook of Hume*, 491–92. Cf. David Hume, *A Treatise of Human Nature: Being an Attempt to Introduce the Experimental Method of Reasoning into Moral Subjects* (London, 1739–1740), 3.2.1; 3.2.2; 3.2.10.

9
Revolution, Once Again: A Freeborn Englishman in the Late Eighteenth Century

Blanket dismissals of the demands for freedom and liberty by the peasants of 1381 were becoming even more difficult in a Europe now faced with the impact of Voltaire and Rousseau coupled with the lauding of an English constitution and a world being transformed by the Industrial Revolution. By the end of the eighteenth century, a Tyler-despising Tory writer like John Gifford (1758–1818) could see the demands of the rebels at Mile End as reasonable ones, with Richard himself understood as reciprocating in the spirit of liberty, reason, and justice (the merely self-interested Tyler was removed from the scene).[1] Elsewhere, it was said that liberty, purchases of freedom blocked by an unfair Act of Parliament, and visible freedoms of town-dwellers inspired peasants 'annexed to the soil,' according to Oliver Goldsmith (c. 1728–1774) in the second volume of *The History of England* (1771; cf. Goldsmith's poem, 'The Deserted Village' [1770]). While still critical of the 'tumultuous rabble,' 1381 was the 'first instance' of 'a knowledge of the rights of humanity, diffusing itself even to the very lowest of the people.' And just as such ideas were taking off, Goldsmith claimed, 'the seeds of discontent were still more cultivated by the preaching of several men, who went about the country, inculcating the natural equality of mankind; and consequently, the right that all had to an equal participation of the goods of nature.'[2] Ball may not be mentioned by name here but the potential for a mainstream comeback was increasing significantly by the end of the eighteenth century, which, as we will see, would be partly driven by changes from below. Yet Ball's comeback, as with Gifford's Tyler, would

---

1 John Gifford, *A Plain Address to the Common Sense of the People of England* (London, 1792), 7–9.
2 Oliver Goldsmith, *The History of England, from the Earliest Times to the Death of George II*, Vol. II (London, 1771), 127–29.

also be accompanied by a new shade of notoriety as the debates around the idea of an English constitution were tested against the startling realities of revolutions in America and France and their reception in Ireland, and then Actually Existing Republicanism. Certainly, the huge ideological clashes between reaction and revolution towards the end of the eighteenth century opened up opportunities for positive evaluations of past revolutionary activities—including violent ones. But Ball, Tyler, and the rebels were not going to be accepted without a struggle.

1381 and Political Unrest toward the End of the Eighteenth Century

Tyler (much more than Ball) and the rebels of 1381 were, of course, a known historical point of reference in public discourse (e.g., in the press) and in Parliament, from antiquarianism through general warning of the dangers of rebellion or the disorderly mob to illustrations and paintings (e.g., Northcote's *The Death of Wat Tyler*; Blake's *Wat Tyler and the Tax-Gatherer* printed in Charles Allen's *A New and Improved History of England* [1798]).[3] But it was a menacing memory that could again be turned against the government, such as in one of the more moderate recorded responses to William Pitt's 'shop tax' in 1785:

3 See, e.g., *Stamford Mercury* (9 November 1775); *Dublin Evening Post* (8, 12. 15, 19, 22 August 1780); *Hibernian Journal* (5 May 1784); *Dublin Evening Post* (25 January 1785); *Oxford Journal* (14 May 1785); *Ipswich Journal* (14 May 1785); *Hereford Journal* (19 May 1785); *Newcastle Courant* (21 May 1785); *Hampshire Chronicle* (14 November 1785); *Caledonian Mercury* (14 May 1787); *Dublin Evening Post* (15 May 1787); *Bath Chronicle and Weekly Gazette* (17 May 1787); *Universal Register* (7 May 1787); *Bury and Norwich Post* (22 October 1788); *The Times* (17 July 1789); *Hampshire Chronicle* (2 May 1791); *Bury and Norwich Post* (15 August 1792); *Kentish Gazette* (24 October 1794) *Kentish Weekly Post* (24 October 1794); *Norfolk Chronicle* (25 October 1794); *Hampshire Chronicle* (November 1794); *Cumberland Pacquet, and Ware's Whitehaven Advertiser* (4 November 1794); *Hereford Journal* (5 November 1794); *Northampton Mercury* (8 November 1794); *Gloucester Journal* (17 November 1794); *Newcastle Courant* (15 November 1794); *Hampshire Chronicle* (17 November 1794). Tyler, Straw, Hob Carter, Jack Shepherd, and Tom Miller featured in an older ballad reprinted by Evans, *Old Ballads, Historical and Narrative*, 280–92. For a discussion of Tyler in *Old Ballads* see Basdeo, *Life and Legend of a Rebel Leader*, loc 1415–1449.

> A bold, but unfortunate, bard, took out his pencil, and wrote on the door of the Court of Requests, leading to Westminster Hall. As follows:
> 'Poor Wat Tyler now is dead,
> And no brave fellow in his stead,
> Or Pitt this day would lose his head;'
> Which he had no sooner done, than an officer belonging to the gentleman usher of the black rod, who observed what he had been doing, seized him by the collar, in the midst of a large mob, and insisted upon his taking the flap of his coat and wiping out the lines before all the people, which he was compelled to do, and was afterwards kicked out of the house.[4]

The fear of the possibility of another Tyler emerging was relatively fresh in the memory after the Gordon Riots (June 1780).[5] The riots had obvious points of comparison, such as the destruction of aristocratic property and springing of prisoners *en masse*, while the anti-Catholic sentiments led by Lord George Gordon and the Protestant Association could tap into old concerns associating 1381 with problematic religion. In the fallout from the riots, Ball himself made an appearance. He turned up, for instance, in a publication of an extract from Carte's account of 1381 which, it was claimed, 'has so striking resemblance to the late insurrection of the lower class of people in and about London.'[6]

The Gordon Riots happened during the American War of Independence, as well as discontents in Ireland and anxieties about republicanism, and this only intensified the sting of 1381. Indeed, sometimes such events, references, or allusions could be combined in reporting.[7] The American situation, though, was not going to be as easily countered as a riot or a mob, yet 1381 remained an obvious comparison. Though the French may ridicule 'English patriotism and English liberty,' they should not be expected to

---

4   *Stamford Mercury*, 17 June 1785. For the longer version of the offending passage, see, e.g., *Saunders's News-Letter* (22 June 1785) and *Dublin Evening Post* (23 June 1785). Cf. *The Times* (11 May 1785); *Northampton Mercury* (13 April 1772).

5   E.g., *Kentish Gazette* (14 June 1780); *Salisbury and Winchester Journal* (19 June 1780); *Caledonian Mercury* (17 July 1780); *Derby Mercury* (16 January 1783). See also John Paul de Castro, *The Gordon Riots* (Oxford: Oxford University Press, 1926), 19–20; Lloyd Rudolph, 'The Eighteenth-Century Mob in America and Europe,' *American Quarterly* 11 (1959): 447–69 (455–56); Linebaugh, *The London Hanged*, 347; Basdeo, *Life and Legend of a Rebel Leader*, loc 1275–1306.

6   *Gentlemen's Magazine* 50 (1780), 469–72 (469).

7   E.g., *Salisbury and Winchester Journal* (19 June 1780); *Dublin Evening Post* (25 January 1785); *Hibernian Journal* (4 October 1784). Cf. *Universal Register* (14 December 1786); *The Times* (23 February 1789); *The Times* (26 April 1790).

subject their trade to 'utter ruin' at the hands of 'the most powerful maritime kingdom in the world' by getting involved with the American colonies, one report contemptuously suggested in September 1776, adding, 'Can it be conceived that a great Prince will enter into an alliance with such men as a Wat Tyler, a Jack Straw, an Adams, or a Hancock? Away then with the ridiculous idea of a treaty between rebels and the sovereign of a large empire.'[8]

The French Problem

The French Revolution and war with France updated the ongoing reapplication of 1381 with the fear of mobs and demagogues intensifying further still.[9] As *The Times* put it in September 1789 while employing the idea of liberty perverted, the 'Parisian insurgents are exactly in that habit of mind which possessed Wat Tyler and his revelling companions, and carrying the idea of liberty into licentiousness, they must in the end be overthrown.'[10] In the press, and in addition to the standard references to Tyler (and, to a lesser extent, Jack Straw), we find occasional allusions to Ball-style teaching[11] and an updating of conventional connections made between ideology of 1381 and Anabaptism for the new era of republicanism.[12] But there are some explicit references to Ball himself and his hanging inspired by the histories of England (on the subtle modifications of describing Ball's death in terms of 'hanging,' see Chapter 8).[13] We even find an imaginative way

---

8 *Leeds Intelligencer* (10 September 1776).
9 E.g., *The Times* (22 August 1789); *The Times* (3 September 1789); *Chelmsford Chronicle* (25 September 1789); *The Times* (18 February 1790); *Bath Chronicle and Weekly Gazette* (4 March 1790); *Norfolk Chronicle* (6 March 1790); *The Times* (1 August 1791); *Stamford Mercury* (18 May 1792); *The Times* (6 July 1792); *The Times* (1 August 1792); *The Times* (3 January 1793); *The Times* (4 July 1793); *The Times* (28 October 1793); *Kentish Weekly Post* (17 June 1794).
10 *The Times* (4 September 1789). Cf. *Bath Chronicle and Weekly Gazette* (4 March 1790) and *Norfolk Chronicle* (6 March 1790): 'Liberty unrestrained, and stretched beyond its proper boundaries.'
11 E.g., *The Times* (14 October 1791) and *Oxford Journal* (15 October 1791): 'The present National Assembly of France reminds us of Wat Tyler's *Free Parliament* on Blackheath, where one Fellow says, Shan't I be a Judge?—and another, Shan't I be appointed a Bishop?'
12 E.g., *Kentish Gazette* (2 February 1790).
13 E.g., *The Times* (4 August 1791).

of directly rebutting Ball's central idea. One writer in the *Bath Chronicle* (November 1797) contemptuously referred to the 'levelling principle' of the French Revolution which had only encouraged plunder and robbery and was now 'industriously propagated by extravagant and profligate people in these kingdoms' who 'have had the effrontery to hold up the proverbial maxim of Wat Tyler, and John Ball, a seditious Priest who was hanged in Richard the Second's reign'. The reader is even given an answer to 'John Ball's seditious text':

>'When Adam delv'd, and Eve span,
>Who was then a Gentleman?'
>ANSWER.
>When naked all, like Eve and Adam,
>Your Joan might be as good as Madam;
>And, tillage then the only trade,
>We all had learnt to use the spade.
>But, tho' mankind are still the same,
>And *equal rights* by nature claim;
>Yet, if no social laws existed,
>And everyman did what he lifted;
>If mankind must dig or spin,
>You'd have no covering but your skin.
>For, who would weave, or be your taylor?
>Who'd be a soldier or a sailor?
>Who'd make your tables or your shelves?
>'Troth! you must make them all yourselves.
>Let each man then assist his neighbour,
>And each perform some useful labour:
>Thus various arts would be invented,
>And those, now poor and discontented,
>Might soon grow rich, by labouring more;
>While *lazy* folks must needs be poor:
>For why should they, who take no pains,
>Rob others of their honest gains?
>While some obey, and some command,
>And each man lends an helping hand;
>While those best skill'd, the vessel steer,
>Each may be happy in his sphere.
>In short, 'tis evident, you see,
>That different ranks there needs must be;
>There must be then, say what you can,
>That *dreadful* thing—a Gentleman![14]

14 *Bath Chronicle and Weekly Gazette* (9 November 1797).

This poetic take on the origins of the social contract and social hierarchy also shows how emerging capitalism (and imperialism) of the sort that might even have made Norman Tebbit blush was now becoming important in how Ball and the revolt would be understood. But as we will see, the changing socio-economic world of the late eighteenth century meant competing ideas, including those concerning Ball and Tyler as men of the hard-working, labouring classes who were poor because the government had exploited them (see, e.g., Southey's *Wat Tyler*, in Chapters 10 and 11).

Tyler may have appeared more regularly in political discourse, but the story of Ball played a significant role in the histories of 1381 (though Tyler and mob violence would take pride of place in accompanying illustrations). The presentations of Ball betrayed anxieties about what might happen with republicanism on the loose—or at least it would not have been difficult to have read them in such a way. Indeed, the same account is repeated in different histories. For example, in William Augustus Russel, *A New and Authentic History of England* (published over 1777–1779) and George Frederick Raymond et al., *A New Universal and Impartial History of England* (published over 1777–1790), among others, the people were said to have already acquired 'some idea of independence,' as well as 'breaking the chains' imposed on them by the 'haughty nobility.' This involved updating a now standard understanding of an excessive Ball: Ball was said to be the key instigator, which allows the narrative to retain some sympathy with the plight of peasants while still condemning revolt. Enthusiasm and awareness of their 'own importance' had been helped by this 'turbulent, but popular preacher' who 'inculcated' various audiences in the kingdom with the 'maxims of equal right and liberty to all the goods of nature' and talked about the 'tyranny of artificial distinctions' introduced by a few insolent rulers. As such 'doctrines' were popular and kindled in the 'minds of the vulgar,' the sparks of rebellion were 'soon blown into a flame' by the 'cruelty' of the tax collectors. Nevertheless, despite acknowledgment of mismanagement, the regicidal tendencies of the rebels were, if anything, heightened. They were cast as 'savage plebeians' who planned to 'murder the king, together with the whole nobility, and bury all government in general anarchy, in order to destroy every species of subordination, and render all men equal.' Furthermore, there is also an emphasis on the retelling of Tyler's death seen also in, for instance, Smollett's *Complete History of Britain*. Here, again, Tyler's actions, like Ball's, are in distinction from the more acceptable rebel demands and help justify the importance of social order: the king was unable to understand the levelling demands of the illiterate Tyler who in response took the king's lack of comprehension as a 'contemptuous refusal' and raised his dagger before Walworth attacked.[15]

Tyler 'now seemed to thirst for blood' and entertained thoughts of murdering the king, with all his nobility, and laying the city of London in ashes,' according to the account in Edward Bernard, *A New, Comprehensive and Complete History of England* (1783).[16] Bernard added the story about the 'fanatic priest' Ball, Jack Straw, and others, and their punishment for 'high treason.' This was a moral for the reader based on the fear of mobs and of more revolutionary rumblings in the present, no matter how respectable their aims, and in contrast to the English constitution:

> From their fate, the people of this age may learn the invaluable estimation of their precious constitution and equal government, and not hastily to engage in riots and popular insurrections, which generally, if not always, end in their own destruction; for popular insurrections, when they have no persons of rank and distinction at their head, who have genius and influence to govern them, and to awaken their attention to the voice of reason, prudence, and humanity, degenerate into licentious mobs. The most daring, vicious, and abandoned, get the lead; cruelty and rapine become wanton sports; all the laws of right, reasons, nature, and justice, are trampled underfoot; and with whatever laudable views they may have been first actuated, every valuable purpose is sure to be defeated; and the more upright in their intentions, will suffer equal punishment with those knaves and fools who have deluded them.[17]

15 William Augustus Russel, *A New and Authentic History of England from the Most Remote Period of Genuine Historical Evidence, to the Present Important Crisis* (London, 1777–1779), 224–25; George Frederick Raymond assisted by Alexander Gordon, Hugh Owen and Others, *A New Universal and Impartial History of England from the Earliest Authentic Records, and Most Genuine Historical Evidence, to the End of the Present Year* (London, 1790), 205–7. See also, e.g., George William Spencer, assisted by Hugh Fitzwilliam, Alex Douglas and other Gentlemen, who have for many Years made the History of this Country their peculiar Study, *A New, Authentic, and Complete History of England, from the First Settlement of Brutus in this Island to the Year 1795* (London, 1794), 197–99. Cf. *Universal Register* (29 June 1786); *The Times* (4 August 1791); Simon Keynes, 'The Cult of King Alfred the Great,' *Anglo-Saxon England* 28 (1999): 225–356 (303–5).

16 Edward Bernard, assisted by Gentlemen of approved Abilities, who have for many Years made the English History their chief Study, particularly Mr Millar, *The New, Comprehensive and Complete History of England from the Earliest Period of Authentic Information, to the Middle of the Year, MDCCLXXXIII* (London, 1783), 198.

17 Bernard, *New, Comprehensive and Complete History of England*, 199.

Ominously, the narrative then turns to the fate of over 1,500 insurgents at the hangman's noose.

Richard Cumberland's Ever Shrinking Ball

Fears were such that even Richard Cumberland's decidedly non-radical opera and love story, *Richard the Second* (1792), was heavily censored and resulted in a heavily rewritten version, *The Armorer*, which was performed in 1793.[18] The broad outline of the uprising in *Richard the Second* was in one sense uncontroversial by the time Cumberland wrote—if anything, Cumberland watered down any potential sympathy with the most famous rebels. The tax gatherer Ralph Rackum threatened to carry away the young Rosamond, though tellingly the blacksmith who killed the tax gatherer was the upright Jerry Furnace rather than Tyler. Tyler was one of the destructive insurgents along with other familiar names, including the bloodthirsty and traitorous Jack Straw who would abandon the uprising in the face of the king's forces. Furnace, the one-time armourer of the Black Prince (Richard's father), was effectively forced by necessity to join the insurgents. He remained loyal to the king throughout and was among those pardoned by him. *Richard the Second* ended with the conventional lauding of the Lord Mayor and, finally, a song embracing national peace. *The Armorer* was a revision of *Richard the Second* to the point of removing the uprising, the Lord Mayor, Sir Robert Knollys, Richard, and the 'Insurgents' Wat Tyler, Jack Straw, Hob Carter, and Tom Miller, while the plot now progressed through the lustful designs of the Earl of Suffolk and the imprisonment of Furnace (now 'Harry').

Ball did not feature in *Richard the Second*. However, it is likely that Friar Dominic—a comic character with somewhat giddy affections for

18 John Larpent Plays (San Marino, CA: The Huntington Library), LA 963. For discussion see, e.g., Jeffrey N. Cox, 'Baillie, Siddons, Larpent: Gender, Power, and Politics in the Theatre of Romanticism,' in Catherine Burroughs (ed.), *Women in British Romantic Theatre: Drama, Performance, and Society, 1790–1840* (Cambridge: Cambridge University Press, 2000), 23–47 (39–42); George Taylor, *The French Revolution and the London Stage, 1789–1805* (Cambridge: Cambridge University Press, 2000), 71–76; David Worrall, *Theatric Revolution: Drama, Censorship, and Romantic Period Subcultures 1773–1832* (Oxford: Oxford University Press, 2006), 107–12. *Richard the Second* and *The Armorer* can be found in Richard J. Dircks (ed.), *The Unpublished Plays of Richard Cumberland: Volume 1* (New York: AMS Press, 1991), 307–61, 363–416.

Rosamond—functioned as a parody of Ball, or it could easily have appeared so to anyone familiar with the history of Ball's reception. Dominic was connected with Tyler, Straw, and the rebels, he was called a 'seditious monk,' he enjoyed a good drink (in this case, metheglin), he had no love for Rackum, and he coolly accepted Rackum's death with a macabre spin (by way of his trademark Latin quips) on Ball's hope for all things being shared in common: *Mors omnibus communis*.[19] When he was called forth among the other rebel leaders by Tyler, Dominic said, 'What wou'd you with me, who am a man of Peace? I exhort you, Brethren to have regard unto the Church.' Tyler then offers him the role as Sudbury's replacement, trusting that he will dedicate his time as archbishop of Canterbury 'to mirth and good fellowship.' This offer immediately changed the fickle Dominic's mind who promised to 'bear it with what grace I may,' and conveniently noted that when he took his vow of poverty he 'saw no prospect that I shou'd ever be rich,' observed that Canterbury's Chair was 'an easy Cushion for an old man to sleep upon, and a nap upon velvet may be to the full as comfortable as early Vigils and a Straw Crib' (I; III:2). But Ball was only a partial parallel. There was no sermon when the rebels gather at Blackheath as Dominic barely featured in the scene and he later talked his way out of execution with another convenient claim that he only preached 'as the Spirit prompts' and that just because people are wicked it cannot be proof that 'their preacher recommends Sin' (III:2). Dominic was retained in *The Armorer* because without the context of the uprising (including, therefore, the omission of the offer to replace Sudbury) and with a new unrelated storyline, there was no obvious reason to connect him or his quips with Ball or the uprising. He was just another comedy priest.

In his memoirs, Cumberland admitted that he 'did not always succeed in entertaining the audience' and one such example was the fate of the story of Tyler: 'When I had taken all the comedy out of it, I was not surprised to find that the public were not very greatly edified by what was left.'[20] But he should also have been unsurprised that such a topic was censored given what had happened in France and thus what could happen in England. Anna Larpent, wife and assistant of the Examiner of Plays, John Larpent, wrote in her diary (8 December 1792) that 'the whole' was 'really written

---

19   Cf. Froissart, *Chroniques* 10.96; *Anon. Chron.* 137; Hume, *History of England from the Invasion of Julius Caesar to the Revolution in 1688: Volume II*, 290, etc.
20   Richard Cumberland, *Memoirs of Richard Cumberland, Written by Himself: Containing an account of His life and writings, interspersed with anecdotes and characters of several of the most distinguished persons of his time, with whom he has had intercourse and connexion: Volume II* (London, 1807), 278.

with taste' but that 'it appears extremely unfit for representation at a time when the Country is full of Alarm, being the story of Wat Tyler the killing of the Tax Gatherer &c. very ill judgd.'[21] And one reason why the country was full of alarm and why the 1381 uprising was so threatening was because Thomas Paine's hugely popular *Rights of Man* was becoming one of the defining texts of the era and would play a famous or infamous role in the reclamation of 1381.

Burke vs Paine

Probably the most famous critical response in English to the unfolding French Revolution was by Edmund Burke (c. 1729–1797) in *Reflections on the Revolution in France*, published in November 1790. *Reflections* was popular in the sense of sales (it sold 7,000 in its first week),[22] the support it gained among certain sections of the conservative and reactionary establishment and property owners, the responses it provoked, and, of course, its intellectual legacy. But it was simultaneously controversial, divisive, and disliked, particularly among radicals and some of Burke's Whig colleagues, including his one-time friend Charles James Fox. Burke believed that the revolution in France begat chaos, anarchy, barbarism, and tyranny, and he was concerned about the collapse of traditional authority in France (e.g., monarchy, nobility, church) and the threat posed to property. Burke instead favoured a system with a kind of pragmatic conservative evolution, one that understood complexity and contradiction and was based on experience. This was to be favoured over a system of dramatic transformation and dedication to theoretical abstraction as was understood to be happening in France. To whatever extent, one of Burke's concerns was that such levelling ideas could take off in Britain and he engaged with polemical debates about the nature of an English constitution from time immemorial, here with a conservative edge and downplaying certain democratising and revolutionary interpretations. What had happened and was happening in France was not, he emphatically stressed, to be mistaken with the

---

21 Quoted in Worrall, *Theatric Revolution*, 110.
22 Gregory Claeys, 'The *Reflections* Refracted: The Critical Reception of Burke's *Reflections on the Revolution in France* during the Early 1790s', in John Whale (ed.), *Edmund Burke's Reflections on the Revolution in France: New Interdisciplinary Essays* (Manchester: Manchester University Press, 2000), 40–59 (41).

'constitution of this kingdom, and the principles of the glorious Revolution' of 1688 which stretched back to Magna Carta, which in turn 'was connected with another positive charter from Henry I and that both the one and the other were nothing more than a re-affirmance of the still more antient standing law of the kingdom.'[23]

From a stay-maker and some Quaker background, Thomas Paine (1737–1809) returned to England from France to counter the criticisms of revolutionary France by his one-time friend Burke. Paine had already achieved fame for his role in the American War of Independence, particularly through his hugely popular pamphlet *Common Sense* (1776).[24] Here, we might crudely summarise, Paine had produced arguments on society and government which form an important context for understanding his later rehabilitation of 1381. Society, he provocatively argued, is 'produced by our wants' and 'promotes our happiness by uniting our affections' while government is a product of 'our wickedness' by 'restraining our vices.' Thus, Paine famously stated, 'Society in every state is a blessing, but Government even in its best state is but a necessary evil; in its worst state an intolerable one.'[25] He discussed the importance of laws, widening representation, and elections because such 'frequent interchange will establish a common

---

23 Edmund Burke, *Reflections on the Revolution in France, and on the Proceedings in Certain Societies in London Relative to that Event* (London, 1790), 2, 47. For a detailed summary of the context and content of *Reflections*, see, e.g., F. P. Lock, *Edmund Burke, Volume II: 1784–1797* (Oxford: Oxford University Press, 2006), 245–65, 282–31. On Burke, 1688 and the constitution, see Ben J. Taylor, 'Reflections on the Revolution in England: Edmund Burke's Uses of 1688,' *History of Political Thought* 35 (2014): 91–120. On Burke and the constitution, J. G. A. Pocock, 'Burke and the Ancient Constitution—A Problem in the History of Ideas,' *Historical Journal* 3 (1960): 125–43, and E. P. Thompson, *The Making of the English Working Class* (London: Penguin, 1963), 97–98, are still worth reading.

24 For detailed summaries of the writing and reception of *Common Sense*, see e.g., John Keane, *Tom Paine: A Political Life* (London: Bloomsbury, 1995), 106–29; Craig Nelson, *Thomas Paine: Enlightenment, Revolution, and the Birth of Modern Nations* (London: Penguin, 2006), 78–100; Mark Philp, *Thomas Paine* (Oxford: Oxford University Press, 2007), 9–15; W. A. Speck, *A Political Biography of Thomas Paine* (London: Routledge, 2013), 27–52.

25 Thomas Paine, *Common Sense* (Philadelphia, 1776), 1. For discussion of the details of, assumptions about, and contexts of, Paine's thinking on social contract, see, e.g., Carine Lounissi, 'Thomas Paine's Reflections on the Social Contract: A Consistent Theory?,' in Scott Cleary and Ivy Linton Stabell (eds.), *New Directions in Thomas Paine Studies* (New York: Palgrave Macmillan, 2016), 175–93.

interest with every part of the community, they will mutually and naturally support each other,' and on this, rather than 'the unmeaning name of king,' depends 'the strength of Government' and 'the happiness of the governed.'[26] Paine also fired at the supposed English constitution. Unlike Burke, Paine thought the complexity surrounding the idea of an English constitution was problematic because it could obfuscate and deflect criticisms and was ultimately the cause of the nation's suffering. Indeed, he even argued that this unwritten constitution was an absurdity. Certainly, such thinking presupposed that a monarch cannot be trusted and will thirst after absolute power while the Commons would provide the necessary checks. But the same constitution also allowed the monarch to check the Commons and reject their bills. As Paine worded it, 'we have been wise enough to lock the door against absolute Monarchy, we at the same time have been foolish enough to put the Crown in possession of the key.'[27]

Echoing Ball's Adam and Eve couplet, Paine used the Bible to undermine monarchy, and then hereditary monarchy (before he subjected the Bible and Christianity to scathing critiques in *The Age of Reason*, of course). He argued that with 'MANKIND being originally equals in the order of creation the equality could only be destroyed by some subsequent circumstance.' To explain the distinction between people in terms of monarchs and subjects, which ran contrary to the 'equal right of nature,' Paine turned to the biblical accounts of kingship. He argued that when the world had no kings, there were no wars and the relative happiness of the first Patriarchs' quiet, rural existence was ruined through the introduction of kingship, first by 'heathens' then mimicked by Israel and later in the 'Christian World.' This might have impressed the devil, but it is contrary to the will of God as declared by Gideon and Samuel because this form of government 'so impiously invades the prerogative of Heaven.' Little surprise, then, that, for Paine, monarchical governments had to gloss over the anti-monarchical biblical passages, and little surprise that an English dynastic claim rested on the foundations of William the Conqueror ('a French Bastard landing with an armed Banditti and establishing himself king of England against the consent of the natives'). In a reversal of Burke, it was 'monarchy and succession [that] have laid…the world in blood and ashes.'[28]

While Paine took up much space in *Common Sense* writing about the American context, his ideas were for wider rethinking about government. 'Written by an ENGLISHMAN' is on its title page while the introduction

26 Paine, *Common Sense*, 3.
27 Paine, *Common Sense*, 6.
28 Paine, *Common Sense*, 7–15.

has the claim that 'the cause of America is in a great measure the cause of all mankind' and that there are 'universal' issues at stake which chime with 'the principles of all lovers of mankind.'[29] The shift to defending revolutionary France against Burke was natural enough. The first part of the *Rights of Man* was published in March 1791—just months after Burke's *Reflections*—and sold out instantly. It went through three editions within March alone and by May had sold a record-breaking 50,000 copies. It was an international success as well as a radical phenomenon in Britain and Ireland.[30] In it, Paine developed his ideas against hereditary monarchy (with one eye on George III) and the aristocrat, and the rejection of the idea of an English constitution.[31] Among other things (including calculating taxation for a system of welfare and education), he argued about how the revolution had dethroned despotism in France. He added that there cannot be a system of government that possesses the 'right or the power of binding and controuling posterity to the *"end of time"*.' Instead, 'Every age and generation must be as free to act for itself in all cases as the ages and generations which preceded it.'[32]

After being expelled from the Whigs amidst the disputes over his criticisms of the French revolution, Burke published *An Appeal from the New to the Old Whigs* in August 1791. While defending his own position in relation to the Whig tradition, he attacked what he perceived as pro-revolutionary Whigs with Paine and *Rights of Man* as a foil. But what is of most significance here is Burke's use of 1381 as a parallel to events in France and a sarcastic assessment of Ball who was cast as a type for, or

29 Paine, *Common Sense*, 'Introduction,' no page number.
30 Keane, *Tom Paine*, 304–10. For further details on the context of the writing and reception of *Rights of Man*, see, e.g., Thompson, *Making of the English Working Class*, 99–110, 114–25; Gregory Claeys, *Thomas Paine: Social and Political Thought* (London: Routledge, 1989), 63–84; Keane, *Tom Paine*, 282–353; Amanda Goodrich, *Debating England's Aristocracy in the 1790s: Pamphlets, Polemics, and Political Ideas* (Woodbridge: Boydell Press, 2005), 56–84; Nelson, *Thomas Paine*, 191–234; Philp, *Thomas Paine*, 39–52; Speck, *Political Biography*, 105–26.
31 As Thomas Paine, *Rights of Man: Being an Answer to Mr Burke's Attack on the French Revolution* (London, 1791), 54, put it: 'Can then Mr Burke produce the English Constitution? If he cannot, we may fairly conclude, that though it has been so much talked about, no such thing as a constitution exists, or ever did exist, and consequently that the people have a constitution to form.'
32 Paine, *Rights of Man*, 11.

ideologically forefather of, Paine (among others), as different writers would similarly do with Tyler and Paine.³³ Furthermore,

> There is no doubt, but that this great teacher of the rights of man decorated his discourse on this valuable text, with lemmas, theorems, scholia, corollaries, and all the apparatus of science, which was furnished in as great plenty and perfection out of the dogmatic and polemic magazines, the old horse-armory, of the schoolmen, among whom Rev. Dr Ball was bred, as they can be supplied from the new arsenal at Hackney.³⁴

The 'Abbé John Ball,' that 'reverend patriarch of sedition' and 'prototype of our modern preachers,' understood the rights of man 'as well as Abbé Gregoire.' He was of the opinion 'with the national assembly' that 'all the evils which have fallen upon men had been caused by an ignorance of their "having been born and continued equal as to their rights".' If the populace had only been able to repeat 'that profound maxim,' Burke cynically continued, then everything would have worked out for them: 'No tyranny, no vexation, no oppression, no care, no sorry…This would have cured them like a charm for the tooth-ach.' However, the ignorant 'lowest wretches' always talk 'such stuff' yet still suffer 'many evils and oppressions, both before and since the republication by the national assembly of this spell of healing potency and virtue.' When the 'enlightened Dr Ball' wanted to push this point, he chose the Adam and Eve couplet, though he was likely not the inventor of this popular 'sapient maxim.' Nevertheless, this saying is 'fully equal to all the modern dissertations on the equality of mankind' but, Burke ridiculed, it has one advantage—'that it is in rhyme'!³⁵

By drawing on a known example of the revolutionary mob, Burke could be certain that parts of his audience would have recoiled in disgust. Indeed, Burke noted that even 'Our doctors of the day are not so fond of quoting

33 E.g., Gifford, *Plain Address*, 7–9; William Thomas Fitzgerald, 'The Sturdy Reformer, A New Song, Exemplifying to the Good People of England, the Doctrines of the Rights of Man' (1792), in *Miscellaneous Poems* (London: J. Wright, 1801), 19–25; *A Dialogue between Wat Tyler, Mischievous Tom, and an English Farmer* (London, 1793), which includes a passing mention of Ball when Tyler wonders where is 'thy Dr *Ball* to back thee' (5); Jonathan Boucher, *A View of the Causes and Consequences of the American Revolution; in Thirteen Discourses Preached in North America between the Years 1763 and 1775* (London, 1797), l–li.
34 Edmund Burke, *An Appeal from the New to the Old Whigs, in Consequence of Some Late Discussions in Parliament, Relative to the Reflections on the French Revolution* (London, 1791), 133.
35 Burke, *Appeal from the New to the Old Whigs*, 132–34.

the opinions of this ancient sage as they are of imitating his conduct,' not least because Ball was a failure.[36] However, by virtue of this taking place in such a polarised debate, Ball and 1381 could equally be seen as a good thing by Burke's enemies. R. B. Dobson went as far as to claim that 'to be attacked by Burke in the years after 1789 was to ensure sympathy for oneself; and perhaps nothing contributed more to the Peasants' Revolt new *réclame* than Burke's heavy sarcasm at its expense.'[37] We get something like a confirmation of this in part two of the *Rights of Man*, published in February 1792 (and even more popular than part one), where the revolutionary framework for Paine's thinking provided the suitable context for radically rethinking 1381. In what would become a famous footnote to anyone with interest in the reception of the uprising, Paine turned the history of the reception of Tyler on its head. He fired at the 'sycophancy of historians, and men like Mr. Burke, who seek to gloss over a base action of the court by traducing Tyler,' adding that 'his fame will outlive their falsehood.' Noting that 'several of the court newspapers' kept mentioning Tyler, he countered that it was hardly surprising that 'his memory should be traduced by court sycophants, and all those who live on the spoil of a public.'[38]

Paine challenged this narrative simply by retelling the story of 1381 with a positive spin, while the case of the poll tax collection—which, of course, had a long history of being condemned—made the task easier. If any favour in law was shown over the collection of the poll tax, 'it was to the rich rather than to the poor.' While poll taxes 'had always been odious,' this was also 'oppressive and unjust' and, with an implicit updating, it 'excited, as it naturally must, universal detestation among the poor and middle classes.' Paine also gave the account of the assault on (Wat) Tyler's daughter. This 'circumstance served to bring the discontents to an issue' as the rebellion gathered momentum when the rebels marched on London with their demands notably summarised as 'an abolition of the tax, and a redress of other grievances.' The court, being in a 'forlorn condition,' was unable to resist and Richard ('at its head') met with Tyler at Smithfield. Instead of Tyler being framed as arrogant and acting above his station, we now have him making 'many fair professions, courtier like.' Paine also reversed the Walworth myth whose actions were now deemed sneaky—he was the 'cowardly assassin.'[39] Paine's assessment of Tyler was that he

36 Burke, *Appeal from the New to the Old Whigs*, 134.
37 Dobson (ed.), *Peasants' Revolt of 1381*, 392.
38 Thomas Paine, *Rights of Man, Part the Second. Combining Principle and Practice* (London, 1792), footnote to page 111.
39 Paine, *Rights of Man, Part the Second*, footnote to page 111. Cf. *Stamford Mercury* (18 May 1792), 'And brave Walworth's entitled a cowardly assassin.'

was likely 'an intrepid disinterested man' but his proposals were 'on a more just and public ground... than those which had been made to John by the Barons.' In other words, the 1381 revolt deserves pride of place over Magna Carta and Paine finished with the comment that would recur in the history of the reception of 1381: 'If the Barons merited a monument to be erected in Runnymede, Tyler merits one in Smithfield.'[40]

Paine's work was dismissed as vulgar and common (which Paine himself played on).[41] He found himself the subject of hostile propaganda and surveillance, as George III's government looked for ways to curb his influence without making him a martyr. Effectively forced out of Britain, Paine was tried in absentia for seditious libel.[42] Nevertheless, no small thanks to Paine, the idea of a sympathetic reading of the 1381 uprising was now out and ready to be exploited in radical circles.[43] And if Wat Tyler's reputation could be restored, then so too could John Ball's.

---

40 Paine, *Rights of Man, Part the Second*, footnote to page 111. For a response to Paine's reclaiming of Tyler, see, e.g., *The Times* (1 August 1792).
41 Cf. *The Times* (3 January 1793): 'Wat Tyler was a slater—Paine a stav-maker—Oliver Cromwell a blacksmith, and most of the present Legislators of France, can neither read nor write.'
42 Keane, *Tom Paine*, 306–5, 327–28, 334–48.
43 Dobson, 'Remembering the Peasants' Revolt,' in Liddell and Wood (eds.), *Essex and the Great Revolt of 1381*, 13.

10

The Second Coming of John Ball: John Baxter, Robert Southey, and Radicalism of the 1790s

Thomas Paine prepared the way for the second coming of John Ball after centuries of an overwhelmingly hostile press, making straight the paths for rethinking political representation and class relations. In the 1790s, reformers and radicals—with ideological connections traceable through (for instance) Wilkes, the Duke of Richmond, the American Revolution, and Irish dissidents—reacted in a range of ways to the French Revolution and the ideas of Paine, not least through the various famous political societies. This involved (but not exclusively) the interests of artisans and working people, and their own understandings and discussions of constitutionalism, political corruption, liberty, religious tolerance, abolitionism, rule of law, absolutism and arbitrary exercise of power, parliamentary reform, annual parliaments, land enclosures, property ownership, universal male suffrage, mass education, poverty alleviation, role of the aristocracy, etc. Whatever the extent of the radicalism and sympathies with the French Revolution, associations and individuals were certainly perceived to be potential Jacobin extremists and a threat to the king, a perception that was increasingly loaded after the French regicide and declaration of war in 1793. Founded in 1792, the London Corresponding Society were one of the most prominent groups associated with English reformism and radicalism of the 1790s. During the treason trials of 1794 and arrests for alleged attacks aimed at the king, members were arrested, with John Thelwall, John Horne Tooke, and founder Thomas Hardy put on trial for high treason for which they were acquitted.[1] Against this backdrop of 1790s radicalism it is

1 For details on 1790s radicalism, London Corresponding Society, etc., see, e.g., Thompson, *Making of the English Working Class*, 19–203; Albert Goodwin, *The Friends of Liberty: The English Democratic Movement in the Age of the French Revolution* (London: Routledge, 1979); Iain McCalman, *Radical Underworld: Prophets, Revolutionaries and Pornographers in London, 1795–1840*

not difficult to see how the story of Ball could now be re-read as a heroic, anti-establishment one.

John Baxter

Among those arrested was the silversmith John Baxter who became chair of the London Corresponding Society in 1794 and a founder member of a splinter group, the Friends of Liberty, in 1795. In the same year, he published a pamphlet on the right of resistance—or at least in theory, hence the opening qualification: 'Do not be alarmed, I respect the Laws and Constitution of my country; and when I speak of Resistance to Oppression, it is not to destroy but to preserve them.' As with earlier constitutional arguments that preceded Baxter, he argued that not all resistance can be classified as 'Rebellion,' though it 'should be in the last resort of a much injured and suffering People.'[2] While the theory might not have been new, the ideological (and socio-economical) position from which Baxter employed it was, because it meant looking back at demands made, for instance, in the 1381 uprising as potentially constitutional, as more reactionary writers were even starting to note. Most significantly for understanding receptions of the uprising, Baxter then published *A New and Impartial History of England* (1796). Baxter promised to hold up the 'crimes of KINGS and MINISTERS to public view' and the 'luxury, ostentation, and corruption of courtiers and placemen,' while prefacing his history with an extended discussion

---

(Cambridge: Cambridge University Press, 1988), 7–25; John Barrell, *Imagining the King's Death: Figurative Treason, Fantasies of Regicide, 1793–1796* (Oxford: Oxford University Press, 2000); Steve Poole, *The Politics of Regicide in England, 1760–1850: Troublesome Subjects* (Manchester: Manchester University Press, 2000), 90–119; Goodrich, *Debating England's Aristocracy in the 1790s*; Michael T. Davis, '"Reformers No Rioters": British Radicalism and Mob Identity in the 1790s,' in Davis, (ed), *Crowd Actions*, 146–62; Jon Mee, *Print, Publicity, and Popular Radicalism in the 1790s: The Laurel of Liberty* (Cambridge: Cambridge University Press, 2016).

2 John Baxter, 'Resistance to Oppression, the Constitutional Right of Britons Asserted in a Lecture Delivered before Section 2 of the Society of the Friends of Liberty, on Monday, November 9th (1795),' in Gregory Claeys (ed.), *Political Writings of the 1790s, Volume 4: Radicalism and Reform 1793–1800* (London: William Pickering, 1995), 439–42 (439–40). Goodwin, *Friends of Liberty*, 369–71, downplays the more violent and radical interpretations of Baxter. Cf. Mee, *Print, Publicity, and Popular Radicalism*, 21–22, 94, 108.

of the importance of the Saxon constitution. 'Much as we respect the opinions of Mr Thomas Paine in many particulars,' Baxter added, 'we cannot agree with him, that we have no constitution.'[3]

A New and Impartial History of England was dedicated to 'the people at large, to the London Corresponding Society in particular, and to the Political Societies of Great Britain in General, associated for parliamentary reform, and the promotion of constitutional information' and with further reference to the treason trials on the title page and in the preface. The preface also includes discussion of the importance of justice for peer and peasant, legal and parliamentary corruption, the significance of political societies under threat, and how 'virtuous characters are in danger of Spies from an overbearing Aristocracy.' Thus, the importance of promoting and interpreting the constitution was emphasised by Baxter; indeed, the very point of such a history is to contrast the free ancient constitution with present times. The preface opens with the claim that this history is motivated by the 'love of our country' and an exposé of 'CORRUPTION AND DESPOTISM through the various periods of our history' and to counter the deception that makes up most histories. The parts of the country's history which relate to the 'RIGHTS AND LIBERTIES OF THE PEOPLE' are to be brought out of the shade and should be seen as a defence of the 'Liberty of the Press.' For Baxter, it was not entirely clear from where the constitution emerged but effectively it was the Saxons and with the Norman Conquest that 'the Saxon laws and constitution were laid prostrate.' Indeed, Paine's mistake, Baxter thought, was not carrying his views beyond the Normans. After that, levels of liberty were dictated by 'policy or necessity.' Norman tyrants attempted to introduce 'absolute despotism' but were resisted by the 'firm spirit of Englishmen' and their attempts to restore the Saxon constitution. The 1688 Revolution expelled a tyrant and confirmed the Saxon laws. This meant that the nation could hold the king to account and law-making and taxation came through the consent of the people via parliamentary representation. The future wellbeing of the Constitution now

---

3   John Baxter, *A New and Impartial History of England, from the Most Early Period of Genuine Historical Evidence to the Present Important and Alarming Crisis* (London, 1796), ix–x. On the context of Baxter's constitutionalism, see, e.g., Benjamin Weinstein, 'Popular Constitutionalism and the London Corresponding Society,' *Albion* 34 (2002): 37–57. Cf. James Epstein, '"Our Real Constitution": Trial Defence and Radical Memory in the Age of Revolution,' in James Vernon (ed.), *Re-reading the Constitution: New Narratives in the Political History of England's Long Nineteenth Century* (Cambridge: Cambridge University Press, 1996), 22–51.

lay in universal suffrage, Baxter claimed, and his history would stand up for the public cause.[4]

With a constitutionalism from below in place, Baxter could re-read 1381 and claim Ball as a hero of English history.[5] It is telling that the story is effectively the same (down to the familiar wording) but now the value judgement changes. Where centuries of dominant interpreters could assume that the actions of Ball and the rebels were a bad thing, Baxter could now assume the opposite. He discussed the poll tax and serfdom but likewise framed it in terms of familiar eighteenth-century debates. Baxter observed the 'high reputation in which this country stands for the enjoyment of civil liberty' but that Froissart instead revealed that 'personal slavery was more general here than in any country in Europe.' Despite some gaining enough wealth to acquire freedom, a 'tyrannical act of parliament' meant this could not happen. At the beginning of the story, Ball emerged, and Baxter explicitly changed Ball's conventional designation: 'who is called a *seditious preacher*, but whom we will denominate a *true philanthropist*.' Ball 'inculcated among his countrymen the principles of the first origin of mankind from one common stock,' an 'equal right to liberty, and to all the goods of nature.' He preached against the 'tyranny of artificial distinctions,' 'the abuses which had arisen from the degradation of the more considerable part of the species, and the aggrandisement of a few insolent rulers.' Such 'doctrines' conformed easily with ideas of 'primitive equality' and (as Hume stressed) are 'engraven in the hearts of all men' and appreciated by the suffering people, among whom the Adam and Eve 'distich' was common. For his views, Baxter explained, Ball was also 'thrown into the Tower.' Given that he was said to have been put in the Tower, Ball later returns in the narrative to be released, as the rebels killed Sudbury et al., among other 'outrages in the city.'[6] Baxter's explicit judgements aside, his wording echoed or could be directly found in previous historians (e.g., Hume, Russel, Raymond, Goldsmith, Gifford), even if Baxter did not always acknowledge his sources. But with his change of emphasis, we might now say that for Baxter's Ball in the 1380s, read Baxter's radical London in the 1790s.

Tyler too. Like Paine, Thelwall had already criticised the unjust 'assassination' of Tyler—a concern that would emerge in Baxter's retelling of Tyler's death—and praised the 1381 uprising, 'notwithstanding the opprobrious epithets of particular historians' because it 'is evidently marked by

---

4   Baxter, *A New and Impartial History of England*, v–xii.
5   Dobson, 'Remembering the Peasants' Revolt,' in Liddell and Wood (eds.), *Essex and the Great Revolt of 1381*, 13–14.
6   Baxter, *A New and Impartial History of England*, 196–97.

the modesty and reasonableness of the demands made by the victorious insurgents.' We also learn about one of these historians: Hume, 'the apologist for tyranny...the obsequious historian.'[7] Baxter's narrative on Tyler follows on from Ball, and his retelling of the London revolt is conventional enough. It is not uncritical; there is a clear ideological distancing from excessive mob behaviour and 'their outrageous violence.' Nevertheless, the narrative is presented in terms of, for instance, an opportunity to take 'vengeance on their tyrants,' to 'vindicate their native liberty,' denials of justice, 'evil ministers,' pillaging the houses of 'many obnoxious individuals.' At Mile End, Tyler wanted the 'abolition of slavery,' freedom of commerce, and fixed rent on lands. At Smithfield, Tyler neither 'intended violence to the king, nor expected it himself' and made further demands, including slaves being set free, 'all commonages...be open to the poor as well as the rich,' and pardons for the latest 'outrages.' These demands, Baxter added, were 'unquestionably reasonable.' Unfortunately, Walworth took offence at Tyler's manner and Tyler was attacked. The nobility and gentry, worried that the rebels would still have too much freedom and thus abolish the feudal system, prompted the king to revoke any promises. Among those killed were Jack Straw and Ball, and strikingly this was done 'without any form or process, in violation of both law and the treaty of general amnesty.' It was such actions that infuriated the largely peaceful rebels.[8]

Baxter ended with a diversion on the lessons of history and hit home what was already explicit enough in his account: 1381 was an abuse of the constitution from above and a defence of the constitution from below. Similarly, Baxter wondered how historians have little animosity towards the insurrection of the barons but do not offer the same generosity to efforts of 'the people to defend themselves from the oppression of the king or his nobility.' The rebels were in the first instance denied justice and then fought for 'native freedom.' These were the reasons why Baxter felt that 1381 required a more substantial account and the rebels required rescuing them from the 'undeserved odium' which had long been cast upon them. Moreover, Baxter invoked William the Conqueror and how he might have (like Richard) bound himself to follow the Saxon laws and customs. William and his successors were known for not fulfilling their oaths, but such duplicity also meant that they did not alter the constitution either.

7   John Thelwall, *The Peripatetic; or, Sketches of the Heart, of Nature and Society; in a Series of Politico-Sentimental Journals, in Verse and Prose, of the Eccentric Excursions of Sylvanus Theophrastus Supposed to be Written by Himself* (London, 1793), 23–28.
8   Baxter, *A New and Impartial History of England*, 197–98.

It would have been pragmatic, therefore, for the people to have insisted on the 'full restoration of the Saxon constitution' and its implementation which would have secured them from future oppression. It was just unfortunate that there was a lack of guidance and influence to develop the public good. The idea of the constitution was more typically implied in previous histories. To begin to clear away this weighty history of interpretation, Baxter's case from below had to strike emphatically.

Robert Southey's Revolutionary Priest

Around this time, another Paine sympathiser had written favourably of 1381. As a nineteen year old at Oxford, the future Poet Laureate Robert Southey (1774–1843) wrote his dramatic poem, *Wat Tyler* (1794). There was good reason why the young Southey would be interested in the subject matter. In addition to quipping that he was some distant relative of Tyler,[9] he was at that time a Jacobin and an admirer of Paine as the treason trials were taking place in London. In other words, these were the exact kinds of sympathies we might expect of someone reclaiming the legacy of Tyler and Ball. Yet there were other, related types of radical influences on Southey. He also read and appreciated William Godwin's *Enquiry Concerning Political Justice and Its Influence on Morals and Happiness* (1793), and in June 1794 he met Samuel Taylor Coleridge at Oxford where they developed and promoted ideas about a 'pantisocracy'. This would be a little republic of reason, with property held in common and liberty for all, which he later claimed would have been the 'foundations of a community, upon what we believed to be the political system of Christianity'.[10] It would also involve emigrating to America and building this new society on the banks of the Susquehanna River, though Southey revised his thinking and proposed testing Wales first before the idea fell through.[11]

9 'Robert Southey to Thomas Southey (6 November 1794)', in Kenneth Curry (ed.), *New Letters of Robert Southey: Volume I* (New York: Columbia University Press, 1965), 85–86; Carol Bolton, *Writing the Empire: Robert Southey and Romantic Colonialism* (London: Routledge, 2007), 261 n. 22.
10 Robert Southey, *A Letter to William Smith, Esq., M.P.* (London, 1817), 20.
11 For details see, e.g., Mark Storey, *Robert Southey: A Life* (Oxford: Oxford University Press, 1997), 44–83; W. A. Speck, *Robert Southey: Entire Man of Letters* (New Haven: Yale University Press, 2006), 42–82; David M. Craig, *Robert Southey and Romantic Apostasy: Political Argument in Britain, 1780–1840* (Woodbridge: Boydell Press, 2007), 33–35. Cf. 'Robert Southey to Thomas

Wat Tyler is a dramatic poem in three acts, which may have included among its sources the accounts by David Hume and Robert Howard.[12] As a piece of romantic medievalism that would become popularly associated with 1381 in the nineteenth century, it begins at a blacksmith's shop with a song, a dance, and a maypole welcoming the month of May. A mournful Tyler lays down his hammer and sits by his door before his old friend Hob Carter asks why he is so sad. Tyler, the 'hard-working' man of an 'unblemish'd character,' explains how he toils but remains poor and what money he has left will be lost to the poll tax (easily read as a commentary on changing labour relations in the late eighteenth-century present). Carter denounces 'our ministers—panders of the king's will' for draining their wealth and forcing boys away into the army. Tyler wonders why a humble blacksmith from Deptford should give all he has 'to massacre the Frenchmen,/Murder as enemies men I never saw!', adding that he could not care less whether 'a Richard or a Charles' wears the crown of France because, while the kings enjoy the spoils, 'we pay—we bleed.' Tyler even goes as far as saying that the sun would still shine and rain would still fall even if 'neither of these royal pests existed.' The youthful Piers asks about what nature provides, to which Tyler answers that nature provides sufficient for all but the strong 'hoards up superfluous stores,/Robb'd from his weaker fellows, starves the poor,/Or gives to pity what he owes to justice.' We learn from Piers that this is what 'our good friend' Ball (who is more prominent than Tyler in the work) had preached, and Alice asks why Ball was imprisoned. After all, he is 'charitable, good, and pious,' preaching that 'all mankind are brethren' and as 'brethren they should love each other.' Tyler explains the spurious reasons for Ball's imprisonment:

> Rank sedition—
> High treason, every syllable, my child!
> The priests cry out on him for heresy,
> The nobles all detest him as a rebel,
> And this good man, this minister of Christ,
> This man, the friend and brother of mankind,
> Lingers in the dark dungeon![13]

Southey (12 October 1794),' in Curry (ed.), *New Letters of Robert Southey: Volume I*, 80–82.

12 Matheson, 'The Peasants' Revolt through Five Centuries of Rumor and Reporting,' 143.

13 Robert Southey, *Wat Tyler* (London, 1817), 2–12.

As with Baxter, obviously read 1790s radicalism in England, the world of the treason trials, and receptions of the French Revolution.[14]

And the allusions do not stop. The poem continues, with Tyler and Piers discussing poverty and the future of Piers and young Alice before the tax collectors make their entrance. We then get an account of the collector's assault on Alice and what will now happen to Tyler, only to hear a cry of 'Liberty! Liberty!—No Poll tax!—No War!' Carter now explains that 'we have broke our chains—we will rise in anger' and overthrow the handful of oppressors. For Piers had rallied the villages to arms 'For Liberty and Justice!' and on to Maidstone to free 'good John Ball,/Our friend, our shepherd.' Whereas other histories had tried to blame Tyler for using the rebellion to escape retribution for killing the tax collector, Tyler explains that the mob should not dwell on the private case of the tax collector but instead think of the oppression they have faced at the hands of the 'destructive tyrants' and how, 'like beasts,/They sell you with their land—claim all the fruits/Which the kindly earth produces as their own.'[15]

The rebels at Blackheath have Ball's Adam and Eve couplet as their song refrain with additional lyrics:

> Wretched is the infant's lot,
> Born within the straw-roof'd cot!
> Be he generous, wise or brave,
> He must only be a slave.
> Long, long labour, little rest,
> Still to toil to be oppress'd;
> Drain'd by taxes of his store,
> Punish'd next for being poor;
> This is the poor wretch's lot,
> Born within the straw-roof'd cot.
> While the peasant works—to sleep;
> While the peasant sows—to reap;
> On the couch of ease to lie,
> Rioting in revelry;
> Be he villain, be he fool,
> Still to hold despotic rule,

---

14 Storey, *Robert Southey*, 68–70; Dunn, 'Wat Tyler: The Many Roles of an English Rebel', 28; Ian Haywood, '"The Renovating Fury": Southey, Republicanism and Sensationalism', *Romanticism on the Net* 32–33 (2003–2004): 1–25 (8–15); Speck, *Robert Southey*, 51–52; Craig, *Romantic Apostasy*, 1 (cf. 27–28 on the fusion of 'Godwinian stoicism with Christian fortitude'); Basdeo, *Life and Legend of a Rebel Leader*, loc 1655–1798.

15 Southey, *Wat Tyler*, 13–20.

Trampling on his slaves with scorn;
This is to be nobly born.

Enter the 'honest priest' Ball. His 'squalid rags' explain his time in prison, while he adds that he was reviled, insulted, and left to languish in a damp dungeon. Nevertheless, he 'bore it cheerily' for he had done his duty and, somewhat Christ-like, 'pitied my oppressors' while feeling sorrow for the 'poor men of England.' Tyler agrees that Ball should address the crowd and remind them of 'their long-withdrawn rights.' Ball gives a long speech ('something like a sermon') calling the Englishmen gathered in 'the cause of freedom.' He explains that though he may be a priest, he is not the sort to exploit the poor. Instead, we get a mention of Jesus, hitherto rare in the history of reception of Ball and here something akin to the burgeoning study of the historical or 'real' figure of Jesus—including Jesus the revolutionary, Jesus the opponent of state and church tyranny, and Jesus the reformer—in the late eighteenth century.[16] Ball preaches and practices 'the law of Christ,' reminding the audience that the 'Son of God' did not come in power but as the 'man from Nazareth,' humble, lowly in heart. Jesus's preaching of mercy, justice, and love involved the woes to the rich and injunctions to sell possessions and give to the poor (Luke 6.24; 18.22; Matthew 19.21; Mark 10.21).[17]

Ball hammers the point home like a prophet. He encourages them to think about justice, the 'lordly baron feasting on your spoils,' the one in comfort on the 'couch of luxury' (cf. Amos 6.4), etc., and why such types should lord it over them, enjoying the fruits of their labour. But the sun shines on all (cf. Matthew 5.45), God's creation provides for all, the pleasant-smelling flora can be enjoyed by all, but the arrogant baron blasphemously claims lordship by birth and nature. In the proud place, 'blood-purpled robes of royalty' feast, lording 'over millions' while turning the labouring classes to poverty (cf. Luke 16.19–31). And there are suggestions that this is tied in with Saxon-style constitutionalism as he encourages his audience to remember their 'long-forgotten rights,/Your sacred, your inalienable freedom.' Tom Miller, Jack Straw, and Carter are somewhat surprised that such a speech could come from a religious person. Alluding to the tradition of

---

16 Jonathan C. P. Birch, 'Revolutionary Contexts for the Quest: Jesus in the Rhetoric and Methods of Early Modern Intellectual History,' *Journal for the Study of the Historical Jesus* 17 (2019): 35–80; Jonathan C. P. Birch, *Jesus in an Age of Enlightenment: Radical Gospels from Thomas Hobbes to Thomas Jefferson* (New York: Palgrave Macmillan, 2019). I am grateful to Jonathan Birch for private discussion of such issues.
17 Southey, *Wat Tyler*, 23–30.

Ball as the new bishop of England, Jack Straw claims that no bishop would 'tell you truths like these,' and even says that he will be made archbishop. Carter goes further still: 'There was never a bishop among all the apostles.' Ball, however, continues, explaining that they are 'all equal by nature.' Later, he simply claims to be 'plain John Ball,' their equal who has come to serve not command (cf. Matthew 20.28; Mark 10.45). Like Tyler, Ball is presented as focusing on the needs of the mob as they favour justice over revenge and are encouraged to remember mercy. As ever somewhat Christ-like, Ball proclaims that they may not have been treated well by their oppressors, but the mob—in an inversion of the popular eighteenth-century cliché—will show them the meaning of humanity![18]

The events in London are retold, including scenes with the king, Walworth, and the archbishop of Canterbury. Ball is present with Tyler at Smithfield and offers relatively pragmatic advice, namely, to endorse seizing the king as a figurehead and for protection but with the qualification that human blood should not be shed, and Tyler likewise emphasises that the king should not be touched. Indeed, he is later disturbed to find that Jack Straw beheaded the archbishop of Canterbury! As Baxter would soon do, this apology for Ball and Tyler is in contrast with centuries of retellings of the story and the rehabilitation presumably functions as a defence against allegations made against radicals in London at the time *Wat Tyler* was being written. Indeed, Ball adds the warning that 'The faith of courts/ Is but a weak dependence! You are honest!' He even argues that it is better to die an honest victim (as Tyler soon does) than live in the face of a 'cold policy that still suspects,' perhaps picking up on earlier hints of martyrdom (with allusions to Matthew 20.28 and Mark 10.45).[19] But Southey went out of his way, and perhaps necessarily so given the weighty reception he was up against. Even after Tyler is stabbed, Ball discourages the un-Christian act of revenge and, dedicated to the cause both he and Tyler wanted, agrees with the king on implementation of freedom and repealing of the tax.

Nevertheless, and again with revolutionary France in the background, Ball and Piers acknowledge that violence such as the beheading of an archbishop is the 'curse of insurrection.' Here we get a philosophy of revolutionary violence as Ball educates the young Piers, explaining that while punishment and revenge is wrong, this is expected collateral damage, or carried out in moments of outrage. Indeed, this should perhaps be expected when those that labour are freed after such repression and not least when

---

18 Southey, *Wat Tyler*, 29–33. On the broader context of the inversion of the mob cliché, see, e.g., Haywood, 'Renovating Fury,' 4, 10, 13.
19 Southey, *Wat Tyler*, 40.

the oppressor is an avaricious, hypocritical 'high-priest.'[20] But still for Ball, revenge and punishment are ultimately wrong—as he illustrates with his anger at the treatment of Tyler—and they eliminate the possibility of repentance. As ever, Ball is acting like Christ, not the hypocritical official church authorities. But he is also aware that Tyler's reputation has been unfairly tarnished and worries that the crowd will now listen to the 'courtly falsehood.'[21] Indeed, when the king reads out his promises, the crowd lap it up while the sceptical Ball knows the people have to remain—peacefully, of course—for it to be confirmed by Parliament. Yet Ball is still troubled and prays to establish whether this is the right decision and whether the alternative might be the only way: to risk blood and slaughter for all things to be equal. Such are the brutal decisions a revolutionary and their supporters must deal with in the most testing of moral circumstances.

Then comes the galling truth as a wounded Piers shows that the 'false monarch' went back on his vow, as Ball tried to heal Piers's wounds rather than flee. Now Ball's reputation over the centuries blots the saintly figure in *Wat Tyler*, as a solider calls him 'that old seditious heretic' and takes away the 'old stirrer-up of insurrection.' Similarly, *Wat Tyler* is also an attack on the popular heroic memory of Walworth. Walworth repeats the seditious label and ridicules Ball's 'strange wild notions/Of this equality,' which the implied reader in the 1790s would know are eminently reasonable. By way of contrast to Ball, Sir John Tresilian, who later repeats the unfair allegations against him, unwittingly voices the dirty hypocrisy behind the claim of 'fair free open trial, where the King/Can chuse his jury and appoint his judges.' Ball is brought in, his preaching (in line with centuries of elite reception)

20 Southey, *Wat Tyler*, 47–48. Southey would develop such views but in a more muted, less violent form ('not by tumult and mad violence/Can peace be forc'd, and Order and Reform,/But by the calm, collected public voice') in 'Inscription. For a Column in Smithfield Where Wat Tyler was Killed,' *Morning Post and Gazeteer* (12 February 1798). There are obvious echoes of Paine's call for a Tyler memorial, which Hone also mentioned in the preface to his 1817 edition entitled, *Wat Tyler; A Dramatic Poem. A New Edition with a Preface Suitable to Recent Circumstances*. Cf. Kenneth R. Johnston, *Unusual Suspects: Pitt's Reign of Alarm and the Lost Generation of the 1790s* (Oxford: Oxford University Press, 2013), 269 ('This is like lecturing Citizen Thelwall in Godwin's voice'); Haywood, 'Renovating Fury,' 17 ('Few radical readers in 1817 would want to dissent from such a measured and enlightened position, at least in public, and the poem seems to carry considerable moral authority. But in the text of *Wat Tyler*, as we have seen, the reader could find a more militant and regicidal extrapolation from contemporary politics').
21 Southey, *Wat Tyler*, 53.

said to be the spark of the revolt, and he gets a kangaroo trial scene worthy of that given to Jesus himself according to the Gospels. He admits he is John Ball but denies he is a rebel and then throws back the allegation at his accusers: they 'Rebel against the people's sovereignty.' Ball claims he is guilty only of preaching equality and opposing oppressive and exploitative structures of society, by repeating the teaching he gave throughout *Wat Tyler*, and he is given the most brutal death as punishment. Ball, of course, takes it like a saint. But like future interpreters, Southey had to deal with the problem that Ball failed. In a way that William Morris's Ball would famously take up differently nearly a century later, Southey's Ball, like a true martyr, promises that his 'truth' will survive and return when it will 'blaze with sun-surpassing splendour' as the 'dark mists of prejudice and falsehood/Fade' and the 'whole world be lighted!'[22]

A World Turned Upside Down—and Back Again?

Southey's Ball was the ideal revolutionary or radical priest—committed, honest, loyal, respected, single-minded, dedicated, pragmatic, nuanced, sceptical, saintly, Christ-like, and a martyr—in stark contrast to the tyrannical state. His republican tendencies and attacks on the economic relations between ruler and ruled may have been part of the known discourses of the 1790s, but they are remarkable when compared with the history of the reception of Ball since 1381. Indeed, was not all this an even more dramatic rehabilitation of Ball than the one Baxter would give a few years later?[23] Yes and no. Clearly, Southey pushed the case further than Baxter, but *Wat Tyler* was not published in the 1790s, despite the publisher James Ridgway, who was imprisoned at Newgate, provisionally agreeing to do so.[24] Instead, *Wat*

---

22 Southey, *Wat Tyler*, 48–69.
23 Dobson, *Peasants' Revolt of 1381*, 397, even claimed that the last scene of *Wat Tyler* 'shows that no one has ever made John Ball seem a more dangerous preacher of sedition to the modern world than the young Southey.'
24 On the legal details and the story of the manuscript, see, e.g., Frank Taliaferro Hoadley, 'The Controversy over Southey's *Wat Tyler*,' *Studies in Philology* 38 (1941): 81–96 (85); 'Robert Southey to Edith Fricker (c. 12 January 1795),' in Curry (ed.), *New Letters of Robert Southey: Volume I*, 90–92; Ralph Anthony Manogue, 'Southey and William Wordsworth: New Light on an Old Quarrel,' *Charles Lamb Bulletin* NS 38 (1982): 105–14; Speck, *Robert Southey*, 170–71;

Tyler would be sensationally published in 1817 by Southey's enemies when Southey was now the Poet Laureate (from 1813) and one of the 'Lake Poets' who had become decidedly reactionary and anti-Jacobin. This spectacular timing may have exposed Southey's seemingly one-hundred-and-eighty-degree ideological shift, but it would also bring about the full inauguration of John Ball as an English hero.

Megan Richardson, *The Right to Privacy: Origins and Influence of a Nineteenth-Century Idea* (Cambridge: Cambridge University Press, 2017), 15–20.

11
After Waterloo: The Poet Laureate's John Ball

There are straightforward reasons why the publication of Southey's *Wat Tyler* in 1817 had an impact; as the subtitle to William Hone's version of Southey's *Wat Tyler* tellingly put it: *New Edition, With a Preface Suitable to Recent Circumstances*.[1] The economic hardships following the Napoleonic Wars and the introduction of the Corn Laws in 1815 led to waves of discontent with reactions ranging from reformist to revolutionary. Comparisons between 1381 and contemporary radicalism remained a point of reference in Parliament, as we might expect. In the discussion of the suspension of Habeas Corpus (26 February 1817), Lord Milton downplayed the threat of the Spenceans and to make his point he still compared them with the dwindling threat of the Anabaptists who had advocated the same principles of all goods in common ('with the battle-axe in one hand, and the Bible in the other') and 1381 which was 'founded on the same principles, but it had no very serious consequences.'[2] But *Wat Tyler* was not used just to embarrass Southey against this sort of backdrop. There was now a degree of identification between the causes of political radicals and the 1381 uprising (especially 1381 as understood via Southey's account) now that the uprising had been reclaimed. As Robert Poole observed, readings of *Wat Tyler* were part of the 'melodramatic' confrontation with authority associated with petitioning Parliament and appealing to the crown which meant that the 'favoured precedent' for early post-war radicalism 'was not the French revolution but the English rebellion of 1381—the so-called "peasants' revolt."'[3]

1   Haywood, 'Renovating Fury,' 17.
2   *Caledonian Mercury* (3 March 1817).
3   Robert Poole, 'French Revolution or Peasants' Revolt? Petitioners and Rebels from the Blanketeers to the Chartists,' *Labour History Review* 74 (2009): 6–26.

Spa Fields

The most immediate context for the Southey outrage was the Spa Fields mass meetings associated with Spenceans James Watson, his son (also James), Arthur Thistlewood, Thomas Preston, and John Hooper, alongside the soon-to-be-revealed disreputable government spy, John Castle. The 'Orator' Henry Hunt agreed to speak at a mass meeting on 15 November 1816 with the condition that the more revolutionary Spencean proposals and actions were not part of the proceedings. Instead, he wanted to focus on issues of annual parliaments and universal suffrage. The second, bigger meeting on 2 December was accompanied by a subgroup marching on the city and some rioting, though not enough to prevent Hunt from giving his speech to sizeable crowds later in the day. Imperfect human memory, contradictory reports, conflicting radical agendas and tactics, crowd chaos, and no small consumption of alcohol on the day, means reconstruction of the events is not always straightforward. Nevertheless, E. P. Thompson's generalisation remains helpful: 'The riots were not a simple drunken outbreak, nor a carefully planned provocation, nor yet a definite attempt to simulate the fall of the Bastille, but they partook in some degree of all three.'[4]

The figure of Wat Tyler emerged in the reporting of the more provocative speeches. It was immediately claimed that during the speech of 'an Orator whose name is said to be Smith,' the allegation that Hunt was 'another Wat Tyler' was embraced ('Wat Tyler was well deserving of the praise of his country, and fulfilled his duty as an Englishman'). The press reporting of a chaotic march on the city no doubt conjured up one memory of Tyler but a counternarrative seems to have been in place: the Spa Fields crowd had a radical take on the ancient constitutionalist position, for 'the Ministers had trifled with our liberties, and refused to grant the people their rights.'[5] The

---

4   Thompson, *Making of the English Working Class*, 696. For a summary of the Spa Fields riots, see, e.g., John Belchem, *'Orator' Hunt: Henry Hunt and English Working-Class Radicalism* (Oxford: Clarendon, 1985), 44–54; John Stevenson, *Popular Disturbances in England 1700–1832* (second edition; New York: Routledge, 1992), 239–43; Mark Storey, *Robert Southey: A Life* (Oxford: Oxford University Press, 1997), 252–54.

5   E.g., *Kentish Gazette* (3 December 1816); *Caledonian Mercury* (5 December 1816); *Cheltenham Chronicle* (5 December 1816); *Belfast Commercial Chronicle* (7 December 1816); *Perthshire Courier* (12 December 1816). On the satirical negative memory of 1381 and Spa Fields radicalism, see *The Dorchester Guide, Or, A House that Jack Built* (London, 1819), 20–21; on the satirical positive

connection between Tyler and the fight for ancient constitutional rights is clearer in other accounts of Spa Fields. In one account, an unnamed speaker was surrounded by an ominous-looking crowd; the speaker told them that 'we have been oppressed for 800 years since the Norman Conquest' and that 'Wat Tyler would have succeeded had he not been basely murdered by a Lord Mayor, William of Walworth—Have Parliament done their duty?—(*No!*)—Has the Regent done his duty?—(*No, no!*),' before adding further comments on hypocrisy and the neglect of poor and starving people in England and Ireland.[6] In this instance, we have reference to the familiar argument about the Saxon liberties destroyed by William the Conqueror and his line, down to the present king. Elsewhere, James Watson (said to be surrounded by those of the 'lowest order—sailors, porters, dustmen, coal-heavers, old women, mechanics of a very mean appearance, and some few of a more respectable order')[7] spoke about the Norman Conquest and was followed by his son, James, who spoke about a 'second Wat Tyler' being a suitable label for his friend, here presumed to be Thomas Preston. Watson Jr was reported to have claimed that this was 'no bad title' because Tyler 'rose for the purpose of putting down an oppressive tax, and would have succeeded had he not been basely murdered by William Walworth, then Mayor of London.'[8]

Two months later, Southey's *Wat Tyler* was published—just as Southey wrote scathingly against parliamentary reform.

---

memory of 1381 and Spa fields radicalism, see *The Black Dwarf* (26 March 1817).

6 E.g., *Morning Post* (3 December 1816); *Dublin Evening Post* (5 December 1816); *Cambridge Chronicle and Journal* (6 December 1816); *Kentish Gazette* (6 December 1816); *Bristol Mirror* (7 December 1816); *Durham County Advertiser* (7 December 1816); *Carlisle Patriot* (7 December 1816); *Suffolk Chronicle* (7 December 1816); *Chester Courant* (10 December 1816); *Lancaster Gazette* (14 December 1816).

7 *Northampton Mercury* (7 December 1816).

8 E.g., *Public Ledger and Daily Advertiser* (5 December 1816); *Northampton Mercury* (7 December 1816); *National Register* (9 December 1816); *Carlisle Patriot* (14 December 1816). *The Trial of James Watson: For High Treason, at the Bar of the Court of King's Bench: Volume 1* (London, 1817), 72, 147–48; *The Trial of James Watson: For High Treason, at the Bar of the Court of King's Bench: Volume 2* (London, 1817), 452.

The Poet Laureate's *Wat Tyler*

Dated to October 1816 but published on 11 February 1817, Southey wrote an anonymous article in the *Quarterly Review* which formed and forms an especially suitable point of contrast to the younger radical Southey.[9] After an emphatic defence of the war with Napoleon's France, Southey gave a conventional establishment attack on more immediate parliamentary reform (universal suffrage, triannual and annual parliaments, increased representation, ballot voting, etc.), radical journalists (e.g., William Cobbett), and speakers (e.g., Hunt). If his earlier position was more Paine, now it was more Burke who was indeed echoed in Southey's discussion of the constitution and gradual political evolution.[10]

Southey's opponents were now presented very much like his younger self's presentation of Ball but now such advocates of radicalism were framed in the traditional negative manner dominant in the history of reception of 1381. Southey returned the mob to its conventional status as a cipher for chaos, disorder, and rebellion, now reemployed to counter popular democracy ('ochlocracy, a mob-government, which is as much worse than anarchy, as the vilest ruffians of a civilized country are more wicked than rude savages').[11] He railed against the 'apostles of anarchy' who imposed upon the 'ignorance of the multitude, flattering their errors and inflaming their passions…exciting them to sedition and rebellion.' Southey was distressed at how the 'populace look for no other qualification in their heroes than effrontery and a voluble tongue.' Now, 'evil-minded and insidious men' have 'laboured more wickedly and more successfully in corrupting them…'[12] In his criticism of the history of striving for a perfect society based on the community of goods, he noted that, 'Such a community prevailed among some of the primitive Christians, though no law of the Gospel enjoined

---

9 *Quarterly Review* 16 (October 1816), 225–78; 'Robert Southey to Thomas Southey (21 December 1816)', in Ian Packer, Tim Fulford, and Lynda Pratt (eds), *The Collected Letters of Robert Southey: Part Five, 1816–1818* (Romantic Circles, University of Maryland, 2016), https://romantic-circles.org/editions/southey_letters/Part_Five/HTML/letterEEd.26.2882.html.

10 On Southey and the constitution, see, e.g., Craig, *Robert Southey and Romantic Apostasy*, 119–20, 203–11.

11 *Quarterly Review* 16 (October 1816), 259. Cf. Kim Wheatley, *Shelley and His Readers: Beyond Paranoid Politics* (Columbia: University of Missouri Press, 1999), 23–27, for analysis of Southey's article and its presentation of the crowd/people/mob in devilish language.

12 *Quarterly Review* 16 (October 1816), 226.

it...In America also it is acted upon by many obscure sects, living inoffensively and industriously in small communities.'[13] He critiqued those who would have been fellow travellers in his younger days, including Thomas Spence and his followers, the London Corresponding Society and Thomas Evans. Indeed, Southey presented Evans's understanding of Jesus in a way reminiscent of Ball's references to Jesus (and Southey's references to Ball) in *Wat Tyler*:

> Though this librarian has affixed the title of Christian Policy to his book, he makes no other pretention to the character of Christian himself than as a Spencean philanthropist, and informs us, that 'this man, Christ, was a Roman slave, crucified as a slave (the mode of execution peculiar to Roman slaves) for preaching the seditious doctrine that God was the proprietor of the earth, and not the Romans; that all men were equal in his sight, and consequently ought not to be slaves to another, nor to the Romans, for which he was crucified by the Romans.' Mr Evans is equally well read in history and in the Gospel![14]

And it obviously followed that now Southey had switched sides, the established church was to be defended against the 'rancour of theological hatred.'[15]

Spicing up the stark comparisons between the younger Southey and the Southey of the *Quarterly Review* article, *Wat Tyler* was republished anonymously about the same time (13 February 1817) by Sherwood, Neely, and Jones, 'an establishment which usually dealt in nothing more sensational than travel literature or *de luxe* editions of Blackstone,' as Frank Taliaferro Hoadley succinctly put it.[16] Southey discovered the pirated publication through a notice in the *Morning Chronicle* which openly mentioned the real author:

> A *curious* dramatic Poem, entitled *Wat Tyler*, by MR SOUTHEY, is just published. The public will be astonished how such a production could come from the pen of the Poet Laureat, and it can only be accounted for on the principles asserted by MR COBBETT, that sentiments so opposite to those which he now professes came from him before he had his view corrected by a more intimate knowledge of the Court. It will be read with

---

13 *Quarterly Review* 16 (October 1816), 264.
14 *Quarterly Review* 16 (October 1816), 269.
15 *Quarterly Review* 16 (October 1816), 272.
16 Frank Taliaferro Hoadley, 'The Controversy over Southey's *Wat Tyler*,' *Studies in Philology* 38 (1941): 81–96 (81).

curiosity by his former admirers, and with astonishment by those who respect his present opinions.[17]

And thus began a public and legal controversy, with friend, foe, Tory, Whig, radical, and reformer arguing about allegations of hypocrisy in the press and in Parliament.[18]

Amidst the mudslinging, Ball too can be seen (just about). He was typically used to make the claim that Southey the establishment man was hypocritical in his handling of radicals and reformers. To highlight Southey's 'inconsistency', William Hone quoted the 'When Adam delv'd...' song from *Wat Tyler*, scathingly adding that Southey was 'until he became Poet Laureate, a Poet' who once held 'not merely reforming opinions, but very wild notions indeed'. However, 'in consideration of a Court pension, he now regularly inflames his muse, in praise of official persons and business... compelled to sing like a blind linnet by a sly pinch, with every now and then a volume of his old verses flying into his face, and putting him out!'[19] William Hazlitt juxtaposed *Wat Tyler* with Southey's *Quarterly Review* article to point out the extremities in his thinking and, again, the perceived hypocrisy and contradictions. Here, Ball functioned as the named point of contrast. The author of *Wat Tyler* was 'an Ultra-jacobin' whereas the author of the *Quarterly Review* article was 'an Ultra-royalist':

> [T]he one was a frantic demagogue; the other is a servile court-tool; the one maintained second-hand paradoxes; the other repeats second-hard common places; the one vented those opinions which gratified the vanity of youth; the other adopts those prejudices which are most conducive to the convenience of age; the one saw nothing but the abuses of power...the other goes the whole length of despotism; the one vilified kings, priests, and nobles; the other vilifies the people; the one was for universal suffrage

---

17 *Morning Chronicle* (12 February 1817); 'Robert Southey to John Murray' (14 February 1817), in Kenneth Curry (ed.), *New Letters of Robert Southey: Volume II* (New York: Columbia University Press, 1965), 149–51.

18 For the details see Hoadley, 'The Controversy over Southey's *Wat Tyler*'; Storey, *Robert Southey*, 256–62; Haywood, 'Renovating Fury', 16–17; Speck, *Robert Southey*, 170–72; Craig, *Romantic Apostasy*, 1–4; Kim Wheatley, *Romantic Feuds: Transcending the 'Age of Personality'* (Aldershot: Ashgate, 2013), 21–56; Ian Packer, 'Robert Southey, Politics, and the Year 1817', *Romanticism on the Net* 68–69 (2017): 1–22; Basdeo, *Life and Legend of a Rebel Leader*, loc 1791–1894; Stephen Basdeo, 'The Critical Reception of Robert Southey's *Wat Tyler*', *Romantic Circles*, https://romantic-circles.org/editions/wattyler/contexts/reception.html. Cf. *London Courier and Evening Gazette* (26 February 1817).

19 *Reformists' Register* (21 February 1817).

and perfect equality; the other is for seat-selling and the increasing influence of the Crown; the one admired the preaching of John Ball; the other recommends the Suspension of the Habeas Corpus, and the putting down of the *Examiner* by the sword, the dagger, or the thumb-screw.[20]

To hammer the point home, a lengthy extract of *Wat Tyler* (featuring Ball) was appended to Hazlitt's article.

Zachary Zealoushead

Southey was parodied in a similar sense in Zachary Zealoushead, *Plots and Placemen* (1817), a pseudonymous drama from Spencean circles.[21] In Scene IV, the 'Poet' (Southey) leads a grand procession and the banner bearing the 'richly emblazoned' arms recalling his youth includes an allusion to Tyler and Ball: 'the arms, field Or, a viper biting a file; crest, a camelion; supporters, a blacksmith and a ragged priest—the motto, which is in *heathen Greek*, means "My boyish errors are renounced".'[22] The hypocritical Poet then gives an address which is, as the accompanying note makes clear, 'John Ball's speech to the Mob' directly taken from *Wat Tyler*, and then turned on its head ('I am a Poet…Not one who riots in the poor man's praise,/Or cares for his opinion. I am one/Who preach the law of Pitt, and in my life/Would practice what he taught,' etc.).[23] And in more hammering home of the point, the parody ends with a comic rendition of Rule Britannia ('Rule Corruption! Rule the knaves,/For Britons shortly will be slaves!').[24]

20 *The Examiner* (9 March 1817).
21 For discussion of *Plots and Placemen*, including suggestions concerning authorship, see, e.g., Worrall, *Theatric Revolution*, 274–309; John Gardner, *Poetry and Popular Protest: Peterloo, Cato Street and the Queen Caroline Controversy* (New York: Palgrave Macmillan, 2011), 113; Robert Poole, '"To the Last Drop of My Blood": Melodrama and Politics in Late Georgian England,' in Peter Yeandle, Katherine Newey, and Jeffrey Richards (eds.), *Politics, Performance and Popular Culture: Theatre and Society in Nineteenth-Century Britain* (Manchester: Manchester University Press, 2016), 21–43 (37).
22 Zachary Zealoushead, *Plots and Placemen, or Green Bag Glory, an Historical Melo Drama, in Two Acts. As Performed at the Boroughmonger's Private Theatre* (London, 1817), 21.
23 Zealoushead, *Plots and Placemen*, 21–23, with reference to Ball's speech in Robert Southey, *Wat Tyler* (London, 1817), 22–24.
24 Zealoushead, *Plots and Placemen*, 23–24.

And so the pillorying continued—even in Parliament. In the House of Commons (14 March), and reported fully in the *Morning Chronicle*, the dissenter, abolitionist, and opposition MP for Norwich (and, incidentally, formerly MP for Sudbury), William Smith, quoted from *Quarterly Review* and *Wat Tyler* again to highlight the radical differences and hypocrisy. Would not the author of the *Quarterly Review* article condemn an inflammatory work such as *Wat Tyler*? Nevertheless, while not naming the author, 'a man was not to be blamed for changing his opinions, but should not throw imputations on those who held the same opinions which he had held.' And to highlight the point of contrast, the revolutionary words of Ball according to this 'renegado' were quoted:

> My brethren, these are the truths and weighty ones:
> Ye are all equal; nature made ye so.
> Equality is your birth-right;—when I gaze
> On the proud palace, and behold one man
> In the blood-purpled robes of royalty
> Feasting at ease, and lording over millions;
> Then turn me to the hut of poverty,
> And see the wretched labourer, worn with toil,
> Divide his scanty morsel with his infants;
> I sicken, and, indignant at the sight.
> 'Blush for the patience of humanity.'[25]

Was this not, Smith joked, a clear example of the virus affecting the public mind that the author of the *Quarterly Review* warned against!

This was enough to provoke an impassioned response from Southey. He denied the charge of being a renegade and rejected the claim that he imputed evil intentions to those who now held the views he once did. The publication, Southey conceded, may well be 'mischievous' and could be 'especially dangerous at this time,' but, he claimed, it was an unpublished work and reflected the 'errors of youth' at a time when republicanism belonged to a 'very small number' of the educated classes. He denied, though, that 'it is a seditious performance' because 'it places on the mouths of the personages who are introduced nothing more than a correct statement of their real principles...The sentiments of the historical characters are correctly stated.'[26] Southey claimed that his ultimate aims at societal improvement had not really changed—just the means of achieving them. Whether any of this constitutes a fair defence is moot—as W. A. Speck

---

25 *Morning Chronicle* (15 March 1817).
26 Southey, *A Letter to William Smith*, 6–7, 15.

put it, 'In 1817 Southey would have sent the author of *Wat Tyler* to Botany Bay'[27]—and Southey's response only generated further debate as the controversy rumbled on.

But, no matter how discredited Southey may now have been among radicals, what this episode did do was to perpetuate a radical take on Ball as the memory of 1381 was on its way to public redemption. When Southey failed in his bid to get an injunction and *Wat Tyler* was not subjected to copyright, radicals like Hone took advantage of the peculiar situation and ensured that the text was republished cheaply and read widely. Such was the notoriety of *Wat Tyler* that it was reported in July 1817 that the dramatic poem was 'actually performed, with very considerable spirit and effect, by a company of strolling Players, at Wittington, in Shropshire, on Thursday week!' The audience was said to be 'numerous and varied' and witnessed 'strongly marked' passages 'allusive to the late and present times' and strongly contrasted with 'Mr Southey's tergiversation.'[28] *Wat Tyler* was even estimated to have sold 60,000 copies, and seven editions emerged in 1817 with more to follow. Unfortunately for Southey, his sympathetic retelling of Tyler, Ball, and the 1381 uprising would become his bestselling work (royalty-free, of course) and arguably matched in fame only by his version of 'The Three Bears.'[29]

After Spa Fields

Post-Spa Fields, Tyler's memory (as well as the warning about his fate) was soon invoked as a point of comparison in the context of the suspension of Habeas Corpus, and the actions of Manchester and Lancashire radicals, notably the proposed march of the Blanketeers in March 1817.[30] Promoted by William Benbow, Samuel Drummond, and John Bagguley, their demands were for constitutional reform and to highlight the plight

27 Speck, *Robert Southey*, 172.
28 E.g., *Chester Chronicle* (25 July 1817); *Oxford University and City Herald* (26 July 1817); *Liverpool Mercury* (8 August 1817).
29 See further, e.g., William St Clair, *The Reading Nation in the Romantic Period* (Cambridge: Cambridge University Press, 2004), 316–19; Worrall, *Theatric Revolution*, 306–7; Speck, *Robert Southey*, 171; Poole, '"To the Last Drop of My Blood"', 21–43.
30 H. W. C. Davis, 'Lancashire Reformers, 1816–17', *Bulletin of the John Rylands Library* 10 (1926): 47–79; Thompson, *Making of the English Working Class*, 702–16; Poole, 'French Revolution or Peasants' Revolt?'

of the workers in the Lancashire cotton industry by having small groups of workers marching from Manchester to London with a blanket and petition for the Prince Regent. Crowds and marchers gathered at St Peter's Field on 10 March, and Bagguley was reported to have made an analogy with 1381 in his speech:

> This is one of the happiest moments of my life to see you all ready to go so virtuous & aplaudable a journey. There never was such a thing done before. If you look through all the annals of history you will not see any like this. In the reign of Richard II. about 40,000 men went to London to demand their rights of the King; & he granted them their rights & they went home again. But they only came a little way from London, they did not go from Manchester.[31]

The march did not succeed. Dragoons soon intervened, some participants were arrested, and virtually all the marchers who did get away from Manchester were stopped en route and sent home or arrested. Spies had infiltrated the radicals and after the proposed march there were claims that insurrectionary disturbances were planned in order to release the imprisoned Blanketeers and to march on London. By the end of March, a number of arrests were made—but this was not the end of unrest in Manchester (culminating, of course, with the Peterloo massacre, 16 August 1819) nor indeed elsewhere (e.g., Pentrich uprising, June 1817). On top of this, there was also, of course, the Cato Street conspiracy (1820) to assassinate the Cabinet. Reference to 1381 continued to be an ongoing and convenient establishment point of reference for the topics of mobs, disturbances, agitators, mass meetings, radicals, reformers, and unrest.[32] But Tyler also continued to have a home among radicals and Hunt himself was reported

---

31 Home Office papers collected in the appendix to Davis, 'Lancashire Reformers,' 64–79 (76–77): H.O. 40.5 (Manchester Papers), No. 11. On Tyler and 1381 among the Blanketeers and Manchester radicals, see also Poole, 'French Revolution or Peasants' Revolt?'

32 E.g., *Evening Mail* (20 June 1817); *Military Register* (25 June 1817); *Durham County Advertiser* (1 November 1817); *Morning Post* (14 August 1817); *Liverpool Mercury* (30 January 1818); *Globe* (23 June 1818); *Morning Chronicle* (23 June 1818); *Statesman* (23 June 1818); *Carlisle Patriot* (18 July 1818); *Carlisle Journal* (25 July 1818); *Leicester Chronicle* (26 December 1818); *Star* (26 June 1819); *Tyne Mercury* (29 June 1819); *Globe* (2 July 1819); *Morning Post* (2 July 1819); *Durham County Advertiser* (24 July 1819); *Carlisle Patriot* (31 July 1819); *Dublin Evening Post* (14 August 1819); *Public Ledger and Daily Advertiser* (17 August 1819); *Saunders's News-Letter* (18 August 1819); *Chester Courant* (24 August 1819); *Exeter Flying Post* (2 September 1819); *Worcester*

as toying with the comparison and even martyrdom at a mass meeting at Smithfield (July 1819)—of all places—after he received assassination threats: 'if necessity called for it, I should, like Wat Tyler, glory in dying at your head.'[33]

Against this sort of background and wider, related (though often loosely connected) networks, radical publications continued to bring up Southey's youthful work, as well as charges of hypocrisy. Extracts from the most provocative parts of *Wat Tyler* (including Ball's speeches) were used to satirise Southey in the 26 March edition of *The Black Dwarf*.[34] On 29 March 1817, *Wat Tyler* was given some space in W. T. Sherwin's radical periodical, *The Republican* (shortly after, the *Weekly Political Register*). The preface focuses mostly on Tyler and an untrustworthy king with a gently positive understanding of the uprising. 'The History of Wat Tyler has always held a distinguished place in the English records,' the preface claims, and 'though some men affect to disapprove of his conduct, all men have concurred in admiring his courage.' Ball was not named but his influence would have been clear enough in the retelling of the myth of the Norman Yoke. 1381 was a time when the nation 'began to rise above the barbarous state into which the conquest, by William the Norman, had plunged it, and to shew strong signs of returning life' as would happen when the human mind is 'left to pursue its natural course without interruption.' The signs of this renewal could easily be read in Sherwin's reforming present and in the context of the Blanketeers, in that the reaction to the costly wars with France

---

    Journal (2 September 1819); *Royal Cornwall Gazette* (4 September 1819); *Hampshire Chronicle* (20 September 1819); *Morning Post* (12 August 1819).
33 Found in, e.g., *Caledonian Mercury* (21 July 1819); *Windsor and Eton Express* (18 July 1819); *Star* (21 July 1819); *Globe* (22 July 1819); *Morning Chronicle* (22 July 1819); *Public Ledger and Daily Advertiser* (22 July 1819); *Star* (22 July 1819); *Statesman* (22 July 1819); *Suffolk Chronicle* (24 July 1819); *Bell's Weekly Messenger* (26 July 1819); *Bristol Mercury* (26 July 1819); *Hampshire Chronicle* (26 July 1819); *Observer* (26 July 1819); *Saunders's News-Letter* (26 July 1819); *Chester Courant* (27 July 1819); *Cumberland Pacquet, and Ware's Whitehaven Advertiser* (27 July 1819); *Dublin Evening Post* (27 July 1819); *Bury and Norwich Post* (28 July 1819); *Bath Chronicle and Weekly Gazette* (29 July 1819); *Derby Mercury* (29 July 1819); *Exeter Flying Post* (29 July 1819); *Liverpool Mercury* (30 July 1819). Cf. *Sun* (23 June 1818); *Stamford Mercury* (26 June 1818); *Manchester Mercury* (27 July 1819); *Public Ledger and Daily Advertiser* (28 June 1819); *Manchester Mercury* (29 June 1819); *Sun* (22 July 1819); *Westmorland Gazette* (24 July 1819); *Bell's Weekly Messenger* (25 July 1819); *Observer* (25 July 1819); *Dublin Evening Post* (27 July 1819).
34 *The Black Dwarf* (26 March 1817).

and the poll tax 'gave rise to a discussion, amongst the people, about the right of the government to adopt such a measure and the result of that discussion was resistance.' And the accompanying motto for the people was the Adam and Eve couplet.[35]

Beyond Southey

While Southey's work was the dominant and most influential dramatic portrayal of Ball and the 1381 uprising, at least in radical circles, it was not the only one. One production was performed at the then Coburg theatre in 1825 and 1831: *Wat Tyler & Jack Straw; or, The Life and Death of King Richard II*.[36] The unusual foregrounding of Wat Tyler and Jack Straw in the story of Richard's life and death further points to the popularity of the 1381 uprising in the light of the pirating of Southey's *Wat Tyler* and recent disturbances. The playbill for the week starting 25 April 1825 advertised *Jack Straw & Wat Tyler* as 'an entirely New Grand Historical Drama...produced with a degree of Splendour & Accuracy equal to any of the former popular Historical Pieces of this Theatre.' While there are perhaps inevitable overlaps with Southey (e.g., Tyler at his forge, the Maypole, Alice and Piers), the play was contextualised more broadly at the beginning of conflict between the houses of Lancaster and York by way of Shakespeare.[37] As the full title already implies, the 'Rebellion of Wat Tyler' presented its own acknowledged chronological problems ('In condensing this vast mass of historical matter, involving a considerable lapse of years, some anachronisms are unavoidable'). While whatever influence Southey may have had was domesticated, what was advertised on the playbill provided a sufficiently broad perspective for an audience of potentially diverse interests. The public presentation of *Wat Tyler & Jack Straw* stood firmly in the now relatively uncontroversial tradition of combining sympathy for the plight of the rebels ('occasions by the tyrannical and oppressive manner in which the exorbitant taxes were extorted'), praise for Tyler's handling of the treatment of his daughter Alice ('nobly resents the insult'), concern about an

---

35 *The Republican* (29 March 1817).
36 See, e.g., Jane Moody, *Illegitimate Theatre in London, 1770–1840* (Cambridge: Cambridge University Press, 2000), 141–46; Frederick Burwick, *Playing to the Crowd: London Popular Theatre, 1780–1830* (New York: Palgrave Macmillan, 2011), 119–20.
37 Moody, *Illegitimate Theatre in London*, 144.

uprising ('its alarming progress'), disdain for leading rebels ('Excessive arrogance of Jack Straw'), and praise for Richard and Walworth in dealing with the rebels ('the firmness of the Mayor of London, and the uncommon presence of mind of the young King'). Ball did not feature on the playbill, but his Adam and Eve couplet was quoted in full.[38]

And, of course, Ball's place in the histories of England continued. Among others, we might note that of the Catholic priest John Lingard (1771–1851), whose *History of England* was published and revised between 1819 and 1830. Lingard's history made extensive use of primary sources, hunting down manuscripts and material from the continent. Lingard's concern for the calm, careful, and disarmingly detached (though hardly without judgement) presentation of data was part of a critical apology for the reasonableness, tolerance, and loyalty of Catholics and Catholicism in England against the backdrop of Catholic emancipation and eventually the Roman Catholic Relief Act (1829). In a letter (18 December 1819), Lingard discussed the importance of subtlety in refutation of arguments, memorably noting that in 'my account of the Reformation I must say much to shock protestant prejudices; and my only chance of being read by them depends upon my having the reputation of a temperate writer. The good to be done is by writing a book which protestants will read.'[39] As his letter suggests, this critical attitude also meant a degree of undermining the more glorious histories of the Reformation, though he hardly remained uncritical of Catholic and Protestant alike.[40] Lingard's histories also engaged with a longer-term history which involved Catholicism and Catholic theology in England and with claims of them having wider international influence that stretched back through the Anglo-Saxons and Augustine of Canterbury.[41]

---

38 *A Collection of Playbills from Old Vic Theatre 1824–1833*, British Library, Digital Store Playbills 175, http://access.bl.uk/item/viewer/ark:/81055/vdc_100022589022.0x000002.

39 Martin Haile and Edwin Bonney, *Life and Letters of John Lingard, 1771–1851* (St Louis, MO: Herder, 1911), 166. Cf. 109.

40 Nevertheless, Lingard's account would be used in William Cobbett's polemical attack on the class interests and state power of the Church of England in *History of the Protestant 'Reformation'* (London, 1829). See, e.g., Peter J. Manning, 'The History of Cobbett's A History of the Protestant "Reformation,"' *Huntington Library Quarterly* 64 (2001): 429–43.

41 For discussion of Lingard and his work, see, among others, Peter Phillips, 'John Lingard and *The Anglo-Saxon Church*', *Recusant History* 23 (1996–1997): 178–89; Peter Phillips, *John Lingard: Priest and Historian* (Leominster: Gracewing, 2008); John Vidmar, 'John Lingard's History of the English Reformation: History or Apologetics?', *Catholic Historical Review* 85 (1999): 383–419;

Lingard's approach to 1381 was distinctive if familiar. In understanding the revolt, Lingard contextualised it broadly in European history among people 'no longer willing to submit to the impositions of their rulers, or to wear the chains which had been thrown round the necks of their fathers by a warlike and haughty aristocracy.' This change involved the 'progressive improvement in society,' spread of knowledge, pressure of taxation, and ongoing wars.[42] In England, the villeins had been in almost the same predicament since the Norman conquest. Progress of emancipation was slow, and improved conditions of others embittered those who remained serfs.[43] Standard immediate causes were included too, such as the tax collection and the account of (Wat) Tyler's daughter.[44] However, Lingard emphasised a crucial ideological component too.

Resistance was encouraged by the 'doctrines so recently taught by Wycliffe, that the right of property was founded in grace' which was notably paralleled with 'itinerant preachers' who 'inculcated the natural equality of mankind, and the tyranny of artificial distinctions.'[45] Wycliffe is important for understanding Lingard's reading of Ball. Before the 1381 uprising was retold in Lingard's narrative, readers were already informed that Wycliffe had been charged with teaching 'heterodox tenets,' involved in 'fierce but ridiculous controversy,' engaged in 'violent hostility to the friars' throughout his life, and known for the 'coarseness' of his invectives.[46] After the discussion of the 1381 revolt, Wycliffe returns to the historical narrative when the insurrection had created hostilities towards him. The 'itinerant preachers' may have improved on the 'lessons of their master' but, if the sources are to be believed, then 'their sermons were calculated to awaken in the people a spirit of discontent and insubordination, and to bring into contempt the established authorities, both in church and state.'[47] Wycliffe was understood as obscure, a 'religious innovator' who 'changed his opinion at will while simultaneously claiming to be 'infallible in every

---

Philip H. Cattermole, *John Lingard: The Historian as Apologist* (Kibworth Beauchamp: Matador, 2013); Hugh Magennis, 'Not Angles but Anglicans? Reformation and Post-Reformation Perspectives on the Anglo-Saxon Church, Part II: Seventeenth and Eighteenth Centuries,' *English Studies* 96 (2015): 363–78 (372–75).

42 John Lingard, *The History of England from the First Invasion to the Accession of Henry VIII: Volume III* (London, 1819), 174–75.
43 Lingard, *The History of England*, 175.
44 Lingard, *The History of England*, 176–77.
45 Lingard, *The History of England*, 175–76.
46 Lingard, *The History of England*, 108, 158, 159, 161.
47 Lingard, *The History of England*, 190.

change' and who feigned 'innocence' to cover his 'most mischievous tendency.' Lingard could certainly praise Wycliffe's character but also (and crucially) saw him as flawed, someone who encouraged indiscriminate and unreasonable invectives against the whole clergy.[48] By making such moves, Philip Cattermole argued that Lingard was able to distance Wycliffe from 'contemporary Anglicanism, and, indeed, from every form of respectable Protestantism. And Lingard's own distaste for the heretic is expressed, significantly, in social as well as doctrinal categories...Wycliffe is not a good Roman Catholic, a courageous Lutheran, or a decent Anglican, he is simply a rogue.'[49]

This was the context in which Ball was likewise understood, and one familiar from the history of reception. Ball was labelled an 'itinerant preacher'—a label Lingard repeated no doubt to keep the Wycliffe parallel in mind—who had been imprisoned for his 'seditious and heterodox harangues.'[50] He was the 'appointed preacher' to the 'lawless and tumultuous multitude' at Blackheath where he gave his sermon on the Adam and Eve couplet. Picking up on the tension between the potential egalitarianism of the sermon and the idea of a proposed alternative hierarchy present among the rebels, the 'infatuated hearers' promised to make Ball archbishop of Canterbury and chancellor 'in defiance of his own doctrines.'[51] The comparison with Wycliffe was also mentioned in a footnote which repeated the claim that Ball was an 'itinerant preacher.' Lingard made the damaging connection with subtlety. He rejected the claims of 'some writers' that Ball was one of Wycliffe's 'disciples' and accepted Knighton's claim that Ball was the precursor. Paralleling the portrayal of Wycliffe as antisocial, the reason was that Ball had taken up the role of an 'itinerant preacher' long before and was 'repeatedly excommunicated' for actions against the Pope, archbishops, bishops, and clergy. Then Lingard added the killer line to undermine Wycliffe: 'When, however, Wycliffe began to dogmatize, he adopted some of the doctrines of the new teacher, and ingrafted them on his own.'[52] In the broader context of Catholic emancipation, Ball and the crazed itinerant preachers beyond the realms of reasonable Catholicism and Protestantism were a useful foil for the implied alternative: the good, loyal subject.

48 Lingard, *The History of England*, 195.
49 Cattermole, *John Lingard*, 129.
50 Lingard, *The History of England*, 177.
51 Lingard, *The History of England*, 178.
52 Lingard, *The History of England*, 177.

Mrs O'Neill's Ball

The popularity of the novel meant that a new type of reception of Ball was also emerging. Alongside popular romantic interest in Robin Hood and medieval England more generally, the cast of characters from 1381 would prove to be an intriguing subject matter for creative writing in the nineteenth century (and beyond), with the novel providing much more scope for new detail. One novel which also functioned as a commentary on post-Waterloo radicalism is (and perhaps was) relatively obscure: Mrs O'Neill, *The Bondman: A Story of the Days of Wat Tyler* (1833), volume five in the Library of Romance series edited by Leitch Ritchie.[53] *The Bondman* took numerous details (particularly the events in London) from the chroniclers or their later interpreters and copiers, as alluded to in the Advertisement prefacing the novel ('if the old chronicles are to be credited...The critical reader...will immediately perceive from whence the information has been derived'). Indeed, despite the obvious fictional elements, the novel made claims about historical accuracy ('all the legal information scattered through the volume, is strictly correct; and every historical event, as nearly so as the machinery of the tale permitted'),[54] while one criticism of the novel was that there was *too much* antiquarian knowledge.[55] This combination of medieval romanticism and concerns for historical accuracy meant that it was not a problem to present Ball as a pious populist Catholic priest and tonsured monk who crossed himself and administered last rites.[56] This line would be developed further by William Morris towards the end of the century with a much more polemical edge in his critique of Protestant-influenced capitalism (see Chapter 15).

Beginning in August 1374 away from the south east at Sudley, *The Bondman* first tells the story of Stephen Holgrave who had been freed from serfdom after saving the life of his lord, the Baron of Sudley, Roland De Boteler. Stephen is in love with the beautiful Margaret and they are married by Margaret's brother, one Father John of the abbey of Winchcombe. Unfortunately for the couple, De Boteler's steward, Thomas Calverley, is also besotted with Margaret, and his dastardly and elaborate plots lead to Stephen being remade a bondman. During his travails, Stephen befriends

---

53 *Caledonian Mercury* (11 May 1833) assumed Ritchie was the author.
54 Mrs O'Neill, *The Bondman: A Story of the Days of Wat Tyler* (London, 1833), 3. Cf. 42. Antiquarian interests were noted in, e.g., *Spectator* (11 May 1833) and *Bell's New Weekly Messenger* (12 May 1833).
55 *Cheltenham Looker-On* (11 May 1833).
56 O'Neill, *Bondman*, e.g., 12, 52, 81–85, 103–4, 129.

the loyal, brave, and physically imposing—though sometimes quick of temper—blacksmith Wat Turner and begins to contemplate ideas of whether lords and serfs are both equally children of God, even to the point of replacing his own dead baby by stealing the infant De Boteler heir who would otherwise grow up to 'trample on his fellow men.'[57] After Stephen escapes with the help of Father John, De Boteler wants Stephen hunted down and, despite strong pressure, neither Wat Turner nor Father John would say anything to betray Stephen. Father John's loyalty (as well as administering the last rites to an excommunicated man) leads to him being cast out and stripped of his position, though he also starts 'to express strange opinions' about the end of serfdom and that it was acceptable for a bondman to escape from the master's authority.[58] As he left the abbey with regret, a weakened Father John finds that he had the sympathy of people 'of different ages and sexes.' Calverley has him arrested (though not without some struggle) and we learn that the outcast is called 'John Ball,' the 'son of a bondman.'[59] A recently released Wat Turner is outraged and leads a group to free the tortured Ball from imprisonment.

Six months later (July 1377), Ball is now living in a humble dwelling in London and witnesses the procession of the new king which only serves to further his radicalisation. He does not like the treatment of the populace by the royal guards and pages and is surprised and saddened to see that his old superior at Winchcombe, Simon Sudbury, is now archbishop of Canterbury. Ball even manages to get to the king to ask for justice, but Sudbury recognises him and, along with John of Gaunt, ridicules Ball, his background, and his 'doctrine that *all* should be free!' But a defiant Ball fires back: 'Triumph not, John of Lancaster, for I say unto you, *all* SHALL be free! You, and it may be the proudest of you all, may yet quail before the base-born!'[60] Ball, unsurprisingly, is ejected. Meanwhile, Calverley discovers the whereabout of Stephen in the Forest of Dean but is effectively trapped as Stephen's fellow free workers and forest dwellers protect him and send a humiliated Calverley away. Nevertheless, Stephen is soon covertly duped by Black Jack (later identified as Jack Straw) and is captured and forced to return to the life of a bondman.

The background of life from below allowed O'Neill to show the impact of the infamous poll tax—presented conventionally as a product of bad advisors to the king and heavy-handed collection—which tellingly 'gave

---

57 O'Neill, *Bondman*, 61.
58 O'Neill, *Bondman*, 79.
59 O'Neill, *Bondman*, 85.
60 O'Neill, *Bondman*, 93.

rise to a sort of coalition among the lower classes.'[61] In St Albans, amidst the discontent in 1381, is Ball, now an established and popular itinerant preacher described as a 'homeless wanderer, never resting under the same roof a second night' and seen by crowds and sympathisers as a 'prophet.' His 'mission was rather to the serf than the freeman.' He is an 'apostle of those who had none to help them.' He preaches freedom for the bondman and about the cruelty and corrupt wealth of the lords and how the 'high ones of authority shall be hewn down, and the haughty shall lick the dust like serpents.' But 'we shall tread them down like the mire in the streets... As the gathering of locusts shall we run upon them.' The badly advised king is likewise in 'bondage.' He must hear the sufferings in the realm and the cruelty surrounding him must be swept away. In this changed world, there will be an end to tithes, the bondman will be enfranchised, rents will be made fairer, the rich will give up their wealth to the poor, and the only priests remaining will be those administering the sacraments.[62] Ball also makes a trip back to Winchcombe, where more and more people listen to his ideas as his reputation and popularity grows further, to the extent that Stephen could escape to the south east.

But it is in Maidstone, 'under the powerful influence of John Ball,' that a particular meeting fomented disorder, organised by Wat Turner (now going under his uncle's name, 'Wat Tyler') and his wife, Bridget, with the entry code 'With King Richard and the true Commons,' though some participants are less keen on the need for a monarch. Here the leaders of the revolt, despite their personal disagreements and ambitions, draw up their demands, which include freeing bondmen, buying and selling in any town or city, and fair rents. They also plan their most dramatic move of marching on London and, despite misgivings (especially Stephen's), this would involve burning targets. Ball emphatically adds that no killing should be done except in self-defence, but it is to little avail as the revolt begins with bloodshed and Tyler is not especially suited to the role of general.

Ball is present at the meeting on the Thames and dragged onto the royal boat after being identified by Sudbury and De Boteler. He is then imprisoned in the Tower of London. This retelling of the revolt allowed O'Neill to explain further why there was destruction of and violence in London despite the intentions of figures like Ball. Ball's disappearance worries Tyler and the Kentish rebels who are waiting for him at Blackheath, so they decide to find him. Sudbury is suspected so the rebels target Lambeth Palace first and destroy its fineries while vowing vengeance on Ball's enemies. They

---

61 O'Neill, *Bondman*, 103.
62 O'Neill, *Bondman*, 103–4.

then march on the Tower as the duplicitous rogue Jack Straw privately negotiates with the king and his assistants,[63] giving them the ideas about insincere promises concerning the charters of freedom for the rebels and to free Ball in order to quell the rising because Ball abhorred violence. Tyler and Stephen eventually free Ball and they are all then shocked (especially Ball) when the traitorous Jack Straw proclaims that, on Ball's command, he had made terms with the king and that the Essex rebels were marching home. Ball still renounces violence and takes time out to pray in the chapel near an initially unaware Sudbury. But Sudbury and Ball are soon arguing about the rights and wrongs of who could worship in such a place, divine authority, and the impact of the poll tax before Sudbury would meet his fate. Ball is despondent and angry as rioting ensues and did not take Sudbury's mitre.

Ball surprisingly returns when De Boteler holds court to pardon Stephen and brokers a deal to restore the De Boteler child in return for the release of all bondmen on the manor. After successfully doing so, Ball approaches the king, saying,

> The work that I strove for has begun, and it will finish; but mine eyes will not live to see that day. From the hour that blood was shed I forsook the cause; but I hid myself from the snares that were laid for me; — for I said, Surely the light shall yet rise up in darkness! And it has risen; and it will grow brighter and brighter: — but John Ball's task is done and he gives himself up to the death that awaits him.[64]

Ball is effectively being made a martyr for the nonviolent and antiviolent cause and the imagery seen in Southey (and later developed by Morris) is used to describe the hoped-for eschatological fulfilment—a brightening light replacing the darkness. But Ball receives the king's clemency, though he only lives two more years and his body is lain at the Cistercian monastery in Burgundy. All wrongs in the story are righted. Jack Straw too gets his comeuppance. He takes Ball's discarded cloak and cowl and escapes, but his luck runs out as he is mistaken for Ball among those who had not known about his pardon. Straw is hanged (just as history told O'Neill that Ball had been) at St Albans, 'as one who had stirred up the bondmen to insurrection.'[65] As Ball had previously said in a famous saying from Matthew 7.2 that in some ways summarises the fate of the different

---

63 Black Jack was mistakenly claimed to be the alias of Jack Cade in *Court Journal* (11 May 1833).
64 O'Neill, *Bondman*, 149.
65 O'Neill, *Bondman*, 152.

characters in the novel, 'with what measure you mete to others, the same shall be meted to you again.'[66]

The Bondman functions as an overview of the pros, cons, and contradictions of post-Waterloo radicalism and reformism.[67] Nonviolence, antiviolence, and concerns about the discipline of the crowd, but with a clear sympathy for rebel demands, collectively form the dominant position in the novel. In a positive take on a tradition developing through Hume onward, O'Neill ensured that the novel works with what had become a standard assumption, namely that serfdom was outdated and wrong. Now, though, it was emphasised that some nonviolent reform was possible more immediately. And presumably reform was thought especially possible in O'Neill's present, hence the novel slips into the language of the poll tax giving 'rise to a sort of coalition among the lower classes' and the agitation of 'the bondmen, and, indeed, all of the labouring class.'[68] Stephen Basdeo points out that it is significant that such sentiments were written in the context of the Great Reform Act of 1832 (and the disturbances that led up to it) which extended the franchise to include men among the growing middle classes while effectively excluding the working class. He adds that we are not presented with a 'mindless rabble' but a 'highly organised band of disenfranchised people, drawn from the working and middle classes, whose leaders have clear political goals,' with the relatively pessimistic ending mirroring the events of 1832 in that the demands of the working classes were not fully realised.[69] While Basdeo is aware that the rebels are not presented as faultless (e.g., some drink too much, they can be overly violent), I would suggest that these assumed faults are an integral part of the novel's argument. *The Bondman* reflects certain middle-class concerns about the working class and their tactics just as Ball was increasingly disillusioned with rebels' behaviour (including Tyler's) as the uprising happens. It is also important that the disciplined and nonviolent Ball was presented as having developed remarkable literacy skills for one from a bondman background which sets him apart from the rebels as a leader, as it did Jack Straw who was presented as abusing this important position. The message of *The Bondman* is this: *do not get too enthusiastic, avoid violence, and beware of the wreckers!* In other words, if there were radical sympathies in *The Bondman*, they are more reformist-journalist than revolutionary-Spencean.

66 O'Neill, *Bondman*, 84, 130. Stephen's transformation of fortunes is, tellingly, compared with Job's.
67 Effectively recognised in, e.g., *Bell's New Weekly Messenger* (12 May 1833).
68 O'Neill, *Bondman*, 103, 105.
69 Basdeo, *Life and Legend of a Rebel Leader*, loc 2591.

This balancing act between radicalism, reformism, and political respectability meant that *The Bondman* was uncontroversial and received positive reviews, often with extracts. These reviews included the now expected acceptance that serfdom had to end, sympathy with the rebels' concerns (including an acceptance of Tyler as a reformer), praise for the characterisation of Ball and other leaders, and a general (although not always uncritical) aesthetic appreciation of the novel.[70] Indeed, the review in the *Spectator* (11 May 1833) rejected the revolutionary reading of 1381 (not least in light of the French Revolution) associated with the young Southey and praised *The Bondman* for getting its history right:

> The subject of Wat Tyler's rebellion has, as our readers know, been already adopted as the vehicle of revolutionary principles, by a poet who has long abjured the ungainful cause of the People: but he misrepresented the epoch, in attributing to the *dramatis personae* of his piece the wild theories of some of the heroes of the French Revolution. *The Bondman* is a far more faithful representation of the spirit of the period, and much more enlightened as to the causes as well as the effects of this great outbreak of the injured operatives of England.[71]

The reception of the revolt with its degree of mainstream acceptance had come a long way in the fifty years preceding the publication of *The Bondman*.

In the Advertisement prefacing *The Bondman*, we see the emphatic rejection of serfdom accepted in the reviews. The old feudal distinctions are dismissed as 'revolting' and the villein as a 'thing that was' with 'the monk' (Ball), credited as 'the first who whispered in the ear of an English serf, that slavery was not his birthright.'[72] Ball thus remains a stoic hero of the novel, and still somewhat ahead of his time.[73] But his characteristics also meant

---

70 *Caledonian Mercury* (11 May 1833); *Cheltenham Looker-On* (11 May 1833); *Court Journal* (11 May 1833); *London Literary Gazette* (11 May 1833); *Spectator* (11 May 1833); *Bell's New Weekly Messenger* (12 May 1833); *Brighton Gazette* (30 May 1833); *Chester Chronicle* (17 May 1833); *Belfast Commercial Chronicle* (20 May 1833); *Morning Advertiser* (25 June 1833).
71 *Spectator* (11 May 1833).
72 O'Neill, *Bondman*, 3.
73 The presentation of Ball is reflective of the emerging mid-nineteenth-century tensions surrounding the constructions of manliness and the (self-)disciplined monk or ascetic. See, e.g., Herbert Sussman, *Victorian Masculinities: Manhood and Masculine Poetics in Early Victorian Literature and Art* (Cambridge: Cambridge University Press, 1995); James Eli Adams, *Dandies and Desert Saints: Styles of Victorian Masculinity* (Ithaca: Cornell University Press, 1995).

196 *Spectres of John Ball*

that Ball functioned as a cipher for the nineteenth-century present and in this respect it is telling how even Ball is presented as struggling with the perceived excesses of the uprising. Certainly, he could take care of himself in a brawl. Fighting when under attack and for an honourable cause (to provide Stephen's mother, Edith, the Christian burial she should have had), Ball dealt with one axe-wielding assailant comfortably. He seems to have seized the assailant's arm with a 'giant grasp,' wrenched the axe from his hands, and 'hurled [him] violently to the earth.' However, this is a classic double-edged construction of lower-order masculinity also seen with Wat Turner/Tyler—masculinity that can heroically protect but also worryingly threaten. Now, a 'strange sensation thrilled through the heart of the excited monk—the impulse to shed blood!' Ball picked up the axe and 'waved it fiercely' around his head as 'nature and religion warred, for in instant, in his bosom' before 'religion' triumphed and the axe was hurled away.[74] When the story reaches 1381, Ball still struggles to contain himself, and the respectable limits of his religion, as his eyes were 'flashing with an enthusiasm perhaps too ardent to be compatible with sound reason.'[75] Ball may not have the ideal ending, and his urges perhaps contributed to his death, but it was certainly better than the bloody fate of those (lower-order) rebels who could not control their temper, violence, enthusiasm, and chaotic 'nature.' The inherited model of the dangerous mob had not entirely vanished.

Ball was presented in terms of recognisable bourgeois ideals of masculinity from O'Neill's industrialising nineteenth-century context.[76] He was honourable, studious, intelligent, hard-working, brave, loyal, decent, disciplined, morally upright, protective, unafraid to die for his beliefs, prepared to stand up to corrupt and bullying authorities, and a staunch defender of Stephen who himself fulfilled certain ideals of masculinity the closer he was to his quiet home life and away from the violence. As Ball grew into his role as the prophet of the uprising, he was calm and eschewed bloodshed. The novel format means that we get a detailed physical description of Ball, which was somewhat reflective of his characteristics. At the beginning of the story, we read that,

74 O'Neill, *Bondman*, 52.
75 O'Neill, *Bondman*, 103.
76 For overviews of constructions of masculinities, see, e.g., John Tosh, 'Masculinities in an Industrializing Society: Britain, 1800–1914,' *Journal of British Studies* 44 (2005): 330–42 (331–35); John Tosh, *Manliness and Masculinities in Nineteenth-Century Britain: Essays on Gender, Family and Empire* (Harlow: Pearson Education, 2005), 13–82; Dustin Friedman, 'Unsettling the Normative: Articulations of Masculinity,' *Literature Compass* 7 (2010): 1077–88.

> Father John was sitting with a book in his hand, and he still wore the white surplice...[he] was a man about thirty-five, of a tall muscular figure, with thick dark hair encircling his tonsure, a thin visage, and an aquiline nose. There was piety and meekness in the high pale forehead; and in the whole countenance, when the eyes were cast down, or when their light was partly shaded by the lids and the projecting brows: but when the lids were raised, and the large, deeply-set eyes flashed full upon the object of his scrutiny, there was a proud—a searching expression in the glance which had often made the obdurate sinner tremble, and which never failed to awe presumption and extort respect. Such was the man whom Calverley was about to address; and from whose quiet, unassuming demeanour at this moment, a stranger would have augured little opposition to any reasonable proposal that might be suggested: but Calverley well knew the character of the monk.[77]

The shape and size of Ball's nose would soon return in the history of his reception (see, e.g., Chapters 14, 15). During the 1381 uprising, we have a further description of Ball, aged a little more:

> as the baroness bent her eyes upon the father, she saw, in the deep marks on the forehead, and in the changed hue of his circling hair, that he had paid the price of strong excitement; but yet she almost marvelled if the placid countenance she now gazed upon could belong to one who had dared and done so much.[78]

However, the significant emphasis on conventional ideals of masculinity attributed to Ball in *The Bondman* served another function. They held back an alternative understanding of threatening working-class masculinity and masculinity from below associated with violence and ideological zeal—a tension which seems to have left physical marks on Ball's head and face and a tension which, presumably, contributed to his death just two years after his pardon.

Beyond the Great Reform Act

When the young Southey wrote *Wat Tyler* in 1794, such a sympathetic and sustained reading of a historically maligned figure like Ball was (potentially) an act of explicit provocation. By the time we get to *The Bondman* and its

---

77 O'Neill, *Bondman*, 12.
78 O'Neill, *Bondman*, 129.

reception in 1833, Ball and Tyler could be distanced from (for instance) the French Revolution and seen in fairly uncontroversial terms as a homegrown precursor to reform and rightly making demands against the puzzling and outdated practice of serfdom and slavery of the English. Though Ball and Tyler could now be appropriated in the less-than-radical circles, their provocative edge was hardly lost: in 1831, for instance, Southey's *Wat Tyler* could be used as a sympathetic point of comparison for the Captain Swing agitation.[79] Thus, the memory of 1381 reflected the ongoing debates over political representation, land reform, and popular discontent. While romantic depictions of Ball and the 1381 uprising would soon take off, O'Neill's novel would not replace Southey's drama as the more recent main point of reference in an industrialising England. Nevertheless, the tensions surrounding the memories of 1381 in *The Bondman*—not least over working-class agitation, drinking habits, and violence—were ones which would come to the fore in the next wave of nineteenth-century radicalism which emerged in the aftermath of the limitations of the Great Reform Act: Chartism.

---

79 Worrall, *Theatric Revolution*, 368.

12
'Peaceably If We May, Forcibly If We Must': Ball among the Chartists

By the 1830s, Ball, Wat Tyler, and the rebels of 1381 were regularly assumed to be on the side of the history of struggles from below. They (and especially Tyler) get passing mentions in the *Poor Man's Guardian*, including in the reports of meetings of the National Union of the Working Classes, with reference to abolitionism, a warning of the consequences of suppressing working-class press, a lesson from history as to what happens if arms are laid down before agreed demands are met, an advert for Southey's *Wat Tyler*, and criticism of Whig attacks on Irish liberty accompanied by a threat of Tyler-style justice for anyone sexually harassing women.[1] The emergence of Chartism at the end of the decade almost inevitably meant new emphases in the reception history of Ball. Chartism marked the largest working-class mass political movement to date and the famous six demands of the People's Charter of 1838 (universal male suffrage; end of property qualification for MPs; annual elections; voting by secret ballot; payment for MPs; equitable representation of electoral districts) moved the public debate beyond the Great Reform Act while dealing with acute concerns about middle-class betrayal. As with earlier radicalism, there were strong social and economic emphases in Chartism, including wage rises, workplace reform, worker representation, and opposition to the New Poor Law (1834). There was parliamentary success in the form of an elected Chartist MP (1847), and tensions in Chartism over issues about 'moral force' versus 'physical force.' Nevertheless, some of the most notable actions associated with the Chartist era—including mass petitions to Parliament (1839, 1842, 1848), widespread strike action (1842), arrests of leaders,

---

1   E.g., *Poor Man's Guardian* (27 August 1831); *Poor Man's Guardian* (4 August 1832); *Poor Man's Guardian* (9 March 1833); *Poor Man's Guardian* (17 August 1833); *Poor Man's Guardian* (5 April 1834).

mass public meetings, heavy-handed treatment from the authorities, riots, conspiracies, insurrectionary activity such as the Newport Rising (1839), and the deportation of prominent Chartists such as William Cuffay following the Kennington Common demonstration (1848)—meant that it was a movement and moment that particularly lent itself to the ongoing reception of 1381.[2]

1381 and the Middle Classes

Tyler is referenced in poetry, including as a ghost from the 1381 uprising commenting on the nineteenth-century present, as a part of an inspirational English radical tradition, and coupled with the then relatively new tradition casting Walworth as villain and Tyler as hero. He was portrayed as a working-class representation of Victorian morality and respectability as part of the Chartist drive for political representation.[3] In London, Chartist localities took names such as the 'Wat Tyler League' and the 'Wat Tyler Brigade,' Isaac Jefferson in Bradford went by the name 'Wat Tyler,' and Tyler was said to feature on banners in Sheffield.[4] R. B. Dobson's curious

2 Chartist historical comparisons were not restricted to 1381, of course, or other national parallels. Revolutionary France also continued to be an important point of reference. See, e.g., Gregory Vargo, *An Underground History of Early Victorian Fiction: Chartism, Radical Print Culture, and the Social Problem Novel* (Cambridge: Cambridge University Press, 2018), 210–11.
3 For a fuller discussion of these presentations of Tyler among Chartists, see Basdeo, *Life and Legend of a Rebel Leader*, loc 2159–2517. On Tyler as ghost, see, e.g., *The Odd Fellow* (18 April 1840); *The Odd Fellow* (21 August 1841); and Charles Cole's poem, 'The Spirit of Wat Tyler,' in *Northern Star* (16 September 1848).
4 David Goodway, *London Chartism 1838–1848* (Cambridge: Cambridge University Press, 1982), 13; John Belchem, '1848: Feargus O'Connor and the Collapse of the Mass Platform,' in James Epstein and Dorothy Thompson (eds), *The Chartist Experience: Studies in Working-Class Radicalism and Culture, 1830–1860* (London: Macmillan Press, 1982), 269–310 (290); Dobson, 'Remembering the Peasants' Revolt,' in Liddell and Wood (eds.), *Essex and the Great Revolt of 1381*, 14; Marc Brodie, 'Free Trade and Cheap Theatre: Sources of Politics for the Nineteenth-century London Poor,' *Social History* 28 (2003): 346–60 (348); Taylor, *London's Burning*, 33–34; Chris R. Vanden Bossche, *Reform Acts: Chartism, Social Agency and the Victorian Novel, 1832–1867* (Baltimore: Johns Hopkins University Press, 2014), 49. See, e.g., *The Times* (31 May 1848); *Northern Star* (16 September 1848); *The Times* (16 September

claim that phenomena such as the Wat Tyler Brigade constituted a 'brief appearance' and that the 'legacy of the Peasants' Revolt to the nineteenth-century working class was rarely relevant and often ambiguous' has, in the face of weighty evidence, been rightly challenged by Stephen Basdeo.[5] However, Dobson's point was not entirely unfounded; for all his popularity among Chartists, Tyler was not always accepted uncritically as his uncouth behaviour or tactical failings were also noted.[6]

Nevertheless, Tyler was typically presented as an important cipher for Chartist propaganda and causes. Tyler and the 1381 uprising were used as part of an attack on the middle classes and accusations of their betrayal of working-class causes. In one definition, the middle classes were not 'servile ministers, clerks, or small farmers' but the 'bullfrog farmers, whose wealth is produced by their men; I mean also brokers, shopkeepers, and I include parsons of every description.' Their 'religion is fanaticism, not pure undefiled religion...it was saying God, God, have we not glorified in thy name; not what we have done in thy name,' their morality 'consists in retail trickery, in lying and cheating,' and their 'system...pretty to the eye, but rotten at the core.' Their drunkenness is kept hidden while preaching temperance to the working classes just as they talk politics and make Chartist-style promises while denying the franchise to 'working men' and throwing around the allegation 'Chartist.' However, 'all struggles originated with the working classes' and examples included the blacksmith Tyler ('one of the noblest') who would have thrived among the working classes of the nineteenth century,[7] an argument found elsewhere in Chartism and well beyond.

Elsewhere, we get fuller historical treatment of the 1381 uprising as a polemic against middle-class betrayal in a popular Chartist article. 'Slavery had nominally been abolished' yet the 'slave-owners' had their own 'clause' for 'promoting their own interests, by ridding themselves of their aged and useless hands, whom they turned out to starve in the name of liberty'

1848); *Examiner* (30 September 1848); *Northern Star* (5 April 1851); Robert George Gammage, *History of the Chartist Movement, 1837–1854* (second edition; Newcastle-on-Tyne, Browne & Browne, 1894 [1854]), 333.

5   Dobson (ed.), *Peasants' Revolt of 1381*, 355; Basdeo, *Life and Legend of a Rebel Leader*, loc 2210. See now Stephen Basdeo, 'Rousing 'the Spirit of Wat Tyler': Chartist Newspaper Portrayals of the Rebel Leader,' in David Matthews and Mike Sanders (eds.), *Subaltern Medievalisms: Medievalism 'from below' in Nineteenth-Century Britain* (Boydell & Brewer, 2021), 110–24. Unfortunately, this essay came out too late to be incorporated properly into this book.

6   E.g., *Northern Liberator* (25 April 1840); *Chartist Circular* (26 September 1840).

7   *Northern Star* (2 April 1842).

and 'extracted the most degrading personal services from those they were pleased to term villains.' The insurgents were aiming for emancipation from 'personal slavery' for 'freedom of trade in market towns, and a fixed rent on lands' (by now widely accepted as reasonable rebel demands). So moderate were such demands that Richard granted them. The real villain of the uprising in this reading was Walworth—a 'London shopocrat,' a 'base and bloody-minded middle-man,' a 'low-minded scamp,' and a 'scheming profit-monger.' Richard had no problem with Tyler, but it was (echoing John Baxter—see Chapter 9) the 'lying middle-class histories' that were to blame for claims about Tyler's alleged insolence towards the king. Instead, Walworth's 'cunning and treachery inescapable from his class' was why Tyler was ultimately killed. Indeed, after Tyler's death the greatest problem for Richard was preventing the mass of 'the *bourgeoisie* or citizen-soldiers' from slaughtering the rebels—'another instance of middle-class sympathy.' Tyler's views were 'of the most exalted and beneficent description.' He held that there was a 'perfect equality among mankind' and sought the 'destruction of superstition and the sophistries by which they had been degraded,' which meant necessarily attacking priests and lawyers as 'the two most formidable instruments in the hands of the oppressor.' In a critical exegesis of Hume's account, the article stresses that rather than the king, it was the 'nation'—that is, 'the mere middle-class'—that was not ready for such moderate demands, and the charters were revoked by 'a board of legal assassins, in the garb of judges, lawyers, priests, and hangmen.'[8]

While Tyler was the more common reference point in Chartism and their retellings of 1381, Ball too turns up. The aftermath of the armed and bloody Newport Uprising (4 November 1839) involved difficulties and disputes over disturbances, potential uprisings, tactical use of violence, trials of Chartist prisoners, conspiracies, and concerns for public credibility.[9] Against this backdrop, and general Chartist debates about 'moral force' and 'physical force,' an article on 'The Progress of Liberty in England' was published in the *Northern Liberator* (April 1840) which gave a critical appraisal of the violence of the 1381 uprising when 'the people,' after putting up with 'every indignity and outrage that cruel tyranny could devise,' finally 'asserted their own rights.' Employing quasi-eschatological language,

8   *Chartist Circular* (16 January 1841).
9   For summary and details, see, e.g., Dorothy Thompson, *The Chartists: Popular Politics in the Industrial Revolution* (New York: Pantheon Books, 1984), 77–87; David V. J. Jones, *The Last Rising: The Newport Chartist Insurrection of 1839* (Cardiff: University of Wales Press, 1999); Malcolm Chase, *Chartism: A New History* (Manchester: Manchester University Press, 2007), 126–40.

the article argues that when the 'day of retribution arrived,' the 'oppressed sometimes retaliated upon the oppressors' but added that this 'even confounded the innocent with the guilty.' There were, therefore, moral lessons to be learned from this 'bad example'—in this case, how instigating retaliatory and excessive violence might turn supporters away and how Christians should 'return good for evil.' Tyler's death was more a tactical error as it was 'probably provoked by his own insolence' and so left the people leaderless 'at a most critical moment' which led them to snatch defeat from the jaws of victory by turning to the hypocritical king. At this point, it was noted in passing that Ball was killed and that he was to be compared (positively) with the popular firebrand preacher associated with Chartism and the fierce denouncer of factory conditions and the New Poor Law (and hardly alien to ideas of violence himself): Joseph Rayner Stephens ('Their preacher, John Ball, the Stephens of his day'). The account moves on to explain how people were then pacified under successive kings until the emergence of Cade and his followers who were given a critical reception in the article. Cade tried 'wholesome restraint,' but the mob burst through with 'violence and plunder' which alarmed the peaceable and sympathetic citizens and turned them against Cade's cause and defeated the cause of liberties for the people.[10]

Southey's Chartist Ball

Ball could be invoked to support (a degree of) nonviolence. In a letter to the *Northern Star* (28 February 1846), Robert Johnstone—a shoemaker from North Yorkshire—wrote in support of the 'National Anti-Militia Society' which he had discovered in a previous edition.[11] The earlier edition reported that, in response to the rumours of war and a Militia Bill, the (here called) 'National Anti-Militia Association' was 'established for the protection of those who have a conscientious objection to the service, and who will not pay others to do that for them which they object to themselves'

---

10 *Northern Liberator* (25 April 1840). On Stephens, see, e.g., Michael S. Edwards, *Purge This Realm: A Life of Joseph Rayner Stephens* (London: Epworth Press, 1994). On Joseph Capper, Primitive Methodism and memories of Ball, in the Potteries, see Charles Shaw, *When I Was a Child* (Firle: Caliban Books, 1977 [1903]), 147–48.
11 *Northern Star* (28 February 1846); *Northern Star* (7 February 1846).

under the title (and a Chartist slogan), 'No Vote! No Musket!'[12] Johnstone's opposition to military service was because he saw no reason to obey their rules and personnel given that he had no voice in their creation or appointment. Additionally, he wrote that he was never fond of fighting nor had the relevant experience and his increasing age was not conducive to learning 'the art and mystery of becoming a human butcher.' And, besides, he had a family, and they took up his time and attention. Johnstone had a more obvious political point: he felt he had no right to take the life of another person 'by any means that a government may think proper to put into my power, under the pretence of serving the Queen and country' and, in line with the earlier report of the association read by Johnstone, he objected to hiring another person to do such work. And Ball (or Southey's Ball) provided an authority for such an argument. The epigraph is a quotation from Ball during his trial in Southey's *Wat Tyler* and the impact of the crown, Parliament, and wars with France on the life of peasants and whether, in their present form, they provide any benefit:

> The people fight and suffer:—think ye, Sirs,
> If neither country had been cursed with chief,
> The peasants would have quarrelled?

We might add that Johnstone had not turned into an extreme pacifist and, like the story of Tyler bashing out the tax-gatherer's brains (though not mentioned in Johnstone's letter, it was still in Southey's account), he would take the life of anyone that threatened his family, even if it were against the law of the land.[13]

Southey was a detailed enough source for various emphases in the ongoing reception of Ball. A *Northern Star* article charged 'Protestant divines and Protestant laymen' with hypocrisy ('their pretended love for religious liberty') for their passivity while 'honest men' were incarcerated for blasphemy—this was in the spirit of the much-maligned Catholic Inquisition, no less. Indeed, the article further criticised the priesthood of all denominations for continuing to keep Europe in the dark on religion and politics and for being the historic tool of the aristocracy (adding some choice words against Burke). The judge's sentence, it was argued, recalled that of Tresilian on Ball according to Southey, picking up on

---

12 *Northern Star* (7 February 1846). Cf. Mark Hovell, *The Chartist Movement* (third edition; Manchester: Manchester University Press, [1918, 1925] 1966), 276.
13 *Northern Star* (28 February 1846).

the martyrological reception history (and Chartist martyrology) with an anticlerical bent:

> Whereas you are accused before us,
> Of stirring up the people to rebellion,
> *And preaching to them strange and dangerous doctrines;*
> And whereas your behaviour to the Court
> *Has been most insolent and contumacious...*
> I condemn you
> To death; you shall be hanged by the neck,
> But not till you are dead—your bowels opened—
> Your heart torn out, and burnt before your face—
> Your traitorous head be severed from your body—
> Your body quartered, and exposed upon
> The city gates—a terrible example!
> *And the Lord God have mercy on your soul.*

This sentiment was given an eschatological twist by way of the Chartist favourite: Shelley's 'Queen Mab'. The article looked to a time (directly quoting Shelley) when 'A brighter morn awaits the human day!' The 'time is coming' (cf. John 4.23; 5.25; 8.31–32; Knighton, *Chron.* 222–224; Walsingham, *Chronica maiora* 546–547) 'when the human race will look back with horror upon the madness, delusion, and slavery of past and present times.' This will be a time 'when tyrants and priests will be known no more' and (again directly quoting Shelley) when 'Falsehood's trade,/Shall be as hateful and unprofitable,/As that of truth is now!'[14] This combination of political martyrdom and eschatological change cast in the language of morning light would be most famously developed at length in William Morris's treatment of Ball (see Chapter 15).

Beyond Southey

Southey's *Wat Tyler* was, therefore, assumed as a standard resource for different Chartist readings of Ball and Tyler, which was hardly surprising given how widely sold and advertised it was in radical and then Chartist

---

14 *Northern Star* (2 December 1843). On the 'immortal Wat Tyler' (e.g., *Northern Star* [27 November 1841]) and martyrdom or suffering for the cause in Chartist memory, see, e.g., *Northern Star* (26 February 1848); *Northern Star* (7 October 1848); *Northern Star* (4 August 1849); Thompson, *Chartists*, 86–87.

circles.[15] Illustrations of Tyler and the tax collector, and Tyler meeting the king, were published on the front page of *Cleave's Penny Gazette* under the title 'SCENES FROM SOUTHEY'S "WAT TYLER"' (John Cleave himself published a pirated version of *Wat Tyler*).[16] The surplus proceeds from a performance of *Wat Tyler* at Darlington Theatre were to be donated for 'the support of Durham political prisoners,'[17] while at Clitheroe, *Wat Tyler* was performed twice to a full house by a theatrical group who were said to be 'all Chartists of the right stamp.'[18] Southey's play was an important part of Chartist social events. At Trowbridge, a recitation from *Wat Tyler* was given at a 'tea party,'[19] while in Coventry at Easter, there were performances from *Wat Tyler* (among other works) in the evening's frivolities at a 'tea and dancing party' held at St George's Inn.[20] Not to be outdone, in London a 'GRAND BALL AND CONCERT' was advertised featuring selected passages from *Wat Tyler* among its evening's entertainment.[21] With Ball's trial, discussions of liberty, the struggles of working people, and the promise of the fulfilment of Ball's hopes for the future, it is not difficult to see why Southey's drama would have been popular among Chartists. Benjamin Brierley's memoirs provide further insight from other Easter tea-party performances, this time at Failsworth:

> From that time we had a tea party and a dramatic performance every Easter Monday for years. Southey's 'Wat Tyler' was our first ambitious effort. After that 'William Tell.' Only fancy two armies meeting, fighting, and subverting a government, on three or four planks; and you will think less of the glories of the battlefield, and the dignities of rulers.[22]

However, Southey was not the only immediate source for learning about 1381. The 'Labour Mechanic' Charles Cole produced poems about Tyler.[23] There were different sources available for Ball too. The *Northern*

15 Taylor, *London's Burning*, 28–29; Gregory Vargo (ed.), *Chartist Drama* (Manchester: Manchester University Press, 2020).
16 *Cleave's Penny Gazette of Variety and Amusement* (10 March 1838).
17 *Northern Star* (31 October 1840).
18 *Northern Star* (19 November 1842).
19 *Northern Star* (16 October 1841).
20 *Northern Star* (9 April 1842).
21 *Northern Star* (29 May 1841).
22 Benjamin Brierley, *Home Memories and Recollections of a Life* (Manchester: Abel Heywood & Son, 1886), 41.
23 E.g., 'Sonnets after Reading a Part of History Relating to Wat Tyler,' in *Cleave's Penny Gazette of Variety and Amusement* (3 July 1841); 'The Spirit of Wat Tyler,' in *Northern Star* (16 September 1848).

Star reported that a speech by Ball was read out at a weekly Chartist meeting in Birmingham (1942) which was taken from the play *Wat Tyler*, written by the Chartist with radical Christian sympathies, John Watkins.[24] Unfortunately, the play is not extant, but we learn a little more about it from a report in the *Yorkshire Gazette*. The play in three acts (with the subtitle, *Or the Poll Tax Rebellion*) was a 'medley of quotations from innumerable works' and performed at Watkins's hometown of Whitby (which Watkins had polemically criticised for its Toryism) on 8 March 1839, with the additional comment that 'a more complete burlesque we never before witnessed.'[25] *The Odd Fellow* described it as a 'great success.'[26]

Egan's Ball

An important resource during the Chartist years came from the novelist Pierce James Egan the Younger (1814–1880), whose cheap, popular, mass-produced penny bloods reveal some radical sentiments, and notably so in his portrayal of the fourteenth century.[27] Working in, and a pioneer of, the Robin Hood literary tradition, Egan used Medieval England to look at issues such as class relations and constitutionalism. Originally in serial form, Egan's *Wat Tyler; Or, The Rebellion of 1381* was published in 1841 with several reprints over the next decade, itself based on or making reference to standard sources such as Froissart, Knighton, Stow, Charles Allen, and Southey. *Wat Tyler* provides an extensive (often violent, sometimes romantic) backstory of a young, strapping, and chivalrous Tyler who shares

---

24 *Northern Star* (10 December 1842).
25 *Yorkshire Gazette* (16 March 1839). A prologue to Watkins's play was written by Ebenezer Elliott in *The Poetical Works of Ebenezer Elliott, the Corn-Law Rhymer* (London, 1840), 163. Cf. *Bath Chronicle* (6 February 1873). On the details of Watkins, see, e.g., Chase, *Chartism*, 117–25. See also the notes to the version of Southey's *Wat Tyler* presented in Vargo (ed.), *Chartist Drama*.
26 *The Odd Fellow* (30 March 1839).
27 J. W. Ebsworth, revised by Megan A. Stephan, 'Pierce James Egan (1814–1880),' *ODNB* (23 September 2004); Anna Vaninskaya, 'Dreams of John Ball: Reading the Peasants' Revolt in the Nineteenth Century,' *Nineteenth-Century Contexts* 31 (2009): 45–57 (48–49); Taylor, *London's Burning*, 37–39; Stephen Basdeo, 'Radical Medievalism: Pierce Egan the Younger's *Robin Hood*, *Wat Tyler*, and *Adam Bell*,' in Stephen Basdeo and Lauren Padgett (eds.), *Leeds Working Papers in Victorian Studies Vol. 15: Imagining the Victorians* (Leeds: Leeds Centre for Victorian Studies, 2016), 48–64.

many of the masculine traits attributed to him and Ball by Mrs O'Neill (see Chapter 11). We also discover the story of his blossoming and (naturally) complicated romance with Violet Evesham in the face of unscrupulous lords and their brigands, and other heroic deeds connected with the Hundred Years' War. *Wat Tyler* (eventually) ends with a familiar retelling of the story of the 1381 uprising.

Chris Vanden Bossche has provided a detailed analysis of why Egan's novel, despite never explicitly mentioning the Chartists, 'deserves a place in the canon of Chartist fiction.'[28] For a start, Tyler and his followers want 'charters' and Tyler makes six demands echoing the six points of the People's Charter. There are similar failures of petitions, similarities with Chartist mass demonstrations, the language of 'enfranchisement,' and claims of the people deserving legislative representation. The extended backstory also allowed Egan to develop Walter Scott's *Ivanhoe* (1820) and the myth of the Norman Yoke with its conflict between Normans and Saxons. But, Vanden Bossche points out, there is not a straightforward opposition between Norman oppressor and Saxon oppressed in Egan's novel. Saxons work with chivalrous Normans and overcome both ethnic difference and the clique of the more lustful and corrupt Norman aristocrats in order to establish the national constitution of fully enfranchised citizens in the mid-fourteenth century. This constitution promotes the 'compassionate ideal' with social mobility and with honour based on chivalric deeds and behaviour rather than on birth. However, this is followed by a period run by a corrupt new aristocracy—not just a clique within the aristocracy—who instead adhere to a class-based version of the Norman Yoke as serfdom takes hold of 'the people' and perverts Merry England. Egan could then present Tyler in 1381 like the Chartists, namely leading a moral revolution with the potential for physical force in an attempt to restore the constitution—as indeed the constitution itself permitted. Tyler wants chivalric restraint in the use of physical violence and fiercely opposes (often in vain) excess, debauchery, and plunder among rebels. This is a crucial part of the political argument underpinning *Wat Tyler* which has one eye on its Chartist present: if the rebels had acted more maturely and more like the example of Tyler, then they might even have succeeded. Crucially, Tyler survives a little longer than the standard histories and points towards a future when the people would be able to enact change.[29]

We can build on Vanden Bossche's analysis with reference to Ball who is not a major character in *Wat Tyler*, though is a prominent leader in the

---

28 Vanden Bossche, *Reform Acts*, 38.
29 Vanden Bossche, *Reform Acts*, 38–49.

section retelling the uprising of 1381. Ball emerges in Egan's narrative at the time of Richard's accession, a time when 'the people...had been ground almost to powder' and are in a 'horrible state of vassalage' but are now beginning to resist unfair taxation, realising that 'they were born to be something else than slaves.'[30] Ball is set against a context where those who reveal the state of submission are denounced as 'scandalous and wicked traytours' and those who oppose serfdom are treated with scornful laughter.[31] The presentation of Ball's overall story is built on a fairly typical presentation of the revolt: the problems of taxation alongside Tyler's daughter (here named 'Rubacelle' after a Flemish maiden), the escape from the Maidstone prison, Ball as one of the leaders of the revolt who (along with Jack Straw) supports Tyler, the march on London, Tyler's (admittedly extended) death, and so on. There are details of Ball arriving from Highbury with Jack Straw before they gallop off to the Tower and of Ball's death, which is due to a betrayal by some of his followers through a 'considerable bribe, and a promise of a free pardon.' Ball is taken to prison, faces a kangaroo court, and is beheaded, with his head placed alongside Jack Straw's and Tyler's on London Bridge.[32]

Ball is presented extremely positively. He is loyal, disciplined, mild, and goodly. His background is that of the 'poor'—'poor as the humblest serf in the kingdom' who dedicates all this time to the poor and is in turn popular among them. His background is also that of a 'mendicant friar,' a 'priest...an enthusiast, who followed religion for religion's sake,' who 'dedicated himself to his fellow-beings, in the service of God' and, in a direct reversal of the historical negative labelling, he is a 'good priest.'[33] Echoing Mrs O'Neill's more substantial treatment (albeit with a more Southey-style radical spin), Ball belongs to and led those who could 'restrain the people in any excess which, in the first excitement of success, they might be disposed to commit,' as happened in the Tower.[34] In his Blackheath speech, Ball further explains that he was more a political thinker than a military strategist: 'I leave to our good leader, Wat Tyler, to explain to you how to obtain your freedom; I but seek to show you the right you have not to submit to oppression and injustice from any body of men.'[35] Ball's discipline even extends to the peo-

---

30 Pierce Egan the Younger, *Wat Tyler; Or, The Rebellion of 1381* (London, 1847 [1841]), 794.
31 Egan, *Wat Tyler*, 795.
32 Egan, *Wat Tyler*, 867.
33 Egan, *Wat Tyler*, 794–95, 819, 820.
34 Egan, *Wat Tyler*, 814, 854.
35 Egan, *Wat Tyler*, 838.

ple wanting to extract bloody revenge for Tyler's death as Ball prevents it on Tyler's orders, which saved the king's life.

As with Tyler, and as with what was becoming a developing theme in the reception of Ball, Egan presented Ball as a figure ahead of his time and whose message and dedication was now suited to the nineteenth-century present. This is made clear in an extended aside on political agitation of which Ball is an exemplar:

> There are always men whose minds are in advance of the times—men who in general are bold and fearless advocates for truth and justice—men who know the relative positions of the rich and poor in the eye of justice, and who fear not to publish it—men who side with the oppressed against the oppressor, the crushed against those who crush, the despised against the despiser—men who think the laborer worthy of his hire, and when they see every effort to take from him his labor without giving him an equivalent, step forth, and with a voice that will be heard, advocate his cause, denounce the injustice, and demand the restitution of his rights.[36]

Indeed, there are further hints of Ball's historical advancement to the extent that it would have been difficult not to recognise his contemporary relevance: he is the type of 'radical' that 'astounded "the powers that were"—an aristocracy so very high in toryism, they could believe no improvement in the people's condition less than a crime, for which there was no punishment bad enough.'[37] Tellingly, the loathsome and exploitative Sudbury imprisons Ball over 'freedom of speech,' a familiar radical fate by the mid-nineteenth century.[38] There is even clearer association with Chartist history of the time. Ball pushes the people to move the king through 'petitions and prayers' and the people listen and did indeed 'send petition after petition' but in vain as 'their appeals and prayers went unheeded.' In contextualising Ball's ideas, Chartist-compatible language of slavery to describe the plight of the workers is emphasised. The nobility 'believed the poor people were born to slave and toil' and they were 'degraded slaves' deserving of 'emancipation from slavery.'[39] Ball's Adam and Eve speech at Blackheath could easily have been a description of a Chartist rally or a mass meeting addressed by a popular nineteenth-century orator, with a Chartist-style take on the need for the threat of mass power to make the ruling class change their ways. It is given to a 'mighty multitude, upon a

---

36 Egan, *Wat Tyler*, 795.
37 Egan, *Wat Tyler*, 794–995.
38 Egan, *Wat Tyler*, 831.
39 Egan, *Wat Tyler*, 795.

platform' alongside the other leaders as he waved his hand to call the adoring crowd to silence. Ball makes demands for 'our rights,' which in this case are very much focused on freedom framed in terms of material needs and material exploitation of many by the few.[40]

The presentation of, and the language in, Ball's extended Adam and Eve speech is strikingly reminiscent of that Chartist parallel to Ball, Joseph Rayner Stephens. Three years prior to the publication of *Wat Tyler*, it was famously reported that,

> The Rev. J. R. Stephens…was received with enthusiastic cheering, which was prolonged for a considerable time…he asked what it was that made this mighty movement of the masses the people of England…[what] brought her sons together in such a mighty assembly?…They were to tell their foes through the land that they were mighty, because they knew their rights, and had the power as well to obtain them…[He spoke of] the principle which acknowledged the right of every man that breathed God's free air and trod God's free earth, to have his home and his hearth, and his wife and his children, as securely guaranteed to him as if any other man whom the Aristocracy had created. This question of Universal Suffrage is a knife and fork question…a bread and cheese question…if any man ask him what he meant by Universal Suffrage, he would answer, that every working man in the land had a right to have a good coat to his back, a comfortable abode in which to shelter himself and his family, a good dinner upon his table, and no more work than was necessary for keeping him in health, and as much wages for that work as would keep him in plenty, and afford him the enjoyment of all the blessings of life which a reasonable man could desire.[41]

Egan's Ball likewise talks of questions of wives and children and complains about how the crowd lack 'pleasant homes or happy families' and lack a 'just share of the proceeds' of their 'toil.' Their labour props up the 'riotous luxury,' the 'extravagance and debauchery' of the few at the expense of the 'starvation of thousands.' It is neither God's will nor a 'law of nature' that the people should have nothing to call their own or that the few have a 'right…to bend a mass of fellow beings to their absolute will' because they were born in a palace. Indeed, there is a further 'right,' the 'right….to enjoy those immunities and privileges which your contributions to the state make your due.' The few are not descended from angels but from Adam and Eve, just like everyone else, and their ancestors were not always noble—a sentiment adorned with the famous Adam and Eve couplet which points to

40 Egan, *Wat Tyler*, 835–36.
41 *Northern Star* (29 September 1838).

a time when all were equal, and all worked to enjoy 'the fruits of his labour.' All people are wounded when hit, shiver when cold, pant when hot, bleed when stabbed, weep if sorrowful, laugh if glad, feel refreshed after sleep, and grow older and die. The ruling few are not, therefore, 'naturally of a higher race,' and God judges by good or evil actions. Instead, the reason why one person might be better than another is because of their upright behaviour: the labouring Cain was better than his labouring brother Abel because he was 'better inclined.'[42]

The tensions in Chartist and radical understandings of republicanism and monarchy and the tensions in pro- and anti-royalism in the long history of the reception of Ball were brought together in Egan's presentation of the Blackheath speech. In the story, it is part of the call for a re-creation of a shared national identity which ought to be indifferent to ethnic differences (at least between Saxon and Norman) and understood in terms of political rights and economic fairness. The critique of the fine living of the few at the expense of the many should even extend to the king (who was strongly criticised in *Wat Tyler*), and is close to the point of undermining the institution of the monarchy itself which was not always the case in Chartism or in other positive receptions of Ball. The people, Ball points out, produce the wealth that props up the nobles *and* the king. This Ball goes a step further in explaining the origins of monarchy: in the earliest time the strongest man did as he pleased, did not work, took from what weaker ones had gathered, and dealt with any discontent by force. When people worked together collectively to overthrow the strong man, another would rise and so the solution to this and other disputes was to have 'one man' to judge, who, upon death, would pass on the duty to the oldest person. Over time, this transformed into passing on the duty not to the 'oldest and wisest' but to the son, irrespective of whether he inherited wisdom 'or was a natural idiot.' The chief's power extended, and he developed a wider circle of influence with some sharing of the wealth 'which was not his, but the people's to share' along with 'power over the people which was not his to bestow.' By this time, the monarch, surrounded by 'parasites and sycophants,' had made the mistake of believing that such a position was a divine right over the support of the people. It may be that, for all the strong language, Egan's Ball attacks the form of monarchy associated with the myth of the Norman Yoke rather than rulership in its ideal form because the monarch is ultimately a servant and the king would 'be taught differently' and 'shown that he is the people's servant, not their master, to oppress and grind them to powder.' Ball even accepts that the despised advisors could

---

42 Egan, *Wat Tyler*, 836–38.

be shown the error of their ways and 'that it is better to guide than drive; that gentleness would have succeeded, where harshness and injustice have compelled rebellion.' But the king had resorted back to the 'strong man of old' while the people finally 'united to throw off your chains' and make the few tremble and wish that they had treated the people better.[43]

Cooper, Cuffay, and National Identity

There were also other summaries of English history that continued among Chartists which, as with Egan's *Wat Tyler*, formed the basis of a national identity grounded not in ethnic homogeneity but a shared political one. Ball, for instance, turned up at meetings in the historical lectures of Thomas Cooper (1805–1892), the Leicester Chartist, shoemaker, and autodidact, who also had a career as (among other things) a Methodist preacher, an educationalist, a poet, a novelist, a speaker, and a journalist.[44] In London (at the George and Dragon on Blackheath Hill, no less), his lecture subject was announced as 'the true character of the insurrection under Wat Tyler, in the reign of Richard the Second.' Cooper talked about the context of England preceding the revolt, the 'spirit kindled by Wickliffe,' European uprisings, the 'grievous and unjust' poll tax, the uprisings in Suffolk (under Lister) and Essex (under Jack Straw), the uprising in Kent under Tyler and the 'Wickliffe or Lollard preacher' Ball, the events in London, and—picking up on what was now an established tradition in the reversal from below of the 1381 narrative—the 'treacherous massacre' of Tyler following the king and his advisers when they broke their promises. What Cooper's lecture further did was to face the issue of the uprising as an ostensible failure by arguing for its longer-term success: it was instead shown 'to have had the effect of commencing the abolition of villainage' despite the opposition of

43 Egan, *Wat Tyler*, 837–38.
44 For Cooper's details, see, e.g., Stephen Roberts, 'Thomas Cooper in Leicester, 1840–1843', *Transactions of the Leicestershire Archaeological and Historical Society* 61 (1987): 62–76; Stephen Roberts, 'The Later Radical Career of Thomas Cooper c.1845–1855', *Transactions of the Leicestershire Archaeological and Historical Society* 64 (1990): 62–72; Stephen Roberts, *The Chartist Prisoners: The Radical Lives of Thomas Cooper (1805–1892) and Arthur O'Neill (1819–1896)* (Oxford: Peter Lang, 2008); Stephen Roberts, 'Cooper, Thomas (1805–1892)', *ODNB* (8 January 2009); Gregory Vargo, 'A Life in Fragments: Thomas Cooper's Chartist *Bildungsroman*', *Victorian Literature and Culture* 39 (2011): 167–81.

king and Parliament. The lecture was then wrapped up (and presumably recontextualised, if even implicitly) with reference to a 'fervid zeal among working men, and to a more hearty and persevering union for the People's Charter.'[45]

In some ways, what was reported of Cooper's lectures involved familiar topics and emphases in the history of the reception of Ball. But one familiar topic was given a distinctive interpretation that would continue steadily and much more explicitly in the nineteenth and twentieth centuries. The *Northern Star* (20 September 1845) reported of a talk in London where Cooper placed Ball and 1381 firmly in the tradition of the Norman Yoke and loss of Saxon liberties, freedoms, constitution, and land, which, as we have seen, still had currency in the Chartist movement and wider mid-nineteenth-century culture, even if such ideas were critically received and there were competing Chartist understandings.[46] Cooper's two-and-a-half-hour lecture discussed acts of William 'the Bastard' and his accompanying 'robbers,' while remembering the Saxon 'rebels.' Much of English

---

45 *Northern Star* (4 October 1845). Cf., e.g., the reference to 'Old Tyler's spirit,' in Cooper's *The Purgatory of Suicides: A Prison-rhyme in Ten Books* 5.12 (London, 1847), and Southey's Wat Tyler in Thomas Cooper, *Two Orations Against Taking Away Human Life Under Any Circumstances; and in Explanation and Defence of the Misrepresented Doctrine of Non-Resistance* (London, 1846), 21.

46 See, e.g., John Belchem, 'Republicanism, Popular Constitutionalism and the Radical Platform in Early Nineteenth-Century England,' *Social History* 6 (1981): 1–32; James Epstein, *Radical Expression: Political Language, Ritual, and Symbol in England, 1790–1850* (Oxford: Oxford University Press, 1994), 1–32; Billie Melman, 'Claiming the Nation's Past: The Invention of an Anglo-Saxon Tradition,' *Journal of Contemporary History* 26 (1991): 575–95; Margot C. Finn, *After Chartism: Class and Nation in English Radical Politics, 1848–1874* (Cambridge: Cambridge University Press, 1993), 84, 191; Malcolm Chase, 'Chartism and the Land: "The Mighty People's Question",' in Matthew Cragoe and Paul Readman (ed.), *The Land Question in Britain, 1750–1950* (New York: Palgrave Macmillan, 2010), 57–73; Eileen Yeo, 'Some Practices and Problems of Chartist Democracy,' in Epstein and Thompson (eds), *Chartist Experience*, 345–80; Josh Gibson, 'The Chartists and the Constitution: Revisiting British Popular Constitutionalism,' *Journal of British Studies* 56 (2017): 70–90; Josh Gibson, 'Natural Right and the Intellectual Context of Early Chartist Thought,' *History Workshop Journal* 84 (2017): 194–213; Matthew Roberts, *Chartism, Commemoration and the Cult of the Radical Hero* (New York: Routledge, 2020), xviii, 40, chapter 4. Christopher Hill's influential essay, 'The Norman Yoke,' in Saville (ed.), *Democracy and the Labour Movement*, 11–66, saw the Norman Yoke as a myth in decline with the advent of socialism but noted its use for Chartists.

history was hastily recounted in order to devote more time to Thomas Becket's struggle with Henry II and Magna Carta building up to 'a lengthened and very striking relation of the insurrection of Wat Tyler, John Ball, Jack Straw, Lister of Norfolk, and their peasant compeers,' before a hasty overview of Reformation England.[47]

While the content of Cooper's talk may be familiar enough by now, the context points to something perhaps less so. This meeting was chaired by another leading Chartist, William Cuffay (c. 1788–1870). Cuffay's grandfather was a slave and his father (Chatham) was born on St Kitts into slavery while among what is known about his mother (Juliana) is that she was said to have been pregnant on the ship to Britain, though William seems to have been born in Chatham. Cuffay was a tailor by trade and would become a dedicated Chartist activist, trade unionist, and musician before being deported to Van Diemen's Land/Tasmania after involvement in the 1848 conspiracy. He was the most prominent black Chartist (others included David Duffy and Benjamin Prophett) and received racial slurs in the press and satirical magazines.[48] That he was involved prominently in a session centred on the English tradition hints at a reception history of Ball that Egan had stressed and which would later become popular in discussion of racial politics: the downplaying of familial lineage and racial or ethnic emphases—or, alternatively, a stress on the inclusion of different ethnicities—and the foregrounding political unity, behaviour, and universalising understandings of rights in the construction of radical English identity and history.

Furthermore, Cuffay's intellectual prowess, demeanour, and command of language were what marked him out in relation to both (and even rising above) race and Englishness according to Thomas Martin Wheeler's *Sunshine and Shadow*, serialised (1849–1850) in the *Northern Star*. This includes reference to this 'diminutive Son of Africa's despised and injured race…son of a West Indian and grandson of an African slave, he spoke the English tongue pure and grammatical, and with a degree of ease and facility which would shame many who boast of the purity of their Saxon or Norman descent.' It was Cuffay who 'in the hour of danger no man could be more depended on.' Cuffay is presented as an example of a wider internationalist

---

47 *Northern Star* (20 September 1845).
48 For biographical details on Cuffay, see, e.g., Norbert J. Gossman, 'William Cuffay: London's Black Chartist,' *Phylon* (1983): 56–65; Peter Fryer, *Staying Power: The History of Black People in Britain* (London: Pluto Press, 1984), 237–46; Chase, *Chartism*, 303–11; Martin Hoyles, *William Cuffay: The Life and Times of a Chartist Leader* (Hertford: Hansib, 2013).

phenomenon that transcended race understood in strict biological terms. He was created from a 'race of free men and free institutions' created by a 'magical breath' and whose tragic fate would now help 'rouse the world.'[49]

We should not, of course, romanticise antiracism in nineteenth-century English radicalism. Antisemitism was present and antisemitic slurs can be found among Chartists, including negative stereotypes about Jews as financiers and moneylenders. This antisemitism was, as Malcolm Chase argued, 'casual and economic rather than racialist or systemic' and was curbed, to some degree, by the 'broadly educative function of Chartism and the widened intellectual horizons of its members.'[50] Chase added that with the 'important exception' of antisemitism, Chartism 'was rarely overtly racist.' There were awkward and even contradictory comparisons made between chattel slavery and wage slavery among Chartists, but the Chartist press and platform was consistent in its opposition to chattel slavery. It was a movement that allied with abolitionists, and prominent members shared platforms with figures such as Frederick Douglass on his visit to Britain in 1846.[51]

That the tradition of the Norman Yoke in English radicalism was being framed predominantly in terms of challenges to the political and economic settlement—rather than (say) the creation of a biologically racialised Victorian English identity—meant that a prominent figure like Cuffay was simply assumed (in the *Northern Star* report at least) to be part of it.[52] Indeed, Norbert Gossman classified Cuffay himself as 'more a backward-looking Cobbett kind of democrat who talked of restoring Anglo Saxon liberties.'[53] There is also a clear parallel with the strong (and also

49 *Northern Star* (6 October 1849). For further discussion, see Vargo, *Underground History*, 203–4.
50 Chase, *Chartism*, 288.
51 Chase, *Chartism*, 307–8. See also, e.g., Thompson, *Chartists*, 189–91; Richard Bradbury, 'Frederick Douglass and the Chartists,' in Alan Rice and Martin Crawford (eds.), *Liberating Sojourn: Frederick Douglass and Transnational Reform* (Athens, GA: University of Georgia Press, 1999), 169–86; Kelly J. Mays, 'Slaves in Heaven, Laborers in Hell: Chartist Poets' Ambivalent Identification with the (Black) Slave,' *Victorian Poetry* 39 (2001): 137–63; Mike Sanders, *The Poetry of Chartism: Aesthetics, Politics, History* (Cambridge: Cambridge University Press, 2009), 93–94; Richard Huzzey, *Freedom Burning: Anti-Slavery and Empire in Victorian Britain* (Ithaca: Cornell University Press, 2012), 89–90; Hoyles, *William Cuffay*, 97–98; Tom Scriven, 'William Cuffay: The Chartists' Black Leader,' *Tribune* (4 July 2020).
52 Cf. *Northern Star* (19 June 1847); *Northern Star* (7 October 1848).
53 Gossman, 'William Cuffay,' 64.

demonised) Irish participation in radical politics in late eighteenth- and nineteenth-century England. Irish Chartists could embrace the language of William as the bastard who introduced feudalism while Alfred the Great, as Chase further noted, was 'potentially a figure in admiration of whom both English and Irish, and Catholic and Protestant, could combine. Blessed with a clean pair of hands as far as Ireland was concerned, he stood for a different concept of English authority, untainted by landlordism.'[54] Certainly, the idea of a racially or ethnically inclusive English radical tradition associated with 1381 and Ball would be taken up much more explicitly in the twentieth century. But it was hardly without precedent.

---

54 Chase, 'Chartism and the Land', in Cragoe and Readman (ed.), *Land Question in Britain*, 60.

13
Haranguing after Chartism: The Making of the Victorian Ball

By the mid-nineteenth century, the 1381 uprising had become a standard historical reference point across classes and tastes. The drama and violence associated with Tyler and Jack Straw in particular made them suitable subjects for penny dreadfuls.[1] Penny dreadfuls also provided visual representations of the revolt which was one of the shared overlaps they had with Egan's *Wat Tyler*,[2] the 1851 edition of which contained sixty-five large illustrations drawn by W. H. Thwaites (engraved by one John Wall, no less) typically focusing on Tyler, as we might expect.[3] An especially important visual representation of Ball came from a different context. The famous illustration of Ball in the Froissart manuscript was copied and presented (in colour) with a subtle Victorian updating in Henry Noel Humphreys's *Illuminated Illustrations of Froissart* (1844–1845), under the title, 'John Ball Preaching.' Humphreys's illustration (featuring a slightly striking nose) was accompanied by basic information about the 'priest' and a description of him as 'one of the chief instigators of the rebellion of 1381.' There is familiar language ('He harangued the people of his village…he preached equality of rank and property, he was popular among the lower orders') and some brief narrative detail, including how Ball and Jack Straw 'concealed themselves in a ruin, but were betrayed by their own men.' There was also a visual antiquarian interest paralleling the common rhetoric of accuracy among historians: that the names of Tyler and Ball were written on the illustration 'in white dresses…would seem to render it probable that they are actual portraits.'[4]

1   For full discussion, see Basdeo, *Life and Legend of a Rebel Leader*, loc 2718–2821.
2   Vaninskaya, 'Dreams of John Ball,' 52.
3   Pierce Egan, *Wat Tyler* (large edition; London: W.S. Johnson, 1851).
4   Henry Noel Humphreys, *Illuminated Illustrations of Froissart: Selected from the MS in the Bibliothèque Royale in Paris and Other Sources* (London: William Smith, 1845), 73–74. Cf. *Northwich Guardian* (5 April 1873). An updated

However, as we have seen throughout this book, antiquarian claims hardly preclude ideological interests, and the overt political constructions of Ball and the revolt continued unabashed. In a story in *Boy's Own Magazine* (1865) about the times of Richard II, we get an image of an athletic, muscular and angry version of Ball and his companions (featuring, as with Humphreys and Mrs O'Neill, a striking nose) which are familiar Victorian stereotypes of masculinity—including often ambiguous and ambivalent stereotypes of working-class masculinity—in a relatively conservative construction of the world.[5] As we might expect, these tensions were reflected in the familiar accompanying story with its familiar accompanying words where Ball was said to have 'harangued the people.'[6] The tension was between Ball the 'hot-headed ecclesiastic' and the Wycliffite Ball's take on the Adam and Eve couplet which was, according to an editorial note, 'the cry of the English people long after Wat Tyler's rebellion was crushed, and until the insecurity upon the throne of a new dynasty caused such a coalition between king and commons, and such a granting of privileges by the one to the other, as smoothed off the rough edges of difference of class, and made the condition of the people more bearable, if not more equal.'[7] This was one typical assessment of its time among others, as different interested parties in post-Chartist Victorian England variously tried to account for the inherited tension between violence and reasonable demands set against the backdrop of the Industrial Revolution and working-class demands. And questions of insurrection (and indeed Englishness) intersected with another tension inherited from the reception of Ball: a monk who may or may not have been a deranged ascetic and who may or may not have been a proto-Protestant ahead of his time.

---

    version of Froissart's illustration of Ball was also found, for instance, in editions of Froissart, e.g., *The Chronicles of Froissart: Vol. I* (London: Henry G. Bohn, 1849), 653–55.

5 Francis Davenant, 'Hubert Ellis: A Story of King Richard's Days the Second,' in *Boy's Own Volume of Fact, Fiction, History and Adventure N.S. 6* (London: S. O. Beeton, 1865), 1–464; Kelly Boyd, *Manliness and the Boys' Story Paper in Britain: A Cultural History, 1855–1940* (New York: Palgrave McMillan, 2003), 2, 5, 8, 28–31, 190.

6 Davenant, 'Hubert Ellis,' 284.

7 Davenant, 'Hubert Ellis,' 291, 454.

Ball the Social and Political Reformer

Chartist influence on the reception of Ball and the revolt had a solid presence and, for some, the association of 1381 and Chartism could seem an obvious point of comparison.[8] Performed at the Royal Victoria Theatre over the Christmas period at the end of 1849/beginning of 1850, the pantomime *Wat Tyler: Or Jack Straw's Rebellion* was advertised with overt political references, including casting Tyler as the Chartist leader of 1381.[9] Egan's *Wat Tyler*, which as we saw portrayed the rebels in clear Chartist language, was, as Stephen Basdeo put it bluntly, 'abridged and virtually plagiarised' in the anonymous *Life and Adventures of Wat Tyler the Good and the Brave* (1851).[10] Here, there is even a vague backstory for Ball who had previously received 'injustice from the hands of some of the retainers of the government' and had further 'perambulated the country and inculcated on the minds of the people, that mankind were derived from one common stock, and explained to them, that it was to support a few in riotous luxury, in extravagance and debauchery, that the many were reduced to starvation.'[11]

Chartism as an obvious point of reference for explaining Ball was presented in *Cassell's Illustrated History of England* (1856–1864), a venture associated with the publishing enterprise of the entrepreneur John Cassell (1817–1865) whose political interests included educating the working class, temperance, and universal suffrage.[12] A fairly conventional economic reading of history was given, alongside standard factors (e.g., taxation), for understanding the uprising. This involved seeing ideas associated with the revolt intertwined with the growth of towns and trade which provided opportunities for liberty and comforts in the face of the familiar 'haughty aristocracy' treating serfs like beasts.[13] Referencing Froissart (especially),

---

8   Harvey P. Sucksmith, 'Sir Leicester Dedlock, Wat Tyler, and the Chartists: The Role of the Iron-Master in Bleak House', *Dickens Studies Annual* 4 (1975): 113–31. Cf. *Heywood Advertiser* (27 November 1858); *Bath Chronicle* (6 February 1873).
9   Brodie, 'Free Trade and Cheap Theatre, 346–48; Jeffrey Richards, *The Golden Age of Pantomime: Slapstick, Spectacle and Subversion in Victorian England* (London: I.B. Tauris, 2015), 190–92.
10 Basdeo, *Life and Legend of a Rebel Leader*, loc 2394.
11 Anonymous, *Life and Adventures of Wat Tyler the Good and the Brave* (H. G. Collins: London, 1851), 161–62.
12 Rosemary Mitchell, 'Cassell, John (1817–1865)', *ODNB* (23 September 2004).
13 *Cassell's Illustrated History of England: New and Revised Edition, Volume I* (London: Cassell, Petter & Galpin, 1865), 410–11.

Knighton, Walsingham, Stow, and Holinshed, the account of the 1381 uprising in *Cassell's Illustrated History* reminded the audience that Ball and 'his doctrines have been described by his enemies.' Instead, Ball 'appears to have been a thorough democrat or Chartist of his day, drawing his opinions from the literal declarations of the gospel that God is no respecter of persons; and addressing these and new startling ideas to the inflamed minds of ignorant and oppressed people.'[14] This is paralleled with Wycliffe's teaching, which is presented just before Ball's as similar in type.[15]

But there are qualifications given. The rebels were 'said to have committed great atrocities' and that 'many outrages were committed is most probable' because it is 'inevitable from so general a rising of an uneducated and oppressed populace smarting under generations of wrongs.'[16] Likewise, Wycliffe and Luther were said to have a parallel reception history.[17] Nevertheless, it was argued that they should be judged by 'their own public demands' presented to the king which were 'most wonderfully simple, reasonable, and enlightened for such a people, under such exasperating circumstances,' a tradition which had been developing in earnest from Hume onward.[18] As we have seen before from other post-Hume reformist perspectives (e.g., Mrs O'Neill), there was a concern not only about violence but a combination of a lack of political awareness and a movement ahead of its time. According to *Cassell's Illustrated History*, sometimes a noble would emancipate the entire estate, but not always, and a preacher

14 *Cassell's Illustrated History of England*, 413. Cf. *Liverpool Standard* (1 June 1852). On Ball, compare also Henry Cooper in the *Birmingham Daily Post* (16 April 1858): 'At Maidstone...the favourite democratic preacher, John Ball, was elected [Tyler's] chaplain, who took for the text of his first sermon the good old rhyme—"When Adam delved and Eve Span, Who was then the gentleman?"'
15 'It has been supposed that the preaching of Wycliffe had no little effect in rousing this storm in England, and there can be no doubt of it. The people, once made acquainted with the doctrines of human right, justice, and liberty abounding in the Bible, and pervading it at its very essence, could only regard the knowledge as a direct call from God to rise, rend the bondage of their cruel slavery, and assume the rank of men' (*Cassell's Illustrated History of England*, 411).
16 *Cassell's Illustrated History of England*, 413.
17 *Cassell's Illustrated History of England*, 411, on Wycliffe and Luther: 'This light, this wonderful knowledge, coming too suddenly upon them, made them, as it were, intoxicated, and overthrew all restraint and tranquillity of mind. They felt their wrongs the more acutely be perceiving their rights, and how basely they had been deprived of them by men professing this religion of truth, justice, and humanity. Such was the case on the preaching of Luther in German afterwards.'
18 *Cassell's Illustrated History of England*, 413.

like Ball with his 'great gospel of freedom' could not be quiet in this context. But while his words were 'only too true,' this was 'a truth coming too suddenly,' and more than people could bear, 'or were disciplined to win, or, if won at once, to maintain.' And, the audience was informed, these 'poor people' did not realise that there was 'growing up that power amongst the people, the shape of Parliament, which should gradually and securely fight their battles, and establish their desires.'[19]

The perceived tension between egalitarianism and hierarchy in Ball's teaching and its reception was exploited to provide a reformist reading of the revolt, even if some could just read the tension as hypocrisy.[20] Such a sympathetic reading of the revolt came from probably the most famous nineteenth-century advocate of social reform. In the serialised version of *A Child's History of England* published in June 1852, Charles Dickens presented a brief and relatively standard overview of the revolt which is largely sympathetic towards the rebels and hostile towards the institution of serfdom. The badly implemented poll tax was unfortunate because the people had 'long been suffering under great oppression,' were 'still the mere slaves of the lords of the land,' and were typically 'harshly and unjustly treated.' Rebel demands at Mile End (the end of slavery, fixed rents, buying and selling in markets, pardons for past offences) are once again seen as fair from a more liberal nineteenth-century perspective ('Heaven knows, there was nothing very unreasonable in these proposals!'). Tyler's defence of his daughter and killing of the collector is simply 'what any honest father under such provocation might have done.' In assessing the meeting of Tyler and the deceitful Richard, it was Tyler who appeared 'in history as beyond comparison the truer and more respectable man of the two' while Walworth's attack was similarly a 'not very valiant deed.' Ball is briefly mentioned as a 'priest,' but Dickens challenged whether the teaching of the rebels (and historically associated with Ball) was fairly presented. Dickens represents an attempt at normalising Ball and the rebels which required decaffeinating insurrectionary ideology associated with their reception. Picking up on the tension between ideals and implementation in the sources and reception, Dickens deemed it unlikely that 'they wanted to abolish all property, and to declare all men equal' because they demanded allegiance to the king and were not 'disposed to injure' those that had done them no harm 'merely because they

19 *Cassell's Illustrated History of England*, 411.
20 Thomas Keightley, *The History of England, Vol. I* (London, 1839), 301, for instance, has a note on the response of the 'multitude' to Ball's Blackheath sermon: 'It is amusing to observe how men cannot divest themselves of their original ideas; while vowing to abolish all ranks and offices they talked of conferring the highest on their leaders.'

were of high station,' even to the point of romanticising the story of Joan of Kent by claiming that she was 'merely to kiss a few dirty-faced rough-bearded men who were noisily fond of royalty.'[21] It is worth adding that the hugely popular Baptist preacher and writer Charles Spurgeon shared very similar views to Dickens on Ball and the revolt.[22]

From Patriot to Abolitionist

Tyler's killing of the tax collector who insulted his daughter (as well as Walworth's killing of Tyler) was used in the press as a nostalgic point of contrast with the present state of Englishmen, who were deemed cowardly and unchivalrous, particularly when it came to protecting or helping women. Since the days of Tyler, there had been a 'strange decline in the personal manliness of the people...Englishmen are changed since Wat Tyler...we are become a milder and meaner people.'[23] By the mid-nineteenth

21 Charles Dickens, 'A Child's History of England: Chapter XVII', in *Household Words* V (1852), 304–8 (304–6).
22 Spurgeon's lecture on the 'Illustrious Lord Mayors' (November 1861, reprinted in *London City Press* [11 November 1867]) echoes Dickens's account. Spurgeon similarly argued that the behaviour of the rebels led by Ball and Tyler towards the queen mother did not involve 'ill-treating her' but 'a few rough and kind salutes'. Though not uncritical of the violence in the London revolt, Spurgeon joined the ranks of those who wanted to reclaim and somewhat tame Ball and the uprising, with one eye on the treatment of 'workers' in the present and hoping for a more conciliatory resolution than one of class conflict ('When will all classes perceive their dependence upon each other, and renounce the attitude of opposition which they are still so ready to assume?'). Spurgeon also wanted to restore the reputation of Ball. Ball the 'priest', the 'warlike chaplain', was assessed as being 'fanatical and enthusiastic enough, but not half so bad as some paint him.' That may not sound as positive as the assessment of Tyler, but Spurgeon had more rescuing to do. 'History', he claimed, 'will yet have more to say about John Ball.' Ball's take on the Adam and Eve couplet meant that he 'inveighed with all his might against the oppressions of the lords, and the haughtiness of the high and mighty ones who taxed and insulted the people.' Ball's teaching might have been 'rather extreme in radicalism' but as it was described by his enemies and as he had faith in the king, 'we have no ground to believe that he preached anarchy, or advocated levelling.'
23 *Tipperary Free Press* (28 September 1853); *Glasgow Free Press* (1 October 1853). On the idea of 'manliness' and uprising, see also, e.g., *Penny Illustrated Paper* (19 October 1861).

century, this expectation of manly behaviour by Tyler (who was consistently a muscular blacksmith) had long been established among friend and foe alike, and the connection with an idealised national identity was an obvious one in sympathetic receptions of the revolt. As with the Chartists before, the idea of the expectation of liberty from serfdom and (some of) the rebels' disciplined expectation of a civil society was something worthy of the label 'patriotism' in nineteenth-century receptions. Tyler could be seen as the 'true patriot' (unlike Jack Straw) who wanted the abolition of bond service and was opposed to plunder.[24] Tyler could also be seen as leading such reasonable 'patriots' to '[liberate] the celebrated priest, John Ball,' who preached his 'remarkable sermon' at Blackheath on the Adam and Eve saying.[25] Spurgeon's reformist reading of the 'warlike chaplain' was connected to the claim that Tyler was a 'patriot' who (echoing Paine) 'never had sufficient honour done to his memory.'[26]

A national or collective identity grounded in ideas of liberty rather than race or ethnicity that we saw with the Chartists and their supporters took on a new dimension when Ball turned up in American abolitionist discourse in the case of James Redpath (1833–1891), the journalist and advocate for John Brown. Brought up in Berwick-upon-Tweed, Redpath trained as a printer before emigrating to Michigan in the 1840s and then working as a reporter in New York. In the 1850s he developed his abolitionist views, not least when he ventured South to report on and see slavery first-hand.[27] In 1854 and 1855 Redpath wrote letters and reports of his travels and interviews with slaves which were published in the abolitionist press under the name 'John Ball Jr.'[28] The use of 'John Ball' as a figure of insurrection was

---

24 *Wolverhampton Chronicle* (5 March 1856). Cf. *Lloyd's Weekly Newspaper* (21 August 1853); *Bath Chronicle* (6 February 1873). *John Bull* (2 September 1876) claimed, perhaps slightly unfairly, of Charles H. Pearson, *English History in the Fourteenth Century* (London: Rivingtons, 1876) and C. Edmund Maurice, *Lives of English Popular Leaders in the Middle Ages: Tyler, Ball, and Oldcastle* (London: Henry S. King & Co.: London, 1875), that Pearson 'has not been persuaded by Mr. Maurice to remove Wat Tyler from the rank of mob leader to that of a genuine patriot.'
25 *Leamington Advertiser* (14 February 1856).
26 *London City Press* (11 November 1867).
27 For biographical details, see John R. McKivigan, *Forgotten Firebrand: James Redpath and the Making of Nineteenth-Century America* (Ithaca: Cornell University Press, 2008).
28 E.g., *Liberator* (4, 11 August 1854; 1, 8 September 1854); *National Anti-Slavery Standard* (14, 21, 28 October 1854; 25 November 1854; 2, 16, 23 December 1854; 27 January 1855; 17, 31 March 1855; 7, 14, April 1855). See also James

made clearer in his extended publication, *Roving Editor* (1859), shortly after in an early instance of the construction of a radical tradition:

> I saw or believed that one cycle of anti-slavery warfare was about to close—the cycle whose correspondences in history are the eras of John Ball, the herald of the brave Jack Cade; of the Humble Remonstrants who preceded Oliver Cromwell, and the Iconoclastic Puritans; and of the Encyclopaedists of the age of Louis the Sixteenth, whose writings prepared the way for the French Revolution. I believed that the cycle of action was at hand. I considered it, therefore, of importance to know the feelings and aspirations of the slaves…I left the South and went to Kansas; and endeavoured, personally, and by my pen, to precipitate a revolution.[29]

As this point in his career the contents of the John Ball Jr letters further show that Redpath would, if necessary, have supported slaves in a violent uprising. Redpath may have thought being obviously British partly helped gain sufficient trust for interviewees to be able to open up and talk, which further illuminates the choice of the 'John Ball Jr' pseudonym.[30] But it was also a Britishness of a certain revolutionary kind and one which was based on claims about equality not limited to those from the country of his birth, Europe, or white America.[31]

Ball the Seditious Reformer

In his 1858 lecture on the history of Maidstone, A. J. B. Beresford-Hope MP gave the usual critique of the provocation of the 'tyrannous conduct of the Government' in causing the 'rebellion of Wat Tyler' but with the likewise common negative qualification that it ended 'like all other lawless attempts, in more trouble and misery than the original cause could have occasioned.' Ball's imprisonment and escape were also mentioned. 'Whether he went to prison for good or bad deeds, does not appear,' Beresford-Hope claimed, but 'judging from what follows, it may be concluded that he was a person

---

Redpath, *The Roving Editor: Or, Talks with Slaves in the Southern States* (New York 1859).
29 Redpath, *Roving Editor*, 299–300.
30 McKivigan, *Forgotten Firebrand*, 14.
31 For an in-depth analysis of the 'John Ball Jr' letters and their attitude towards slavery and violent uprising, as well as their possible influence, see McKivigan, *Forgotten Firebrand*, 10–18, 26, 27, 41, 44–45, 207 n. 106.

of somewhat loose principles.' Ball (also labelled a 'priest' and given the title 'Rev.') became 'chaplain of [Tyler's] forces' and was on a promise to be made archbishop of Canterbury if Tyler became king, but his Adam and Eve couplet, Beresford-Hope joked, was 'certainly not to be found in scripture.' The death of Tyler and Ball brought an end to 'his expectations of the archbishopric' which, the *Maidstone Journal* reported, was greeted by cheers.[32]

In other words, the negative memory of the revolt did not disappear and the positive one was not left uncontested after the heyday of Chartism, and not least at Fishmongers' Hall where Walworth was still lionised.[33] The rehabilitation of the 1381 revolt was also parodied (e.g., George Augustus Sala, *Wat Tyler, M.P.: An Operatic Extravaganza* [1869]) as the rebels (especially Tyler) turned up in comic theatre,[34] and we even get mention of 'John Baw' alongside Straw and the 'insolent' Tyler in Nelson Lee's pantomime, *Harlequin Wat Tyler: or Love, War, and Peace*, performed at Christmas in 1867.[35] But even if Tyler could sometimes be deprived of the full force of his former menace, it hardly vanished and his associations with unpalatable radical or violent positions, or as one of the historic threats to the capital itself, lingered.[36] In the case of Ball, one children's history of England still

---

32 *Maidstone Journal* (9 November 1858). Cf. *South Eastern Gazette* (9 November 1858).
33 E.g., *Northern Star* (5 June 1852); *Lloyd's Weekly Newspaper* (6 June 1852); *Hampshire Advertiser* (12 June 1852); *Sussex Advertiser* (20 March 1855); *Morning Advertiser* (30 April 1857); *London City Press* (6 March 1858); *London City Press* (9 November 1861); *Morning Post* (13 February 1863); *Holborn Journal* (1 April 1865); *London City Press* (10 October 1863); *London City Press* (21 October 1865); *Globe* (21 August 1873); *Grantham Journal* (2 January 1875); *Pall Mall Gazette* (18 April 1879).
34 Alastair Dunn, 'Wat Tyler: The Many Roles of an English Rebel,' *History Today* 51 (July 2001): 28. Cf. *The Press* (8 October 1853); *Staffordshire Advertiser* (24 January 1857); *Liverpool Daily Post* (18 June 1857); *The Era* (1 March 1863); *London City Press* (5 August 1865); *Morning Post* (21 December 1869); *Illustrated Times* (25 December 1869); *Penny Illustrated Paper* (25 December 1869); *The Graphic* (1 January 1870); *Daily Telegraph* (25 January 1870).
35 E.g., *Clerkenwell News* (27 December 1867); *Lloyd's Weekly London Newspaper* (29 December 1867). The conventional 'Ball' was reported in, e.g., *Morning Advertiser* (27 December 1867). Elsewhere, Ball was said to have later changed his name to 'Jack Straw' and may have been born in Offham, Kent (*Dover Express* [13 November 1868]). He was also called a 'priest of Coventry' in the *Herts Advertiser* (7 August 1869).
36 Cf. *The Era* (11 December 1859). On the different invocations of the memory of Tyler as a potential threat, see, e.g., *Cardiff and Merthyr Guardian* (17 May 1851); *Halifax Courier* (18 June 1853); *London Daily News* (17 February 1855);

saw fit to provide a counterargument to Ball's perceived levelling theology and couched it in terms of what now looks like cliched Victorian capitalism:

> With much truth there is some falsehood in this reasoning. In one sense all men are equal in the eyes of their Creator, and all who will labour to produce the fruits of the earth have a right to a share of them. But God has not been pleased to make all men equal in personal gifts; some possess intellect, learning, and industry, while others are weak-minded, ignorant and idle; and it is therefore impossible to keep them on an equality, even for a single day...This is not an artificial state of society but the result of the natural laws of the world, and all attempts at defeating it only end in failure and confusion. But the poor ignorant men that John Ball preached to did not understand these things, and as he was possessed of a certain uncultivated eloquence, his harangues excited them to a state of enthusiasm.[37]

Not all critiques shared or required this paternalistic tone. One satirical attack was on the apparent connections between Radicalism, pretentions to stimulate another Tyler and Straw, and the role of the enigmatic 'mystic.' 'Mystic' was here understood as a figure drawn to sentimentality, 'deep intentions,' impracticality, chain smoking, hats, beards, tufts, coffee, philosophy, asceticism, vegetarianism, art, and 'peculiar views of marriage'— and taking on the role of 'Father Ball of Pantheism.' This only required one response: 'Ancient Pantheism, seeing the Divine in everything, and

---

Sheffield Independent (24 February 1855); *Wiltshire Times* (17 January 1857); *Staffordshire Advertiser* (7 February 1857); *West Surrey Times* (14 February 1857); *Examiner* (22 August 1857); *Coventry Standard* (30 April 1858); *Star of Gwent* (18 December 1858); *Shoreditch Observer* (29 March 1862); *London Daily News* (2 July 1862); *London Evening Standard* (17 September 1863); *Pall Mall Gazette* (18 September 1865); *Shipping and Mercantile Gazette* (27 November 1863); *Islington Gazette* (27 October 1865); *Kilkenny Journal* (16 March 1867); *Leeds Times* (4 May 1867); *Newcastle Daily Chronicle* (7 May 1867); *Londonderry Sentinel* (4 June 1867); *Globe* (11 July 1867); *Globe* (6 August 1867); *Sheffield Daily Telegraph* (13 February 1869); *Sheffield Daily Telegraph* (15 February 1869); *Bell's Life in London* (19 February 1870); *Liverpool Mercury* (19 March 1870); *Framlingham Weekly News* (2 April 1870); *Illustrated London News* (14 May 1870); *Chester Chronicle* (8 April 1871); *Yorkshire Post* (Tuesday 25 April 1871); *Clerkenwell News* (27 June 1871); *Globe* (26 July 1873); *Taunton Courier* (17 December 1873); *Sheffield Independent* (15 January 1874); *Tavistock Gazette* (23 January 1874); *Royal Cornwall Gazette* (14 February 1874).

37 Henry Tyrrell, *A History of England for the Young, Vol. I* (London: London Printing and Publishing Company, c. 1853), 334–35.

cultivating an universal symbolism, led at last to the worship of the baboon; modern Pantheism has this notable difference—it *begins* with it!'[38]

This line of attack does not seem to have been typical. In the case of Ball-the-priest, lingering sinister radicalism could be used to reapply the old debates about the extremes of religion or Protestant reform and claims about its association with insurrection, though this time in a setting of growing distance from, and outright disgust with, the institution of serfdom. Charles Knight's *Popular History of England* (1855–1862) was a conventional Whiggish history grounded in Saxon constitutionalism and the basic arguments were standard enough. In addition to accepting that (Wat) Tyler's daughter had been mistreated, he continued the argument that the expectation of liberty was reasonable but violence was not going to work: 'The insurrection of 1381, like most other attempts to obtain political justice by a tumultuous appeal to arms, was set on foot for the assertion of moderate demands, and became an occasion for havoc and bloodshed.'[39] Ball 'the itinerant preacher' did not get *directly* bad treatment from Knight, but as a signatory to the famous letters, he was seen to be an organiser (along with Jack Milner, Jack Carter, and Jack Trueman) acting in a 'remarkable manner.' There was a near inevitability of violence connected with the organisation associated with Ball when the 'course of the insurgents was marked by the accustomed atrocities of ignorant men with weapons in their hands.'[40] This allowed Knight, like others before him, to criticise the rebellion in favour of a different model of greater cooperation between the classes and to hold the view that the demands were reasonable but violent disruption was not, a view he likewise applied to his nineteenth-century present.[41] In what Knight saw as a particularly brutal age from top to bottom, it was therefore unlikely that 'these rustics would exhibit the virtue of mercy which the lords of chivalry never cultivated.'[42]

Where *Cassell's Illustrated History* wanted to rescue both Ball and Wycliffe, the violent insurrection associated with Ball's organisational

---

38　*The Press* (10 December 1853). Cf. *Northwich Guardian* (5 April 1873), via Froissart, which reports on Ball as the 'crazy priest.'
39　Charles Knight, *The Popular History of England: An Illustrated History of Society and Government from the Earliest Period to Our Own Times, Volume II* (London: Bradbury and Evans, 1857), 5.
40　Knight, *Popular History of England*, 6. One review of Knight's *Popular History of England* added that 'An itinerant preacher was rendered a highly useful though a reckless instrument in the hands of Wat Tyler to accomplish his purposes' (*Southern Reporter* [29 September 1856]).
41　Rosemary Mitchell, 'Knight, Charles (1791–1873),' *ODNB* (3 January 2008).
42　Knight, *Popular History of England*, 6.

abilities functioned as a sharp point of contrast for Knight's Protestant apology for the innocence of Wycliffe's theology. Such social and theological tensions were an ongoing subplot in the reception of the revolt from the attack on Wycliffe by the Catholic historian and priest John Lingard (see Chapter 11) to James Anthony Froude's pro-Reformation retort in *History of England from the Fall of Wolsey to the Death of Elizabeth*, the first two volumes of which came out in 1856 and similarly saw the insurrection in terms of 'bloodshed, destruction, and a ferocity natural to such outbreaks.' Froude did not mention Ball by name but he was no doubt implied in the reference to the 'two priests' who 'accompanied the insurgents' and who emphatically were 'not Wycliffe's followers, but the licentious counterfeits of them, who trod inevitably in their footsteps, and were inevitably countenanced by their doctrines.'[43] But, as this also implies, there was still a tension between Wycliffe's theology and its social implications, so while for Froude it 'would be absurd to attribute this disaster to Wycliffe…it is equally certain that the doctrines which he had taught were incompatible, at that particular time, with an effective repression of the spirit which had caused the explosion.' Wycliffe's 'ambiguous language' brought 'discredit on his nobler efforts' and had taught 'the wiser and better portion of the people to confound heterodoxy of opinion with sedition, anarchy, and disorder.'[44] These tensions between theological heterodoxy and social disorder were hardly confined to genre of history; they resulted in two of the most extended discussions of Ball in the years following the Chartist era: the novels *Alice of Fobbing* and *Merry England*.

Alice of Fobbing

Working in the long-established tradition of high ecclesiastical receptions of Ball was the Tractarian clergyman and prolific High Church novelist

---

43 James Anthony Froude, *History of England from the Fall of Wolsey to the Death of Elizabeth: Volume II* (London: John W. Parker and Son, 1856), 17. In a later work, which was more muted in its hostility towards the rebels (though not towards Catholicism), Froude directly named Ball and then referred to a fellow leader of the revolt as 'a second priest, named Jaques or Jack Straw' and called them both the 'two priests'—James Anthony Froude, 'Annals of an English Abbey,' *Scribner's Monthly* (November–December, 1873): 91–101, 187–99, 282–93 (199, 287). The essay was republished in James Anthony Froude, *Short Studies on Great Subjects* (third series; London: Spottiswoode and Co, 1877), 1–89.
44 Froude, *History of England*, 17–18. Cf. *Galway Vindicator* (8 September 1852).

William Edward Heygate (1816–1902).[45] Heygate's reading of Ball in *Alice of Fobbing; or, the Times of Jack Straw and Wat Tyler* (1860) was part theological propaganda, part anti-revolutionary conservatism,[46] regularly providing explanations with reference to Piers Plowman, Froissart, Walsingham, Knighton, and Wilkins. Indeed, the antiquarian interests, not unlike Humphreys's presentations of Froissart's alleged portrait of Ball, included the suggestion that Froissart used sources for Ball's teaching from contemporary 'short-hand writers.'[47]

The novel worked with standard explanations for the 1381 revolt (or *revolution*, in the case of *Alice of Fobbing*), including the costly wars with France, French plundering of the coast, the poll tax, the tyrannical officials and heavy-handed tax collectors, the plight of serfs desiring freedom, and the story of (Wat) Tyler's daughter. A degree of sympathy with these issues had long been a feature of more conservative anti-revolutionary receptions of the 1381 uprising and Heygate was no exception. Nor was he an exception in his conclusion that violence and revolution was the inappropriate response, no matter how bad the treatment. Heygate acknowledged that 'oppression rouses rebellion' but with the crucial qualification that 'one wrong gives birth to another'—hence the novel stresses the violence and drunkenness of the revolt. He was aware (how could he not have been?) that historians now took sides and now fight the 'old battle over again with sharp words' but 'angry passions stain the bright blade of justice' and, ultimately, 'all truly were wrong.'[48] Heygate's presentation of the treatment of Tyler's daughter is a case in point. Heygate acknowledged the wrongdoing and moral dilemma of how to react but claimed that Tyler's turn to rebellion meant that, from then on, 'we can no longer feel for poor Wat,' who now appeared a 'desperate insurgent, drunk with success, and not desirous of peace.' It was a dark day that 'changed the peaceful tiler of Dartford into a shedder of blood, a fierce rebel; and then a bleeding and despised corpse, lying like a dead dog in Smithfield!'[49] After Tyler's death when the life was

---

45 For biographical details see, e.g., S. A. Skinner, 'Heygate, William Edward,' *ODNB* (23 September 2004); George Herring, 'W. E. Heygate: Tractarian Clerical Novelist,' *Studies in Church History* 48 (2012): 259–70. Heygate's paternal uncle was, incidentally, once MP for Sudbury (1818–1826).

46 Vaninskaya, 'Dreams of John Ball,' 49–50. On 1381 understood as revolution, cf. William E. Heygate, *Alice of Fobbing; or, the Times of Jack Straw and Wat Tyler* (London: J. H. and J. Parker, 1860), 6: 'rebellion from one end of the land to the other.'

47 Heygate, *Alice of Fobbing*, 21.

48 Heygate, *Alice of Fobbing*, 98.

49 Heygate, *Alice of Fobbing*, 23–24.

stamped out of the 'broken pieces of the serpent,' the uprising would then be remembered as another of the many 'proofs of history that an unsuccessful struggle for liberty only rivets the chains of those who serve, and that re-action from fear is cruel.'[50]

If the bondage of serfs and violent reaction were both wrong answers, then what could be the right one? Heygate's broader conservative and somewhat Tractarian solution to his problem came through his discussions of morality, corruption, and decay of a church in need of revitalisation. This included reflection on the inevitable corruption of the church and clergy which should be seen alongside the importance of dutiful service to God and praying that God will purify the hearts of others, including the church, in God's own time and manner.[51] This further included ideas about Christians suffering wrong before drawing the sword, while not excusing the behaviour of the wrongdoer and oppressor.[52] While 'scandalous cases' are more likely to be well known, according to Heygate's account, attention should be directed toward the 'bright examples,' those who are 'retiring and humble as true piety is.'[53] A similar logic is at work in Heygate's ambivalent presentation of Wycliffe, whose teaching 'probably…to some extent' helped to 'fan the flame of discontent,' though this was not intentional. And the lack of intentionality, and Wycliffe's 'moderation' and likely lack of support, meant that there were some constraints to the influence of his teaching.[54]

The figure of Ball is used (among others) in the story to explain why revolution and uprising are the seemingly easy but wrong path. The discussion of the sermons of Jack Straw and Ball include the remark that 'all persons do enjoy a sermon which lets them off, and heartily abuses the vices of which they are not guilty.'[55] The story may follow Alice Baker and how her life intersects with the revolt and its aftermath, but Ball's revolutionary teaching is a recurring problem in the novel, and one addressed at the very beginning. The tranquil scene of the church at Fobbing is contrasted with a group of worshippers with 'scowling looks' and 'sullen expression' congregating in the churchyard and led by Thomas Baker and his 'fierce, scornful manner.' They talk about their burdens and with reference to Ball's controversial 'allegorical' letters, 'the circulars by which the emissaries of

---

50 Heygate, *Alice of Fobbing*, 69–69.
51 Heygate, *Alice of Fobbing*, 29–31.
52 Heygate, *Alice of Fobbing*, 81–83.
53 Heygate, *Alice of Fobbing*, 10.
54 Heygate, *Alice of Fobbing*, 9. Cf. *Cumberland and Westmorland Advertiser* (12 November 1867).
55 Heygate, *Alice of Fobbing*, 9.

revolution were inciting their countrymen in dark enigmatical sentences.' Strange though they may seem, the gist of the letters is 'plain enough to enable the missives to accomplish the work they were intended to do.'[56]

The detailed aside on Ball's career and imprisonments serves the purpose of showing Ball as a perversion of the ideal function of the church, assuming he even properly belonged to the church in the first place. Heygate went as far as to claim that 'whether John Ball was ever in holy orders or not is more than doubtful.' Referencing Wilkins in support, he noted that Ball was labelled a 'pretended priest, and a vagabond.' The charges against Ball involved 'preaching contrary to the will of the incumbents in churches and churchyards against the archbishop, bishops and pope, and of preaching other "enormities".' Instead, then, he concluded that Ball was 'the apostle of rebellion in Kent.'[57] Sudbury ('a learned man and good') in the Tower provided a suitable point of comparison for Heygate, for 'the mob burst in, Wat, and Jack Straw, and Ball, and the fiercer of the rebels, and began to glut their revenge.' This especially violent mob insulted the 'once Fair Maid of Kent' and attacked 'England's chief shepherd, the Archbishop.' Following Walsingham (*Chronica maiora* 424–431), Sudbury was effectively accorded the status of martyr as he 'set the example of the act and place,' he took eight blows to kill, and his corpse lay unburied all day. Unlike Ball's rowdy mob, Sudbury had just 'celebrated Mass before the King' and pleaded for 'Death by which alone a Christian dies in peace and hope' but was instead 'dragged forth to execution.' We also get a telling comparison with none other than another hero of anti-revolutionary High Church thought, Archbishop Laud, who on Tower Hill 'subsequently perished with equal constancy, temper, and injustice.'[58]

Merry England

More polemical still was the popular Victorian novelist William Harrison Ainsworth in his three volume (and previously serialised) *Merry England: Or, Nobles and Serfs* (1874). As a younger man, Ainsworth published commercially successful novels about infamous criminals (e.g., *Rockwood* [1834], *Jack Sheppard* [1839]) and historical novels (e.g., *Guy Fawkes* [1840], *The Tower of London* [1840]), which meant the 1381 revolt was a relatively

---

56 Heygate, *Alice of Fobbing*, 1–3. It is, perhaps, worth noting that 'Hob the robber' became 'Bob the robber.'
57 Heygate, *Alice of Fobbing*, 23, referencing David Wilkins, *Concilia Magnae Britanniae et Hiberniae: Volume III* (London, 1737), 164.
58 Heygate, *Alice of Fobbing*, 66.

unsurprising topic, even if his reputation had declined by the time of *Merry England*.[59] The sources and influences are the familiar chroniclers or historians (e.g., Froissart, Walsingham, Knighton, Grafton, Holinshed, Stow, and possibly Lingard), as well as more recent examples such as Egan.[60] Like Egan's *Wat Tyler*, Ainsworth's *Merry England* is closely connected to the Robin Hood tradition. Ball is a seditious conspirator close to Jack Straw who is explicitly compared with, and a type of, Robin Hood. This may explain why Ball is regularly called 'friar' and the opening chapter heading is 'The Smith, the Friar, and the Outlaw' which would hardly have been out-of-place in a Robin Hood story.[61] There would, however, be little in the way of romanticising friar Ball and the rebels in *Merry England*.

Despite being brought up in a 'strict atmosphere of Whiggism and Nonconformity,' Ainsworth developed Tory and (somewhat anachronistically) Jacobite 'principles.' Moreover, it was recalled that he 'identified himself with the Church of England, of which he was a staunch supporter, although like most artistic natures, he acknowledged the attraction of the gorgeous ritual and sensuous music of the Roman Church.'[62] Moreover, Ainsworth's views on toleration of loyal Catholics and Catholicism came through clearly in his earlier work, including his preface to *Guy Fawkes* which further references the history of John Lingard, a fellow Lancastrian local (see Chapter 11).[63] Basdeo suggests that it is 'difficult to know who the reader is supposed to sympathise with in the novel' and that Ainsworth's novels 'rarely…seek to make a political point,' though Basdeo notices the revolutionary rage of the rebels and how Tyler 'grows haughty and full of ambition.'[64] There are, however, some clear indications in *Merry England* of Ainsworth's ideological tendencies, as well as further indications of who

---

59 For further details, see, e.g., Sheldon Goldfarb, 'Ainsworth, William Harrison,' *ODNB* (23 September 2004); Stephen Carver, *The Author Who Outsold Dickens: The Life and Work of W. H. Ainsworth* (Philadelphia: Pen and Sword History, 2020).

60 William Harrison Ainsworth, *Merry England: Or, Nobles and Serfs, Volume 1* (London: Tinsley Brothers, 1874), vii. Cf. Basdeo, *Life and Legend of a Rebel Leader*, loc 2625–2732.

61 Ainsworth, *Merry England: Or, Nobles and Serfs, Volume 1*, 3, 13–18.

62 S. M. Ellis, *William Harrison Ainsworth and His Friends, Vol. I* (London: John Lane, 1911), 24–25. Cf. Goldfarb, 'Ainsworth'; Carver, *Author Who Outsold Dickens*, 13, 15, 19, 21, 34, 119–21, 124–27.

63 William Harrison Ainsworth, *Guy Fawkes; or, The Gunpowder Treason, Volume 1* (London: Chapman and Hall, 1840), 6–8; Carver, *Author Who Outsold Dickens*, 124–26.

64 Basdeo, *Life and Legend of a Rebel Leader*, loc 2732.

was and was not a worthy recipient of sympathy. We see this in the presentation of Ball and the rebels who represent anything but conservatism and have little respect for Catholic heritage.

Certainly, failures from above are explicitly acknowledged, as we would expect. The usual reasons are given for the causes of the revolt (problematic advisors, poll tax collection, wars with France, nobility abusing their privileges), though with some distinctive emphases, such as the poll tax being 'farmed to a rich company of Lombard merchants, then resident in the City of London.'[65] Nevertheless, while Tyler's (supposed) daughter Editha features extensively in the story (including her surprise love interest, Richard II),[66] Tyler's intense hatred of the wealthy and the nobility and desire for redistribution of property among the 'lower classes' is introduced earlier.[67] And herein lay a particular problem because it was a view which meant the revolt could not be purely blamed on nobles failing in their idealised roles and so it was also the wrong reaction associated with the revolutionary and apostate thought epitomised by Ball.

Ball is presented as excessive in his religious zeal, as well as giving his familiar 'inflammatory preaching' which provokes the oppressed peasantry into revolt. Additionally, we get mention of Ball's letter to the 'head man' in each village, which is a rewritten version of the familiar letter from Knighton and now with explicit revolutionary implications and eschatology, that age old establishment categorisation of overenthusiastic religious belief:

> John Ball greets you well;
> Soon you'll hear the signal bell.
> When it sounds, rise suddenly:
> And, as you would freemen be,
> Hold together steadfastly,
> In brotherhood and unity.
> Nothing fear,
> The end is near—
> The end you hope for—Liberty.[68]

65 Ainsworth, *Merry England: Or, Nobles and Serfs, Volume 1*, 18–19. Cf. Henry Cooper in the *Birmingham Daily Post* (16 April 1858): 'the tax was farmed out to some of the favourite courtiers, who again farmed it out to foreign vampires, whose hired collectors proceeded to collect it with a degree of harshness and insolence which the people could not bear.'
66 This love story between Richard and Tyler's differently named daughter was known elsewhere, including Lee's *Harlequin Wat Tyler*.
67 Ainsworth, *Merry England: Or, Nobles and Serfs, Volume 1*, 6–7.
68 Ainsworth, *Merry England: Or, Nobles and Serfs, Volume 1*, 11–12.

The description of Ball is minimal (particularly when compared with other characters), probably hinting at the idea of him as a religious fanatic in his asceticism—he wears a grey gown with a cord belt and walks barefoot throughout the Kentish villages.[69] And the language of religious excess gets progressively stronger from beginning to end. When Sudbury had Ball imprisoned at Canterbury, he then looked upon him as a 'half-crazed enthusiast, affected by the heresies of Wycliffe' and would have had him killed if he knew his full intentions.[70] By the end of Ball's story, he becomes a fully crazed enthusiast bent on misguided destruction of wealth and presented as taking on elevated roles usually reserved for the wildest of egotist.

Tyler, Jack Straw, and Ball are the cold, calculating rulers of the destructive mob.[71] On their march to Rochester, the rebels plunder the wealthier houses and slay anyone who resists them ('like a swarm of locusts, did the insurgents sweep on, devouring all before them and spreading terror and confusion throughout the country'). The leaders, however, do nothing to 'check ferocity and licence.'[72] But this is presented in terms of a perversion of religious authority in a world turned upside down, even to the point of being a kind of outrageous imitation of not just the archbishop of Canterbury but arguably Christ and God, perhaps even hinting at Ball being a type of antichrist. After Ball is freed (by Wycliffites) at Canterbury, 'they presently beheld him riding on a mule, at the head of a vast multitude.'[73] At Blackheath, speaking from his 'lofty pulpit' to a huge, adoring 'host,' Ball 'commenced one of his fiery harangues' concerning the destruction of the nobles and seizure of their wealth but with an additional prophetic denunciation (and tapping into the long tradition of the revolt as a threat specifically to the capital): 'Nineveh was a great city…an exceeding great and proud city, but it was not spared. Neither shall great and proud London be spared, by reason of its iniquities!' (cf. Jonah 3–4; Nahum 2.8; 3.7; Zephaniah 2.13; Matthew 12.41).[74]

---

69 E.g., Ainsworth, *Merry England: Or, Nobles and Serfs, Volume 1*, 10; William Harrison Ainsworth, *Merry England: Or, Nobles and Serfs, Volume 3* (London: Tinsley Brothers, 1874), 4.
70 Ainsworth, *Merry England: Or, Nobles and Serfs, Volume 1*, 12.
71 Ainsworth, *Merry England: Or, Nobles and Serfs, Volume 1*, 260.
72 William Harrison Ainsworth, *Merry England: Or, Nobles and Serfs, Volume 2* (London: Tinsley Brothers, 1874), 30–31.
73 Ainsworth, *Merry England: Or, Nobles and Serfs, Volume 1*, 247. Cf. Froude, 'Annals of an English Abbey,' 289, on recalling Ball in London at Ball's trial and echoing Jesus's arrival in Jerusalem (i.e., the 'triumphal entry' of Matthew 21.1–11; Mark 11.1–11; Luke 19.28–44; John 12.12–19): 'a month and two days after his triumphal entry into London.'
74 Ainsworth, *Merry England: Or, Nobles and Serfs, Volume 3*, 16–17.

At the archbishop's palace at Canterbury, the presentation of Ball's enthusiasm as an act of religious demagoguery becomes plain to see. Ball's elevation (second only to Tyler's) recalls Christ's position next to God (cf. Matthew 22.44; 26.64; Mark 16.19, Luke 22.69; Acts 2.34; 5.31; 7.55–56; Romans 8.34; Ephesians 1.20; Colossians 3.1; Hebrews 8.1; 10.12; 12.2; 1 Peter 3.22; Revelation 3.21. Cf. Psalm 110.1). Tyler proclaims his authority by sitting on the throne 'while John Ball took a place on his right, and the Outlaw on his left.' From their 'elevated spot' the three leaders 'surveyed the lawless proceedings of the throng' while Tyler even had his foot on a stool (cf. Isaiah 66.1–2; Psalm 132.7; 1 Chronicles 28.2; 2 Chronicles 9.18; Matthew 5.35). They preside over a kangaroo court as the old seneschal Siward is brought before them 'for judgment.'[75] Ball's strange dark-Christ persona is clearly another way of denoting religious excess and zeal. He takes his mule to the top of a 'mound' which rose from the flat plain (cf. Luke 6.17; Matthew 5.1; 8.1) and 'from his elevated position preached a sermon to the vast assemblage.' He then speaks on the Adam and Eve couplet with a 'loud, mocking voice' which was 'increasing in fervour.' This is shown as a 'very singular and striking picture' with his 'features inflamed by excitement.'[76]

Ball even starts to use a 'portable pulpit...which was more than twenty feet high' which he 'ascended' to preach to the crowd. With his 'stentorian voice' he could make himself heard at a 'considerable distance.' After his sermon, he invites the insurgents to join him in prayer and, again echoing the implied perverted Christ role he is given in the novel, 'the entire host knelt down' and there was the stirring spectacle of the 'vast kneeling multitude' (cf. Philippians 2.9–11). The accompanying hymn 'in which thousands of rude, untutored voices joined, was sublime.'[77] That this was more in league with the satanic is also made clear. When Ball threw his hood back during the events in London, he has 'an almost demoniacal expression,' and when Tyler is killed, Ball rides forward on his mule 'with the looks and gestures of a demoniac.'[78] This is the moment, at peak zeal and madness, when he finally turns on the king and is killed by Sir John Philpot as the 'apostate monk' falls from his trusty mule.[79]

---

75 Ainsworth, *Merry England: Or, Nobles and Serfs, Volume 1*, 262–65; Ainsworth, *Merry England: Or, Nobles and Serfs, Volume 3*, 146.
76 Ainsworth, *Merry England: Or, Nobles and Serfs, Volume 2*, 27–29.
77 Ainsworth, *Merry England: Or, Nobles and Serfs, Volume 3*, 4–5.
78 Ainsworth, *Merry England: Or, Nobles and Serfs, Volume 3*, 219, 232.
79 Ainsworth, *Merry England: Or, Nobles and Serfs, Volume 3*, 232. Cf. 1.77, when Ball was initially opposed not to the king but the king's advisors.

Part of the purpose of the demonic Ball is to present him as a foil for critiquing what laid beyond the established church, much in the same ways as we saw Church of England writers did during the Reformation, particularly those hostile to the more radical Reformation. In this case, the connection between Ball's zeal and his devotion to Wycliffe is important in implicitly constructing excessive Protestantism. Chaucer has a role in the novel and learns from Ball himself about his adherence to 'Wycliffe's doctrines.'[80] The old concerns so prominent in the Reformation are also present in *Merry England*. Chaucer learns that Ball is effectively a proto-reformer who claims that a 'religious insurrection was at hand' and that 'ecclesiastical hierarchy must be abolished' but that this would soon develop into sharing property in common and, ultimately, a full revolt.[81] Ball's unfortunate claims to religious authority and political sedition become clearer as the novel progresses. In one of his 'fierce and inflammatory harangues' he calls on the people to rise up, proclaims that Sudbury must die, and that 'neither the King nor the kingdom ought to submit to any episcopal see…no bishop or other ecclesiastic ought to hold an important civil office.' Ball also rejects papal authority, 'like my master, John Wycliffe.'[82]

Merry England presents two martyrdoms as contrasts with Ball. First is Siward's judgement before Ball, Straw, and the enthroned Tyler. On seeing Ball and the multitude at the palace, Siward immediately criticises Ball 'with unabated courage,' calling him a 'renegade priest' worthy of hanging for stirring up 'all this mischief.' He even fires a bolt at Ball which is merely laughed off.[83] In the judgement scene, after the palace was 'invaded by a furious throng,' Siward is prepared to die before betraying the archbishop. The 'brave old man' tries to block out the furious cries on the bloodthirsty mob and he 'cast a look upwards at the golden angel on the spire' and 'murmured a prayer' before being beheaded by a 'ferocious ruffian.'[84] This was a death surely worthy of any staunch supporter of the Church of England with Catholic aesthetics and sympathies.[85]

More elaborate still is the presentation of Sudbury as martyr, again based on Walsingham's account, which also included the claims of devilish influence. On the brow of Tower Hill, on his loyal mule, Ball watches 'the

---

80 Ainsworth, *Merry England: Or, Nobles and Serfs, Volume 1*, 129.
81 Ainsworth, *Merry England: Or, Nobles and Serfs, Volume 1*, 130.
82 Ainsworth, *Merry England: Or, Nobles and Serfs, Volume 1*, 248–51.
83 Ainsworth, *Merry England: Or, Nobles and Serfs, Volume 1*, 255–56.
84 Ainsworth, *Merry England: Or, Nobles and Serfs, Volume 1*, 265. Cf. Froude, 'Annals of an English Abbey,' 284.
85 Cf. Carver, *Author Who Outsold Dickens*, 125–27.

painful march of the victims, and exulted in the indignities to which they were exposed' before riding down to meet the archbishop. Ball greets him in a 'scoffing tone' and tells him he was to reap the reward of his crimes. Sudbury's trial hints at the story of Barabbas, as Ball explains to the crowd that Sudbury had 'wronged the people' and deserved to die, to which the crowd responded with 'one voice' that 'He shall die!'[86] Sudbury does not know what wrong he has done but, like a good martyr, does not plead for his life. Sudbury's defence promotes a kind of proto-High Church civic paternalism as he explains that he had expended money on the people and partly rebuilt Canterbury, which Ball rejects as false speaking. Sudbury functions as a representative for the true church, paralleling (and against) Ball who functions as a representative of its perversion, notably by Sudbury having a voice which matches Ball's in being able to command a crowd. In 'a voice that awakened attention,' Sudbury warns them of the consequences of their actions and claims that England will be under an Interdict.[87] But Ball, naturally rejecting Catholic hierarchy, refuses to acknowledge the Pope's authority. Not fearing death, Sudbury had already prepared for his fate by spending the night in (tellingly) 'prayer and confession' but unleashes a prophetic condemnation of Ball, who he accuses of abandoning his 'religion' and inciting rebellion for which he would shortly appear before the (proper) 'Judgment Seat.' The crowd may have been howling like wolves but Sudbury (like Siward before him) remains calm, forgives his executioner (who took several strokes to complete the act), and gives the appropriately Catholicising response: raising up his hands to heaven, he calls on the assistance of the prayers of the 'blessed angels and saints.' And just in case we are not clear, Sudbury concludes after the first failed swing of the axe that 'Heaven wills that I should be ranked among the martyrs!'[88]

The Wheel Is Going to Keep Turning

But English Protestantism of course had an alternative theological reading of history to counter anything with Catholic tendencies, not least when it came to Wycliffe. In an 1859 lecture on 'Wycliffe the First Great English Protestant' given in Hyde (as well as elsewhere, over many years) and

---

86 Ainsworth, *Merry England: Or, Nobles and Serfs, Volume 3*, 188–89.
87 Ainsworth, *Merry England: Or, Nobles and Serfs, Volume 3*, 191–92. Cf. Froude, 'Annals of an English Abbey,' 284.
88 Ainsworth, *Merry England: Or, Nobles and Serfs, Volume 3*, 191–92.

hosted by the Rev. A. Read, the Chartist and radical Henry Vincent set the scene of a pervasive Catholic influence in English politics, claiming that since the time of William the Conqueror there had been a movement to 'overthrow the civil power of papal dominance.' This was the context for his discussion of Wycliffe's teachings and the influence of the Bible 'upon the public mind.' The only other historical event reported concerned the state of England up to the time of Richard II, 'paying a high compliment to Wat Tyler, as being instrumental in abolishing slavery in England.'[89] The influence of the idea of Ball as a negative theological foil likewise had its limitations; Cassell's theological reclaiming of Ball as a figure proclaiming 'the literal declarations of the gospel that God is no respecter of persons' was hardly unusual.[90]

Indeed, Ball and his supporters as radical biblical or theological interpreters was a recurring theme, even if less prominent than his political proclamations. At the advent of Chartism, Thomas Keightley (1789–1872) wrote in his *History of England* (1839) that opposition to serfdom had been spreading throughout society partly because of the Bible. The 'equal and beneficent spirit which the Gospel breathes had,' Keightley argued, 'imperceptibly penetrated all ranks.' Thus, kings and nobles 'had been gradually emancipating their serfs,' clergy favoured emancipation, and 'religious teaching frequently dwelt on the equality of all portions of a sinful race on the eyes of a just and beneficent Deity.'[91] While Ball may have been 'fanatical and enthusiastic enough,' one of Spurgeon's reasons for believing that he was 'not half so bad as some paint him' was an implicitly Protestant (or an implicitly anti-Catholic) reading of Ball: he was excommunicated for 'holding the doctrine that all men are equal, which was very horrible heresy in the judgment of the Church of Rome.'[92]

Despite the negative readings of Ball, then, the momentum in favour of the revolt was not slowing as the reception history headed toward the end of the nineteenth century. Indeed, the internal tensions in the negative readings of the revolt always provided the potential for more sympathetic

---

89 *Glossop Record* (5 November 1859). Cf. *Bolton Chronicle* (20 September 1856); *Derbyshire Advertiser and Journal* (25 September 1857); *Derby Mercury* (30 September 1857); *Surrey Comet* (23 September 1865); *Surrey Comet* (7 October 1865); *London City Press* (14 October 1871); *Whitby Times* (21 August 1874); *Peterborough Advertiser* (28 November 1874). The *Sheffield Daily Telegraph* (13 November 1874) reported that Vincent had even talked about 'Wycliffe's overthrow of English serfdom.'
90 *Cassell's Illustrated History of England*, 413.
91 Keightley, *The History of England*, 300.
92 *London City Press* (11 November 1867).

retellings. The lauding of Tyler's defence of his daughter was virtually ubiquitous in receptions of 1381 and, incidentally, we even find the impressive verbal form, 'to Wat Tylerise,'[93] which took its place alongside the more general 'to be Wat Tylered.'[94] Even if some writers disliked insurrection and the violent response, condemnation of serfdom and praise of basic liberty was also ubiquitous in mid-nineteenth-century receptions. As ever, a simple reversal of whether lower order insurgency was a good or bad thing meant that the 1381 revolt could always elicit certain sympathies, being, as it was, associated with the working class, strikes, trade unionism, protests, unjust taxation, political reform and representation, the pursuit of liberty and justice, and freedom from slavery.[95] In this context, the reclaiming of Ball, including critiquing the derogatory remarks of the chroniclers and historians, continued to be relatively normalised. As one critique of Froissart's assessment of Ball put it (and echoing Hume), the 'generous sentiments of natural equality are so deeply ingraven on the human heart, and so inseparably blended with the dictates of reason and conscience, that no appeal to them can be wholly vain; their power over those who grievously suffer from their violation never can cease to be great.'[96]

93 *Worcestershire Chronicle* (2 January 1867).
94 *Illustrated Times* (29 August 1857).
95 See, additionally, e.g., *The Advocate* (8 January 1851); *South Eastern Gazette* (20 April 1852); *Kentish Mercury* (25 December 1852); *South Eastern Gazette* (28 February 1854); *Bell's Weekly Messenger* (17 March 1856); *Bristol Mercury* (29 November 1856); *Staffordshire Advertiser* (7 February 1857); *Illustrated Times* (21 February 1857); *Rochdale Observer* (22 May 1858); *Rochdale Pilot* (5 June 1858); *Preston Chronicle* (4 September 1858); *Star of Gwent* (18 December 1858); *Saint James's Chronicle* (9 July 1863); *London Evening Standard* (15 August 1863); *London Evening Standard* (1 October 1863); *Shoreditch Observer* (2 December 1865); *Newcastle Daily Chronicle* (2 February 1867); *Hereford Times* (16 February 1867); *Wakefield Free Press* (16 February 1867); *Penny Illustrated Paper* (16 February 1867); *West London Observer* (16 February 1867); *Yorkshire Post and Leeds Intelligencer* (23 March 1867); *Morning Advertiser* (17 April 1867); *Carlisle Patriot* (19 April 1867); *Huddersfield Chronicle* (20 April 1867); *Manchester Courier* (23 April 1867); *Illustrated Times* (10 August 1867); *Manchester Courier* (18 November 1867); *Eddowes's Journal* (20 November 1867); *Somerset County Gazette* (14 December 1867); *Sheerness Times Guardian* (11 April 1868); *Herts Advertiser* (7 August 1869); *Gloucester Journal* (18 November 1871); *Bath Chronicle* (6 February 1873); *Manchester Evening News* (2 June 1873); *Knaresborough Post* (7 November 1874); *Northampton Mercury* (28 November 1874); *Burnley Gazette* (3 July 1875); *Kentish Independent* (8 April 1876); *Barnsley Independent* (7 July 1877).
96 *South Eastern Gazette* (1 July 1851).

14
Class Struggle among the Historians

Beyond plenty of snippets, more extended hagiographical lectures on Ball turn up from towards the end of the nineteenth century. In November 1882, the *Herts Advertiser* reported on one such lecture given by the Rev. William Urwick on 'John Ball, the Lollard Martyr'. Ball was not only 'the Lollard martyr' and the 'first Protestant martyr in England' who 'refused to retract his so-called heresies or to deny his Heavenly Master and Lord,' he was apparently even treated the same way Paul had been treated by the 'Jerusalem Jews,' and, in a more elevated comparison still, like 'his Heavenly Master he died in the midst of foes'. The 'patriot of Blackheath' was further 'refused the right of Englishmen'—trial by jury—and the trial itself was a perversion of justice. Ball's politics were presented in a relatively benign manner, not to be confused (as they were) with the violence of Wat Tyler or Jack Straw. It was for good reason that, apparently, 'among the poor, the weak, the down-trodden, and oppressed people of England in his time, there were many hearts that beat in sympathy with John Ball,' and 'many a sigh was heard, many a tear shed, in many a poor home in England, when the news reached it that John Ball, the Lollard preacher and people's friend, was hanged.' Urwick was reported to have claimed that it was Walsingham who gave Ball's sermon a 'political tone' whereas the reality was (citing Isaiah 58.6) that the 'politics he preached are only the politics of gospel liberty as against oppression and robbery,' particularly against the poor.[1]

But this relative de-politicising of Ball was not happening elsewhere, including in the numerous talks given by various lecturing clergy. As Tyler was associated with Radicalism and Liberals,[2] so Ball was similarly a 'democratic priest' whose famous couplet 'suggests that principle of equality

---

1   *Herts Advertiser* (4 November 1882). Cf. *Bath Chronicle* (6 February 1873).
2   E.g., *Bedfordshire Mercury* (24 November 1877); *Batley Reporter and Guardian* (30 November 1878); *Eastern Daily Press* (26 July 1883).

which lies at the root of democracy.'[3] But from the 1860s and 1870s onwards, and in the light of the five-hundredth anniversary of the revolt,[4] friend and foe were increasingly agreeing that Ball was associated with something a little stronger in an era when the ideas of Marx and Engels were becoming better known. In his lecture (1878) on Wycliffe to the Brighouse Liberal Club, Rev. Galbraith argued that Wycliffe's views on church property would 'even now be considered radical and revolutionary' and, in lamenting the influence of the 1381 uprising, claimed of it that 'a spirit of semi-religious communism mingled strangely with the secular element in the movement.' Ball's 'stirring sermon' at Blackheath was, in fact, an example of 'preaching socialism.'[5] In a talk in Dudley (1880), Rev. Fox argued that socialism had a long history and (as well as Anabaptism after him) was associated with the 'reforming priest of the name John Ball,'[6] while in 1882 the much travelled Rev. Clark spoke in Boston (Lincolnshire) of 'the agitation of John Ball, the socialist.'[7] In other parts of the press we find statements about Ball teaching a 'simple communism of the disaffected agriculturalists' expressed in the Adam and Eve couplet ('doggerel rhyme'),[8] while the 'agrarian character' of the revolt was also attested in Ball's couplet and formed the basis for 'its theory of Communism.'[9] Sudbury was even 'beheaded by the Communists under Wat Tyler.'[10]

Even in receptions of Ball where socialism was a problem, such connections were becoming difficult to deny. *Extracts from the Flying Roll* by the Southcottian James Jershom Jezreel (formerly James White) received a

3 *Reynolds's Newspaper* (8 September 1878). Cf. *Kentish Mercury* (30 March 1883): 'John Ball the friar, excited the armed host by his democratic sermons.'
4 Very little was made of the anniversary in the English press beyond casual, passing, and typically copied mentions, cf. e.g., *Leighton Buzzard Observer* (1 February 1881); *Newcastle Courant* (4 February 1881); *Lake's Falmouth Packet* (12 February 1881); *Whitstable Times* (12 March 1881); *West Somerset Free Press* (26 March 1881); *Weston Mercury* (26 March 1881); *Reading Mercury* (19 March 1881); *Preston Chronicle* (26 March 1881); *Liverpool Daily Post* (12 November 1881). Dobson, 'Remembering the Peasants' Revolt,' in Liddell and Wood (eds.), *Essex and the Great Revolt of 1381*, 15, likewise wrote of 'the somewhat remarkable silence which greeted the quincentenary of the rebellion.'
5 *Brighouse News* (6 April 1878). Cf. *Hampstead & Highgate Express* (28 October 1876).
6 *Dudley and District News* (24 January 1880).
7 *Boston Guardian* (30 September 1882).
8 *Globe* (5 January 1881).
9 *Globe* (11 November 1881); *Huddersfield Chronicle* (14 November 1881).
10 *Bath Chronicle* (28 December 1882); *Nottinghamshire Guardian* (29 December 1882).

polemical review in the *Record* which effectively brought together and then split and reapplied the positive and negative receptions of Ball. Worryingly, Jezreel was understood to use the English language 'of the good county of Kent, the county of John Ball and plain speaking,' and the county associated with the invention of the 'awkward' Adam and Eve question. Once again, thoughts about Adam and Eve had returned in Kent but this was not the 'mad priest' and 'pure-blooded Englishman and an honest Christian' of the fourteenth century. But even the problematic side of Ball's nineteenth-century reputation was not enough to undermine him—Ball may have been 'a Socialist we fear' but even this could be countered by claiming that he still had 'the best elements of Mr. Spurgeon and Joseph Arch.' The old, negative portrayal of the seditious Ball were now attributed to his unworthy heir. This latter-day Kentish 'mad priest' was probably foreign and not really an Englishman given his use of the English language with its 'occidental twang,' dubious spelling, and grammatical inconsistencies. Worst still were his heretical tendencies (Gnosticism in particular), a 'grotesque jumble,' full of 'absurdity,' 'vulgarity,' and 'madness.'[11]

By the 1880s it was commonplace to find the revolt, and Ball especially, alongside labels relating to 'socialism' and 'communism.'[12] In the background to all this was, of course, Marx and Engels and their influence in England. This was observed in the press. Certainly, a 'good deal of attention has been directed at the Socialistic movement at the East-end of London,' and there has been 'an energetic crusade against capitalists and landowners' in Regent Street, according to a report in 1883 under the title 'Clerical Socialism.' Even more startling ('very noteworthy') were not only the involvement of 'clergymen reputed to belong to the High Church party' but also the accompanying principles of the Democratic Federation, no less. One lecture on socialism, it was added, looked at examples from the past which included Ball (naturally), whose Adam and Eve couplet was met with 'a responsive cheer from the audience.' The principle that labour is

---

11   *Record* (11 December 1885), discussed in P. G. Rogers, *The Sixth Trumpeter: The Story of Jezreel and His Tower* (London: Oxford University Press, 1963), 57–58. I am grateful to Michelle Fletcher for this reference.

12   See also, e.g., *London Evening Standard* (15 August 1863); *Herts Advertiser* (7 August 1869); *Pall Mall Gazette* (26 April 1872); *Bath Chronicle* (6 February 1873); *Taunton Courier* (4 June 1879); *Daily Telegraph* (9 June 1881). Jane Cowan, *Newcastle Chronicle* (9 June 1883), similarly claimed that Ball taught as thorough a transformation of the 'social system as ever did the revolutionaries of a more enlightened time.'

the source of value may have been adopted by 'Carl Marx,' but it was 'not unknown' to Ball.[13]

And such associations between Ball and socialism or communism were not just short reports or brief remarks in the popular press on public lectures. In an extended essay in *Scribner's Monthly* (1873), shortly republished as a book of collected essays, James Anthony Froude, later regius professor at Oxford (1892–1894), used language of eighteenth-century France to describe Ball's teachings. Continuing his earlier analysis of Wycliffe (see Chapter 13), Froude claimed that Ball was 'said to be infected with Wickliffe's heresies—infected at any rate with impatience of wrong-dealing, and with visions of the contrat social' and preached 'liberty, equality and fraternity.'[14] The association between Ball and revolutionary thinking was updated further by Froude. Discussions surrounding Wycliffe and the uprising likewise involved the 'elemental rights of man,' the result of which was 'an explosion of communism.'[15] Indeed, Froude further claimed that Tyler, Straw, and Ball were planning on governing England in Richard's name 'on communist principles.'[16] What the emerging professionalisation of history—which Dobson saw as the 'first golden age in the academic historiography of the Peasants' Revolt'[17]— also provided was more expanded accounts in books and articles which tried to understand in more detail the place of Ball in the bigger historical picture, from causes to consequences. This included, as we will see, a dialectical materialist model associated with Marxism and explanations of the transformation from feudalist to bourgeois society but also developments of the Whiggish view of history, theories on the growth of the English state, and the place of Ball (and indeed religion) within them. All the while, the spectre of communism haunted the analysis of even the most dispassionate historian.

Religious Socialism among the Dons

Like much of the story of the reception of 1381, some basic details could be agreed across the ideological spectrum with the differences emerging

---

13 *Reynolds's Newspaper* (18 November 1883).
14 Froude, 'Annals of an English Abbey,' 198. Cf. *Norwich Mercury* (24 January 1874).
15 Froude, 'Annals of an English Abbey,' 196.
16 Froude, 'Annals of an English Abbey,' 286.
17 Dobson, 'Remembering the Peasants' Revolt,' in Liddell and Wood (eds.), *Essex and the Great Revolt of 1381*, 17.

in the longer-term historical evaluation or value judgements placed upon them. Ideas of failure, social potency, and historical development in relation to Ball were likewise understood from left to right. One of the most authoritative conservative interpretations was from Anglican priest (and later bishop), Tory, regius professor at Oxford (1866–1884), and dominant figure among the emerging professional historians, William Stubbs (1825–1901). In his landmark volumes, *The Constitutional History of England in Its Origin and Development* (1874–1878), Stubbs presented the familiar and varied causes for the 'revolutionary rising of 1381', deemed to be 'one of the most portentous phenomena to be found in the whole of our history.'[18] However, he also provided a distinct downplaying of overall ideological coherency among the varied and ignoble agendas:

> it would seem as if all men who had or thought they had any grievance had banded together... No common political motive can be alleged: but just as in court and parliament, forgetful of the older and nobler war-cries, men were intriguing and combining for selfish ends, year by year altering their combinations and diversifying the object of their intrigues;- so the general discontent and trouble in the humbler classes...produced a rebellion with many causes and many consequences, having perhaps a common organisation, but not animated by any one principle except a wish to shake off the particular burden.[19]

Ball appears as (and, indeed, merely in) a footnote to this history, the 'most conspicuous' of the clergy complaining about the church and presented among those 'taking advantage of the popularity of Wycliffe's order of poor priests' who were 'spreading through the country perverted social views in the guise of religion.'[20] If Walsingham was correct, Stubbs

18 William Stubbs, *The Constitutional History of England in Its Origin and Development, Vol. II* (Oxford: Clarendon Press, 1875), 449.
19 Stubbs, *Constitutional History of England*, 450–51.
20 Stubbs, *Constitutional History of England*, 450–52, including n. 2. A more toned down version of this argument is found in, e.g., Henry de Beltgens Gibbins, *English Social Reformers* (London: Methuen & Co., 1892), 5–6, 25: the 'revolt...was encouraged and stimulated, indirectly perhaps, but none the less certainly, by the teaching of Wiklif and his followers, the "poor priests"... No doubt the order of the wandering friars that Wiklif founded may have gone further in their direct teaching than did their great master; but such doctrine... must have greatly encouraged those who rebelled against the undue exactions of their lords...Of their preaching we shall have an example in the sermons of John Ball...His teaching was wrong and one-sided...John Ball was an enthusiast, violent and mistaken, but yet rousing our sympathy by his evident

surmised, then Ball's 'doctrines...were a perversion and practical application of Wycliffe's theories, but probably bearing to the practical teaching of Wycliffe much the same relation as those of the Anabaptists did to Luther's.'[21] But Wycliffe was not without fault and, with clear foreshadowing of his treatment of Ball, the ambiguities (and selfishness) in his ideas could lead to failure and even socialism:

> Wycliffe himself was a deep thinker and a popular teacher; but his logical system of politics, when it was applied to practice, turned out to be little else than socialism; and his religious system, unless its vital doctrines are understood to be thrown into the shade by its controversial tone, was unfortunately devoid of the true leaven of all religious success, sympathy, and charity.[22]

The use of the idea of a perversion of Wycliffe, of Protestantism, and of religion, as well as the inbuilt dangers of a complicated Wycliffe, built on a long-established tradition, and one which was live in Stubbs's mid-late nineteenth-century context, not least in the case of Froude (see also Chapter 13). In his treatment of 1381, Stubbs's understanding of long-term national growth and his own take on Whiggish history and constitution harked back to the tradition that Ball represented some sort of aberration but whose contribution to the progression of English history involved generating reaction from above in dealing with such threats. If Ball's ideas foreshadowed socialism, then this was something to be dealt with or warned against rather than embraced in the national story.

Shortly after Stubbs's *Constitutional History of England*, the importance of the Bible in the revolt and for Ball was promoted differently in another landmark work: that of the influential professor (at KCL and Oxford) of economics and political economy, political radical, campaigner for the Liberal Party, MP, occasional biblical scholar, and lapsed Tractarian priest, James Thorold Rogers (1823–1890) in *Six Centuries of Work and Wages: The History of English Labour* (1884). Rogers likewise focused on the influence of Wycliffe's 'religious opinions' where they interacted with 'social

---

earnestness and good faith.' For a positive spin on the poor priests in similar language, see, e.g., *Brighouse News* (6 April 1878). Cf. Pearson, *English History in the Fourteenth Century*, 253, 264 ('John Ball, who, if not one of Wycliffe's "poor priests," preached doctrines very similar to theirs...John Ball and John Wrawe had done more to destroy Wycliffe's work than the whole church establishment could have effected').

21 Stubbs, *Constitutional History of England*, 451–52.
22 Stubbs, *Constitutional History of England*, 440.

and political theories' and this involved establishing the barefooted poor priests to counter the influence of the begging friars devoted to the pope.[23] Wycliffe's poor priests were active around the country and organised 'resistance among the serfs' and 'honeycombed the minds of the upland folk with what may be called religious socialism.' But while there were obvious similarities with Stubbs's understanding of the basic details, the evaluation was quite different. These 'Bible men' had been,

> introduced to the new world of the Old Testament, to the history of the human race, to the primeval garden and the young world, where the first parents of all mankind lived by simple toil, and were the ancestors of the proud noble and knight, as well as of the down-trodden serf and despised burgher. They read of the brave times when there was no king in Israel, when every man did that which was right in his own eyes, and sat under his own vine and his own fig-tree, none daring to make him afraid...But, most of all, the preacher would dwell on his own prototype, on the man of God, the wise prophet who denounced kings and princes and high-priests...[24]

With the revitalised old book, we now have a causal explanation for the emergence of a historical type: the 'peasant preacher' who could stir up resistance and reapply the biblical stories to their predicament. These preachers could sometimes be 'denounced, detected, and imprisoned' and one such example was, of course, Ball, 'one of the most active and

---

23 James E. Thorold Rogers, *Six Centuries of Work and Wages: The History of English Labour* (New York: G. P. Putnam's Sons, 1884), 249–51.

24 Rogers, *Six Centuries*, 254–55. Cf. *Bath Chronicle* (6 February 1873); *Brighouse News* (6 April 1878). See also J. J. Jusserand, *English Wayfaring Life in the Middle Ages (XIVth Century)* (transl. Lucy Toulmin Smith; London: T. Fisher Unwin, 1899 [1884]), 284–85, 290, 294: 'Those whom Wyclif sent to popularize his doctrines, his "simple priests," or "poor priests," did just what others had done before them; they imitated their forerunners, and no more confined themselves to expounding the difficult and not always democratic theories of their master than the mendicant friars, or monks, or secular priests, friends of the revolution, strictly kept to the precepts of the gospel. Their sympathies were with the people, and they showed it in their discourses...The revolutionary leader John Ball was a secular priest, and so was the well-known Lollard, William Thorpe...What made Ball powerful was that he found his best weapons in the Bible; quoting it he appealed to the good sentiments of the lowly, to their virtue, their reason...Certain it is that many friars, in their roaming career, preached in the market place, just like John Ball, the new doctrines of emancipation.'

outspoken' of the poor priests who was imprisoned because of 'his violent harangues.'[25]

John Richard Green

An influential combination of a homegrown radicalism—indeed 'socialism'—and rethinking of the periodisation of history came from the popular and influential, 800-plus page, *A Short History of the English People* (1874) by John Richard Green (1837–1883). His sources for the uprising tellingly included Rogers's earlier work on the 'condition of land and labour at this time' alongside the chroniclers Knighton and Walsingham, who were 'the fullest and most valuable,' though he cited Froissart too.[26] Holding liberal and radical political and theological views, Green had worked as an Anglican priest (notably in the East End slums) before devoting his time to history where he was able to continue these interests. Green was also a friend of Stubbs (and Stubbs's successor at Oxford, E. A. Freeman) and likewise worked in the standard tradition of the importance of Anglo-Saxon liberties in the retelling of English history. But Green, rhetorically at least, had a strong focus on non-traditional history in other ways. Not without wider internationalist and comparative interests, Green's was a patriotic history that stressed the importance of how the English people had periodically stood up against oppressive rule. This history from below (as we might now call it) was to be retold alongside the social and cultural life of individuals (e.g., Chaucer, Shakespeare) and the people more generally rather than kings and battles, even to the point of controversially downgrading the periodisation of history based on monarchs.[27] This emphasis

---

25 Rogers, *Six Centuries*, 255. Rogers (261) also noted a 'letter of an enigmatical but sufficiently intelligible kind addressed by one Schep, formerly a priest of York, but latterly of Colchester, to the confederates.' Cf. Jusserand, *English Wayfaring Life*, 288: 'We may gain an idea of their speeches by recalling the celebrated harangue of the priest John Ball, the most stirring of these travelling orators.'
26 John R. Green, *A Short History of the English People* (London: Macmillan and Co., 1874), 237.
27 For biography and analysis of the context and content of *A Short History* see, e.g., John Kenyon, *The History Men: Classic Work on Historians and Their History* (second edition; London: Weidenfeld and Nicolson 1993), 164–70; Anthony Brundage, *The People's Historian: John Richard Green and the Writing of History in Victorian England* (Westport: Greenwood, 1994).

on 'people' was explained in the preface to *A Short History* and illustrated with the example of, among others, Ball:

> It is a history not of English Kings or English Conquests, but of the English People....I have preferred...to dwell on...that constitutional, intellectual, and social advance in which we read the history of the nation itself...I have devoted more space to Chaucer than to Cressy, to Caxton than to the petty strife of Yorkist and Lancastrian, to the Poor Law of Elizabeth than to her victory at Cadiz, to the Methodist revival than to the escape of the Young Pretender...If I have said little of the glories of Cressy, it is because I have dwelt much on the wrong and misery which prompted the verse of Longland and the preaching of Ball...In England, more than elsewhere, constitutional progress has been the result of social development...I have endeavoured to point out, at great crises, such as those of the Peasant Revolt of the rise of the New Monarchy, how much of our political history is the outcome of social changes; and throughout I have drawn greater attention to the religious, intellectual, and industrial progress of the nation itself than has, so far as I remember, ever been done in any previous history of the same extent.[28]

In practice, Green may not have been as consistent in avoiding elite history as he claimed but the point was clear enough. Not only was Green's *A Short History* a hugely popular book (it sold 32,000 copies in its first year), it was used, as Anthony Brundage added, in classes sponsored by the Workers' Educational Association and influenced the first generation of Labour MPs.[29] Honourable mention must also be made of Green's use of the term 'Peasant Revolt' (and the years 1377–1381 were organised under the hitherto uncommon title) which may have been the most influential use of the famous label as it was starting to take off.[30]

28 Green, *A Short History*, iii–iv.
29 Brundage, *The People's Historian*, 157.
30 Dobson, 'Remembering the Peasants' Revolt', in Liddell and Wood (eds.), *Essex and the Great Revolt of 1381*, 16; Paul Strohm, 'A "Peasants' Revolt"?' in Stephen J. Harris and Bryon Lee Grigsby (eds.), *Misconceptions about the Middle Ages* (New York: Routledge, 2008), 197–203 (201–2); Prescott, 'Great and Horrible Rumour', in Firnhaber-Baker and Schoenaers (eds.), *Routledge History Handbook of Medieval Revolt*, 78, 97. Prescott speculates that Green may have been inspired by the work of Joseph Arch and the formation of a union for agricultural workers which was presented, for instance, in Edwin Goadby's article under the title 'Peasants' Revolt' in *New Monthly Magazine* 153 (1873), 36–40. In addition to the examples provided by Dobson and Prescott, we might note the familiar 'Peasants' Revolt' was used, e.g., in the *Herts Advertiser* (4 November 1882), while similar labels included, e.g., the 'peasant insurrection'

Green gave a history of the social organisation of rural England including the emergence of serfdom, the seeds of its undoing, the significance of long-term social mobility among the peasantry, the rise of the wealthier tenant and the free labourer, the availability of an alternative life in towns, and accompanying class struggles dramatically intensified by the labour shortages and parliamentary reactions following the Black Death. This generated the 'impulse towards a wider liberty' which was manifest in the 'spirit of social revolt.'[31] The growth of a fierce 'spirit of resistance' involved strikes among lower craftsmen and collaboration between free labourers and 'villians' and between fugitive serfs and wealthier tenantry. In this context, the 'cry of the poor' found a 'terrible utterance' in the words of Ball, noting (in scare quotes) how the 'courtly' Froissart called him 'a mad priest of Kent.' 'Mad' he may have been labelled, but, Green argued, it was through Ball's preaching that 'England first listened to knell of feudalism' and, in a striking turn of phrase which connected Ball with the revolutionary future, 'the declaration of the rights of man.' Indeed, Green's present became further infused with Ball of the past in the claim that it was the 'tyranny of property that then as ever roused the defiance of socialism.' Ball's 'levelling doctrine' as found in the Adam and Eve rhyme was spreading when a 'fresh instance of public oppression fanned the smouldering discontent into a flame,' namely the poll tax and the 'desperate struggle in which the proprietary classes...were striving to reduce the labourer into fresh serfage.'[32]

But this reading of history and Ball in terms of economics and class struggles was connected to the importance of changes in religious belief through Green's earlier presentation of Wycliffe, and with a distinctive Protestant bias. Wycliffe—presented in near hagiographical terms—was 'the first Reformer' who asserted the 'freedom of religious thought against the dogmas of the Papacy.' This was precisely the point when the medieval church 'had sunk to its lowest point of spiritual decay' but also as its 'extortion and tyranny...severed the English clergy from the Papacy' while 'their own selfishness severed them from the nation at large.'[33] The wealthier and higher clergy were more interested in political office and were 'severed

---

in the *Yorkshire Post* (14 June 1877) and the 'peasant rising' in the *Todmorden Advertiser* (15 December 1882). By 1902, George Kriehn, 'Studies in the Sources of the Social Revolt in 1381,' *American Historical Review* 7 (1902): 254–85 (254 n. 1), was rejecting what he called the 'usual title *Peasants' Rising*' on the now familiar grounds that the rebellion was not made up exclusively of peasants.

31 Green, *A Short History*, 240.
32 Green, *A Short History*, 243.
33 Green, *A Short History*, 229–30.

from the lower priesthood' by 'scandalous inequality'.[34] Wycliffe's philosophical critique of the church involving arguments about the dominion of God undermined the mediating priesthood of the medieval church and permitted the seizing of ecclesiastical property. Allegations of turning serf against lord may have been dismissed with disdain by Wycliffe, but he 'had to bear a suspicion which was justified by the conduct of some of his followers'. And in this context, Green noted that Ball was claimed to be 'one of his adherents' and Wycliffe's ideas were now 'attached to the projects of the socialist peasant leaders'.[35] Though Wycliffe became tainted with such ideas, he nonetheless distanced himself from the support of 'wealthier classes'. Wycliffe had already established his poor preachers with their 'coarse sermons' who provided a widespread network among all classes, including among the 'peasantry of the country-side'. But, in the 'first of such a kind in our history', he appealed to 'England at large' with tract after tract 'in the tongue of the people itself' and was 'transformed into the pamphleteer' as he became the 'father of our later English prose', albeit 'rough, clear, homely English…the speech of the ploughman and the trader of the day…coloured with the picturesque phraseology of the Bible'.[36]

This presentation of Wycliffe the religious *and* social reformer and transformer of England provided Green with another connection to Ball. For Green, the 'religious revolution' of Wycliffe certainly gave a 'fresh impulse to a revolution of even greater importance, which had for a long time been changing the whole face of the country'.[37] But there are clear linguistic connections between Wycliffe and Ball in *A Short History* assisted by Green's approach to history. In addition to summarising the 'things will never go well in England' speech, Green suggested that Ball's twenty-year preaching had been 'a Lollardry of coarser and more popular type than that of Wyclif'.[38] Green's emphasis on a history from below meant that Ball's letters ('quaint rhymes') could be reclaimed and foregrounded. They 'served as a summons to the revolt' and in the 'rude jingle of these lines began for England the literature of political controversy' which were the predecessors of the pamphlets of Milton and (surprisingly) Burke. The letters may have been 'rough', but they expressed 'clearly enough' (no nonsensi-

---

34 Green, *A Short History*, 231.
35 Green, *A Short History*, 233. Cf. Jane Cowan's claim presented in the *Newcastle Chronicle* (9 June 1883) that where Wycliffe 'gained a hearing among the upper classes', his 'disciple' Ball 'expounded a more advanced Lollordism [sic?] in simple language, to suit the ears of his unlearned audience'.
36 Green, *A Short History*, 234–35.
37 Green, *A Short History*, 238.
38 Green, *A Short History*, 243.

cal or incomprehensible dark riddles here!) the 'mingled passions which met in the revolt of the peasants,' namely their 'longing for a right rule, for plain and simple justice; their scorn of the immorality of the nobles and the infamy of the court; their resentment at the perversion of the law to the cause of oppression.'[39]

Charles Edmund Maurice

There was already enough momentum behind Green's history, but it gained more from Charles Edmund Maurice (1843–1927), son of the Christian socialist F. D. Maurice and brother-in-law of the famous social reformer, Octavia Hill, who also moved in F. D. Maurice's circles.[40] Maurice's *Lives of English Popular Leaders in the Middle Ages: Tyler, Ball, and Oldcastle* (1875) was very much in the genre of what we would now recognise as academic history writing. This included thanking professors, textual emendations, regular referencing of primary sources to support arguments, primary sources assessed against each other for likely reliability, discussions of immediate and more long-term causes, interplay of national and regional histories, questions of social mobility, extensive discussion of social and religious backgrounds, and some myth-busting ('John of Gaunt, the Duke of Lancaster, whom the prejudice of Protestants, and the genius of Shakespeare, have done their best to turn into an enlightened reformer, was seen by the men of his own generation in a very different light').[41] Maurice also looked at the legacy and achievements of Ball and Tyler, including

---

39 Green, *A Short History*, 243–45.
40 For an overview see, e.g., Astrid Swenson, 'Founders of the National Trust,' *ODNB* (24 May 2008); Gillian Darley, 'Hill, Octavia,' *ODNB* (24 May 2012); Stephen Basdeo, 'An Early Socialist History of the Peasants' Revolt: Charles Edmund Maurice's "Lives of English Popular Leaders of the Middle Ages" (1875),' in *Here Begynneth A Lytell Geste of Robin Hood* (15 July 2015), https://gesteofrobinhood.com/2017/07/15/an-early-socialist-history-of-the-peasants-revolt-charles-edmund-maurices-lives-of-english-popular-leaders-of-the-middle-ages-1875/. Cf. C. Edmund Maurice, 'Preface,' in C. Edmund Maurice (ed.), *Life of Octavia Hill as Told in Her Letters* (London: Macmillan, 1913).
41 Maurice, *Lives of English Popular Leaders in the Middle Ages*, 170. A similar point is noted in Vaninskaya, 'Dreams of John Ball,' 51–52. Vaninskaya rightly adds the qualification that we should not generalise about these professional affectations at the end of the nineteenth century, and nor were they confined to

the argument that they taught 'serfs and the workmen to stand together, and depend upon themselves...which was remembered afterwards.' This helped shift thinking on constitutional freedom and restraints on the king's power, and influenced ideas relating to the 'Reformation' in that the dangers Wycliffe now posed were fully recognised by the nobles and Lollardy was effectively forced to spread 'among the poor and oppressed of the nation.'[42] This meant that Ball's letters deserved to be rescued from obscurity or hostility and taken seriously as historical evidence in reconstructing the life of Ball. The letters 'illustrate at once the spirit of his preaching and of his influence on this movement' while the 'tone and phraseology of these letters are to a great extent derived from the "Vision of Piers Plowman",'[43] a comment that could have been made at almost any time in the history of modern, critical historical scholarship. None of these issues were unprecedented, of course, but collectively Maurice's style is indicative of how far history writing had moved since the time of Hume a century earlier.

Maurice read Ball and the 1381 uprising emphatically in terms of class struggle and an extensive dialectical reading of history. He looked at how the fortunes of the 'poorer classes' were driven by the 'struggles' between towns and monasteries and the merchants and 'workmen' so that the 'growing antagonism between class and class forced them into the independent and aggressive position which they assumed in the fourteenth century, and which naturally found its logical result in the insurrection of Tyler and Ball.'[44] The context of the 1381 revolt is preceded by a discussion under the heading '*The Class Struggle in Richard II's Reign*' and framed in terms of the growing strength of the serfs and the 'labouring classes.'[45] Maurice's detailed history of class relations in England also involved an analysis of such relations 'with the earlier religious movements,'[46] in order to understand the role of Ball. Indeed, when Maurice got to Ball, his preaching was narrowed down to the precise manifestations of class struggles in Essex in order to understand why the people of Essex 'were particularly ready to listen to insurrectionary preaching at this time.'[47] The letters associated with Ball were likewise understood in explicitly class-based terms. The language

---

non-fiction. Nevertheless, they still formed a recognisable style in the emerging professionalisation of history.

42 Maurice, *Lives of English Popular Leaders*, 195–99.
43 Maurice, *Lives of English Popular Leaders*, 157, 159. See also, e.g., Gibbins, *English Social Reformers*, 14–15, 20–21.
44 Maurice, *Lives of English Popular Leaders*, 3.
45 Maurice, *Lives of English Popular Leaders*, 128–29.
46 Maurice, *Lives of English Popular Leaders*, 2.
47 Maurice, *Lives of English Popular Leaders*, 143.

of grinding small in the 'Jakke Mylner letter' may be accounted for, Maurice argued, by the bitterest of struggles between 'monks and their dependants' which turned on the dependants' claim 'to grind their own corn.'[48]

We get the various details of Ball's life, including use of sources beyond the chroniclers, which we would now expect of a biography. Ball came from York to Essex and devoted himself to Colchester in particular, he attracted the attention of archbishops of Canterbury, he was imprisoned and excommunicated some time before 1381, and his behaviour was noted by Edward III. But the details of Ball's life were again typically analysed by Maurice in terms of class struggle. Ball's preaching, it seemed, began 'between 1350 and 1360' at a time 'when the lords and poorer gentry were struggling in every way to prevent the villeins from rising to the freer position which seemed to be open to them after the plague, and to prevent the workmen from gaining higher wages.'[49] Ball belonged to the 'class then known as parochial chaplains,' a 'class which…seems to have corresponded among churchmen to the ordinary artisan class among the laity.' These parochial chaplains had risen in importance after the plague of 1348 and 'like other labourers' had 'taken advantage of the greater need for their services to ask for higher salaries at this time.' In turn, this led such clergy into conflict with the archbishop, who would threaten to remove them from office.[50] Certainly, Maurice could see other explanations that were not so obviously rooted in class. Maurice thought much of Ball's preaching 'seems to have had a purely moral object' which included an insistence on the 'necessity of marriage' (Maurice's reading of the bastards saying) and, 'like Wyclif,' the necessity of voluntary priesthood 'because that institution would enable the people to confine their support to those who deserved it.' Nevertheless, class struggle was never that far away and, after mentioning Ball's teaching on tithes, Maurice noted ('finally') that he 'denounced the slavery under which the commons of Essex were labouring.'[51]

It is certainly clear that Ball was given an elevated status. Ball was 'the real hero of the insurrection,' who gave 'wise advice' and was one greater than Tyler.[52] Ball was a 'remarkable man who, even more than Tyler, was the moving spirit in the insurrection of 1381,' and once Ball was freed from Maidstone prison, 'the great work was done' because if Tyler was more and more 'recognized as the head of the movement, Ball was undoubtedly its

---

48 Maurice, *Lives of English Popular Leaders*, 160.
49 Maurice, *Lives of English Popular Leaders*, 145–46.
50 Maurice, *Lives of English Popular Leaders*, 143.
51 Maurice, *Lives of English Popular Leaders*, 144.
52 Maurice, *Lives of English Popular Leaders*, iii, 165.

heart.'⁵³ Unsurprisingly, the revolt itself was understood in similarly heroic terms. It was 'the most formidable democratic movement which had ever been known in England at that time' against a broader backdrop of the myth of the Norman Yoke.⁵⁴ While hardly a straightforward case, Maurice's presentation of Ball (much like Green's presentation) can be viewed alongside the nineteenth-century biographies of Great Men, including 'religious' figures such as Jesus, who were understood in relation to (or beyond) issues of the emerging nation and nation state. Echoing the Chartists, then, this construction of English identity foregrounding a history of shared class or political interests over ethnic or racial characteristics was present even if not as explicit as Egan's presentation (see Chapter 12). But more so than Egan, Maurice pushed for religious characteristics. He argued that the 'insurrection of Tyler and Ball' was more than just a 'general democratic movement of the fourteenth century'; it received its 'colouring' and was 'coloured by, that religious movement which was so essentially English in its character.'⁵⁵ This was effectively a Protestant or proto-Protestant religious colouring because Ball's teaching was, according to Maurice, based on an acceptance of the 'doctrines of the great reformer' Wycliffe, though as ever Maurice gave the historian's qualification that this understanding helps to explain why Ball was prohibited from preaching in churches.⁵⁶ Though not uncritical of the history of the Protestant Reformation, Maurice still lauded its 'champions of real freedom, and the effect of which Henry VIII was unable to destroy' and the book concludes (with reference to John Oldcastle) in praise of puritanism.⁵⁷

By giving Ball and the revolt heroic status, Maurice was faced with the problem some of his predecessors had in reclaiming 1381: the association of violence. Maurice made a familiar move by downplaying the idea that Ball and Tyler would have embraced extreme violence and mob terror. As ever, this was done in the language of the critical historian. If Tyler ('as his enemies said') wanted the 'general destruction of the nobility and lawyers' then there was plenty of opportunity to do so but the only violence needed was in exceptional situations, notably including the rescue of Ball from Maidstone. Certainly, there were exceptions to the exceptional situations, but as with Egan and others, these could be explained as exceptions that happened away from Tyler's personal, disciplined influence.

---

53   Maurice, *Lives of English Popular Leaders*, 143, 157.
54   Maurice, *Lives of English Popular Leaders*, 181.
55   Maurice, *Lives of English Popular Leaders*, 1.
56   Maurice, *Lives of English Popular Leaders*, 148.
57   Maurice, *Lives of English Popular Leaders*, vii, 281.

Unlike attempts to explain away the actions against Joan of Kent in terms of rowdy familiarity (e.g., Dickens, Spurgeon), there was 'at least one act of brutal ruffianism (an insult to the mother of the king).'[58] Ball himself was like Tyler in his restraint and so when the chroniclers claimed Ball gave 'more ferocious advice,' this could be 'fairly set aside.' Needless to say, this was critically justified. Maurice argued that there was no call to violence in Ball's letters, that even Froissart noted that Ball appealed to the king for justice, that the Essex rebels conducted themselves honourably, and that Walsingham did not mention such charges in his presentation of Ball's trial.[59] Even Ball's interpretation of the Adam and Eve couplet ('his sermon on that curious text') was brought into service of the idea of mass, disciplined power. 'The drift of the sermon,' Maurice added, 'was a discourse on the natural equality of man and an exhortation to be bold in maintaining the demands which should recover this equality.'[60]

Historians of the Peasants' Rising

Maurice was a sign of things to come. At the turn of the twentieth century, and as was noted and assessed at the time, historians were beginning to produce works more specifically focused on the revolt itself, rather than a chapter or section in a history of the nation, but also with increased use and publication of unpublished or difficult-to-access primary sources.[61] The modern, critical historical study of the revolt had now arrived, or at least had one of its most important periods in the history of such scholarship. *Le soulèvement des travailleurs d'Angeleterre en 1381* (1898) by André Réville and edited by Charles Petit-Dutaillis has all the hallmarks of such familiar history writing. Réville initially wrote a thesis on the revolt in Hertfordshire, Suffolk, and Norfolk, and then visited London and Cambridge to examine and transcribe various documents but, after becoming a professor in Paris (1891), he died from a sudden disease in 1894, aged just 27.[62] The thesis and

---

58 Maurice, *Lives of English Popular Leaders*, 182.
59 Maurice, *Lives of English Popular Leaders*, 145.
60 Maurice, *Lives of English Popular Leaders*, 169.
61 Kriehn, 'Social Revolt in 1381'.
62 André Réville with Charles Petit-Dutaillis, *Le soulèvement des travailleurs d'Angeleterre en 1381* (Paris: A. Picard et fils, 1898), i–xviii; Anon., 'The Peasants' Rising of 1381,' *Edinburgh Review* CCCXCI (1900): 76–107 (76–77); Oman, *Great Revolt of 1381*, iii–v.

various documents were published by Petit-Dutaillis who developed and added a substantial introduction on the issues surrounding the 1381 revolt.

Despite its title pointing to an interest in workers, Ball in *Le soulèvement des travailleurs d'Angeleterre en 1381* did not feature in the ways he had among English historians and their class interests relating to socialism. As we might expect, Ball featured little in the main body of the text beyond the basic narrative. We thus get Ball as one of the rebel leaders around London and initiators of the revolt, the capture and death of Ball, authorship of the letters, and his stubbornness in the face of execution. There is also some discussion of the levels of restraint shown by the crown and comparative torture and punishment practices in France.[63] The introduction explains the downplaying of the connection between the rebellion and Wycliffe or the Lollards and stresses instead that preachers like Ball attacked the failings of the higher clergy as opposed to involvement in doctrinal matters like transubstantiation.[64] But in the case of Ball himself, the introduction does not provide much detail or commentary beyond the basics of the narrative and is typically mentioned in passing, including the story of his preaching for twenty years and his role as the 'prêtre vagabond,' his teaching on tithes, his release from prison, the letters, the 'dicton populaire' which he took as his text at Blackheath for his 'harangue révolutionnaire,' the violent content of his Blackheath preaching which fired up the rebels, the revolt in London, and his death.[65] There is mention of the many agitators and discussion of the involvement of clergy besides 'le fameux John Ball.'[66]

We might speculate that the English cultural heritage was not enough to make Ball such a contentious figure for French historians. But we should, as ever, resist any urge to suggest that by virtue of sharing familiar traits with critical historians, such writers were immune from political and economic tendencies. With the major English publications of the time, and whatever the merits of their reconstructions of 1381, some of the contemporary rhetoric relating to the prominence of the labour movement remained. Edgar Powell's *The Rising in East Anglia in 1381* (1896) may have featured extensive appendixes on poll tax lists and various documents but the framing of the book is instructive. In the introduction, he outlined the economic

---

63 Réville with Petit-Dutaillis, *Le soulèvement des travailleurs d'Angeleterre*, 4, 150–51, 159.
64 Réville with Petit-Dutaillis, *Le soulèvement des travailleurs d'Angeleterre*, lxiii–lxiv, lxvii–lxviii.
65 Réville with Petit-Dutaillis, *Le soulèvement des travailleurs d'Angeleterre*, lxi, lxii, lxvi, lxxix n. 7, lxxxi, lxxxix, cxxi n. 3, cxxxi.
66 Réville with Petit-Dutaillis, *Le soulèvement des travailleurs d'Angeleterre*, xlix, cf. lxvi.

causes of the revolt (e.g., scarcity of agricultural labour, demands for higher wages, and landowners' refusal to meet them) and strikingly referred to the rebels as 'working-classes' who had 'arrived as a class.' Indeed, Powell openly used language drawn from the development of the labour movement to describe the rebels:

> Already do we find that in self-defence the working-classes had begun to form confederate clubs, the prototypes of our modern trades-unions, whose object was to resist with a strong hand the claims for customary labour due from the holders of servile lands, which it appears the landlords owing to the scarcity of labourers were now trying to enforce to the utmost.[67]

Powell added that 'in the struggle that eventually ensued we do not find that the working-classes were left to fight alone' and that 'the popular party had obtained the active support and sympathy of a considerable proportion of the country gentry' who had 'a genuine sympathy for the working-classes.' Powell further stressed ideas about the complexity of class interests and bourgeois social democratic concerns. Combined with a common aversion to the poll tax, he argued, 'may possibly account for some of the better class giving their active assistance to the revolutionary party, but the movement was distinctly against their interests as a class,' and some may have hoped that their efforts could have brought about the 'better governance of the realm.'[68] It is striking that this sort of emphasis was muted in the main body of Powell's text and analysis but then returned in the conclusion. Indeed, here are the closing words of Powell's argument (excluding appendixes):

> In looking back across the five centuries that separate us from the portentous outbreak of 1381, when the great working class of England, roused to fury by the goad of relentless taxation, turned so fiercely to bay, we cannot, even while justly condemning their violence, withhold a large measure of sympathy both for the ideas which prompted, and for the results which followed their action.
>
> And though the attempt was then frustrated and the rising crushed, and that to the great and unquestionable advantage of the nation as a whole,

---

67 Powell, *The Rising in East Anglia in 1381*, 1–2. Cf. Gibbins, *English Social Reformers*, 5: 'The spirit of the revolt which is thus evident among the working-classes...'
68 Powell, *The Rising in East Anglia in 1381*, 3.

yet, apart from the objects which were more consciously pursued, the effort marks an important epoch.

It emphasized to the country at large, in a way there was no possibility of mistaking, the fact that the working classes had arrived at a position of great power; and though perhaps in disclosing that power they had also disclosed their inability, as yet, to use it to the greatest effect, yet their strength and position had been shown to be such as no rulers could with safety ignore.[69]

At the heart of Powell's framing of his argument was Ball, whose criticisms of church and state were said to have 'found an eager audience among the working-classes, and, being carried through the length and breadth of the country, left men's minds unsettled and expectant in every department of life.'[70] There may also be an implicit Protestantizing of Ball, though Powell was cautious in his judgement. He suggested that Ball was a kind of Lollard ('himself, it is said, a disciple of Wiclif')[71] while carefully not being too explicit about such close identification given that such a close identification with Wycliffe was used for polemical purposes by the chroniclers.

Along with George Macaulay Trevelyan, Powell published a collection of previously unpublished documents as an appendix to Trevelyan's *England in the Age of Wycliffe*, published the same year (1899). This collection of documents includes a song attributed to rebels in Yorkshire in a trial from 1382 which, Powell and Trevelyan claimed in the introduction with an allusion to Ball's letters, 'opens a narrow window through which we gain a glance into the hearts and minds' of those who rose in revolt, believing that 'the King's son of heaven should pay for all.' They added that the Yorkshire song was not as 'religious' in its sentiment as the letters of Ball and more a 'preliminary to murder and rebellion,' but it still proves that such rioters were 'inspired by an ideal of independent manhood which could not tamely endure slavery and wrong.'[72] That this again echoes nineteenth-century battles for working-class democratic representation that we saw in *The Rising in East Anglia in 1381* is unsurprising and doubly so given that the collection of documents functioned as an appendix to a book by Trevelyan, the famous and popular Whig historian, Liberal, nostalgist, and later regius

---

69 Powell, *The Rising in East Anglia in 1381*, 66.
70 Powell, *The Rising in East Anglia in 1381*, 3.
71 Powell, *The Rising in East Anglia in 1381*, 3.
72 Edgar Powell and George Macaulay Trevelyan (eds.), *The Peasants' Rising and the Lollards: A Collection of Unpublished Documents Forming an Appendix to "England in the Age of Wycliffe"* (London: Longmans, Green, and Co., 1899), x.

professor at Cambridge (1927–1943), whose ideological leanings were never too difficult to detect.

England in the Age of Wycliffe was published at the beginning of Trevelyan's career and was originally a dissertation for a fellowship at Trinity College, Cambridge, where he acknowledged his debt to Réville and Powell on the 'Peasants' Rising.'[73] With its themes of religious tolerance, constitutionalism, individual liberty, and hostility to (Catholic) despotism anticipating seventeenth-century blooming, the book was, as David Cannadine argued, 'in some ways the most Whiggish piece of history he ever wrote.'[74] Trevelyan did not conceal comparisons with more recent history to make his point. He compared the uprising with the French Revolution (which he was sympathetic towards at this stage of his career). Ball's Adam and Eve couplet, that 'famous catchword,' 'seems to have corresponded in importance and popularity to "Liberté, Egalité, Fraternité".' Ideas of personal freedom, Trevelyan argued, were soon seen to be in accordance with Christianity by the peasantry and 'their humbler religious pastors,' and the 'religious persons who were most directly in touch with the labouring classes.' These tendencies were associated with the important but flawed figure of Ball as a precursor to Wycliffe's ideas.[75] Such instigators of the rebellion were comparable to 'some parish priests at the beginning of the French Revolution.'[76] But this bid for freedom, in Trevelyan's Whiggish reading, was not to be equated with communism, and he used the mindset of a critical historian to show it. 'The attempt to picture the Rising as a communistic movement,' he argued, 'ignores the plainest facts.' Froissart's report of Ball's preaching was criticised as 'that of a prejudiced person in full sympathy with the upper classes, and shocked by the startling horrors of the Rising.' Thus, Trevelyan could question whether Ball

---

73 George Macaulay Trevelyan, *England in the Age of Wycliffe* (London: Longmans, Green, and Co., 1899), v. David Cannadine, *G.M. Trevelyan: A Life in History* (London: HarperCollinsPublishers, 1992), 97, adds the influence of Stubbs.

74 Cannadine, *G.M. Trevelyan*, 97–99.

75 Trevelyan, *England in the Age of Wycliffe*, 195–96. Ball likely promoted 'murders' as the Blackheath sermon suggests, Trevelyan argued, while his dogged, unflinching personality 'had won the hearts of the classes he had long loved and served' (224–25). Elsewhere, Ball was an example of one of the 'irresponsible individuals' preaching Wycliffe's 'doctrines' before Wycliffe had sent out any of his friends (363). But he was still a precursor to Wycliffe, and Trevelyan even entertains the idea that Ball was indeed critical of transubstantiation, though ultimately Ball himself should remain 'responsible for the good and evil he did' (196, 363).

76 Trevelyan, *England in the Age of Wycliffe*, 195–96.

and the 'agitators' believed in having 'all things in common' and added that when the rising did take place, there was no such request. Now in a firmly established tradition of (partially) rescuing the uprising from above, Trevelyan claimed that their 'very practical demands' were about 'personal freedom' and reasonable rents which were accepted by most of the rebels who then went home, and even those who stayed 'produced no scheme of speculative communism, but confined themselves to practical illustrations of the theory by carrying off everything on which they could lay their hands.' Nevertheless, he provided telling rule of thumb in his creation of a reasonable ideological centre: whenever there is a 'labour movement,' there will always be a few 'communists' and 'the conservative classes will always give an unfair prominence to the extreme idea.'[77]

We should not see Trevelyan and his penchant for more recent historical analogies as simply an attempt to counter anachronistic communist or socialist readings of the past. Trevelyan's liberal alternative is clear enough. That he began by calling the uprising 'an organic part of the history of labour' which 'throws more light on the aspirations and qualities of the working class than any other record of medieval times' is a further indication that *England in the Age of Wycliffe* can be read against the backdrop of the ideological battles over the labour movement on the eve of the twentieth century.[78] The levelling tendencies of 'the Christian spirit' grounded in the idea of common origins from Adam and Eve did not just form 'very real and valid' arguments against hereditary serfdom but were 'democratic.'[79] For Trevelyan, then, the general tone of the uprising was 'that of Christian Democracy,' led and theorised by the 'chief agitator' Ball and friars while Lollards were accused (probably fairly, he added) of carrying on 'Ball's work.'[80] Trevelyan believed Ball's letters have been 'preserved for us in their original words' and 'bear the stamp of genuineness on their face.' The chroniclers could not have invented them as their message 'breathes the deep and gallant feeling that led the noblest among the rebels to defy gallows and quartering block in the cause of freedom.'[81] This is Trevelyan's reading of an indigenous English democratic movement which is, effectively, more akin to parliamentary democracy than revolutionary overthrowing of the state.

77 Trevelyan, *England in the Age of Wycliffe*, 197–98.
78 Trevelyan, *England in the Age of Wycliffe*, 182.
79 Trevelyan, *England in the Age of Wycliffe*, 196.
80 Trevelyan, *England in the Age of Wycliffe*, 202.
81 Trevelyan, *England in the Age of Wycliffe*, 203–4.

Such a politicised presentation of Ball would gain further support in perhaps the early landmark publication in the modern historical study of the revolt by Charles Oman in *The Great Revolt of 1381* (1906). Oman—a student of Stubbs, a military historian, conservative, and Chichele professor at Oxford (1905–1946)—acknowledged his appreciation of Trevelyan's 'brilliant sketch,' as well as acknowledging Réville and Powell.[82] Oman certainly took issue with the portrayal of Ball as Lollard. Against Rogers (and others), Oman strongly denied that Ball was in league with the Poor Preachers or had been a dedicated follower of Wycliffe—indeed, Oman downplayed the influence of Wycliffe on the rebellion as a whole.[83] Instead, Ball and his allies ought to be seen against the backdrop of the 'old doctrine of evangelical poverty' associated with the Franciscans.[84] But this move still allowed Oman to present Ball in similar political categories as those associated with Trevelyan and Powell. Oman cast Ball as a 'visionary and a prophet rather than organiser' who had 'spread discontent' through his itinerant preaching over the twenty years.[85]

This prophetic categorisation is significant given that Oman stressed, despite involvement of figures like Ball, that the motives of the rebels were 'essentially secular' rather than religious, with 'practical grievances' rather than 'fanaticism or disinterested zeal for a spiritual transformation.'[86] The designation 'prophet' and its claimed connection with broader popular appeal allowed Oman to keep Ball's interests more 'secular' than overly religious to the point of fanaticism, hence:

> Ball was a prophet in the ancient Hebrew style—a denouncer of the wickedness of the times, and more especially of the wickedness of the higher clergy...But evil secular lords and their oppressions were not omitted in his objurgatory sermons. He was a kind of modern Jeremiah, hateful to the Pashurs and the Zedekiahs of 1381...when he was liberated by the rioters...was certain of an audience far larger than he had ever before addressed, and audience, too, which was in entire sympathy with his views.[87]

This framing of Ball also dovetailed into Oman's political categorisation. Ball's daily 'harangues' involved what he thought was 'the actual commencement of that reign of Christian democracy of which he had so longed

---

82 Oman, *Great Revolt of 1381*, iii–v.
83 Oman, *Great Revolt of 1381*, 19–20.
84 Oman, *Great Revolt of 1381*, 20, cf. 42.
85 Oman, *Great Revolt of 1381*, 12.
86 Oman, *Great Revolt of 1381*, 21.
87 Oman, *Great Revolt of 1381*, 42–43.

dreamed.' This involved the removal of 'social inequalities' by which Oman meant the end of 'rich and poor...lords and serfs' and 'spiritual wickedness in high places.'[88] But it is also striking what such a levelling attitude was *not* for Oman, as we see in his handling of the Blackheath sermon and Ball's 'famous jingling couplet.' These may have been drawn in 'the most lurid colours' and likely exaggerated the murderous intent but probably reflected Ball's ideas. And these ideas were 'democracy and not communism' and the rebels 'wanted to become freeholders, not to form phalansteries and hold all things in common.'[89]

Engels, Marxism, and Hyndman

Fears about the spectre of communism among historians were not, of course, unfounded—and not just because of events happening across Europe in the nineteenth century. Notions of class struggle in driving historical change were most famously developed earlier by Marx and Engels, who in turn provided a distinctive framework for understanding failure and influence of medieval movements in relation to the emergence of capitalism. Indeed, Engels—a keen observer of Chartism—even mentioned the example of Ball when reflecting on the failure of the German revolution of 1848–1849 through a comparison with the Peasant War of 1525. Written in London in 1850, and following Marx's treatment of the aftermath of the 1848 French Revolution, Engels's *Peasant War in Germany* would eventually become a key text in the emergence of materialist readings of history and religion with its emphasis on the importance of class struggle and explaining the complex shifts from feudalism to capitalism, as the preface to the 1870 edition made clearer still.[90] Engels understood Ball

---

88 Oman, *Great Revolt of 1381*, 43.
89 Oman, *Great Revolt of 1381*, 51–52. Cf. Emily Cooper, *The History of England from the Landing of Caesar to the Reign of Victoria: Volume 1* (London: Simpkin, Marshall and Co., 1877), 236: 'Although the insurrection was a political rather than a religious movement, yet the priest Ball passing for a disciple of Wyclif, whose followers continued to increase, the excitement was connected with the spread of his doctrines.' See also the Victorian off-handedness in response to Ball's alleged levelling tendencies: on the Adam and Eve couplet, she quipped, 'And probably no one replied by comparing the advantage of civilised life with the existence of a savage.'
90 Frederick Engels, 'Preface to the Second Edition (1870),' in *The Peasant War in Germany*, https://www.marxists.org/archive/marx/works/1850/peasant-war-germany/index.htm.

and the 1381 uprising, as well as Wycliffe's movement, partly in terms of medieval peasant insurrections and revolutionary opposition to feudalism, with their radical demands based on ideas of being children of God and the restoration of radical equality associated with the early church. Such demands included political equality, equality of property, and an end to compulsory labour, ground rents, and various privileges. In the fourteenth and fifteenth centuries, such peasant and plebeian heresy took an independent stand alongside the town-based heresies of the growing middle class which opposed church wealth, privilege, and power. According to Engels, more fanatical movements and groups such as the Lollards continued the revolutionary tradition during the times of suppression.[91]

The fate of this tradition in plebeian hands highlights some of Engels's influential interests in the longer-term consequences of historical development. Representing people with neither privilege nor property, plebeians were the only class that functioned beyond, and was ignored by, feudalism and urban associations and, as a propertyless faction, questioned the fundamental views and institutions of the wider class-based society. In this sense, plebeian heresy was both a symptom of the decay of feudalism and the urban associations and a precursor of modern bourgeois society. Plebeian opposition could not stop at fighting feudalism and middle-class associations, and its fantasies reached even beyond the bourgeois society of the future, not least through millenarian understandings of early Christianity. This fantastical vision was invariably violent but historical constraints meant that the spectacular demands were dramatically narrowed and translated into charity, equality before the law, and republican governments as the hope of communism became instead an anticipation of modern bourgeois society.[92] While Engels had his own interests in focusing on such apocalyptic trajectories in *Peasant War in Germany*, it was the importance he and Marx put on longer term, historical materialist implications that would have a lasting influence in the reception of Ball. And one of the more prominent and popular advocates of an explicitly *English* socialist history which included Ball came from the socialist and founder of the Democratic Federation in 1881 (from 1884, the Social Democratic Federation), and not uncritical disseminator of Marx's ideas: H. M. Hyndman.

Hyndman's view of socialism was grounded in ideas of a form of English or British exceptionalism, as he outlined in his 1881 essay, 'Dawn of a Revolutionary Epoch,' which looked at 'The English tendency...to build up

---

91 Engels, *Peasant War in Germany*, chapter 2.
92 Engels, *Peasant War in Germany*, chapter 2.

from the bottom, to improve the conditions of life below.' He qualified discussions concerning the extent of the need for class conflict with a degree of reformism and gradualism ('the conditions of life for the multitude do need reform, even if it be brought about by some sacrifice of the ease and comfort now the sole appanage of the wealthier classes…The wiser heads admit that the realisation of this their materialist Utopia must be gradual'). This was understood in contrast to 'the fanatics of the new Socialist gospel' who hold that 'their day shall be to-morrow', that proceeding slowly was 'cowardice', and that a 'social revolution' must proceed with 'violence to start with'. By contrast, Hyndman's arguments were presented as being tied in with an English or British uniqueness and collaboration and compromise between the classes (overlapping here with other interpreters of Ball, e.g., Spurgeon—see Chapter 13). Britain and 'Anglo-Saxon communities', in contrast to the Continent, had long secured the right to public meetings, freedom of the press, and hard forms of personal liberty, and worked out problems 'without that dangerous excitement which has attended the endeavour to solve them elsewhere', adding that 'we shall be able to satisfy the legitimate claims of the many without trenching upon the rights or the privileges of the few'. In England, unlike elsewhere, there was no 'envy of wealth' and, as the working classes got their demands met through constitutional means, 'they have no mind to try the subversionary doctrines of the Continental agitators'. The 'English people…respect their natural leaders' and are ready to follow them 'politically and socially in orderly fashion' which presupposes that the upper classes are prepared to lead not for their own selfish gain but for 'the benefit of that class which, as has been well said, is really the nation'. Nevertheless, this calm gradualism depended on the 'amount of consideration which they receive' and so, in the northern towns, there were 'all the elements of the fiercest and, under certain conditions, of the most uncontrollable democracy the world has ever seen.'[93] While the legitimacy of the idea of tying in Hyndman with Conservativism or Tory radicalism from Engels onwards has been challenged, it is not difficult to see how such perceptions could emerge from a reading of 'The Dawn of a Revolutionary Epoch.'[94]

93 H. M. Hyndman, 'Dawn of a Revolutionary Epoch', *Nineteenth Century* (January 1881): 1–18, available at https://www.marxists.org/archive/hyndman/1881/01/revolutionary-dawn.htm. See also, of course, H. M. Hyndman, *England For All* (London: E. W. Allen, 1881). While critical of Ball's tactics and alleged extremism, a similar argument on the duties of the 'rich' to bring about change see, e.g., Gibbins, *English Social Reformers*, 25.
94 Seamus Flaherty, 'H. M. Hyndman and the Intellectual Origins of the Remaking of Socialism in Britain, 1878–1881', *English Historical Review* 134

Ball appears in *The Historical Basis for Socialism in England* (1883) where Hyndman provided an analysis of social and economic developments and the production and distribution of wealth in England since the fifteenth century and presented it as (again, what we might call) a history from below in its contrast to 'middle-class' histories. He acknowledged his debt to Marx and Engels (and others), and to the French translation of *Capital* in particular.[95] The tension between gradualism, demands from below, and the behaviour of the upper classes in Hyndman's earlier essay came through in his treatment of Ball as an indigenous hero of progression. Violence was downplayed and the revolt itself was 'put down at the moment by treachery and false promises' but effectively it 'really secured freedom for the mass of the people.' Ball had 'genuine grievances to point to and definite reforms to propose when he addressed his stirring speeches to tens of thousands of his stalwart countrymen.' To highlight how Ball supported 'great social and political principles,' Hyndman specifically cited Ball's speech beginning, 'things cannot be well for us in this England of ours.' And if that was not clear enough, then an accompanying note explicitly made the key point about homegrown socialism in defence against the apparent slur of foreign infiltration:

> It is well to show that the idea of socialism is no foreign importation into England. Tyler, Cade, Ball, Kett, More, Bellers, Spence, Owen, read to me like sound English names: not a foreigner in the whole batch. They all held opinions which our capitalist-landlord House of Commons would denounce as direct plagiarisms from 'continental revolutionists.' We islanders have been revolutionists however, and will be again, ignorant as our capitalists are of the history of the people. Edmund Burke, with his fine sophistical Whiggery, of course sneered at coarse, vigorous John Ball. But then, so far as we know, Ball did not sell himself to the nobles as Burke did.[96]

Hyndman was writing in a context where a number of themes surrounding Ball had been promoted to lesser or greater extent towards the end of the nineteenth century: working-class masculinity, class conflict, romantic

(2019): 855–80, has challenged the Tory radical reading and has contextualised Hyndman in Liberal traditions, *contra* other major readings concerning the nature of influence, e.g., Chushichi Tsuzuki, *H. M. Hyndman and British Socialism* (London: Oxford University Press, 1961); Mark Bevir, *The Making of British Socialism* (Princeton: Princeton University Press, 2011), 65–84.

95 H. M. Hyndman, *The Historical Basis for Socialism in England* (London: Kegan Paul, Trench & Co., 1883), vii–x.

96 Hyndman, *Historical Basis*, 3–4.

medievalism, political visionary ahead of his time, the extent of justifiable violence, a heroic failure, martyrdom, and an English identity grounded not only in political liberty and change but ideas of socialism and communism. Yet Hyndman was also a controversial figure among socialists and the focus of a split in the Social Democratic Federation in 1884—not least over allegations of jingoism,[97] while Hyndman's patriotism and promotion of Anglo-Saxon blood was 'verging on chauvinism and racism.'[98] Among the dissenters was one of the most influential socialists and readers of Ball: William Morris. As the influence of Southey had waned,[99] Morris would now run with Hyndman's Ball and establish the standard fictional account for decades to come, grounded in historical materialism—even if Morris's interpreters would not always acknowledge this.

---

97 *Justice* (31 January 1885).
98 Bevir, *Making of British Socialism*, 75.
99 Southey's *Wat Tyler* turns up sporadically in the second half of the nineteenth century, e.g., *Kentish Mercury* (23 August 1862); *Examiner* (21 May 1864); *Illustrated London News* (21 January 1865); *Liverpool Daily Post* (15 September 1869); *Barnsley Independent* (7 July 1877); *Reynolds's Newspaper* (8 September 1878); *Exeter and Plymouth Gazette* (13 November 1878); *South London Press* (13 November 1880); *Sheffield Independent* (2 April 1881); *Sheffield Independent* (24 December 1881); *Acton Gazette* (11 February 1882); *Northwich Guardian* (15 March 1882); *Daily Telegraph* (10 August 1882); *Royal Cornwall Gazette* (5 January 1883); *Derbyshire Courier* (6 October 1883). Southey is also referenced in Charlotte M. Yonge's novel on the revolt, *The Wardship of Steepcoombe* (London: National Society, 1896), 197, 242.

15
William Morris: Delaying Ball's New World

Such is the influence of the writer, poet, artist and designer, medievalist, translator, and socialist, William Morris (1834–1896) in the history of the reception of Ball that it rivals that of Ball himself and likewise requires a dedicated chapter. Morris's *A Dream of John Ball* was first serialised in *Commonweal* in 1886–1887 (later as a book in 1888, and then with his own publishing house Kelmscott Press in 1892) and, like his famous *News from Nowhere* (serialised in *Commonweal* [1890]), is a dialectical materialist reading of English history in fictional form. Certainly, there is some antiquarian interest (e.g., poll tax, the story of Tyler's daughter) but it is marginalised in Morris's story which foregrounds medieval aesthetics, failure, martyrdom, and an extended socialist vision of the future cast in the language of an eschatological or apocalyptic seer. Some of these themes came through in a letter Morris wrote to the *Manchester Guardian* in 1884, where he defended himself against recent criticisms cast in the language of 'heresy'. He explained that his audiences at Ancoats, 'one of which was almost wholly composed of working men, and the other much made up of them,' would not have agreed as he explained to them 'who John Ball was,' and that,

> he preached the enfranchisement of labour as he understood it, and that to him it meant the abolition of serfdom first, and good life to the labourer next…John Ball was murdered by the fleecers of the people many hundred years ago, but indeed in a sense he lives still, though I am but a part, and not the whole of him…Nor will he quite die as long as he has work to do; and I am not yet convinced that even in Manchester he has no work to do…your correspondents' letters…seem to take for granted that my opinions are eccentric and solitary—died with John Ball in fact; but I can hardly believe them to be so ignorant of current events as not to know that all over Europe Socialism is alive and growing.[1]

1   *Manchester Guardian* (7 October 1884).

To understand what Morris was doing with Ball, we need, then, to understand his views on religion, socialism, and the fusion of both, in more detail.

Religion

Catholic, medieval, and romantic aesthetics were important for Morris, even if he had long given up life as a believing Christian by the time of *A Dream of John Ball*.[2] Brought up a strict Anglican, Morris appreciated the antiquated architecture of churches—whether visits to old churches and cathedrals (including Canterbury) or taking brass rubbings—which would inform his work and ideas throughout his life.[3] However, there was a more specific strand of Anglicanism which was more influential than others. In 1848 Morris went to Marlborough College, Wiltshire, where he came into more sustained contact with the world of Anglo-Catholicism which would form part of the romantic influence on him. Before he finished his pre-university schooling, and after he and others were removed from Marlborough, Morris was also privately tutored by the Rev. Frederick B. Guy, which further exposed him to High Church tendencies and the architecture of old churches.[4]

Morris went to Exeter College, Oxford University, in 1852 to study the classics. There, he met his lifelong friend Edward Burne-Jones with whom, among other things, his medieval, Arthurian, Romantic, and Anglo-Catholic and Tractarian interests developed not only in his aesthetics but also in his critique of the Victorian present and the brutality of industrialisation.[5]

2   My emphasis on Catholic aesthetics does not, of course, exclude the possibility of certain Protestant influences on Morris, including issues relating to ethics, art, and work as argued by Bevir, *Making of British Socialism*, 88–89, 95–96, 99, 104–5. However, Morris's emphasis on Catholic aesthetics and his critique of Protestantism are, as we will see, crucial for understanding *A Dream of John Ball*.
3   E. P. Thompson, *William Morris: Romantic to Revolutionary* (New York: Pantheon Books, [1955] 1977), 4–5; Fiona MacCarthy, *William Morris: A Life for Our Time* (Kindle edition; London: Faber & Faber, [1995] 2010), loc 287, 579–633.
4   Thompson, *William Morris*, 23–29; MacCarthy, *William Morris*, loc 1066–1103, 1146, 1171, 1178.
5   MacCarthy, *William Morris*, loc 1314–1357, 1750; Phil Katz, *Thinking Hands: The Power of Labour in William Morris* (UK [city unknown]: Hetherington Press, 2005), 9–13, 109–24.

John Ruskin too would continue to be an ongoing and related fascination and influenced Morris's similarly famous ideas about societal decay, morality, beauty, nature, and the alienation of Victorian working patterns in contrast to the freedom of individual expression for medieval workers. Morris and Burne-Jones further developed an interest in Christian Socialism and critiques of poverty, class, and capitalism, including the works and ideas of Charles Kingsley and F. D. Maurice.[6] While Morris would lose his religion, Christian language and imagery remained. His ongoing appreciation of Anglo-Catholicism, Ruskin, and Christian Socialism was partly because they represented a welcome protest against establishment Puritanism and Protestantism and what he saw as its accompanying moral and economic hypocrisy, its misery, and its historic role enabling capitalism.[7] Certainly, when he fully embraced the socialist cause in the 1880s, its atheistic connotations may have caused controversy and certainly he criticised the established church and Christianity of hypocrisy and for being moulded by capitalism. Nevertheless, he still formed alliances and connections with church groups and retained some admiration for Christian Socialists.[8]

Morris, Socialism, and Communism

Morris's success in business and design was accompanied by a problematic truth: Morris was producing works not for the proletariat but the wealthy. Morris's politics and related activities became associated with the left wing of liberalism, but he would become increasingly disheartened and saw such liberalism as too closely aligned with the interests of capitalists and capitalism. Morris tried, with limited success, to improve working conditions on his own premises but understood that the capitalist world constrained the development of socialist models. By the 1880s Morris's politics became aligned with anti-imperialism, working-class interests, revolution, and socialism, the latter of which he would describe as,

6   MacCarthy, *William Morris*, loc 1444–1460, 1541–1607, 3908.
7   Ruth Kinna, *William Morris and the Art of Socialism* (Cardiff: University of Wales Press, 2000), 36–37.
8   See, e.g., Thompson, *William Morris*, 25–26, 699–700, 710–11; MacCarthy, *William Morris*, loc 1806–1815, 2227, 4000–4018, 5925, 8737, 8822–8831, 8972, 8979, 9055, 9085, 9166, 9211, 9283, 9952–9961; Stephen Williams, 'Morris, Christianity and Socialism: An Episode,' *Journal of William Morris Studies* 21 (2015): 38–45.

a condition of society in which there should be neither rich nor poor, neither master nor master's man, neither idle nor overworked, neither brain-sick brain workers, nor heart-sick hand workers, in a word, in which all men would be living in equality of condition, and would manage their affairs unwastefully, and with the full consciousness that harm to one would mean harm to all—the realization at last of the meaning of the word COMMONWEALTH.[9]

Morris moved away from liberalism towards the smaller socialist movements and socialist and radical literature, including the ideas of Engels and Marx (though he found parts of *Capital* particularly hard going), Sergius Stepniak, and William Cobbett.[10] Morris described this change in more sudden terms and in the language more typical of religion: it was, he said, a 'conversion.'[11] In 1883, he joined the newly formed Democratic Federation established by Hyndman, and became involved in its bureaucracy as well as a regular speaker, propagandist, publisher, and, of course, designer. The manifesto of June 1883, *Socialism Made Plain*, was an attempt to challenge 'this miserable huckster's society, where poverty and prostitution, fraud and adulteration, swindling and jobbery, luxury and debauchery reign supreme.' It critiqued the 'organised brute force of the few' which had 'for generations robbed and tyrannised over the unorganised brute force of the many' and the parliamentary system for being 'maintained in the interests of those who rob and oppress you.' It called on the 'men and women of England' to ask themselves whether they should 'bow down in slavish subjection' before the governing classes and whether they should demand the 'full fruits' of their labour and become the governing class themselves. It demanded 'complete adult suffrage for every man and woman in these islands,' the 'abolition of all hereditary authority,' and that the land 'in towns, mines, parks, mountains, moors should be owned by the people for the people, to be held, used, built over and cultivated upon such terms as the people themselves see fit to ordain.' Further demands included affordable housing, compulsory education with the 'provision of at least one

---

9   William Morris, 'How I Became A Socialist,' *Justice* (16 June 1894).
10 On Morris's turn to socialism, and the much-debated nuances of his positions, see, e.g., Thompson, *William Morris*, 243–74, and Thompson's famous Postscript, 763–816; MacCarthy, *William Morris*, loc 8737–9128, 9157–9523; Kinna, *William Morris*, 1–31, 107–21, 157–212; Hassan Mahamdallie, *Crossing the 'River of Fire': The Socialism of William Morris* (London: Redwords, 2008); Katz, *Thinking Hands*, 112–13, 215–66; Bevir, *Making of British Socialism*, 85–105.
11 Morris, 'How I Became A Socialist.' Cf. Thompson, *William Morris*, 274.

wholesome meal a day in each school,' an eight-hour working day, the end of the national debt, state appropriation of the railways, and the establishment of national banks.[12]

The Democratic Federation became the Social Democratic Federation in 1884 and there was the split over the role of parliamentary socialism and British imperialism—Morris was hostile to both, which led to his departure. By the end of the year Morris established the Socialist League and, amidst different factions (anarchist, parliamentarian), he pushed a non-parliamentary, internationalist, and revolutionary road to socialism with close connections to working-class interests and culture. Whatever else he may have said, he could still claim in October 1885 that he was 'beginning to hope that I may live to see the great change.'[13] At this time, Morris was a signatory to the *Manifesto of the Socialist League* of February/March 1885, which was revised for October 1885 by Morris and a former member of the Social Democratic Federation, Ernest Belfort Bax. The manifesto explains exploitation and class conflict, including examples such as open rebellion, strikes, and even crime. This 'veiled war' could also take place within classes, including among workers themselves for 'bare subsistence.' Quoting the *Communist Manifesto* there is a description of how the pursuit of profit forces wares and cheap goods on the market irrespective of whether there is any demand. The impact of the promotion of bourgeois civilisation has resulted in desperate lives of 'its slaves, the working class.' Only socialism—and not mere administrative tweaking—can remedy this, and with echoes of Acts 2.44–45 and 4.32–35 and Marx, all means of production and distribution of wealth 'must be declared and treated as the common property of all,' with workers receiving the full value of their labour 'without deduction for the profit of a master.' Working hours would need to be dramatically reduced and then everyone 'will have abundant leisure for following intellectual or other pursuits congenial to his nature.'[14]

---

12 Executive Committee of the Democratic Federation, *Socialism Made Plain: The Social and Political Manifesto of the Democratic Federation* (June 1883), 3–7.

13 William Morris, 'To John Burns (27 October 1885),' in Norman Kelvin (ed.), *The Collected Letters of William Morris: Volume II, Part B: 1885–1888* (Princeton: Princeton University Press, 1987), 475.

14 'The Manifesto of the Socialist League,' *Commonweal* 1.1 (February 1885), revised by William Morris and E. Belfort Bax, *The Manifesto of the Socialist League* (London: Socialist League Office, 1885). Cf. Ernest Belfort Bax, *Religion of Socialism: Essays in Modern Socialist Criticism* (second edition; London: Swan Sonnenschein & Co, 1890), 78: 'insuchwise that each citizen shall obtain

The *Manifesto of the Socialist League* also popularised a dialectical materialist reading of history or what we might alternatively think of as a post-Christian theory of eschatology, which, as we will see, was developed by Bax and Morris in 'Socialism from the Root Up' (*Commonweal* 1886–1888) and was essential for understanding Morris's presentation of Ball. In the most basic sense, the dialectical reading of history in the manifesto claimed that just as 'chattel-slavery passed into serfdom, and serfdom into the so-called free-labour system, so most surely will this latter pass into social order.' To help bring about this change, the Socialist League would endeavour to educate people in the 'principles of this great cause' and so 'when the crisis comes,' there will be a body of people 'ready to step into their due places and deal with and direct the irresistible movement.' This would involve solidarity or 'close fellowship' and a 'steady purpose for the advancement of the Cause,' including 'equality and brotherhood for all the world' to bring about the necessary organisation and discipline. But there would be no distinctions of rank or dignity because selfish ambitions of leadership previously weakened the workers' cause.[15]

Indeed, in his 1893 lecturing, Morris would start to use the language of 'communism' in the development of his ideas and reading of history where a more federalized communism would be the successor to socialism and the state.[16] Perceptions of the machinery of socialism, including the administration of public facilities and higher wages, certainly brought improvements but did not always bring their benefits to the working classes. Socialism, however, needed to go a stage further in 'converting' workers to a complete socialism: communism. For Morris, there was no difference between *complete* socialism and communism but rather communism would exist when socialism 'ceases to be militant and becomes triumphant.' Communism will foreground the resources of nature (e.g., land), which should be owned by 'the whole community for the benefit of the whole' so that people (for there will be no classes) have their necessities and 'reasonable comforts' satisfied. Echoing (among others) Marx, Bax, and Acts 2.44–45 (cf. Acts

---

the full advantage of the improved processes of production, inasmuch as each citizen shall have to contribute his share to the necessary work of society.'

15 *Commonweal* 1.1 (February 1885).

16 Morris's lecturing on 'Communism (1893)' was published as *Communism* (Fabian Tract 113; London: Fabian Society, 1903) and is available now at https://www.marxists.org/archive/morris/works/1893/commune.htm. Cf. William Morris, 'Where Are We Now?,' *Commonweal* 6 (15 November 1890). For summaries of Morris and the shifts towards and in socialism and communism, see, e.g., Kinna, *William Morris*, 118–19; Ruth Levitas, 'More, Morris, Utopia…and Us,' *Journal of William Morris Studies* 22 (2016): 4–17 (8–12).

4.32–35), people for certain positions will be chosen because they are 'fit for the work' and not because they must have a job found for them. They will do their 'work for the benefit of each and all.'[17]

The Religion of Socialism

As Morris put it concerning England's future in his poem collected in *Chants for Socialists*, 'The Day is Coming' (1884), 'There more than one in a thousand in the days that are yet to come…That the Dawn and the Day is coming.'[18] This language took an eschatological turn of a different variety towards the end of the 1880s. In the aftermath of Bloody Sunday—defeat in the face of police violence used in the demonstration about unemployment at Trafalgar Square (13 November 1887)—Morris now rethought the imminence of the Great Change and looked to a more patient growing of working-class consciousness. Thus, in his 1893 lecturing, he noted in biblical-sounding language of end times that while 'hope of the new-birth' (cf. Mark 13.8; Romans 8.22–24) was growing, some believed that a sudden change was 'close at hand' (cf. Isaiah 13.22; Jeremiah 48.16; Micah 7.4; Zephaniah 1.7; Matthew 3.2; 4.17; 10.7; Mark 1.15; Luke 10.9, 11). But like St Paul and his imitators before him, Morris even admitted that his younger self believed in the 'inevitableness of a sudden and speedy change' (cf. Philippians 1.20; 2 Timothy 4.6–8). Like plenty of other preachers of

---

17 This is an issue that turns up elsewhere in Morris's thinking, e.g., 'True and False Society [1887],' in *The Collected Works of William Morris with Introductions by His Daughter May Morris, Volume XXIII; Signs of Change: Lectures on Socialism* (London: Longman Green, 1915), 215–37. Cf. William Morris on 'Artists and Artisan as an Artist Sees It,' in *Commonweal* 3 (10 September 1887): 'The long and short of it is this, a decent life, a share in the common life of all is the only "reward" that any man can honestly take for his work, whatever he is; if he asks for more, that means that he intends to play the master over somebody. When the workers have made up their minds to be free, he won't get that, so he may make himself easy, and get amusement out of his work as he can, if he is a "superior person". Well, I end as our comrade, with the word "equality", which will one day become a real thing and no mere word, and so cure all our troubles.' On the political context of Morris's position on contribution according to ability and providing according to needs, see, e.g., Kinna, *William Morris*, 116–18.

18 *Justice* 1.11 (5 March 1884); William Morris, *Chants for Socialists* (London: Socialist League Office, 1885), 3–5.

imminent upheaval faced with the realisation of failure, from 1887 onward Morris was wary of the timing of the Great Change and warned that we should remember how hard it was for other tyrannies to die and that social democratic changes were mere alleviations of the 'present days of oppression.'[19] Slowness of change will even lead to a 'period of great suffering and misery' and so Morris hoped for the advent of the change to be speedy and less painful (cf. Mark 13.17–20). Instead of giving up hope, educating the workers should be done by any means possible and be supplemented by the aims of socialism and 'a longing to bring about the complete change which will supplant civilization by communism.'[20]

His use of eschatological and apocalyptic allusions, and appropriation of language we might generally associate with religion, was not accidental. The *Manifesto of the Socialist League* openly concludes with a call for 'single-hearted devotion to the religion of Socialism, the only religion which the Socialist League professes.' This idea of socialism as the new or alternative religion, and one which was to retain a 'religious' or 'ethical' sense of responsibility to one another—and put the evangelising consciousness-raising, propagandistic, and revolutionary potential of popular education at its heart—had some resonance towards the end of the nineteenth century and beyond.[21] Naturally, the 'religion of socialism' was an idea in opposition to the 'religion of capitalism' which was developed elsewhere independently and in both similar and different ways by Bax and Morris.[22] As Morris proclaimed in *Justice* (1884), 'while theologians are

19 Morris, 'Communism (1893).' See also Kinna, *William Morris*, 157–59.
20 Morris, 'Communism (1893).'
21 On the rhetoric of the 'religion of socialism' in context, see, e.g., Stephen Yeo, 'A New Life: The Religion of Socialism in Britain, 1883–1896,' *History Workshop* 4 (1977): 5–56; Kinna, *William Morris*, 42, 173 (cf. 92, 99, 107); Anna Vaninskaya, *William Morris and the Idea of Community: Romance, History and Propaganda, 1880–1914* (Edinburgh: Edinburgh University Press, 2010), 7, 62, 83–84, 140–46, 156–58, 160–65, 175–86, 198–99 (with 55–56 covering Morris's use of apocalyptic language in the mid-1880s); Seamus Flaherty, *Marx, Engels and Modern British Socialism: The Social and Political Thought of H. M. Hyndman, E. B. Bax, and William Morris* (New York: Palgrave Macmillan, 2020), 141–61.
22 Williams, 'Morris, Christianity and Socialism,' 38, 41–42. Cf. William Morris, 'To George Bainton (2 April 1888),' in Norman Kelvin (ed.), *Collected Letters of William Morris: Volume II, Part B*, 763–65; Bax, *Religion of Socialism*. On the differences between Bax and Morris, see Ruth Kinna, 'Time and Utopia: The Gap between Morris and Bax,' *Journal of William Morris Studies* 18 (2010): 36–47. Compare also MacCarthy, *William Morris*, loc 1103 (cf. loc 9113): 'Morris flung himself into the religious life at Marlborough with an extremism

disputing about the existence of a hell elsewhere, we are on the way to realising it here: and if capitalism is to endure, whatever may become of men when they die, they will come to hell when they are born. Think of that and devote yourselves to the spread of the RELIGION OF SOCIALISM.'[23] Nevertheless, the 'religion of socialism' as presented in the *Manifesto of the Socialist League* reflects signatories' views that a degree of human agency, ideals, ethics, ideas, persuasion, and even utopianism is needed. People must 'strive' and educate for the goal of 'realising the change towards social order' while incorporating experiences of defeat and thus being prepared to make 'sacrifices' to 'the Cause.'[24]

This was something Morris developed in relation to a dialectical reading of history. 'Let it be admitted,' Morris claimed in 1890, 'that Christianity, like all religions which include a system of morality, has something in common with socialism.' Nevertheless, the 'contrast between real and actual Christianity' is meaningless because 'real (I should call it ideal) Christianity has never existed at all.' Instead, Morris argued, 'Christianity has developed in due historic sequence from the first, and has taken the various forms which social, political, economic circumstances have forced on it,' and when 'this beggarly period has been supplanted by one in which Socialism is realized, will not the system of morality, the theory of life, be all-embracing, and can it be other than the Socialistic theory? Where then will be the Christian ethic? — *absorbed in Socialism*.'[25] Before we turn to *A*

---

that was both opposed to and inherent in his family and which was to resurface in his passionate adherence to the other religion of the Socialist cause.'

23 *Justice* (12 April 1884). The 'spread' of this religion was put in stronger language still, even if certain 'zealots' were thought to be wreckers: E.g., William Morris, 'To Georgiana Burne-Jones (26 August 1883),' in Norman Kelvin (ed.), *The Collected Letters of William Morris: Volume II, Part A: 1881–1884* (Princeton: Princeton University Press, 1987), 219: 'the aim of Socialists should be the founding of a religion, towards which end compromise is no use, and we only want to have those with us who will be with us to the end.'

24 *Commonweal* 1.1 (February 1885); cf. *Commonweal* 1.2 (March 1886); Chapter 17 ('How the Change Came') in William Morris, *News from Nowhere* (London: Longmans, Green and Co., 1908 [1890, 1892]). See also, e.g., Thompson, *William Morris*, 721–23, 786; Raymond Williams, *Culture and Materialism: Selected Essays* (London: Verso, 1980), 204–5; Perry Anderson, *Arguments within English Socialism* (London: Verso, 1980), 159–60; Kinna, *William Morris*, 16–18, 98–114, 172–76; Kinna, 'Time and Utopia,' 42; Vaninskaya, *William Morris and the Idea of Community*, 84, 125, 178. As Phil Katz put it, that 'the path to socialism would be a long one, dotted with setbacks amidst advances' (*Thinking Hands*, 243).

25 William Morris, 'Christianity and Socialism,' *Commonweal* 6 (8 March 1890).

Dream of John Ball, we need to look further at Morris's reading of history and religion, and Ball's place within this schema.

Religion and History according to Bax and Morris

The transformation of Christianity touched upon in the *Manifesto of the Socialist League* was part of Morris's dialectical reading of history which underpins *A Dream of John Ball*.[26] More precisely, *A Dream of John Ball* can be read in light of Bax's particular reception of Marx, Engels, and others but more precisely still, as Nicholas Salmon rightly stressed, through Bax and Morris's contemporaneous explanation in 'Socialism from the Root Up,' serialised in *Commonweal* (1886–1888) and revised and incorporated into their *Socialism: Its Growth and Outcome* (1893).[27] Here, despite the differences they held, Morris and Bax provided a generalised history of human society up to the period of capitalism, though looking beyond to a new order yet to come which will be reached through socialism. Indeed, this is an understanding of history where the present and future have been shaped by the struggles of the past and the 'struggle towards change' has 'forced us whether we will it or not, to help forward that change.'[28]

Because of its importance for understanding *A Dream of John Ball* (and its ongoing reception), it is worth outlining the arguments presented in

26 For discussions of Morris's dialectical history in context, including the range of influences, see, e.g., John Goode, 'William Morris and the Dream of Revolution,' in John Lucas (ed.), *Literature and Politics in the Nineteenth Century: Essays* (London: Methuen, 1971), 221–80; Marcus Waithe, *William Morris's Utopia of Strangers: Victorian Medievalism and the Ideal of Hospitality* (Cambridge: D. S. Brewer, 2006), 118–42; Vaninskaya, *William Morris and the Idea of Community*, 75–134; Bevir, *Making of British Socialism*, 85–105; Flaherty, *Marx, Engels and Modern British Socialism*, 205–29.
27 Nicholas Salmon, 'A Reassessment of *A Dream of John Ball*,' *Journal of the William Morris Society* 14 (2001): 29–38. Cf. Stephen F. Eisenman, 'Communism in Furs: A Dream of Prehistory in William Morris's *John Ball*,' *The Art Bulletin* 87 (2005): 92–110 (95–97, 106); Vaninskaya, *William Morris and the Idea of Community*, 78–81. For 'Socialism from the Root Up,' I reference the collection of the *Commonweal* articles in William Morris, *Political Writings: Contributions to Justice and Commonweal 1883–1890* (ed. Nicholas Salmon; Bristol: Thoemmes Press, 1994), 495–622.
28 Morris and Bax, 'Socialism from the Root Up,' 497.

'Socialism from the Root Up.' Early human existence involved satisfying the immediate needs of the individual but gave way to primitive communism as human beings realised that they could go beyond basic needs of food and shelter and harness nature to produce a livelihood, with some tilling the ground. Increasing human wealth brought with it change. Land may not have been the property of individuals, but it was also not common to allcomers and so 'primitive society' developed with exclusive groups and hostility towards other groups, thereby producing the conditions for war and warrior-leaders. Greater powers of production meant greater disposable wealth and a greater share of the wealth for the warrior-kings—and so primitive communism transformed into individual ownership.

This led to the rise of the larger group, the tribe, where the blood relationship became the norm and land was distributed according to various arbitrary arrangements, even if ownership was not admitted to individuals. Tribal society also developed slavery, which meant that a class-based society had begun. The tribe then became a collection of tribes, or the people, and then transformed into ancient civilisation, where the city became important and where slavery developed rapidly. With the city, political life emerged as did a systematising of received beliefs into regular worship of the ancestors of the tribe which was the 'first universal religion' whereby the 'universe was conceived of as a system of animated beings to be feared and propitiated by man.' This grew into 'religion of the city' patriotism which marked the progressive peoples (or at least in their most progressive moments), including the Greeks, Romans, and 'the Hebrew.'[29]

As it was among the tribes, so hostilities between cities continued. But among the Greeks, individual struggles for pre-eminence eroded city patriotism thereby allowing military domination, political intrigue, and confusion until the independence of the Greeks was taken away by a similarly corrupted Roman power. Internal Roman struggles among its tribes led to the development of a middle class, living off the profits made from slave labour. The old city republic gave way to the formation of an empire built on slavery with tax gathering and commercial interests. This was the victory of individualism and the defeat of public spirit. The wealth of the empire would consequently suffer through commercial greed as even slave labour became unprofitable and taxes could not be paid. Soldiers once 'religiously devoted' to the city became too-costly mercenaries.[30] The Barbarians would take over and their inherited tribal communism meant

---

29 Morris and Bax, 'Socialism from the Root Up,' 499.
30 Morris and Bax, 'Socialism from the Root Up,' 500.

a renewed antagonism of individual and common rights as Barbarian and Roman ideas would come together to form the Middle Ages.

In theory, the accompanying feudal system had a hierarchical order of service from serf upwards with the ruler providing the protection even for the serf. God was the owner of the land with authority given to rulers and further devolved to feudal lords downwards until the serf. For the serf, the local lord was the 'incarnation of the compulsion and protection of God, which all men acknowledged and looked for.'[31] Of course, Morris and Bax were well aware that theory did not always match reality and abuses of the system led to continual rebellion. Nevertheless, such ideals meant that the medieval system was tied in with its own religious system which was inherited from early Christianity. Under Roman rule, Christianity would be individualistic in that it pushed for a reward theology and compensation in the next life, alongside obedience to the ruling powers. This theology was muted in medieval Christianity which 'brought the kingdom of heaven to earth' and infused temporal power. Put another way, the 'Church was political and social rather than religious,' while the 'State was at least as much religious as it was political and social.'[32]

The ideas of primitive communism among the tribes were absorbed into the medieval system but they also fed into associations for mutual aid which developed (with some resistance) into trade associations and then corporations of the free towns and craft-guilds who were used by bureaucratic kings to counter the power of nobles and the church. The life of the medieval serf was duly changed, and significantly so. In the early Middle Ages, the serf did both field work and handicrafts, but the latter was now dominated by the guilds.

By the mid-fourteenth century, craft-guilds were triumphant and mark the end of the first part of the Middle Ages for Morris and Bax. Serfs began to accept the changes, some moved to towns and became associated with the guilds, some became free even if living on unfree tenured lands. The breakdown of serfdom was 'marked by the peasant's war in England led by Wat Tyler and John Ball in Kent, and John Litster in East Anglia, which was the answer of the combined yeomen, emancipated and unemancipated serfs, to the attempt of the nobles to check the movement.'[33] This was explained elsewhere by Morris in *Commonweal* 1888 under the title 'Revolutionary Calendar: Wat Tyler.' Here, Morris argued that, despite the failure of the revolt, the 'inevitable movement' of the 'extinction of serfdom

---

31 Morris and Bax, 'Socialism from the Root Up,' 501.
32 Morris and Bax, 'Socialism from the Root Up,' 502.
33 Morris and Bax, 'Socialism from the Root Up,' 504.

in England went on faster and faster.'[34] In Bax and Morris's joint history, they explained that the developments of craft-guilds and freed serfs moving to towns led to the emergence of the free labourer who was compelled to be affiliated with the guild. As the guilds dominated alongside developments in trade, so came the rise of the privileged and unprivileged worker and the beginnings of the present middle class and the proletariat. Labour would eventually become 'a commodity to be bought and sold in the market as the body of the chattel-slave once had been.'[35]

With the emergence of printing technology and new or revived learning beyond the medieval church, the next transformation towards a commercial society based on capital and wage-labour began which would break up the old hierarchies. Medieval Christianity and its corporate ethics and divinely justified hierarchy was not suited to this transformation to commercialism. God no longer owned the land, and the individualist ethics of early Christianity and the removal of religion from worldly business were revived or brought to the fore again and epitomised by Protestantism. This also meant the return to prominence of reward theology to quieten people's discontents. Where this new or revived religion was different was that, unlike early Christianity, it actively assisted in oppression and advocated against rebellion. But this religion was now on the wane and subservient to the power of the state.

Though less so than *A Dream of John Ball*, the details of the future transformation were necessarily vague—these things were, Morris and Bax argued, no more easily foreseeable than to those living at the beginnings of the commercial period. Among the speculations they gave was the future of religion, and to do this they gave a redefinition of the term. The popular connection between religion and supernatural beliefs needed to be qualified: rather than an essential aspect of religion, supernatural beliefs should be seen more as an accessory. In its early history, religion was concerned with kinship and society. In this early period, religious belief made no distinction between human beings, animals, or inanimate matters as all these were considered 'conscious and intelligent.' The development of civilization into both a possessing, dominating, and slave-holding class, and a non-possessing and dominated one, provided the possessing class time for reflection. The upper class developed ideas about distinguishing human beings from the rest of nature, between the familiar and the

---

34 William Morris, 'Revolutionary Calendar: Wat Tyler,' *Commonweal* 4.126 (9 June 1888). See also William Morris, *Signs of Change: Seven Lectures Delivered on Various Occasions* (London: Reeves and Turner, 1888), 80.
35 Morris and Bax, 'Socialism from the Root Up,' 511.

relatively unknown. In nature, a distinction could also be drawn between visible objects understood as unconscious and a power which acted from behind the scenes and was 'conceived of as manlike in character, but above mankind in knowledge and power, and no longer a part of the things themselves, but without them, and moving and controlling them.'[36] Alongside this, other binaries emerged: the distinction between the individual and society and the distinction within the individual between the body and soul. And this is how Bax and Morris argued that religion became associated with the supernatural.

As customs based on an idea of nature full of conscious beings became irrelevant or even repugnant, a new explanatory system emerged. This included the importance of a future existence for the soul and grew into 'universal or ethical religions' such as Buddhism and Christianity. Whereas older tribal societies kept loyalties inside the tribe, the new morality held a duty to all people beyond specific communities. However, these were vague injunctions which could be explained away when necessary because morality was grounded in a deity and this deity could reveal themselves to the individual conscience. This development in morality took time but would reach its final development in Christianity. In the present, it was a system that 'has now under the influence of competitive economics taken the final form of the devil-take-the-hindmost doctrine and practice of modern society.'[37]

The future form of this moral consciousness will, they argued, involve some kind of return to the older ethics but on a 'higher level.' This time the narrow scope of kinship will disappear, and the individual will completely identify with social interests broadly understood in terms of humanity. In fact, this new ethic was understood to have inspired thousands in or around their present, such as the 'heroic devotion' of the working classes in the Paris Commune of 1871 to the 'idea of true and universal freedom.'[38] But they also believed this feeling was spreading in the home of bourgeois bureaucracy—England. This was the result of class struggle which was now approaching the crisis that will abolish all classes. The hope for economic change and an improved existence has allowed this new ethic to be understood.

---

36 Morris and Bax, 'Socialism from the Root Up', 619.
37 Morris and Bax, 'Socialism from the Root Up', 621.
38 Morris and Bax, 'Socialism from the Root Up', 621.

A Dream of John Ball

A Dream of John Ball is a partial retelling of this history in story form. It seems that one notable and immediate prompt to write this story was the Lord Mayor's Show in London where, Morris complained, the death of Tyler ('the ruffianly agitator') was celebrated against a 'dark background of foolish and ignorant armed peasants.' Turning to Froissart (with a few digs at him), Morris explained that the rebels were in fact objecting to serfdom and exploitation, and summarised (while reading between Froissart's lines) a more positive account of thousands of rebels, Jack Straw, Tyler, and Tyler's 'worthier associate' Ball (including his sermon about everything in common)—and their downfall. Morris stressed that neither Tyler nor Ball 'died for nothing,' though gave little in the way of detail as to the value of their deaths.[39] *A Dream of John Ball*, however, did.

A Dream of John Ball starts with the Man from Essex (effectively Morris himself) dreaming about the past as a kind of 'architectural peep-show' (Ch. I) but ends up in an especially lucid dream about being in Kent in 1381 during the revolt. The Man from Essex meets the Kentish rebels, including Will Green who was 'one of the wealthier' yeomen (Ch. VIII). Green is quizzical when confronted by the idea that someone has no master, joking that the Man from Essex must have come down from heaven before whispering a coded message from the opening of Ball's letters in Knighton:

39 William Morris, 'The Lord Mayor's Show,' *Justice* (15 November 1884). Froissart was a key source for *A Dream of John Ball*, and others have noted sources and wider influences such as Holinshed, Knighton, and Walsingham, as well as historians from Morris's time (e.g., Edward Freeman, John Richard Green, James Thorold Rogers). Morris was also friends with Charles Edmund Maurice. See, e.g., Carole Silver, *The Romance of William Morris* (Athens, OH: University of Ohio Press, 1981), 124; Michael Holzman, 'The Encouragement and Warning of History: William Morris's *A Dream of John Ball*,' in Florence Boos and Carole Silver (eds), *Socialism and the Literary Artistry of William Morris* (Columbia: University of Missouri Press 1990), 98–116 (102); Peter Faulkner, *William Morris and the Idea of England: Kelmscott Lecture 1991* (London: William Morris Society, 1992); Salmon, 'A Reassessment,' 29–38; Vaninskaya, 'Dreams of John Ball,' 50–52; Vaninskaya, *William Morris and the Idea of Community*, 125–29; Ingrid Hanson, 'The Living Past and the Fellowship of Sacrificial Violence in William Morris's *A Dream of John Ball*,' in Kate Mitchell and Nicola Parsons (eds.), *Reading Historical Fiction: The Revenant and Remembered Past* (New York: Palgrave Macmillan, 2013), 204–19 (206–7); Julia Courtney, 'Versions of the Past, Problems of the Present, Hopes for the Future: Morris and Others Rewrite the Peasants' Revolt,' *Journal of William Morris Studies* (2015): 10–25 (11–12).

'John the Miller, that ground small, small, small.' In response, the Man from Essex mouths another of the coded references: 'The king's son of heaven shall pay for all' (Ch. I). Reference to the famous sayings from the revolt are more prominent still when they head to a church with a cross where they all gather and mingle, accompanied by a banner with a picture of 'a man and a woman half-clad in skins of beasts seen against a background of green trees, the man holding a spade and the woman a distaff and spindle rudely done enough, but yet with a certain spirit and much meaning' with the famous words, 'When Adam delved and Eve span/Who was then the gentleman?' (Ch. III). This description would, of course, be made especially famous by Burne-Jones's frontispiece etching of Adam and Eve for the Longman editions of *A Dream of John Ball*.

The scene is set for Ball to address the crowd, and we get a description of the charismatic man himself. Ball is described as 'tall and big-boned' whose 'not very noteworthy' face was shaven and consisted of a 'big but blunt chin,' a 'big' mouth, a 'longish upper lip,' grey eyes which were 'well opened and wide apart,' and a 'ring of dark hair' around his 'priest's tonsure.' He also had that 'big...clear cut' nose with 'wide nostrils,' the notable size of which may have been standard by the time Morris was writing (see Chapters 11, 13), and Morris may have been influenced by Humphreys's collection of Froissart pictures and their reception.[40] Ball's eyes (which have something of a reception history themselves) could alternately light up his face with a 'kindly smile,' look 'set and stern,' or appear as if looking at something in the distance, 'which is the wont of the eyes of the poet or enthusiast' (Ch. III). These features, including those relating to being a monk, may have broadly complemented certain prominent manly stereotypes in Victorian England, but, as we will see below, Morris had much more to say on issues of Ball and gender which he saw as pointing far beyond the present.[41]

The rebels emotionally and tearfully receive Ball's preaching from the cross. Ball references the rebels rescuing him from prison, the importance of fellowship and solidarity, the difficulties of committed revolutionary activity, the sorry state and fate of the rich lords and oppressors, and the

---

40 Morris gave a copy of Humphreys's illustrations to Louisa Macdonald which is still preserved with a note dating to 1857. See Norman Kelvin (ed.), *The Collected Letters of William Morris: Volume I, 1848–1880* (Princeton: Princeton University Press, 1984), 136 n. 1.

41 On the broader questions of Morris and Victorian constructions of manliness, see, e.g., Jan Marsh, 'William Morris and Victorian Manliness,' in Peter Faulkner and Peter Preston (eds), *William Morris: Centenary Essays* (Exeter: University of Exeter Press, 1999), 185–99; Susan Mooney, 'William Morris and Manliness,' *Eras* 15 (2014): 1–23.

benefits peasants will receive in fellowship when they lack masters. During this, the Man from Essex delivers his famous words (influential too in the history of the reception of Ball) about the longer-term implications of the revolt and the histories of defeat and new struggles, and so anticipating the finale of *A Dream of John Ball*:

> But while I pondered all these things, and how men fight and lose the battle, and the thing that they fought for comes about in spite of their defeat, and when it comes turns out not to be what they meant, and other men have to fight for what they meant under another name—while I pondered all this, John Ball began to speak again in the same soft and dear voice with which he had left off. (Ch. IV)

Before this theme is expounded in the latter chapters, the rebels, with Ball's blessing and with the banner of Adam and Eve, go on to win the battle of Township's End. With Jack Straw taking centre stage, they manage to chase the knights out and kill, among others, the sheriff, lawyers, and bailiffs. Ball now talks up the imminent and monumental march on London to the enthusiastic crowd with a reminder of the importance of their fellowship and, somewhat prophetically, to stand firm and keep their wits about them when faced with devious opponents who 'shall lead you astray' (Ch. VII; cf. Matthew 24.4, 24; Mark 13.5–6, 22; Luke 21.8).[42]

Ball and the Man from Essex then retire to Will Green's house for supper before they both head to the (extensively described) moonlit church amidst the battle's dead, pondering mortality, fidelity to the Fellowship, and talking of the 'Days to Come' (Ch. X), the 'days that are to be on the earth before the Day of Doom cometh' (Ch. IX). The Man from Essex tells of the fate of Ball and the uprising in London, which Ball stoically accepts knowing that 'I live now and shall live' (Ch. X), but also of a future where villeinage would soon wither away 'so that your lives and your deaths both shall bear fruit.' But while things would improve, this would not, as Ball hoped, usher in an era where those who labour would no longer be exploited, would live happy lives, and would enjoy 'the goods of the earth without money and without price.' This era, Ball is informed, would not come for a long time. Before then would be an era of exploiters and exploitation and the 'more that is made in the land the more shall they crave' (Ch. X).

---

42 Anxieties about being 'led astray' are common in biblical texts. See, e.g., Psalms 14.3; 40.4; 95.10; 119.67, 118; Proverbs 10.17; 12.26; Isaiah 9.16; 30.28; 35.8; 44.20; 47.10; 53.6; Jeremiah 8.4; 23.13; 50.6; Ezekiel 14.11; 20.30; 44.10, 15; 48.11; Hosea 4.12; Amos 2.4; Micah 3.5; 1 Corinthians 12.2; 2 Corinthians 11.3; Galatians 2.13; Titus 3.3; Hebrews 3.10; 2 Peter 2.15.

Here we get an explanation of the rise of capitalism—effectively a version of the argument presented in 'Socialism from the Root Up'—cast in the language of prophetic prediction of the 'wondrous seer' (Ch. XI). The Man from Essex explains that 'in the time to come,' lords will see that labourers have more than they need and would demand their surplus, and 'in those days' trade will increase and land use will alter to remove corn and people for more sheep and more wool to sell to the 'Easterlings' (Ch. X). There may be no more villeins in England (much to Ball's puzzlement), but so-called free people will produce for the market by selling their labour to the masters and earning enough to live.

Surely, Ball naively suggested, those that labour 'under the whip like the Hebrews in the land of Egypt' will fight and resist! But the Man from Essex says that few wars will be fought over these issues and instead will continue to be fought for as they have been—for some king or lord, or indeed 'some usurer and forestaller of the market' (Ch. XI). People may 'feel the plague and yet not know the remedy' and their livelihood will gradually decline as they grow increasingly helpless while feeling times are like the 'kingdom of heaven,' even if these are but moderate improvements (Ch. XI). And rather than being forced to work under the whip, this new system, with its technological developments (Ch. XXII), will produce more workers than masters and so workers will undercut one another so lords will never lack in willing slaves. 'In the latter days,' Ball explains, in a world of monopolists, there may still be 'times of famine' even in 'times of plenty.' Goods and bread may be cheap 'in those days' but people will pray for prices to rise so profits increase, and some wealth might trickle down (Ch. XI).

So, Ball wearily asks against the symbolic backdrop of a church increasingly lit from the 'first coming of the kindly day,' would people think that things must be so forever, or would they think of a remedy? As Ball's death contributes to what he strove for, the pair discussed, so those in the latter and worse times will seek different ways to remedy their situation, and not always successfully in the face of mightier, more numerous, and often hidden masters. Workers would not always be aware of their shared interests but 'in the end' they will come to this knowledge and bring about the remedy and it will be seen that struggles were not for nothing. The Man from Essex comforts Ball with the knowledge that the 'Change beyond the Change' will come and the 'Fellowship of Men shall endure' despite the 'tribulations.'

By the end of *A Dream of John Ball*, the white poppy that the Man from Essex picked up at Will Green's house may eventually have 'seemed…to have withered and dwindled' (Chs. IX, XI, XII) but Morris's dialectical understanding ensured that hope continued. Picking up on earlier symbolism of light and dark (e.g., Southey, Mrs O'Neill, Chartists), the glimmer brings day out of the night and in the same way 'wise men and valiant souls' will see the remedy. The complaints of the poor will be heeded until one day they will become a threat to the rich. In the end times, there will be those who have conquered fear of change and look to the times that will come rather than to the dream that failed, despite all the threats, murders, strife, doubts, failures, disagreements, and dangers, even within the Fellowship. But there will be victory and this time there will be the 'end of all' and people will enjoy the 'fruits of the earth and the fruits of their toil... without money and without price.' And the 'time will come' when Ball's dream will come to fruition and John Ball's name will be remembered and inspire hope for this future change (Ch. XII).

England: From Each according to Their Abilities

As is widely recognised, Morris's interests in this future change focused primarily on socialism and communism *in England* and such impulses in English history. *A Dream of John Ball* implicitly advocates how such ideas belong in English tradition. They are certainly compatible with Morris's understanding of English, Germanic, and Northern European aesthetics and language,[43] a view echoed in different ways by his contemporaries (see Chapters 14, 16). His reading was likewise in the tradition of radical takes on the myth of the English constitution.[44] Morris elaborated on the history of the English constitution in detail, but the basic point was that the socialist future would restore some of what was lost. 'In the new Society,' as Morris claimed in a lecture first delivered in 1887, 'we should form bodies like municipalities, county-boards and parishes, and almost all practical public work would be done by these bodies' and 'everybody who had any capacity for such work would have to do his share of it.' But he also told his audience that they 'must remember that this is no new idea after all, but is the ancient constitution of the land, which [was] gradually corrupted and overlaid by officialism of one sort or other.'[45]

---

43 On language, see, e.g., Will Abberley, '"To Make a New Tongue": Natural and Manufactured Language in the Late Fiction of William Morris,' *Journal of Victorian Culture* 17 (2012): 397–412.
44 Vaninskaya, *William Morris and the Idea of Community*, 106–11.
45 William Morris, 'What Socialists Want,' available at https://www.marxists.org/archive/morris/works/1887/want.htm.

Like others before and alongside him, Morris was updating this radical English myth in the face of competing myths which foregrounded different understandings of race, ethnicity, class, and shared history. Julia Courtney located *A Dream of John Ball* against the backdrop of what Krishan Kumar called a 'moment of Englishness'. This was when Britain's industrial strength was challenged, and imperial anxieties were provoked by America and Germany. In response, there was a cultural and intellectual drive to examine the national history, its people, and its prospects.[46] Morris's 'oppositional' version of what England could and should be was, of course, emphatically anti-capitalist and against what the British state stood for.[47] The importance of fellowship for Morris meant that it had obvious affinities with the ideas about English political identity we saw associated with, for instance, the Chartists, Egan, Redpath, and even Maurice. As it was put in *Commonweal* (1885) in answer to the question, 'Will the social family take the place of the private family?'—

> It is surely clear that Socialism could never assent that a family should be confined to blood-relations; for the rest there would be no hard and fast line as to what a family should be; it would be what people might choose, what they might find convenient according to the circumstances.[48]

But, as this obviously implies, with Morris there was another angle to this understanding of familial or blood ties largely overlooked in the history of the reception of Ball but one that was coming to the fore with socialist understandings of the development of human history: rethinking the function of gender roles in human history and beyond capitalism.

---

46 Courtney, 'Versions of the Past', 10, following Krishan Kumar, *The Making of English National Identity* (Cambridge: Cambridge University Press, 2003), 224. Note also the qualifications about Morris's rhetoric in relation to nationalism in Vaninskaya, *William Morris and the Idea of Community*, 38, and broader comparative analysis in Anna Vaninskaya, '"A True Conception of History": "Making the Past Part of the Present" in Late-Victorian Historical Romances', in Hugh Dunthorne and Michael Wintle (eds), *The Historical Imagination in Nineteenth-Century Britain and the Low Countries* (Brill: Leiden, 2013), 151–67.

47 On 'oppositional Englishness', see, e.g., Paul Ward, *Red Flag and Union Jack: Englishness, Patriotism and the British Left, 1881–1924* (Woodbridge: Boydell Press, 1998); Stephen Yeo, 'Socialism, the State and Some Oppositional Englishness', in Robert Colls and Philip Dodd (eds.), *Englishness, Politics and Culture, 1880–1920* (second edition; London: Bloomsbury, 2014), 331–88.

48 *Commonweal* 1.9 (October 1885).

Stephen Eisenman showed how Burne-Jones's Adam and Eve frontispiece highlighted the idea of a communistic impulse in humanity and in England found in *A Dream of John Ball*. This was done by harking back to the example of the earliest stages of human social evolution and primitive communism while foreshadowing aspects of what will come, as found in, for instance, 'Socialism from the Root Up.' The etching of Adam and Eve in their furs, with their children, and carrying out their respective digging and spinning may be less interested in the curse of the Genesis story and the fate of Cain and more in the 'hard but satisfying labor in conditions of equality and mutual aid.'[49] These workers were not alienated from their labour and, crucially, the division of labour was along gendered lines—from each according to their gendered abilities (Adam dug, Eve spun). This was in line with Morris's gendered vision for the future (and understanding of the distant past) which reflected his broader vision for societal change.[50] In an interview with Sarah A. Tooley published in 1894, Morris hoped that the 'time may soon come when there shall be no question of rivalry between the sexes,' and stated that he was in favour of suffrage for adult women, women's involvement in local governing bodies, and women being granted university honours and the opportunities of public speaking, all connected with a general understanding of fairness and 'one moral law, the same for both sexes.'[51] But he also tended to believe there were roles more typically (and physiologically) suited to either men (e.g., handicrafts) or women (e.g., housekeeping).[52] Morris hardly escaped Victorian stereotypes about gender and domesticity but here we can see how they were rethought more in terms of his gendered understanding of 'from each according to their ability':

> In a properly organised society, viz., under a socialist system, opportunity would be given to all persons for doing the work most suitable to them. The economical position of women would be the same as that of men;

---

49 Eisenman, 'Communism in Furs,' 93, 95.
50 See further, e.g., Kinna, *William Morris*, 130–37, 152–53.
51 Sarah A. Tooley, 'A Living Wage for Women: An Interview with William Morris,' *The Women's Signal* (19 April 1894), in Tony Pinkney (ed.), *We Met Morris: Interviews with William Morris, 1885–96* (Reading: SpireBooks, 2005), 89–95 (94–95).
52 Tooley, 'Living Wage for Women,' 93–94, where Morris was remembered as claiming that the art of housekeeping was especially important and difficult to master, adding 'People lift their eyebrows over women mastering the details of the higher mathematics; why, it is infinitely more difficult to learn the details of good housekeeping.'

they would take their place in production according to their capacities, whatever these might turn out to be in a state of things so much improved from our present conditions.[53]

The prominence of the Adam and Eve banner in *A Dream of John Ball* can likewise be understood in such terms.

But Morris's view of equality by way of a gendered division of labour did not mean everything fit dominant late-nineteenth-century gender stereotypes—indeed, Morris's anticipated future by way of medieval England would involve some significant behavioural shifts. As Fiona MacCarthy pointed out, some conventional nineteenth-century understandings of masculinity and femininity were implicitly critiqued in *A Dream of John Ball* as men were moved and cried into their beards and women looked straight back at men rather than fluttering or flirting.[54] Morris himself may also have inherited various earlier discourses about the monk and monastery in relation to artistic manhood in earlier Victorian England of the sort Herbert Sussman analysed in detail, namely male anxieties surrounding the changes brought about by industrialisation and emerging middle classes in early Victorian England. Sussman argued that it is,

> this tension in bourgeois masculinity between the homosocial and the heterosexual that energizes the Victorian idealization of monasticism. For those middle-class male writers dissatisfied with the demands of this hegemonic valorization of domesticity, marriage, and even heterosexuality, the monastery as a sacralized, celibate all-male society safely distanced in time provides a figure through which they could express in covert form, or as an open secret, their attraction to a world of chaste masculine bonding from which female has been magically eliminated, an attraction that clearly resonated with the longings of their middle-class male readers.[55]

Yet Morris's homosocial association with Burne-Jones and Dante Gabriel Rossetti was one thing; Morris's forward-thinking Ball was something else. Ball may have been living in a monastery, but this did not stop him falling in love (with a woman) and nor was it in a way that supported bourgeois models of family life. When Ball and the Man from Essex later talked about the future, we learn that Ball had an 'unwedded wife with whom I dwelt in love after I had taken the tonsure' but who had since died

---

53 Tooley, 'Interview with William Morris,' 260–61.
54 MacCarthy, *William Morris*, loc 10305. Cf. Eisenman, 'Communism in Furs,' 100.
55 Sussman, *Victorian Masculinities*, 5 (cf. 141 on Morris).

(Ch. X). Morris was likely envisaging an idealised past foreshadowing the hoped-for future, based on his own strong criticisms of marriage. A useful parallel to Morris's use of medieval England is his discussion of the history and traditions of Iceland and the 'North.' Here, Morris claimed that the 'position of women was good in this society, the married couple being pretty much on an equality,' citing as evidence 'many stories told of women divorcing themselves for some insult or offense, a blow being considered enough excuse.'[56]

Morris's socialist understandings of marriage and gender relations were, clearly, tied in with his understanding of capitalism and history. As he put it in a letter to George Bernard Shaw, abolishing wedlock 'while the present economical slavery lasts would be futile.' It was the case that 'as long as women are compelled to marry for a livelihood real marriage is a rare exception and prostitution or a kind of legalized rape the rule.'[57] The change in the relations of production and distribution, so he claimed in the *Manifesto for Socialist League*, would mean everyone could live decently, 'free from the sordid anxieties for daily livelihood which at present weigh so heavily on the greatest part of mankind.' The collapse of economic slavery would transform 'social and moral relations' and orientate duty towards the community. In this context, the *Manifesto* added some indication about the idea of free love undermining a rigid understanding of marriage. Or, as the *Manifesto* put it more colourfully, 'Our modern bourgeois property-marriage, maintained as it is by its necessary complement, universal venal prostitution, would give place to kindly and human relations between the sexes.'[58] He further suggested that the downgrading of marriage in the socialist order would lead to communal support for children and help them move away from potentially abusive parents.[59] In

---

56 William Morris, 'The Early Literature of the North—Iceland,' lecture at a meeting sponsored by the Hammersmith Branch of the Socialist League at Kelmscott House (9 October 1887), https://www.marxists.org/archive//morris/works/1887/iceland.htm.
57 William Morris, 'To George Bernard Shaw (18 March 1885),' in Norman Kelvin (ed.), *Collected Letters of William Morris: Volume II, Part B*, 404. Cf. *Commonweal* 3.82 (6 August 1887).
58 *Commonweal* 1.1 (February 1885).
59 Kinna, *William Morris*, 152–53. Cf. William Morris and E. Belfort Bax, *Socialism: Its Growth and Outcome* (London: Swan Sonnenschein & Co, 1893), 299–301; William Morris, 'To William Sharman (April 1886),' in Norman Kelvin (ed.), *Collected Letters of William Morris: Volume II, Part B*, 546–47 (cf. 584–85). Issues of family and marriage in the future world to come were famously taken up in *News from Nowhere* (e.g., chs. 5, 9, 26). See, e.g., John

some ways, all of this is not what we might expect to be associated with a monkish character like Ball. But if we think of this new religion of socialism acting as a fictive kinship, then it is hardly that alien to the history of monastic and Actually Existing Religious Practices. Put another way, the old will again be absorbed into the new.

The Eschatology of Socialism

Christianity and the religion of socialism in *A Dream of John Ball* even went as far as incorporating Ball's take on the language of Jesus and application to his present.[60] Ball talked authoritatively in terms of: 'I say to you' (e.g., Chs. IV, VI, X; cf. Matthew 5.17–48); the perils of being led astray (Chs. IV, VII; see above); the possibility of repentance (Ch. IV; cf. Luke 15); a suggestion that 'in these days are ye building a house which shall not be overthrown' (Ch. VII; Mark 14.58; Matthew 26.61; Acts 7.47–50; Revelation 21); and a warning to bury the dead now in the light of their urgent mission, for 'after tomorrow let the dead abide to bury their dead' (Ch. VII; Matthew 8.22; Luke 9.60). By virtue of being so obviously Christianised is a strong indication that the time was not right for Ball's revolt to work. It is notable that it was the more knowledgeable Man from Essex who now took on the language of Jesus once the future was being explained and Ball's lack of knowledge was exposed, effectively signalling the shift to the new religion of socialism. It was Ball who asked the authoritative seer to explain 'what shall befall' (Ch. X; cf. Matthew 24.3; Mark 13.3–4; Luke 21.7) and it was the Man from Essex who understood what things will be like 'in those days' and made predictions of great wars arising 'in the beginning of these evil times' (Ch. XI; cf. Matthew 24.6–8; Mark 13.7–8; Luke 21.9–10). He even got the 'I say...' sayings when addressing Ball (Ch. X).

Bellamy Foster, 'William Morris's Romantic Revolutionary Ideal: Nature, Labour and Gender in *News from Nowhere*', *Journal of William Morris Studies* 22 (2017): 17–35 (26–32).

60 See also Hanson, 'Living Past', in Mitchell and Parsons (eds.), *Reading Historical Fiction*, 211–12, on biblical echoes and the Christ comparison, and their importance for issues of martyrdom and sacrifice in *A Dream of John Ball*. On the 'chiliasm' of Ball in relation to the socialist reading of the future in *A Dream of John Ball*, see also, e.g., Joe P. L. Davidson, 'Between Utopia and Tradition: William Morris's *A Dream of John Ball*', *European Legacy* 25 (2020): 1–15.

For all that Ball's idea of fellowship was Christian, it also looked to something more secularised, as one of the most famous passages from *A Dream of John Ball* reiterated:

> Forsooth, ye have heard it said that ye shall do well in this world that in the world to come ye may live happily for ever; do ye well then, and have your reward both on earth and in heaven; for I say to you that earth and heaven are not two but one; and this one is that which ye know, and are each one of you a part of, to wit, the Holy Church, and in each one of you dwelleth the life of the Church, unless ye slay it. Forsooth, brethren, will ye murder the Church any one of you, and go forth a wandering man and lonely, even as Cain did who slew his brother? Ah, my brothers, what an evil doom is this, to be an outcast from the Church, to have none to love you and to speak with you, to be without fellowship! Forsooth, brothers, fellowship is heaven, and lack of fellowship is hell: fellowship is life, and lack of fellowship is death: and the deeds that ye do upon the earth, it is for fellowship's sake that ye do them, and the life that is in it, that shall live on and on for ever, and each one of you part of it, while many a man's life upon the earth from the earth shall wane. (Ch. IV)

This fellowship, then, pointed to the religion of socialism that was to come. Indeed, the very act of communion between Ball and the Man from Essex—with their solidarity, critical dialogue, and shared interests—was, as Florence Boos framed it, an instance of fellowship across time, including shared interests with a more secularised context.[61] Unlike capitalism, where workers and individuals were to be pitted against one another and the rich oppress, fellowship was communal and its communal strength was what would propel it to victory, someday. It was for the lonely or imprisoned to 'dream of fellowship' while those 'of a fellowship' to do what needs to be done (Ch. IV).

This fellowship was, on one level, a fourteenth-century Christian version of 'all things in common.'[62] When the lords were gone, when the people lacked masters, they would not lack for fields they have tilled, houses they have built, nor clothes they have woven. They will not mow the 'deep grass for another' while 'his own kine lack cow-meat.' The one who sows will reap and the reaper will 'eat in fellowship the harvest that in fellowship

---

61 Florence S. Boos, 'Alternative Victorian Futures: "Historicism," Past and Present, and A Dream of John Ball,' in Florence S. Boos (ed.), *History and Community: Essays in Victorian Medievalism* (New York: Garland Publishing, 1992), 3–37. See also, e.g., Hanson, 'Living Past,' in Mitchell and Parsons (eds.), *Reading Historical Fiction*, 212–13, 217.
62 Cf. Vaninskaya, *William Morris and the Idea of Community*, 130.

he hath won,' the one who built a house will live in it with 'those that he biddeth of his free will,' and in the tithe barn will be 'wheat for all men to eat of when the seasons are untoward.' This of itself did not have to be understood as 'Christian,' of course, but the text added that everyone will 'keep the holidays of the Church in peace of body and joy of heart' and that the saints in heaven will be glad that 'man shall help man' (Ch. V). The Man from Essex could, tellingly, see further than 'beyond this church' (Ch. X) and promise a time when there would be no abbeys, no priories, no monks, no friars, and, indeed, nothing religious (Ch. XIII). Shorn of its religious trappings and potential opposition, this more secularised version of the fellowship and all things held in common was implied. This would be a time, in the distant future, when 'all men shall work and none make to work, and so none shall be robbed,' when 'all men labour and live and be happy, and have the goods of the earth without money and without price' (Chs. X, XIII).

The romanticised and extensively described fourteenth-century society and people in *A Dream of John Ball* of course contrasted sharply with the misery of the Man from Essex's wretched capitalist present. *A Dream of John Ball* took the example from the fourteenth-century past to speculate about future possibilities. As Morris wrote, the story, with its extensive explanation of post-Ball history, was primarily designed to place stress on socialism and the future. 'When I wrote my little book,' Morris noted, 'I did it more with the intention of bringing in the Socialistic dialogue at the end rather than of dealing with the literary and dramatic side of the story.'[63] Thus, in the final chapters of *A Dream of John Ball*, the authoritative seer naturally appropriates Morris's own prophetic and eschatological language in the service of paving the way for the religion of socialism. Indeed, the ominous setting for the conversation between Ball and the Man from Essex is set in the church with a 'chancel arch the Doom of the last Day, in which the painter had not spared either kings or bishops, and in which a lawyer with his blue coif was one of the chief figures in the group which the Devil was hauling off to hell.' It is here that Ball wishes to 'talk of the days that are to be on the earth before the Day of Doom cometh' (Ch. IX). This eschatology is, of course, secularised in accordance with Morris's reading of history. Ball's dreams of fellowship were not going to happen in the fourteenth century as the transformation to capitalism was only just beginning. It was instead the readers and hearers of *A Dream of John Ball* who might see capitalism give way to a better world. And, as *News from Nowhere* would

---

63 William Morris, 'To Chris Healy (6 October 1894),' in Norman Kelvin (ed.), *The Collected Letters of William Morris, Volume IV: 1893–1896* (Princeton: Princeton University Press, 1996), 212.

further suggest, this socialist or communist future might even have a heady dose of fourteenth-century aesthetics.[64]

But it still had to be done, of course. It was now down to the socialists and revolutionaries under capitalism to fulfil Ball's vision for which there was more 'scientific' justification for its time being nigh. The example of Ball showed the kind of revolutionary attitude, determination, and heroism now required in the late nineteenth century—but with the qualification that there would always be defeats.[65] Ball and the other leaders may have been daring 'before their time,' as Morris put it in a lecture on 'Feudal England' (1887), but there was still something in their message for the present. Morris added (in language that might stand at odds with the more inclusive notions of fellowship he was associated with) that the 1381 'revolt was put down with cruelty worthy of an Irish landlord or a sweating capitalist of the present day.'[66] Whatever Morris's ambiguities concerning violence may have been, he thought that where in 1381 there was turning of 'our plough-shares into swords and our pruning-hooks into spears' (*A Dream of John Ball*, Ch. VIII) so a disciplined use of violence was needed to counter violence or the threat of violence to keep the workers in their place. His presentation of Ball and the rebels as martyrs was part of the connection between past failure and future success with communally shared fellowship, solidarity, and martyrological violence across the ages. As Ingrid Hanson put it, Morris's account presents an important historical example of sacrificial violence which functions as 'emotionally engaging propaganda' for the readers' present and, where it is designed to be acknowledged, that organised, disciplined violence is required for 'social transformation and the paradoxical price of equal and harmonious community.'[67]

Ball the Catholic/Non-Protestant

One of the most distinctive features of Morris's presentation of religion and the revolt in *A Dream of John Ball* is that this world is emphatically

---

64 Cf. Eisenman, 'Communism in Furs,' 92.
65 Cf. Kinna, *William Morris*, 41–42, 114, 97, 98–99, 130, 138, 162–63, 174–77. Cf. Eisenman, 'Communism in Furs,' 93.
66 Morris, *Signs of Change*, 80.
67 Hanson, 'Living Past,' in Mitchell and Parsons (eds.), *Reading Historical Fiction*, 205, 209, 219. Cf. Vaninskaya, *William Morris and the Idea of Community*, 84–86; Ingrid Hanson, *William Morris and the Uses of Violence, 1856–1890* (London: Anthem Press, 2013), 131–66.

Catholic.[68] Morris was clear in his Catholicising of the priest which equally clearly reflected Morris's aesthetic, political, and historical interests. For instance, Ball talks of the 'blessed saints and the angels' (Ch. IV), looks forward to a time when 'Faithfully and merrily then shall all men keep the holidays of the Church in peace of body and joy of heart' (Ch. IV), and is understood to 'say mass' (Ch. VIII). This is a setting where the 'priest blessed the meat in the name of the Trinity' prompting the natural response from the Man from Essex and his company: 'we crossed ourselves and fell to' (Ch. VIII). Indeed, Ball elsewhere 'crossed himself' and provides 'holy water' (Ch. IX).

Ball was also presented by Morris in terms of what we might describe as a Catholicism-from-below. Ball is the 'rascal hedge-priest' (Ch. IV) and 'another sort of priest' when compared with the local parson who had scuttled off 'to his monastery with the two other chantry priests who dwelt in that house'. The people—especially women—were glad Ball instead would now be saying mass (Ch. VIII). As we saw above, Morris viewed the revolt as an indication of the long-term breakdown of serfdom and the rise of the guilds. But there is another angle to his understanding of the development of medieval history that helps us understand his take on Catholicism-from-below in *A Dream of John Ball*. As we also saw, for Morris and Bax medieval Christianity effectively infused the spirit of the kingdom of heaven into the temporal power thereby instilling a system of protection for the social order, including serfs. Nevertheless, they argued, the system could be abused, and this provoked ongoing protest movements against authority, and, in England, it was the 'chronic rebellion of the Foresters, which produced such an impression on the minds of the people', particularly in the 'ballad epic' of the mythical hero Robin Hood.[69] Medieval society may have been changing by the end of the fourteenth century in the Bax-Morris schema, but this tradition of protest was inherited by Morris's Ball. Indeed, a ballad of Robin Hood is sung in *A Dream of John Ball* in order to usher in Ball himself (Ch. II).[70]

This Catholicising is emphatic and what we should expect from Morris and his understanding of history and the emergence of Protestantism. For Morris, Protestantism, particularly Puritanism, was full of hypocrisy and played a significant role in the rise and consolidation of capitalism which

---

68 Vaninskaya, *William Morris and the Idea of Community*, 130–33.
69 Morris and Bax, 'Socialism from the Root Up', 502–3.
70 Cf. Salmon, 'A Reassessment', 33. On Robin Hood traditions and *A Dream of John Ball*, see Stephen Basdeo, 'William Morris's References to the Outlaw in *A Dream of John Ball* (1888)', *Journal of William Morris Studies* 23 (2019): 52–63.

was just starting its transformation in Morris's late fourteenth century. In the fourteenth-century England of *A Dream of John Ball*, the proto-Protestants of popular memory—the Lollards—might even have been co-opted by the lords in their ambitions to bring back serfdom, in sharp opposition to what many of Morris's contemporaries were arguing:

> So let us get the collar on their necks again, and make their day's work longer and their bever-time shorter, as the good statute of the old king bade. And good it were if the Holy Church were to look to it (and the Lollards might help herein) that all these naughty and wearisome holidays were done away with; or that it should be unlawful for any man below the degree of a squire to keep the holy days of the church, except in the heart and the spirit only, and let the body labour meanwhile; for does not the Apostle say, 'If a man work not, neither should he eat'? And if such things were done, and such an estate of noble rich men and worthy poor men upholden for ever, then would it be good times in England, and life were worth the living. (Ch. II)

If Ball was a sign of things to come, then so too were the Lollards. This Catholicising or even anti-Protestant tendency in *A Dream of John Ball* is striking because of how proto-Protestant Ball was typically assumed to be at this point in the history of reception and what was to come in the history of reception, despite the profound influence of Morris on the history of reception.

Indeed, Anna Vaninskaya noted a reading list from F. J. Gould and the Young Socialist Education Bureau around the turn of the twentieth century which recommended *A Dream of John Ball* in the discussion of the 1381 revolt. The reading list simultaneously claimed that the revolt was assisted by the spread of new religious ideas through the 'Preaching Friars' or Lollards which in turn would be developed in the tradition of Puritanism, Nonconformity, and Free Churches! Vaninskaya commented that Morris 'would not have welcomed being associated with such an interpretation, but by the 1900s the invocation of his name in this context had become an inevitability', to which we can add more examples of Morris-inspired works which maintained the Wycliffe/Lollard/proto-Protestant connection as if Morris had never challenged the issue.[71] The Protestant heritage

---

71 Vaninskaya, 'Dreams of John Ball', 54–55. Other early receptions of, or works explicitly inspired by, Morris and/or *A Dream of John Ball* which connected Ball with Wycliffe/Lollards, or saw them as representing complementary movements, include, e.g., *Labour Leader* (30 September 1899); Annie Nathan Meyer, *Robert Annys, Poor Priest: A Tale of the Great Uprising* (London: Macmillan, 1901), e.g., 5–6; Keir Hardie, *From Serfdom to Socialism* (ed. John Callow;

and Nonconformist influence on the emerging labour movement was too strong to be dislodged even by Morris. But it remained that the invocation of Morris's name was a near inevitability in discussions of the revolt and, about a century on from Southey, a new dominant reference point for understanding Ball had been established in the form of *A Dream of John Ball*.

London: Lawrence and Wishart, 2015), 74, 122; James Leatham, *The Peasants' Revolt, or The Tragedy of a Nation* (London: Twentieth Century Press, n.d.), 4, 14–15; H. M. Hyndman, *John Ball: Priest and Prophet of the Peasants' Revolt* (London: Twentieth Century Press, 1909), 4.

16
Still Dreaming of John Ball

By the time of the formation of the Labour Party in 1906, Ball was a familiar point of reference, buoyed by a socialist subculture infused with what Raphael Samuel called 'Marxist Mediaevalism'.[1] Another important figure added his authority to this tradition: Keir Hardie, a founding figure and first parliamentary leader of the Labour Party. In *From Serfdom to Socialism* (1907), Hardie argued that the early church believed that communism was the ideal, most Christian form of social organisation. Christianity may have become the official religion 'of the State,' but the 'great semi-religious semi-political' movements in medieval Europe 'had a Communistic basis,' and this included, of course, 'the Peasant Revolt in England—led by John Ball, "the mad Priest of Kent"' which 'drew its inspiration from the Communistic teachings of Wycliffe' and was 'led by a Communist'.[2] Grounded in Rogers's analysis of living standards in the fifteenth century, Hardie lamented the sorry fate of workers and the communal village since then and the rise of the 'selfish creed of each for himself' with the Protestant Reformation. And thus, it was 'not for nothing that John Ball and Wat Tyler taught the peasantry of England the doctrine of the dignity of manhood and emptiness of titles'.[3] The appendix also included Ball's famous speech from Froissart.

Hardie was not alone. Coming from a Fabian and Independent Labour Party (ILP) background, Frederick John Shaw, under his usual pseudonym Brougham Villiers, framed his *The Socialist Movement in England* (1908) against the backdrop of the formation of the Labour Party.[4] In the preface, Villiers was keen to show how the English are 'no more insensible than others' to the universal appeal of socialism. However, for a generation, he

1 Raphael Samuel, 'British Marxist Historians, 1880–1980: Part One,' *New Left Review* 120 (1980): 21–96 (28).
2 Hardie, *From Serfdom to Socialism*, 85, 122.
3 Hardie, *From Serfdom to Socialism*, 91–92.
4 For biographical details, see Mark Bevir, 'Shaw, Frederick John [*pseud.* Brougham Villiers] (1863–1939),' *ODNB* (22 September 2005).

argued, socialism (at least in party-political terms) had made no obvious progress in England and anti-socialist politicians flattered themselves that socialism was un-English. Villiers's aim was, then, to show that the English past supported the developments in the English present, and that 'from the days of John Ball to those of Owen, there is enough in our history' to show that this perceived gap 'is not due to any special anti-Socialist bias in the English character.'[5] In his chapter on 'Medieval Socialism,' he further argued that More's *Utopia* was not new, and its ideas were even in retreat. Rather, *Utopia* expressed popular ideas that had thrived in Christendom and gave the example of the 'Peasants' Revolt' and its 'eloquent spokesman in John Ball,' adding that whether most of those who participated 'shared his communistic faith or not, there was certainly a Socialist element present.'[6]

This idea of a history or canon of English radicalism and Ball as a supporter of socialism or communist ideas belonged to a convenient and pre-existing story for a newly formed party as leading lights pointed to its deeper radical roots.[7] But there was something else going on here. In Villiers's preface, he warned of a stark alternative—'fellowship or death'— and the Labour Party had to make the case for fellowship. In his chapter on medieval Christianity, he opened with a reference to 'Anglo-Catholic Socialists and democratic members of the arts and crafts societies' looking back to the Middle Ages 'with a certain regret' because 'art was a living social fact, not a mere pastime of the cultured few.'[8] He continued with a typical enough late nineteenth-century romantic reading of medieval Christianity, the decoration of Gothic buildings, altar cloths, and church vessels by 'village craftsmen…artistic and capable,' and how in this 'ancient form of municipal Socialism,' men and women would meet annually to discuss parish affairs (secular and religious) and appoint their churchwarden.[9] And so on. Much more could be said about Villiers's position but by now it should be clear that his reading of English socialism and his discussion of Ball would have resonated with anyone familiar with Ruskin and/or

5   Brougham Villiers, *The Socialist Movement in England* (London: T. Fisher Unwin, 1908), vi.
6   Villiers, *Socialist Movement in England*, 19.
7   See, e.g., Claire V. J. Griffiths, 'History and the Labour Party,' in Claire V. J. Griffiths, James J. Nott, and William Whyte (ed.), *Classes, Cultures and Politics: Essays on British History for Ross McKibbin* (Oxford: Oxford University Press, 2011), 292–301; Antony Taylor, '"The Pioneers of the Great Army of Democrats": The Mythology and Popular History of the British Labour Party, 1890–1931,' *Historical Research* 91 (2018): 723–43.
8   Villiers, *Socialist Movement in England*, 19.
9   Villiers, *Socialist Movement in England*, 23–24.

Morris—or, indeed, with Robert Blatchford's nostalgic and hugely popular *Merrie England* (1893) which was mentioned alongside Ball in passing by Villiers.[10] But Villiers later devoted much more space to Morris than Blatchford, not only as the 'first and greatest' of his generation dedicated to 'shaping Socialism into something more in keeping with English ideas,' but even as 'the greatest personality that has ever been connected with Socialism in England, or perhaps in the modern world.'[11]

On this Villiers was not alone either. The broad rhetorical overlaps between Hardie and Morris are evident in what was cited above, and there was the shared romantic and popular medievalism. Hardie likewise saw Ball as part of a homegrown socialist tradition stretching from Wycliffe to Morris by way of luminaries such as Winstanley, More, Owen, and Maurice, and paralleled with international traditions which kept the dream alive ('the workers of Greece had their Solon, of Stata their Lycurgus, of Italy their Spartacus, of Germany their Huss'), all sharing a common goal of overthrowing a system of greed and woe irrespective of race.[12] As with Villiers (and plenty of others), Morris was given an especially elevated position in socialist history. Though aware of their differences over parliamentarianism and revolution, Hardie viewed Morris as 'the greatest man whom the Socialist movement has yet claimed in this country.'[13] From the times when the 'still small voice of Jesus the Communist stole over the earth,' there have been those who have stood as witnesses to socialism against the forces of selfishness and capitalism, and in the late nineteenth century the 'imposing form of William Morris the Communist stood lonely and grand like a beacon on a mighty rock in the midst of a storm-tossed sea warning the people of England.'[14] The implication of this is that the reception of Ball now invariably involved the reception of *A Dream of John Ball* and its celebrated author.

The Influence of Morris

But this needs qualification. Anna Vaninskaya noted that Morris's late romances reached their widest audiences through trade publishers like Longmans and Green, and Reeves and Turner, yet 'comparatively speaking,

10 Villiers, *Socialist Movement in England*, 134.
11 Villiers, *Socialist Movement in England*, 108.
12 Hardie, *From Serfdom to Socialism*, 74–75, 123–24.
13 Hardie, *From Serfdom to Socialism*, 72.
14 Hardie, *From Serfdom to Socialism*, 123.

they never sold well' and by 1920 the print run of *A Dream of John Ball* was just over 15,000. The expensive Kelmscott versions were not mass produced and reached a small niche audience, and *Commonweal* did not have a wide circulation and struggled for its very survival. These romances were,' Vaninskaya remarked, 'always a minority taste.'[15] And even those minorities could complain that there was still not sufficient understanding of Morris. 'How many have *read* "The Dream of John Ball"?,' asked the *Clarion*, a regular and staunch promoter of *A Dream of John Ball*.[16] This remark might have applied to the obituary writer of *The Times* who infamously misspelled the title as 'A Dream of John Bull' when listing Morris's prose romances that should not be forgotten.[17] However, such an error only reinforced the importance of *A Dream of John Ball* for H. M. Hyndman in his obituary for Morris in *Justice*:

> The verses which he wrote from time to time for the Socialists are in quite another style. Naturally enough, their great merit is overlooked by men who think that his reputation would have been greater if he had died before he became active in the Socialist movement. To such people the 'Dream of John Ball'—the Times calls it the 'Dream of John *Bull*'—is doubtless a weak and effective piece of prose! We know better.[18]

Indeed, it was thanks in no small part to *A Dream of John Ball* that Ball could even make it into a list of 'Famous John Balls' who 'dreamed many wonderful things,' though unlike his sporting namesake 'did not dream that a John Ball would win the Amateur Golf Championship eight times.'[19]

Certainly, early discussions of *A Dream of John Ball* were predominantly (but not exclusively) to be found in the socialist press and socialist circles, and this was an especially important network for keeping Ball's memory alive. Indeed, there is good evidence that Morris's reading of Ball was becoming part of socialist or democratic memorialising and propaganda of different ideological shades (Marxist, revolutionary, parliamentary, Fabian, suffragette, etc.). Occasionally the seemingly incidental details like Morris's Ball having a 'big nose' were still pointed out or even illustrated based on this description, though others were available.[20] That Morris

15 Vaninskaya, *William Morris and the Idea of Community*, 43.
16 *Clarion* (21 April 1894), italics original. Cf. *Clarion* (13 January 1900).
17 *The Times* (5 October 1896).
18 *Justice* (10 October 1896), obituary dated to 6 October. Italics original.
19 *Liverpool Echo* (21 June 1912).
20 *Justice* (14 April 1888); Annie Nathan Meyer, *Robert Annys, Poor Priest: A Tale of the Great Uprising* (London: Macmillan, 1901), 57. The socialist Quaker journal *The Ploughshare* (February 1916) provided a specially commissioned

presented Ball in martyrological terms was important for such propagandizing, as we will see further below. A review in *To-day* suggested that Morris's 'memorialising' had done justice to a true hero and rescued the memory of the 'loyal priest and martyr' from centuries of derision and for the 'people's cause'.[21] Among socialists it was hoped, then, that *A Dream of John Ball* could spread their ideas and make Ball known once again.[22] Memorialisation could take the form of memorisation as parts of the story were recalled with seeming ease, making it ideal material for propaganda according to at least one reader: 'I can repeat almost the whole of the sermon...I need scarcely point out to our orators how well the book lends itself to quotation.'[23] Morris's Ball could be quoted at length as a positive reminder of the aims of fellowship to readers of the suffrage publication *Votes for Women*, while Morris and *A Dream of John Ball* influenced the socialism of Emily Wilding Davison, who would herself be understood as a martyr after her death at the 1913 Derby.[24] Up and down the country, and

---

illustration by Joseph E. Southall directly based on Morris's description to accompany an article by William J. Holland. The picture is available at 'The Ploughshare, Voice of Quaker Socialism,' *Quaker Strongrooms* (4 March 2013), https://quakerstrongrooms.org/2013/03/04/the-ploughshare-voice-of-quaker-socialism/. The cover for H. M. Hyndman's pamphlet for the SDF's house publisher, *John Ball: Priest and Prophet of the Peasants' Revolt* (London: Twentieth Century Press, n.d.), includes a picture (signed by Grenville Manton) of Ball dressed as a monk with his cowl up. He is portrayed with the now typical chiselled jaw and strong cheekbones inherited from the nineteenth-century constructions of Ball's masculinity but there is no obvious emphasis placed on the size of his nose. There are two versions of this pamphlet, one anonymous and undated (which I use here, though I will name Hyndman for convenience) and one with Hyndman as named author and dated to 1909. I am grateful here to Phil Katz, Antony Taylor, and John Stephen Enderby for discussion, as well as to Katz for providing me with a copy. It should be noted that a substantial-looking Ball more akin to the Friar Tuck tradition was known from around the time in a postcard from a 1907 St Albans pageant, a picture of which is available at 'The Red Dagger, Part 1,' *International Times* (December 2013), http://internationaltimes.it/the-red-dagger-pt-1/.

21 *To-day* (June 1888); Hanson, 'Living Past,' in Mitchell and Parsons (eds.), *Reading Historical Fiction*, 204. Cf. *Westminster Gazette* (21 August 1914); *Chelmsford Chronicle* (28 August 1914).
22 *Clarion* (20 August 1892).
23 *Clarion* (2 June 1894). Cf., e.g., Robert Blatchford, *My Favourite Books* (London: Clarion Office, 1900), 106–7; *Labour Leader* (18 November 1910).
24 *Votes for Women* (8 August 1913); Carolyn P. Collette, '"Faire Emelye": Medievalism and the Moral Courage of Emily Wilding Davison,' *The Chaucer Review* 42 (2008): 223–43 (239–39).

particularly at various Clarion social clubs, there were public lectures on it, public readings from it, and even singing of its words—indeed Morris himself read or chanted it at meetings, drawing comparisons between Morris and Ball ('as though it were John Ball himself who was speaking').[25] Quotations from *A Dream of John Ball* found their way on to banners and decorations at branches of the ILP and SDF while National Clarion Cycling Club carried as its motto, 'Fellowship is Life, Lack of Fellowship is Death,' which could likewise be used as a rallying cry for unity among workers.[26]

A Dream of John Ball was effectively endorsed by, and associated with, leading socialists. It was read at the packed funeral of Tom Maguire (d. 1895) in the Labour Church, Leeds, which 'made a most feeling reference to the gentleness and faithfulness of the deceased as a friend' in a ceremony which appreciated the 'unusual high esteem' in which the deceased was held and 'his genius and labours on behalf of Socialism.'[27] *Clarion* founder Robert Blatchford included *A Dream of John Ball* in his list of favourite books,[28] while leading Fabian Beatrice Webb (then Potter) wrote about *A Dream of John Ball* in her diary entry on the romantic frolics she had on the late train from Sheffield to London with her future husband Sidney, 'indulging on the unwonted luxury of first-class, S.W. telling me the story of his examination triumphs and reading me to sleep with *John Ball's Dream*. The tie stiffening!'[29] Katharine Glasier, among the founders of the ILP and later editor of *Labour Leader*, used familiar imagery in the same paper to contrast Morris with Tolstoy's gloomy world of disease and suffering. To stop the causes of such misery, she added, 'I would far rather have the sun-lit pictures of "News from Nowhere" and "The Dream of John Ball." We can run to meet the sun, where, at best, we can only crawl away from the

---

25 E.g., *Clarion* (14 July 1900); *Clarion* (11 August 1900); *Clarion* (20 April 1901); *Clarion* (23 January 1903); *Justice* (14 October 1905); *Clarion* (19 April 1907); *Rugby Advertiser* (10 September 1910); *Clarion* (22 March 1912); *Labour Leader* (13 February 1913). Quotation from J. Bruce Glasier, *William Morris and the Early Days of the Socialist Movement* (London: Longmans, Green, and Co., 1921), 40. Cf. *Labour Leader* (4 December 1913), where *A Dream of John Ball* was given as a gift.
26 Vaninskaya, *William Morris and the Idea of Community*, 121, 171, 191–92; *Daily Citizen* (12 November 1912).
27 *Labour Leader* (16 March 1895). Cf. *Yorkshire Evening Post* (11 March 1895).
28 Blatchford, *My Favourite Books*, 106–16.
29 Beatrice Webb, *The Diary of Beatrice Webb, Volume One (1873–1892): Glitter Around and Darkness Within* (ed. Norman and Jeanne MacKenzie; London: Virago Press, 1982), 340.

darkness.'[30] By the First World War, then, the intellectual, ideological, and cultural credibility of Morris's reading of Ball had long been established in socialist circles. Whether Morris would have approved of all such appropriations is, of course, another question, though it was an issue that would be reviewed (see Chapter 17).

A Dream of John Ball: So Good It Should Be True

This memorialising brought with it, of course, different appreciatory emphases. Even if such an advocate like Blatchford could be critical of the lack of characterisation (including Morris's presentation of Ball), there was, as we might expect, plenty of high praise, particularly concerning the aesthetic qualities of the story and the writer (e.g., 'exquisite', 'probably his best effort in prose', 'beautiful', 'beautiful story', 'beautiful prose', 'most exquisite prose', 'beautiful as much of his poetry is…his prose still better', 'beauty of phrasing', 'quaint and delicious prose [masterpiece]', 'strong and great thoughts and a strong and vigorous utterance', 'bonniest story of medieval England ever penned', 'glorious…imaginative prose', 'the faculty of conjuring up sights and sounds', 'the author's faculty of picturesqueness is here at its best…beautiful').[31] Even among non-socialists or those more sceptical of the politics in *A Dream of John Ball* (and even the figure of Ball himself), similar praise could be found. 'There will of course be many opinions' about Morris's understanding of 'Ball's character' (who, incidentally, still 'harangues') and 'treatment of social problems', wrote one review, 'but as to the literary beauty of this book, and as to the earnestness of his desire to be of service to his fellows, there can be but one.'[32] The political discourses may be 'simply dull' and 'scarcely…convincing', according to another review, but 'the romance—ah, that is a different affair! So far as it

30 *Labour Leader* (25 September 1908).
31 E.g., *Eastern Daily Press* (14 May 1889); *Leicester Daily Post* (14 May 1889); *The Queen: The Lady's Newspaper* (12 November 1892); *Clarion* (24 November 1894); *Yorkshire Post* (11 May 1895); *Clarion* (13 July 1895); *Northern Echo* (5 October 1896); *The Sketch* (7 October 1896); *Clarion* (10 October 1896); *Clarion* (10 April 1908); *Labour Leader* (18 November 1910); *Scotsman* (6 October 1913); *Airdrie & Coatbridge Advertiser* (28 February 1914); Blatchford, *My Favourite Books*, 106, 108–10. Cf. *Clarion* (24 May 1912).
32 *The Graphic* (12 January 1889).

goes, it is full of the vision and the faculty divine...Mr. Morris has a genius for suggesting beautiful things.' This even led the reviewer to provide a re-reading of the image of Adam and Eve based on the lack of practicality. Burne-Jones's frontispiece design provided a new reading: 'Who was then the husbandman?' Why? Because 'anything more amateurish than the grand old gardener's manner of digging it would be hard to conceive.' Nevertheless, it was a 'graceful design' and 'his spade is primitive only in the sense of being ineffectual.'[33] A review in the *Manchester Courier* was upfront about the ideological differences ('fortunately, there is a great gulf fixed between the Conservatives and the Socialist') but 'still every person must admit the charm of Mr. Morris's style' and that 'as a poet and a writer of poetical prose he is likely to be remembered when the opinions which he advocates—no doubt with sincerity—give place to some other fad, or panacea, for the cure of all social evils.'[34]

A Dream of John Ball was becoming a point of reference for understanding the revolt itself, alongside historical books like Green's *Short History*. In one report on the Norwich diocese and its history, the 'episcopal tyrant' Henry le Despenser 'supressed with cruelty the rising of the wretched East Anglian peasants described by William Morris in his "Dream of John Ball."'[35] But writers and readers (or at least some of them) were not unconsciously blurring fiction and nonfiction; rather, the aesthetics of *A Dream of John Ball* were thought to be too good to lose out to mere history books. Blatchford made what at first sight looks like a somewhat gullible statement about Ball's speech at the cross in *A Dream of John Ball*: 'How much of the speech is historical and how much original I cannot say.' After all, he added, much was absent from what was presented in Green's *Short History*, not least the famous 'fellowship is heaven, and lack of fellowship is hell' line. However, we should probably attribute a degree of wiliness on Blatchford's part when he less-than-innocently claimed, 'I am constrained to think that Ball's eloquence at the cross owes a very great deal to William Morris, the Socialist poet.'[36] That it might have been as much a product of Morris's creative imagination as historical record did not undermine its significance because Blatchford claimed he could not give an authority for Green's version of the speech—somewhat unfairly, perhaps, given that Green did

---

33 *Pall Mall Gazette* (16 March 1888).
34 *Manchester Courier* (21 June 1890).
35 *London Daily News* (7 February 1910). Cf. *Chelmsford Chronicle* (28 August 1914).
36 Blatchford, *My Favourite Books*, 110–11.

acknowledge sources[37]—and questioned whether we even know that Ball wrote the sermons attributed to him. And with that move, Blatchford was able to elevate Morris's authority to the level of the critical historian and 'rejoice with Morris that the honest historian, Green, ferreted out the truth about the peasant revolt, and cleared the people's memory from the slanders which class prejudice had heaped upon it.'[38]

In *Robert Annys: Poor Priest A Tale of the Great Uprising* (1901), Annie Nathan Meyer—the American writer with a background in the New York Sephardic Jewish community and liberal Judaism—justified using Morris because of his aesthetic qualities by likewise appealing to the possibilities of capturing something of the words of the historical 'mad priest of Kent.' In the note to the reader prefacing the novel, Meyer argued that 'certain bits of Morris's imaginative work were too fine and true to be spared in any attempt to set the blunt old poor priest before the modern reader' and 'just as a few of the sayings of John Ball bear the marks of authenticity too clearly upon them to be mistaken for mine, so such as are taken from Morris are as clearly distinguished by the marks of supreme beauty and genius.' Meyer acknowledged that the personal description of Ball was taken from Morris, including the claim that 'his nose was big.' Parts of his sermon were also taken from Morris, including the famous saying 'friendship is heaven and lack of fellowship is hell—fellowship is life, and lack of fellowship is death.'[39] We might add that the use of Morris also included the location of the cross and the banner bearing the Adam and Eve couplet and 'a picture of a man and a woman rudely clad and with bare legs and feet seen against a background of green trees, the man holding a spade, the woman a distaff and spindle, rudely enough drawn, yet with great spirit and meaning.'[40] As this novelistic account of the 1381 revolt also involved (of course) a love story, the idea that Ball preached that 'all priests should be as other men, even to the taking of a wife' is important for the plot and Robert Annys's personal turmoil.[41]

---

37 As Vaninskaya, *William Morris and the Idea of Community*, 122, put it of Blatchford's reading of Green: 'By no means a naïve, though maybe an inattentive, reader...'
38 Blatchford, *My Favourite Books*, 110–15.
39 Meyer, *Robert Annys*, 57, 63–64.
40 Meyer, *Robert Annys*, 56–57, 65–66.
41 Meyer, *Robert Annys*, 136–37, 243. In Edward Gilliat, *John Standish, or The Harrowing of London* (London: Seeley & Co, 1889 [1888]), 242, there is a discussion about Ball being smeared by allegations that even wives were to be shared in common.

Meyer's *Robert Annys* may have been praised in reviews for its historical knowledge, research, and realism,[42] but James Leatham's pamphlet *Peasants' Revolt* was explicitly positioned as a work of critical historical reconstruction and still managed to incorporate *A Dream of John Ball*. Leatham—a socialist and trade unionist influenced by Morris with a background working with the SDF, ILP, and Labour and who developed ideas about nationalisation, local government, and political representation[43]—criticised previous accounts of the revolt for having been 'treated in the flimsiest way by all the historians', with Green being a notable exception (and even his narrative was deemed too brief) and Rogers acknowledged for providing valuable contextual information. The chroniclers were contradictory, with 'many obvious inaccuracies as to matter of fact' and 'strongly and often amusingly' biased against the rebels. It was further unfortunate that we have to rely on Froissart who himself relied on 'second-hand' information and whose 'naïve prejudices are corrected only by his medieval love of a good tale.' Leatham did present his work in terms of weighing and assessing evidence but also provided a striking qualification of his own work, namely that 'absolute accuracy' cannot be claimed for his own account.[44] And if there is one obvious instance where this might be the case then it is where Leatham wrote about the ongoing relevance of Ball in the present but still with hints that there was a possibility of overcoming historical anachronism. Leatham encouraged readers to apply the words 'put into the mouth of John Ball by a great artist who lived in the fourteenth almost as much as he lived in the nineteenth century' and quoted from *A Dream of John Ball* about the ongoing importance of fellowship in the face of failures.[45]

England's Dreaming of John Ball

The lauding of Morris's aesthetically pleasing reconstruction of the world of Ball was tied in with romantic ideas of England.[46] Its language 'had just

---

42 E.g., *Bognor Regis Observer* (1 May 1901); *Sheffield Daily Telegraph* (22 May 1901); *Brighouse News* (7 June 1901); *North Devon Journal* (6 June 1901); *London Daily News* (13 June 1901); *Yorkshire Post* (21 August 1901).
43 Robert Duncan, 'Leatham, James (1865–1945)', *ODNB* (23 September 2004). Cf. James Leatham, *William Morris: Master of Many Crafts* (Peterhead: Sentinel Office, 1899).
44 Leatham, *Peasants' Revolt*, 2.
45 Leatham, *Peasants' Revolt*, 16.
46 Cf. *North Wilts Herald* (17 October 1913).

enough of the old-world forms of speech to complete its wonderful verisimilitude as a brief word-picture of fourteenth century England at the time of the famous agitation of the so-called Crazy Priest of Kent.'[47] There is probably something of this attitude when an American reprint of *A Dream of John Ball* was praised for the careful presentation that 'recalls the illuminated manuscripts of the Middle Ages' with further claims that it was 'particularly fitting that the first American edition of this Socialist romance should appear in so lovely a form.'[48] The connections or blurring between England past and present (and future) were picked up in a lecture (1901) at the Technical Institute, Norwich, by C. F. G. Masterman on Morris and the revival of medievalism. Masterman took *A Dream of John Ball* and the future presented in *News from Nowhere* to show how Morris's England could be read as 'an idealised picture of the 14th century' where 'all ugliness was banished' with the 'sturdy independence of the English yeoman... decoration on the church, the banqueting hall, and the village cross.' But this reading meant Morris's vision of England went hand-in-hand with the political radicalism of a 'village community with its free artists' and a 'free giving of gifts,' a 'consciousness of the pleasantness of work,' and the 'substitution of fellowship for mastery.' Notably, we get the relatively uncommon explicit connection with gender and sexuality in this 'frankly medieval' atmosphere where 'it has been said that the chief occupation of the men and women of that time seemed to be love-making and haymaking...The children were brought up in a kind of woodland picnic development.'[49]

This romantic vision of the past partly explains why *A Dream of John Ball* received positive receptions from ideologically different quarters, which is also important for understanding the C/conservative reception of Morris.[50] The appeal of *A Dream of John Ball* could fairly typically be associated with the 'delightful...picture of the Kentish hamlet' and the influence of the lovingly studied 'sagemen.'[51] We can, perhaps, see why the socialist valorising of England from Hyndman through to the splits over support for the First World War could sometimes lead to allegations of imperialism and jingoism.

47 *Cheltenham Chronicle* (15 June 1907).
48 *Labour Leader* (23 July 1898). Cf. *Labour Leader* (19 November 1898).
49 *Norwich Mercury* (26 October 1901); *Lowestoft Journal* (26 October 1901). Cf. *East Anglian Daily Times* (19 October 1901).
50 Michelle Weinroth, *Reclaiming William Morris: Englishness, Sublimity and the Rhetoric of Dissent* (Montreal: McGill-Queen's University Press, 1996).
51 *Pall Mall Gazette* (16 March 1888).

But a romantic vision of the past among ideologically sympathetic readers of *A Dream of John Ball* could also be used in anarchist and libertarian traditions less connected with ideas of the state and nationalism and more connected with the generic 'people'. If not portrayed in explicitly patriotic terms, then a discussion in *Freedom* could still talk in terms of collective agency about how readers who did not know Morris personally 'will get some idea of his intense love of the people by reading *A Dream of John Ball*.'[52] In his later recollections of a tradition of English libertarian socialism and its connections with Yiddish and Jewish anarchism in the East End, Rudolf Rocker could even use *A Dream of John Ball* to support his eyebrow-raising claim that Morris 'had no patience with Marxism'. The reasoning Rocker gave was grounded in his reading of Morris and books like *A Dream of John Ball* which went beyond 'scientific economic theory' and looked to a 'new community life, where people would be free and would be able to express themselves freely in life, in art, in culture and civilisation. Man's free spirit was what mattered to him most.'[53] But on other parts of the Left more interested in using the state for the purposes of socialism, there was also an ongoing anticapitalist understanding of the people and nation. This was made clear in the commemoration of Morris's death on 1 October 1905 at the Kelmscott Club which included a talk on *A Dream of John Ball* and reflections on Ball's phrase (reported in more idiomatic English), 'For verily the day of the earth has come' (Ch. XII). This, it was reported in *Justice*, involved 'the tendency to return to a more natural life on the soil' and 'saw that the hope for workers was bound up with the nationalisation of the land.'[54]

A century on from the outburst of political radicalism of the late eighteenth century, Ball (via Morris) could be invoked in the development of a national radical tradition which would become popular in twentieth-century presentations of an alternative national story. In her 1898 lecture on comradeship and *A Dream of John Ball*, one 'Miss P. Mellor' argued that 'John Ball, the people's preacher,' who was imprisoned for 'inciting land labourers to rebel against the injustice and tyrannies of the nobles,'

52 *Freedom* (1 August 1900).
53 Rudolf Rocker, *The London Years* (Nottingham: Five Leaves, 2005 [1956]), 102–3. With respect to the anti-Marxian reading of Morris, it is worth noting that Rocker first saw a sickly Morris in 1895 and Rocker described his own English as 'poor' at that time and so they 'could not converse much.'
54 *Justice* (14 October 1905). On the revolt in relation to broader questions of land and land nationalisation see also, e.g., Harold Cox, *Land Nationalisation* (London: Methuen and Co., 1892), 22–23; Christopher Turnor, *Land Problems and National Welfare* (London: John Lane, 1911), 116–18.

addressed a mass meeting of labouring men on a 'village green in Kent' and that the 'spirit of comradeship, of good fellowship, human brotherhood' was epitomised by the phrase 'Fellowship is life, and lack of fellowship is death.' Mellor saw this as 'a most powerful impulse in social evolution' and the driving force behind 'nearly all the political and social reforms, from the signing of the Magna Charta to the passing of the Factory Acts.' This sense of fellowship ('or love for others') has 'abolished the torture, witchcraft persecutions, slavery, and many other such unrighteous customs' and enabled 'the hospital movement, the lifeboat movement, and the organisation of such bodies as the Societies for the Prevention of Cruelty to Animals and to Children.' This sentiment was an increasingly powerful 'factor in the social evolution of our land during the last century or so...in spite of the navies arming, and the newspapers preaching their dreadful doctrine of war.'[55] Such a connection between Ball and a hostility to war or anti-imperialism would gain momentum in the twentieth century. But it was not unprecedented (see Chapter 12) and was found among other socialists of the time, such as Lady Warwick (Daisy Greville).[56]

With 'fellowship is life, lack of fellowship is death' on its front cover, Hyndman's pamphlet, *John Ball: Priest and Prophet of the Peasants' Revolt*, was more forthright still in its construction of a deep-rooted English socialist or radical tradition. Ball himself was 'undoubtedly the first great English propagandist for the cause of the people' and in the future, people will look back upon Ball and Tyler along with Cade, Kett, More, Vane, Blake, and Harrison as part of the heroic tradition. But it is a tradition clearly aware of its nineteenth-century heritage, including the Chartists, Bronterre O'Brien, Ernest Jones, and 'the great' Robert Owen.[57] As we will see, this was a tradition tied up with ideas of martyrdom and sacrifice, and figures like Ball are presented as 'noble self-sacrificing heroes of the workers' movement' but representative of much bigger indigenous social and ideological forces.

55 *Whitby Gazette* (2 December 1898).
56 At an ILP meeting in 1909, Warwick similarly invoked a 'voice that roused the Eastern Counties, the voice of John Ball' which 'was heard all along the roads and countryside.' This was, naturally, Ball via Morris and the labour movement as his voice 'roused the conscience of the workers with the watchword, "Brethren, fellowship is heaven, and the lack of fellowship is hell."' And reflecting on this, she looked to a time when 'the blot upon our country of starving little children is removed' and 'when men realise it is better to abolish destitution than to build armaments.' See: *Chelmsford Chronicle* (10 September 1909); *Barking, East Ham and Ilford Advertiser* (11 September 1909).
57 Hyndman, *John Ball*, 8, 19. See also a similar tradition constructed in Hyndman's article in *Justice* (14 June 1884).

They were among the 'thousands of English toilers who met the most heinous opposition of the governing classes with a courage and determination worthy of the best traditions of our people' and it is the poverty-stricken wage-earners rather than the rich or the well-to-do who 'are really the great English nation.'[58] There are echoes here of Hyndman's earlier work, as we would expect, but while the pamphlet cannot escape the charges of including certain demographics in its tradition, there is stronger evidence of an internationalism at play. The work of 'the great German' William Liebknecht on the English working-class movement is not only duly noted but Liebknecht himself is praised as one who 'fought and suffered so much for the workers of Germany.'[59] Claims about having 'enough patriotism left to hope that this country will yet take the lead in this great movement' are part of the same argument that looked to America and the 'men who broke down negro slavery—John Brown, Lloyd Garrison, Wendell Phillips, and their friends.' There are echoes of certain Chartists and their awkward framing of such issues in that the pamphlet ultimately promoted fighting for a 'greater cause than theirs,' namely the 'emancipation of the workers throughout the whole civilised world.'[60]

Eschatology of Socialism, Still

As we saw at the end of the previous chapter, Morris's Catholic Ball and critical attitude towards Lollardy could not stop the constant association between Ball and proto-Protestantism and Wycliffe/Lollards at the turn of the twentieth century.[61] We even get a version of Ball via Morris from socialist and pacifist Quaker circles which would not have a serious influence at the time, but a softened version would arguably be the most dominant popular reception of Ball at the turn of the twenty-first century (Chapters 22, 23). In an article on Ball in *The Ploughshare* (February 1916) as the war was underway, this Ball held in contempt the 'lords and courtiers, and the host of vampires that battened and fattened on the toil

---

58 Hyndman, *John Ball*, 1, 9.
59 Hyndman, *John Ball*, 13.
60 Hyndman, *John Ball*, 8, 19.
61 Those connecting Ball and Lollards/Wycliffe include, e.g., *Labour Leader* (30 September 1899); Meyer, *Robert Annys, Poor Priest*, 5–6; Hardie, *From Serfdom to Socialism*, 74, 122; Leatham, *Peasants' Revolt*, 4, 14–15; Hyndman, *John Ball*, 4.

of the poor.' Though accompanied by a monkish Ball from Morris, it was explained that Christ too was reviled by such oppressors for distinctly Quaker reasons coupled with Morris's famous imagery. For it 'has ever been the lot of him who would strike the shackles from men's souls and bid them look upon the Light whereby man lives.' Ball himself was 'mad...but in the divine sense, exalted with an overwhelming love and pity, inspired with an irrefragable faith in the equality of all men in the sight of God, a joyous, forward-looking apostle of Universal Brotherhood.'[62]

But such sharp (albeit typically unacknowledged) divergences from Morris's Catholic Ball did not stop further discussion about religion, the religion or eschatology of socialism, and its relationship to his dialectical reading of history. The blurring of religion dominant in the past with the socialism of the present is clear enough, for instance, in Hyndman's Morris-inspired pamphlet, *John Ball*. Before Ball at Blackheath 'was the finest of all congregations—a mass of comrades in the cause...his message of human solidarity must have been voiced with splendid eloquence.'[63] As the full title of the pamphlet (*John Ball: Priest and Prophet of the Peasants' Revolt*) also stated, Ball was understood in prophetic terms alongside labels such as 'revolutionist.' Perhaps owing something to another source, Charles Oman (see Chapter 14), 'prophet' was understood in the sense of daring social critic ('John Ball was a prophet of the old Hebrew style'), though the pamphlet itself used prophetic language in the sense of looking at the future, here as encouragement (e.g., 'In the days that are to be, when art will spring out of the life of the people,' 'their day of triumph came, as ours is surely coming').[64] Hyndman and Oman were hardly alone. *A Dream of John Ball* itself was elsewhere understood to be 'couched in the form of a prophecy,'[65] while Hyndman's sometime rival, Andreas Scheu, acknowledged that Morris 'showed religious feeling' in *A Dream of John Ball*. Scheu added that this was necessary so that a sympathetic conversation with Ball could take place and Morris did not confuse this with the 'religious feeling' which 'modern respectability exacts.'[66]

A different analysis put it somewhat esoterically: in *A Dream of John Ball* the earthly paradise may have been fixed in the past while in *News from Nowhere* it may have been placed in the future but, in reality, there

---

62 *The Ploughshare* (February 1916).
63 Hyndman, *John Ball*, 8, 19.
64 Hyndman, *John Ball*, 4, 6, 19.
65 *Pall Mall Gazette* (16 March 1888). See also, e.g., *Justice* (2 September 1911); *Daily Herald* (28 November 1914).
66 *Justice* (17 October 1896).

was no difference between the two because it was Morris' own method of removing what he loved out of space and time in order to view it in the light of Eternity.'⁶⁷ The blurring and reading of past, present, and future history was an important legacy in the early reception of Morris (and influenced too by the historians and socialists of the late nineteenth century). Both Mellor and Warwick likewise picked up on the need for the will to change the present in light of the future. For Mellor, the words on comradeship become part of the 'effect of our deeds living on and on for ever, and influencing generations yet unborn…one of the grandest incentives to a noble life that one can possibly have.' Echoing Morris's symbolism of light and dark (as others did) and urging the eschatological moment, Warwick suggested that the 'dream of John Ball may ere long be realised, for to us the star of our hopes grows ever brighter, the goal ever nearer' when 'this curse of poverty is ended.' God may grant this possibility but there is a clear emphasis on human action to realise this goal 'quickly and now.' To loud applause Warwick said this could be done if the workers would follow Marx and Engels's famous call to arms: 'Workers of the world, unite! You have nothing but your chains to lose!'⁶⁸

Hyndman's *John Ball* provided a relatively detailed and now familiar dialectical reading of English history. From William the Conqueror to just prior to the Peasants' Revolt, the struggles in English history required the 'workers' but the nature of the struggles meant that the 'common people' would play a role in supporting a given section of the ruling classes. While the masses began with 'no real consciousness of their own interests,' their regular participation helped develop 'class consciousness' and for them to select their own leaders and help their own material advancement, rights, and freedoms against their masters. As towns and industry developed, merchants and artisans started organising themselves into guilds while the poorer workers started hiring themselves out as wage labourers. The Black Death was also an important factor in this decline of feudalism in that higher wages and lower rents were demanded as labour became scarce and the fear of empty land was not unfounded. This also led to increasing social strife that, Hyndman argued, 'corresponds somewhat to the modern state of "hostile confrontation of Capital and Labour".'⁶⁹ As this class

---

67 *Morning Post* (28 December 1908).
68 *Chelmsford Chronicle* (10 September 1909). On Morris's imagery of light and dark, particularly with reference to growing awareness and hope for the future, see, e.g., *Chelmsford Chronicle* (10 September 1909); *Barking, East Ham & Ilford Advertiser* (11 September 1909).
69 Hyndman, *John Ball*, 1–4.

conflict was escalating, Wycliffe and the poor priests emerged in the retelling. The poor priests won the confidence of the peasants with whom 'they helped to combine in secret trade unions, acting as messengers between different parts of the country, and as treasurers to the societies, helping in many ways to fan the flame of revolt that was kindling among the people.' Hyndman claimed that the 'priest-agitator' Ball with his 'revolutionary' messages may have been similar to the 'communist section of the Lollards' but nevertheless emerged earlier and his 'doctrine' of human equality went further than Wycliffe's in that it 'denounced the whole system of society based on class and social distinctions, and on the individual ownership of land and wealth which is socially produced.'[70]

According to Hyndman in *John Ball*, the revolt was 'the first great conscious struggle of the English workers against personal oppression and social forms' while the immediate outcome of the revolt was that it 'constituted the workers a class,' hastened the decline of feudalism, and (in line with Rogers) led to a century of relative prosperity not seen since. It effectively inaugurated class-conscious struggle through the demand to sell produce in markets which led to the emergence of a capitalist class and the wage system and, by doing so, the peasant demands unconsciously helped generate the two opposing classes of modern society.[71] At the turn of the twentieth century, Hyndman noted, there was no longer the need for material poverty. Once the masses understand this history of English development, 'then the dream of John Ball will soon be realised.'[72]

Leatham's reading of English historical development was more critical of Ball. Certainly, a similar and indeed typical framing of Ball as communist was used in his pamphlet, *Peasants' Revolt*, which included a section (citing Rogers at length) on the influence of the Bible on the 'communistic rising' and connected the 'communist doctrines and practice' of the early Christians' and Wycliffe's Bible with the 'Communism' of the 'prophet-priest' Ball and other preachers of the time.[73] The connections between past and present were clear throughout *Peasants' Revolt*. The 'harangues' (a term used with some sarcasm by Leatham) of preachers like Ball with his 'communistic doctrines' (including the Adam and Eve couplet) were 'canvassed at meetings of London citizens.'[74] The poll taxes were 'farmed out to

---

70 Hyndman, *John Ball*, 4–5.
71 Hyndman, *John Ball*, 8, 9, 10, 14; on the prosperity of the fifteenth century, and a text cited in *John Ball*, see also Gibbins, *English Social Reformers*, 35.
72 Hyndman, *John Ball*, 17–18.
73 Leatham, *Peasants' Revolt*, 14–15.
74 Leatham, *Peasants' Revolt*, 3–4, 14–15.

capitalistic harpies' while 'the price of labour' had not only risen because of the Black Death but also as the result of 'widespread trade unionism among labourers and artizans' inspired by the 'communistic oratory' of the russet priests.[75] But this is not simply, of course, another case of the language of the present constructing the past. There was a major issue emerging from *A Dream of John Ball*: Ball's dream failed to emerge in the fourteenth century because it *could not* have emerged in the fourteenth century. This point was often overlooked or ignored but it was less easy to do so for those providing a history of England and class struggle. Leatham, however, wanted to bring this issue to the fore and probably did so more than any other socialist presentation from the first decade of the twentieth century.

The reason why Leatham so emphatically presented the revolt as a *tragedy* was not simply because of the loss of life but also because 'with no political principle behind the rising, it could not succeed' and the 'time was not ripe' for a successful revolt. Parliamentary government had not then been established as the 'register of the popular will' and Parliament then was overshadowed by the crown and the Executive which would hardly have achieved the economic goals of the peasantry. Moreover, the 'revolting peasants' were in a 'low state of enlightenment' and the leaders were not familiar with alternative political methods from Greece and Rome where government could be localised and detached from the king. They lacked the awareness; enacting constitutional change and taking the word of a king was flawed because the monarch could not make changes to the law and property without the consent of Parliament. Moreover, the 'priestly inspirers' may have been 'Christian Communists' but, like the rebels more generally, provided no political arrangements for the transition to, and the securement and administration of, communism beyond socialism.[76]

But given that Morris was a guide of sorts for Leatham, there was still something to be salvaged from the failure, no matter how starkly put. Leatham's *Peasants' Revolt* included an epigraph from *A Dream of John Ball* which concerned the memory of those defeated and others having to 'fight for what they meant under a different name'.[77] This meant that the rebels, for all their failings and lack of political and tactical insight, did not die in vain. At the very least it was 'right to protest and rebel against injustice gross and palpable' while errors remain inevitable as reason and progress compromise relentlessly with the 'tyranny of existing circumstances'.[78]

75 Leatham, *Peasants' Revolt*, 2–3.
76 Leatham, *Peasants' Revolt*, 12–13.
77 Leatham, *Peasants' Revolt*, 1.
78 Leatham, *Peasants' Revolt*, 15–16.

Even the failed revolt still stood as a 'deterrent to the worst extremes of oppression,' as witnessed by the first half of the nineteenth century which 'represents the most miserable phase through which labour has passed in the history of Britain.'[79] But Leatham went further in employing a Morris-style martyrology. Rational public spirit and commitment to the common good were grown through 'all tradition of heroism and self-sacrifice that has come down to us' while the 'Tree of Liberty and Right' was nurtured by 'the blood of martyrs.' Such dramatic dedication may not be expected in the twentieth century but to hand on this heritage of a commitment to the public good, the examples of those who faced more dangerous circumstances must never be forgotten, which Leatham supported through the authority of *A Dream of John Ball*.[80] Leatham's open criticism of the revolt may have differed from other presentations, including that in Hyndman's *John Ball*, but a shared martyrology remained in this eschatology of socialism from Morris. For Hyndman, Ball's name came down to us across the centuries 'to be revered, a beacon to light us...an instructive revelation of the cruel and brutal methods by which the governing classes keep the mass of our people in poverty and subjection.' Through his 'martyrdom,' Ball deserved his place in 'our calendar of heroes,' never-to-be-forgotten and indeed rendered imperishable by the noble poem of William Morris, "A Dream of John Ball."'[81]

England's Road to Socialism

Whatever Morris would have made of it, a shifting of his dialectical reading of history towards parliamentary democracy, or parliamentary democracy as one avenue among others, was common enough and a parliamentarian reading of Morris and Ball would continue in the Labour Party throughout the twentieth century. Against the backdrop of the uneasy relationship between Hyndman and SDF and the newly evolved Labour Party, Hyndman's *John Ball* looked to a 'complete social revolution' to protect the modern worker, and this involved parliamentary representation. The 'mission' of the socialist movement, he argued, was for 'workers to use their vote, and their right to organise in the interests of their class.' Only the socialists properly understood the 'truth of John Ball's prophecy, "that

---

79 Leatham, *Peasants' Revolt*, 14.
80 Leatham, *Peasants' Revolt*, 16.
81 Hyndman, *John Ball*, 1, 8.

things will not go well in England till all things be held in common", and to bring about such a revolution would require a system of renumeration for labour that was fairer than the competitive wage system: the collective and democratic ownership and control of the means of production. And workers had now begun to organise themselves seriously 'and have at last made their voice feebly heard in the House of Commons.'[82]

For Leatham (who would become a Labour councillor in 1923), the present generation and 'democracy to-day' can now make good on the promises of the fourteenth-century past through the 'power of governance' and will learn to use it not only for the greatest number of people but 'in the ultimate highest interests of all.'[83] *A Dream of John Ball* was similarly invoked for parliamentary reform early on in its reception. With swipes at the 'anti-democratic' Froissart, an article in the *Clarion* (1894) claimed that while Morris's Ball may have known what 'the people needed,' the 'ignorant mob were deceived, as they always are' by duplicitous promises of 'liberty,' just as 'people's cry for food is still turned by cunning politicians into a cry for Votes.' Instead, what was needed was something beyond free parks and public libraries: a permanent overcoming of the 'trade of the old Parliamentary hands' by teaching the 'great mass of the poor people' that neither 'liberty' nor votes will feed the hungry or clothe the naked. What was now required to remedy such 'social evils' was returning to Parliament a 'formidable phalanx of resolute social (as opposed to political) reformers.'[84]

There were also notable differences of emphasis in the reception of Ball and Morris, and in some cases the Marxism and violent revolution were toned down. In Meyer's *Robert Annys*, for instance, the 'poor priest' Ball was more closely connected to Wycliffe than Morris would ever have accepted, even if Meyer presented him as an extremist manifestation of Wycliffite thinking of which Wycliffe himself disapproved because it undid 'the peace of the realm' through the 'reckless violence' of Ball's language and 'the revolutionary quality of his theories.'[85] Indeed, alongside the tensions between corruptions in the established church, proto-Protestant reform, and the concerns of the people, *Robert Annys* contrasts the perceived extremism of Ball and the near inevitable excessive violence of the mob with a peaceful, reformist, and gradualist agenda. The novel effectively replaces the kind of Marxism of Morris's model of historical progress and acceptance of the violence of 1381 as a link to the present. It is telling

82 Hyndman, *John Ball*, 11.
83 Leatham, *Peasants' Revolt*, 16.
84 *Clarion* (24 November 1894).
85 Meyer, *Robert Annys*, 5–6.

what kind of spectre stalks behind 'the rusty, cracked weapons of the mob.' It is not the spectre of communism that terrifies even the most hardened warriors but the 'spectre of a coming Democracy.'[86] The novel ultimately concludes that the 'Uprising had failed because the people were not yet ready for success' but that the 'very failure of the Uprising had within it something precious' and 'no historian may ever tell of the end of the Great Uprising, for it had no end, but it goeth ever on and on.'[87] A review in *The Scotsman* claimed not unreasonably that the book discusses a 'strange and terrible uprising, premature, but very real, of the voice and the power of Demos in England.'[88] But whether Meyer's understanding would have been perceived in England or the UK to be in conflict with the slippery uses of the term 'socialism' is moot. A loose Fabian definition of the time held that state socialism in an English context means 'the community democratically organized for collective purposes, whether parochially, locally, or nationally,'[89] so we should not be surprised that a positive review of Meyer's book could still, for instance, casually refer to 'the great Socialist movement of the Lollards.'[90]

Dialectical History as a Rhetorical Tactic

The dialectical logic of Ball's place in English history included the idea that the potential for change was presently at a low ebb which served an obvious rhetorical or propagandistic function: to try and provoke action in the present. This is a familiar logic of reverse psychology along the lines of secretly hoping change can happen by hectoring everyone about how terrible everything is and how no one is doing anything. This encouragement for action in the present was predictably coupled with nostalgia for an England lost and used in the service of damning the present to provoke action. 'Alas there are no John Balls nowadays and few Will Greens or Jack Straws,' decried Frederick Keddell in a *Justice* (1888) review. Yet, amidst the gloom, Morris's description of Ball's preaching at the cross was strangely reminiscent of 'meetings that I have seen in small villages' at the time of a General Election when the villagers hear 'some audacious London Radical

---

86 Meyer, *Robert Annys*, 274.
87 Meyer, *Robert Annys*, 346–47.
88 *The Scotsman* (13 May 1901).
89 Sidney Ball, *The Moral Aspects of Socialism* (London: Fabian Society, 1896), 1.
90 *London Daily News* (13 June 1901).

or Socialist inveigh against the rule of the Squire and the Parson.' But even if the sense of suffering and being wronged provided the context for change and historical advancement, still for Keddell the 'feeling of despair and hopelessness…paralyses every effort.' Indeed, it got worse. Morris's work even functioned as a warning about the future because the 'tyranny of these days' may only lead 'to another and harder tyranny,' just as it did after the end of villeinage. Nevertheless, this was a reading that still required hope, and, despite the pessimism, the real question was whether the present system 'is now rotten enough to be the cause of its own destruction or must be endured for a few more years,' not that it mattered too much for those seeking its overthrow. And just in case the Great Change may be later rather than sooner, Keddell had more immediate interests in forcing change, namely the hope that Morris would find a way to reduce the price of *A Dream of John Ball* to a more affordable shilling edition (which did indeed happen) so that those most interested could buy it.[91]

In *Peasants' Revolt*, with all its emphasis on the need for savvy and enlightened leadership, Leatham lamented that while the 'commons' now had the power to force change, the suffering of those who have resisted past tyrannies was now being valued lightly. This disrespect to the past was shown by half of the people not bothering to record their votes in elections, and those who did use the hard-fought gains did so 'to return to power the classes with whom their ancestors contended in deadly strife.'[92] Leatham had certainly been more explicit still in his critiques, but he was also prepared to deliver a public dressing down to audiences for not listening to socialist thinkers and leaders like himself.[93] In an earlier pamphlet, *The Class War* (1892), which was previously delivered as a lecture in Glasgow and Aberdeen, Leatham effectively put himself in the tradition of leaders like Ball whose teachings had been overlooked by followers too easily swayed by their masters' vision of the world. Leatham was scathing in his attitude towards working-class surrender to political economists, trade unionists, and Liberals who, unlike socialists, think workers need to 'bring good times to their masters' in order to improve their own lot.[94] The lecture was not just a polemic against reformists but a sustained harangue against

---

91 *Justice* (14 April 1888). Cf. *Clarion* (7 July 1894); *Freedom* (1 August 1912). On the one-shilling Reeves and Turner edition, see Vaninskaya, *William Morris and the Idea of Community*, 43–44.
92 Leatham, *Peasants' Revolt*, 16.
93 Vaninskaya, *William Morris and the Idea of Community*, 124, 166.
94 James Leatham, *The Class War: A Lecture* (sixth edition; London: Twentieth Century Press; orig. Aberdeen: James Leatham, 1892), 3.

those members of his audience 'who believe that there is no necessary antagonism between landlord and tenant, between capitalist and labourer, between rich and poor' and who were satisfied 'with Trade Unionism,' instead of the forward march of Socialism, even to the point of telling them that it is 'little wonder if at times we get sick of talking to you.' Not one to let sentimentality get in his way, Leatham informed his audience that, whether they liked it or not, 'we will preach, and you will hear us, and ultimately you will be forced to recognise that the Class War exists.'[95]

Fortunately, Leatham pointed out, there was a tradition of those who had fought the good fight and kept alive the flame of hatred of oppressive systems. In Britain, Ball, Tyler, and Cade were the 'forerunners of Socialism' and a tradition was as much international (including Irish) as homegrown up to Marx ('intellectually rigorous, morally incorruptible, living for the Revolution'), Hyndman, Blatchford, Hardie, and, of course, Morris, the 'artist-prophet of the new society.' And just in case anyone wondered whether some of his list were undeserving, Leatham cited Ball's speech about things going well (or otherwise) in England from Froissart.[96] The English manifestation of the Class War should have been settled in those days. The rebels of 1381 had the numbers and had the southern and midland counties at their mercy. But this war failed, Leatham claimed, because people did not 'cherish the class hatred as John Ball cherished it, and did not see as clearly as he saw what [was] required to be done.' Just as rebels believed in Richard II and 'neglected their own leaders,' so to do those among the working class who believe in the Liberal Party and William Booth of the Salvation Army fame. And so Leatham's haranguing continued ('The trouble is the same to-day. You don't want enough; and you don't want it definitely enough. You are too humble, too easily satisfied') but with the recommendation that they become more educated about their plight, start consorting with poets, historians, scientists, economists and philosophers, and toughen themselves up for the Class War.[97]

A quite different kind of rhetorical tactic was used in *Labour Leader* in 1899, then edited by Keir Hardie. Amidst the clamour for a new party of the working class, Morris's Ball was resurrected in an attempt to recruit John Burns, veteran of the 1889 London Dock Strike with a socialist and trade union background and now an independent parliamentarian. Ball returns from the grave to tell Burns a truth 'and to ring your bell and call you out.' The coded names in Ball's letters are given an updating for workers at the

---

95 Leatham, *Class War*, 2–3.
96 Leatham, *Class War*, 9–10.
97 Leatham, *Class War*, 10–11.

end of the century. In addition to Jack Miller, we now have Jack Docker, Jack Miner, Jack Tailor, Jack Clerk, etc., who 'bid you come out to them and finish and make a good end of that you began at the Docks in August now ten years gone.' The ghost of Ball recalls the tireless work Burns did back in 1889, encouraging the 'starving multitudes' and preaching 'unto them anew and with power my Gospel of the Fellowship of the Poor,' much as Ball, Tyler and Wycliffe had roused 'the workers' in the fourteenth century. Burns's famous booming voice, very similar to Ball's famous booming voice, managed to wake the long-dead Ball and, indeed, the 'whole world' to 'brotherhood' and 'fellowship.' In those days, Ball was present among the crowds and in *A Dream of John Ball* the 'poet' was given prophetic knowledge of his coming a year later and of days to equal those of the summer of 1381. This is, effectively, the solidarity of the fellowship over the centuries of *A Dream of John Ball*. But in some ways Burns is even better, because unlike Ball and Tyler he is able to command restraint among his followers; in others, however, there are worrying similarities. Gone is the 'expectation of the quick coming of the kingdom' as the short-lived triumph turned into a nightmare and provoked Ball to rise from his grave again. Tyler- or Ball-style leadership from among the workers is now lacking as candidate after candidate has fallen to allure of the ruling classes and abandoned the people, and the people now blame Burns. However, in a telling rhetorical twist, and because Burns had 'erred, not sinned,' two remaining members of the fellowship still have faith in Burns: Burns and Ball. Ball refuses to believe the rumours that Burns had been sweet-talked by the lords and 'representatives of the rich' but now is the time for Burns to find, as Wycliffe did, his 'simple priests' and Lollard movement and come back from his 'withdrawal' because (in a piece of double-edged encouragement) 'you have... not deserted them.' And this is crucial because the lesson Ball gives from history is that dark times will follow failure if leaders stay gagged and 'no one else but you has the power of impassioned speech which can create in the hearts of the people The New Party, The New Industry, The New Education, The New Religion...and quicken the workers with the sense of their combined might and the right...found a new party.'[98] Unfortunately for the ghostly Ball, hopes of a rousing success for the fellowship, and Hardie's ongoing attempts to bring Burns onside, the double-edge flattery would fail and Burns would work with the Liberals, (in)famously accepting cabinet rank in 1905.[99]

---

98 *Labour Leader* (30 September 1899).
99 Kenneth D. Brown, 'Burns, John Elliott (1858–1943),' *ODNB* (26 May 2016).

Beyond Morris

Morris may have dominated the reception of Ball in the years following *A Dream of John Ball* but there were plenty of exceptions where Morris at least was not directly invoked. We find the odd antiquarian reference to Ball, his familiar place in radical histories or sympathetic reconstructions, his association with violent and communistic anarchism, and his role the occasional pageant.[100] 'John Ball's Strike' took its place in the history of labour struggles, while an Engels-style analysis of Ball and European peasant uprisings in a historical materialist schema was noted by one of the leading figures of Irish socialism, James Connolly.[101] Though we should not forget that this was also the era of the popular works of Trevelyan and Oman (see Chapter 14), whose work on the revolt was promoted in public lectures,[102] the radical memory of Ball was strong in other popularising (and sometimes politicising) historians, where Ball was given at least a passing and positive acknowledgment.[103] Particular mention should be made of the Christian socialist Joseph Clayton. Clayton may not have contributed anything especially new to the reception of Ball but through a publishing burst this 'custodian of radical memory,' as Antony Taylor put it, made the revolt and related traditions 'integral to the mythology of the Independent Labour Party.'[104] Elsewhere, the idea of Ball as the true Christian against the plutocrat was taken up by the radical journalist John Morrison Davidson,

---

100 See, e.g., *Labour Leader* (19 October 1906); W. G. Wilkins, *The Rise and Progress of Poverty in England from the Norman Conquest to Modern Times* (London: Headley Brothers, 1907), 3–6; *Kentish Independent* (8 October 1909); Ernest Alfred Vizetelly, *The Anarchists: Their Faith and Their Record Including Sidelights on the Royal and Other Personages Who Have been Assassinated* (London: John Lane, 1911), 5–6; Bede Jarrett, *Mediaeval Socialism* (London: T. C. & E. C. Jack, 1913), 32–35; E. N. Bennett, *Problems of Village Life* (London: Williams & Norgate, 1914), 18–23. Cf. Taylor, *London's Burning*, 23, 183, n. 15.
101 *Labour Leader* (3 November 1911); James Connolly, *Socialism Made Easy* (Chicago: C. H. Kerry & Co. Chicago, 1909), 21.
102 E.g., *Morning Post* (9 August 1898); *London Daily News* (23 January 1905); *St James's Gazette* (23 January 1905); *Morning Post* (23 January 1905).
103 See, e.g., J. J. Jusserand, *English Wayfaring Life in the Middle Ages (XIVth Century)* (trans. Lucy Toulmin Smith; London: T. Fisher Unwin, 1899 [1884]), 284–94; Richard Heath, *The English Peasant: Studies, Historical, Local and Biographic* (London: T. Fisher Unwin, 1893), 13–14.
104 Taylor, *London's Burning*, 25–26. See Joseph Clayton, *Wat Tyler and the Great Uprising* (London: Francis Griffiths, 1909); Joseph Clayton, *Leaders of the People: Studies in Democratic History* (London: Martin Secker, 1910), 139–70,

who criticised the 'thousand defamatory pens [that] have lied away the characters of Ball and Tyler,' and then moved onto Shakespeare who 'shamelessly travestied, in the interest of "the classes," two distinct historic events—viz., Tyler's rebellion (1381) and Cade's rebellion (1450)—in order to produce a single odious character, totally unlike either of these popular leaders' (see Chapter 5). Instead, Ball and Tyler lived their lives as an example with their modern principles, while the principles of 'Wyclif and Ball travelled to the Continent, and took root in Bohemia' with Huss and the idea of a 'Democratic Republic and of a system based on Communism.' Ball asserted Christianity in its 'primitive purity' and preached the 'Gospel of the Poor and the oppressed,' not of 'profit' but 'sacrifice' which had not been asserted since 'its capture and prostitution by the vile Emperor Constantine and his sinister pack of Pagan priests and Imperial officials.' Instead, the 'Peasants' Revolt' aimed to 'reorganise the State on the basis of Christian Communism.'[105]

While nowhere near as influential as Morris's account, there were more novels and stories set against the backdrop of the revolt, such as Edward Gilliat's *John Standish, or The Harrowing of London* (1888), William Minto's *The Mediation of Ralph Hardelot* (1888), Harriette E. Burch's *Dick Delver: A Story of the Peasant Revolt of the Fourteenth Century* (1889), as well as another from America, Florence Converse's *Long Will: A Romance* (1903). In addition to the standard discussions of Wycliffe, proto-Protestantism, socialism, communism, and threatening mobs, we get the usual descriptions of pony-riding Ball the 'haranguing' preacher of 'fiery orations,' such as those associated with his ragged clothes, thick hair (aside from the tonsure), piercing eyes, impressive voice, lean face, and sinewy body.[106]

335; Joseph Clayton, *The Rise of Democracy* (London: Cassell and Company, 1911), 13, 66–78.

105 J. Morrison Davidson, *The Annals of Toil. Being Labour-History Outlines, Roman and British. Part I* (London: William Reeves, 1899), 120–21, 134–41.

106 In William Minto, *The Mediation of Ralph Hardelot: Vol. II* (London: Macmillan and Co, 1888), 204, 'He was rather over the middle height, of spare sinewy figure, the face lean. He was not of imposing bulk, and yet when he began to speak he at once conveyed an impression of indomitable force. Fiery energy beamed from the eyes, and there was a suggestion of strength in the firm muscles of the lower part of the face and the square angular head. The hair grew thick round the forehead, and the tonsure was obviously artificial.' Harriette E. Burch, *Dick Delver: A Story of the Peasant Revolt of the Fourteenth Century* (London: The Religious Tract Society, 1889), 56, 108, has Ball the 'haranguing' preacher of 'fiery orations,' 'a poor, barefooted priest… in russet gown with arms extended and flashing eyes…declaiming in a voice

There were also two novels which had connections with Morris, but in a different way to how we have seen so far: *The Wardship of Steepcombe* (1896) by the Tractate apologist Charlotte Mary Yonge, and *The Banner of Saint George* (1901) by Mary Bramston, both analysed in some detail by Julia Courtney.[107] Yonge's earlier work with its chivalrous message had once influenced Morris, while in Bramston's novel the bearded Essexian and 'leader of the Socialists' of mild, reasonable, peaceful but impractical persuasion, John Kirkby, appears to have been based on Morris.[108] Both novels, however, provided presentations of Ball different from Morris's, yet familiar in the history of reception. While sympathetic to the plight of the rebels, *The Wardship of Steepcombe* worked with moralistic and broadly conservative assumptions of human society and is likewise sympathetic with the predicament in which Richard found himself. In another established move, the novel presents Ball as an extreme or misguided version of Wycliffe. For all the nostalgic medievalism in the novel, the church was in 'decay' at the time, Yonge claimed in the preface, and figures like Wycliffe and Bishop William of Wykeham did their part to 'purify' the church. But followers, she added, can go beyond their leader, as Luther found out, and so the 'insurrection of Wat Tyler' owed something to the 'poor priests' of Wycliffe coupled with 'intolerable oppression.'[109] The 'poor priests' sent out by Wycliffe to preach 'the higher and purer doctrine…which was truly Catholic' had, in the case of figures like Ball, become 'almost crazed with

---

that reached to the farthest corner of the graveyard.' According to Gilliat, *John Standish*, 240–41, 'Ball was habited head to foot in black; his hood was drawn over his head; round his waist was a girdle of leather, which held up a gipsire or large purse on his left side. His face was thin, and his brow careworn, but there was a look of resolute daring about his mouth…raising his clear voice in ringing tones, and with fiery look, he cried, "…Things shall never go well in England…"'

107 Courtney, 'Versions of the Past.' On other stories, including penny dreadfuls, see Basdeo, *Life and Legend of a Rebel Leader*, chapter 6; Stephen Basdeo, 'Youthful Consumption and Conservative Visions: Robin Hood and Wat Tyler in Late Victorian Penny Periodicals,' in Rachel Bryant Davies and Barbara Gribling (eds.), *Pasts at Play: Childhood Encounters with History in British Culture, 1750–1914* (Manchester: Manchester University Press, 2020), 125–41.

108 Courtney, 'Versions of the Past,' 13, 18–19; Mary Bramston, *The Banner of Saint George: A Picture of Old England* (London: Duckworth, 1901), 51–52.

109 Charlotte M. Yonge, *The Wardship of Steepcoombe* (London: National Society, 1896), v–viii.

the sight of oppression around them' which led to their preaching of revolutionary views.[110]

Bramston's *Banner of Saint George* foregrounded another leader of the 'Peasant Revolt,'[111] William Grindecobbe, who she portrayed sympathetically and heroically because of his restraint, moderation, and law-abiding attitude, in contrast to, for instance, the one figure in the reception of the revolt who struggled to shake off his deceitful or crazed association: the 'Anarchist' leader Jack Straw. Indeed, with Grindecobbe as its model of noble masculinity, the novel works with a Whiggish view of history and progress of the English nation with an accompanying view of the grimness of Medieval life.[112] Ball's description is a familiar one inherited from the nineteenth-century constructions of muscular masculinity in that he was a 'swarthy, powerfully built man' but with a hint of excessive zeal in 'black eyes' which 'glowed with fire' when his 'oratory expressed his own feelings' (again, a common description in Ball's reception).[113] Even when he was older, haggard, and grey with his shoulders slumped, his 'eyes still blazed, and his voice had its old ring when he grew excited with his subject.'[114] This description probably reflects the degree of ambiguity in the presentation of Ball's message. Ball's ideas represent what a lot of people were thinking and were popular enough to warrant a contrast with John the Baptist, even though someone like William Langland could not approve of Ball.[115] Ball's preaching is sufficiently cryptic to lead to divergent interpretations, even if he should be properly understood as a more moderate rebel.[116] Ball's cryptic writing, with its 'allegorical style,' had its drawbacks. On the one hand, Alan Harding of St Albans had enough experience of Ball's verses to know that they included a warning 'not to mar the good cause by violence and robbery, and not to be led on by the knaves in the Borough to use their strength for unlawful ends.' However, and reflecting a long running debate in critical scholarship on the revolt, some believed the reference to Hob the Robber was a call to chastise the lords for their tyranny 'so that Ball's Good advice hardly had all the effect intended.'[117] As with the Morris-like Kirkby, Ball is contrasted with the half-crazed Straw who wants to take

110 Yonge, *Wardship*, 199.
111 Bramston, *Banner*, v.
112 Courtney, 'Versions of the Past,' 17.
113 Bramston, *Banner*, 39–40.
114 Bramston, *Banner*, 76.
115 Bramston, *Banner*, 40, 47–48, 158. See also, e.g., Gilliat, *John Standish*, 241–43, 276–80.
116 Bramston, *Banner*, 125–26.
117 Bramston, *Banner*, 81–82.

Ball's moralistic words in the direction of revolutionary violence. In Ball's preaching on the eschatological weeds, Straw nodded but impatiently turns away when Ball claims that the worst weeds were not the lords and lawyers but the seven deadly sins as Ball ends with a 'moral exhortation.'[118] Indeed, Ball is closely associated with the Morris-like Kirkby as Ball too 'was essentially Socialist' and, fittingly, Kirkby is in sympathy with him. Thus, not only is Straw the Anarchist leader contrasted with Morris the Socialist leader, but he is also not among 'Ball's men.'[119]

The more conservative readings of the revolt that had gathered momentum from Hume onward were updated for the age of Victorian imperialism, among which we might include Henry Newbolt's Anglo-centric version of Froissart.[120] G. A. Henty, apologist for the Empire, turned his attention to the revolt in *A March on London* (1897). Henty pushed the familiar line both in the preface and through the character of Edgar that rebel demands (end to serfdom, reduction of land rent, the liberty to buy and sell in fairs and markets, pardon for past offences) were reasonable but that violence and the attitude of leaders like Tyler were wrong. The novel pushes hard old negative stereotypes about the mob against the backdrop of anxieties about the emerging labour movement, as Antony Taylor has noted.[121] We might also add that the preface states that the rebels 'felt that they were not free men, and were not even deemed worthy to fight in the wars of their country' which, as Stephen Basdeo has suggested, is a hint of Henty's imperial propaganda coming through: people just wanted to serve the Empire![122] Ball's influence lurks in the background of Henty's presentation of the uprising. Sir Ralph had heard of 'one John Ball, a pestilent knave, who preaches treason to them, and tells them that as all men are equal, so all the goods of those of the better class should be divided among those having nothing, a doctrine which pleases the rascals mightily.'[123] There is even a discussion of the Adam and Eve couplet and the reinforcing of traditional gender roles, tied in with the importance of male military service, but at some ideological distance from Morris's socialism. Of the Adam and Eve couplet (the basis for Ball's 'harangues'), Dame Agatha remarks, 'You see, one did the rough part of the toil, the other sat at home and did what

---

118 Bramston, *Banner*, 77–78.
119 Bramston, *Banner*, 51.
120 Henry Newbolt, *Froissart in England* (London: James Nisbet & Co, 1900).
121 G. A. Henty, *A March on London, Being a Story of Wat Tyler's Rebellion* (New York, C. Scribner's Sons, 1897), 41–48; Taylor, *London's Burning*, 41–42.
122 Basdeo, *Life and Legend of a Rebel Leader*, loc 2856.
123 Henty, *A March on London*, 108.

was needful there, and so it has been ever since. You know how you shared our feelings of delight that your brother had grown stronger, and would be able to take his own part, as his fathers had done before him, to become a brave and valiant knight, and assuredly it is not for you to repine now that a fair opportunity offers for him to prepare for his career.'[124]

In more sympathetic circles, Ball's name could of course be invoked without any obvious hint of Morris's influence, whether understood as rightfully standing up to tyranny or heavy taxation, part of a Wycliffite, Nonconformist, or Protestant tradition with an interest in workers' rights or social democracy, part of a Paine-like hope for alternative commemorative statues, or simply of general blessed memory.[125] The 'Red Week' (7–14 June 1914) of the relatively recently formed British Socialist Party (BSP) happily coincided with the five-hundred-and-thirty-third anniversary of the 'Peasants' Revolt' when Ball and Tyler brought to fruition their decades of labour. The BSP hoped that their 'Red Week' would be successful, just as the 1381 rebels shook the authorities to such an extent that in the century that followed, 'the working class had a rough plenty that they have not seen before or since.'[126] The propagandistic significance of the location of a suffragette meeting at Blackheath in 1912 was not lost to the reporter in *Votes for Women*, who noted that Tyler and the 'people's priest, John Ball' likewise met there with 60,000 men 'to demand the abolition of serfdom and the right, for every man and woman, to be free.'[127] But while these exceptions are, to lesser or greater degree, important, Morris's influence was hard to escape when Ball's name was raised, particularly in any sustained discussion. And this was only going to continue.

---

124 Henty, *A March on London*, 196–97. More 'harangues' can be found in Gilliat, *John Standish*, 239.
125 E.g., *Norwich Mercury* (2 June 1900); *Clarion* (21 April 1905); *Sheffield Independent* (27 April 1908); *Labour Leader* (6 January 1911).
126 *Justice* (4 June 1914). Cf. *Labour Leader* (7 June 1912).
127 *Votes for Women* (21 June 1912).

17
Red John? Ball after the Great War

An English Tragedy?

Decorated in floral patterns and with a promise to use only words originating in Middle English, William Chandler's play *Thirteen Eighty One: An English Tragedy* (1927) shows that Morris's legacy of reading Ball was still going strong after the Great War.[1] And the comparisons hardly ended with its literary and pictorial ornamentation. The play itself was dedicated to Morris. Among its listed influences under the subheading 'Vision' are *A Dream of John Ball* and Southey's *Wat Tyler* (Green, Froissart, and various other works on background material are listed under 'History'). The rebels even have a familiar banner featuring Adam with a spade and Eve with a child (II.II) and chant 'When Adam delved and Eve span...' (I.III). Paralleling the early copies of *A Dream of John Ball*, Chandler's play was a good quality production limited to 250 copies, which raised the ire of *Freedom* for being too expensive for working-class readers.[2] We might even note the usual quiet betrayal of Morris over Ball's Catholicism. While Ball regularly crosses himself, and Dominican and Franciscan priests are among the rebels, Ball and Tyler are associated with Wycliffe and there is a strong anti-papal theme running throughout. Indeed, the author's note at the beginning of the play claimed that 'About this time occurred the first expression of English Non-conformity.'

But there was something different about *Thirteen Eighty One*: the backdrop of war, whether the context in which it was written or the events described within. Ball explains the causes of the revolt and, among the deeper causes (in addition to the Black Death and the Statue of Labourers), notes the 'waste of blood & treasure in French wars' (I.II). The play begins with discussion about the horrors of war which, as Mrs Wender (the

---

1 William Chandler, *Thirteen Eighty One: An English Tragedy* (London: Stylus Press, 1927).
2 *Freedom* (1 October 1927); Taylor, *London's Burning*, 31.

mother of the veteran Tom) implies, leads to the behaviour of 'Each against all, and each one for himself,' even if she thought the war necessary to stop the enemy from 'laying waste our land.' Tom, on the other hand, says he saw 'the sacrifice of man for man...beneath the darkling wings of death.' Mrs Wender even explains to 'Tommy boy' that she is but concerned for her son who has come back from France only to go fighting again, even if this time it is for liberty from enemies at home (I.I). Against the advice of his mother and his love, Mary, Tom goes and, of course, dies. But this is violence that could have been prevented had people listened to the wise and astute Ball (who, knowing the political manoeuvrings and ramifications behind the scenes, even tries to save Sudbury) and not the ill-disciplined and rowdy pillaging rebels or the impatient, quick-to-act Tyler, a theme which by now was old in the reception of the revolt.

Chandler developed Morris's understanding of the future as a counter to the general gloomy atmosphere of his *English Tragedy*. The Ball of *Thirteen Eighty One* can be understood as taking on the role of Morris's Man from Essex who helped educate Ball about the future in *A Dream of John Ball*. Tyler even asks Ball, 'Come you from the clouds?', to which Ball answers 'No, not from Heaven, where I hope to go. I come from Essex' (I.II). Ball is described as one who speaks like a 'seer' (II.I) and who exits the stage '*as one seeing a vision*' (II.II), presumably as a visual indication of his prophetic (in socialist terms) status. He regularly 'dreams,' to Tyler's bafflement (II. II), of 'fair Liberty/Chained in a gloomy prison' (I.III), a future of 'Peace, Brotherhood, and general kindness,/And Fellowship of heaven and earth' (II.II), and an England where 'Mine and Thine' ceases to be and all things are held in common (II.II; cf. I.II). People are baffled by what Ball meant by the end of 'Mine and Thine' (the 'root of all troubles' I.I) throughout and this is because, like Morris's Man from Essex, he was pointing to a distant future change beyond the present when no one will work for another but for all and will not be in need of sustenance, a time of 'plenteous worth' (II.III). *Thirteen Eighty One* presents Ball as having the unenviable knowledge of knowing that the revolt may very well be a catastrophic failure but that the hope still continues throughout the centuries. This hope is often unseen, but the 1381 uprising will stand out like a beacon, inspiring people towards justice and truth. It is precisely this foreknowledge that made people think Ball was 'mad,' something beyond the standard explanation of the time where he was typically deemed 'mad' because he challenged the class system. The epilogue includes a discussion between Past, Present, and Future, confirming Ball's understanding, and ends with Liberty as a young woman chained in a 'blood-drenched cell,' imprisoned by Ignorance, Lust, and Power, but who remembers Runnymede and thinks of 'Flames yet afar, beyond my ken,/The world-wide brotherhood of men.'

Thirteen Eighty One, then, still acts as an encouragement that things will change, no matter how desperate the present seems. Jack Straw and Ball die not unlike how Tom remembers fallen soldiers—hands clasped, eye-to-eye as martyrs—but they do so in the knowledge that whatever else happens, the future, ultimately, 'bringeth full abiding peace' (II.III). And the change envisaged is not just liberty and freedom but socialism. The author's note stresses (as the epilogue does and Jack Straw later does in the play; I.III) that the revolt was when 'the voice of organised Labour was first heard in England' and that around this time appeared 'the first Socialist in England, John Ball.' That Ball was a socialist and a martyr was hardly uncontroversial after the war (see below). But what *kind* of socialist *was*. The ideological appropriation of *A Dream of John Ball*, the analyses of the miseries of capitalism, and the acceptance of Morris's Marxism now varied according to political persuasion in a world further shaken up not just by a world war but by the Russian Revolution, the General Strike of 1926, and the economic and political crises of the 1930s. Labour (with the Fabians and the Independent Labour Party [ILP]) were the movement in the ascendency but the Communist Party of Great Britain (CPGB; founded in 1920) sharpened the debate over Morris's Marxism, and while the war dealt a huge blow to anarchism in London, it still continued to make its own claims on Morris's legacy.

The Battle for *A Dream of John Ball*

While we cannot establish numbers, it seems that *A Dream of John Ball* was popular among sections of the working class. At the end of his life, John Bruce Glasier (d. 1920), friend of Morris and later a leading ILP figure, wrote of how socialism had transformed the lives of miners as well as their bookshelves where *A Dream of John Ball* and *News from Nowhere* sat alongside works by Plato, Plutarch, Mill, Carlyle, Spencer, Darwin, Huxley, and others.[3] Over a decade later, in 1934, Harold Laski—LSE professor of political science, lecturer, writer, Labour Party activist and thinker, and, by the mid-1930s, a Marxist—made a similar claim with reference to more desperate circumstances:

---

3   J. Bruce Glasier, *The Meaning of Socialism* (National Labour Press: Manchester, 1919), 220.

I went last week to the coalfields of Cumberland, and I saw again, in house after house of the miners there, the tattered pages of the paper-bound "A Dream of John Ball" and "Songs for Socialists." Make no mistake, the song that Morris sang is more profoundly in the hearts of the working class than at any time in his own lifetime.[4]

Whatever the extent of the popularity of *A Dream of John Ball* among miners and the working class more generally, it was influential (or at least widely cited or referenced) in the Labour Party and for its assorted personalities. Laski himself was an admirer of *A Dream of John Ball*,[5] as was the future Prime Minister Clement Attlee with whom Laski had a famous spat over allegations that Laski supported violent revolution in certain circumstances. Attlee's favourite passage was the most famous one about fellowship and lack of fellowship.[6] Through Attlee's older brother Tom, Morris's work would be an influence throughout Attlee's life, even if there was some awareness that political compromise and the age of the machine sat at odds with *News from Nowhere* and *A Dream of John Ball*.[7] Whilst Mayor of Stepney (1919–1920) in the post-war East End, Attlee wrote *The Social Worker* (1920). After giving advice on the imperceptibility of change and the benefits of cheerfulness in the face of pessimism when doing community work, he quoted approvingly, and tellingly, from *A Dream of John Ball* on fighting, losing, and victory, 'when it turns out not to be what they meant, and other men have to fight for what they meant under another name.'[8]

Attlee and Laski were hardly alone. Even with due differences sometimes acknowledged, Morris was a reference point for a generation of Labour politicians, thinkers, and activists from among different tendencies (e.g., Ramsay MacDonald, R. H. Tawney, G. D. H. Cole).[9] *Justice* even called

---

4   Quoted in Eisenman, 'Communism in Furs', 105, from John Drinkwater, Holbrook Jackson and Harold J. Laski, *Speeches in Commemoration of William Morris* (Walthamstow, 1934). I have not been able to access the original.
5   E.g., *Daily Herald* (6 August 1932).
6   Kenneth Harris, *Attlee* (revised edition; London: Weidenfeld and Nicolson, 1995), 23–24.
7   John Bew, *Citizen Clem: A Biography of Attlee* (Kindle edition; London: Riverrun, 2016), loc 1278–1308, 1826–1858, 10767–10798.
8   C. R. Attlee, *The Social Worker* (London: G. Bell and Sons, 1920), 137, quoting *A Dream of John Ball*, ch. IV. These were words he would critically discuss with Tom. Bew, *Citizen Clem*, loc 10806.
9   E.g., Bevir, *Making of British Socialism*, 86. Cf. G. D. H. Cole, *A History of Socialist Thought, Volume II: Marxism and Anarchism 1850–1890* (London: Macmillan, 1954), 417–20.

for the 'splendid episode' of the 'Peasants' Revolt' and the inspiring story of Ball and Tyler, with its potential for rural appeal, to be commemorated among the Labour parties of the South East, claiming *A Dream of John Ball* was effectively written for 'us' to read and to induce others to read.[10] More generally still, *A Dream of John Ball* and its ideas of fellowship continued to be a recognised point of reference from the First World War to the Second, whether on the Left (especially), in overviews of Morris's life, or for the cultured reader.[11] It could be referenced for its invocation of handicrafts and a lost pride and joy in work over against the age of the machine and the misery of the capitalist system.[12] Indeed, by contrasting the seemingly more plentiful fourteenth century, *A Dream of John Ball* could elsewhere be used to convey shock at the state of the twentieth, where there is no lack of food but there is a lack of will to feed the hungry.[13] Like Morris's Ball, the anarchist newspaper *Freedom* was incredulous at the idea that people could still be starving while warehouses were stacked with food or that people were unemployed while acres of England required tilling. Like Ball, they also thought that there was an alternative where food, clothing, and shelter were available to all and people would 'no longer listen to the glib-tongued leaders and politicians who tell them that these things have always been and must always be.'[14] One suggestion at solving problems of hunger and food shortages after the First World War was the continuation of the communal kitchen and community meals, based on the presentation of a better life in *A Dream of John Ball* and *News from Nowhere*.[15]

There is also explicit evidence of receptions of the Russian Revolution intertwining with receptions of *A Dream of John Ball*. Between the

10 *Justice* (22 May 1924).
11 E.g., *Clarion* (19 February 1915); *Labour Leader* (29 July 1915); *Labour Leader* (29 July 1915); *Labour Leader* (29 July 1915); *Justice* (3 February 1916); *Westminster Gazette* (20 August 1918); *Westminster Gazette* (23 January 1919); *Leeds Mercury* (25 January 1919); *Justice* (19 May 1921); *Illustrated London News* (19 April 1924); *The Sketch* (19 November 1924); *West London Observer* (4 May 1928); *Blyth News* (7 January 1929); *West Middlesex Gazette* (11 October 1930); *Middlesex County Times* (24 March 1934); *Yorkshire Post* (24 March 1934); *Western Daily Press* (31 December 1936); *Coventry Evening Telegraph* (19 January 1938); *Chelmsford Chronicle* (8 April 1938); *Birmingham Mail* (21 August 1939).
12 E.g., *Daily Herald* (14 September 1926); *Lancashire Evening Post* (24 March 1934).
13 *Cornish Guardian* (22 February 1934).
14 *Freedom* (1 January 1921).
15 *Uxbridge & W. Drayton Gazette* (30 November 1917).

February and October revolutions, ILP MPs hosted a delegation from the Russian Workmen's and Soldiers' Council in July 1917 as part of a mission 'to hasten a democratic world peace'. Robert Williams recalled discussions ranging from how *A Dream of John Ball* impressed to how the House of Commons did not.[16] In a post-October Revolution polemic against the capitalist class, *The Communist*, the first weekly of the Communist Party of Great Britain (CPBG), ran the headline 'Workers and Workless! Read the handwriting on the wall. It spells your doom or the doom of capitalism' with an accompanying quotation about 'foul swine' from *A Dream of John Ball*. The 'foul swine' were responsible for producing chaos and more specifically were interpreted as 'all the Allied nations whose people were to bask in the rays of a new dawn after the war,' but such countries have become 'homes of starvation'.[17] A less antagonistic perspective on class war and *A Dream of John Ball* (as ever, we leave aside what Morris might have made of such a move) was presented in the *Sunday Mirror*, where Morris's story was used as a prophetic prediction of the 'hopeless industrial warfare,' and the reviewer hoped 'employer and employed' could come to understand one another.[18] Yet another attempt at getting lambs to lay with wolves and lions came from the Rev. Harold Hurst (St James's, Northampton), who preached on Ball's words about fellowship in *A Dream of John Ball* as a challenge against the lack of fellowship among different sects both in the church and in socialist politics (rival unions, SDF, ILP, Fabians), due to jealousy, snobbery, pettiness, class feelings, etc. Thus, before 'sons of labour and sons of light could take fellowship with each other they must be sure of fellowship amongst themselves.'[19]

The centenary of Morris's birth in 1934 was a flashpoint in the differing appropriations of Morris and thus *A Dream of John Ball*, not least when Conservative leader Stanley Baldwin spoke at the opening of the exhibition at the Victoria and Albert Museum. This, and the varied appropriations of Morris on the Left, provoked a damning response from one of the founding members of the CPGB, Robin Page Arnot. Arnot defended the revolutionary nature of Morris's writings (including *A Dream of John Ball*) and attacked those who had made Morris (using Lenin's words) a 'harmless saint,' depriving him of his revolutionary Marxist credentials. And two particular myths of Morris needed destroying: 'the bourgeois myth on the one hand and the Labour Party-ILP myth on the other.' Baldwin and his

16 *Daily Herald* (11 August 1917).
17 *The Communist* (27 January 1921).
18 *Sunday Mirror* (24 February 1924). Cf. *Cornishman* (5 March 1924).
19 *Northampton Chronicle and Echo* (28 April 1924).

reception in the press formed Arnot's exemplar of the bourgeois myth: Morris as the great artist, great poet, great craftsman, with no mention of Morris the dedicated socialist. The debunking of the Tory Morris was done with reference to 'these foul swine' in *A Dream of John Ball*—that is, the Tories as 'representative of the capitalist class'. The Labour-ILP myth was epitomised by Ramsay MacDonald and Bruce Glasier and his circle, and it downplayed Morris's Marxism, economics, and class antagonism in the name of a more 'ethical' socialism instead. The 'early mythmongers of the ILP' were anti-Marxist while later some even tried to rethink Marx along the same lines as they rethought Morris. Arnot accepted (via Engels) that Morris could make tactical errors, but this never meant that Morris's Marxism and class antagonism were to be downplayed or ignored. Only 'those so blind' could not 'see the results of a study of Marx in John Ball'. He challenged those who read *A Dream of John Ball* only for its beauty and romance whilst not thinking through the point of the contrast between now and then, its revolutionary call to the workers of the present, its dialectical reading of English history, and what it might say about the future. But Arnot also contextualised *A Dream of John Ball* in Morris's reading of Marx's *Capital*, and further added that Morris's story can be summarised by the opening words of the *Communist Manifesto*: 'the history of all human society, past and present, has been the history of class struggles.'[20]

Ball almost beyond Morris

Ball as a figure beyond Morris's reception, or at least beyond just overt reference to Morris, was of course still found during and between the world wars, including other critiques of the proto-Protestant reading of the revolt and medieval heresy.[21] And Ball (almost) beyond Morris remained a figure more likely to be found and discussed in interwar communist, socialist, or democratic mythmaking. Discussions might include associations with socialism generally, Wycliffite or proto-Protestant socialism, communism, English radicalism, a class-conscious working class, working-class history, labourers, hostility towards the ruling class and aristocrats, martyrdom,

---

20 Robin Page Arnot, *William Morris: A Vindication* (London: Martin Lawrence Ltd, 1934), available at https://www.marxists.org/archive/arnot-page/1934/03/morrisvindicated.htm.
21 E.g., G. K. Chesterton, *A Short History of England* (London: Chatto and Windus, 1917), 128–29.

martyrdom for the 'religion of humanity', anti-oppression, fighting against squalid conditions, constitutionalism, rights, struggles for liberty, voting Labour, and opposition to the dread of war, alongside the odd hope for a memorial or the occasional reference to the Ball of Green's history and even Southey's *Wat Tyler*.[22] Ball was also given an update in line with reference to contemporary events, including the General Strike of 1926 and the hunger marches.[23] There were limits to the praise in some instances. In an otherwise hagiographical account of Ball, Hugh Broadbridge fell back on an old criticism of the revolt to criticise a certain kind of violence. Embittered by the suffering he had endured, Ball made 'only one mistake,' Broadbridge claimed, and that was when he 'incited the mob to violence… he advocated murder of all who opposed.' For those few days, Ball had his heel on the government's neck, and dreadfully he used the opportunity.'[24]

The democratic associations also included local government in the case of Bernard Fleetwood-Walker's *John Ball and the Peasants' Rising of 1381* (1938), a mural for the Council Chamber at Essex Country Hall, Chelmsford, where it still hangs today next to a portrait of the queen.[25] Ball is sat on a white horse in white and black robes, finger raised, preaching to the crowd with a St George's Cross hanging in the corner. With his now familiar (see Chapter 16) though extremely gaunt face (and, arguably,

---

22 See, e.g., *Buckinghamshire Examiner* (2 June 1916); *Forward* (20 January 1917); *Motherwell Times* (16 November 1917); *Coventry Evening Telegraph* (18 March 1920); *Chester-le-Street Chronicle* (2 July 1920); *Justice* (12 May 1921); *Justice* (19 May 1921); *Gloucestershire Echo* (6 March 1923); *Freedom* (1 June 1923); *Birmingham Daily Gazette* (5 September 1924); J. C. Hardwick, *Master and Man: A Tale of the Peasants' Revolt* (London: Sheldon Press, 1924), 154; *Nottingham Journal* (26 January 1927); *Chelmsford Chronicle* (17 May 1929); *Clarion* (1 February 1931); *Daily Worker* (28 August 1931); *Daily Worker* (6 June 1932); *Daily Worker* (23 October 1935); *Yarmouth Independent* (26 October 1935); *Daily Herald* (8 August 1936); Hugh Broadbridge, 'The Turning of the Worm,' in *Fifty Mutinies, Rebellions and Revolutions* (London: Odhams Press Ltd, 1938), 371–84; *West Middlesex Gazette* (27 August 1938); *Daily Worker* (2 September 1938); *Uxbridge & W. Drayton Gazette* (10 February 1939); *West Middlesex Gazette* (18 February 1939); *Chelmsford Chronicle* (16 June 1939); *Bedfordshire Times and Independent* (21 February 1941); *Daily Worker* (20 October 1942); *Daily Worker* (3 September 1943); *Leamington Spa Courier* (28 January 1944). Cf. *Taunton Courier* (28 February 1942); *Suffolk and Essex Free Press* (11 February 1943). Cf. Taylor, *London's Burning*, 29, 32–33.
23 E.g., *Daily Herald* (6 September 1926); *Daily Herald* (22 February 1934).
24 Broadbridge, 'Turning of the Worm,' 376–77.
25 The picture can be viewed at http://www.fleetwood-walker.co.uk/public-collections/.

a large nose), Fleetwood-Walker's Ball also resembles the description given in Halcott Glover's popular play, *Wat Tyler: A Play in Three Acts* (1921), where he is 'thin and pale' in prison and not much different after his escape, with the additional detail that he is 'white-faced and weak'.[26] Ball does not, however, appear to be quite as weak in Fleetwood-Walker's painting, though perhaps not as swashbuckling as the fit, talkative, jailbreaking, and dog-owning Ball of J. C. Hardwick's *Master and Man* (1924).[27] Not only has Fleetwood-Walker's Ball had time to recover, but he represents certain democratic ideals. As Marie Considine has shown, the mural scenes were chosen by Essex County Council and designed to present important events in Essex's history. Ball was presented as a preacher of rights whose popularity was contextualised against the backdrop of serfdom and the inability of labourers to seek higher-paid work. Considine further notes that Ball as the central character on the horse was associated with regal portraiture but, strikingly, the horse's head is bowed low, 'suggesting a people's hero with humility.' That Essex County Council identified itself with Ball in such a way may have been to reassure people that their local council had the interests of the ratepayers at heart, while domesticating the revolt into the ideology of the ruling class.[28]

Ball's place in the relatively flexible canonising of English radical history continued to be normalised. But it was a tradition regularly updated, often along party-political lines, and the familiar narrative of history from dispossessions of the Saxons through the Peasants' Revolt to the labour movement was disseminated through networks such as the Plebs League and the Workers' Educational Association.[29] Sometimes depending on the leftist

26 Halcott Glover, *Wat Tyler: A Play in Three Acts* (London: Bloomsbury Press, 1921), 27, 32.
27 Hardwick's Ball is still relatively familiar, if bearded: 'He was a man of middle age, clothed in a jerkin of brown worsted with a black hood over his head, by which his face was partly hidden. He had a short beard; his cheeks were lean and brown, his eyes were lively and keen, set deeply in his head, and of singular blue colour…his voice was deep and mellow…the dog followed behind obediently. Indeed, it was a shepherd's dog, and excellently disciplined…thrusting forth his hand, he took mine in a strong grip…He was indeed…a very copious talker…He marched with a steady swing that carried him mile after mile without weariness' (Hardwick, *Master and Man*, 15–18). Later he is said to have a particular manner of 'waving his hand in a peculiar [*sic*?] way' (57).
28 Marie Considine, 'The Social, Political and Economic Determinants of a Modern Portrait Artist: Bernard Fleetwood-Walker (1893–1965)', (PhD Thesis; University of Birmingham, 2012), 66–67, 114–15.
29 Examples include, Gibbins, *English Social Reformers*; Geo Guest, *An Introduction to English Rural History* (London: Workers' Educational

persuasion of a given paper, writer, or activist, Ball now stood variously alongside Harry Quelch, Keir Hardie, the Suffragettes, Ben Tillett, and/or Tom Mann. With these new additions, Ball also stood alongside the previously rarely connected Tolpuddle Martyrs and the increasingly popular figures from the English Revolution, as well as traditional favourites such as Tyler, Cade, Kett, Milton, Shelley, Owen, O'Brien, certain Chartists, Jones, and Morris.[30] Such was the obviousness of connecting Ball with later trade unionism and Labour that it found its way into R. M. Freeman's parody of Dr Johnson's afterlife in *The New Boswell* (1923). When rambling through the Elysian fields, Johnson, Goldsmith, and Boswell came across two troublesome types—'the Reverend John Ball and Mr Wat Tyler'—who are the centre of attention in the chapter dedicated to the Labour Party. Much to Johnson's horror, Ball spoke of his satisfaction of how well England was now doing and how England would do better yet if those 'most worthy successors,' Robert Smillie and Mr Ramsay MacDonald, have any say in the matter. This is because they are 'sworn to have the land for the people, and the mines also, and everything else that justly belongs to them.' To Johnson's even greater horror, Ball said that if the present owners did not hand them over, then 'the people will exercise their just rights and take

---

Association, 1920), 20–23; Raymond Postgate, *A Short History of the British Workers* (London: Plebs League, 1926). For discussion and summary of the WEA and Plebs League and the English radical tradition and history, see John Stephen Enderby, 'The English Radical Tradition and the British Left 1885–1945' (PhD Thesis; Sheffield Hallam University, 2019), 286–334.

30 E.g., *Justice* (21 December 1916); *Labour Leader* (1 November 1917); Clement J. Bundock, *Direct Action and the Constitution* (London: Independent Labour Party, 1920); *Worker's Dreadnought* (20 August 1921); *Daily Herald* (6 September 1926); *Daily Herald* (12 January 1934); *John Bull* (30 January 1937); *Daily Worker* (6 October 1936); *Daily Worker* (7 November 1938); *Daily Worker* (6 September 1940); *Daily Herald* (28 January 1943). Cf. Samuel, 'British Marxist Historians,'; Clare V. J. Griffiths, *Labour and the Countryside: The Politics of Rural Britain 1918–1939* (Oxford: Oxford University Press, 2007), 44–48; Taylor, *London's Burning*, 26–27, 31, 37; Taylor, '"The Pioneers of the Great Army of Democrats".' The developing commemoration of the Tolpuddle Martyrs in the twentieth century, see, e.g., Clare V. J. Griffiths, 'Remembering Tolpuddle: Rural History and Commemoration in the Inter-War Labour History,' *History Workshop Journal* 44 (1997): 144–69; Clare V. J. Griffiths, 'From Dorsetshire Labourers to Tolpuddle Martyrs: Celebrating Radicalism in the English Countryside,' in Quentin Outram and Keith Laybourn (eds.), *Secular Martyrdom in Britain and Ireland: From Peterloo to the Present* (New York: Palgrave Macmillan, 2019), 59–84.

them.' Johnson resorted to an old type of comparison for Ball: by retorting that this was the same method as used by Dick Turpin.[31]

The internationalist aspect of Ball and a native radical tradition was also stressed, whether invoked to provoke support for Belgian workers deported to Germany in the First World War, a comparison with Mexican revolutionary unrest, opposition to fascism home and abroad, or as an understanding of a manifestation of the 'Angel of Revolt' found in different local, national, and continental traditions (e.g., German, Irish, French, Welsh, Scottish).[32] While there was the reassuring discovery of a John Ball Rambling Club in Kent,[33] there was also a repeated worry that the Garden of England had lost its radical edge and its connection with trade unionism, and so needed to be reminded of its revolutionary past to jolt them back into action.[34] One promoter of the Kentish radical tradition, the socialist councillor Fred H. Gorle, took particular offence at the Prime Minister Lloyd George's visit to the county in 1921 and his reference to Ball ('a sort of Socialist leader of his day') and his suggestion that his friend Jack Jones (the Labour MP for Silvertown) would enjoy being compared with Ball, Tyler, and Cade. Gorle told the story of the 'first English socialist' Ball and the revolt, arguing that just as the rebels fought against the tyranny of serfdom, so socialists fight a different form of class tyranny—wage slavery. But whereas the rebels had little option but to use force, 'peaceful revolution' could be done through the ballot box with people stirred into action by the 'voice of John Ball.' He imagined Ball listening to 'this parody of a statesman' and reminding everyone how liberties remained under threat. Ball might perhaps have preached on Adam and Eve, 'if Lloyd George's police allowed him.' But, Gorle concluded, what would be worthwhile was for Ball's memory to be kept alive, a commemoration to be held, and Jack Jones to join in. And Gorle recommended that Conrad Noel give a sermon

---

31 R. M. Freedman, *The New Boswell* (London: John Lane, 1923), 27–33. The Dick Turpin comparison also turned up in Parliament. See, e.g., *Birmingham Daily Gazette* (5 September 1924).
32 E.g., *Justice* (21 December 1916); *Labour Leader* (1 November 1917); *Daily Worker* (7 November 1938); *Daily Worker* (1 June 1939); Jack Lindsay and Edgell Rickword (eds.), *A Handbook of Freedom: A Record of English Democracy through Twelve Centuries* (New York: International Publishers, 1939), vii, xi–xiii, 26–44.
33 *Daily Worker* (27 July 1939).
34 *Justice* (19 May 1921); *Sevenoaks Chronicle* (27 February 1925); *Kent Folkestone, Hythe, Sandgate & Cheriton Herald* (9 June 1934). Cf. also Griffiths, *Labour and the Countryside*, 46; Taylor, *London's Burning*, 27.

on Blackheath as part of 'a glorious gathering to commemorate the martyrdom of John Ball.'[35]

Ball and the Red Vicar of Thaxted

As 'Wat Tyler Road' in Blackheath became a very real possibility,[36] Ball would get his own memorial of sorts not too far from Kent. Indeed, it was through the catholicising Anglican vicar Conrad Le Despenser Roden Noel (1869–1942) himself that the Chapel of Blessed John Ball Priest and Martyr 1381 was established at the parish church in Thaxted, Essex, where Noel was vicar (1910–1942). This interest in Ball was part of the Red Vicar of Thaxted's revolutionary Christian socialism, which was influenced by, among others, F. D. Maurice, Stewart Headlam and the Guild of St Matthew, and the Church Socialist League. This was a socialism that stressed the importance of the 'Commonwealth of God' and a Mass celebrated 'as prelude to the New World Order in which all would be justly produced and equally distributed.'[37] In 1918 he pushed these ideas further still and established the revolutionary Catholic Crusade which backed the Russian Revolution and was hostile towards the British Empire. Among the numerous revolutionary pronouncements in its manifesto was a plea for a 'free England' and to 'break up the present world & make a new, in the

---

35 *Justice* (19 May 1921). Cf. *Justice* (12 May 1921); *East Kent Gazette* (14 May 1921); *Justice* (26 May 1921).
36 Taylor, *London's Burning*, 22.
37 Conrad Noel, *An Autobiography* (London: J.M. Dent & Sons, 1945), 91. Noel's story has been repeatedly told and for the details of his life that follow, see, e.g., Reginald Groves, *Conrad Noel and the Thaxted Movement: An Adventure in Christian Socialism* (London: Merlin Press, 1967); Jack Putterill, *Conrad Noel: Prophet and Priest, 1869–1942* (Cambridge: E. & E. Plumridge, 1976); Kenneth Leech (ed.), *Conrad Noel and the Catholic Crusade: A Critical Evaluation* (Croydon: Jubilee Group, 1993); Andrew Robinson, 'Thaxted: Conrad Noel and Now', *Anglican and Episcopal History* 63 (1994): 285–89; Mark D. Chapman, *Liturgy, Socialism and Life: The Legacy of Conrad Noel* (London: Darton, Longman and Todd, 2001); Arthur Burns, 'Beyond the "Red Vicar": Community and Christian Socialism in Thaxted, Essex, 1910–84', *History Workshop Journal* 75 (2013): 101–24; Katie Palmer Heathman, '"I Ring for the General Dance": Morris and Englishness in the Work of Conrad Noel', in Michael Heaney (ed.), *The Histories of the Morris in Britain* (London: English Folk Dance and Song Society & Historical Dance Society, 2018), 115–31.

power of the Outlaw of Galilee.' Also included in its outlaw tradition were 'the Catholic Clergy who led the 1381 rebellion,' who proclaimed (echoing Ball's famous words) 'that things cannot go well in England till the rich disgorge and there be neither master nor man.'[38]

Noel also had a background in the ILP, though in 1911 he briefly joined the British Socialist Party and was a supporter (but not a member) of the CPGB. But the Catholic Crusade would become associated with the Trotskyite split in the 1930s and Noel became a critic of Stalin and then founder of the Order of the Church Militant before his death in 1942. His political radicalism caused predictable controversies, perhaps none more infamous than the Battle of the Flags. After hanging the Allies' flags during the First World War, things soon got controversial in 1921 when the Red Flag, the Sinn Féin flag, and the St George's flag were hung in the church, much to the horror of certain Cambridge students. These flags epitomised Noel's combined nationalism and internationalism, from the motto 'He hath made of one blood all nations' on the Red Flag to his preference for the cross of St George over the imperialist Union Jack. But Noel's socialist politics and sacramental theology were also influenced by Morris and Ruskin, and his time at Thaxted was also remembered for his liturgical preferences for English and medieval romanticism, folk traditions, floral beauty, aesthetics, music, popular participation, processions, and, of course, morris dancing, started by Noel's wife, Miriam. The Thaxted folk traditions were emerging around the time Cecil Sharp was collecting, reviving, and creating an English tradition of folk music and dance (including morris dancing), and Sharp himself would regularly visit Thaxted.[39]

As we will see, folk music and notions of Englishness would become an important context for understanding the reception of Ball later in the twentieth century (see Chapters 22, 23). Noel likewise developed notions of a specifically religious English radical tradition in this respect. The 'revolutionary teaching at Thaxted,' Noel claimed, was found not only in books and in the pulpit but also in 'the life of a group and the expression of that life in worship.' Noel saw it as alternative to the 'sluggish routine and conventionalism of much modern Nonconformity and of the "C. of E."' The distinction and labelling are important here because they explain the tradition in which he placed Ball. The 'C. of E.' was distinguished from the 'Church of England' in that 'C. of E.' was but another name for the Establishment and 'the Establishment is the religion of the ratepayer, and

---

38 The manifesto is republished as Reginald Groves (ed.), *The Catholic Crusade, 1918–1936* (London: Archive One, 1970).
39 Noel, *Autobiography*, 104–5; Chapman, *Liturgy, Socialism and Life*, 23.

the religion of the ratepayer is not a religion but a disease.' By contrast, the 'Church of England' tradition includes not only those deemed precursors to socialism but lively communal worship with sufficiently catholicising tendencies, hence the otherwise surprising (at least in the history of the reception of Ball) inclusion of Laud: 'she is the Church of Anselm, of Becket of those such as Langton and John Ball who fought for the freedom of the people, the Church of Laud in his fight against a narrow Calvinism and the oppression of the poor, and still in modern times, the church of Maurice and Kingsley, of Scott Holland and Stewart Headlam.'[40]

In *Socialism in Church History* (1910), Ball was likewise contextualised in a history of the church in England which owed something to (among others) Hyndman, though Noel (as was implied throughout the manifesto of the Catholic Crusade) was especially keen to stress the importance of the impact of aspects of the church and theology rather than concentrate on materialist readings of history, which reflected his broader interests in having God and socialism intertwined.[41] As was now typical, the fifteenth century was elevated by Noel as an example of the quality of life in medieval England ('a merry England in fact and in deed').[42] Referencing Ruskin and Morris, he stressed the ways in which life from work to architecture was better in the fifteenth century than the capitalist present and, ideally, there was a 'Collective Catholicism' with a reciprocal relationship between the people and the monarch.[43] But, he asked, 'even if Church thought and Church legislation modified and corrected secular law in a socialist direction,' what about counter evidence such as the 'peasants' rising' (even if, as he reasonably noted, it predated the fifteenth century)?[44] Noel responded that this kind of counter argument does not understand the nature of revolt because 'slums never revolt' and the idea that 'oppression and misery cause revolutionary impatience' is a popular fallacy. But when people know that better days have been restrained by the yoke, then 'rebellion is inevitable.' In the case of the peasants' uprising, this was as much about holding the ideals of medieval England to account. 'Church tradition' was also in their favour and set against 'landed plutocracy and ecclesiastical officialdom.'[45] The revolt was fittingly led by 'priests and friars' like Ball 'who, if they knew little of Canon law, knew much of the Gospel to which itself appealed.' For

40 Noel, *Autobiography*, 90–91.
41 Chapman, *Liturgy, Socialism and Life*, 16–17.
42 Conrad Noel, *Socialism in Church History* (London: Frank Palmer 1910), 167.
43 Noel, *Socialism*, 163–87.
44 Noel, *Socialism*, 187–88.
45 Noel, *Socialism*, 188.

over twenty years, Ball and 'other priests' had been preaching 'up and down the countryside' while three archbishops opposed them. Ball signalled the uprising in the name of the Trinity in his letter and the interconnected 'peasant clubs' organised throughout the counties 'was for the most part the work of the clergy of the English Church.'[46]

Glover's Inspired Prophet

Folk music pervades the background of Glover's play, *Wat Tyler* (1921), coupled with certain notions of religiosity. There are echoes of Morris's dreamer, but Glover went beyond Morris, beyond what Chandler would soon do with the dreamer Ball (see above), and beyond the standard explanations for the label 'mad.' In Glover's presentation, Ball echoes biblical notions (discussed in biblical scholarship of the time) of the prophet, ecstatic prophecy, prophetic deprivation, and the potential for these phenomena to be classified as madness, as well as recalling the behaviour of recognisable interwar religious virtuosi in an era of Theosophy, Spiritualism, mediums, occultism, and Panaceans that crossed the political spectrum.[47] Glover's near saintly Ball has 'dreams' and 'visions' and describes himself as a 'seeing man.' This behaviour is trance-like, something akin to a 'fit,' for when he does have a vision he is described as *'possessed...his ringing utterance is that of a prophet'* and *'lifting his wasted arms, his voice ringing out loud and inspired.'*[48] This partly accounts for the description of Ball as 'mad,' though his imprisonment drove him to madness and fever-like

---

46 Noel, *Socialism*, 188–89.
47 Jenny Hazelgrove, *Spiritualism and British Society between the Wars* (Manchester: Manchester University Press, 2000); Georgina Byrne, *Modern Spiritualism and the Church of England, 1850–1939* (Woodbridge: Boydell Press, 2010); Brad E. Kelle, 'The Phenomenon of Israelite Prophecy in Contemporary Scholarship,' *Currents in Biblical Research* 12 (2014): 275–320 (282–90); Alastair Lockhart, *Personal Religion and Spiritual Healing: The Panacea Society in the Twentieth Century* (Albany, NY: SUNY Press, 2019), 51–62. For biblical references compare, e.g., Numbers 11.24–30; 1 Samuel 10.6–13; 19.20–24; 1 Kings 22.19–23; 2 Kings 3.13–20; 5.26; 6.17; Isaiah 6; 20.1–6; 61.1; Jeremiah 16.1–9; 23.16–40; 29.26–27; Ezekiel 1; 2.1–2; 3.12–15; 4–6; 8; 10–12; 24.15–27; 37.1–14; 40–48; Hosea 9.7; Amos 3.7; 7.1–8.3; 9.1–3; Joel 3.1–2; Micah 3.8; Zechariah 1–6; Mark 1.6–11; 1 Corinthians 12–14; 2 Corinthians 12.1–5.
48 Glover, *Wat Tyler*, 41–45.

dreaming and he only comes around once he hears the familiar Adam and Eve rhyme and is sprung from prison. But Tyler cannot comprehend these visions and this incomprehension points to a now more familiar conflict in the history of the reception of the revolt: the disciplined, wise Ball who advocates nonviolence against those who do not act violently versus the physical, hot tempered, and slightly dim-witted Tyler. Violence and chaos naturally follow, epitomised by drunken rebels slurring Ball's Adam and Eve rhyme, including a new debauched version 'When Adam delved and Eve span...Beer for every Englishman,'[49] echoing that old spin on levelling ideas associated with the likes of Ball (see, e.g., Chapters 5, 8).

Glover's play seems to have been popular and was revised for open-air performances,[50] which might further explain the need for such a striking visual presentation of Ball in terms of visual and recognisable prophetic behaviours. Audiences were especially vocal in their enthusiasm, while in 1923 it was performed amidst the 2500 visitors to the annual Commemoration of the Community and College of the Resurrection at Mirfield.[51] There is clearly sympathy for the plight of the rebels, and the play foregrounds the taxation for war, the Statute of Labourers, and wage demands as prime causes of the discontent and conflict. As several reviews noted, this was clearly a play with contemporary implications with one eye on unresolved tensions in the present labour movement.[52] According to the *Sunday Mirror*, while the play 'takes place in the twelfth century[!], the theme itself is essentially modern. The Middle Ages had their "Labour problem"; we have ours! And that problem remains to-day what it has always been. "Wat Tyler" states the problem, but makes no attempt to solve it.'[53] While one review argued that Glover's rebels 'were not of the Red Flag, Communist type,'[54] we should not lose sight of violent Tyler's symbol in a play performed in the aftermath of the Russian Revolution—the hammer. Indeed, while acknowledging the dangers of historical parallels, a review in the *Liverpool Echo* differently argued that 'Ball, Tyler, and their followers, militant and spiritual, were not Labour, but Communist. The worker

---

49 Glover, *Wat Tyler*, 60.
50 E.g., *Liverpool Echo* (8 June 1923); *Rugby Advertiser* (28 June 1929).
51 *The Era* (16 November 1921); *Truth* (23 November 1921); *Yorkshire Post* (16 July 1923).
52 E.g., *Pall Mall Gazette* (15 November 1921); *The Era* (16 November 1921); *Hull Daily Mail* (17 November 1921); *Nottingham Journal* (21 November 1921); *Rugby Advertiser* (28 June 1929).
53 *Sunday Mirror* (20 November 1921).
54 *Aberdeen Press and Journal* (15 November 1921).

and his hammer figure on half of the emblems of Soviet Russia.'[55] That this connection was made should not be surprising because Ball was elsewhere brought into the contemporary debates about the Soviet Union and, in the run up to the Second World War, the Communist Party of Great Britain provided its own distinctive contribution to, and influence on, the ongoing reception of Ball to which we now turn.

---

55 *Liverpool Echo* (8 June 1923).

18
Bolshevik Ball

In one review of Halcott Glover's *Wat Tyler*, it was stated that,

> It is fortunate, perhaps, that the management, and all concerned at the Old Vic are not transported back in James I days. That monarch had an unpleasant habit when events on the stage showed an odious comparison with things in politics of clapping the actors into gaol or fining them…With the rumoured prospect of a further increase in the amount of Income Tax in the next Budget, the Old Vic revives this gory method of protest of 1381![1]

As the slightly tongue-in-cheek tone implies, some of the sting had been removed from the legacy of the revolt by the interwar years. Nevertheless, ideas of Ball as a (wrong sort of) seditious threat, so dominant for centuries in the reception history of the revolt, did not disappear entirely, and the perceived Bolshevik threat provided the opportunity for reuse. In *The People*, Charles Lowe updated the old slur that Ball was a 'demagogue' who originated the theories of 'social reform' associated with the French Communists of 1870 'and with which the Bolshevists are now in turn seeking to create a new Heaven and a new earth, though the result is only an intensified Hell.' Ball, who first asked the 'communistic question' about Adam digging and Eve spinning, was bordering on promoting something distinctly un-British and he 'is not to be confounded with our patron-saint, John Bull,' claimed Lowe.[2] We also find an updating of the once dominant theme in the reception of the revolt, namely the fear of the mob and threats to the stability of the capital.[3] Arthur Shadwell happily reported a 'general slump in Bolshevism and Direct Action' but was still concerned with a 'persistent proletariat unrest that strives for raising the status of the worker in the mass.' Shadwell picked up on the typical anti-Irish slur ('wild Irishmen')

1 *Nottingham Journal* (21 November 1921).
2 *The People* (14 January 1923).
3 For the interwar updating of this theme, see Taylor, *London's Burning*, 20–45, 75–104.

and threats to London through arson plots, and from those causing 'mischief' by 'taking advantage of the prevailing unemployment.' He grudgingly accepted that guild socialism was a more acceptable route for discontent because it is 'entirely pacific and anti-slavery, which the Bolshevik movement is not.' And in this context, he noted that the last time 'a mob seized the City' was under Wat Tyler and 'the mad priest, John Ball.'[4]

The question of violence in 1381 and its appropriateness in the present was not dissimilarly updated in light of the Russian Revolution in left-wing anti-Bolshevism. The 'Peasants' Revolt' may indeed be a 'warning to the governing classes presently in power,' claimed an article in *Justice*, but Ball and the rebels had no franchise, unlike the workers of the present. The franchise gives the workers the opportunity to overthrow the 'evils of the present system of industrial exploitation' as readers are asked whether they will use this power to 'succumb to the wiles of "Communists" and agents-provocateurs, and fail, as did your forefathers, and bind bonds still more tightly?'[5] But the Russian Revolution was a vexed question on the Labourite left as the definition of democracy and the potential for violence could be in the eye of the beholder. In an Independent Labour Party (ILP) pamphlet attacking the Liberal coalition government's clandestine policy against Soviet Russia (*Direct Action and the Constitution* [1920]), Clement Bundock accepted that history had progressed beyond the use of physical force to make political demands.[6] Instead, the weapon workers now had mass withdrawal of labour in the form of a general strike and parliamentary representation. Bundock turned the tables on those who criticised supporters of Soviet Russia by arguing that, despite his denunciations of dictatorship abroad, Lloyd George had in fact begun creating a dictatorship in Britain and acted unconstitutionally and undemocratically in intervening against Russia through secret decision making. Alternatively, Bundock argued, Labour was defending the British constitution and thereby continuing a now long-established tradition of left-wing understandings of the old Whiggish argument. Labour was honouring the memory of those who built the constitution, who provided the 'measure of liberty' now enjoyed and wrested from the ruling class, and who maintained the 'best of our traditions.'[7] 'Direct action' has deep roots in English history and one example was the Peasants' Revolt and the 'Bolshevik of the Fourteenth Century,' by

---

4 *Exeter and Plymouth Gazette* (19 January 1921).
5 *Justice* (7 July 1921).
6 For further discussion of the pamphlet, see, e.g., Enderby, 'English Radical Tradition,' 130–36.
7 Bundock, *Direct Action and the Constitution*, 5.

which Bundock meant that the 'mad priest of Kent' would now be called a 'Bolshevik agent', for Ball and the rebels denounced 'social inequalities' and demanded 'better rule' and justice.[8] Thus, if Labour were forced to take direct action, it would be in 'defence of the constitution' and 'in line with history,' even if it would be better if the British public would vote to secure political action.[9]

As we might expect, strong support for a Bolshevik Ball was found from the Communist Party of Great Britain (CPGB).[10] Presumably in the tradition of using 'Wat Tyler' or 'Jack Cade' as a *nom de plume*, one 'John Ball' was the regular writer of 'Industrial Notes' for *The Communist*, the short-lived newspaper (1920–1923) of the Communist Party whose editors included T. A. Jackson, the working-class intellectual brought up on Victorian medievalism and a regular Ball advocate (see also Chapter 19).[11] *The Communist* also included articles by Alexander John on the 'Peasants' Revolt' as part of a history of 'English revolutions,' including a retelling of Ball who 'was preaching Communism to the masses for about 20 years' and 'died in a way worthy to his great revolutionary life.'[12] More specifically, Ball was a 'utopian Communist' and, like Glover's play, more 'an agitator and idealist' than a 'man of action'. While he was not a pacifist, he was a 'prophet and not a soldier' who was prepared to suffer for his 'Communistic doctrines' over harming aggressors or even leading a 'revolutionary campaign.' Brave, compassionate, and likely a 'wonderful speaker,' he stood by his deeds during the 'revolution' even as he was about to die. Nevertheless, and in a way now familiar enough, John argued that the 1381 revolution was not 'religious' and its real driving force was a 'social

---

8   Bundock, *Direct Action and the Constitution*, 9–10.
9   Bundock, *Direct Action and the Constitution*, 16.
10 Indeed, from around this time, there was a Russian pamphlet on 1381: Andrei Globa, Уот Тайлер: Поэма [*Wat Tyler: Poem*] (Петербург, 1922). It features images of a tonsured and not insubstantial Ball leading the masses alongside Wat Tyler and Jack Straw. Unfortunately, I am unable to read the Russian text. I am grateful to Stephen Basdeo for drawing my attention to this.
11 See further, e.g., T. A. Jackson, *Solo Trumpet: Some Memories of Socialist Agitation and Propaganda* (London: Lawrence and Wishart, 1953); Vivien Morton and Stuart Macintyre, *T. A. Jackson—Revolutionary and Working Class Intellectual: Centenary Appreciation 1879–1979* (London: Central Books, 1979); Kevin Morgan, Gidon Cohen, and Andrew Flinn, *Communists and British Society 1920–1991* (London: Rivers Oram Press, 2007), 50, 201, 237–38; Philip Bounds, 'The Marxist Outsider: T. A. Jackson as Autobiographer and Critic,' *Socialism and Democracy* 31 (2017): 122–44.
12 *The Communist* (1 July 1922).

revolution necessitated by economic changes.' Whatever doctrinal issues may have constituted the definition of 'religious,' the alternative definition of the driving force behind the revolt was again broad enough to incorporate the 'prophetic' Ball, the ablest speaker of the 'earthly, but noble ideas of the social revolutionaries.' The people of the fourteenth century were moved by 'Communistic ideas' but, in a move expected of Marxists (like Morris) with an interest in historical materialism, John located Ball as a figure before his time. His communistic ideals were 'beautiful, no more than ideal dreams' but 'this prophetic forerunner among Communistic agitators, should be held in grateful memory by the British labouring masses.'[13]

Ball against Fascism

The most influential presentation of Ball from interwar Communist Party circles came at the end of the period, between 1934 and 1939. The hostility towards Labour, the ILP, and social democrats in the 'Class against Class' line gave way to a sharply different emphasis in the face of rising fascist power. The Communist Party identified the rise of fascism as capitalism's latest desperate weapon, imperialism at its most reactionary, and a hindrance to the suitable conditions for a shift towards socialism. Prompted by Georgi Dimitrov's address to the Seventh Congress of the Comintern,[14] the Popular Front strategy of the late 1930s involved defending democratic states against the threat of a fascist takeover and collaboration partly through developing national, anti-fascist resistance movements. This further meant that the Communist Party, like others in the wider labour movement, were to use homegrown radical traditions to combat fascist appropriations, or those traditions threatened by fascism, and place them into the cultural life of the nation while critiquing the narratives of the ruling class. Nations were to link revolutionary movements of the past with present-day struggles, and infuse national struggles with socialist content, as was happening in the Soviet Union.[15] Political compromises involved

---

13 *The Communist* (24 June 1922).
14 See Georgi Dimitrov, *The Working Class against Fascism* (London: Martin Lawrence, 1935).
15 For summaries of Popular Front strategy, including its relevance for English and British cultural life, and the CPGB in this era, see, e.g., Samuel, 'British Marxist Historians,' 41–42; Noreen Branson, *History of the Communist Party of Great Britain 1927–1941* (London: Lawrence and Wishart, 1985), 110–264;

in upholding the Popular Front manifested themselves in foregrounding the overlaps with the radical religious, liberal, and Whiggish traditions of English history and downplaying the rhetoric of Marxism-Leninism.[16] Interests in the progressive movements tended to focus on *the people* rather than the *proletariat* alone.[17] Nevertheless, Communist propagandizing remained. As the Communist Party historian James Klugmann would later recall shortly before his death in 1977, 'We became no longer just the critics of the insufficiencies of Wat Tyler seen through the eyes of a card-holding peasant...We became the inheritors of the Peasants' Revolt... it linked us with the past and gave us a more correct course for the future.'[18] However, the polemical edge of Robin Page Arnot's reclaiming of Morris and *A Dream of John Ball* in 1934 (see Chapter 17) would, for now, more likely be blunted—at least where it concerned other groups on the English Left.

English Pageantry

Theatrical performance, music (notably 'folk') concerts, and historical or civic pageants (where Ball and the rebels of 1381 were already a known example) were an important and effective part of CPGB propaganda and

---

Kevin Morgan, *Against Fascism and War: Ruptures and Continuities in British Communist Politics 1935–41* (Manchester: Manchester University Press, 1989), 33–68; Francis Beckett, *Enemy Within: The Rise and Fall of the British Communist Party* (Woodbridge: Merlin Press, 1998 [1995]), 60–70; Stephen Woodhams, *History in the Making: Raymond Williams, E.P. Thompson and Radical Intellectuals 1936–1956* (London: Merlin Press, 2001), 23–34; Ben Harker, '"Communism is English": Edgell Rickword, Jack Lindsay and the Cultural Politics of the Popular Front,' *Literature and History* 20 (2011): 16–34; Thomas Linehan, 'Communist Culture and Anti-Fascism in Inter-War Britain,' in Nigel Copsey and Andrzej Olechnowicz (eds.), *Varieties of Anti-Fascism: Britain in the Inter-War Period* (New York: Palgrave Macmillan, 2010), 31–51.

16 Enderby, 'English Radical Tradition,' 191–202; Morgan, *Against Fascism and War*, 40–41.
17 Bill Schwarz, '"The People" in History: The Communist Party Historians Group 1946–56,' in Richard Johnson, Gregor McLennan, Bill Schwartz, and David Sutton (ed.), *Making Histories: Studies in History Writing and Politics* (London: Hutchinson, 1982), 44–95 (55).
18 James Klugmann, 'The Crisis of the Thirties,' in Jon Clark, Margot Heinemann, David Margolies, and Carole Snee (eds.), *Culture and Crisis in Britain in the Thirties* (London: Lawrence and Wishart, 1980), 13–36 (25).

propagandizing of radical traditions in the Popular Front era.[19] Part of the Festival of Music in April 1939, *Music for the People* was a pageant at the end of the era performed at the Royal Albert Hall. It was designed to popularise classical and folk music against high cultural and jingoist dominance and to show that rather than an escape from oppression, music is integral to the long historical and ongoing tradition of fighting oppression for a better future.[20] The idea of the pageant owed much to Alan Bush (who later produced an opera about 1381—see Chapter 19), and featured prominent contributions from, among many others, A. L. Lloyd, the Workers' Music Association, Paul Robeson, and Randall Swingler. The pageant included a Popular Frontist sweep of English, British, European, and American radical history, touching on, for example, Medieval peasant life, Levellers, Diggers, Winstanley, the growth of industrial England, the French Revolution, songs from prisoners in Nazi concentration camps, black American slaves, Chartists, Russian struggles for freedom, Morris, Tom Mann, the (Red) Dean of Canterbury (Hewlett Johnson), and Fred Copeman and International Brigades. Amidst this was an episode dedicated to the Peasants' Revolt led by the revolutionary leaders Ball and Tyler (accompanied by the song, 'Cutty Wren'), effectively representing the beginning of this popular tradition.[21]

19 On pageants, concerts, and rallies, see, e.g., Mick Wallis, 'Pageantry and the Popular Front: Ideological Production in the Thirties,' *New Theatre Quarterly* 38 (May 1994): 132–56; Mick Wallis, 'The Popular Front Pageant: Its Emergence and Decline,' *New Theatre Quarterly* 11 (1995): 17–32; Mick Wallis, 'Heirs to the Pageant: Mass Spectacle and the Popular Front,' in Andy Croft (ed.), *Weapon in the Struggle: The Cultural History of the Communist Party in Britain* (London: Pluto, 1998), 48–67; Raphael Samuel, *The Lost World of British Communism* (London: Verso, 2006), 111; Griffiths, *Labour and the Countryside*, 45; Enderby, 'English Radical Tradition,' 225–39; Tom Hulme, 'Historical Pageants, Neo-Romanticism and the City in Interwar Britain,' in Angela Bartie, Linda Fleming, Mark Freeman, Alexander Hutton, and Paul Readman (eds.), *Restaging the Past: Historical Pageants, Culture and Society in Modern Britain* (London: UCL Press, 2020), 158–79. On Ball and 1381 in historical pageants, music, and performance, see, e.g., *Norwood News* (29 February 1924); *Thanet Advertiser* (8 May 1934); *Thanet Advertiser* (13 July 1934); *Thanet Advertiser* (17 July 1934); *Daily Worker* (6 October 1936); *Gloucester Journal* (19 March 1938); *The Stage* (8 June 1939); *Birmingham Daily Post* (2 August 1939); *Daily Worker* (6 September 1940).
20 Wallis, 'Heirs to the Pageant,' in Croft (ed.), *Weapon in the Struggle*, 58–61.
21 For details, discussion, and synopsis of the pageant, see Angela Bartie, Linda Fleming, Mark Freeman, Tom Hulme, Alex Hutton, and Paul Readman, 'Music for the People,' *The Redress of the Past: Historical Pageants in Britain*,

Prior to this, the Communist Party report to the Central Committee in September 1938 noted the popularity and importance of historical pageants, referencing events in Manchester, Liverpool, Burnley, Glasgow, Dundee, Newcastle, and other towns.[22] Perhaps the most famous was the 'March of History' commemoration in Hyde Park, 20 September 1936.[23] The *Daily Worker* reported between 4,000 and 5,000 people in the procession stretching through London and between 15,000 and 20,000 in Hyde Park. The theme of the Peasants' Revolt begun a history of 'people who have always known when to revolt against tyranny and will always know in the future' and the banners included slogans about fighting for democracy and progress and how the Communist Party 'fights for peace and Socialism and a merry England.'[24] There were banners dedicated to various heroes, including from the revolt and the labour movement.[25] While there was an element of festivity about such pageants, they could also be used for the kinds of martyrological purposes we have seen with understandings of the rise of English socialism. The procession at Hyde Park culminated with the Red Flag and the Spanish flag and a portrait of Felicia Browne, a Communist Party activist who died fighting in Spain. While there were exceptions like Morris, what united much of the radical tradition in the procession was martyrdom at the hands of an oppressive power—though this was hardly a topic alien to Morris. As Thomas Linehan put it, 'the tradition and community represented in the 20 September London pageant…was one that came into being, to a large degree, through the blood sacrifice,' with Browne's portrait endowing 'her blood sacrifice with eschatological purpose, whereby her sacrifice was presented as an important,

---

https://www.historicalpageants.ac.uk/pageants/1132/. For contrasting assessments in the press, see, e.g., *The Times* (3 April 1939); *Manchester Guardian* (6 April 1939); *Daily Worker* (10 April 1939). Cf. *Daily Worker* (3 April 1939); *Daily Worker* (4 April 1939).

22 Communist Party of Great Britain, *Report to the Central Committee to the Fifteenth Party Congress*, Birmingham (16–19 September 1938), available at https://www.marxists.org/history/international/comintern/sections/britain/central_committee/1938/09/report.htm. For discussion of regional and local pageants, see Wallis, 'Heirs to the Pageant,' in Croft (ed.), *Weapon in the Struggle*, 50–52, 57–58.

23 See the Communist Party pamphlet from London District Committee, *The March of English History* (London: Communist Party of Great Britain, 1936). Ball is mentioned on page 4. I am grateful to Phil Katz for giving me access to this pamphlet.

24 *Daily Worker* (21 September 1936).

25 Cf. Samuel, 'British Marxist Historians,' 41–42; Wallis, 'Heirs to the Pageant,' in Croft (ed.), *Weapon in the Struggle*, 48.

even necessary element in that long historical struggle towards arriving at the final liberating goal of freedom from tyranny, whether feudal, Victorian capitalist, or fascist.'[26]

In the late 1930s, Jack Lindsay (1900–1990) brought together ideas of pageantry, performance, poetry, and culture in relation to Popular Front, Englishness, and the appropriation of Ball. Lindsay was born in Melbourne in 1900 and came to London in 1926. He seems to have become a member of the Communist Party in 1941, though from 1936 saw himself as a fellow traveller and there is even the possibility that he joined the party around then.[27] Lindsay was particularly irked by a dismissive *TLS* review of a book on Chartism written by the *Daily Worker* journalist Allen Hunt. The review claimed that a Communist could not understand the English people to which Lindsay replied in the form of a long dramatic poem, 'Not English?' (1936) (soon changed to 'Who Are the English?'), published in *Left Review* and popular enough to be republished as a pamphlet and performed as a Mass Declamation at Unity Theatre, London.[28] In the poem, Lindsay produced an alternative history of leaders and movements and how the ruling class have tried to silence them or put the working class in their place. And the first name called up from history as being defined by the ruling class as not English is Ball who, after giving his Adam and Eve rhyme, is further dismissed as a mere 'peasant.' The poem counters this with talk of avengement and rising up and an English tradition of Cade, Lollards, Anabaptists, Levellers, Muggletonians, Luddites, Chartists, Morris, modern-day workers, General Strike, etc., and calls for workers of the world to unite and for a Socialist or Soviet Republic of England.[29]

---

26 Linehan, 'Communist Culture and Anti-Fascism in Inter-War Britain,' in Copsey and Olechnowicz (eds.), *Varieties of Anti-Fascism*, 45–46.

27 For biographical details, see, e.g., Paul Gillen, 'Jack Lindsay's Romantic Communism,' *Westerly* 36 (1991): 65–77 (65); Harker, 'Communism is English,' 19; Simon Meddick, Liz Payne, and Phil Katz (eds.), *Red Lives* (Croydon: Manifesto Press, 2020), 125–26. Adrian Caesar, *Dividing Lines: Poetry, Class, and Ideology in the 1930s* (Manchester: Manchester University Press, 1991), 211–22.

28 For the story of 'Who Are the English?,' see, e.g., Colin Chambers, *The Story of Unity Theatre* (London: Lawrence and Wishart, 1989), 80–82; Caesar, *Dividing Lines*, 217–21; Wallis, 'Pageantry and the Popular Front,' 141–42; Jack Lindsay, *Who Are the English? Selected Poems: 1935–1981* (Middlesbrough: Smokestack Books, 2014), 9–12; *Morning Star* (28 October 2014); Harker, 'Communism is English,' 22–26.

29 'Who Are the English?,' in Lindsay, *Who Are the English?*, 28–34. 'Soviet' is used in the version in *Left Review* 2 (May 1936), 353–57 (357). Cf. the title of

While there are nods to other nations of Britain (with notable reference to the Clyde and to Rhondda miners), this is an English-centred vision, perhaps reflecting suspicions of Scottish and Welsh nationalism and the imperialism associated with Great Britain.[30]

This was a topic taken up elsewhere by Lindsay (along with Edgell Rickwood) in the late 1930s as part of the socialist or Communist spin on the story of the 'freeborn Englishman' defined in terms of class and political interests rather than some inherent racial qualities.[31] As the war broke out, *England, My England* (1939) was published with the fitting subtitle, *A Pageant of the English People*, which Lindsay claimed not only sold 80,000 copies but also 'had a strong effect in the factories.'[32] Lindsay's pageant in written form pitted the long history of the England of the workers against the England of the rich landowner and ruling class who had done everything to destroy communal forms of living. This was a romantic vision of England and its landscape and culture, and the England of Ball who spoke on village greens, in smoky alehouses, and in churchyards.[33] It was an internationalist vision of an England that had emotional links with people in other lands while national rivalries had come about through capitalism. But there was telling threat from the ruling classes of other countries, no doubt with contemporary resonances. When William and the Normans conquered England, the peasantry were now 'subject aliens as well as a suppressed class' faced with increasingly violent and corrupt lords and a period of English history marked by domination of the land and slavery through serfdom. This was the 'kind of England that the ruling classes have always wanted' and so the school history books do not tell of the 'most important fact in the history of these years': that the land had been stolen from the English.[34]

Lindsay's presentation of the history of resistance to the ruling class has much in common with Communist Party presentations of the time, including the downplaying of the connection between Ball and Wycliffe and the Lollards (who otherwise retain their place in the understanding of the uprising) and the construction of a tradition that not only included Cade, Kett,

---

the programme for the CPGB, *For Soviet Britain* (London: Communist Party of Great Britain, 1935).
30 So Harker, 'Communism is English,' 25–26.
31 Lindsay and Rickword (eds.), *A Handbook of Freedom*, vii, xi–xiii, 26–44.
32 Jack Lindsay, *Fanfrolico and After* (London: Bodley Head, 1962), 274. Cf. Wallis, 'Pageantry and the Popular Front,' 142; Harker, 'Communism is English,' 22
33 Jack Lindsay, *England, My England: A Pageant of the English People* (London: Fore Publications, 1939), 10.
34 Lindsay, *England, My England*, 7–9.

Winstanley, Diggers, Lilburne, Levellers, Paine, Blanketeers, Tolpuddle Martyrs, Chartists, abolitionists, and Morris, but also Tom Mann, Harry Pollitt, and the General Strike. Indeed, for Lindsay, the Communist Party had now appeared, and it represented the 'real tradition of the working class of England, with renewed scientific insight.' But this tradition was now under threat in the imperialist epoch and an increasing encroachment of the 'police-state' and 'the prelude of the English type of Fascism' enabled by capitalism to 'smash the free trade unions.' Nevertheless, there have been new things learned, not least through the struggles of the Soviet Union and in Spain, and now the state has to be used in the period of transition in cooperation with trade unions to safeguard the communal spirit. And it is in England 'as nowhere else' that there has been a 'solidly persisting communist tradition' and, Lindsay concluded, it is time to pick up this tradition of the English people because 'Communism is English.'[35]

The peasants under Ball's leadership also desired communism.[36] And Ball, of course, played an important part in inaugurating this English tradition, and a desire for communism, by fighting a version of this fight, a 'grand united protest of Englishmen against the feudal lords.' He was a 'poor priest' rejected by the 'smug clergy who denied him their pulpits.' He was driven, persecuted, but resolute in his efforts to rouse the English to understand the injustice of class oppression and he wanted 'all enslaved Englishmen' to be free. But for a state of peace to reign in the world, classes must be 'altogether abolished.' Ball was betrayed and killed, like so many others, by those defending private property but faced his accusers with 'all the courage of a great revolutionary' and his memory, the 'true English tradition,' was carried on for centuries after his death. In Lindsay's presentation this had contemporary relevance. The slayers of people like Ball were now 'condemning millions to the dark misery of unemployment, piling up fortunes out of rearmament-programmes, aiding Fascism here and elsewhere, hurling the world once more towards the shambles of war.' There was a simple choice: stand with the England of defiant, staunch freedom or stand with those who would have watched the bowels ripped out of Ball—stand with the workers John Nameless, John the Miller, Jack Carter, Piers Plowman, and John Trueman, against Hob the Robber![37]

---

35 Lindsay, *England, My England*, 62–64.
36 Lindsay, *England, My England*, 19.
37 Lindsay, *England, My England*, 9–16.

A People's History

Part of the broader Popular Front cultural agenda and its interest in English radical history was publishing, including the formation of the popular Left Book Club in 1936. While the seventeenth century was an important reference point for this sort of Popular Front construction of national traditions, Ball and 1381 certainly had a presence. A landmark book in British Marxist and Communist Party history writing (and beyond) and Popular Front propaganda, and a probable inspiration for *Music for the People*, was A. L. Morton's *A People's History of England* (1938) which through Left Book Club networks was distributed to 40,000 members as its monthly choice for May 1938.[38] The epilogue to the first edition was written in light of the seemingly imminent war and criticised British foreign policy for compromises with fascist aggression. But Morton, while aware of what was likely to come, still hoped war could be averted if the workers of Britain especially could unite enough to force its government to stop encouraging such aggressions and stand with France and the Soviet Union to ensure global peace. 'This book ends,' Morton concluded, 'at one of the most critical moments in our history, when more than ever before their own fate and the fate of the world lies in the capacity of the people for right judgment followed by right action.'[39]

There are indications of similar interests at play in Morton's handling of Ball and the 'Peasants' Rising' but which did not lose sight of the bigger Communist picture. Morton stressed that in the face of the Statute of Labourers, the Great Society[40] arose and was an organised 'nation-wide body' which 'prepared a programme of demands that gave a unified character to the rising.' The letters of Ball provided cryptic 'but well understood' messages pointing to careful organisation. It was also a rising that, unlike earlier peasant risings, was not borne out of despair but 'the work of men who had already won a certain measure of freedom and prosperity and were demanding more.' The rebellion gave rise to the peasantry being treated with more respect, to a greater sense of their power and 'common

---

38 Ben Harker, 'Morton, (Arthur) Leslie (1903–1987),' *ODNB* (11 October 2018). On Morton and the pageant, see 'Music for the People.'
39 Morton, *People's History of England*, 527, reflecting the views of the Communist Party. See, e.g., Morgan, *Against Fascism and War*, 57–66.
40 The 'Great Society' was and is a term associated with the revolt dating back to 1381, the significance of which (if any at all) has long been disputed. It remains a contested term among political appropriations of the revolt—see, e.g., Chapter 23.

interests as a class,' and to the longer-term shift from serfdom to free peasant farmers and wage labourers. This standard historical materialist reading was continued in his reading of communism and religion as part of the natural expression of a revolt under feudalism. In addition to the immediate demands of the peasants (end of serfdom, fair rents, and the end to the Statute of Labourers), the rising had a 'background of primitive Communism, strongly Christian in character,' though Morton downplayed the influence of Wycliffe and the Lollards. One of these known 'preachers of Communism' was, of course, Ball. Morton stressed that Ball's prestige among the rebels was 'unquestionably great' but there are hints of Popular Front compromise in Morton's reading, and not just in the repeated national character of the rising. Ultimately, he argued that there was 'no trace of Communism in the demands they presented' and these immediate demands 'were probably a minimum upon which all were agreed.'[41] Indeed, this focus on the agreed rebel demands could likewise assume a shared sympathy among Marxists and non-Marxists alike in Morton's own time, as the history of interpretation strongly supports. It may be significant that the title page to *A People's History of England* has a quotation from *A Dream of John Ball*, appreciating the great transformation in the more distant future despite how the present looks ('Ill would Change be at Whiles, were it not for the Change beyond the Change').[42]

Fagan's *Nine Days that Shook England*

Another publication from the world of the Left Book Club was published the same year and dealt directly with the revolt: *Nine Days that Shook England* (1938) by Hyman Fagan, a CPGB activist from the Jewish East End of London.[43] *Nine Days* is a detailed Marxist analysis of the revolt,

41 Morton, *People's History of England*, 119–20, 124. See also, e.g., A. L. Morton, *The English Utopia* (London: Lawrence & Wishart, 1952), 27.
42 For Morton on *A Dream of John Ball*, see, e.g., Morton, *English Utopia*, 202, 208; A. L. Morton (ed.), *Three Works by William Morris* (London: Lawrence & Wishart, 1968), 22–24.
43 Graham Stevenson, 'Fagan, Hymie,' *Encyclopedia of Communist Biographies* (19 September 2008), https://grahamstevenson.me.uk/2008/09/19/hymie-fagan/; Morgan, Cohen, and Flinn, *Communists and British Society 1920–1991*, 194, 258–59; Megan Ainsworth, 'Hyman Isaac Fagan,' *Writing Lives: Collaborative Research Project on Working-Class Autobiography* (2013–14), http://www.writinglives.org/category/hyman-fagan.

its political social and economic contexts, and its place in the shift from feudalism to capitalism, as well as foregrounding the significance of the Statute of Labourers in causes of the revolt, as was becoming common in such ideological circles. There is also a sustained analysis of religion. To challenge feudalism, Fagan argued, a heretical alternative to established church teachings was required. And the fourteenth century was ready for such challenges as the church was hated on all sides: the barons coveted the wealth of the church, burghers and knights were in competition with the church for workers, and the peasantry saw the church as a ruthless oppressor. Struggling to keep up with the beginnings of the emergence of capitalism, the church became the symbol of all things reactionary. Wycliffe, and his views on dominion and confiscation of church lands, was especially suited to these times and ready to be appropriated by different sides. Fagan stressed that Wycliffe himself supported the baronage and the king and denounced revolutionary readings of his teachings, while his views would take off among burghers in towns and form part of the middle-class heresies in Europe. Like Morton, Fagan downplayed direct connections between the peasants and Wycliffe, but related ideas were found useful in undermining the church. The peasants preferred a return to primitive Christian equality, 'to abolish all divisions in rank and wealth' and to have 'one bishop who would be concerned with only his people and little else,' which would, of course, translate into the demands that Ball be made bishop of England.[44]

But Fagan's book always had an eye on the present, and not just implicitly in the ways in which he framed Ball and the revolt. Throughout the book there are repeated comparisons with twentieth-century issues, movements, and figures, including the Russian Revolution, Bolsheviks, Lenin, vanguardism, royal and ecclesiastical extravagance, British Communists, Versailles, fascism, Hitler, Franco, Spanish Civil War, anti-fascist fighters in Spain and Germany, the General Strike, 1930s unemployment, and monopoly capitalism, to name but few. The very title echoes John Reed's famous account of the 1917 revolution, *Ten Days That Shook the World* (1919). There is also a distinctive feature in the reception of Ball and the revolt: a concern for the fate of Jews. As part of his background analyses, Fagan noted the expulsion of Jews under Edward I for economic reasons, carried out with brutality and malice, including the story of Jews being left to drown by a shipmaster.[45] Fagan wrote of scapegoating and blaming of

---

44 Hyman Fagan, *Nine Days that Shook England: An Account of the English People's Uprising in 1381* (London: Victor Gollancz, 1938), 55; cf. 149, 159.
45 Fagan, *Nine Days*, 26.

Jews in the context of the Black Death, from stories of Jews poisoning wells to 12,000 Jews 'slaughtered in Mainz alone.' The inclusion of a Germanic location might be significant, but he added ominously that the only reason there were no pogroms in England was because Jews had been expelled.[46] With memories of Cable Street still relatively fresh in the popular memory, readers at the end of the 1930s would no doubt have picked up on the threat to Jews at home as well as in central Europe.

As we might expect, Popular Front sentiment is another constant in Fagan's understanding of 1381, particularly in his foregrounding of the Great Society. The Great Society is presented as a highly organised and diverse movement formed in the light of the Statute of Labourers with headquarters in Colchester and then London, bringing together 'bands and confederacies' and able to provide advice and guidance, to discuss tactics, and to run often illegal meetings.[47] The society developed from among those seeking work and higher wages, or fighting worsening conditions, who were 'independent craftsmen,' 'mainly artisans such as tylers, carpenters, slaters, sheepshearers and others.'[48] The society included both wealthier peasants and serfs, anticipating an argument about the different social types among the rebels he would make with his co-author Rodney Hilton. Fagan also distinguished between the plutocrat and the small merchant so that even the Fishmongers' Guild could include members not only in some tension with the wealthy Walworth but with connections to and even within the Great Society.[49] By the time Tyler led the people ('almost to victory'), this was a unified movement of peasants, workers, merchants, and knights 'marching under one banner,' struggling against the 'great lords, bishops and plutocrats,' and with one goal: 'a free and happy England.'[50] Leaders were respected and emerged as local figures with popular support and by the time of the revolt there is a 'Revolutionary Committee' calling for a 'united attack upon power, privilege, corruption and mis-rule, and for the defence of the lives of the common people of England.'[51] Explicit connections are made with the present and not just the Bolsheviks. The book ends with reference to the 'great responsibility' resting on the shoulders of 'all progressive peoples': they must save England from being destroyed by another 'decaying ruling class' and turn it into a 'land of peace, freedom

---

46 Fagan, *Nine Days*, 57.
47 Fagan, *Nine Days*, 101.
48 Fagan, *Nine Days*, 20.
49 Fagan, *Nine Days*, 84.
50 Fagan, *Nine Days*, 106, 143.
51 Fagan, *Nine Days*, 146; cf. 184–86.

and social equality.' And this patriotism, of course, inspired the 'greatest English patriots' like Ball.[52]

Ball was a central figure for Fagan, one of the respected leaders and the 'greatest theoretician and agitator' of the movement.[53] Indeed, he also published a summary article in the *Daily Worker* the same year under the title 'Britain's First Revolutionary' which featured a picture of a stern, well-fed Ball, quite the opposite of the under-fed Ball of Fleetwood-Walker's mural from the same year, though not unprecedented.[54] We might add that the *Daily Worker* picture does not follow Morris's physical description (including nose size), quoted in *Nine Days*.[55] But if the physical description of Ball was hardly Fagan's driving interest, the *Daily Worker* headline was: Fagan's Ball was indeed the first great English revolutionary and preacher of class struggle in *Nine Days*. In numerous purples passages, Fagan lauds Ball's preaching of class struggle, organising, agitation, steadfastness in the face of death, for providing hope for those suffering and stirring up a belief in a better future.[56]

Through the figure of Ball, Fagan arguably developed something running throughout *Nine Days*: an implicit case for Communist leadership of the diverse movement in the present. The diversity of the fourteenth-century movement was both a great strength and a great weakness, he argued. The common bond 'forged a unity' which made for a 'powerful force' while there were often antagonistic, conflicting interests. Ball's speeches may have expressed the discontents but there was still no dominant class 'able to take the leadership and to provide that theoretical basis which might have overcome the existent divergent views.'[57] It is striking that Fagan compared Tyler with Harry Pollitt (General Secretary of the CPGB) and William Gallagher (CPGB founder member and MP), Ball with Tom Mann (CPGB founder member with an International Brigades battalion named after him), and the 1381 leadership with Communist leadership before the General Strike. After all, both Ball and Mann (of whom Ball would have been 'rightly proud') were framed by the authorities, arrested under similar laws, answered their persecutors bluntly, and, as part of this

---

52 Fagan, *Nine Days*, 278.
53 Fagan, *Nine Days*, 142.
54 E.g., the Friar Tuck-style Ball on a postcard from a 1907 St Albans pageant, available at 'The Red Dagger, Part 1,' *International Times* (December 2013), http://internationaltimes.it/the-red-dagger-pt-1/.
55 *Daily Worker* (19 July 1938); Fagan, *Nine Days*, 109–10 (cf. 105).
56 Fagan, *Nine Days*, 75–76, 103, 109, 112.
57 Fagan, *Nine Days*, 117.

'organic link with the insurrection of 1381,' both functioned in similar economic crises.[58]

Ball's letters were even compared with Lenin's ideas and actions (which feature regularly in *Nine Days*). The letters may have been written in the 'mystical phraseology of the period' and 'steeped in religious sentiment' but they still clearly gave 'practical revolutionary advice' and even indirect calls for 'armed insurrection of the English masses.' Their coded nature was necessary for covert organisation and the 'combination of legal and illegal methods, upon which Lenin was so insistent.'[59] For Fagan, the most obvious historical point of comparison for Ball's letters was 'those urgent letters of advice and instruction sent by Lenin to the Bolsheviks when he was forced to hide in the Finnish marshes.' Ball's letters played a similarly urgent role in that he moved the 'English masses' into action.[60] But there were further comparisons made between the discipline promoted in Ball's John Shepe letter and semi-feudal societies of Fagan's present, notably Spain, and the importance of the right kind of leadership. Fagan stressed that it was important for revolutionaries, especially from the peasantry, to have one leader, strict discipline, and 'politically reliable comrades' rather than 'dozens of self-elected busybodies all giving confusing and conflicting orders.' The Great Society functioned as the vanguard for this disciplined movement in the fourteenth century. But then Fagan immediately turned to examples like Spain of chaotic fighting and retreating, provinces fighting for themselves 'without bothering about the rest of the country as a whole.' The revolution instead needs to bring victories together against a united ruling class and this is why 'a disciplined unified party of the working class is so necessary if the modern proletarian movements are to carry out their historic tasks.'[61]

From World War to Cold War

The ongoing influence of Popular Front thinking went far beyond 1939, even after the fallout from the Soviet-Nazi non-aggression pact, and a

58 Fagan, *Nine Days*, 125–26, 145. Pollitt himself reviewed *Nine Days* in the *Daily Worker* (10 August 1938).
59 Fagan, *Nine Days*, 129–30.
60 Fagan, *Nine Days*, 134–35.
61 Fagan, *Nine Days*, 131–32. Compare the conclusion to the review of *Nine Days* in *Labour Monthly* (December 1938) with echoes of Morris: 'Let the leaders of the labour movement have faith in the labouring class that the dream of John Ball may become at last reality.'

broadly understood radical tradition on the Left was already firmly established. When the Second World War was underway, the example of Spain was hardly forgotten. One war-time letter defended the International Brigades in Spain and those who died or were injured 'in that glorious attempt to stem the tide of Fascism.' They fought in 'a country strange to them for their ideals' and this internationalism belonged to the 'same fundamental principles as John Ball and Wat Tyler fought for more than five centuries before.' All the while, the 'democratic nations' led by Britain not only applied non-intervention rather than support the legally elected Spanish government but also prevented the Spanish government from buying weapons for self-defence.[62] And, of course, there were obvious continuities between Popular Front thinking about the English radical tradition and the idea of the People's War.[63] Against the backdrop of bombed towns and Coventry in ruins, Ball, Tyler, and 'the martyrs of Smithfield'—alongside the tradition from the 'barons at Runnymede' through the age of Cromwell to the Tolpuddle martyrs, thousands of unnamed trade unionists and Morris—were now invoked by the socialist and spiritualist Hannen Swaffer in support of the war effort. Now was the time, he encouraged, to follow the predecessors in envisaging, no matter how dimly, a better future and to become part of that very tradition for the 'children of the unborn years.'[64] But the Popular Front era directly influenced our next stage of the reception of Ball after the Second World War and understandings of an English radical tradition emerging from the Communist Party Historians' Group, of which Morton was a central figure. Yet the Cold War also meant that Communist interpretations were now going to be especially sensitive amidst the post-war competing understandings of the legacy of 1381.

---

62 *Mid-Sussex Times* (20 February 1940). A retort claimed that the Spanish government would have in fact killed Ball and Tyler: *Mid-Sussex Times* (27 February 1940).
63 Cf. Chambers, *Unity Theatre*, 228–62; John Field, 'Survival, Growth and Retreat: The WEA in Wartime, 1939–45', in Stephen K. Roberts (ed.), *A Ministry of Enthusiasm: Centenary Essays on the Workers' Educational Association* (Pluto Press, London, 2003), 131–52 (131–32).
64 *The People* (24 November 1940). For an overview of Swaffer, see Linton Andrews, 'Swaffer (Frederic Charles) Hannen (1879–1962)', *ODNB* (14 November 2018).

19
Cold War Ball

From an East End Jewish background, for cab driver, wartime firefighter, socialist, and popular historian Charles Poulsen (1911–2001), the 1930s were relatively conventional.[1] He started the decade in the Young Communist League (YCL) followed by the Communist Party of Great Britain (CPGB), and he stood against the British Union of Fascists at Cable Street. He even helped start the League of the Militant Godless, though his attitude towards religion would mellow. And, of course, he was interested in Ball, the 1381 revolt, and the English radical tradition, an interest which remained throughout his life.[2] After an argument with a fellow firefighter about English history, the constitution, popular representative democracy, and violent revolution, Poulsen wrote about this period of the English radical past, completing some of it on stolen toilet paper.[3] *English Episode* was published in 1946 and reworked as a play, *The Word of a King*, for Unity Theatre (1951), starring Colin Pinney as Ball and David Evans as Wat Tyler.[4] The play added to Unity's interest in a homegrown radicalism with Poulsen wanting to show that 'revolutionary ideas were not foreign to Britain' and 'Ball's speeches as the first in Europe to propound a socialist

---

1 See, e.g., *Guardian* (14 December 2001); Graham Stevenson, 'Poulsen, Charles', *Encyclopedia of Communist Biographies* (20 September 2008), https://grahamstevenson.me.uk/2008/09/20/charles-poulsen/; John T. Connor, 'Historical Turns in Twentieth-Century Fiction', in Robert DeMaria Jr., Heesok Chang, and Samantha Zacher (eds.), *A Companion to British Literature, Volume 4: Victorian and Twentieth-Century Literature, 1837–2000* (Oxford: Wiley-Blackwell, 2014), 314–32 (317–18).
2 See, e.g., Charles Poulsen, *The English Rebels* (London: Journeyman, 1984), 1–44.
3 Andy Croft, 'Writers, the Communist Party and the Battle of Ideas, 1945–1950', *Socialist History* 5 (1995): 2–25; Connor, 'Historical Turns in Twentieth-Century Fiction', in DeMaria, Jr., Chang, and Zacher (eds.), *A Companion to British Literature, Volume 4*, 314–32 (317–18).
4 Charles Poulsen, *English Episode: A Tale of the Peasants' Revolt of 1381* (London: Progress, 1946).

and egalitarian vision of society.'[5] The play's title was part of a now established tradition of Richard II's deceit and he was not the first (nor the last) to include Chaucer, reported as 'telling fruity stories at Richard II's court.'[6] In some ways, this was nothing new in socialist readings of 1381. Yet there was something distinctive about the publicity it received in the post-war *Daily Worker*'s advocacy of homegrown culture. Barbara Niven stressed in her promotion of the play that part of its aim and of Unity was to 'go deep under Yankee skins' and be 'equally painful to Yankee yes-men of this country.' *The Word of a King*, she claimed, 'brings out in all its colour and force our national fighting tradition, with its story of the Peasants' Revolt of 1381 and of Wat Tyler and John Ball.' This fight to 'maintain our progressive cultural tradition these days' also involved supporting the *Daily Worker*, which 'alone among British newspapers ... defends national independence and fights back with facts and comment against the poison of Yankee "culture".'[7] New enemies would now dominate as the world moved towards the Cold War and as Britain was experiencing ever more American cultural influence.

But the world in which the revolt was now going to be framed was changing in other ways. Stephen Basdeo argued that from the Second World War onwards, Tyler 'almost disappears from popular culture,' speculating that Attlee's Labour government, and its social and economic reforms and establishment of a longer-term post-war political consensus carried on by the Conservatives under Anthony Eden and Harold MacMillan, meant that there were 'fewer reasons for the radical ghost of Tyler to emerge during the mid-twentieth century.'[8] This needs some qualification, and certainly if we are to apply this argument to Ball. For a start, there was a steady stream of post-war novels set against the backdrop of the revolt or which discuss Ball in some way.[9] Moreover, in 1948 the Labour Party published

5   Chambers, *Unity Theatre*, 323. Cf. *Daily Worker* (2 March 1951); *Daily Worker* (3 May 1951); *The Stage* (10 May 1951); *Daily Worker* (18 May 1951); *Kensington Post* (25 May 1951).
6   *Truth* (11 May 1951).
7   *Daily Worker* (13 June 1951). 'The USA threat to British culture' was the title of a conference held on 29 April 1951, under the auspices of the CPGB's National Cultural Commission, the proceedings being published in *Arena*, New Series 2.8 (June/July 1951) and edited by Jack Lindsay. I am grateful to Martin Levy for pointing this out.
8   Basdeo, *Life and Legend of a Rebel Leader*, loc 3320.
9   E.g., Neil Bell [Stephen Southwold], *The Immortal Dyer: A Novel of the Life and Times of Jeff Lister, King of the Commons, the Pride of Norfolk* (London: Redman, 1964 [London: Robert Hale, 1948]); William Woods, *Thunder on*

a 'New Appreciation' of the *Communist Manifesto* by Harold Laski for its centenary. The foreword by the Labour Party has Ball at the beginning of a British socialist tradition geared firmly toward Labour and with the familiar internationalist connections:

> The British Labour Party has its roots in the history of Britain. The Levellers, Chartists, Christian Socialists, the Fabians and many other bodies, all made it possible to carry theory into practice. John Ball, Robert Owen, William Morris, Keir Hardie, John Burns, Sydney Webb, and many more British men and women have played outstanding parts in the development of socialist thought and organisation. But British socialists have never isolated themselves from their fellows on the continent of Europe. Our own ideas have been different from those of continental socialism which stemmed more directly from Marx, but we, too, have been influenced in a hundred ways by European thinkers and fighters, and, above all, by the authors of the Manifesto.[10]

The Prime Minister Clement Attlee himself provided the foreword to Francis Williams's *Fifty Years' March: The Rise of the Labour Party* (1949), where it was claimed that the 'history of socialism in Britain goes back through the soil of the centuries…to the Christian communism of John Wyclif, to John Ball, the hedge priest' who 'died on the gallows' as a lesson to those 'who should ask disturbing questions.'[11]

Saturday (London: Andrew Melrose, 1952); Anya Seton, *Katherine* (London: Hodder and Stoughton, 1954); T. H. White, *Candle in the Wind* (London: Collins 1958); Philip Lindsay, *The Golden Cage* (London: Robert Hale, 1961); Prudence Andrew, *The Earthworms* (London: Hutchinson, 1963); Charles E. Israel, *Who Was Then the Gentleman?* (London: Macmillan and Co, 1963); H. E. Priestley, *Swords over Southdowne* (London: Frederick Muller, 1964).

10 Harold J. Laski (ed.), *Communist Manifesto: Socialist Landmark* (London: George Allen and Unwin, 1948), 6.

11 Francis Williams, *Fifty Years' March: The Rise of the Labour Party* (London: Odhams Press, 1949), 111. Ball could also resonate among Irish socialists and writers. Seán O'Casey (followed by Dominic Behan) criticised George Orwell for (among other things) a lack of originality, claiming that *Animal Farm* owed much to another man of the English establishment, John Gower. In *Vox Clamantis*, O'Casey noted, Gower revealed how 'he was frightened near to death by the peasants led by Wat Tyler and John Ball' (see Chapter 3). See Seán O'Casey, *Sunset and Evening Star* (New York: Macmillan, 1954), 139–140. For Dominic Behan's use of O'Casey, see *Irish Times* (13 October 1972). I am grateful here for the help of Frankie Gaffney.

Williams, of course, included Morris in his Labour mythology.[12] The incorporation of Morris was nothing new, nor in Labour's intellectual circles was the use of that Attlee favourite, *A Dream of John Ball*. G. D. H. Cole's *History of Socialist Thought* (1954) presented Morris in tension with anarchism and hostile to parliamentarism, claiming instead that he 'began to build up a political movement more closely related to the actual claims and interests of the workers enrolled in the new Unions of the gasworkers, dockers, and other less skilled groups.' Moreover, Cole argued that Morris somewhat grudgingly accepted that state socialism might have to be a part of a necessary transitional stage, comparable to the Leninist notion of the withering away of the state. But, in contrast to Lenin, this 'Morrisite Socialism,' Cole suggested, 'has much in common, not with Anarchism pure and simple, but with Anarchist-Communism' in that it looks to a society when 'governmental institutions will have totally disappeared, and such organisation as survives will arise out of the spontaneous activities of free groups.' Morris's socialism according to Cole arose out of a 'deep passion for fellowship and social equality' as expressed in Ball's sermon at the cross in *A Dream of John Ball*.[13] As Cole's reading already implies, Morris and Ball continued to have wider currency on the Left. We might, for instance, note that the English translation of an extract of Rudolf Rocker's memoirs of his time at the heart of anarchism in the East End of London—where he claimed Morris and *A Dream of John Ball* for an English libertarian socialist tradition—was published in 1956.[14]

It was, however, Communist Party members who were especially active in promoting Ball's memory, including via Morris and through the activities of Robin Page Arnot (see Chapter 17).[15] Arnot continued to stress that Morris was a 'revolutionary socialist' and used *A Dream of John Ball* (among other evidence) to counter 'the bourgeois myth' of Morris-the-great-Victorian and the now relabelled 'Menshevik myth' (formerly the 'Labour Party-ILP myth') of Morris as a 'gentle socialist.'[16] *A Dream of John Ball* 'is revolutionary' and Arnot made clear that it provided a historical materialist and Marxist argument in promoting 'faith in the struggle of the

---

12 Williams, *Fifty Years' March*, 51–62.
13 Cole, *A History of Socialist Thought, Volume II*, 418–19.
14 Rocker, *The London Years*, 102–3.
15 On Morris's memory among Arnot and the CPGB in the 1950s, see, e.g., Helen E. Roberts, 'Commemorating William Morris: Robin Page Arnot and the Early History of the William Morris Society,' *Journal of William Morris Studies* 11 (1995): 33–37.
16 R. Page Arnot, *William Morris: The Man and The Myth* (London: Lawrence and Wishart, 1964), 10–12.

workers and their ultimate victory.'[17] The *Daily Worker* also continued the tradition in the socialist press of promoting Ball (and Morris), not least through the efforts of T. A. Jackson.[18] There was also a wider interest in Ball beyond Morris in the *Daily Worker*. In one column, Andrew Rothstein noted the significance of the location of the Marx Memorial Library, pointing out that Clerkenwell Green was the same area where 'the rebel peasants of East Anglia in 1381, led by Jack Straw and John Ball, burned St John's Priory.'[19] Ball was again compared with the stories of Robin Hood—both, it was claimed in one article, sharing the English tradition of primitive communism.[20] A Rodney Hilton article in the *Daily Worker* gave Ball another political spin as Hilton critiqued monarchy as a relic of feudalism (part of a series critiquing the queen's coronation) accompanied by a picture of the lino-engraving by Ern Brooks ('The Freeing of John Ball') featuring peasants freeing a bearded and determined-looking Ball from prison.[21]

However, it remains clear at least from newspaper searches that the interest in Ball in the wider press did diminish sharply from the 1940s onward. Ball may have been popular in the radical press but that was past its heyday, leaving his legacy mainly to the *Daily Worker/Morning Star*. Otherwise, the most typical reference to Ball is found with reference to general antiquarian and local history interests, popular history books, the occasional pageant, and even a light-hearted school play.[22] Basdeo may have a point that Attlee's post-war consensus played its part. Indeed, the socialism or communism associated with Morris (and thus Ball) in many

---

17 Arnot, *William Morris: The Man and The Myth*, 123.
18 E.g., *Daily Worker* (31 July 1950); *Daily Worker* (28 June 1950); *Daily Worker* (9 November 1950); *Daily Worker* (3 March 1953). Cf. *Daily Worker* (3 October 1946).
19 *Daily Worker* (22 April 1953).
20 *Daily Worker* (21 November 1953).
21 *Daily Worker* (11 May 1953). Cf. *Daily Worker* (23 April 1952). On earlier republican interpretations of 1381, see Taylor, *London's Burning*, 183 n. 15. As ever, versions of the illustration of Ball from the Froissart manuscript, with a striking nose, continued, see, e.g., G. R. Kesteven, *The Peasants' Revolt* (London: Chatto & Windus, 1965), 41.
22 E.g., *Essex Newsman* (17 June 1947); *Chelmsford Chronicle* (20 June 1947); *Thanet Advertiser* (23 January 1948); *Taunton Courier* (22 May 1948); *Leicester Chronicle* (21 July 1961); *Taunton Courier* (25 August 1962); Kesteven, *Peasants' Revolt*, 13, 31, 47, 48, 74, 85–86. Cf. *The Times* (28 July 1949); *Guardian* (16 May 1951); *The Times* (13 June 1960). Tyler and the revolt were also given sympathetic treatment in the children's educational magazine *Look and Learn* (14 July 1962), where the rebels even have Soviet-looking sickles.

of the influential receptions of Ball sat uneasily with Labour Party understandings, hence Attlee's critical reflections and awareness of the tensions between Morris's *A Dream of John Ball* and Attlee's world of political compromise and technological development.[23] This tension was exposed, for instance, when Morgan Phillips tried to explain his famous quip about British socialism owing more to Methodism than to Marxism by bringing Morris into the discussion of such a non-revolutionary 'ethical' and 'religious' tradition. Phillips was soon met with Communist rebuttal from Jackson, who pointed not only to Morris's Marxism but also to Ball as an exemplar of an English revolutionary tradition now continued by the Communist Party.[24] Others associated with Labour tried to hold the ideological tensions together, as the example of Cole's reading of Morris and *A Dream of John Ball* noted above shows.

The association with Communism became particularly problematic as the Cold War was underway, and this too may have contributed to the declining public presentations, as we will see. There may also have been basic generational issues involved in this 'decline': a generation that were brought up on Morris and Victorian and Edwardian medievalism were dying out (Jackson, for instance, died in 1955 and Cole in 1959) while Rocker's reminiscences—including the influence of Morris—were largely of East End Yiddish anarchism of a bygone era towards the end of Rocker's life. In his centenary edition of Morris's works (1934, and republished in 1948), even Cole was already wondering whether the 'medieval setting' of *A Dream of John Ball* 'puts some of us off in these days; for we cannot quite believe in Morris' Middle Ages.'[25] In 1944, Mary Epstein doubted whether the 'majority of working people have drawn much inspiration' from the 'ancestors of the British Communist Party' such as Ball, Thomas More, and the Levellers, whose presence looked 'artificial' amidst the 'history which the average person remembers.'[26] Perhaps the reviewer of Philip Lindsay and Reg Groves's *The Peasants' Revolt 1381* (1950) was not alone in thinking that the cast of characters was now but 'names vaguely remembered from one's schooldays.'[27] Yet however we measure the extent of this 'decline,' it remains that popular presentations of Ball were continuing after the war in

23 Bew, *Citizen Clem*, loc 1278–1308, 1826–1858, 10767–10798.
24 *Daily Worker* (28 June 1950); *Daily Worker* (31 July 1950).
25 G. D. H. Cole, 'Introduction,' in William Morris, *Selected Writings* (ed. G.D. H. Cole; London: Nonesuch Press, 1934), xi–xxiv (xviii).
26 Mary Epstein, 'Our National Traditions,' *Party Organisation and the Invasion* (London: Communist Party of Great Britain, 1944), 21.
27 *Truth* (17 November 1950).

different strands of the Left. While the influence of the Popular Front era remained, they were now shifting and transforming, particularly in light of developments in the Soviet Union and the emerging Cold War.

Cider with Balle

Though famed among a generation of teenage schoolchildren for *Cider with Rosie* (1959), Laurie Lee wrote a near forgotten verse play in six scenes about 'John Balle' and the uprising, *Peasants' Priest*, which was performed between 21 and 28 June 1947 at the post-war resurrection of the Canterbury Cathedral Festival.[28] As with Poulsen and his reception, the world of pre-war anti-fascism and the emerging Cold War had to be navigated accordingly. Following his somewhat whimsical journey to Spain with his violin (1935–1936), Lee soon returned wanting to fight fascism and join the International Brigades. This meant that Lee was inevitably connected with Communist Party networks and he was recognised as a reliable comrade and communist. But while he would become associated with progressive causes in his life, his activity in Spain was not, as his biographer Valerie Grove put it, because he was 'politically obsessed,' and he later claimed he went because of guilt about what was happening to his Spanish friends.[29] Of his return to London, Jane Mack speculated Lee might have seen *Music for the People* in 1939 (see Chapter 18), additionally noting that the International Brigades commander Fred Copeman, who featured in the pageant, had organised a strike at a building site where Lee had worked and had also inspected Lee's contingent in Spain.[30] Irrespective of whether we can make precise connections with his time in Spain and associations with British Communism, this background played its part in Lee's handling of a subject so central to Communist propaganda in the Popular Front era.

In some ways, *Peasants' Priest* is a conventional explanation of the causes of uprising (Black Death, foreign wars, undefended coasts, poll tax,

---

28 Kenneth W. Pickering, *Drama in the Cathedral: The Canterbury Festival Plays 1928–1948* (Worthing: Churchman Publishing, 1985), 267–87 (on Lee's dislike of the play and its lack of revival since 1947, see 267–68); Jane Mack, 'Introduction,' in Laurie Lee, *Three Plays* (Cheltenham: Cyder Press, 2003), i–xvi.

29 Valerie Grove, *Laurie Lee: The Well-Loved Stranger* (London: Viking, 1999), 90–99, 105–110, 293, 378, 431–32, 484, 517, quotation 90.

30 Mack, 'Introduction,' in Lee, *Three Plays*, iii. Cf. Laurie Lee, *As I Walked Out One Midsummer Morning* (New York: Atheneum, 1969), 38–42.

resentment towards inequality, etc.) and the presentation of the rebellion itself, with the potentially ill-disciplined rebels gathering around the banner of St George and in need of their leaders. Among the king's advisors, Salisbury acknowledges that these are the 'country hands of England' who joined a 'solemn purpose' to redress 'a list of ancient wrongs' (Scene 5), perhaps hinting at the constitutionalist tradition of the Norman Yoke and lost Anglo-Saxon rights. We likewise get a conventional understanding of Balle. We hear of a priest and preacher of equality who was a 'poorly man, lean as a stave,/rough as a wolf, and brilliant of eye' (Scene 1).[31] Balle himself ('the sainted man,' Scene 4) is stoic, resolute, and undaunted in the prison and in his arguments with the jailor Friar—a notable contrast to the near-broken imprisoned Ball of Halcott Glover's *Wat Tyler* but a nonetheless familiar trait in the literary history of the presentation of the revolt. Balle has a devoted following and the teaching of the peasant priest permeates the rebellion, including the regular allusions to the language of his letters. The final words of the play are from the arresting Sergeant who proclaims that the 'Rebellion's bread was leavened by this yeast:/take him away, he was the peasants' priest' (Scene 6). Thus, if Tyler (who is not a character, at least not when alive) represents the sword of the revolt, then Balle is its sceptre (Scene 2). Whether the play can be strictly categorised as pro-Protestant is debateable but there is a strong attack on the perceived greed and corruption of popes and bishops, on the use of doggerel Latin, and on the splendour of the physical church which is contrasted with the church of the people, peasants, serfs, and poor who have Christ as their brother (Scenes 2, 4, 6). Nevertheless, in keeping with the letters associated with Ball, Mary is still invoked on different occasions (e.g., Scenes 2, 6).

The play also takes seriously the problem of failure of honourable ideals in need of future fulfilment and, like its famed Festival predecessor (T. S. Eliot's *Murder in the Cathedral* [1935]), *Peasants' Priest* deals with the struggles of an archbishop of Canterbury (portrayed with some sympathy by Lee) and the issues of martyrdom, in this case Balle's. The interlude at the end of the fourth scene has the comic Green Mask and the tragic Yellow Mask foretell the inevitable tragic failure of the revolt. The hopes and fears for the future are cast in the conventional language of light and dark ('Look to your hopes and keep them bright…weep not for his day's dark ending') and tied in with the equally conventional understanding of

---

31 A photograph of Bernard Miles as Balle is available in Pickering, *Drama in the Cathedral*, 287. Quotations are taken from Lee, *Three Plays*, 1–57. On the editing of the wording by the producer Martin Browne, see Pickering, *Drama in the Cathedral*, 268–69, 280–81.

Balle as martyr—indeed the play ends with Balle being arrested and taken away. In his discussion with Martha, who is worried about his safety, Balle explains that even if they kill him, or indeed all of them, they cannot kill the real heart of the rebellion, pointing to the analogous example of Christ's redemptive suffering. To add to the dramatic decisions of the martyr, Balle (quite the opposite of the lustful rebels of earlier receptions) turns down the offer of love and the opportunity to flee with Martha. After ensuring she escapes, Ball finishes by framing the question 'What have we won?' in terms of a lesson for the future, no matter how dimly lit hope may appear. Like foxes emerging from holes, 'we've proved/the sun is up, the angels walk the grass,/that there's still heaven to be won on earth.' 'Love' might be the trick needed to win but for now it means hiding away again, a retreat back to the darkness (Scene 6).

No doubt Lee's experiences in Spain were entangled with his understanding of Balle and no doubt the recent war experiences of the audiences were too. But there are the other nuances to the presentation of Balle's ideas worth noting. When Balle speaks about equality, lost freedoms, and Adam and Eve, there is a familiar turn of phrase. Echoing Rousseau's famous words, people are now 'laying in chains' despite the claim that 'Man was born free' (Scene 4), and a 'slave once free, though for a day,' has tasted the air of emancipation which will 'keep him forever free, though he be chained/far heavier than before' (Scene 6). But while the general Popular Front background (which included the representation of revolutionary France in *Music for the People*) would have provided an important influence, we do not get the implicit propagandistic subtext of the pageant or publications of the 1930s. Kenneth Pickering detected hints of reference to 'international and industrial relations' (e.g., in Salisbury's duplicity) yet concluded that '*Peasants' Priest* does not contain specific social comment but it is certainly there by implication.'[32] Put another way, Lee's critique of feudal oppression does not point to a precise ideological tendency and should probably be located broadly in the liberal and radical traditions. Among the constraints of the setting felt by Lee,[33] his presentation of Balle would have helped in negotiating a conservative setting like Canterbury Cathedral which also hosted the controversial 'Red Dean' of Canterbury and supporter of the Soviet Union, Hewlett Johnson.

---

32 Pickering, *Drama in the Cathedral*, 286.
33 Pickering, *Drama in the Cathedral*, 267–68.

Tankie or Trot? Legacies of Thaxted

The Thaxted experiment, and the accompanying appropriation of Ball, did not cease with the death in 1942 of that other controversial red clergyman Conrad Noel (see Chapter 17), though its legacy did split into two major ideological tendencies on the Left: Marxism-Leninism of the Soviet Union and Trotskyism. Noel's successor at Thaxted (from 1942 to 1973), the socialist Jack Putterill (1892–1980), maintained and developed the distinctive worship tradition combined with political engagement (fittingly he was a Labour activist and chaired a branch of the National Union of Agricultural Workers). Where he differed from Noel was that he continued to be impressed with developments in the Soviet Union in the Stalin era (and beyond), including leading prayers for Stalin in 1953 and supporting Soviet actions in Hungary and Czechoslovakia.[34] More mundanely, when recalling Thaxted, Putterill mentioned a woodcut by Burne-Jones illustrating Ball's Adam and Eve saying and the brass lamp in the John Ball Chapel inscribed with a dedication to Catholic Crusader Desmond O'Neill and also featuring the couplet.[35] He also recalled his time as a Labour councillor on Essex County Council and the 'huge picture of John Ball' (Bernard Fleetwood-Walker's *John Ball and the Peasants' Rising of 1381*—see Chapter 17) which 'particularly pleased' him, though he thought Ball was inaccurately made to look like a Dominican friar (at this point in the history of reception, Ball's Catholic dress was typically presented in terms of its 'medieval-ness' rather than consistency over, or precise interest in, affiliation). He wished the Tory-dominated councillors could have heard one of Ball's sermons so that they might 'read, learn and digest' Morris's *A Dream of John Ball*.[36]

Putterill located Ball and Thaxted in a long English tradition (note the title of his pamphlet: *John Ball and the Dragon*)[37] and internationalist tradition of striving for the kingdom, fellowship, and justice, from the Bible through Lenin and the Soviet Union and pointing to a distant future when 'final perfection is achieved.'[38] He also provided a general Morris-style

---

34 See further Arthur Burns, 'Putterill, John Cyril [Jack] (1892–1980),' *ODNB* (4 October 2012).
35 Putterill, *Thaxted Quest for Social Justice: The Autobiography of Fr Jack Putterill, Turbulent Priest and Rebel* (Marlow: Precision Press, 1977), 33, 82.
36 Putterill, *Thaxted Quest for Social Justice*, 101–2.
37 Jack Putterill, *John Ball and the Dragon* (Saffron Walden: Rev. J. C. Putterill, 1964).
38 Jack Putterill, *Thaxted Quest for Social Justice*, 132–49.

historical materialist framework for understanding the ongoing significance of Ball who had 'died a martyr in the cause of emancipation of the people in their fight against the Dragon of Exploitation.' This was part of a changing England as serfdom gradually disappeared and, with the transformation to capitalism, peasants were 'no longer tied to the land' but instead began to live 'by selling their labour' which proved 'a cruel struggle' involving 'hunger unemployment, starvation and the gallows.' The only response to this was the creation of trade unionism started by the Tolpuddle six and continued through to the National Union of Agricultural Workers. But, Putterill argued, struggling for better pay and conditions for workers was not enough; what was needed for workers was the 'rightful ownership and control in the land of their birth.' Thus, he could add to Ball's famous saying about things not going well in England until all things were held in common, and continuing the connection with the feudal fourteenth century in the future transition to socialism: 'until, that is, the Dragon of EXPLOITATION in every form and disguise has been overthrown and slain.'[39]

In addition to his background with Noel in the Catholic Crusade and Christian socialism, and an ongoing desire to perpetuate the ideals and memory of Thaxted,[40] Reginald Groves (1908–1988) was involved in the bitter Trotskyite split from the Communist Party in the 1930s and would retain a hostility to the CPGB and to all things Stalin, as well as having a lifelong but uneasy relationship with Trotskyism. He later recalled his role in the split as a 'confused, and certainly hopeless protest...Yet it is right that it should be recorded; and the names remembered of the handful who spoke out against the destruction of true socialism and communism.'[41] This combination of near unattainable ideals and heroic failure was a theme elsewhere in his political life. Groves worked with and for the Labour Party, even standing as a prospective parliamentary candidate in 1938 (coming third) and again in 1945, 1950, 1951, and 1955 (repeatedly coming second). Despite never likely to win outright, they were all deemed credible performances given the constraints. As part of his concern to develop socialism in the countryside, his interests in these constituencies were precisely because they were rural and difficult seats to win.[42] This theme of a

---

39 Putterill, *John Ball and the Dragon*.
40 Groves, *Conrad Noel and the Thaxted Movement*.
41 Reg Groves, *The Balham Group: How British Trotskyism Began* (Pluto: London, 1974), foreword.
42 John McIlroy, 'Groves, Reginald Percy (Reg) (1908–1988): Communist, Trotskyist, Christian Socialist, Labour Historian and Labour Party

heroic struggle/failure against odds came through in his publications on rural struggle, notably in *The Peasants' Revolt 1381* (1950), co-written with Philip Lindsay, and where Ball features strongly. As John McIlroy put it, 'If he [Groves] was no more successful than the long line he venerated, from John Ball through Julian Harney to Conrad Noel, his consolation was that he would be remembered as a worthy member of the distinguished fellowship of English revolutionaries.'[43]

Peasants' Revolt 1381 is a romanticised narrative history which stands in some contrast to the detailed historical-materialist framing of *The English Rising of 1381* by Communist Party historians Hyman Fagan and Rodney Hilton, also published in 1950 (see Chapter 20). Indeed, the Christ-like portrayal of Ball is arguably the most hagiographical in the history of Ball's reception and one of the clearest examples of Ball in the tradition of the Great Man of history. In the absence of a portrait, the reader is encouraged to 'picture him as he desires,' as the authors seemed to. Ball was probably 'lean' because of a lack of 'fattening food or rich wine.' His eyes 'would have shone bright with the faith that upheld him.' His skin was probably 'brown' and leathery because he walked 'in all weathers' with his stained, threadbare, ragged, and patched frock. 'Like a god' he must have appeared to peasants as he blessed them and 'talked of freedom.'[44] He was, following the standard claims, 'eloquent,' and his voice 'carried far across the crowded ranks.'[45] At Maidstone prison, Ball 'did not despair,' knowing his followers were waiting, even if he emerged 'enfeebled by weeks of confinement, pale, blinking at the bright June sunshine after the gloom of the dungeon.'[46]

Ball was the 'great man of the revolt, even more so than Tyler (who, the book claims, was likely converted by Ball).[47] The rebellion was carefully planned and organised, with Ball's widely dispersed letters emphasising 'loyalty to chosen leaders.' Over the years, Ball, 'that man of action,' along with his 'comrades,' had been 'preaching, whispering, uniting the people' through his 'call to a commonwealth of equals.' Ball's Blackheath sermon had serfs and workers of all kinds in attendance and Froissart is said to show Ball 'preaching his Christian communism to great crowds who

---

    Parliamentary Candidate,' in Keith Gildart and David Howell (eds.), *Dictionary of Labour Biography, Vol. XII* (New York: Palgrave Macmillan, 2005), 106–19.
43 McIlroy, 'Groves, Reginald Percy,' 119.
44 Philip Lindsay and Reg Groves, *The Peasants' Revolt 1381* (London: Hutchinson and Co., 1950), 73.
45 Lindsay and Groves, *Peasants' Revolt 1381*, 74, 101.
46 Lindsay and Groves, *Peasants' Revolt 1381*, 75, 86.
47 Lindsay and Groves, *Peasants' Revolt 1381*, 73–74; cf. 82–83.

listened gladly.'[48] In the classic rhetoric of the nineteenth-century Great Man in relation to his time and place, it is Ball 'who towers over all men of this period,' who 'we think when we recall the heroic people marching,' who we see 'with his staff and shaven poll trudging, through sun or rain… wherever he can find the oppressed and can lift up their hearts with the courage of his words and the urgency of his spirit, with that magic which we call personality.' Referencing Morris, Ball is understood as 'more than a man,' he was 'a symbol, a saviour, the embodiment of a people's aspirations.' It was 'as though he drew into him the longings of the outcast, as though these longings took flesh in him, took voice when he spoke and called for action.' Ball represents one of the 'moments in history when history takes, it would seem, physical shape' and is the kind of person who arises in every revolution, knowing 'the exact words to use,' speaking 'straight to the heart so that the listener almost believed it was his own heart speaking,' and drawing 'from untutored minds half-conscious aspirations and gave them form so that the listener felt that he himself had thought and said these things.'[49] Lindsay and Groves's historical account shifts into creating their own martyrology, fitting for a hagiography and the tragic fate of a Great Man. It is in 'the early morning light' when Ball, 'strong heart and poet of the rebellion,' mounted the scaffold to have a last look at the town and landscape as 'many must have sobbed and prayed' around him. He must have died slowly and in 'terrible pain.' But in addition to the gore, we get a death infused with value and meaning: Ball's 'dream did not die with his flesh.' As the bloodstained hand of the executioner lifted up Ball's 'great heart,' the onlookers would 'not forget, and their children would not forget, and their children's children, for that heart yet beat for them. John Ball had ceased to live as a man; he became instead a greater thing, a symbol, never to be forgotten.'[50]

Peasants' Revolt 1381 effectively functions as a new myth of origins and provides a founding personality to counter Stalin; as Mark O'Brien put it, *Peasants' Revolt 1381* was 'about establishing a non-Stalinist tradition of English revolutionary writings.'[51] We might add that this English revolutionary tradition was given familiar theological proto-Protestant characteristics. While the ideas of Wycliffe and the Lollards may have overlapped

---

48 Lindsay and Groves, *Peasants' Revolt 1381*, 17, 72, 74, 86–87, 157.
49 Lindsay and Groves, *Peasants' Revolt 1381*, 73.
50 Lindsay and Groves, *Peasants' Revolt 1381*, 152.
51 Mark O'Brien, *When Adam Delved and Eve Span: A History of the Peasants' Revolt of 1381* (second Kindle edition; London: Bookmarks Publications, 2016), loc 1361.

with Ball's, he was thought to be independent of them; nevertheless, Lindsay and Groves claimed that Ball accepted Wycliffe's view of the Eucharist. Ball was also deemed to be a critic of the 'pope and papal corruption,' acted like the 'true apostles of Christ,' and spoke a 'simple truth' and a dream of freedom in his Adam and Eve 'rime.'[52] But this English revolutionary tradition was also given a Trotskyite spin with ideas about world revolution. In the final words of the book there is a clear hint of the Trotskyite opposition to the idea of socialism in one country and the Trotskyite slogan associated with Groves and his circle during their split from CPGB: 'Not National Socialism but World Revolution.'[53] Lindsay and Groves ended by listing the 'great figures, the symbols of freedom' who stood for 'the inarticulate commons who followed them.' These were Jack Straw, the Dartford Tyler, William Grindecobbe, Geoffrey Lister, Wat Tyler, John Shirle, and 'above all, imperishably imprinted in our history and our literature, living on as the voice of the disinherited and the prophet of God's kingdom on earth, John Ball himself talking quietly on the steps of a village cross to men of all centuries and all lands of the great fellowship of the poor.'[54] While internationalism is hardly alien to socialist receptions of Ball, when compared with the historical materialist and Popular Frontist arguments from the Communist Party historians, this dramatic conclusion is strikingly distinctive in its emphasis and must owe something to British Trotskyism.

Ball among the Bushes

But there were bigger threats to the Communist Party, and their readings of Ball, than British Trotskyism. Another product of the Popular Front era, and a driving force behind *Music for the People*, nailed his ideological convictions to the mast and reveals a new era in the reception of Ball: the Cold War. The example of Alan Bush (1900–1995)—a professor at the Royal Academy of Music from 1925 who had also joined the CPGB in 1935 and was a founder of the Workers' Music Association in 1936—might seem, on the surface, nothing new in socialist or even liberal readings of 1381. His opera, *Wat Tyler*, with the libretto written by his wife Nancy Bush (1905–1991), was one of the winners of a competition for new operas hosted by the Arts Council of Great Britain as part of the 1951 Festival of

---

52 Lindsay and Groves, *Peasants' Revolt 1381*, 60–62, 70–71; cf. 150–51.
53 Groves, *The Balham Group*, chs. 3 and 4.
54 Lindsay and Groves, *Peasants' Revolt 1381*, 176.

Britain.⁵⁵ The sources used were relatively standard (*Anonimalle Chronicle*, Froissart, Stow, Jusserand, and Trevelyan), with the Communist addition of Fagan's *Nine Days That Shook England*.⁵⁶ Throughout we get the background of folk song (e.g., the inclusion of 'Cutty Wren,' as with *Music for the People*) which was characteristic for Bush's understanding of homegrown socialism as it now was in the ongoing reception of Ball.⁵⁷

Liberties given by artistic license notwithstanding,⁵⁸ the ideological presentation of Ball in the Bushs' opera was relatively standard fare on the Left (and indeed much of the post-eighteenth-century reception) generally and complemented the now familiar presentations of a homegrown English radicalism. Before we meet Ball, his influence pervades the world of the rebels, even if not always recognised. Tax collectors are identified with Hob the Robber, memorable names and sayings from Ball's coded letters are discussed, and Tyler sings the Adam and Eve couplet, and after Ball is introduced by the Chorus (representing the voice of the people) he too sings about Adam and Eve and the bell being rung. Ball is presented (at least by the rough and raw Tyler) as one with his familiar commanding voice and as a fellow leader of the rebels who commands their respect and indeed reverence as some of the peasants fall on their knees. Indeed, in the pictures from the 1974 stage production, the heavily bearded Richard Angas as Ball looks part-monk, part-Charlton Heston's Moses, part-biblical prophet of popular imagination.⁵⁹ Ball talks about people being created equal in the beginning, the human creation of tyranny and distinction, how things will

55 *Alan Bush's "Wat Tyler": Berlin Première of British Opera*, available at https://jbpsc.arts.gla.ac.uk/digital.php?ref=PSC/1/2/2/250. The revised version was published as Nancy Bush and Alan Bush, *Wat Tyler: Opera in Two Acts with a Prologue* (Richmond: R. W. Simpson, 1956). For biographical details, see, e.g., Nancy Bush, *Alan Bush: Music, Politics and Life* (London: Thames Publishing, 2000); Richard Stoker, 'Bush, Alan Dudley (1900–1995),' *ODNB* (3 October 2013); Meddick, Payne, and Katz (eds.), *Red Lives*, 26–27.
56 Bush, 'Preface,' in Bush and Bush, *Wat Tyler*, 1. For wider possible influences, see Joanna Bullivant, *Alan Bush, Modern Music, and the Cold War: The Cultural Left in Britain and the Communist Bloc* (Cambridge: Cambridge University Press, 2017), 191–217.
57 See Bullivant, *Alan Bush*, 160–65, 176–90, 201–3, for a discussion of Bush on nationalism, folk, and 'Cutty Wren.'
58 Nancy Bush, 'Preface,' in Bush and Bush, *Wat Tyler*, 1–2 (1). Worth noting here is that Tyler's daughter is called 'Jennet' and his wife 'Margaret.'
59 Photographs are available at http://www.alanbushtrust.org.uk/music/operas/wat_tyler.asp. Cf. Jane Lane, *A Summer Storm* (London: Peter Davies, 1976), 29: 'he roamed the countryside for the past twenty years in the manner of an Old Testament prophet.'

not go well in England until everything is held in common and high and low are levelled out. The standard Morris allusions are present, notably reference to 'fellowship is Heaven and lack of it Hell', and there is Morris-like symbolism of light and dark, including a future 'world of light/That like a vision burns'. There is, perhaps, some Catholicising of Ball, or at least no obvious Protestantising, as Ball crosses himself and utters a version of the Trinitarian formula in Latin (I.3). We do not get the death of Ball, but he is distraught at Tyler's death and he and the other rebels mourn over Tyler's body. After Richard reneges on his promise, light glows from the stage right until the Peasants are 'bathed in warm light' and the opera ends optimistically in recognition of the importance of changing perceptions and how all that is great in people 'once again shall rise' (epilogue, later designated Act II.3).

Certainly, anyone familiar with the more socialist or Marxist traditions might note Ball's place in the transformation from feudalism through capitalism to the socialist and communist future. But this alone was not new as Morris and his imitators had pushed this line—and much more explicitly. The most serious point of controversy was context. The first performances of the opera were not in Britain but were instead successfully performed in the German Democratic Republic (GDR) as *Wat Tyler* was broadcast on Berlin Radio in 1952 and first on stage in Leipzig (1953), Rostock (1955), and Magdeburg (1959).[60] In the setting of the newly-formed GDR, the opera and this familiar English tradition with its familiar claims took on different meanings in a socialist state, with the traditional heroic masculinity of Tyler playing into German communist constructions of worker-heroism and Wat and Margaret as presiding over a new kind of model family replacing fascist constructions of family values.[61] But in Britain, as reviewers noted, Bush's operas, including *Wat Tyler*, were relatively ignored. While a version was broadcast by the BBC in December 1956, *Wat Tyler* was not performed on stage in the UK until 1974 by the Workers' Music Association and a troupe performing operas that had gone largely unnoticed.[62] One likely reason for this (as regularly noted) was because of associations with Soviet Communism and the GDR, just as the Soviet Union was becoming especially controversial in public discourse after Khrushchev's speech

---

60 Nathaniel G. Lew, *Tonic to the Nation: Making English Music in the Festival of Britain* (New York: Routledge, 2017), 149–52. Cf. Bush, *Alan Bush*, 65–68; *Daily Worker* (8 September 1953); *The Stage* (29 November 1956); *Guardian* (1 December 1960).
61 Bullivant, *Alan Bush*, 230–32.
62 Bush, *Alan Bush*, 68–72; Lew, *Tonic to the Nation*, 153–54.

denouncing Stalin and intervention in Hungary in 1956.[63] In a letter to *The Stage*, Dennis Arundell distanced himself from claims that he was to produce *Wat Tyler* for the 1956 BBC production. Although he said he believed in the 'theory that art is beyond politics,' he could not be associated with the opera because of 'the Communist brutalities in Hungary' and because 'in this opera history seems to me to have been distorted for propaganda purposes.'[64] Bush responded, particularly to defend Nancy against charges of propaganda. He pointed to the sources used (*Anonimalle Chronicle*, Froissart, Stow, Jusserand, and Trevelyan—tellingly, the Communist Fagan was not mentioned) and argued that if there was a propagandistic purpose it was to 'celebrate in operatic form one of the many episodes in history in which English men and women fought for freedom against oppression.'[65]

But such associations remained an issue for Bush and *Wat Tyler* and were almost inescapable in Cold War Britain. Some criticisms were blunt. In a review published at the time of the six-hundredth anniversary of the revolt (June 1981), Paul Griffiths accused Bush of being 'blind to the truth of Soviet-style socialism' and so 'has to be treated with a certain amount of caution.' His operas, Griffiths noted, were 'studies of the rise of oppressed peoples' and were 'all allowed, even encouraged, by their composer to commit the perversion of being used by that shining light of liberty the German Democratic Republic.'[66] Others were more subtle in their critique. In a generally positive review of his 1961 concert, *The Times* labelled Bush as 'Britain's leading communist composer' inspired by 'Marxist idealism.' Typically, however, Bush's 'creative temperament' was not overly problematic for the reviewer because Bush appeared to be 'studious and introvert rather than rabble-rousing' and in such cases the music was 'too well bred to start revolutions.' But the flip side of this was the more overtly revolutionary case of *Wat Tyler*, where Bush 'cultivates simplicity and a rousing extravert vein,' for here he was understood to be at 'his least spontaneous and least distinguished.'[67] Margaret Davies had a more positive understanding of *Wat Tyler* and the relatively obscure 1974 performance but there was a shared ideological logic with *The Times* review thirteen years previous. It was precisely because of its 'decorous pace and lack of variety' that it could

---

63 Already, in the *Yorkshire Post* (11 April 1953): 'Bush's political sympathies are well known and—probably because of that—it is not so well known that he really is one of our best composers.'
64 *The Stage* (6 December 1956).
65 *The Stage* (20 December 1956).
66 Paul Griffiths, '80+,' *Musical Times* 122 (June 1981), 390.
67 *The Times* (20 November 1961).

not 'kindle into any hint of revolutionary fervour.' Davies was surprised that such a well-constructed work was neglected in Britain and acknowledged that this might have been because of Bush's 'Communist sympathies' but *Wat Tyler* 'preaches no political message today' and she was content to conclude that its 'interest is historical.'[68]

Certainly, perceptions of *Wat Tyler* being un-English or un-British were part of the reasons why it was relatively neglected. But the construction of English and British national identity was more complex than a straightforward dominance of a certain type of post-war or Cold War jingoism.[69] The story of 1381 was long embedded in the national story by the mid-twentieth century, Bush himself retained some respect among musicians and critics, and there was no blanket dismissal of its compatibility with British or English identity. Indeed, John Falding in the *Birmingham Post* wrote of the 1974 performance as an 'overdue recognition of such an essentially English work.'[70] Of the 1974 performance, *The Stage* review similarly thought it 'incredible' that Bush's opera had to wait so long for its British stage premier, seeing it as 'a thoroughly English work, with the praiseworthy theme of struggle against tyranny…inspired by John Ball's preaching of the brotherhood of man.'[71] Nevertheless, *Wat Tyler* was hardly going to avoid claims of being too closely allied to foreign interests, even if implicitly.[72] And this almost inevitably meant that the old hostile readings of the revolt in relation to the state could likewise be invoked, even if somewhat toned down since the ages of Bancroft, Cleveland, Hume, and Burke. Trevor Gee, protesting perhaps a little too much, wrote that while his objection was 'not political,' the BBC performances 'dispel the notion [that] this politically-inspired opera was some neglected masterpiece,' adding that Tyler and the revolt was a worthy enough topic in itself, even if 'peasant behaviour and Tyler's dubious character have been carefully whitewashed.'[73]

---

68 *Illustrated London News* (1 September 1974).
69 Bullivant, *Alan Bush*, 191–217; Lew, *Tonic to the Nation*, 153.
70 *Birmingham Post* (21 June 1974).
71 *The Stage* (27 July 1974).
72 Cf. *Kensington Post* (7 January 1972): 'Quite apart from their musical worth it is understandable that the Bush operas would find an audience in East Germany.'
73 *Truth* (14 December 1956).

Ball's Pursuit of the Millennium

Cold War England saw the old hostile reading of the religious (over)enthusiast, including Ball, acquire an important academic updating through the influential work of Norman Cohn (1915–2007), particularly on issues relating to millenarianism, apocalypticism, extremism, and genocide, and how modern radical ideologies (particularly Communism and Nazism) were part of a longer ideological tradition inherited from the Middle Ages. Cohn was born in London to a German Jewish father and German Catholic mother with a South African upbringing. During his wartime service he developed his thinking about (or against) the Soviet Union and the ideological drivers behind Nazism and totalitarianism which would become central to his long academic career from 1946 until his retirement in 1980. Cohn was made Astor-Wolfson Professor of History at the University of Sussex (1973) and later a Fellow of the British Academy (1978). At the University of Sussex, Cohn became the director of the Columbus Centre for Studies of Persecution and Genocide (1966–1980), initially funded by David Astor (owner of the liberal newspaper, the *Observer*) as the Centre for Research in Collective Psychopathology. *The Pursuit of the Millennium*—first published in 1957, revised and expanded for a third edition in 1970, and translated into several languages—brought him popular and cross-disciplinary academic recognition and brought to the intellectual fore claims about how medieval behaviours and modern political violence, racism, and genocide were socially, psychologically, and historically connected.[74]

As the critical study of millenarianism and apocalypticism was in its infancy, Cohn provided one of the most lasting political or liberal frameworks for explaining figures like Ball that effectively functioned (and still function today) as an alternative to the socialist and Marxist ones we have seen. *Pursuit of the Millennium* may have been a history of major millennialist movements and moments in medieval Europe (and their biblical roots), but it was the interpretation and relevance of these for understanding Nazism and Bolshevism, particularly in its famous conclusion, that gave the book its lasting fame.[75] As he put it in the revised edition, Cohn

---

74 For the biographical details on Cohn, see, e.g., William Lamont, 'Norman Rufus Colin Cohn 1915–2007', *Proceedings of the British Academy* 161 (2009): 87–108; Lorenzo Ferrari, 'The Pursuit of Humanity's Inner Demons: The Reception of Norman Cohn's Intellectual Journey', *Storia della Storiografia* 75 (2019): 59–82.

75 Norman Cohn, *The Pursuit of the Millennium* (London: Secker & Warburg, 1957), 307–14. There was forewarning in the Foreword too (xiv–xv).

wanted to show that millenarianism flourished among the unorganised, marginalised, 'rootless poor' (rather than 'simple poor' or peasantry at large) of Western Europe between the eleventh and sixteenth centuries. They received these ideas from 'would-be prophets or would-be messiahs,' many from the lower clergy, and usually against the backdrop of disaster (e.g., plague, famines, sharp rises in prices).[76] Medieval ideas about transforming lives became, Cohn argued, 'transfused with phantasies of a world reborn into innocence through a final, apocalyptic massacre,' with evil ones identified with Jews, the clergy, and the rich, who would be exterminated before the establishment of a kingdom without sin or suffering. With 'such phantasies,' revolts could spread beyond local concerns to be interpreted as an event of unique, cataclysmic importance, the recurring essence of which Cohn labelled 'revolutionary millenarianism.'[77]

Cohn further argued that such millenarian movements were the 'true precursors' of the revolutionary movements of the twentieth century.[78] Cohn ended with a stark warning about the history of influence. Ideas of a final struggle and overthrowing of world tyranny by a chosen people continued dimly over the centuries and occasionally flared up between the sixteenth and twentieth centuries with 'naïve and explicit supernaturalism' gradually replaced by a secularised orientation which claimed to be scientific, guided now by the purposes of History. Even so, the grand demands of purifying the world remained, with some targets likewise remaining (e.g., 'the Jews') and some modified accordingly (e.g., 'the bourgeoise'). This 'apocalyptic fanaticism,' Cohn claimed, was inherited by Lenin and Hitler. Nazi ideas about global Jewish conspiracy stood 'only one remove from medieval demonology' and such inherited apocalypticism accounts for the 'otherwise incomprehensible decision' in the middle of a war to murder six-million Jews. Whereas Nazi ideology was obscurantist, Communist ideology claimed to be scientific and progressive, yet both, Cohn claimed, shared a 'murderous hatred' of similar political enemies in their final historic struggle. What Marx ultimately passed on was his unconscious acquisition of a 'quasi-apocalyptic phantasy' with capitalism as Babylon and the masters as Antichrist who were to go under a 'sea of blood and fire' in order to clear the way for the 'egalitarian Millennium.' But by secularising this vision, Marx ensured its survival. However, Cohn argued that its future

---

76 Norman Cohn, *The Pursuit of the Millennium: Revolutionary Millenarians and Mystical Anarchists of the Middle Ages* (revised and expanded edition; Oxford: Oxford University Press, 1970), 16. Quotations are all from the 1970 edition.
77 Cohn, *Pursuit of the Millennium*, 11, 16–17.
78 Cohn, *Pursuit of the Millennium*, 15.

went well beyond what Marx would have expected and that it was not the industrial workers of highly developed capitalism who bought into this apocalyptic vision, but instead it penetrated into 'economically backward countries such as Russia and China.' Crucially, this construction of the history of ideas also has a kind of normative or acceptable centre. In Cohn's case, what united Communists and Nazis was 'their murderous hatred of Liberals and Socialists and reformers of every kind.' Indeed, as he said in one revealing statement, 'There are aspects of Nazism and Communism alike that are barely comprehensible, barely conceivable even, to those whose political assumptions and norms are provided by a liberal society, however imperfect.' And, for Cohn, this was because the strangeness of such beliefs was 'rooted in an earlier and forgotten age,' yet this 'subterranean medieval fanaticism' remained the 'source of the giant fanaticisms which in our day have convulsed the world.'[79]

Ball and the rebels of 1381 were, then, a precursor to these regimes according to Cohn's schema. For Cohn, the 1381 uprising was part of the shift in belief from 'a society without distinctions of status or wealth…a Golden Age irrecoverably lost' to a Golden Age instead 'preordained for the immediate future.' But it was in the ideas of Ball where 'one finds the myth' as 'most of the insurgents' were not obviously influenced by it. Most of the peasants and artisans were, he argued, concerned with 'limited and realistic objectives' and he pointed to the conventional evidence for such an argument: the agreement at Mile End. Here there was 'nothing at all to hint at any impending miraculous restoration of an egalitarian State of Nature,' even if 'such phantasy' might still have been present among some insurgents.[80] Irrespective of whether Ball preached the sermons attributed to him verbatim, for Cohn it remained likely that such ideas were being disseminated. When Wycliffe's teaching was decontextualised and the nuances removed from their scholastic context, then his claims about all things in common 'were barely distinguishable from the mystical anarchism of the Free Spirit.' But to make the 'phantasy of the egalitarian State of Nature' take off, a 'social criticism of a more personal and passionate kind' was required. Cohn's explanation here turned to the 'virulent criticism' reserved for the rich and powerful and the idea of the Last Judgement as 'a day of vengeance of the poor.' Such prophecy could then be turned into a 'revolutionary propaganda of the most explosive kind' to bring the Last Judgement nearer, as seen in Walsingham's presentation of Ball and in the letters attributed to Ball. Here, Ball was proclaiming the imminent

---

79 Cohn, *Pursuit of the Millennium*, 285–88.
80 Cohn, *Pursuit of the Millennium*, 198–99.

fulfilment of the prophecy and encouraging the 'common people, as the children of the Kingdom,' to bring about the 'annihilation of the demonic powers which was to usher in the Millennium.' This would be an imminent Millennium 'cleansed of sin,' particularly those associated with the rich, and a recreation of the 'primal egalitarian State of Nature, a second Golden Age.'[81]

The reason why the English Peasants' Revolt had this millenarian flavour was because of the inclusion of lower clergy and 'apostates and irregulars' like Ball—those people 'always eager to assume the role of divinely inspired prophets.' With reference to Froissart, Cohn claimed that Ball's 'most enthusiastic followers' were among excluded workers, the unskilled and poor Londoners who envied the rich and noble. In this milieu, the 'fanatical *prophetae*' mixed with the 'disorientated and desperate poor' was 'bound' to produce 'utmost violence' and a belief that society was being made anew. From this, Cohn tentatively suggested that 'millenarian expectations' may have underpinned the burning of the Savoy and the destruction of London.[82] This was, Cohn added in his famous conclusion, representative of a wider phenomenon in a nation-wide revolt when 'somewhere on the radical fringe, a *propheta* with his following of paupers' was 'intent on turning this one particular upheaval into the apocalyptic battle, the final purification of the world,' with Ball content to be a precursor to or prophet of the returning Christ.[83]

We can locate Cohn in the tradition of a historic and developing discourse about fanaticism in relation to the political centre as examined by Alberto Toscano, and its relation to the history of political understandings of apocalypticism, millenarianism, and similar ways that deviance is constructed in liberal political discourse with reference to the language of religion.[84] Following Toscano's presentation, the fanatic has been constructed as someone thought to be beyond tolerance, rationality, compromise, and political debate, someone who looks to the removal of all rival views. Fanaticism might be closely connected with abstract notions of universalism and egalitarianism. In this discourse, the fanatic is an ahistorical and monolithic threat with formal likenesses prioritised over political and

---

81 Cohn, *Pursuit of the Millennium*, 199–203.
82 Cohn, *Pursuit of the Millennium*, 203–4.
83 Cohn, *Pursuit of the Millennium*, 284.
84 Alberto Toscano, *Fanaticism: On the Uses of an Idea* (London: Verso, 2010); James Crossley, *Cults, Martyrs and Good Samaritans: Religion in Contemporary English Political Discourse* (London: Pluto, 2018), 131–62; James Crossley, 'The End of Apocalypticism: From Burton Mack's Jesus to North American Liberalism,' *Journal for the Study of the Historical Jesus* (forthcoming).

historical context in such understandings. We have seen similar understandings of Ball as fanatic in earlier chapters, but in the twentieth century such discourses were updated as understandings of fanaticism were thought to be found in totalitarianism, whether understood as German Nazism or Soviet Communism, both effectively understood (as Toscano might put it) as political religions. As fanaticism could also represent terror and the irrational opposition to the West, this sort of labelling was also applied to Islam as a particularly potent totalising fusion of religion and politics. Indeed, Soviet Communism and Islam have a history of being compared to one another as similar universalising phenomena. In other words, liberal discourses around fanaticism become part of constructing what stands outside liberal-democratic capitalism.

Whatever the rights or wrongs of Cohn's argument and understanding of 1381, *The Pursuit of the Millennium* functions as a classic example in the history of fanaticism. Cohn (as he himself recognised) did not have a significant influence on the scholarly study of medieval religion, and while his understanding of Ball is certainly noted, it is rarely developed in any detail.[85] However, he has had a major influence on the ways in which apocalypticism, extremism, and fanaticism have been understood which continues to this day in popular intellectual discourse, and which continues to have an advocate in the public intellectual John Gray.[86] We might reasonably speculate, then, that the tainting with such hard apocalypticism of a long-politicised figure like Ball (not least through the academic and cultural credibility of a popular intellectual like Cohn) further contributed to the declining interest in, or public presentation of, Ball and the rebels in Cold War England. That there were obvious religious connotations of such language was hardly going to help in a country where church attendance and commitment, and sensitivities towards political uses of biblical language, were becoming increasingly alien in public discourse (see Chapters 22, 23). Nevertheless, Ball the revolutionary priest with millenarian tendencies

---

85 For a critique of Cohn's emphasis on millenarianism in relation to Ball, see Richard Firth Green, 'John Ball's Letters,' in Hanawalt (ed.), *Chaucer's England*, 181, 186.

86 John Gray, *Black Mass: Apocalyptic Religion and the Death of Utopia* (London: Allen Lane, 2007); John Gray, 'The Recurrent Dream of an End-Time,' *A Point of View* (BBC Radio 4; 20 December 2019), https://www.bbc.co.uk/sounds/play/m000c8rz. Gray also wrote an obituary for Cohn—see John Gray, 'Professor Norman Cohn,' *Independent* (29 September 2007). For other prominent advocates, see also, e.g., Ian McEwan, 'The Day of Judgment,' *Guardian* (31 May 2008); Giles Fraser, 'To Islamic State, Dabiq is important—but it's not the end of the world,' *Guardian* (10 October 2014).

was not going to go away just yet, even if somewhat modified. He still had culturally credible Marxist allies in Cold War England, and perhaps none more so than Rodney Hilton.

20
Rodney Hilton: Ball at the End of Historical Materialism?

Perhaps no one gave the 1381 uprising more popular academic credibility in the second half of the twentieth century than the historian of medieval feudal society, Rodney Hilton (1916–2002), who wrote one of the defining books on the revolt: *Bond Men Made Free: Medieval Peasant Movements and the English Rising of 1381* (1973). Hilton hailed from Middleton, Lancashire, from a Nonconformist and socialist family, including parents active in the Independent Labour Party (ILP). In correspondence and interviews with Harvey Kaye and Dennis Dworkin, Hilton was reported as highlighting his connections with the labour movement in Lancashire and the politically radical traditions in Middleton, including retelling a story that his grandfather lived in a cottage which commemorated the place where Samuel Bamford was arrested in 1819 after Peterloo.[1] Hilton was part of the 'mobile working class,' as Dworkin put it,[2] and after attending Manchester Grammar School went to the University of Oxford (1935–1938) on a scholarship to study history at Balliol. In 1946, after serving in the war (in North Africa, Syria, Palestine, and Italy), he would become one of the most distinguished medieval historians of his era. He became a lecturer in the School of History at the University of Birmingham where he remained for his career, becoming Professor of Medieval Social History in 1963 and retiring in 1982. Throughout his career, his politics and Marxism remained integral to his work and his influence on the Left beyond the academic study of medieval history. Monitored by MI5, Hilton joined the Communist Party at Oxford in face of the rise of fascism and crises of capitalism and remained a member until 1956 when, like many others, he left

---

1 Harvey J. Kaye, *The British Marxist Historians* (Cambridge: Polity Press, 1984), 265, n. 4; Dennis Dworkin, *Cultural Marxism in Postwar Britain: History, the New Left, and the Origins of Cultural Studies* (Durham and London: Duke University Press, 1997), 264 n. 11.
2 Dworkin, *Cultural Marxism*, 14.

in the aftermath of Khrushchev's denunciation of Stalin and the Soviet intervention in Hungary. Hilton nevertheless remained a Marxist and was politically active, as a trade unionist, in the Labour Party, and again in the Communist Party of Great Britain in its final years (at least under the CPGB title) in the 1980s.[3]

Historical Materialism

His background in the Communist Party and the work of the Communist Party Historians' Group (1946–1956) is crucial to understanding the emergence of Hilton's take of the revolt and Ball, with the Popular Front mentality central as Hilton and his fellow Historians' Group members navigated both academia and Marxist politics.[4] The Historians' Group

---

3   I owe the biographical details to Edward Miller, 'Introduction,' in T. H. Aston, P. R. Coss, Christopher Dyer, and Joan Thirsk (eds.), *Social Relations and Ideas: Essays in Honour of R. H. Hilton* (Cambridge: Cambridge University Press, 1983), ix–xiii; Kaye, *British Marxist Historians*, 71–72; Dworkin, *Cultural Marxism*, 14–16; Chris Wickham, 'Rodney Hilton,' *History Today* 52 (2002): 6–7; Christopher Dyer, 'Obituary: Rodney Hilton,' *Guardian* (10 June 2002); Christopher Dyer, 'A New Introduction (2003),' in Hilton, *Bond Men Made Free*, ix–xiii; Christopher Dyer, 'Rodney Howard Hilton 1916–2002,' *Proceedings of the British Academy* 130 (2005): 52–77; Christopher Dyer, 'Introduction: Rodney Hilton, Medieval Historian,' in Christopher Dyer, Peter Coss, and Chris Wickham (eds.), *Rodney Hilton's Middle Ages 400–1600: An Exploration of Historical Themes* (Oxford: Oxford University Press, 2007), 10–17; Rosamond Faith, 'Rodney Hilton (1916–2002),' *History Workshop Journal* 55 (2003): 278–82; Terence J. Byres, 'Rodney Hilton (1916–2002): In Memoriam,' *Journal of Agrarian Change* 6 (2006): 1–16; E. J. E. Hobsbawm, 'Hilton, Rodney Howard (1916–2002),' *ODNB* (8 January 2009); Aglaia Kasdagli, 'Medieval History and Marxism in England, 1950–1956,' *Past and Present* 242 (1) (2019): 1–43 . Cf. Peter Coss, 'R. H. Hilton,' *Past and Present* 176 (2002): 7–10.

4   For discussion, see, e.g., Eric Hobsbawm, 'Communist Party Historians' Group 1946–56,' in Maurice Cornforth (ed.), *Rebels and their Causes: Essays in Honour of A. L. Morton* (London: Lawrence & Wishart, 1978), 21–48; Schwarz, '"The People" in History,' in Johnson, McLennan, Schwartz, and Sutton (eds.), *Making Histories*, 44–95; Kaye, *British Marxist Historians*, 10–18; David Parker, 'The Communist Party Historians' Group,' *Socialist History* 12 (1997): 33–58; Sam Ashman, 'Communist Party Historians' Group,' in John Rees (ed.), *Essays on Historical Materialism* (London: Bookmarks, 1998), 145–59; Matt Perry, *Marxism and History* (London: Palgrave MacMillan, 2002), 88–94; David

(featuring a number of future prominent historians such as Christopher Hill, Eric Hobsbawm, and E. P. Thompson) had planned to discuss a revision of Morton's *A People's History of England* (see Chapter 18), though they would collaborate and divide the division of labour into historical periods in their mapping out of popular national traditions. The 1381 uprising became a conventional starting point for their understanding of homegrown English radicalism. Dona Torr, an especially popular and influential figure in the Historians' Group, noted in her posthumous and incomplete book *Tom Mann and His Times* (1956) that Mann realised that capitalism was not eternal by way of William Morris and his story of the 'seditious priest John Ball' and the Adam and Eve couplet, locating this as part of an 'English revolutionary tradition':

> Our story of the struggle for freedom begins with the great Rebellion led by Wat Tyler and inspired by Ball's 20 years' preaching…The defeated revolutionaries who at their execution spoke so proudly of their cause were the first Englishmen who have told their rulers and judges that they were glad to suffer for freedom…the ideas of the Levellers and Diggers have their place in the English revolutionary tradition which extends from John Ball to Tom Mann.[5]

In a festschrift for Torr (1954), Hill published one of the most important examinations of the development of a distinctly English radicalism both for the Historians' Group and more widely in academia as he traced the early modern development of the myth of the Norman Yoke through to the working-class movement showing how it was subsumed into socialist theories. While he accepted that the myth may have had a continuous history since 1066, he effectively skipped over the medieval period. Nevertheless, Hill contextualised ideas of the Norman Yoke in broader theories relating to a lost Golden Age and how societies explain the origins of exploitation

---

Renton, 'Studying Their Own Nation without Insularity? The British Marxist Historians Reconsidered,' *Science and Society* 69 (2005): 559–79; Francis King, 'Editorial: Our History,' *Socialist History* 47 (2015): 1–13; Willie Thompson, 'From Communist Party Historians' Group to Socialist History Society, 1946–2017,' *History Workshop* (10 April 2017), https://www.historyworkshop.org.uk/from-communist-party-historians-group-to-socialist-history-society-1946-2017/; Jonathan White, *Making Our Own History: A User's Guide to Marx's Historical Materialism* (Glasgow: Praxis Press, 2021), 103–11.

5   Dona Torr, *Tom Mann and His Times: Volume One (1856–1890)* (London: Lawrence and Wishart, 1956), 98, 110.

and project hope for future equality. The Adam and Eve couplet from 1381 was the first example Hill gave.[6]

Following the lead of pre-war Marxist histories, the Historians' Group (including Torr and Hill) wanted to explain the transition from feudalism to capitalism in historical materialist terms which, contrary to a common academic reception, continued throughout the careers of figures like Hill, Hilton, Hobsbawm, and even Thompson. As Jonathan White points out, 'If they are subsequently seen as having rejected historical materialism or having been more interested in "history from below," it is...because subsequent historians have failed to understand the historical conditions within which they made their own history.'[7] The stress on history from below over historical materialism in the reception of the Historians' Group would have consequences for the reception of Ball, as we will see in later chapters. Nevertheless, the Historians' Group inherited and worked with the notion that the 1381 uprising was an important example of such class conflict as a moment illuminating the tensions, contradictions, successes, failures, and resolutions involved in the transition from feudalism to capitalism.

Hilton would become the figure most associated with the study of 1381, but it was, crucially, part of his wider study of class struggle in feudal England. There were developments over his career, of course, but broadly speaking Hilton's distinctive arguments focused on the exploitative relationship between landowner and peasant, with the former powerful enough to extract the surplus from the latter. In terms of the landlord-tenant relationship, Hilton saw the importance of the peasantry as a wider category that incorporated serfs, agricultural labourers, and artisans, and this was important for understanding the different social backgrounds of the 1381 rebels. But Hilton went much further than simply establishing social status because for him the struggle involved in the landlord-tenant relationship was the motor of historical change. What marked this struggle was the extraction of rents and competing demands and conflict manifested in differing ways over time in medieval Europe—and indeed increasing over time with the growth of trade and the reach of the state. Such resistance and demands for freedoms and liberties led to the freeing up of peasants and artisans for a new type of economic relationship to emerge in agrarian

---

6 Hill, 'The Norman Yoke,' in Saville (ed.), *Democracy and the Labour Movement*, 11–12. On Torr, Hill, and the Norman Yoke among the Historians' Group, see Schwarz, '"The People" in History,' in Johnson, McLennan, Schwartz, and Sutton (eds.), *Making Histories*, 44–95; Kaye, *British Marxist Historians*, 69–74.

7 White, *Making Our Own History*, vii, cf. 110–11.

capitalism which would morph into industrial capitalism. This explains the place of Ball and the rebels in Hilton's schema as they contributed to the declining attitudes of deference towards ruling class ideas, effectively ending the feudal reaction after the Black Death. In helping curb the power of the lords, they contributed to the emergence of commodity production in the more market-orientated South East.[8]

Fittingly, Hilton's early publication on the revolt during the Historians' Group years—*The English Rising of 1381* (1950)—was with Hyman Fagan (see Chapter 18). Together, they wanted to challenge the inadequacy of received views of feudal society, and this gave Hilton a platform to present some of his key ideas. Fagan was responsible for almost all of Part II, which focused on the revolt itself and was a revision of his *Nine Days That Shook England* (1938) but with a specific focus on the familiar narrative from the summer of 1381 and which naturally included his understanding of Ball.[9] Hilton, however, was responsible for Part I and the final chapter (XII) where he examined the 'superstructure of ideas and institutions which had evolved from the mode of production in this society' and the role of the landlord-peasant relationship in the transition from feudalism to capitalism.[10] As we might expect, there was also a familiar propagandistic element to the publication. In the introduction (and perhaps exaggerating the

---

8   This a summary of numerous publications by Hilton, including: (with Hyman Fagan) *The English Rising of 1381* (London: Lawrence and Wishart, 1950); *The Decline of Serfdom in Medieval England* (London: Palgrave Macmillan, 1969); *The English Peasantry in the Later Middle Ages: The Ford Lectures for 1973 and Related Studies* (Oxford: Oxford University Press, 1975); *Bond Men Made Free: Medieval Peasant Movements and the English Rising of 1381* (London: Routledge, 2003 [1973]); 'The Rebellion of 1381', in David Rubinstein (ed.), *People for the People* (London: Ithaca Press, 1973), 18–23; 'Wat Tyler, John Ball and the English Rising', *New Society* (30 April 1981), 171–73; 'The English Rising of 1381', *Marxism Today* (June 1381): 17–19; *Class Conflict and the Crisis of Feudalism* (revised edition; London: Verso, 1990). For more detail on influences Hilton's understanding of the transition from feudalism to capitalism, and the various debating partners and influences on him (e.g., Maurice Dobb, E. A. Kosminsky), see, e.g., Kaye, *British Marxist Historians*, 73–98; Dyer, 'Rodney Howard Hilton 1916–2002'; S. R. Epstein, 'Rodney Hilton, Marxism, and the Transition from Feudalism to Capitalism', in Dyer, Coss, and Wickham (eds.), *Rodney Hilton's Middle Ages 400–1600*, 248–69; Kasdagli, 'Medieval History and Marxism', 8–9, 16–29; White, *Making Our Own History*, 103–11.
9   Fagan and Hilton, *English Rising*, 96–102, 110–13. Fagan also continued to publish on Ball and the revolt elsewhere, e.g., H. Fagan, *The Commoners of England: Part One* (London: Lawrence and Wishart, 1958), 9–31.
10 Fagan and Hilton, *English Rising*, 12, 13–89, 189–96.

situation), they explained that their intention was to correct previous accounts which 'have been influenced by the bias shown against the rebels by all the sources, literary and official' through reconstructing the motives and aims of 'the oppressed.' More specifically, this was for a targeted audience. They stressed that *The English Rising of 1381* was not only a popular (rather than strictly academic) book but one that presented 'to the British people one part of their own tradition of struggle for popular liberties.'[11] As Hilton concluded his major section of *The English Rising of 1381*, Ball emerged at the beginning of such homegrown radicalism as Hilton argued that the songs and ballads of Robin Hood deserved to take their place in the 'literature of revolt' alongside Ball's sermon and 'the literature of the English Revolution, and of the modern working-class movement.'[12]

Given his background, it is no surprise that Hilton was also aligned with Marxist understandings of Morris and Morris's understanding of Ball. This comes through in arguments in passing, such as Hilton's claim that Ball's programme was 'entirely incapable of realisation, given the historical forces at work in the late middle ages,' even if there may have been a fleeting moment when the ideas of the ruling class ceased to rule.[13] More precise connections were made by Hilton when he delivered the Kelmscott Lecture in 1989 with the telling title 'The Change beyond the Change: *A Dream of John Ball*', which he published a year later. In it, Hilton recalled a family friend from the ILP who, in the 1930s, believed the socialism of the ILP was that of Morris rather than Marx. As Robin Page Arnot had done (see Chapters 17, 18), Hilton challenged such utopian readings of Morris and, by way of his old Historians' Group colleague E. P. Thompson, stressed Morris's Marxism. And this corrective included Marx's influence on Morris's historical schema, hence the lecture's focus on 'the change beyond the change.'[14] Yet Hilton was not only prepared to note the inevitable historical inaccuracies in *A Dream of John Ball* but also to critique (though sympathetically) Morris's historical schema in that the implication of social and economic evolution over five centuries ending in the destruction of capitalism might be simplistic. Hilton accepted that this might have been a reasonable vision in the 1880s with the rapid development of industrial capitalism, an organised working class, and socialist movements. Yet Hilton still accepted the basic validity of this historical materialist

---

11 Fagan and Hilton, *English Rising*, 9–10.
12 Fagan and Hilton, *English Rising*, 89.
13 Hilton, 'English Rising of 1381,' 19.
14 Rodney Hilton, *The Change beyond the Change: A Dream of John Ball* (London: William Morris Society, 1990), 5–6.

approach, adding that Morris's 'linking of changing economic and social structures with the complex history of successes and defeats shows shrewd insights' and remained relevant nearly a century later. Hilton did not only look forward; given his reading of class conflict under feudalism, it made sense for him to look back and qualify Morris further in arguing that Ball and 1381 was the continuation of previous successes and defeats. But even if we can read Hilton as extending schema backward and forward in light of unfulfilled eschatological expectations, he still saw his task less to correct and more to 'justify and extend his [Morris's] vision.'[15]

But if Norman Cohn's critique of Communism contributed to the success of his reading of medieval millenarianism (See Chapter 19), then why would Hilton-the-Marxist become arguably the most prominent academic interpreter of 1381 in the Cold War period? Should this not have made him anathema? Perhaps not. For a start, anti-Communist sentiments were not entirely dominant; as William Lamont put it of Cohn's *Pursuit of the Millennium*, 'nothing gave greater offence than his seeming equation of Nazism with Communism. Even some admirers wished away that last chapter.'[16] Moreover, while the CPBG may have been near fatally wounded in the public imagination by the events of the 1950s, prominent members of the Historians' Group were still able to thrive, whether they left (like Hilton, Thompson, and Hill) or remained (like Hobsbawm). E. P. Thompson's hugely successful, influential, and near canonical *The Making of the English Working Class* (1963) had paved the way for the relative prominence of Hilton's most famous book, *Bond Men Made Free* (1973). In the 1950s, Hilton the academic may have been, as Christopher Dyer put it, 'a rather isolated figure' in studying peasant rebellions, with little sympathy found towards Marxism and uprisings, but shifting contexts would allow the former Historians' Group members to thrive and in doing so help reframe the reception of Ball. As Dyer added in his contextualising of Hilton, the 1960s saw social democratic revivals in Britain, Europe, and America, the emergence of the New Left, student uprisings and unrest (including at the University of Birmingham), increasing political interest in peasant economies, and the significance of peasant resistance in Vietnam against America's claims to be fighting Communism.[17] And, while always wary of anachronism, it is striking how Hilton ended *Bond Men Made Free*:

15 Hilton, *Change beyond the Change*, 8–9, 17–18.
16 Lamont, 'Norman Rufus Colin Cohn 1915–2007', 89.
17 Dyer, 'A New Introduction', in Hilton, *Bond Men Made Free*, x–xi; Dyer, 'Rodney Howard Hilton 1916–2002', 67–68. Cf. Dobson, 'Remembering the Peasants' Revolt', in Liddell and Wood (eds.), *Essex and the Great Revolt of 1381*, 17.

'Clearly, the tasks of leadership in contemporary peasant society have nothing in common with the tasks of the past, except in the recognition that conflict is part of existence and that nothing is gained without struggle.'[18]

Hilton's Apocalypse

Hilton's historical materialism, and his association with the Historians' Group, meant his reading of religion provided an alternative narrative to Cohn's reading of medieval apocalypticism and radicalism. Apocalypticism and millenarianism in the hands of the former Historians' Group members (and, of course, deriving from Engels) were certainly handled differently to Cohn's treatment, though there were shared assumptions about premodern precursors to socialism and Communism. Around the same time that Cohn was developing his ideas, Hobsbawm was publishing his take on millenarianism and rural unrest, particularly in *Primitive Rebels* (1959) and *Bandits* (1969). Focusing on agrarian contexts in southern Europe and Latin America, Hobsbawm saw rural banditry and the combination of millenarianism and social agitation as 'primitive' and 'pre-political' in the sense that they were pre-capitalist forms of resistance: these pre-political rebels could once have provided some defence against a world of unjust princes, tax collectors, and landlords, while millenarians could promise a dramatic new world free from injustices of the present order. But such phenomena were further understood as pre-political in the sense that they had to come to terms with a new world and be absorbed into more organised and bureaucratised resistance to capitalism, such as socialist or Communist parties. Indeed, it was this hope for a radical transformation that, Hobsbawm argued, could feed into revolutionary politics of the twentieth century.[19] Hill's famous treatment of the English Revolution

---

18 Hilton, *Bond Men Made Free*, 236.
19 Eric J. Hobsbawm, *Primitive Rebels: Studies in Archaic Forms of Social Movement in the 19th and 20th Centuries* (Manchester: Manchester University Press, 1959); Eric J. Hobsbawm, *Bandits* (London: Weidenfeld and Nicolson, 1969). Cf. e.g., Eric J. Hobsbawm, 'Social Banditry: A Reply', *Comparative Studies in Society and History* 14 (1972): 503–5; Eric J. Hobsbawm, 'Social Banditry', in Henry A. Landsberger (ed), *Rural Protest: Peasant Movements and Social Change* (New York: Macmillan, 1973), 142–57; Eric J. Hobsbawm, 'Peasants and Politics', *Journal of Peasant Studies* 1 (1973): 3–22; Eric J. Hobsbawm, 'Peasant Land Occupations', *Past and Present* 62 (1974): 120–52.

saw seventeenth-century English religious radicalism in a similar way.[20] While the successful revolution was bourgeois in its consequences in that it created a state ready for capitalist development and imperialism, the unsuccessful revolution from below was more radically democratic and generated ideas from proto-Communism through free love to questioning ideas about a creator God and the existence of hell. Hill argued that the radical revolution was important for carrying out regicide and a bourgeois revolution but once power was consolidated it then had to be suppressed.[21]

In a complementary way, Hilton stressed how ideas of freedom, liberty, and egalitarianism owed as much to peasant and insurgent claims against feudalism as to later bourgeois claims. Moreover, any medieval social philosophy would obviously have been cast in terms of Christianity: Christianity and the Bible provided both the ideological legitimisation for the feudal system and the ideological legitimisation for peasant resistance against it. Priests would preach that peasants 'should accept servility, labour services, high money rents, high jurisdictional profits for their lords,' yet peasants 'resisted ideologically in unexpected ways, especially by taking over ideologies that were not intended to help them.' Such resistance might involve accusations that lords were failing in their duties of protection. But it might also involve using the 'contradictions and ambiguities of the Christian religion' to support rebellions. Selected emphases, Hilton noted, involved 'brotherhood of man, equality before God, etc.,' to which he added the famous Ball quip about Adam and Eve which he simply described as a 'well-known peasant slogan of the fourteenth century' because it was so deeply embedded in peasant ideology.[22]

Certainly, the communal life of the peasantry provided cohesion from the poorest to the most prosperous peasant, as well as the possibilities of class identification against the lords. But Hilton could even view 1381 as an example of shared interests and class consciousness among peasants and other producers, with not just demands but a longer-term vision beyond feudal relationships articulated by the lower clergy who were described by Hilton as the 'medieval equivalent of a radical intelligentsia.'[23] In the revolt, the major example of this radical intelligentsia was, of course, Ball. Hilton was keen to stress that Ball was of his time and that no matter how

---

20 See James Crossley, *Harnessing Chaos: The Bible in English Political Discourse since 1968* (revised edition; London: T&T Clark/Bloomsbury, 2016), 37–69.
21 See especially, Hill, *World Turned Upside Down*.
22 Hilton, *Class Conflict*, 9–10. See also Hilton, *Bond Men Made Free*, 211–12.
23 Hilton, 'English Rising of 1381,' 18. See also Hilton, 'Wat Tyler, John Ball,' 171–72.

naïve his views may now seem, in fourteenth-century England he was seen as a threat by the ruling class because he challenged their received thinking. Hilton was suspicious about whether Ball really preached 'primitive communism' as this was 'not a normal, or natural peasant demand,' and fell back on a recurring claim in the history of the reception of the revolt (and a similar one made by Cohn for different reasons) that there was no such example in the 1381 programmes. Strikingly, Hilton did note that such thinking otherwise 'might occur in the millenarian visions of some Christian heretics,' but this still meant putting even more distance between Ball and a Cohn-style reading of 1381.[24]

Heresy was integral to Hilton's understanding of religion and uprisings. Contra conservative historians, heresy was not merely to be explained as spiritual 'rebellions against orthodoxy' but also as a means to convey social discontents.[25] Hilton's treatment of heresy in the case of South-East England in 1381 illustrates his thinking on the matter. The comparatively prominent role of the lower clergy among the rebels was potentially explicable because of the 'peculiarly retarded development' of popular heresy in England. Hilton argued that between 1166 and the Lollard movement at the end of the fourteenth century, there is minimal evidence for a heretical *movement* in England despite a history of social tensions, criticisms of ecclesiastical practices, and speculations about Christianity. For Hilton, the seemingly sudden emergence of Lollardy after the 1381 rebellion should perhaps now be seen as coming from 'several channels' of discontent, and the apparent absence of heretical movements meant the clergy compensated by expressing themselves in the social and political movements of 1381.[26] In other words, the concepts were present even if the movements were not.

Hilton devoted much space in *Bond Men Made Free* to explaining the broader historical background to such heretical thought in medieval Europe. Heretical thinking (or potentially heretical which could be used by the church when required) could take shape in the form of millenarianism, imminent eschatology, the coming of Antichrist, the Second Coming, and the Last Judgement, and most famously developed in the elaborate and historically deterministic schema of Joachim of Fiore and his followers.[27] But this was also a positive vision of an alternative society and could form a system of belief which provided 'firm organisation' necessary for survival

---

24 Hilton, 'English Rising of 1381,' 19; Kaye, *British Marxist Historians*, 93.
25 Hilton, *Class Conflict*, 10. Cf. Hilton, *Bond Men Made Free*, 97.
26 Hilton, *Bond Men Made Free*, 212–13. Hilton, *Change beyond Change*, 13.
27 Hilton, *Bond Men Made Free*, 104–9.

against the odds. For Hilton, the echoes of Marxist language in his descriptions of these systems of belief and their role in class struggle meant that they were not simply described in the language of esoteric speculations about the spiritual church of the final historical stage. With the Second Coming of Christ, a community of property might be envisaged which would bring together marginalised groups in society, including those in bigger towns.[28] In times of 'mass enthusiasm,' Hilton claimed, 'concepts of hierarchy tended to be blurred: the tripartite society must dissolve in the face of Antichrist.'[29]

Although Hilton stressed anticlericalism in his accounts of peasant resistance, he also viewed the (relative) outside leadership of the lower clergy (or even 'clerical proletariat')[30] as important in, for instance, articulating apocalyptic aims in their role as the radical intelligentsia. They were thought to be particularly important 'where movements have aims going well beyond the satisfaction of immediate social and political demands or the expression of immediate resentment of social oppression.'[31] Sympathetic clergy, Hilton stressed, were more literate than peasants and knew the tradition of sermons denouncing the rich. And the more they knew the Bible and church fathers (notably St Ambrose of Milan), the 'more explosive the mixture of social and religious radicalism was likely to be'—the most obvious case being Ball.[32] And if, as *Piers Plowman* satirised, they did not know the Bible or the tradition as well as they should and instead preferred ballads of Robin Hood, then these tales too were 'socially subversive enough.'[33]

Like other members of the Historians' Group, Hilton's Nonconformist background further helps us understand his political and historical interests.[34] More precisely, Hilton came out of a Unitarian background but described his upbringing more in terms of 'cultural' Nonconformity in

---

28 Hilton, *Bond Men Made Free*, 105; Hilton, *Class Conflict*, 10.
29 Hilton, *Bond Men Made Free*, 99.
30 A turn of phrase Hilton also used in his popular presentation of the uprising, e.g., Hilton, 'English Rising of 1381,' 18.
31 Hilton, *Bond Men Made Free*, 124.
32 Hilton, *Bond Men Made Free*, 210.
33 Hilton, *Bond Men Made Free*, 211. Hilton, of course, examined the tales of Robin Hood in such a manner in detail. See Rodney Hilton, 'The Origins of Robin Hood,' *Past and Present* 14 (1958), 30–44. Cf. Fagan and Hilton, *English Rising*, 84–89.
34 On Nonconformity and the Communist Party Historians' Group, and British Communism more generally, see, e.g., Raphael Samuel, 'British Marxist Historians,' 41–55; Kaye, *British Marxist Historians*, 9–10; Dworkin, *Cultural Marxism*, 13–15; Crossley, *Harnessing Chaos*, 46, 53–69.

his reminiscences about Christopher Hill: 'I think that many had a strong Nonconformist upbringing, or (as in my case) deliberately irreligious, though with all the cultural attributes of Nonconformity. In fact, it was not difficult for people with this sort of background to become Communists.'[35] We might speculate that this background had an influence on Hilton's presentation of religion, much as it did on Hill's understanding of religious radicalism in the seventeenth century.[36] Anticlericalism was a significant emphasis in Hilton's understanding of Christian language among peasant uprisings and there are some indications that his understanding complements a certain kind of Protestant Nonconformity which once held some influence on the British Left and in presentations of Ball. If the millenarian tradition was relatively muted according to Hilton, another was not, and it was one cast in more familiar Protestant language. Hilton could talk of movements which were 'simply evangelical in inspiration,' drew on stock ideas from the 'evangelical strand' of the European heretical tradition, and wanted the church to return to the 'simple poverty and equality of the age of the Apostles, which looked to the authority of the Bible rather than to that of the church.' Such movements, Hilton argued, also criticised the 'wealth and power and political involvement of the existing church' and 'in varying degrees rejected the organized priesthood and the sacraments which the priest controlled.' Certain groups (e.g., Waldensians) might instead stress the 'direct relationship between God and man.' This, for Hilton and his interest in class conflict and religion, constituted a radical or revolutionary challenge to the social order, whether proponents knew it or not.[37]

Hilton's treatment of Wycliffe and Lollardy also complements this background, as well as showing clear similarities with the tensions and uneasy comparisons between Ball and Wycliffe in Communist readings (e.g., Lindsay, Morton, Fagan; see Chapter 18) where historical materialist approaches did not require a strict identification with a precise movement in order to work (see Epilogue). Hilton was a critical reader of the primary sources and would not have taken statements about the connection

---

35 Rodney Hilton, 'Christopher Hill: Some Reminiscences,' in Donald H. Pennington and Keith Thomas (eds.), *Puritans and Revolutionaries: Essays in Seventeenth-Century History Presented to Christopher Hill* (Oxford: Oxford University Press, 1978), 6–10 (7).
36 Crossley, *Harnessing Chaos*, 37–69.
37 Hilton, *Bond Men Made Free*, 102–3, 109, 227. Cf. Hilton, *Change beyond Change*, 12–13: 'They were, in fact, concepts of freedom and equality which could find justification in the Bible, especially in the New Testament. There were many heretical strands, some of which could be called "evangelical", deriving their ideas from the Gospels.'

between Lollardy and the 1381 rising at face value. He was naturally aware that Walsingham's claim about Ball sharing the doctrines of Wycliffe was designed to discredit Wycliffe and that there is no strong evidence of Ball being concerned about shifting understandings of the Eucharist. However, by understanding heresy in structural terms, Hilton did not come to reject such a connection with Lollardy either ('not after all so mistaken...If he [Walsingham] had said Ball was a Lollard he might have been nearer to the truth'). Instead, Hilton tied Lollardy and the rebels in with his understanding of English heretical ideas and a lack of a heretical movement by suggesting that we broaden the definition of Lollardy beyond that of a follower of Wycliffe. To support this, he noted that Ball was imprisoned for his preaching in the 1360s. Hilton could thus even claim that it 'would not be unreasonable to regard Ball as a sort of proto-Lollard.'[38] In this way, Hilton provided the most serious intellectual justification on the Left for the popular identification of Ball with Lollardy and, implicitly, the ongoing assumption of a Protestantised or proto-Nonconformist Ball among certain sections of English socialism.

1968

Finally, there was arguably another function of this major emphasis on religion in *Bond Men Made Free* and it relates to Marxist reactions to the social upheavals of the 1960s. The occasionally irreverent student uprisings of 1968 caused a problem for an ageing Marxist intellectual establishment: on the one hand, they might be seen as an obvious cause for a Marxist to support; on the other, the protests could be seen as overly romantic, ill-disciplined, ultra-left radicalism. In Germany, Theodor Adorno was being treated by some as a relic of a best forgotten past and he himself analysed the situation as the unwelcome return of atheoretical anarchism.[39] In Britain, Hobsbawm likewise worried that 1968 had ushered in the return

---

38   Hilton, *Bond Men Made Free*, 213, 227–28. Cf. Fagan and Hilton, *English Rising*, 72–76.
39   Theodor W. Adorno, 'Resignation (1969)', in *Critical Models: Interventions and Catchwords* (New York: Columbia University Press, 2005), 289–93. Cf. Lorenz Jäger, *Adorno: A Political Biography* (New Haven: Yale University Press, 2004), 192–208; Stefan Müller-Doohm, *Adorno: An Intellectual Biography* (Cambridge: Polity, 2005); Detlev Claussen, *Theodor W. Adorno: One Last Genius* (Cambridge, MA: Belknap Press of Harvard University Press, 2008), e.g., 1–2, 10, 201, 332–39.

of anarchism and with it failure and a lack of theoretical insight.[40] For those like Hobsbawm, Hill, and Hilton who had become Communists in the 1930s, the fragmentation of the Left in the 1960s and the popularity of 1968 was further a threat to the dominance of Marxism-Leninism, a theoretical background which led Hilton and Hill to be suspicious of more disorganised rebellion. Despite sympathies, the student unrest of 1968 was still a social world quite removed from the ideals of disciplined seriousness and respectability of those with a background in British Communism and Nonconformity, though it should be added that Hilton was known to be much more at home with wine and in less-than-puritanical settings.[41] To add to the contradictions posed by rebellious students, by 1968 Hilton, Hill, and Hobsbawm were fast becoming distinguished. Indeed, Hill became Master of Balliol at Oxford while Hilton, we recall, became professor at Birmingham in 1963 and, less than a decade after 1968, a Fellow of the British Academy (1977), despite his sometime disdain for academic and university management.[42]

Nevertheless, while neither uncritical of nor naïve about the claims coming from the 1968 generation, members of the Historians' Group could, to some degree, embrace the changing world and be embraced by it. I have argued elsewhere that Hill's famous *The World Turned Upside Down* (1972) was a product of these tensions which partly account for its prominence and popularity. The book covers various radical groups and individuals, from Ranters to Winstanley, and accompanying topics included

---

40 For Hobsbawm's ambivalence concerning the radicalism of the 1960s and 1968, see, e.g., his essays 'Reflections on Anarchism (1969)', 'Revolution and Sex (1969)', and 'May 1968 (1968)', in Eric Hobsbawm, *Revolutionaries* (New York: New Press, 2001), 97–108, 256–60, 279–91, and his book, *Interesting Times: A Twentieth Century Life* (London: Abacus, 2002), 246–62.

41 See, e.g., Samuel H. Beer, 'Christopher Hill: Some Reminiscences', in Pennington and Thomas (eds.), *Puritans and Revolutionaries*, 1–4; Woodhams, *History in the Making*, 103–4, 106; Dyer, 'Obituary'; Dyer, 'Rodney Hilton', 12; Dyer, 'Rodney Howard Hilton 1916–2002', 67–68; Penelope J. Corfield, '"We are All One in the Eyes of the Lord": Christopher Hill and the Historical Meanings of Radical Religion', *History Workshop Journal* 58 (2004): 111–27; Samuel, *Lost World of British Communism*, 185–200; Hobsbawm, *Interesting Times*, 132–33; Hobsbawm, 'Hilton'.

42 Hugh Stretton, 'Christopher Hill: Some Reminiscences', in Pennington and Thomas (eds.), *Puritans and Revolutionaries*, 10–17; Maurice Keen, 'Christopher Hill: Some Reminiscences', in Pennington and Thomas (eds.), *Puritans and Revolutionaries*, 17–21; Dyer, 'Obituary'; Dyer, 'Rodney Hilton', 12; Dyer, 'Rodney Howard Hilton 1916–2002', 64, 75.

antinomianism, land redistribution, class consciousness, and, perhaps most tellingly, sexual freedom and the significance of youthful revolutionary enthusiasm. But this was made more credible and serious, I argued, through the constant reference to the Bible (often concluding a paragraph) as a serious and rational framing of radical ideas and as a means to explain the importance of communal interpretation over individualistic interpretation.[43] The next year, Hilton published *Bond Men Made Free*. Partly constrained by his source material, Hilton did not have such obvious connections to make between the 1380s and the 1960s but *Bond Men Made Free* was nevertheless a sustained book about a major uprising and was likewise published in the aftermath of 1968. Colonial struggles abroad are at least as important for understanding the book in context and it was for good reason that with the death of Franco (1975) Hilton became a popular figure among Spanish radical historians.[44] Though not a major emphasis in *Bond Men Made Free*, there is also some indication of his interest in the area of women's history which was similarly growing from the 1960s onwards. Here we might note Hilton's comment that among 'heretical sects' were 'a high proportion of women' and that the topic of women in the village was a feature of Hilton's 1973 Ford Lectures published in *The English Peasantry in the Later Middle Ages* (1975).[45] Moreover, issues of gender were becoming more mainstream in academic and radical history, helped in no small part by a younger generation associated with the old Historians' Group, notably Sheila Rowbotham who published *Women, Resistance and Revolution* in 1972. Perhaps this tension between radicalism and respectability is best seen in the fact that Hilton, Hill, and Rowbotham gave their seemingly fringe academic subjects with their seemingly bizarre beliefs a significant degree of academic and even popular credibility.

But the 1960s and 1968 in particular would mark another turning point in the story of both the reception of the British Marxist historians and Ball. While Rowbotham was influenced by her older contemporaries, her career would involve engagement with and influences from a wider range of radical and countercultural ideas (including anarchism). More broadly, Communist and Marxist influences towards the end of the twentieth century were among other similarly prominent competing and (sometimes) overlapping influences, tendencies, and affiliations (human rights, animal rights, anarchism, direct action, Trotskyism, women's liberation, antiracism, environmentalism, etc.) on an increasingly fragmented Left. In

---

43 Crossley, *Harnessing Chaos*, 53–69.
44 Dyer, 'Rodney Howard Hilton 1916–2002', 68, 70–72.
45 Hilton, *Bond Men Made Free*, 107; Hilton, *English Peasantry*, 95–110.

the postmodern era, Marxist and Communist totalising claims became unfashionable or distrusted even on the Left, or at least among those who might be identified with the Left, as ideas of resistance and subversion were celebrated in everyday acts removed from ideas of working-class power. Ironically, it was such ideas that gave cultural or subcultural credibility to emerging neoliberalism where the 1960s antibureaucratic rhetoric of freedom, liberty, and personal responsibility was appropriated by the Thatcherite Right with its stress on economic liberalism, deregulation, and entrepreneurialism, alongside contradictory anxieties surrounding nostalgia, counterculture, radicalism, social liberalism, post-imperialism, consumerism, patriotism, and conservatism also coming out of the 1960s. At the turn of the twenty-first century, and with the Soviet Union gone, New Labour fused the rhetoric of social and economic liberalism together, seemingly quelling the influence of socialism and union power.[46] In some ways Hilton's reading of Ball in historical materialist terms may have been the most learned and sustained of such readings but it was also arguably the last great presentation of its kind in a Marxist tradition which had gathered momentum since Engels, Morris, and Hyndman. As the historical materialist readings of Ball went into decline, Ball was more likely to be seen as an example of an almost quaint 'history from below.' Yet while this may have been an English radical tradition often distanced from historical materialism, the final decades did see versions of Ball kept alive on the Left in the battles against Thatcherism—and not least by Hilton himself.

46 See further Crossley, *Cults, Martyrs, and Good Samaritans*, 10–29.

21
Ball after 1968

In the 1970s, references in the press to Ball and the revolt continued to be rare and occasional and are most typically found with reference to theatrical performances (see below). Nevertheless, when they do turn up, they still have their uses in understanding the changing reception of Ball. In a *Coventry Evening Telegraph* column on 'Other People's Homes' (1977), we get a tour of the 'quiet dignity' of Bettie Anstey's house. Through the heavy oak door and up the staircase, there was a stained-glass window featuring Tyler and Ball. Where it came from Mrs Anstey did not know, but the accompanying words beneath Ball were the Adam and Eve couplet, while under Tyler were 'But he who marches in the front rank must fall for the glory of the cause.' That these words were presented by the article as 'intriguing' only adds to the overall sense of how forgotten the popular memory and knowledge of Ball was becoming.[1] Beverley Cross's *The Great Society* (1974)—a performance at the Mermaid Theatre, London, of Richard's final two hours imprisoned at Pontefract Castle where the revolt is recalled through flashbacks—seems to have united different reviewers precisely over the point that J. C. Trewin lamented: 'I doubt whether a chronicle of the peasants' revolt at the opening of Richard II's reign will be generally popular; too many theatregoers share Henry Ford's poor opinion of history.'[2] Such was the perception that this was a memory lost that Charles Lewsen in *The Times* felt the need to remind readers that 'The Great Society of Beverley Cross's title is not that which Lyndon Baines Johnson hoped to create in America, but that which the visionary priest John Ball hoped to bring about by means of the Peasants' Revolt.'[3] Herbert Kretzmer in the *Daily Express* seemed to assume that Ball himself had become a particularly unmemorable figure from history, even among the rebels of 1381,

1 *Coventry Evening Telegraph* (14 March 1977).
2 *Birmingham Post* (21 May and 22 May 1974).
3 *The Times* (21 May 1974).

as he did not mention Ball by name (unlike other characters) but simply referred to 'a raging old priest on the rebel side'.[4]

Of course, neither Ball nor his reception were entirely forgotten, and were still being updated accordingly.[5] Generational tensions emerging from the 1960s were manifesting themselves in the ways Ball was visualised. Some references to Ball reveal a changing social world with reference to a favoured choice of personal grooming (or not). A letter to the *Kent & Sussex Courier* (1970) responded to, and attempted to undermine, the polemical contrast between 'long-haired layabouts' and 'Kent's good old farming stock'. To do this, Ball, Tyler, and Cade were praised as belonging to Kent's farming stock and should take their place alongside fellow long-haired layabouts Robin Hood, King Arthur, John the Baptist, Jesus, and indeed 'most of the heroes of our folk history'.[6] Whether fans of the short-back-and-sides approved or not, it seems that by the 1970s Ball's hair had grown with the times, as further indicated by Bernard Miles's somewhat feral-looking Ball in Cross's *The Great Society* and Richard Angas's similarly hirsute Ball in a production the same year (1974) of Alan Bush's opera *Wat Tyler* (see Chapter 19).[7] But it was not just Ball's physical appearance that was changing; as all this already implies, appearance and ideology went hand-in-hand.

4 *Daily Express* (21 May 1974).
5 As ever, novelists in the UK and North America continued to find the revolt a helpful backdrop or a point of reference. See, e.g., Martha Rofheart, *Cry 'God for Glendower'* (London: Talmy, 1973); Jane Lane, *A Summer Storm* (London: Peter Davies, 1976); John Attenborough, *The Priest's Story* (London: Hodder and Stoughton, 1984). Cf. Taylor, *London's Burning*, 31, 188 n. 69. Some of the description of Ball provided in Rofheart's *Cry 'God for Glendower'* goes against some of the traditional descriptions (e.g., arm movement, eyes), though provides another example of a more sizeable Ball: 'His habit was patched but clean, of a gray wadmal-stuff, girded up over bare feet and legs. He had a mild face and quiet manner, standing quite still, a stocky man upwards of forty, holding up his hand for silence. When he spoke, his voice was low and his words full of reason; low and calm he spoke, but all heard, for not a skirt rustled. He did not wave his arms about or flash his eyes, but like a rock he stood and spoke as one man to another' (14).
6 *Kent & Sussex Courier* (13 February 1970).
7 *The Times* (21 May 1974). For photographs of Bush's opera, see http://www.alanbushtrust.org.uk/music/operas/wat_tyler.asp. Cf. Lane, *A Summer Storm*, 29: 'he roamed the countryside for the past twenty years in the manner of an Old Testament prophet'. *A Summer Storm* also refers to the familiar 'famous bellow' (70, cf. 92) and 'fiery eloquence' (164) of Ball.

Ball and Politics after 1968

From the Left and liberal wings of political culture, the overturning of the old establishment (whether political, military, economic, church, or trade union) was helped by youth movements and the 'Satire Boom' featuring satirists such as David Frost, Peter Cook, Dudley Moore, Jonathan Miller, Alan Bennett, John Bird, and John Fortune. This would give Thatcherism an often unintentional assist, as well as preparing the way for the Anglicised version of postmodernity and the challenge to all (but especially Marxist) metanarratives.[8] As noted, anti-establishment (and later anti-Thatcherite) critique was no longer dominated by Marxist questions of class but rather by a range of fractured interests closer to radical liberalism. Thus, what emerged as dominant discourses on the Left was not necessarily connected with class conflict or Marxism.

That Ball's relation to political radicalism was being rethought after the 1960s was already being laid out in 1970 by Rev. Gordon Wilson in the *Crewe Chronicle*. Wilson noted, and cautiously celebrated, that the age of deference was ending, and people were increasingly vocal about their equality with one another, as students, strikers, pop groups, sports stars, mini-skirted girls, and boys with long, flowing hair 'loudly proclaim their total indifference to sacred custom or august authority.' In Communist countries, Wilson argued, equality was an abstract notion imposed from above and only resulted in creating distinctions of privilege. In contrast, the reactions against deference from below were a 'kind of spontaneous rebellion...a much more natural phenomenon' which was less a reaction against all authority and more about reaction against 'forms and attitudes.' Certainly, such behaviour could be unpleasant and uncouth, for true equality requires respect for the individual which, incidentally it seems, also accounted for the 'failure of totalitarian communist regimes' to achieve equality. Indeed, Wilson even alluded to Orwell's *Animal Farm* to warn against the anti-deference revolution taking a wrong turn. While respect for each other and not our betters was a communist 'ideal,' it was also a Christian one, he argued, and the Christian route was preferable because Christian respect is grounded in love and love 'springs from the source of life itself.' Moreover, the 'rugged individualism' which had 'long been a feature of the English character' originated in the Christian ideal and the present revolt against deference begun six hundred years prior, at least, with Wycliffe and Ball. Ball's Adam and Eve couplet was a critique of deference

---

8   See Crossley, *Harnessing Chaos*, 95–152.

and Ball himself 'was, after all, executed for his lack of deference.' Wilson went on to fire at social distinctions in cricket and then racial distinctions involved in those who wanted to play another test match against White South Africa.⁹ Ball as both liberal Cold War warrior and opponent of Apartheid would return more prominently eleven years later (see below).

Memories of Ball could sometimes be hazy, even when promoted by his most prominent advocates in the late twentieth century. Paul Oestreicher (b. 1931), priest of the Church of the Ascension at Blackheath, suggested that Morris's Ball and the Ball of the chroniclers could still be difficult to disentangle—even to the point of them being assumed to be one and the same. In the *Church Times*, Oestreicher defended keeping church doors open at all times, recalling the bad (e.g., youths creatively using the pulpit as a toilet) and the good (e.g., long conversations with young people from the 'high days of hippy-dom' who had come to meditate and sing). On the noticeboard through the unlocked doors, the words of Ball illustrated the point of fellowship and the importance of Holy Communion, fittingly on Corpus Christi ('the Feast of the Blessed Sacrament'). What is notable is that these were the words of Morris's Ball ('Fellowship...is heaven, and lack of fellowship is hell...') which Oestreicher instead claimed were preached by Ball to the rebels camped on Blackheath.¹⁰

As we will see, Oestreicher became an influential figure in the reception of Ball, and his interests in antiracism and peace activism reflect, or tell a story about, some of the major political and cultural changes in post-1960s England and beyond (see Chapters 22, 23). To this day, the Church of the Ascension invokes Oestreicher and Ball and puts them into a broader tradition with a clear focus on gender, sexuality, and human rights. As their brief statement of belief puts it:

> We are fully supportive of human rights in this church and are active in campaigning for changes in attitudes towards LGBT+ people in the wider church. We see ourselves as in the radical tradition of Wat Tyler and John Ball, who led the Peasants' Revolt. Wat Tyler Road is in the parish. More recently, Rev. Paul Oestreicher was a founding member of Amnesty International in 1961 and of the Movement for the Ordination of Women. Deaconess Elsie Baker was one of the first women ordained to the priesthood in the Church of England and was ordained in her 85th year.¹¹

---

9   *Crewe Chronicle* (28 May 1970).
10 *Church Times* (11 April 1975).
11 https://www.ascension-blackheath.org/page/32/what-we-believe.

Though such specific notions of gender and sexuality would become more clearly associated with Ball sometime later, the 1960s onwards saw the steady foregrounding of often (but not always) marginal associations between Ball and different notions of equality aside from, alongside, or as part of, understandings of class and political representation. The epigraph for David Rubinstein's edited collection of short pieces on British radicalism (*People for the People* [1969]) is a quotation from *A Dream of John Ball* about future battles fought under a different name. The opening main essay is from Rodney Hilton on Ball, and followed the radical tradition which includes traditional favourites (Levellers, Owen, Peterloo, Chartism, Morris, etc.), but also Janet Blackman's 'The First Women's Liberation Movement.'[12]

As with anti-Apartheid readings, racialised readings were being updated and foregrounded. Around the same time as *People for the People*, an educational film for the Learning Corporation of America—*Medieval England: The Peasants' Revolt* (1969), starring Anthony Hopkins as a typically rugged Tyler—took the ideas associated with the revolt in the direction of democratic representation and racial politics.[13] A wise, solemn, unkempt, and stubbly Ball (played by Christopher Logue) provided an expanded version of the Adam and Eve discussion which was a more fully biblical and theologically informed sermon. Nevertheless, it is still a broadly familiar narrative of the revolt also featuring a presentation of conflict between master and serf (or the 'free and the unfree'), a brutal feudal system, and hope for the Great Society. Yet it was still a revolt that was, so the narrator claims, the 'first collision between capital and labour.' Somewhat puzzlingly given this statement, the narrator (Patrick Allen) later claims that feudalism would later give way to 'systems of trade and commerce.' But the film's ending is especially striking. The narrator stresses that in the middle ages, 'basic human rights' were denied to the majority but that 'western civilisation claimed back most of them; the democratic process replaced the feudal system.' Today, it seems to be the minorities rather than majorities who, like the peasants before them, 'cry out against the iron glove in the gut' and this is cut with footage from street uprisings, including footage of civil rights protests and police brutality against black protesters.

---

12 Rubinstein (ed.), *People for the People*.
13 The film is available on YouTube: https://www.youtube.com/watch?v=3IJsIfGyiWA.

Class Remains

But such broader emphases would take time to become embedded in the reception history of Ball while the reading of Ball and the revolt in relation to class and class-conflict remained another strand in the reception of Ball and the revolt in the 1970s, even if it did not dominate as it had for decades. After the work of Hilton (see Chapter 20), one of the most sustained and developed representations of Ball in the early 1970s in relation to such issues came from a popular fringe theatre performance, *Will Wat, If Not What Will?* at the Half Moon Theatre on Alie Street in the East End of London (26 May–24 June 1972). It featured a ten-strong cast playing different roles and written (in collaboration with the cast) by Steve Gooch (b. 1945), a playwright associated with socialist and community theatre and people's history, which included writing an unpublished play on the Lollards (*Passed On* [1978]) which begins in the aftermath of Ball's death.[14] While elite positions are represented or deliberately caricatured (Chaucer gets a firm sending up), *Will Wat* is part of such people's history and it accordingly focuses most attention on the peasantry, presenting their predicament and noting where the decisions of the ruling class had a direct impact on them. Starting in 1340, *Will Wat* moved through different historical scenes in the fourteenth century (e.g., peasant life, Black Death, Edward III and Alice Perrers, returning soldiers, Statute of Labourers, Parliament of Northampton, the revolt itself), which echoed Gooch's understanding of how to represent on the stage historical change and the effects of class struggle over time and place—and the resulting victory of the merchant class.[15] This included audience participation: the Half Moon production involved audience tongue inspections to test for the plague; a third of the audience told they had died of the plague; Parliament sat among the audience; and the king's charters were handed out to the audience,

---

14 Of *Passed On*, Gooch said in Michael Punter, 'Steve Gooch: A Playwright's Progress', *Contemporary Theatre Review* 23 (2013): 602–5 (604), 'I tried to tell the story of a group belief, the non-conformism which, though fiercely suppressed, continues today as one of the most powerful, if now secular, reflexes of protest in English public life.' I am grateful to Steve Gooch for giving me access to *Passed On*.

15 Simon Shepherd, 'An Interview with Steve Gooch', *Renaissance and Modern Studies* 21 (1977): 5–36 (20–21); Steve Gooch, *All Together Now: An Alternative View of Theatre and the Community* (London: Methuen, 1984), 82.

all under the eye of a giant picture of Richard II based on his portrait at Westminster Abbey.[16]

But while entertainment and fun were meant to be part of the experience, there remained serious ideological issues at play and the background to these are worth more discussion. Gooch believed that Britain did not have a strong Marxist tradition, but he saw strengths in a culture of communal experiences and collaboration. As he put it in an interview with Simon Shepherd published in 1977, a more socialised theatre invited people 'to participate fully, both emotionally and intellectually, in the totality of the subject that is being dealt with' so the audience could emotionally engage with the arguments.[17] Gooch explained that he saw himself as part of a socialist theatre which belonged to a broader alternative theatre tradition emerging from the late 1960s and the associated politics. Gooch's tradition was aimed at providing theatre for, or including, a working-class audience and understanding that culture 'is a reflection of the class struggle generally.'[18] Community theatre involved talking not so much about geographical location but more generally about the working class as a community of shared ideas, interests, and experiences, hence workers, trade unionists, and socialists could travel some distance to the Half Moon and still be understood as belonging. But success among working-class audiences could also involve local interest stories and an accompanying popular mythology (as in the case of performances at the Half Moon). The significance of such theatre, he argued, was to present an alternative view of society to that presented in established theatre and the dominant culture. For Gooch, such theatre involved 'exposing the contradictions of capitalist society,' 'presenting a critique of the various ways in which capitalist society may act against the interests of the working-class,' and 'understanding the political forces in people's lives and the cultural issues which affect us all.'[19] Indeed, of the Half Moon production, Irving Wardle in *The Times* noted that Ball's brief appearance linked 'Richard II's Blackheath to the Alie Street of today (an area of small business in the shadow of the Mint), adding that

---

16 Reviews, interviews, photographs, etc., are conveniently collected at 'Will Wat, If Not, What Will? (1972),' *Stages of Half Moon*, https://www.stagesofhalfmoon.org.uk/productions/will-wat-if-not-what-will-1972/. See also Gooch, *Will Wat*, i. On notions of audience more generally, see Gooch, *All Together Now*, 37–38.
17 Shepherd, 'Interview,' 34–35.
18 Shepherd, 'Interview,' 17.
19 Shepherd, 'Interview,' 11.

the famous words that "things won't go well in England till all is held in common".[20]

The language of *Will Wat* played an important part in terms of class positions and identity—and as a potential means of avoiding the familiar cliches of middle-class theatrical language. Gooch was aware of the limitations (including limitations of knowledge) in representing fourteenth-century English on the stage and saw little option but to write in accessible idiomatic English and focus on the material conditions of the characters to show the difference between peasants and the ruling class.[21] The 'Writer's Note' prefacing the published version of *Will Wat* stresses the importance of informality and contact with the audience, adding 'it is no good "playing" this. They should be like people getting up at a family party and doing their turn'—and that the Half Moon was particularly conducive to this. The Note also explains that in avoiding 'Mummerset' acting in the Half Moon production, 'a kind of medieval rural dialect of our own' was developed to show something of the 'physical nature of language in those days.' While a French-style accent was tried for the nobility, it turned out that 'straight "posh" worked very well for them.'[22] In *Will Wat* there is plenty of swearing on both sides (e.g., 'cunt,' 'fucking hell,' 'bollocks,' etc.) which is worth noting if only because such language is so unusual in the history of the reception of Ball and the revolt.

Nevertheless, Gooch was aware that some working-class audiences could use swear words at school or work while shunning such language in other formal settings,[23] and this may perhaps explain why the key religious figures of Ball (played by Maurice Colbourne) and the Ball-like preacher do not use such language in *Will Wat*. Ball instead is known in the play for his preaching about inequality and things not going well in England 'till all things are in common,' presenting a sermon on St Paul and the social body, and providing a familiar version of the Adam and Eve sermon at Blackheath.[24] But even if Ball provides the revered ideological foundations of the uprising, he is hardly distanced from the bloody realities of it. The Blackheath sermon explicitly uses the parable of the wheat and the tares to call for the archbishop, lawyers, and the good and the great to be dispatched 'out of the land' as the king and his entourage (Salisbury, Sudbury,

---

20 *The Times* (16 June 1972).
21 Shepherd, 'Interview,' 19; Punter, 'Steve Gooch,' 605.
22 Steve Gooch, *Will Wat, If Not What Will?* (London: Pluto, 1974), i–ii. Cf. Gooch, *All Together Now*, 53.
23 Shepherd, 'Interview,' 28.
24 Gooch, *Will Wat*, 25, 40–41, 52–53.

Hales, and Walworth) approach on the barge. But even more explicit is Ball's first entrance, where 'He carries the head of a nobleman on a spear.' Ball continues by giving his sermon on solidarity and the importance of the cohesion of the Pauline social body. The severed head serves as an example of someone who 'decided to place himself above other men,' who 'refused to join you,' who 'refused to give up his wealth and possessions to the common good. He wished to remain aloof. Now he is aloft.' The imagery of the head and body is used to explain the role of the king as the 'head that serves the body,' a somewhat ominous explanation given the difficult discussions of regicide that will soon take place in the play.[25]

This is not to say that because Gooch focused on class relations, he avoided discussion about, for instance, race or gender, as his work in the 1970s shows (e.g., the deported women in *Female Transport* [1974] or the background fascism and the National Front in *Backstreet Romeo* [1977]). With *Will Wat*, Gooch is a rare example of a writer bringing the expulsion and drowning of Jews under Edward I into the narrative of the revolt (see also Hyman Fagan; Chapter 18).[26] Nevertheless, it remains that overt issues of class were foregrounded in the Half Moon production. Moreover, the old questions of industry, pay, and conditions—and Ball's role in them—did not go away so easily from wider public debate, at least not when there were prominent analogies in the 1970s.[27] Douglas Orgill may have written a light-hearted article in the *Daily Express* (1977) on the horrors of the medieval toilet and the joys of the modern flush-toilet, but in pointing out the similarities between past and present it is telling what he noted. There was the equivalent of strikes and 'trouble about wages and class distinction' which he highlighted with reference to the Adam and Eve couplet to an audience assumed to be unfamiliar with this past ('People knew their places in those days, didn't they? Well, no they didn't'). Ball's preaching, Orgill claimed, launched the revolt which fuelled 'a festering row about an agricultural wage freeze, and was led by Tyler, who'd been annoyed by the tax men.' Today, he noted, 'we still have wage restraint, and an Inland Revenue,' but no Tyler 'now that David Frost copped out and joined the Establishment.'[28] Reviewers of Cross's *Great Society* had detected similar analogies a few years earlier. R. B. Marriot commended the place for 'the likeness of the Revolt to Industrial events today...indicated without undue

---

25 Gooch, *Will Wat*, 40, 48–49.
26 Gooch, *Will Wat*, 6.
27 Cf. Lane, *Summer Storm*, 24–25.
28 *Daily Express* (14 December 1977).

stress.'²⁹ This point was echoed in Lewsen's review in *The Times* where he 'rather [got] the impression that the peasants were demonstrating against an earlier Industrial Relations Act, as it were, fretting about wages being frozen and not having the right to strike,' adding that the play had further contemporary relevance (that Gooch also touched upon), as it showed 'Flemish immigrants entering the country as cheap labour and being made scapegoats for the peasants' frustration.'³⁰

This also meant that the connection between Ball and socialism was retained in public discourse, including in the reviews of *Great Society*. It was explained in another review in *The Times* that the revolt 'led by Wat Tyler, John Ball, Jack Straw and Thomas Farringdon, almost overthrew the government to establish the first socialist society in Europe.'³¹ The long-established anxieties surrounding the revolt, mob violence, and a threat to the capital were also given an updating.³² In his review, Kretzmer claimed that at 'a time when any London street may blow up under a terrorist's bomb, and mindless violence is at the helm, it is instructive, if not reassuring, to be reminded that the city has long known the cry of innocents' slaughtered in the name of vengeance.' But he qualified this by observing that the London rebels were 'yelling for a socialist utopia' and that in the 'crude slogan shouting of the violent mob we may hear the ancestral echoes of today's wild men of the Maoist left, the ancient thirst for vengeance of the I.R.A.'³³ And if there was one politician on the post-1960s English Left associated (rightly or wrongly) with these sorts of threats, it was another influential interpreter of Ball: Tony Benn.

Tony Benn

Tony Benn (1925–2014) represented the last significant peak for the Labour Left before his mentee Jeremy Corbyn won the Labour leadership election in 2015. In some ways, Benn and Bennism were the closest to something approaching canonical status for the Labour Left of the late-twentieth century and so Benn's remarks should be taken as an important indicator of some of the assumptions about the reception of the revolt. In *Arguments*

29 *The Stage* (30 May 1974).
30 *The Times* (21 May 1974).
31 *The Times* (20 May 1974).
32 Cf. Lane, *A Summer Storm*, e.g., 30, 70–72, 91, 94–95, 101–2, 107–10, 133.
33 *Daily Express* (21 May 1974).

for Socialism (1979), a collection of lectures, speeches, and articles from the 1970s which sold over 75,000 copies,[34] Benn grounded the claims of the Labour Left in the long familiar English radical tradition, including 1381 as the earliest British example (excluding the Bible and Christ, if they be deemed British):

> democratic socialism...is very much a home-grown British product which has been slowly fashioned over the centuries. Its roots are deep in our history and have been nourished by the Bible, the teachings of Christ, the Peasants' Revolt, the Levellers, Tom Paine, the Chartists, Robert Owen, the Webbs and Bernard Shaw who were Fabians, and occasionally by Marxists, Liberals and radicals who have all contributed their analysis to our study of society. The Labour Party comprises within its ranks representatives of a wide range of opinions.[35]

Benn's arguments were developed further in a follow-up collection of material, *Arguments for Democracy* (1981). With this biblically inspired tradition, Benn argued, came anti-establishment teachings which, when interpreted in the sense of 'social imperatives' should be seen as revolutionary. However, in Benn's argument, these teachings inevitably became 'a vague and generalised injunction' to the 'rich and powerful' to be kind while 'the poor' were prompted to return love by being 'patient and submissive.' This is why 'the authorities' had to keep the Bible away from the laity, otherwise the 'radical interpretation of the teachings of Jesus' would continue to spread.[36] Ball and the Peasants' Revolt, alongside Wycliffe and the Lollards, were unsurprisingly part of this radical tradition for Benn. Unlike some on the Left of the Labour Party with Bennite sympathies and in some ways close to certain Marxist readings, Benn kept Ball and the Lollards/Wycliffe distinct. Nevertheless, they were seen as part of the same phenomenon:

> The radical interpretation of the message of brotherhood and the resulting anti-establishment agitation has surfaced time and again throughout our history. Wycliffe and the Lollards were engaged in it. So was the

---

34 Graham Dale, *God's Politicians: The Christian Contribution to 100 Years of Labour* (London: HarperCollins, 2000), 194.
35 Tony Benn, *Arguments for Socialism* (ed. Chris Mullin; London: Jonathan Cape, 1979), 146. For further discussion on Benn and the Bible, see Crossley, *Harnessing Chaos*, 20–26.
36 Tony Benn, *Arguments for Democracy* (ed. Chris Mullin; London: Penguin, 1981), 123–24.

Reverend John Ball whose support for the Peasants' Revolt cost him his life in 1381.³⁷

Benn further described Wycliffe and the Lollards as being persecuted 'for encouraging people to read the Bible, undermining the authority of the bishops and priesthood, the King and the landlords.'³⁸ Under the heading 'The secularisation of the Christian ethic,' this reading was part of Benn's case to bridge Christianity and 'humanism' (and, more widely in Benn's ideas, to counter the claim that atheism was central to socialism). And over this bridge came 'revolutionary ideas deriving from the Bible and the carpenter of Nazareth,' and these ideas influenced people for whom 'neighbourly love within a common humanity is more immediately apparent than the value of mysticism, liturgies and creeds.'³⁹

His idea of radical interpreters of the Bible as understood to be against 'mysticism, liturgies and creeds' pointed to an inherited, albeit more implicit, influence of a particular understanding of Nonconformity in the labour movement and a dominant strand in the interpretation of the revolt, though Benn also explicitly referred to the significance of Congregationalism (Benn's own tradition) and the Quakers. This construction of the stifling established church interested in theological obfuscation is one Benn pushed hard in this same context. 'Generations of churchmen,' he argued, 'have formulated creeds and liturgies, discussed the mystical aspects of theology and worked within ecclesiastical hierarchies to interpret the word of God for the faithful, supported by various disciplines designed to secure their compliance.'⁴⁰ The flip side of this might be a lingering (and unconscious) anti-Catholicism in Benn's argument, and the history of such rhetoric cannot be ignored in understanding such language. In this respect, it is telling that Benn gave Ball the title 'Reverend' rather than the potentially Catholicizing 'Priest.'⁴¹ However, there is something

---

37 Benn, *Arguments for Democracy*, 124.
38 Benn, *Arguments for Democracy*, 244 n. 2.
39 Benn, *Arguments for Democracy*, 125.
40 Benn, *Arguments for Democracy*, 123.
41 'Reverend' is repeated in his talk at the Cambridge Folk Festival, 2000, available as Tony Benn and Roy Bailey, *The Writing on the Wall* (Fuse Records, 2004). Benn does refer to Ball as 'priest' in Tony Benn, *Fighting Back: Speaking Out for Socialism in the Eighties* (London: Hutchinson, 1988), 38–39, but it is an exception that proves the rule in that it alludes to the saying associated with Henry II's exasperation with Thomas Becket, an occasional hero in the English radical tradition: 'John Ball, that turbulent priest—now they would call him a militant, of course.'

else going on in Benn's argument. He also attacked what might be seen as an obvious case of Protestantism in this context, as he did with evangelicals or the archbishop of Canterbury elsewhere,[42] when he criticised churches past and present for being 'more concerned with the task of personal salvation than with the social imperatives spelled out in Jesus' reply [Mark 12.29–31].'[43]

This implicit cross-denominational critique was crucial not just for Benn's attempt to provide a bridge between revolutionary Christianity and humanism for common neighbourly love for all. To make his argument work, it was important for Benn not to have a particular denomination singled out as the oppressor because the argument is a generalisation about democratic resistance to power, hence he elsewhere talked about 'prophets against the kings' or opposing the orders of the Labour Party hierarchy.[44] This dissenting tradition was emphatically collective for Benn and, moreover, one he tied in with the Peasants' Revolt and the interpretation of Acts 2.44–45 and 4.32–35 and all things in common. By the end of the 1980s, Benn's issues of 'common ownership espoused by many generations from John Ball to Lloyd George' were seen in terms of emerging 'ecological movement' reacting against 'the rape of our environment,' an issue seen alongside race, women's rights, and the peace movement in Benn's leftism.[45] But more traditional economic concerns were also at play. In a later debate in the House of Commons, Benn suggested that,

> The Bible has led to many revolutionary ideas—for instance, that we were and are all equal in the sight of God—which is why, in 1401, the House of Commons passed the Heresy Act, which condemned any lay person reading the Bible to be burned at the stake for heresy. The Bible has always been a controversial document. At the time of the Peasants' Revolt and the English revolution, people started thinking of common ownership,

---

42 Tony Benn, *Free at Last! Diaries 1991–2001* (London: Hutchinson, 2002), 17; Tony Benn, *Dare to Be a Daniel: Then and Now* (London: Arrow Books, 2004), 4. Cf. Tony Benn, 'The Power of the Bible Today,' *Sheffield Academic Press Occasional Papers: The Twelfth Annual Sheffield Academic Press Lecture, University of Sheffield, March 17, 1995* (Sheffield: Sheffield Academic Press, 1995), 1–13 (4).
43 Benn, *Arguments for Democracy*, 123.
44 Benn, 'Power of the Bible Today,' 3–5, 7–8; Tony Benn, *Free Radical: New Century Essays* (New York: Continuum, 2003), 226; Benn, *Dare to Be a Daniel*, 4.
45 Benn, *Fighting Back*, 269–70.

based on the life of the apostles...The idea of socialism is of common ownership and that things are best done by co-operation.⁴⁶

In this speech Benn talked about common ownership in relation to nationalisation but in opposition to the top-down sense of nationalised industry and media, as well as against unaccountable corporate interests. Instead, he argued, representation was needed, and progressive change must be driven from below. This line of thought was foundational to Benn's democratic socialism, as it would be for Corbynism (indeed, Corbyn spoke in support of Benn shortly after this speech). Elsewhere, Benn pushed the idea of common ownership and Acts with reference to Clause 4 (a commitment to common/public ownership or nationalisation) of the Labour Party constitution. Benn claimed that 'anyone who really thinks that Clause 4 and common ownership was invented by Karl Marx, and I think there are some people quite high up in the Labour Party who think that, might go back to the Acts of the Apostles for the idea of all things in common.'⁴⁷

But Benn was speaking here about all things in common in relation to Clause 4 just as Tony Blair was removing it from the Labour Party constitution. By the mid-1990s, Benn and Bennism was, it seemed, a spent political force within Labour. The beginning of the decline was, arguably, when Benn narrowly lost the Deputy Leadership election to Denis Healey in a year of some significance for the reception of Ball: 1981. 1981 was not only the year when *Arguments for Democracy* was published, it was also the six-hundredth anniversary of the revolt which, despite the declining public discussion since the War, brought Ball and the revolt firmly back into public debate, even if temporarily. Yet for all its popularity on the Left, the six-hundredth anniversary would, as with Benn's political prominence, instead mark one of the last great hurrahs for the post-war Left in the twentieth century as Thatcherism began to dominate British politics.

---

46 'Economic System,' Hansard (16 May 2000), https://publications.parliament. uk/pa/cm199900/cmhansrd/vo000516/halltext/00516h01.htm. Also cited and discussed in Benn, *Dare to Be a Daniel*, 268–78 (269).
47 Benn, 'Power of the Bible Today', 7.

22
1381/1981

On Bank Holiday Monday on 4 May 1981, a few months before Tony Benn's unsuccessful attempt to become Deputy Leader of the Labour Party, a six-hundredth anniversary celebration of the revolt took place at Blackheath (of course). With a sizable crowd and sold out within an hour, it was an event remembered as part political rally, part festival, with music from Squeeze, Frankie Armstrong & Leon Rosselson, Traitors Gait, Rubber Johnny, Bluebird, and Icarus.[1] There were stalls raising funds for homeless people, unemployed agitators, and Ban the Bomb, while Colin Brown, in his slightly sarcastic article in the *Guardian* perhaps lacking a little in self-awareness, quipped how the 'predominantly middle-class Blackheath peasants were supplied with vegetarian food from a van.'[2] The 1381 Committee included representation from Labour members, the Communist Party, and local community and Co-operative groups. As Stephen Williams outlines, a week prior included a lecture by Rodney Hilton held at Paul Oestreicher's Church of the Ascension. Oestreicher himself was a speaker at the Blackheath rally, as were Tony Benn, Joan Maynard (Labour MP, Sheffield Brightside), and Alan Fisher (National Union of Public Employees general secretary). Also present was the Labour MP for Blackburn Jack Straw who, Williams recalls from memory, was only there because of his namesake. Promotion of the labour movement was put at the heart of the event, including parallels between the Statute of Labourers and pay and conditions in the present.[3] The event material was headed by Ball's couplet and accompanied a picture of Adam and Eve being

---

1 'Tony Benn, Allan Boesak & Squeeze commemorate Peasants Revolt on Blackheath 1981,' *Transpontine* (31 July 2016), http://transpont.blogspot.com/2016/07/tony-benn-allan-boesak-squeeze.html; Stephen Williams, 'Radical Objects: The Peasants' Revolt Badge,' *History Workshop Journal* (19 April 2017), https://www.historyworkshop.org.uk/radical-objects-the-peasants-revolt-badge/.
2 *Guardian* (5 May 1981).
3 Williams, 'Radical Objects.'

tempted by the snake in Eden (presumably an unintentional confusion with the later time when Adam dug and Eve span).[4] Ball unsurprisingly came up in speeches. It was reported that Benn quoted from 'Wat Tyler's chaplain' ('Matters will not be right in England until all things are held in common') and compared the treatment of Ball with the press treatment of Bennites. Jack Straw (the Labour one) also said that the struggle for 'equality, justice, and peace' with which Ball, Tyler, and his namesake were involved has 'yet to be won' and compared it with the march of unemployed people from Liverpool who were united, he claimed, 'across six centuries by common ideas and the common belief in the rightness of their cause and the ultimate triumph of socialism.'[5]

As this already suggests, the various events, commemorations, morris dancing, advertisements, publications, newspaper articles, and parliamentary quips celebrating or alluding to the sixth centenary brought together a number of the different (and often overlapping) ideological tendencies surrounding Ball in an era when he was, seemingly, being increasingly forgotten.[6] In the arts, there was a spike in interest in 1381. A mural promoting a festival on 13 June 1981 was painted in six weeks at Bow Common Lane by Mile End Fields and designed by Ray Walker, who would soon be involved in the famous Cable Street mural. The Bow Common Lane mural featured the flaming words PEASANTS REVOLT in mock-medieval script and a painting of threatening rebels holding aloft burning scrolls with the words 'Serfdom,' 'Bondage,' and 'Feudalism,' with the king and his advisors hiding behind castle walls, though with the fate of the archbishop made clear enough.[7] 1981 also saw a recurring portrait of Ball by David Simkin. The portrait is based on the Froissart illustration and is accompanied by the famous fourteenth-century illustration of serfs in the field from the Queen Mary Psalter. '1381' is presented in a mock-medieval font and paralleled with '1981' in a digital font fit for a country on the eve of the age of the ZX Spectrum. The connection between the two dates was, presumably,

---

4 A picture is available at '1981 Squeeze Gigs,' *Packet of Three: The Squeeze Archives*, http://www.packetofthree.co.uk/html/1981_squeeze_gigs.html.
5 *Guardian* (5 May 1981).
6 In Parliament, Michael Stewart (Lord Stewart of Fulham) even referenced a rarely cited Ball saying, 'Let skill go before will.' See 'Ecc 21St Report: Development Aid Policy,' *Hansard: Volume 420* (3 June 1981), col 1297.
7 Hannah Awcock, 'The East End's Radical Murals,' *Turbulent London* (24 September 2015), https://turbulentlondon.com/2015/09/24/the-east-ends-radical-murals/. Photographs are available at 'Ray Walker—Peasants Revolt—1981,' *For Walls with Tongues*, https://www.forwallswithtongues.org.uk/projects/ray-walker-peasants-revolt-1981/.

through the accompanying quotation: Ball's speech about 'things cannot go well in England until all property is in common...'[8]

There were innovations in the reception of Ball in the performing arts too. The Mercury theatre in Colchester hosted a musical play by Maureen Lee (who would later become a prolific bestselling author), *When Adam Delved and Eve Span*, with Daryl Webster bringing out the 'earthy appeal' of the 'hero' Tyler and Bernard Finch playing the 'super-hero of the uprising' and local of St James's Church with 'touching dignity.' The revolt was even given an aesthetic makeover for the late twentieth century as the play was accompanied by music from Pauline Green 'in a variety of pastiche styles ranging from Jolson to Coward to heavy rock,' as well as 'ballads and numbers more in period.'[9] Other works written at this time include Christopher Beddow's play, *1381*, which looked at the interplay between the recovery of Tyler (the 'once courageous soldier...now more and more devoted to ale'), Jack Straw ('the cold but unselfish strategist' experiencing 'desperate hysterical fits'), and a more familiar Ball: 'the spiritual leader, who is an individual enough to disregard the material advantages of being a cleric and questions not God, but the way the ruling classes have turned him to their advantage.'[10]

Ball: Unsuccessful and Sour

Amidst the celebrations, however, a once influential conservative reading of the revolt was given a platform in the *Spectator* which published four articles by the journalist, foreign correspondent, Anglican, contrarian, and later Chaucer biographer, Richard West (1930–2015).[11] The first article even gave us another example of the tradition of typos, with a reference to 'John Bull' (which was likely a mere slip by someone, given that 'Ball' was used throughout the rest of the article and articles). In this case, West was criticising 'several trade unions, far removed from physical toil' for bandying about the Adam and Eve couplet, as well as the 'ineffable Mr Tony

---

8   A version of the picture is available at 'The Peasants' Revolt of 1381,' *Spartacus Educational*, https://spartacus-educational.com/Peasants_Revolt.htm.
9   *The Stage* (19 November 1981).
10 *The Stage* (19 May 1983).
11 On West, see the profiles and obituaries in, e.g., *Spectator* (6 May 1989); *Spectator* (26 April 2015); *Daily Telegraph* (26 April 2015); *Guardian* (27 April 2015).

Benn' trying to 'present himself as a new Wat Tyler.'[12] Ball was once again dismissed and treated as a malign influence or, at best, a man of disreputable disposition. Ball was an 'unsuccessful clergyman' whose levelling talk was aimed at the 'potentates of the Church rather than secular lords.'[13] His 'levelling sermons' that 'appeal to our modern socialists' were in fact quoted by people like Froissart 'to show up what they considered Ball's absurdity.' Yet such equal division of goods 'was not a popular or approved idea, even among the most radical 14th century thinkers.'[14] While little may be known of Ball, 'it is safe to guess he was rather a sour fellow' and Sudbury 'might have been wiser to have Ball hanged, for he in turn hunted and murdered the Archbishop.'[15] Nevertheless, Sudbury was more the hero of this retelling. He had often been forgotten and most visitors to Canterbury turned to the famed Thomas Becket who was thought by West to be 'a much less worthy archbishop.'[16] John Wraw fared worse than Ball in this retelling as he was, West claimed, 'by a long shot, the nastiest person active in 1381...a sour, greedy fellow, both cruel and cowardly but he knew how to exploit other people's envy and lust for power.'[17]

West's polemic was a version of Burke's conservatism (see Chapter 9) for the late twentieth century. West, for instance, criticised the flippancy of TV programmes sugar-coating the past with in-jokes and contemporary relevance, including a 'bright young TV lady' announcing that 'peasants were flexing their industrial muscle.'[18] The flipside of this lack of respect for the past was that it was complicit in denigrating the Middle Ages and perpetuating an ignorance of fourteenth-century England, 'the age of some of our greatest cathedrals, of Chaucer, of Richard II's court, of full and constant intercourse with the art and scholarship of all Christian Europe.'[19] The fourteenth-century establishment did not carry out the punishments with vengeance but rather the legal proceedings were carried out 'with patience and justice.'[20] By contrast, this England had now been replaced by 'the House of Commons, the Civil Service and the trade unions, which now wield greater and more arrogant power than any mediaeval king.'[21] An

12 *Spectator* (30 May 1981).
13 *Spectator* (6 June 1981).
14 *Spectator* (20 June 1981).
15 *Spectator* (6 June 1981).
16 *Spectator* (6 June 1981).
17 *Spectator* (13 June 1981).
18 *Spectator* (30 May 1981).
19 *Spectator* (30 May 1981).
20 *Spectator* (20 June 1981).
21 *Spectator* (20 June 1981).

England lost and replaced by something far worse and faintly revolutionary forms a key theme over West's articles. The fate of the memory of Sudbury was reflective of the 'saddening town' of Canterbury, much of it destroyed by the war and rebuilt with a less-than-aesthetic shopping piazza, and its streets crowded by 'punk rockers in hair of virulent orange and green.'[22] The inhabitants of modern Cambridge have remained like their rebellious forebearers 'in their hatred of learning, the university and its fine buildings,' with some Cambridge dons 'not far removed from Margery Starre' (see Chapter 1), whether they be the 'preposterous "structuralists"' who 'have been taking over the English faculty' or the colleges which have acted as 'recruiting grounds for the KGB.'[23]

The articles echoed West's wider lament about the state of English politics, culture, and morality published the same year,[24] and echoed a theme that would come to dominate the English right-wing press of the more middle-class or aspiring middle-class variety (e.g., *Mail*, *Telegraph*): discontent caused not by poverty but moral failings of, or decisions made by, the middle classes. West used the argument that, after the Black Death, economic conditions improved and 'people grow more rebellious as their condition improves' while 'affluence also produces hostility to taxation.' This was tied in with the argument that the rebellion was not started or led by peasants but by 'craftsmen and artisans' with leadership coming from 'clerics, landowners, above all the "burghers" of the towns, or what one would now call the bourgeoisie.'[25] In Cambridge and Bury St Edmunds it was 'prosperity [that] fostered the greed of the middle class and envy of the material wealth of the church'[26] and the rebellion itself 'was really a middle-class rather than a peasants' rebellion.' Some old conservative tendencies die hard, however, for the London revolt was judged to have been marked by unruly activities from below, namely 'fighting amongst the working class,' as well as 'hostility towards foreign immigrants.'[27] Nevertheless, today, some of the 'spirit' of the revolt could still be seen in bad manners of relatively comfortable people, illustrated by examples which included an early version of complaints about political correctness. In Fobbing, West recalled, 'a girl came trotting up on a horse and I wouldn't get out of the

---

22 *Spectator* (6 June 1981).
23 *Spectator* (13 June 1981).
24 Richard West, *An English Journey* (London: Chatto & Windus, 1981).
25 *Spectator* (30 May 1981). Cf. *Spectator* (6 June 1981); *Spectator* (13 June 1981).
26 *Spectator* (13 June 1981).
27 *Spectator* (20 June 1981).

way for her, so she said "Do what you f---ing well like!" A girl! If I'd said that I'd have been reported, wouldn't I?'[28]

Ball: CPGB or SWP?

What did not come across in West's *Spectator* series was an overlapping view on the role of artisans, burghers, richer peasants, etc., in the historical materialist understandings of Marxists like Hilton and old Communist Party Historians' Group alumnus A. L. Morton. This may have been an oversight, avoidance, an intellectual inconvenience, or even an indication that in an age of Benn such readings did not carry sufficient menace to warrant an attack by West. Whatever the reason, 1981 certainly provided an opportunity for Hilton and Morton to present their readings of Ball and the revolt. In addition to his lecture at Oestreicher's church, Hilton, noting that with the anniversary 'there has for the first time been a considerable popular manifestation of interest,' published his long-established historical materialist approach to Ball and 1381 in relatively popular fora (*Marxism Today, New Society*).[29] Morton also published a pamphlet on behalf of the CPGB in May 1981 (*When the People Arose: The Peasants' Revolt of 1381*), stressing from the outset how 'class conflict...is a thread running through our history, taking different forms at different times, but never absent... an age-long battle for greater freedoms and a saner way of organising our world.'[30]

Morton's historical materialist approach likewise remained coupled with the argument that the history of struggles involves failures necessary for understanding future hopes. About half the pamphlet involves discussion of the role of the peasant in feudal society, the conflict over wages following the Statute of Labourers, how the lord extracted surplus from the peasant by violent means because (unlike the worker under capitalism) peasants owned their means of production and produce of their labour, and how the lord had dominant legal rights over the peasant. But, with reference to Hilton, Morton stressed that this relationship was not static and tensions in this class relationship involved a growing market for farm

---

28 *Spectator* (30 May 1981).
29 Hilton, 'Wat Tyler, John Ball,' 171–73; 'The English Rising of 1381,' *Marxism Today* (June 1381): 17–19 (quotation 17).
30 A. L. Morton, *When the People Arose: The Peasants' Revolt of 1381* (London: Communist Party of Great Britain, 1981), 1.

produce at odds with the traditional feudal relations. These class struggles underpinned the 1381 revolt and were presented in an argument similar to Hilton's. Though there may have been differing demands among rebels, Ball (with an accompanying sketch 'adapted' from Froissart) was calling for the land held by the lords to 'become the collective property of the cultivators...not one of common ownership but of an England of free and equal peasants, without lords or gentry.'[31] Morton suggested that the outcome of the revolt could not really have been different because of military inferiority and insufficient class strength. But, as we might expect from a Marxist like Morton, the longer term mattered, and the revolt was an important moment in improving the lot of the peasantry and in the decline of feudalism and the growth of capitalism—a new kind of exploitation. To show how the struggle continues, Morton ended—of course—with reference to *A Dream of John Ball* and the idea of others fighting for the cause under a different name.[32]

Familiar this historical materialist argument may now have seemed—and the celebrations provided a high-profile context to give it another airing—but in some ways 1981 also marks a sharp slowing down of its influence on the Left. 1981 saw other claimants for the legacy of Ball and the revolt which would start to dominate the history of reception, particularly a relatively new force on the extra-parliamentary Left from the Trotskyite tradition which was now in the ascendancy: the Socialist Workers' Party (SWP).

The SWP ran a rally in Skegness in the spring of 1981 also celebrating the six-hundredth anniversary of the revolt which included a lecture (published as a pamphlet in June 1981) by arguably the most famous radical journalist of the late twentieth century, Paul Foot.[33] As we might expect, Foot placed class conflict at the fore throughout his retelling of the revolt. The church was presented as part of class power but, Foot explained, excommunicated monks and priests were beginning to challenge the ideas of the church. This started with Wycliffe and his polemics against priestly corruption but for twenty years prior to the revolt, 'wandering preachers' were also speaking out in village meetings against the earls and prelates, the most famous being Ball, about whom we get additional biographical

---

31 Morton, *When the People Arose*, 17–19.
32 Morton, *When the People Arose*, 30–31.
33 Paul Foot, *'This Bright Day of Summer': The Peasants' Revolt of 1381* (London: Socialists Unlimited, 1981). An audio of the lecture is available: Matthew Siegfried, 'Paul Foot Speaks! The Peasant's [sic] Revolt of 1381,' YouTube (23 May 2015), https://www.youtube.com/watch?v=JvEGNnL5IZo. I quote from the written version unless otherwise noted.

information that he was a parish priest at St James's Church, Colchester (a point, we might note, local historian and Anglican priest Brian Bird was beginning to popularise at the time—see Chapter 23).[34] Ball challenged the theological justification for human distinction, in particular the idea that the uneducated people at the bottom of society were the descendants of Cain while the respectable gentlemen were descended from Seth.[35] Ball's Adam and Eve couplet, Foot claimed, wiped this argument clean by pointing to a time where there was no class distinction. In keeping with the reception of Ball on the Left in relation to gender and feminism, the Adam and Eve couplet had another meaning: it questioned whether 'the man was superior to the woman.'[36] Ball was also said to preach 'simple, elementary equality' within the framework of religion but crucially coupled with the idea of organisation, which was seen in other people just like Ball going around villages, appointing representatives, and connecting town and country. Ball's letters had a similar function in that they functioned 'like Party circulars mobilising the membership.'[37]

Where Morton used Hilton as his main scholarly reference point, Foot's arguments have a clear dependence on Philip Lindsay and Reg Groves's *The Peasants' Revolt 1381* (1950), which, as we saw, was the major publication of the revolt associated with British Trotskyism (see Chapter 19). Foot quoted from the conclusion to Lindsay and Groves's account on the significance of organisation. But the additional comments made are striking. Foot added that *Peasants' Revolt 1381* was a 'marvellous book on this subject…by far the best book, by the way, about the Peasants' Revolt.'[38] The spoken version of Foot's lecture includes an aside to the SWP-sympathising audience that 'Reg Groves will be well known to readers of *Socialist Worker* [which Foot once edited] and the *Socialist Review* and other publications—very fine writer.'[39] That the book by Lindsay and Groves was chosen as 'by far the best book' is notable given that the standard and most celebrated Marxist work might otherwise have been understood to have been written by a main speaker at Blackheath with a CPGB background: Hilton. In this respect it is perhaps significant that Foot's lecture attacks 'professors' generally, though particular reference is made to Charles Oman. There are, however, further

34 Foot, 'This Bright Day of Summer', 8–9. Cf. Bird and Stephenson, 'Who Was John Ball?'; Bird, *Colchester Rebel*.
35 Compare the frontispiece to Lindsay and Groves, *Peasants' Revolt 1381*, e.g., 46. Foot was, as we will see, clearly dependent on this book.
36 Foot, 'This Bright Day of Summer', 9.
37 Foot, 'This Bright Day of Summer', 13.
38 Foot, 'This Bright Day of Summer', 17.
39 Siegfried, 'Paul Foot Speaks!'

indications of Trotskyite tendencies and mythmaking in Foot's lecture with possible digs at the tradition associated with Hilton while standing in notable contrast to Morton's contemporaneous pamphlet. Foot polemically attacked the tendency 'perhaps especially' among Marxists 'who think about history' in order to,

> divide it into sealed compartments...say that the peasant comes from a different age, is separate from us, has nothing to do with us, and that history moves by stages, scientific stages, and the peasant is one stage, and the workers are in another...nothing therefore to do with us what happened six hundred years ago, in a quite different sort of economy. We can leave it on one side. We're not peasants, we're very advanced people, we've been an industrial working class burrowing away for years and we've got pretty well nowhere, but we're terribly important and we're much more important than any peasant.[40]

Foot criticised this thinking as 'reactionary', 'wrong', 'insulting', and even 'paralysing' because of the idea that history determines and 'paralyses' our action, thereby omitting the human activity at the heart of the revolt. While acknowledging the differences between now and then, Foot preferred to stress the similarities and particularly how the past and present are united by class struggle. What this also almost inevitably meant was that Morris too had to be onside and Foot concluded by citing *A Dream of John Ball* as supportive evidence—as Hilton himself did, as Morton's pamphlet did, and as Communist Party members long had in their distinctive way. Whether Foot's assessment of his implied Marxist rivals is fair is another question, but it was clearly a rhetorical move which distanced Foot's SWP-inspired Marxism from opposing tendencies. It is also worth noting that this emphasis on a tradition held together by shared class interests *minus* (or a watered-down version of) the accompaniment of the kind of historical materialism associated with Hilton, Morton, and the Communist Party tradition,[41] would become dominant on what remained of the English

---

40 Foot, 'This Bright Day of Summer', 18–19.
41 Hilton is used as a negative foil in an article for the post-SWP group, Counterfire, though in keeping with Counterfire's tendency towards collaboration with other socialist groups, Hilton's work receives some praise. Nevertheless, as with Foot's critique of 'deterministic' Marxists, Hilton (along with Hobsbawm) is similarly accused of lapsing 'into a view of peasant struggles as being unconscious, primitive, and essentially mechanically determined.' While the article turns to the work of 'the left-wing early-medievalist, Nicholas Brooks,' there are clear echoes of the ideas about organisation of the Great Society (downplayed by Hilton) associated with the otherwise unmentioned

Left as the SWP had begun to replace the CPGB as the most high-profile extra-parliamentary socialist party until a rape scandal hit their reputation in the 2010s.

Mass on the Heath

Foot opened his lecture to the SWP rally with a couple of mock announcements. The first was said to have come from Lambeth Palace explaining that the archbishop of Canterbury 'will *not* be attending this year any of the celebrations which are being held to commemorate the Peasants' Revolt,' whether they be at Canterbury, Blackheath, Mile End, or St Albans.[42] It is perhaps unfair to contrast a comedic preamble with the activities of the archbishop of Canterbury during the spring and summer of 1981 but the then incumbent Robert Runcie did in fact celebrate Holy Communion 'from an articulated lorry on Blackheath Common.' An altar was placed on the trailer as Runcie led the worship with clergy distributing 'specially baked brown rolls' among a crowd of around one-thousand people and set against the backdrop of a banner proclaiming: 'Let the Oppressed Go Free: 1381–1981.' The event was organised by the 'radical young clergy' in the South London Jubilee Group and, as we might expect, Oestreicher to commemorate the six-hundredth anniversary at the alleged site of Ball's 'famous sermon' on all being held in common, though in good post-war Church of England style, Canterbury Cathedral also hosted a service commemorating Sudbury which Oestreicher explained as an essential contradiction (see below). It was an ecumenical service in keeping with receptions of Ball towards the end of the twentieth century, with representatives from the Black Pentecostal Churches, the Catholic Church, and the Methodists.[43]

But this was not mere ecumenicalism; Oestreicher would later refer to the Mass on the Heath more as a celebration of 'radical, holy diversity'

Groves as part of the article's case that 'the study of past rebellions show how history is made from below.' See Dominic Alexander, 'Peasant Movements and Political Agency,' *Counterfire* (6 September 2009), https://www.counterfire.org/theory/57-history-of-resistance/1733-peasant-movements-and-political-agency. Cf. Brooks, 'Organization and Achievements,' in Mayr-Harting and Moore (eds.), *Studies in Medieval History*, 247–70.

42 Foot, *'This Bright Day of Summer,'* 3.
43 *Church Times* (12 June 1981).

in connection with its anti-Apartheid message.[44] The anti-racist and anti-slavery connotations of the 'Let the Oppressed Go Free: 1381–1981' banner were always likely to be noted but were even less likely to be missed after the sermon from anti-Apartheid church leader Allan Boesak (b. 1946).[45] Ball, Boesak claimed, spoke to a 'vast crowd' who consisted of 'the poor, the dejected, the empty-handed populace of England, those with "no name in the streets," who long had been oppressed by the rich and the powerful.' Ball inspired the hearers 'to listen, to believe, and for one glorious moment to throw off their despair and hopelessness, to stand up and challenge the seemingly unshakable order of the world.' Ball managed this feat by his 'vision' of a day 'when they would all be recognized as human beings created in the image of a God,' when there would be no master or serf, and when all would share 'the goods of God's earth.' This was the vision of a prophet like Habakkuk, 'rooted always in the cry of the poor and oppressed…that moves the heart of God,' and a vision, no matter how slow it may seem in coming, that will be realised.[46] This was a vision Boesak illustrated by way of Calvin and biblical texts and applied to El Salvador, Nicaragua, Guatemala, and Chile. But it also inspired South African youth 'to face dogs, tear gas, detentions without trial, and gunfire for the sake of liberation.'[47] The English peasants, he added, were faced with a church that did not prioritise justice, peace, and reconciliation and rejected its Lord as it preferred the 'rich and powerful' and made an 'unholy pact with the nobility and the military'—a situation comparable with the behaviour of the Dutch Reformed Church in South Africa. Instead, Boesak suggested, Ball was more likely to be the true image of the church in a similar way to Martin Luther King or those resisting Apartheid in South Africa. And to not participate in this struggle and not to maintain such a prophetic witness would be to dishonour the memory of Ball and make a mockery of the commemoration of the Peasants' Revolt.[48]

In addition to being one of the key organisational figures behind the 1381 commemorations, Oestreicher was already known for his interest in reconstructing and thinking about Ball and the Mass on the Heath.

---

44 Paul Oestreicher, '1968—Year of Shame, Year of Grace,' *Ecumenical Review* 70 (2018): 179–93 (193).
45 *Church Times* (5 June 1981); *Church Times* (12 June 1981). Boesak's sermon from 6 June was published in Allan A. Boesak, *Black and Reformed: Apartheid, Liberation, and the Calvinist Tradition* (ed. Leonard Sweetman; Eugene, OR: Wipf and Stock, 1984), 62–69. All quotations are taken from this.
46 Boesak, *Black and Reformed*, 62–63.
47 Boesak, *Black and Reformed*, 65.
48 Boesak, *Black and Reformed*, 67–68.

His understanding reflected the kinds of politics and theology in which he had been involved. In addition to being an ecumenicist, a supporter of the ordination of women, an anti-racist campaigner, chair of Amnesty International (1975–1979), and Vice President of the Campaign for Nuclear Disarmament (joined 1959), he was, in his own words, 'a child refugee from Hitler's Germany and is a white male Anglican priest and Quaker, a student of politics, a pacifist, and an inhabitant of England who grew up in New Zealand.'[49] Oestreicher was involved in Marxist-Christian dialogue including dialogue with Christians behind the Iron Curtain and the Christian Peace Conference (CPC). Before an assembly in Prague, 1968, he had been pressured to resign, which he said was in turn due to Soviet pressure on the general secretary of the CPC, Jaroslav Ondra. This and Soviet intervention in Prague had hardened his attitude towards what he called 'Stalinism.' Yet he was also critical of Western imperialism and propaganda, and saw a parallel in the classic narratives of betrayal: just as Marx, communists, and socialists were betrayed by party leaders, so Jesus was betrayed by 'the churches' alliance with mammon' as the churches had failed to challenge 'the prevailing capitalist orthodoxy of the West.' He further claimed that the 'boundary between liberation theologians and radical socialists was wafer thin, though, as ever, he was careful to qualify this in terms of difference from perceived extremes, in this case 'Doctrinaire Marxists and the Vatican.'[50]

Indeed, in his preview of the Mass on the Heath for the *Church Times*, Oestreicher classified Ball's preaching as 'liberation theology' whose 'revolutionary sermon' received hostile treatment from the 'monastic priests with a vested interest in the status quo,' and compared this to Latin American theologians in the twentieth century where the parallel with the 'almost landless poor' against the 'land-owning oligarchy' is 'very close.' And, whether in Latin America, South Africa, or fourteenth-century England, he argued, the church found itself on both sides and Ball was the equivalent of the sympathetic clergy in Latin America, preaching a

49 Oestreicher, '1968,' 180. Cf. *Irish Times* (28 November 2000); '60 Faces: Paul Oestreicher,' *Campaign for Nuclear Disarmament*, https://cnduk.org/60-faces-paul-oestreicher/; Merrilyn Thomas, 'Paul Oestreicher—an inspirational peace campaigner,' *Merrilyn Thomas* (2 December 2017), https://merrilynthomas.com/paul-oestreicher-inspirational-peace-campaigner/.
50 Oestreicher, '1968,' 183–84. Cf. Paul Oestreicher, 'Preface' and 'Christians and Communists in Search of Man: Fifty Years after the Russian Revolution,' in James Klugmann and Paul Oestreicher (eds.), *What Kind of Revolution? A Christian-Communist Dialogue* (London: Panther Books, 1968), 9–13, 192–206.

theology of the Kingdom in the here and now, rejecting 'any pie-in-the-sky dualism.' Ball's preaching was, for Oestreicher, primarily about 'freedom for all,' though 'economic justice was inextricably tied up with it.' In six hundred years, some things had changed little as most Christians still faced 'divisions of class (and race).'[51] And yet, as we would expect, this was not liberation theology with hard Marxist characteristics. Certainly, familiar language could be used. 'Although John Ball had visions of a socialist society,' Oestreicher claimed, 'this, from the evidence available, was not an objective of the Peasants' Revolt' as it was not 'the poorest who were taking up arms but those with something to lose…it was more a bourgeois than proletarian revolt.' But this language was not quite being used in the throughgoing historical materialist sense as we might find with Hilton or Morton. Rather this identification of the rebels was used to link not to the present proletariat but to those who organised the event 'from the security of English vicarages' and to ask uncomfortable questions about whose liberation: 'The Blackheath bourgeoise's or the Brazilian peasants'?'[52]

Oestreicher was hoping Boesak might help answer these questions, though as we saw, Boesak's class identification between the rebels and the present was slightly different. But Oestreicher was also negotiating his potentially controversial views in an establishment state church of mixed classes and divergent interests. And so rather than a 'wild rabble-rouser,' Oestreicher's Ball was a 'thoughtful preacher advocating a new kind of society' with this theme of 'equality of all God's children.' There was 'total respect' for the king, and rebel demands were in favour of a king and one archbishop, both representing God with 'equal citizens' under them. It is striking that Oestreicher also claimed that neither Sudbury nor Ball were personally 'particularly saintly or particularly evil' and both, if anything, were 'victims.' This was all part of the contradiction of the Blackheath service and the commemoration of Sudbury at Canterbury and, more broadly, of the struggle to hold together a church that incorporated pacifists like Oestreicher, opposed to nuclear weapons, and those who believe in the right to kill for 'a good cause (like defending one's nation),' who tend to side with the rich and powerful. This tension was explained theologically as a struggle between the 'Christ who divides and the Christ [who] reconciles, the God of judgment and the God of grace.' Indeed, his old hostilities towards the Soviet Union and 'Stalinism' could still be felt as Oestreicher ended his article by wondering how far the Blackheath Eucharist would be from the 'Mass that so amazed the world, when striking workers in the

---

51 *Church Times* (5 June 1981).
52 *Church Times* (5 June 1981).

shipyards of Gdansk fell on their knees to receive the Body and Blood of Christ.'[53]

Everyone Can Sing John Ball!

It is one of the great contradictions of the modern reception of Ball that, despite first being known as a preacher of violence, his memory now owes much to not one but two pacifists who commemorated Ball's death six hundred years later. As part of the Mass on the Heath, Sydney Carter (1915–2004) wrote 'a new folk hymn specially written for the occasion' called 'Sing John Ball' (or variants, e.g., 'Sing, John Ball,' 'John Ball'), and sung the same year by John Kirkpatrick and Carter on an album of various artists performing Carter's songs (*Lovely in the Dances: Songs of Sydney Carter* [1981]).[54] If Ball was the same John Ball who had beaten up and broken the leg of a student (see Chapter 2), then a further tension (or not, depending on your didactic perspective) is that Carter was responsible for various songs that people of my generation had to sing or mime in school assemblies, such as 'One More Step,' 'When I Needed a Neighbour,' and 'Lord of the Dance,' though never in my experience was 'Sing John Ball' sung or mimed. In terms of his religion, Jesus and the Christian tradition were certainly foregrounded in Carter's hymns but he understood them alongside ideas of doubt and in broader interfaith or humanitarian terms: he would, for instance, enjoy singing with rabbi Lionel Blue while 'Lord of the Dance' was partly inspired by a statue of the Hindu god Shiva on his desk.[55] As Oestreicher put it of his friend, 'if any church could come to holding Sydney's allegiance, it was the Society of Friends, with its rejection of dogma, and its reliance on personal experience and social activism, and its affirmation of God's presence in every human being.'[56] Carter's religious ideas were closely aligned with his politics. He would, like Hilton and Christopher Hill, end up at Balliol College, Oxford, in the 1930s but Carter's political and Nonconformist path would involve a different kind

---

53 *Church Times* (5 June 1981).
54 *Church Times* (12 June 1981). For the album details, see 'Mainly Norfolk: English Folk and Other Good Music,' https://mainlynorfolk.info/folk/records/sydneycarter.html.
55 *Guardian* (14 March 2004); *Daily Telegraph* (16 March 2004).
56 Paul Oestreicher, 'Sydney Carter,' *Guardian* (17 March 2004).

of radicalism, more akin to Oestreicher's.[57] Like Hilton and Hill, he would experience the Second World War but for Carter it was rather among fellow pacifists in the Friends Ambulance Unit in the Middle East and Greece. Carter would later become a notable figure in the folk revival of the 1960s, including writing songs for others, such as the anti-war 'Crow on the Cradle' and 'I Want a Little Bomb Like You.'

With 'Sing John Ball,' we have a song about relatively vague concepts of being ruled by love for one another and the general expectation of light coming in the morning, and such imagery of light and morning echoes a long tradition in the reception of Ball, and not least associated with Morris, which, as we saw, turned up earlier in Quakerism (see Chapter 16).[58] But clearly, the influential (among some liberals and leftists at least) postwar pacifism and the overlaps with church groups and school assemblies meant violent understandings of Ball were downplayed. Both 'Sing John Ball' and Carter's hymns more generally with their themes of social justice, nondenominational vagueness, and association with both churches and (non-church) school assemblies tell something of the story of postwar Christianity in England. In the late-twentieth and early twenty-first centuries, there has been an ongoing slump in church attendance with an accompanying political and public discourse about religion that avoids details of dogma and belief in an era where there is some cultural embarrassment associated with identifying as Christian (and notably so in popular music). In public and political discourses, we are more likely to find vague statements when it comes to religion and the Bible which are both typically aligned with broadly agreeable but necessarily ill-defined sentiments like 'freedom,' 'tolerance,' 'love,' etc.[59] Gooch's Bible-quoting Ball holding a noble's head on a spear this is not.

While some of the lyrics of Carter's hymns are hardly shorn of explicit Christian imagery, the lyrics of 'Sing John Ball' chime with Matthew Engelke's notion of religion in England today as 'ambient.' By this, Engelke meant that in public presentations of religion (Christianity in particular), people can engage, ignore, or be apathetic, and all justified in terms of a theology of choice,[60] perhaps fitting for an era of neoliberal or Thatcherite

---

57 For Carter's biographical details, I am dependent on his obituaries, e.g., *Daily Telegraph* (16 March 2004) and Oestreicher's in the *Guardian* (17 March 2004).

58 The lyrics are found in Sydney Carter, *In the Present Tense: Songs of Sydney Carter Volume 5* (London: Stainer & Bell, 1983).

59 I have discussed this in detail elsewhere, with detailed bibliography. See, e.g., Crossley, *Harnessing Chaos*; Crossley, *Cults, Martyrs and Good Samaritans*.

60 Matthew Engelke, *God's Agents: Biblical Publicity in Contemporary England* (Berkeley: University of California Press, 2013), 62–63.

capitalism. We can reword Engelke's argument for a folk setting: religion is there if the listeners want it but it remains sufficiently vague if they have no interest and just want to belt out a tune. We might even say that Carter provided the soundtrack to the fate of the church in England in the late-twentieth and early-twenty first century—and brought Ball along with him. Beneath the polemic, Jonathan Meades's description of the 'cheery new hell' of post-war Christianity contains an element of truth which we might accordingly tweak with reference to Ball. Ball's old religion of 'mumbo-jumbo and God-the-Powerful' has now been replaced by one featuring the 'cardigan-wearing' English God—'God the nice bloke,' 'God the softie'—now housed in cosy architecture rather than in the old seats of God's power which provided the illusion of omnipresence 'as strong as the rock which bears Peter's name.'[61]

As this suggests, perhaps the more significant context for understanding the perpetuation of Ball's memory goes beyond Carter. Indeed, 'Sing John Ball' has thrived in the world of folk music where it has become a popular and widely covered singalong. It has been covered by artists such as the Waterdaughters, Chris Wood, Grace Notes, Danny Spooner, Jon Boden, Melrose Quartet, Sound Tradition, and The Young'uns. While only so much can be read into renditions of the song, we do have various artists giving explanations of Ball collected on *Mainly Norfolk: English Folk and Other Good Music* with commentary by Bob Hudson (to which I refer unless otherwise indicated).[62] General notions of Englishness are significant, at least for the performers. The connection with English history is, as we might expect, repeated with uses of the more archaic language when quoting Ball's couplet ('Adam dalf...,' or variants—e.g., Danny Spooner, Lynda Hardcastle, Sound Tradition). Equally expected is reference to a non-exclusive English identity. We might note, for instance, that for The Young'uns (who have regularly promoted inclusive, more egalitarian, and non-racialised ideas about England), 'John Ball' features on an album (*Never Forget* [2014]) framed by anti-fascist songs about how the far-right English Defence League (EDL) were greeted in their protest outside a mosque in York (2013) not with hostility but peacefully with

---

61   From Jonathan Meades's documentary, 'The Absentee Landlord' (1997; dir. Russell England). See also James G. Crossley, 'Borges's God, Jonathan Meades's Precursor,' in Richard Walsh and Jay Twomey (eds.), *Borges and the Bible* (Sheffield: Sheffield Phoenix Press, 2015).
62   *Mainly Norfolk: English Folk and Other Good Music*, https://mainlynorfolk.info/john.kirkpatrick/songs/johnball.html.

biscuits and tea, two of the most famous symbols of a certain kind of contemporary Englishness.[63]

Folk music has, and continues to have, a history of constructing an implicit or explicit English identity, perhaps most famously epitomised by Billy Bragg among older generations of liberals or leftists.[64] Topics like the Peasants' Revolt, alongside Peterloo, the deportation of a thief to the Australian penal colonies, or any number of topics from agrarian history or reflection on some part of the English landscape, are among the many instances of contemporary inventions of an English tradition. And any invention of an English tradition in the late-twentieth and early twenty-first centuries is sensitive because it is in competition with right-wing, ethnically essentialist and ethnonationalist narratives of English and Britishness which are less at home in contemporary folk music circles. Indeed, folk traditions have been taken up by the far right (including the British National Party) which has built upon implicit and unintentional constructions of English identity that can, with a switch of context, come across as white notions of Englishness or Britishness tied in with dramatic landscapes, supressed histories, and so on. Against this backdrop (incorporating the interrelated contexts of devolution and Brexit), inclusive, pluralistic, multicultural, and multi-ethnic English cultural identities have been emphatically stressed among contemporary folk artists and supporters. Indeed, contemporary English folk music has even been packaged as a kind of 'world music,' and as a genre or movement that should seek inspiration from Irish, Scottish, Celtic, or any other seemingly less embarrassed ownership of national or pan-national mythmaking beyond the British Isles.[65]

---

63 See the interview with The Young'uns by Mark Dishman, 'The Young'uns' David Eagle on New Album *Never Forget*, Anti-fascism, Dodgy Reviews and Biscuits,' *Folk Witness* (19 March 2014).

64 See, e.g., Billy Bragg, *The Progressive Patriot: A Search for Belonging* (London: Bantam Books, 2006). Unsurprisingly, Bragg writes about the English radical tradition with reference to the Peasants' Revolt, and familiar claims such as that when he was at Miners' Strike rallies, he 'learned that the freedom which I enjoyed had had to be fought for' and that 'we were part of a long tradition of struggle in which the people won their rights from a ruling class that had oppressed them all the way' (14).

65 On folk music and Englishness, see, e.g., Trish Winter and Simon Keegan-Phipps, *Performing Englishness: Identity and Politics in a Contemporary Folk Resurgence* (Manchester: Manchester University Press, 2013); Lee Robert Blackstone, 'The Aural and Moral Idylls of "Englishness" and Folk Music,' *Symbolic Interaction* 40 (2017): 561–80. Cf. John Mullen, '"We Need Roots"—Englishness and New Folk Revival,' *Open Democracy* (13 July 2010).

With the possibility that some people simply enjoy singing duly acknowledged, part of the ongoing popularity of 'Sing John Ball' (at least among some of those who have covered it) is that it belongs to a world of inclusive English or British mythmaking. What this national history has more precisely involved is further illuminated by the words of the performers collected on *Mainly Norfolk*, including some familiar understandings of Ball. Ball is, for instance, identified in connection with Wycliffe (e.g., Danny Spooner, *Brave Bold Boys* [2008]).[66] Sound Tradition, in their notes for their album *Blackbird* (2014), while not mentioning Lollardy or Wycliffe explicitly, did describe Ball in a way that echoes some of the Protestantising common in his reception: 'Seen as a major threat to the establishment, Ball's striving for social equality and reforms in Western Christianity was rewarded by his execution in 1381' (Sound Tradition, *Blackbird* [2014]). There are no obvious indications, at least in any public presentations, of any overt anti-Catholicism or even overt-Protestantism (indeed, note the generic 'Western Christianity') and we should probably see this as either the typically unacknowledged and lingering heritage of English Protestantism or broader notions of a problematic 'established religion.' But whatever subtle religious identification there may be, there is sufficient medieval or historic mystique for it not to be too evangelical or anything else deemed culturally problematic in mainstream political discourse.

The attractiveness of Ball's preaching was the primary reason for his imprisonment and death, and this is sometimes presented as unfair by modern standards, akin to popular receptions of (for instance) Jesus dying for his decency and advocacy of human equality (or Sound Tradition's claims about Ball being executed for striving for social equality and reforms). For Danny Spooner, Ball saw 'the hope of an egalitarian England' and through 'Wycliffe's English translation of the Bible had led him to believe that nowhere did it advocate monarchy or aristocracy.' This outright anti-monarchical reading of Ball is rare in the history of reception—the more typical view in republican readings has been to contextualise pro-monarchism as something of its time and culture or how Ball and the rebels were duped. But it is effectively for his republicanism and egalitarianism that Ball was now imprisoned and ultimately, after the rebellion was 'unfortunately'

---

66 Reporting on Sweet Liberties and 'Sing John Ball' at Parliament in 2015, James MacKinnon referred to Ball in terms of the 'Lollard priest's central role in Wat Tyler's Peasants' Revolt of 1381.' See James MacKinnon, 'Sweet Liberties Launch, Speaker's House, Palace of Westminster, 16th November,' *Folk Radio* (19 November 2015), https://www.folkradio.co.uk/2015/11/sweet-liberties-launch-speakers-house-palace-of-westminster/.

defeated, 'John Ball died for his beliefs' (Danny Spooner, *Brave Bold Boys* [2008]).⁶⁷ Certainly, a little more menace in Ball's beliefs can be hinted at. For Dave Webber, this 'character from English history' was 'imprisoned for his incitement of the people' (Dave Webber on Dave Webber and Anni Fentiman, *Together Solo* [1993]). Nevertheless, Carter's pacifism continues to haunt the song's reception and when violence was mentioned by Lynda Hardcastle from Grace Notes, her addition of brackets and exclamation mark further flags up how alien the concept is: 'He preached common property, equality and the extermination of the nobility (!).' Bob Hudson's commentary also picked up on these understandings of Ball and places them explicitly into another kind of broader tradition. He argued that Ball used Wycliffe's English translation of the Bible for progressive purposes and class politics ('John Ball himself was a priest who found in Wycliffe's translation of the Bible into English new hope for an egalitarian England… Ball was executed in 1381 for his efforts in [*sic*] behalf of English working people'). But he added that Ball had become a folk hero to the extent that he is potentially the source of an English-language folk tradition: 'Some modern scholars claim that the few fragments of John Ball's verse that survive are, in fact, the first flowering of political poetry and protest song in English. He is, in a sense, the direct literary ancestor of such modern figures as Woody Guthrie, Allen Ginsberg, Ewan MacColl, and Bob Dylan.'

As we have seen over several previous chapters, these folk traditions relating Ball to an inclusive, non-racialised English tradition grounded in some sort of political radicalism belong to a history of interpretation developed over the previous two centuries. Precisely where we place receptions of 'Sing John Ball' will depend on the singers and their audiences (see also Epilogue) but we should probably not be surprised to find the tendency towards non-violent interpretations appropriated by those traditions that see Ball and the English radical tradition feed into parliamentary democracy. Sweet Liberties—a project featuring Nancy Kerr, Martyn Joseph, Sam Carter, and Maz O'Connor—was commissioned by (among others) the English Folk Dance and Song Society (EFDSS) to look at 800 years 'in pursuit of democracy' since Magna Carta. Tellingly launched at Westminster in November 2015, this included common types of historic examples and themes in folk (struggles for democracy, contrasts between rich and poor,

---

67 Similarly, in a commentary on Carter's songs, including 'Sing John Ball,' John Davies explains that Ball 'was a Lollard priest thrown out of the church for suggesting that all men were equal in God's sight.' See John Davies, 'Sydney Carter—Reflections,' *John Davies*, http://www.johndavies.org/SydneyCarter-talk.pdf.

slavery, etc.). Prominent among the chosen songs was 'Sing John Ball,' which opened and rounded off the launch which also featured songs about homelessness and the problems of meritocracy, the NHS and the hero of the Labour Left Nye Bevan, and the abolition of slavery.[68] This familiar but somewhat domesticated reception of Ball in the twenty-first century was launched just two months after the return of a more radical form of parliamentary democracy in the form of Corbynism where Ball would, just about, be given new interpretations. But, with a fear of media hostility and party-political pressures, they would be interpretations where the tensions between conformity and oppositional politics were more pronounced.

---

68 James MacKinnon, 'Sweet Liberties Launch, Speaker's House, Palace of Westminster, 16th November,' Folk Radio (19 November 2015), https://www.folkradio.co.uk/2015/11/sweet-liberties-launch-speakers-house-palace-of-westminster/; Jonathan Luxmoore and Christine Ellis, 'Not talkin' bout a revolution: where are all the protest songs?,' in *Guardian* (22 February 2016).

23
Twenty-First Century Ball

From Poll Tax to a Memory

The Community Charge required of every adult first in Scotland (1989) then England and Wales (1990) provoked wide-ranging opposition from parliamentary opposition through non-payment to rioting. This new Poll Tax almost inevitably provoked comparisons with 1381, and Wat Tyler in particular.[1] The *Daily Express* explained the comparison under the headline 'Peasants Revolt' and provided a new version of the threatening mob: 'rebellion is being whipped up by the hard-Left...hi-jacked by militants and Left-wingers...Peaceful demonstrations turned into mob rule.'[2] The Peasants' Revolt analogy was taken up by some protestors, and not least in certain anarchist circles. In an account included in the pamphlet *Poll Tax Riot* (1990), published by ACAB Press no less, 1381 was used to indicate (against Thatcher, Kinnock, etc.) that there was a long tradition of 'violent struggle in our history' and a time when people 'rose up against poverty and tyranny' with a familiar 'common declaration': 'We are men formed in Christ's likeness and we are kept like beasts.'[3] In another account published in *Organise!*, the famous Trafalgar Square Poll Tax riot (31 March 1990) was used to show how groups like Class War, the Anarchist Communist Federation, and (to lesser extent) the Direct Action Movement, and their advocacy of class violence, meant that they were the heirs to the Peasants' Revolt and 'Watt Tyler.' They were now the voice of the working class and to be distinguished from (and the enemy of) not only the British government, the ruling class, and the police but also 'middle-class

---

1 Taylor, *London's Burning*, 23; Basdeo, *Life and Legend of a Rebel Leader*, loc 3386–3424.
2 *Daily Express* (2 March 1990).
3 'From 1381 to...,' in *Poll Tax Riot: 10 Hours that Shook Trafalgar Square* (London: ACAB Press, 1990), 18–20 (18). The back cover of the pamphlet mentions a tradition 'of resistance to the ruling class and its laws, an unbroken line from 1381 to the present day. AVENGE WAT TYLER!!'

lefties' or state-collaborators like the Labour Party, the All Britain Poll Tax Federation, the trade unions, the TUC, bourgeois democracy, SWP, Trotskyists, Bolsheviks, Militant, CND, anti-Apartheid, and practically anything on the Left, whether 'reformist' or 'revolutionary'.[4] The discontent associated with the Poll Tax provided opportunities in the press for the occasional reminder of Ball and (especially) Tyler, both of whom were said to have wanted, for instance, 'an end to the feudal slavery of the peasants and called for a communist-style society'.[5] The Poll Tax also inspired a play, *Man of Straw*, which was performed at Willesden Green (London), 9 March 1990. Ball was understood as a 'priest from Colchester' and one of the 'leaders of the revolution' in a play that used 'dance-based movement, live music and improvisation to create stories of immediate relevance to today's world'.[6]

The Poll Tax and the accompanying riots were an indication of subcultural or countercultural contexts where the revolt would have occasional resonance at the end of the century: popular protests movements (e.g., among New Age Travellers, Reclaim the Streets, against the Criminal Justice Act, etc.).[7] Into the twenty-first century, there was still occasional updating in light of political and economic events, such as the Iraq War and the financial crisis of 2008.[8] Nevertheless, and as we might except, Ball and the uprising were very rarely discussed in the press at the end of the twentieth century and the first decades of the twenty-first. In the telling omission of representatives of the revolt in the BBC's discussion of voting on the top 100 Britons in 2002, Jeff Sawtell in the *Morning Star* asked, 'would it have been asking too much to remember the Peasants' Revolt of 1381 led by Wat Tyler and John Ball?'[9] As had now become customary, it fell to the *Morning Star*, Britain's only remaining socialist daily, to preserve Ball's memory. As Rodney Hilton had once done in *Morning Star*'s predecessor, the *Daily Worker* (see Chapter 19), so Paddy McGuffin's column

4 *Organise!* (May–June 1980).
5 *Reading Evening Post* (27 February 1990).
6 *Pinner Observer* (8 March 1990).
7 George McKay, *Senseless Acts of Beauty: Cultures of Resistance Since the Sixties* (London: Verso, 1996), 178–79; Taylor, *London's Burning*, 23.
8 Bringing some of these tendencies together is the performance of Heathcote Williams's 'The Red Dagger: Wat Tyler, John Ball and Johanna Ferrour: The Peasants' Revolt and the City of London Weapons of Mass Destruction,' four parts, YouTube (19 December 2013), https://www.youtube.com/watch?v=SCAiqSRofGY&feature=youtu.be.
9 *Morning Star* (29 October 2002). Morris too, Sawtell noted, was a 'glaring omission'.

critiqued the monarchy with reference to the revolt, in this case arguing that the monarchy has historically done everything it can to prevent 'any form of social justice manifesting itself, including murdering John Ball and Wat Tyler.'[10] While the era of Hilton, Hyman Fagan, and A. L. Morton may have long gone, the *Morning Star* still provided detailed historical articles relating to the revolt with echoes of the heyday of such popular presentations. On the five-hundredth anniversary of the Reformation (2017), Jenny Farrell explained how, from the fourteenth century, opposition to feudalism occurred in the form of heresy and armed rebellion and they were 'class wars despite their religious guise' because 'radical anti-feudal sentiment could only be expressed in theological terms at the time.' Plebian demands could involve 'restoration of early Christian equality of all members of the community—to include civil equality, equity of property of all, and the abolition of ground rents, taxes and privileges.' These ideas represented the interests of a 'separate new class' and the first major peasant uprising under the leadership of preachers like Ball.[11]

The *Morning Star* also ran commemorations of the end of the revolt on 15 June in the form of an advertisement and, in an era where such language has been largely jettisoned on the Left (see below), with faint echoes of older traditions of socialist martyrdom and the accompanying hope for the future. 630 years after what the *Morning Star* now labelled the 'People's Revolt' (echoing its own self-description as the People's Paper and the Popular Frontist tradition associated with the Communist Party) and 'the cruel deaths' of Ball, Tyler, and others, it was suggested that we 'applaud and remember all attempts to achieve freedom, egalitarianism and a better world!'[12] A year later (2012), the commemoration focused on Tyler at Smithfield and Ball and other members of the People's Revolt and their demands for 'equality,' which were then connected to 'ongoing efforts to achieve a better world for all peoples!'[13] The following year, the centre of attention was the 'judicial murder of John Ball' whose connection with the present-day working class was emphasised. He worked for the 'creation of a fairer society,' travelled 'through England talking to the poor and oppressed workers,' and his head was fixed at London Bridge 'as a warning to other workers.' There are further echoes of the old radical tradition in that there is an implicit connection with the Chartists as 'Ball with others set out the People's Charter' and there is a need to transform the present because

10 *Morning Star* (10–11 July 2010).
11 *Morning Star* (31 October 2017).
12 *Morning Star* (15 June 2011).
13 *Morning Star* (15 June 2012).

today's workers are 'still oppressed' and having 'their rights eroded by the elite. We need a new Peoples' Charter and we need it now.'[14] Whether we are still dealing with a tradition of English socialist martyrs is a moot point, but no doubt there are connections with past socialist propaganda where such language was more prominent and more likely recognisable in the world of the *Morning Star*.

Memorialising Ball

There is a John Ball Primary School at Blackheath (opened in 1953) where Ball is described as 'a rebel who played a prominent part in the Peasants' Revolt of 1381, and who famously preached on Blackheath,' accompanied by the illustration from Froissart. Such promotion of local history with broader national impact is a recurring feature in memorials for Ball (see below) but the framing of Ball here gives some indication of how his memory continues to be understood. The information about Ball is immediately followed by a comment on the 'most distinctive characteristic' of John Ball Primary School, namely the 'exceptionally diverse economic, social and cultural backgrounds of the children and the community it serves.'[15] Of course, these issues are significant ones for schools today so we should not read too much into this in terms of the ongoing reception of Ball. Nevertheless, that such a statement could be made in the context of a discussion of the history of the school and its name is certainly in line with ideas of inclusivity associated with a long history of interpretation of Ball. Of course, there remains a variety of ideological frameworks in which Ball is placed (typically Left or sometimes liberal), while the media formats where Ball is commemorated and memorialised likewise vary. In addition to the ongoing popularity of Carter's folk song 'Sing John Ball' and popular histories, Ball turns up in documentaries, poetry and spoken word, makeshift posters, Facebook groups (e.g., Radical English Tradition, Let's Put Up a Statue to John Ball in Colchester), tweets, online videos, and so on. But those that have, comparatively speaking, drawn most public attention as events in their own right have involved the unveiling of plaques and related memorials in his hometown of Colchester and in London. For all their similarities, both have distinctive emphases particular to each location.

14 *Morning Star* (15 June 2013).
15 'The History of John Ball,' John Ball Primary School, https://www.johnball.lewisham.sch.uk/our-school/history/.

Colchester

Colchester has been one of the main centres of Ball memorialising, particularly through the activities of local historian and priest Brian Bird and now the John Ball Society, recently founded by another local historian, David Grocott. Apart from providing the historical detail, Bird's presence in the remembering of Ball has meant that the religious angle of his reception has been a recurring feature. Ball has occasionally been commemorated in churches and pamphlets (especially Bird's) and such details of his life are found in churches in Colchester and Essex.[16] The most notable example of this is the church of St James the Great, Colchester, which Bird identified as Ball's home church. When I last checked in 2019, there was Bird's pamphlet, a photocopy of the opening of the first chapter from *A Dream of John Ball*, and a woodcut based on the illustration from Froissart with the words: *In memory of John Ball. Sometime chaplain at this church. Co-leader of the peasants' revolt. Executed at St Albans on 15th July, 1381*. Another card (*John Ball—Born 1331 Died 1381*) explained more about Ball which tied in this figure of local history with wider historical fame ('He was a national character') and the Christian nature of progressive politics ('it might be said that the first effort at Social Reform led by the Church in this country originated by the preaching of John Ball on Christian democracy').

Bird himself was involved in persuading Colchester Borough Council to name walkways after Ball and Tyler on a housing estate in the old Dutch Quarter which Bird identified (with characteristic confidence) as 'practically on the site of the tenement he inherited from his deceased father in 1350, at the age of nineteen.'[17] As Bird knew, even Colchester residents were rarely familiar with the name of Ball, and even if there was a vague awareness that street names (John Ball Walk, John Ball Alley) had been named after a historical figure, the religious connections were (and are) not obvious. Bird, however, added his own biblical allusion when recalling the street-naming commemorations of Ball, Tyler, and (in Norwich) Kett: 'These prophets will now not be without honour in their own country.'[18] Such is the influence of Bird, perhaps, that today outside the toilets at the Colchester Wetherspoon's pub, there is a picture (including a version of the Froissart illustrations) retelling Ball's early life, as reconstructed by Bird, and Ball's life as a 'chaplain,' his 'Curacy of St James' Church,' a preacher of

---

16 Bird, *Colchester Rebel*. See also Bird, *Rebel before His Time*, 135–37, for examples of commemorations.
17 Bird, *Rebel before His Time*, 136.
18 Bird, *Rebel before His Time*, 137.

a 'subversive doctrine of social equality...in and around Colchester,' and, giving the local history national significance, 'the ideologue of the Peasant's [sic] movement' working with Tyler on 'planning the Peasants' Revolt from Colchester.' Even Tyler was understood (as he sometimes is) as 'another Colchester man' and should not be confused with the Tyler of Dartford in Kent because, the Wetherspoon's picture informs us, 'reputable historians tell us that the leaders of the Peasants' Revolt both came from Colchester.'[19]

Bird's influence as a historian and priest can be seen in other public memorials. On the corner on John Ball Walk there is now a plaque that adds such religious qualifications while maintaining a clear connection to local history: *JOHN BALL of Colchester, Priest. A leader of the Peasants Revolt. Executed at St Albans, 15th July 1381*. Bird had previously commissioned a plaque for the six-hundredth anniversary of Ball's death (15 July 1981) which was attached to a house. However, the resident had it removed and so it was put into storage. It was lost, found, restored by Collins and Curtis Masonry Ltd, lost again, and found again, before the unveiling of 'this memorial to one of the most important men in the history of our town—and our country.'[20] In line with the political and cultural connotations Ball had been accruing in recent decades, and combined with Colchester's distinctive contribution to the modern reception of Ball, the new plaque was unveiled on the 15 July 2017 (the anniversary of Ball's death, now named as John Ball Day) by the bishop of Colchester (Roger Morris) and the human rights campaigner and peer Shami Chakrabarti, accompanied by singing and a John Ball Motet played by Lizzie Gutteridge. Dorian Kelly also acted the part of Ball, combining humour, politics, religion, and antiquarian interests. Kelly opened with a discussion of Adam delving and Eve spinning, emphasising that Ball spoke for 'truth, justice and the word of God.' The religious angle was strong, albeit contextualised safely in medieval England. Kelly had Ball retell the story of the Israelites under Pharaoh and proclaim, 'Let me be your Moses!' While the political emphases were likewise firmly contextualised in medieval England, contemporary echoes remained ('A good day's pay for a good day's work. That's

19 This is not the only Wetherspoon's pub where Ball has a presence. At The William Morris in Hammersmith, London, one of the many Morris-related pictures is the Burne-Jones frontispiece to the Kelmscott edition of *A Dream of John Ball*, with the accompanying Adam and Eve couplet.

20 'John Ball Plaque,' *Colchester Civil Society* (19 January 2017), https://www.colchestercivicsociety.co.uk/2017/01/19/john-ball-plaque/; Rosemary Jewers, 'List of Plaques: John Ball' (14 March 2018), on the website *Colchester Plaque Trails*, http://www.placecheck.info/maps/view/index.php?display=comments&map=104. Cf. Bird, *Rebel before His Time*, 137.

all we want') and, as with 'Sing John Ball' and plenty of public presentations of Ball close to Parliament (recall the event was hosted by a Baroness and a Bishop), violence was not an obvious feature of the performances.[21]

Islington

Predictably, perhaps, outside of church settings and away from the influence of Bird, the overt references to Christianity continued to fade, while the politics were emphasised according to context and in familiar ways. On 11 June 2011, and to a gathering of about 200 people, Tony Benn unveiled the Peasants' Revolt plaque on the outside wall of the pub, The Highbury Barn (26 Highbury Park, London) in Jeremy Corbyn's Islington North constituency. Voted for by locals, the 'Islington People's Plaque' commemorated the attack on Robert Hales's Highbury residence specifically and the Peasants' Revolt more generally. The green plaque reads: NEAR THIS SITE DURING THE PEASANTS' REVOLT 1381 HIGHBURY MANOR WAS BURNT AND DESTROYED. At the unveiling, the story of the revolt was retold by Benn and Corbyn.[22] Most extensively in the *Camden New Journal*,[23] Benn was reported to have compared the uprising to the Arab Spring. This involved a typical democratic framing of the revolt:

> What happened here in 1381 is what is happening in Egypt today and all over the Arab world...People are standing up for their rights. They are not going to be oppressed by dictators. The Peasants' Revolt was the first of a

---

21 'John Ball', *Colchester Civil Society*, https://www.colchestercivicsociety.co.uk/what-we-do/commemorative-plaques/john-ball/. See also *Daily Gazette* (20 July 2016); *Daily Gazette* (7 March 2017). For Lizzie Gutteridge on Ball, see Lizzie Gutteridge, 'When Adam Delved—a song for John Ball by Consort of 1' (9 July 2017), *YouTube*, https://www.youtube.com/watch?v=BS1BM1gB6Nw. For ongoing details on all things Ball, see the website of the John Ball Society, https://www.johnballsociety.org.

22 For the details, see, e.g., Rob Bleaney, 'Tony Benn to unveil peasants' plaque in Highbury', *Islington Gazette* (6 June 2011), https://www.islingtongazette.co.uk/news/environment/tony-benn-to-unveil-peasants-plaque-in-highbury-1-913299; Andrew Johnson, 'Left-wing veteran Tony Benn unveils plaque to 1381 Peasants' Revolt that saw Highbury Manor burnt down', *Camden New Journal* (17 June 2011), http://camdennewjournal.com/article/left-wing-veteran-tony-benn-unveils-plaque-1381-peasants-revolt-saw-highbury-manor-bu?sp=20&sq=bench.

23 Johnson, 'Left-wing veteran Tony Benn unveils plaque to 1381 Peasants' Revolt'.

long series of campaigns to secure freedom and democracy in Britain. We haven't finished yet. There's a lot to do.

But Benn was also reported as emphasising the economic and class aspects of the revolt, how it was caused by freezing agricultural labourers' wages after wage rises following the Black Death, adding,

> In order to stop the wages going up, the government introduced the first-ever pay policy—the Statute of Labourers…The government got in an economic mess and so introduced the poll tax, the most unfair of all taxes. Everyone has to pay the same amount so the poor end up paying the majority of it.

Benn was reported as talking further (with an allusion to Ball) about how the 'land was owned in common but then it was enclosed and sold off.' In line with his understanding of Ball, Benn was said to have applied such arguments to the contemporary world, arguing that 'the wealth was in the land and that's why we have the society we have today' with most people sweating 'their guts out' while 'the wealth is held by a handful of people.' And so, in the reporting at least, it was Ball who was the most prominently featured individual (accompanied by Benn's favoured clerical title for Ball) and, because of Benn's influence, the Bible just about remained:

> The Reverend John Ball said at the time: 'This will not go well in England until all things are held in common. Why should the rich be rich and the poor be poor—where in the Bible will you find the story of a gentleman? Where is the authority for a class-ridden society?'

Benn, as ever, implicitly constructed the revolt as the inaugural campaign in an English or British tradition of campaigning for social justice which led to democracy and greater fairness, in line with the Civil War, the Chartists, the Suffragettes, and the 'great 1945 revolution' of the Labour government. Indeed, the 'great lesson' to be taken from this is that change must come from below ('if you want justice you have to do it yourself') and that this struggle is ongoing and repetitive, and necessarily so because if people 'do not fight the same battles' then 'everything will be taken away from you.' All this is familiar from what we know of Benn, but we should note for now that, despite the suggestion in the plaque itself of the historic violence associated with the revolt, such connotations were not overt in Benn's commentary, a point to which we return below.

Smithfield

The other prominent memorial in London is a slate triptych at 57A West Smithfield, on the wall of St Bartholomew's hospital.[24] The lowercase lettering includes an outline of the local events and reads:

> At this place on 15th June 1381 Wat Tyler, John Ball and other representatives of the Great Rising met King Richard II to finalise terms for ending the Rebellion. The King had agreed to all the political reforms aimed at alleviating the plight of the people. However he and his advisors later reneged on that agreement after killing Tyler in the process near this spot. John Ball and many others of the Revolt were also later executed.

The lowercase is alternated with the following uppercase lettering which gives us Ball's ideas on the state of England:

> THINGS CANNOT GO ON WELL IN ENGLAND NOR EVER WILL UNTIL EVERYTHING SHALL BE IN COMMON, WHEN THERE SHALL BE NEITHER VASSAL NOR LORD AND ALL DISTINCTIONS LEVELLED · JOHN BALL

The accompanying brass plaque provides the general information about its origins: *This memorial commemorating The Great Rising of 1381 was commissioned by Matthew Bell, carved by Emily Hoffnung and unveiled by Ken Loach on 15th July 2015.* There were some difficulties involved in establishing a physical memorial to the rebellion. Bell, a Smithfield resident, tells us that for a 'couple of years' he tried to get permission for the memorial 'where the denouement of the revolt and the death of Wat Tyler took place' but, after 'much bureaucratic to-ing and fro-ing, I was able to get permission from The City of London, English Heritage and St Bartholomew's Hospital.'[25]

That another memorial has been put up is perhaps a good indication that the story of Ball, Tyler, and the revolt no longer holds the threat it once did and this is only further supported by the additional famous quotation on the brass plaque from an even more famous Tyler-sympathiser: *'If the*

---

24 For further details, see, e.g., Matt Brown, 'Peasants' Revolt Plaque Unveiled in Smithfield,' *Londonist* (16 September 2016), https://londonist.com/2015/07/peasants-revolt-plaque-unveiled-in-smithfield; Michele Woodger, 'Smithfield, EC1: Memorial to the Peasants' Revolt,' *Lettering in London* (no date given), https://letteringinlondon.com/portfolio/smithfield-001/.

25 Quotation from the 'About' section of Bell's blog dedicated to the memorial (Matthew Bell, *The 1381 Revolt Smithfield Memorial*, http://revolt1381.blogspot.com/): https://www.blogger.com/profile/10624007353115934584.

Barons merited a monument to be erected at Runnymede, Tyler merited one in Smithfield.' Thomas Paine, 1791. The inclusion of Paine implicitly locates Ball, Tyler, and the revolt in an English radical tradition while socialist connections were made clear at the unveiling, which involved the prominent left-wing filmmaker Ken Loach and the presence of the left-wing politician (and former Mayor of London) Ken Livingstone. Its connections with public history are provided by the presence of arguably the most culturally credible promoter of the revolt today, Melvyn Bragg (see below).[26] But this is a history and tradition which is presented as something beyond mere antiquarianism—these are deaths that must have ongoing relevance with faint hints of martyrdom surrounding the interpretation of the memorial. On the two-year anniversary of the memorial, Bell captioned a photograph of the memorial, providing a connection with contemporary struggles including gender inclusivity: 'June 15th 2017. In memory of the men and women who fought in 1381 and would have been fighting now.'[27] In his reporting of the unveiling of the memorial with a potted history of the revolt, Glyn Robbins argued that the 'Parallels for today are too obvious to mention' but also that there is a danger in commemorating 'our history' when 'we romanticise it and freeze it in aspic.' Thus, he concluded, we should not spend 'too much energy on the fight for a better past!' Instead, 'if we want to truly remember the Peasants' Revolt, we should follow their example.'[28]

As this suggests, this is a history and tradition which looks to a potential end time or goal, hence Ball's uppercase words on the memorial about looking to a time when things go well, when everything is in common, and when distinctions are levelled. In other words, we have a cluster of ideas (memorialising of the dead, ongoing relevance of the death, potential goal of history through heroic deaths, the importance of the example, etc.) that may be called a soft martyrology where the popular connotations of excessive 'religion' have been significantly drained—indeed, the rebels themselves were never likely to be labelled 'martyrs.' Moreover, the Christian or religious aspect of the revolt is only there for those with ears to hear or eyes to see an allusion to Acts 2.44–45 and 4.32–35, while the casual visitor

26 Photographs of the unveiling on 15 July 2015 are provided by Bell, *The 1381 Revolt Smithfield Memorial* (17 December 2015), http://revolt1381.blogspot.com/2015/12/4pm.html.
27 Bell, *The 1381 Revolt Smithfield Memorial* (17 June 2017), http://revolt1381.blogspot.com/2017/06/june-15th-2017.html.
28 Glyn Robbins, 'Remembering the Peasants' Revolt,' *Housing Matters* (16 July 2015), https://glynrobbins.wordpress.com/2015/07/16/remembering-the-peasants-revolt/.

to the memorial is not given any obvious indication of the occupation of Ball. Nevertheless, the location of the memorial is worth noting in that it potentially highlights a kind of comparative martyrology. It is sandwiched between a memorial to William Wallace (aka Braveheart) who was killed nearby in 1305 and, more strikingly still, a Protestant memorial from 1870 commemorating the 'Marian Martyrs' with more traditional martyrological language (*Blessed are the dead which die in the Lord. The noble army of martyrs praise Thee!* and *Within a few feet of this spot, John Rogers, John Bradford, John Philpot, and other servants of God, suffered death by fire for the faith of Christ, in the years 1555, 1556, 1557*).

Whatever we make of the location of the 1381 memorial, a cluster of similar soft martyrological ideas remain, even if the language is made more palatable for post-Christian public discourse or in a world where 'martyrs' might be too closely associated with ISIS or al-Qaeda or something a little too Oriental. After all, when one sympathetic blogger said of the history of the revolt that it had now been 'immortalised,' there is no indication that we should be thinking that Ball, Tyler, and the rest are in for an eternal life of bliss in the heavens for righteous murder.[29] Indeed, part of the implicit remembrance of death is the implicit innocence of the rebels, hence the language of them being the *recipients* of violence, a common theme in contemporary receptions of Ball and memorialising of the revolt. In the lowercase text of the Smithfield memorial, the rebels are betrayed and 'executed' while the royal powers are directly involved in 'killing' Tyler. As Bell similarly captioned the memorial on one of his blog posts: 'In Memoriam; Wat Tyler and those many more who were murdered following the end of the revolt on this day in 1381.'[30] It is also worth noting that the violent actions of the rebels are relatively downplayed in the memorial. The uppercase words of John Ball do not point to any endorsement of violence and beheadings. The violence is not entirely ignored; the engraved text is flanked with medieval weaponry on one side and agricultural equipment on the other, which can also double up as weaponry, of course, as suggested in the engraving. But it is hardly a prominent feature. This downplaying of violence in certain circles (and the uplaying in others) requires further explanation.

29 Metro Girl, 'Memorial to Wat Tyler and the Peasants' Revolt 1381 in Smithfield,' *Memoirs of a Metro Girl* (17 December 2015), https://memoirsofametrogirl.com/2015/12/17/wat-tyler-memorial-london-peasants-revolt-1381-smithfield-st-bartholomew/.

30 Bell, *The 1381 Revolt Smithfield Memorial* (15 June 2016), http://revolt1381.blogspot.com/2016/06/in-memoriam-wat-tyler-and-those-many.html.

Fear of a Violent Ball

The relative prominence of the commemorations of, and memorials for, Ball can be seen as a sign that their memory needs to be preserved because it might be lost. Moreover, it could also be understood as an indication of the historic weakness of the Left for whom Ball has so long been a reference point. Before expanding on this, it is worth establishing some recent prominent attempts to utilise Ball on parts of the Left and how the absence of violence in their retellings is one of the most distinctive features, particularly when contrasted with broader mainstream retellings or a long history of retellings where there are (emphatically) no such qualms. For a start, we can again recall one of the most prominent transmitters of Ball's memory for the Left, namely (the pacifist) Carter's 'Sing John Ball' and its reception (see Chapter 22). As we saw, the song is not about decapitating the lords or putting their heads on spikes, but a hope about being ruled by love for one another. Similarly, another popular rendition in a related context is a recording of Benn's talk in a joint show with the folksinger Roy Bailey at the Cambridge Folk Festival, 2000, where Benn summarised his views on the revolt (see Chapter 21) and the only violence mentioned was the gruesome fate of Ball.[31] It is worth noting too that Bailey is also known for the 'Song of the Leaders' (from the album *Hard Times* [1982]) which includes reference to Ball. The song indicates mass threat posed by the rebels and an emphasis on their discipline in attacking the Savoy Palace and the lawyers' books but the physical violence against people is more implied than explicit—indeed, when it is explicit, it is violence against Wat Tyler. Such tendencies are paralleled on the contemporary Left, and clearer still when a given interpreter is close or attached to the parliamentary Labour Party.

Owen Jones, for instance, used his popular *Guardian* column in 2014 to promote the English radical tradition and Ball's familiar role at its beginning to challenge the promotion of 'British values' and a certain kind of history associated with David Cameron's government. Cameron's history and the 'Tory view of history,' Jones argued, was about 'empire, aristocracy, monarchy, the established church, exploitative employers, and so on.' Against this, Jones promoted another history of a struggle against power by 'ordinary people who are airbrushed from history' which 'goes back to the Peasants' Revolt of 1381, when ordinary folk rose in rebellion at a poll tax.' In line with developing emphases on inclusion on the Left (and beyond), Jones notes that the revolt 'wasn't just led by men,' citing the

---

31 Benn and Bailey, *Writing on the Wall*.

example of Johanna Ferrour. In a way that might further evoke a contemporary mass demonstration with Jones as a speaker or protestor, tens of thousands ('ranging from roofers and bakers to millers and parish priests') marched on Blackheath 'where the Lollard priest John Ball publicly questioned the class system: "When Adam delved and Eve span, who was then the gentleman?"' This was the beginning of a radical tradition which continued through the English Revolution, the Tolpuddle Martyrs, Chartists, Suffragettes, and the first LGBT demonstration in London. The point of this tradition was not just to counter Cameron's history but to provide inspiration and emulation as it 'underpins my values' and 'helps drive me to oppose the values underpinning Cameron's administration.' But what is missing from Jones's history is also important. As with 'Sing John Ball,' conspicuous by its absence is the violence in Jones's presentation of similarities across time. Ball 'publicly questioned' the class system, and what followed in the seventeenth century was 'widespread defiance' and a king simply 'deposed' (!) while 'radical movements like the democratic Levellers and socialistic Diggers flourished.'[32]

Jones's position as a *Guardian* journalist and Labour Party activist close to certain MPs no doubt goes a long way to explaining why he might be less likely to promote the significance of extreme violence in the English radical tradition; teasing out the contemporary relevance of beheading the archbishop of Canterbury was always going be a difficult ask. This may be an obvious point, but the assumed social and political constraints have always been important for understanding the history of reception of Ball. The downplaying of violence is also (unsurprisingly) a common issue when Ball and the revolt are used in Labour circles, with Benn's most famous presentations being an especially important example. Indeed, given the close association with peace campaigning and democratic socialism on the Labour Left in the late twentieth and early twenty-first centuries, it should be even less of a surprise that physical violence against the elites did not get foregrounded either in these public presentations. There are several other examples which would support this general point. The electoral threat from UKIP in 2017 led Sam Tarry (head of Corbyn's 2016 campaign to be re-elected Labour leader) to talk of 'freedoms' being fought for 'by the Peasants' Revolt, the Tolpuddle Martyrs, the Chartists, the suffragettes and others.' This 'radical tradition' too was understood as 'our history' which can be 'an English Labour party that demonstrates that a socialist vision is a patriotic one, because nothing is more patriotic than building a society for

---

32 *Guardian* (15 June 2014).

the many; not the few.'[33] What is less likely to be stressed are the methods sometimes used by the rebels in trying to achieve their goals.

Corbyn sympathiser and Benn's close ally Dennis Skinner had earlier taken Ball in different but complementary ways. What makes the example of Skinner noteworthy is that he heightened the stress on class conflict and confrontation yet still avoided anything overly violent. Skinner gave standard mention of Ball's Adam and Eve couplet as pointing to equality among people and he ratcheted up the language of class conflict when he paraphrased Ball's argument, saying, 'they've got it rich and we're living in poverty...they were next door to being slaves,' while dealing with the 'ideology of these two contrasting groups of people.'[34] Skinner here was presenting Ball for a BBC educational programme, *English File*, and accordingly his emphasis was primarily on the use of language. Skinner's analysis provided modern-day analogies (e.g., Thatcher's Poll Tax) but most significantly he argued that revolutionary statements had to be made without being 'too smart.' Ball, Skinner suggested, would not have been good in the House of Commons today because 'they all talk in yuppie language and they use political jargon that goes over people's heads.'

With Skinner, then, we find him picking up on the theme of the importance of a common English language against the elites in the reception of Ball. But there is another angle to this beyond cutting through jargon. Skinner's reading of Ball was connected with his speaking at, and experiences of, political rallies and his trade union and mining background (the chapter he wrote in his memoirs on the importance of public speaking with the telling title, 'Never Be Dull,' approximately maps onto his exposition of Ball's techniques).[35] The reasons given for Ball's 'fairly simple language' are that a straightforward message cannot be ambiguous and that he had to convey a message in basic form that broke down the ways in which class relations had been masked. There are 'a lot of you, there are not too many of the bosses,' Skinner paraphrased Ball. In this respect, Skinner noted that Ball used a pattern of contrasting pairs (e.g., clothed in velvet versus poor cloth) and three statements ('we have no sovereign to whom we may complain, nor that will hear us, nor do us right') to build up to a climax

---

33 *Guardian* (18 July 2017).
34 'John Ball's Speech to Peasants—Analysis from Dennis Skinner (pt 1/2),' BBC English File (3 August 2012 [original 1996]), https://www.bbc.co.uk/programmes/p00wwk82; 'John Ball's Speech to Peasants—Analysis from Dennis Skinner (pt 2/2)' BBC English File (3 August 2012 [original 1996]), https://www.bbc.co.uk/programmes/p00wwkgn.
35 Dennis Skinner, *Sailing Close to the Wind: Reminiscences* (London: Quercus, 2014), chapter 9.

which was the 'real challenge to be made.' The structure of the speech was understood to have shown from the beginning that 'you're all together in this battle. That there are no sort of leaders and the led. And that you're all going to battle together.' The use of the first-person plural 'we' was to enhance this communal identification so that 'people felt strong' and everybody should be onside. A speech ought to be finished in a way that 'not only inspired people and made them think' but also convinced them to 'follow him as well.' This again meant a clear and precise climax so people can both understand and take notice at the heart and passion of a good speech—with just a hint of potential violence in the BBC's accompanying presentation as the peasants head off with their tools hoping for 'remedy by fairness or otherwise.' But still, Skinner did not (on this BBC schools programme at least) talk about beheading the bosses in this battle, nor did he breakdown the structure of the wording attributed to Ball by Walsingham: 'They must do this first, by killing the most powerful lords of the realm, then by slaying the lawyers, justiciars, and jurors of the land, and finally, by weeding out from their land any that they knew would in the future be harmful to the commonwealth' (*Chronica maiora* 546–557). For Skinner, future change ended at phrases such as a 'real challenge to be made,' which is general enough to apply to the present with little difficulty, just as with other similar presentations such as 'the message of brotherhood and the resulting anti-establishment agitation' (so Benn), 'John Ball publicly question[ing] the class system' (so Jones), or hope for the light coming in the morning and being ruled by the love for one another (so 'Sing John Ball').

Ball, Violence, and Public History

By stark contrast, Ball and/or the revolt have not only been a regular point of reference when history has been popularised (and academic history), but they have also been presented in their dramatic, class-divided, violent, and bloody otherness, including high-profile, academically-informed and popular TV programmes (and now YouTube videos), including: *Horrible Histories* (CBBC; Series 1, Episode 8, 2015); Tony Robinson's *The Peasants' Revolt* for *Timeline* (Channel 4, 2004); and an episode of Simon Schama's *History of Britain* (BBC; Series 1, Episode 5, 2000), where the revolt is not only presented explicitly as a class war but Ball, understood as a radical Lollard leading the retribution, was paralleled by Schama with one of the infamous three figures of Death. We can say similar things about some of the most popular historical books on the revolt, including Alastair

Dunn's *The Peasants' Revolt: England's Failed Revolution of 1381* ([2002] 2004), Juliet Barker's *England, Arise: The People, the King and the Great Revolt of 1381* (2014), and Dan Jones's tellingly titled, *Summer of Blood: The Peasants' Revolt of 1381* (2009).[36]

Perhaps as much as anyone, Melvyn Bragg has been responsible for a sustained public presentation of the academic history of the revolt and Ball in particular, such as on his BBC Radio Four programme *In Our Time* (2006), in his BBC2 TV programme *Radical Lives* (2014), and in his novel *Now Is the Time* (2015).[37] *Now Is the Time* is a particularly good example of Ball in his full medieval otherness. Indeed, packed with close attention to historical detail and antiquarian accuracy, the novel brings together centuries of familiar reception. In addition to a backstory for Tyler, the details of Ball's upbringing are close to those presented by Bird.[38] Ball's physical description is likewise familiar. He is shabbily dressed, tall, lean, thin-lipped, and, of course, bearer of a strong nose. He is a master orator and his voice again carries in the open air, with its chant-like qualities taking it beyond mere speech.[39] Ball is clever, composed, charismatic, full of conviction, dedicated, a man of the workers and common people, and strikes up a close relationship with his jailor (cf., e.g., Chapters 17, 19). There are even hints of Ball being brought up with favoured imagery of Morris-style coming daylight.[40] Ball and the rebellion are partly driven by stories of liberties and an oppressive Francophone nobility, echoing the myth of the Norman Yoke. In line with the contemporary updating of the reception of 1381, women (particularly Johanna Ferrers) are given prominence and agency in *Now Is the Time*, and we even get a women's camp among the rebel army.

In the case of Ball, what we also get is a character fuelled by supernaturalist religion and class conflict to the point that the two categories are almost inseparable. This is a relatively rare Ball in the history of reception (cf.

---

36 To which we might add poetry and spoken work which can incorporate violence. See, e.g., Steve Ely, 'John Ball,' in *Oswald's Book of Hours* (Middlesbrough: Smokestack Books, 2013), available at https://www.poetryinternational.org/pi/poem/24865/auto/0/0/Steve-Ely/JOHN-BALL/en/tile. Cf. Zack Wilson, 'Steve Ely: Poet of Sunday Leagues and Sainted Rebellion,' *Lone Striker* (19 November 2012), http://zackwilsonlonestriker.blogspot.com/2012/11/steve-ely.html.
37 Cf. Virginia Blackburn's review of *Radical Lives* in the *Daily Express* (4 August 2014): "'They executed people,' said Bragg sombrely, a pronouncement that was startlingly illustrated by shots of modern butchers cutting up meat.' Butcher shots were also used in Robinson's *Timeline* documentary.
38 Melvyn Bragg, *Now Is the Time* (London: Sceptre Books, 2015), 19–20.
39 Bragg, *Now Is the Time*, 22, 105, 107.
40 Bragg, *Now Is the Time*, 18–19.

Chapter 17), though perhaps more likely to be found in a novel with strong historical interests. Ball the religious virtuoso engages in spiritual exercises, meditations, intense contemplations, dreams, ecstatic experiences, visions, and trances. He is rumoured to be a prophet and miracle-worker and known as a mystic who even visited Julian of Norwich.[41] But this Ball is no wet liberal: he preaches total obedience to God's demands and even accuses Johanna Ferrers of blasphemy in a disagreement over the fate of prostitutes.[42] The novel opens with Ball's asceticism and it is immediately contrasted with the wealth of Sudbury and the aristocracy. Indeed, Ball's hostility to the church is primarily constructed in terms of such class conflict and he sees such ostentatious wealth as contrary to the Bible. While he was attracted to the mystery and holiness of church life and a desire to help the poor as Christ had done, he was soon wounded by his experiences training to be a priest as he was mocked for his accent, rough mannerism, and humility.[43] There is some presentation in what might previously have been understood as a proto-Protestant construction of Ball. He is sympathetic to Lollards and does not believe that the Bible sanctions the position of pope and archbishop.[44] But Ball is also a recognisably Catholic figure who goes to Mass immediately on being freed from jail, makes the sign of the cross, and engages enthusiastically with the traditions of Corpus Christi.[45] This tension is perhaps related to Ball inaugurating something new. Ball is close to being a Christ-like figure not just in imitation (e.g., blesses, breaks and shares bread, rumoured miracle worker, teaches how to say the Lord's Prayer, delivers his Blackheath sermon from a small mound, pithy Gospel-style sayings, effectively becomes the cross itself) but also in that he inspires something close to a breakaway religious movement as he has a scriptorium set up and scribes make copies of his verses and sermons not in Latin but in English.[46]

Bragg's Ball is even a kind of apocalyptic prophet of end times (note, in this respect, Ball's saying in the novel's title: *Now Is the Time*) who believes God is directing the path through London, the results of which are labelled as Ball's Apocalypse.[47] He talks in terms of the end of the world, punishment, and the recovery of a lost Eden in England. Crucially, Ball

---

41 Bragg, *Now Is the Time*, 21–25, 137, 150, 173, 193, 226.
42 Bragg, *Now Is the Time*, 125, 173–74.
43 Bragg, *Now Is the Time*, 24–25.
44 Bragg, *Now Is the Time*, 116.
45 Bragg, *Now Is the Time*, 104, 137–38, 193, 251.
46 Bragg, *Now Is the Time*, 102–3, 118, 125–26, 135, 137–38, 140.
47 Bragg, *Now Is the Time*, 191, 197.

is explicit in his promotion of divinely sanctioned violence. In response to Tyler's question about whether killing is acceptable in light of the Ten Commandments, Ball explains that Genesis shows that God has killed when necessary and that, in the fourteenth century, in a time of plague, all will die unless wickedness is cleared away. God also commanded his agents (e.g., Saul, Israelites) to kill, and the rebels of 1381 are also the chosen people—after all, the true commons of England had been visited by Joseph of Arimathea and the spirit of the Son of God—and as the chosen people before could kill their own, so too could they.[48] Not one to flinch from his responsibilities, this Ball pushes for the killing of the king's traitorous councillors, encourages the execution of the devilish Sudbury, anticipates the necessity of disciplined violence in London, and maintains Tyler's confidence to kill when required.[49] His saying about knowing friend from foe was nothing less than the talk of war.[50]

While much of the history of reception of Ball can be a fairly straightforward reading of an author's political preferences onto their history or fiction, we need to be especially wary of this in the case of culture and ideology today. To state the obvious, we do not expect Bragg to be too ideologically wedded to the revolt. Whatever sympathies he may have with Ball, we do not expect Bragg to be advocating religious violence and we do not imagine that he has designs on taking over the state, whatever the merits of such a leader might be. More broadly, when a documentary from Bragg, Schama, or Robinson presents religious and class-based violence, no matter how enthusiastically, we do not imagine that any of them in their role as historians are actually endorsing such views—in fact, there would probably be disappointment and incredulity if they did not present such views. The flip side of this is that it would be difficult for Owen Jones to endorse an anti-Conservative reading of history from below by celebrating the execution of the good and the great in the name of class conflict and the words of a borderline religious fundamentalist. So why can violence, extremist religion, and class conflict in English history be discussed not just among the extra-parliamentary Left but also in the heart of mainstream popular culture?

No doubt the willingness to foreground gore and death is related to ideas that such extreme violence belongs to the past where things were done differently in an era of TV where such themes are popular. Odd though it may sound, the idea that the political radicalism associated with Ball and

48 Bragg, *Now Is the Time*, 114–15, 150.
49 Bragg, *Now Is the Time*, 145, 170–71, 192–93, 201–2.
50 Bragg, *Now Is the Time*, 125–26.

the revolt should be found to flourish in mainstream media culture rather than the constrained parliamentary Left is entirely in keeping with the presentation of violence and class conflict under neoliberal capitalism. Radical critique and anti-capitalist and anti-imperialist rhetoric has been absorbed into TV and film and has, as Slavoj Žižek put it, 'lost its subversive sting.'[51] Žižek also gave the example of the film *Avatar* (2009), observing that at the same time as *Avatar* was generating one billion dollars in under three weeks, there was in fact something resembling its plot happening in the Indian state of Orissa. Here, land was sold to mining companies which provoked an armed rebellion. Consequently, there were propaganda and military attacks from the Indian state and a vicious conflict ensued. Žižek added:

> So where is Cameron's film here? Nowhere: in Orissa, there are no noble princesses waiting for white heroes to seduce them and help their people, just the Maoists organising the starving farmers. The film enables us to practise a typical ideological division: sympathising with the idealised aborigines while rejecting their actual struggle. The same people who enjoy the film and admire its aboriginal rebels would in all probability turn away in horror from the Naxalites, dismissing them as murderous terrorists. The true avatar is thus *Avatar* itself—the film substituting for reality.[52]

We might say similar things about Ball and the revolt in popular culture where the presentation of Ball as a full-bloodied, violent, class warrior further permits, if need be, the performance of anti-capitalism and political radicalism at a safe cultural and historical distance.[53] However, whether Žižek continues to be right in claiming that the subversive sting has been lost might at least need some qualification. Whatever original contexts gave meaning to a film like *Avatar*, a documentary by Robinson, or a folk song by Carter, these works are now the material for future interpreters to provide new readings. And in the case of the history of the reception of Ball, precedents are plentiful.

---

51 Slavoj Žižek, 'Do We Still Live in a World?,' http://www.lacan.com/zizrattlesnakeshake.html. See also, e.g., Mark Fisher, *Capitalist Realism: Is There No Alternative?* (Winchester, UK: Zero Books, 2009); Colin Cremin, *Capitalism's New Clothes: Enterprise, Ethics and Enjoyment in Times of Crisis* (London: Pluto Press, 2011).
52 *New Statesman* (4 March 2010).
53 Cf. Fisher, *Capitalist Realism*, 12.

An Exception that Proves the Rule

Yet it remains that against this general backdrop, and paradoxical though it may seem, the contemporary Left has struggled to promote a full-fat version of Ball and the revolt *because of* a fear of this dramatic and violent class conflict, a fear found elsewhere on the Left.[54] But in the case of remembering Ball, there are other important reasons. One is probably straightforward—not many people have heard of Ball (see below). In terms of the problem of violence and historical and cultural difference, it is also because the historical materialist readings of Ball from Morris to Hilton went into decline from the 1960s onward as the Communist Party lost its influence and numbers. Historical materialist readings provided a framework which could account for significant historical and cultural difference (including violence) while simultaneously placing Ball in an ongoing tradition of class struggle. But the idea of a radical English tradition without this framework, and one closely connected to parliamentary democracy (unlike, say, Class War, Anarchist Communist Federation, SWP), effectively has to downplay anything strange, weird, or violent to make the connections between past and present more palatable in trying to make itself appear sufficiently unthreatening and culturally credible.

As a rule of thumb, we might say that the further away from the expectations of Labour parliamentary politics in public discourse, the more likely a violent version of Ball and the revolt can thrive on the Left or in publications that would find sympathies or interest on the Left.[55] A striking example is the work of the photographer and co-founder of Rock Against Racism (1976), Red Saunders. Beginning in 2008, his photographic project HIDDEN 'recreates great moments in the long struggle for rights and representation in Britain' with the aim of recreating 'historic scenes involving the dissenters, revolutionaries, radicals and non-conformists that have often been hidden from a history dominated by Kings, Queens and

---

54 Crossley, *Cults, Martyrs and Good Samaritans*, 162–99.
55 E.g., Christopher Hampton (ed.), *A Radical Reader: The Struggle for Change in England, 1381–1914* (London: Penguin, 1984); J. F. C. Harrison, *The Common People: A History from the Norman Conquest to the Present* (London: Croom Helm, 1984); Poulsen, *English Rebels*; David Horspool, *The English Rebel: One Thousand Years of Troublemaking from the Normans to the Nineties* (London: Viking, 2009); O'Brien, *When Adam Delved and Eve Span*; Frank McLynn, *The Road Not Taken: How Britain Narrowly Missed a Revolution 1381–1926* (London: Bodley Head, 2012).

military battles.'[56] Pictures of this radical tradition, contextualised as 'epic photographs reimagining decisive but overlooked events in Britain's struggle for democracy and social justice,' are typically presented as an inclusive history (i.e., not just white male), featuring, e.g., Leveller women, Thomas Paine, Mary Wollstonecraft, William Cuffay and the Chartists, Swing Riots, and scenes from the Peasants' Revolt. A bearded and scruffy Ball is presented preaching to his peasant audience in a field flanked by a makeshift cross (*John Ball [Hedgerow Priest] 1338–1381*) while Tyler's menacing and blood-splattered army carry a very dead head on a spike and look to the viewer as the city burns in the background (*Wat Tyler and the Peasants' Revolt, 1381*).[57]

In this respect, it is telling where Corbyn *could* be associated with a more violent reading of Ball: when he was positioned closer to extra-parliamentary socialism. When Labour leader, Corbyn was (uniquely) still associated with extra-parliamentary socialism and, with both these contexts in mind, he provided the foreword to an account of a British radical tradition in graphic book format—a genre where extreme violence is, of course, commonplace. Sean Michael Wilson and Robert Brown's *The Many Not the Few: An Illustrated History of Britain Shaped by the People* (2019) is presented as a discussion between a veteran trade unionist, Joe, and his granddaughter, Arushi, once again an implicit acknowledgment of belonging to this tradition irrespective of racial or ethnic background. The violence of the revolt is pictured and not only in illustrations of London aflame; the claim that the 'hated figures of corrupt power were dealt with severely' is accompanied by the heads of Hales and Sudbury on spikes with drops of blood—and nor did Brown (the illustrator) hold back when drawing the decapitated Tyler.[58]

The ideological positions of the graphic story are presented in the tradition of the more radical histories of the revolt, broadly understood. The opening chapter on the Peasants' Revolt begins with a quotation from Ball's

56 'Red Saunders—The Agreement: The Story Behind The Work,' *Cynthia Corbett Gallery* (22 August 2015), https://thecynthiacorbettgallery.wordpress.com/2015/08/22/red-saunders-the-agreement-the-story-behind-the-work/. I am grateful to Gordy Cullum for discussion of Red Saunders's work.

57 'Red Saunders: Hidden,' Impressions Gallery, https://www.impressions-gallery.com/event/red-saunders-hidden/. For the processes involved in capturing the images, see, e.g., 'Red Saunders at Impressions Gallery,' 1 September 2011), *YouTube*, https://www.youtube.com/watch?v=qPmjRDbJMCo.

58 Sean Michael Wilson and Robert Brown, *The Many Not the Few: An Illustrated History of Britain Shaped by the People* (Oxford: Workable Books, 2019), 21–22.

speech about how things cannot go well in England until all goods are held in common and until there is neither serf nor gentleman. Joe gives a standard account of the causes of the revolt, including demands for better pay and conditions after the Black Death and the class conflict that followed, as well as claiming that peasants were getting generally 'bolshy'.[59] Ball himself is introduced preaching 'against corruption in both the church and the state' and whose 'radical' Adam and Eve couplet was both 'anti-class and anti-sexist'.[60] In terms of anti-sexism, it is notable that Joan of Kent was merely 'mocked but not harmed' in class terms with no discussion of the tradition that she was sexually harassed, though not all problematic issues are omitted (e.g., the attack on Flemish immigrants is noted).[61] Ball's Blackheath sermon about all things in common is described as a 'revolution of ideas as to how the country should be governed' and, the editorial aside claims, there were even 'discussions about anarchist-style village councils to run things instead'.[62] Despite the failure of the revolt, the longer-term consequence of the revolt was an improvement on the ways in which the peasants were treated, a familiar theme in socialist and Marxist readings.

The Many Not the Few may not have developed a historical materialism in the style of a Morris, Fagan, or Hilton, but it is hardly incompatible with such a tradition. Corbyn's foreword, with its emphasis on the role of the working classes in driving historical change, echoes some of the more overtly Marxist accounts from yesteryear. Working-class history, 'like black history,' Corbyn argued, has often been neglected in the school curriculum and how 'our rights and freedom are hard won by the sacrifices and advances made by people's movements.' These victories, he continued, require ongoing defence and extension and generations present and future will continue to learn 'from the long road travelled by the working classes' and inaugurated by the Peasants' Revolt.[63] In response to Arushi's comment that all this must have put fear into the lords, Joe even suggests that 'we could do with some of that nowadays, too!'[64] There is also awareness that not only were the rebels supportive of the king because they thought the king was appointed by God, but also that this is a lingering tradition even today ('It's not so easy to shake that stuff off'), echoing explanations given by Hilton (see Chapter 19) and in the *Morning Star* (see above).[65]

59 Wilson and Brown, *The Many Not the Few*, 10–11.
60 Wilson and Brown, *The Many Not the Few*, 15.
61 Wilson and Brown, *The Many Not the Few*, 18, 20.
62 Wilson and Brown, *The Many Not the Few*, 18.
63 Wilson and Brown, *The Many Not the Few*, 5.
64 Wilson and Brown, *The Many Not the Few*, 19.
65 Wilson and Brown, *The Many Not the Few*, 22.

But we should not make precise connections with specific socialist traditions. Instead, it would be more useful to label the context in which the book is framed more generically as equating to the pre-and post-Corbyn extra-parliamentary Left. Wilson himself has published graphic books covering violent topics and radical politics.[66] *The Many Not the Few* was published under auspices of the General Federation of Trade Unions (GFTU) and features an afterword on resources by the GFTU General Secretary (and historical advisor to the book) Doug Nicholls, recommending, among other things, the Marx Memorial Library and the *Culture Matters* website (linked to the *Morning Star*).[67] The book itself mentions figures like Chomsky, and the bibliography includes a number of references to people from different perspectives across the far Left (e.g., Mary Davis, Engels, Eric Hobsbawm, Christopher Hill, Jack Lindsay, A. L. Morton, Charles Poulsen, John Rees, E. P. Thompson, Ellen Meiksins Wood, etc.). The final chapter of *The Many Not the Few* provides, as we might expect, examples of contemporary relevance with reference to the importance of unions and unionising the gig economy, hostility to neoliberalism, and support for Corbyn. But there are precise indications of ideas that are those most associated not with the soft Left of Labour but variously with the old Bennite Left, the *Morning Star*, certain unions, the Communist Party of Britain (CPB), and some post-SWP groups like Counterfire. Indeed, Joe (like Nicholls himself) is a supporter of the socialist case for leaving the EU, the very sort of associations that caused Corbyn so many difficulties from centrist and soft-Left parts of the Labour Party. Though Arushi is sceptical, Joe provides familiar 'Lexit' arguments, including criticisms of EU trade union laws, EU austerity, and the possibility of an EU army, and the case for being able to develop sustainable industries and international working-class solidarity outside the EU.[68] When placed at a further ideological distance from the constraints of the Labour Party, Corbyn could still be tied in with a more caffeinated Ball and related interpretation—even when he was leader of the party.

---

66 See his website, *Sean Michael Wilson: A Graphic Novel Writer from Scotland*, https://seanmichaelwilson.weebly.com/.
67 Wilson and Brown, *The Many Not the Few*, 127.
68 Wilson and Brown, *The Many Not the Few*, 117–25.

24
Epilogue

A Chaotic and Less Chaotic Ball

If we list some of the ways Ball has been understood in the history of his reception, the situation looks chaotic. He has been presented as a forerunner to Wycliffe, a Lollard, a proto-Protestant martyr, an Anabaptist of sorts, a Nonconformist, a Catholic, a Catholic of this or that order, a heterodox Catholic, a millenarian, a mystic, and even some kind of violent fundamentalist. He has been seen as a threat to national security, a perverter of the constitution, a radical or even moderate constitutionalist, a patriot, a violent revolutionary, a hater of political violence, a political reformer, a proto-parliamentarian thinker, a theocratic leader, a mob leader, a monarchist, and a republican. He has been an implicit or explicit supporter of the French Revolution, abolitionism, Chartism, workers' rights, suffragettism, socialism, communism, anarchism, trade unionism, radical liberalism, the Labour Party, the Communist Party of Great Britain, Trotskyism, antiracism, anti-sexism, anti-discrimination, love, and an English or British radical tradition. Temperamentally, he has been viewed as mad, wild, violent, possessed, calm, wise, a naive dreamer, a careful thinker, and a selfless leader prepared to sacrifice his life for the cause. He has even been ignored. His relationship with Wat Tyler likewise differs. They can be two characters who provide the creative tension in narratives of the revolt, they can be at odds with one another, they can be comrades-in-arms, they can be in complete agreement, they can be seen as the complementary ideologue and soldier heading the revolt, they can be seen as the soul (Ball) and the brawn (Tyler) of the revolt, and one can sometimes take pride of place over the other. Although the illustration from the Froissart manuscript still dominates visual depictions and his eyes regularly sparkle and his voice constantly carries, even Ball's physical appearance differs from interpreter to interpreter, from near emaciated to well-fed, from heavy drinker to ascetic, from clean shaven to bearded, from striking nose to nondescript nose. Despite the size of this book, more on his physical depictions still needs to be done and a history of his visual portrayals is one that could provide plenty of data for another reception history of Ball. While visual portrayal of Ball's clothing typically involve Ball looking 'medieval,' further research into the sources concerning monkish dress, which have (often unintentionally) guided the portrayal of Ball as belonging to a given mendicant order, could prove fruitful.

Such is to be expected in discussions of the reception history of a given figure over centuries. But only when decontextualised does his reception appear so chaotic. Unlike the reception history of Jack Straw (a full version of which also needs doing), the reception history of Ball is relatively stable, often predictable, and some generalisations can be made. Following the economic changes after the Black Death, Ball emerged as a Bible-wielding, soft millenarian critic of the lords and church hierarchies, expecting an imminent political, religious, and social transformation whereby peasants and the lower orders would be represented justly and fairly and have access to the fruits of the land. He was soon vilified and presented as a heretic like Wycliffe and the Lollards in order to discredit both Ball himself and Wycliffe. He was often ignored in late medieval retellings of the revolt because his role as devilish ideologue sat uncomfortably with explanations of the breakdown of idealised social roles from above and below. While there is some evidence that his ideas were common enough in popular resistance and while there is good evidence he was seen as a proto-Protestant martyr, his potency as a seditious threat meant he was reintroduced as a warning from history about excessive religion during the English Reformation. This was taken up in seventeenth-century polemics in revolutionary England with some enthusiasm.

But the century that followed the English Revolution saw the beginning of Ball's revival. As ideas about an English or British constitution were developing and capitalist democracy was emerging, criticisms of an increasingly anachronistic institution of serfdom were more and more difficult to dismiss. Nevertheless, Ball as violent mob leader was an ongoing theme that meant he could continue to be used as a warning about social and political instability. In the aftermath of the American and French revolutions, this anxiety remained but simultaneously opened up the possibility for reclaiming Ball. By the late eighteenth/early nineteenth century, Ball was back and well on his way to being an inspirational figure after 400 years of a hostile press. He was soon taken up in revolutionary and reformist circles, and by the emerging working class, abolitionist, liberal, and socialist movements of the nineteenth century, and was typically (but not exclusively) associated with Nonconformity and/or a romanticised medievalism. While the history of the interpretation of Ball has unsurprisingly been dominated by men, the nineteenth and early twentieth centuries also seem to have been a peak in the number of women involved. We might speculate that the reasons for this involved the novel being a notable platform for women in Victorian England, and the emergence of feminism and suffragettism could utilise Ball and the revolt as one of the established emancipatory models before the development of an extensive feminist canon in the twentieth century. Negative readings did not disappear but by the end of the nineteenth century, his reputation was usually positive, if not heroic. He was understood as a founding figure of English radicalism and his memory was perpetuated by different socialist and communist groups (anarchist, Labour Left, Communist Party of Great Britain [CPGB]). The Cold War allowed his reputation to flourish simultaneously as both a pro-Soviet figure and an anti-Soviet founder of English socialism, as well as providing occasional opportunities to revive the negative presentation of Ball as a political threat.

By the turn of the millennium, class interests partly gave way to, or were complemented by, a range of political issues to be associated with equality and diversity. But Ball was becoming an increasingly unthreatening figure, no doubt as the working-class labour movement and the Left had long lost its previous potency. On the parliamentary Left, a somewhat liberalised Ball certainly lost his violent edge and medieval otherness. Likewise, the religious connotations of Ball, should they be found in leftist circles, are now most likely to be vaguely Protestant or opposed to 'established' religion as he is most likely to be seen as a promoter of love, tolerance, freedom, etc. The fate of Christianity and the church in England and public discourse shares the same story: religion is vague enough to ignore it but there if you want to see it, vague enough to deny being overly religious, and vague enough that it is unlikely to be presented excessively.

Ball in Culture and Politics

Nevertheless, an understanding of Ball as a violent figure associated with class-conflict continues on the extra-parliamentary Left, even if its influence is not what it was even 75 years ago. Of Tyler and the revolt, Stephen Basdeo argued that it is 'usually at times of social and political upheaval that his "spectre" appears,' adding that the future for Tyler's legacy 'does not look good' while also noting that, 'on the other hand,' there are popular histories of Tyler and the revolt.¹ There is some truth to this, but it is an explanation that should be qualified. In the case of Ball and Tyler, I hope this book has shown that while their presence has certainly been invoked in times of obvious upheaval, it is not limited to such times. Indeed, that Ball (and Tyler) recurs in novels, plays, popular histories, and documentaries beyond contexts not obviously related to riots or strikes needs explanation. This is why it is important to note that the journalistic Left or parliamentary Left today have struggled with presenting the violence, religion, and class conflict of 1381, in sharp contrast to the presentation of Ball the violent priest which has thrived in popular history and fiction. One reason for the unproblematic presentation of the full-fat version of Ball in popular culture is the same reason why anticapitalism and anticolonialism have thrived in TV and cinema in an era of neoliberalism: such agitation is absorbed and performed in popular culture, without the threat of change or overthrowing of the system in reality (Chapter 23). To understand the ongoing reception of figures like Ball, we need to understand something about our current cultural and ideological contexts, how they have changed and differ from previous ones, and how they deal with oppositional politics and ideology. And dealing with oppositional politics today is not always heavy-handed bludgeoning of subversion.

Indeed, throughout this book, it should be clear that Ball's changing reception is part of the broader historical, political, and social changes over the past 600-plus years, including changes driven partly by mass movements. But it is still helpful to single out some figures as indicative of the major changes and filters through which Ball has been understood. Obviously, the first chroniclers have had a profound influence, if only by virtue of presenting us with a dominant narrative for Ball. Because of Thomas Walsingham and Henry Knighton, the regular claim that Ball was a Lollard or supporter of Wycliffe continued and continues to this day. But more than that, the chroniclers provided the most memorable words of Ball which were originally presented to discredit him. We cannot know for sure whether the historical Ball uttered words with which he became synonymous (e.g., 'When Adam delved and Eve span...,' things 'not well to pass in England, nor shall do till everything be common'), but, if nothing else, the evil chaplain of 1381 bolsters the principle that the devil gets the best tunes, as R. B. Dobson put it in a related context.²

1   Basdeo, *Life and Legend of a Rebel Leader*, loc 3279–4321.
2   Dobson, 'Remembering the Peasants' Revolt,' in Liddell and Wood (eds.), *Essex and the Great Revolt of 1381*, 12. For Dobson, the writer of *The Life and Death of Jack Straw* and Lord Berners's translation of Froissart at the beginning of the sixteenth century were 'inadvertently giving the devil the best tunes.'

Unintentionality would play another important role in spreading the Ball legend. Despite or because of his ideological change of heart, the youthful Robert Southey's presentation of a radical Ball would hold sway for much of the nineteenth century and was near inescapable in discussions of the revolt, certainly among movements like Chartism. The medievalism, radical politics, and even imagery of light and dark, fed into (even if indirectly) the most influential modern presentation of Ball by William Morris, whose *A Dream of John Ball* would in turn hold sway for much of twentieth-century reception. Readings of Morris's reading of Ball could go in different ideological directions on the Left and one area where difference has been most acutely felt is Morris's Marxism. While Morris explicitly gave a historical materialist reading of Ball and located him in Marxist understandings of the transition from feudalism to capitalism, and then to socialism and communism, this did not stop the idea of Morris as a romantic English/British socialist distanced from Marx and Marxism from taking off.

And in some ways, this debate adds further insight into our understanding of the contemporary reception of Ball. Historical materialist readings of Ball associated with Morris, the early British Marxists or interpreters of Marx, the CPGB, and Rodney Hilton, which dominated mid-twentieth century discussions, could accommodate the violence of a medieval figure precisely because medieval England was a place where they did things differently. However, in seeing Ball and 1381 as part of the historical processes driven by class conflict and changing modes of production, they could also accommodate Ball as part of an English or British radical tradition which has dramatically changed, modified, and adapted with the emergence of capitalism and opposition to it. Once the theoretical underpinning of a historical materialist perspective was (largely) lost on the Left, then an English or British radical tradition remained with a weakened dialectical understanding of the past. In using Ball, the relevance of the connection between past and present still had to be explained with the decline of historical materialism, and it is striking that it is in the post-Hilton, post-Cold War, neoliberal era when the vagueness of Ball's relevance and message starts to dominate on the Left. Fittingly, the major reception of Ball here is from Sydney Carter's song and the hope that we will be ruled by the love of one another. From the 1980s onwards, this Ball became a figure who stands in the tradition of *general* shared values and practices associated with the contemporary Left (e.g., social equalities, democracy, anger at the government, A to B marches) and gives 'inspiration,' bolsters 'values,' or provides stories about 'ordinary lives.' To repeat the rule of thumb from Chapter 23: the closer to the *parliamentary* Left, then the less likely Ball's otherness will be entertained. This is not to denigrate the intentions behind such sentiments, of course. But it remains that we are now quite removed from Morris's Ball struggling to understand how radically different the future would be and what would be required to reach a time when all will be held in common.

Nevertheless, these are the receptions waiting to be taken up by the next generations of Ball's interpreters, wherever that may lead. No matter how vague sentiments are about Ball in contemporary folk music and no matter how ideologically different a documentary might be from (say) a young socialist, these are the resources being used to reinterpret Ball and take his reception in new directions. Yet as things stand, Ball is widely unknown today, perhaps surprisingly given how dramatic the events of 1381 were. It is in niche areas where he continues to be a figure of fascination (history, novels, folk music, socialist politics), and where his ongoing legacy is being forged. And if there is one question that has been integral to his reception since 1381 to this day, it is this: What should England be?

Bibliography

Nb: publisher names typically not given for publications from before the mid-nineteenth century.

'60 Faces: Paul Oestreicher.' No Date. *Campaign for Nuclear Disarmament.* Accessed 30 January 2021. https://cnduk.org/60-faces-paul-oestreicher/

Abberley, Will. 2012. '"To Make a New Tongue": Natural and Manufactured Language in the Late Fiction of William Morris.' *Journal of Victorian Culture* 17 (4): 397–412. https://doi.org/10.1080/13555502.2012.728148

Adams, James Eli. 1995. *Dandies and Desert Saints: Styles of Victorian Masculinity.* Ithaca: Cornell University Press. https://doi.org/10.7591/9781501720437

Adkins, Mary Grace Muse. 1949. 'A Theory about *The Life and Death of Jack Straw*.' *The University of Texas Studies in English* 28: 57–82.

Adorno, Theodor W. 2005. *Critical Models: Interventions and Catchwords.* New York: Columbia University Press.

Aers, David. 1999. '*Vox populi* and the Literature of 1381.' In *The Cambridge History of Medieval English Literature*, edited by David Wallace, 432–53. Cambridge: Cambridge University Press. https://doi.org/10.1017/CHOL9780521444200.020

Ainsworth, Megan. 'Hyman Isaac Fagan.' 2013–2014. *Writing Lives: Collaborative Research Project on Working-Class Autobiography.* Accessed 30 January 2021. http://www.writinglives.org/category/hyman-fagan

Ainsworth, Peter, and Godfried Croenen, eds. 2013. *The Online Froissart: Version 1.5.* Sheffield: HRIOnline. http://www.dhi.ac.uk/onlinefroissart

Ainsworth, William Harrison. 1840. *Guy Fawkes; or, The Gunpowder Treason, Volume 1.* London: Chapman and Hall.

Ainsworth, William Harrison. 1874. *Merry England: Or, Nobles and Serfs.* 3 vols. London: Tinsley Brothers.

Alexander, Dominic. 2009. 'Peasant Movements and Political Agency.' *Counterfire* (6 September). Accessed 30 January 2021. https://www.counterfire.org/theory/57-history-of-resistance/1733-peasant-movements-and-political-agency

Allan, David. 2013. 'Reading Hume's *History of England*: Audience and Authority in Georgian England.' In *David Hume: Historical Thinker, Historical Writer*, edited by Mark G. Spencer, 103–20. University Park: Pennsylvania State University Press. https://doi.org/10.5325/j.ctt32b9wf.10

Almond, Philip C. 1999. *Adam and Eve in Seventeenth-Century Thought.* Cambridge: Cambridge University Press. https://doi.org/10.1017/CBO9780511585104

Anderson, Perry. 1980. *Arguments within English Socialism*. London: Verso.
Andrew, Prudence. 1963. *The Earthworms*. London: Hutchinson.
Andrews, Linton. 2018. 'Swaffer, (Frederic Charles) Hannen (1879–1962).' *ODNB*.
Archer, Ian W. 2004. 'John Stow, Citizen and Historian.' In *John Stow (1525–1605) and the Making of the English Past: Studies in Early Modern Culture and the History of the Book*, edited by Ian Gadd and Alexandra Gillespie, 13–26. London: British Library.
Archer, Ian W. 2013. 'Social Order and Disorder.' In *The Oxford Handbook of Holinshed's* Chronicles, edited by Ian W. Archer, Felicity Heal, and Paula Kewes, 389–410. Oxford: Oxford University Press.
Archer, Ian W., Felicity Heal, and Paula Kewes, eds. 2013. *The Oxford Handbook of Holinshed's* Chronicles. Oxford: Oxford University Press.
Archer, Ian W., Felicity Heal, and Paula Kewes. 2013. 'Prologue.' In *The Oxford Handbook of Holinshed's* Chronicles, edited by Ian W. Archer, Felicity Heal, and Paula Kewes, xxix–xxxvii. Oxford: Oxford University Press.
Archer, Ian W., Felicity Heal, Paulina Kewes, and Henry Summerson. eds. 2008–2013. *Holinshed Project*. Accessed 30 January 2021. http://english.nsms.ox.ac.uk/holinshed/
Arnold, Jonathan. 2014. '"Polydorus Italus": Analyzing Authority in Polydore Vergil's *Anglica Historia*.' *Reformation and Renaissance Review* 16 (2): 122–37. https://doi.org/10.1179/1462245914Z.00000000053
Arnot, Robin Page. 1934. *William Morris: A Vindication*. London: Martin Lawrence Ltd.
Arnot, Robin Page. 1964. *William Morris: The Man and The Myth*. London: Lawrence and Wishart.
Ashman, Sam. 1998. 'Communist Party Historians' Group.' In *Essays on Historical Materialism*, edited by John Rees, 145–59. London: Bookmarks.
Aston, Margaret. 1994. 'Corpus Christi and Corpus Regni: Heresy and the Peasants' Revolt.' *Past and Present* 143 (1): 3–47. https://doi.org/10.1093/past/143.1.3
Aston, Margaret. 1993. *Faith and Fire: Popular and Unpopular Religion: 1350–1600*. London: Hambledon Press.
Aston, Thomas. 1641. *A Remonstrance, against Presbitery. Exhibited by divers of the nobilitie, gentrie, ministers and inhabitants of the county palatine of Chester with the motives of that remonstrance. Together with a short survey of the Presbyterian discipline*. London.
Attenborough, John. 1984. *The Priest's Story*. London: Hodder and Stoughton.
Attlee, C. R. 1920. *The Social Worker*. London: G. Bell and Sons.
Aughterson, Kate. 1998. *The English Renaissance: An Anthology and Sources and Documents*. New York: Routledge.
Awcock, Hannah. 2015. 'The East End's Radical Murals.' *Turbulent London* (24 September). Accessed 30 January 2021. https://turbulentlondon.com/2015/09/24/the-east-ends-radical-murals/
Aziz, Jeffrey H. 2007. 'Of Grace and Gross Bodies: Falstaff, Oldcastle and the Fires of Reform.' PhD Thesis: University of Pittsburgh.

Baker, Richard. 1643. *A chronicle of the Kings of England, from the time of the Romans I* [sic] *unto the raigne of our soveraigne lord, King Charles containing all passages of state or church, with all other observations proper for a chronicle.* London.

Ball, Sidney. 1896. *The Moral Aspects of Socialism.* London: Fabian Society. https://doi.org/10.1086/205422

Bancroft, Richard. 1593/2003–2009. *A suruay of the pretended holy discipline. Contayning the beginninges, successe, parts, proceedings, authority, and doctrine of it: with some of the manifold, and material repugnances, varieties and vncertainieties, in that behalfe.* Ann Arbor, MI: Text Creation Partnership.

Barker, Juliet. 2014. *England, Arise: The People, the King, and the Great Revolt of 1381.* London: Little, Brown.

Barney, Stephen A. 2006. *The Penn Commentary on Piers Plowman, Volume 5: C Passus 20–22; B Passus 18–20.* Philadelphia: University of Philadelphia Press. https://doi.org/10.1484/J.YLS.2.302581

Barrell, John. 2000. *Imagining the King's Death: Figurative Treason, Fantasies of Regicide, 1793–1796.* Oxford: Oxford University Press.

Barron, Caroline M. 1981. *Revolt in London: 11th to 15th June 1381.* London: Museum of London.

Bartie, Angela, Linda Fleming, Mark Freeman, Tom Hulme, Alex Hutton, and Paul Readman. n.d. 'Music for the People.' *The Redress of the Past: Historical Pageants in Britain.* Accessed 30 January 2021. https://www.historicalpageants.ac.uk/pageants/1132/

Basdeo, Stephen. 2015. 'An Early Socialist History of the Peasants' Revolt: Charles Edmund Maurice's "Lives of English Popular Leaders of the Middle Ages" (1875).' *Here Begynneth A Lytell Geste of Robin Hood* (15 July). Accessed 30 January 2021. https://gesteofrobinhood.com/2017/07/15/an-early-socialist-history-of-the-peasants-revolt-charles-edmund-maurices-lives-of-english-popular-leaders-of-the-middle-ages-1875/

Basdeo, Stephen. 2016. 'Radical Medievalism: Pierce Egan the Younger's *Robin Hood, Wat Tyler,* and *Adam Bell*.' In *Leeds Working Papers in Victorian Studies Vol. 15: Imagining the Victorians,* edited by Stephen Basdeo and Lauren Padgett, 48–64. Leeds: Leeds Centre for Victorian Studies.

Basdeo, Stephen. 2018. *The Life and Legend of a Rebel Leader: Wat Tyler.* Barnsley: Pen and Sword History.

Basdeo, Stephen. 2019. 'William Morris's References to the Outlaw in *A Dream of John Ball* (1888).' *Journal of William Morris Studies* 23 (2): 52–63.

Basdeo, Stephen. 2020. 'Youthful Consumption and Conservative Visions: Robin Hood and Wat Tyler in Late Victorian Penny Periodicals.' In *Pasts at Play: Childhood Encounters with History in British Culture, 1750–1914,* edited by Rachel Bryant Davies and Barbara Gribling, 125–41. Manchester: Manchester University Press.

Basdeo, Stephen. 2021. 'Rousing "the Spirit of Wat Tyler": Chartist Newspaper Portrayals of the Rebel Leader.' In *Subaltern Medievalisms: Medievalism 'from* below' in Nineteenth Century Britain, edited by David Matthews and Mike Sanders, 110–24. Boydell & Brewer. https://doi.org/10.1017/9781787448575.007

Bax, Ernest Belfort. 1890. *Religion of Socialism: Essays in Modern Socialist Criticism*. Second edition; London: Swan Sonnenschein & Co.

Baxter, John. 1796. *A New and Impartial History of England, from the Most Early Period of Genuine Historical Evidence to the Present Important and Alarming Crisis*. London.

Baxter, John. 1995. 'Resistance to Oppression, the Constitutional Right of Britons Asserted in a Lecture Delivered before Section 2 of the Society of the Friends of Liberty, on Monday, November 9th (1795).' In *Political Writings of the 1790s, Volume 4: Radicalism and Reform 1793–1800*, edited by Gregory Claeys, 439–42. London: William Pickering.

Beckett, Francis. 1998 [1995]. *Enemy Within: The Rise and Fall of the British Communist Party*. Woodbridge: Merlin Press.

Beer, Barrett L. 1985. 'John Stow and the English Reformation, 1547–1559.' *The Sixteenth Century Journal* 16 (2): 257–71. https://doi.org/10.2307/2540915

Beer, Barrett L. 1998. *Tudor England Observed: The World of John Stow*. Stroud: Sutton Publishing.

Beer, Barrett L. 2004. 'English History Abridged: John Stow's Shorter Chronicles and Popular History.' *Albion* 36 (1): 12–27. https://doi.org/10.2307/4054434

Beer, Samuel H. 1978. 'Christopher Hill: Some Reminiscences.' In *Puritans and Revolutionaries: Essays in Seventeenth Century History Presented to Christopher Hill*, edited by Donald H. Pennington and Keith Thomas, 1–4. Oxford: Oxford University Press.

Belchem, John. 1981. 'Republicanism, Popular Constitutionalism and the Radical Platform in Early Nineteenth-Century England.' *Social History* 6 (1): 1–32. https://doi.org/10.1080/03071028108567493

Belchem, John. 1982. '1848: Feargus O'Connor and the Collapse of the Mass Platform.' In *The Chartist Experience: Studies in Working-Class Radicalism and Culture, 1830–1860*, edited by James Epstein and Dorothy Thompson, 269–310. London: Macmillan Press. https://doi.org/10.1007/978-1-349-16921-4_9

Belchem, John. 1985. *'Orator' Hunt: Henry Hunt and English Working-Class Radicalism*. Oxford: Clarendon.

Bell, Matthew. 2015–17. *The 1381 Revolt Smithfield Memorial*. Accessed 30 January 2021. http://revolt1381.blogspot.com/

Bell, Neil [Stephen Southwold]. 1964 [1948]. *The Immortal Dyer: A Novel of the Life and Times of Jeff Lister, King of the Commons, the Pride of Norfolk*. London: Redman.

Bengtson, Jonathan. 1997. 'Saint George and the Formation of English Nationalism.' *Journal of Medieval and Early Modern Studies* 27 (2): 317–40.

Benham, W. Gurney. 1907. *The Oath Book or Red Parchment Book of Colchester*. Colchester: Essex County Standard Office.

Benn, Tony. 1979. *Arguments for Socialism*. Edited by Chris Mullin. London: Jonathan Cape.

Benn, Tony. 1981. *Arguments for Democracy*. Edited by Chris Mullin. London: Penguin.
Benn, Tony. 1988. *Fighting Back: Speaking Out for Socialism in the Eighties*. London: Hutchinson.
Benn, Tony. 1995. 'The Power of the Bible Today.' *Sheffield Academic Press Occasional Papers: The Twelfth Annual Sheffield Academic Press Lecture, University of Sheffield, March 17, 1995*. Sheffield: Sheffield Academic Press: 1–13.
Benn, Tony. 2002. *Free at Last! Diaries 1991–2001*. London: Hutchinson.
Benn, Tony. 2003. *Free Radical: New Century Essays*. New York: Continuum.
Benn, Tony. 2004. *Dare to Be a Daniel: Then and Now*. London: Arrow Books.
Benn, Tony and Roy Bailey. 2004. *The Writing on the Wall*. Fuse Records.
Bennett, E. N. 1914. *Problems of Village Life*. London: Williams & Norgate. https://doi.org/10.5962/bhl.title.31107
Bennett, Michael. 2018. 'John Gower, Squire of Kent, the Peasants' Revolt, and the *Visio Anglie*.' *The Chaucer Review* 53 (3): 258–82. https://doi.org/10.5325/chaucerrev.53.3.0258
ben Saddi, Nathan, a Priest of the Jews. 1740. *The Chronicle of the Kings of England Written in the Manner of the Ancient Jewish Historians*. London.
Bernard, Edward, assisted by Gentlemen of approved Abilities, who have for many Years made the English History their chief Study, particularly Mr Millar. 1783. *The New, Comprehensive and Complete History of England from the Earliest Period of Authentic Information, to the Middle of the Year, MDCCLXXXIII*. London.
Betteridge, Thomas. 1999. *Tudor Histories of the English Reformations, 1530–83*. Aldershot: Ashgate.
Bevir, Mark. 2005. 'Shaw, Frederick John [*pseud*. Brougham Villiers] (1863–1939).' *ODNB*.
Bevir, Mark. 2011. *The Making of British Socialism*. Princeton: Princeton University Press. https://doi.org/10.23943/princeton/9780691150833.001.0001
Bew, John. 2016. *Citizen Clem: A Biography of Attlee*. London: Riverrun.
Birch, Jonathan C. P. 2019. *Jesus in an Age of Enlightenment: Radical Gospels from Thomas Hobbes to Thomas Jefferson*. New York: Palgrave Macmillan. https://doi.org/10.1057/978-1-137-51276-5
Birch, Jonathan C. P. 2019. 'Revolutionary Contexts for the Quest: Jesus in the Rhetoric and Methods of Early Modern Intellectual History.' *Journal for the Study of the Historical Jesus* 17 (1–2): 35–80. https://doi.org/10.1163/17455197-01701005
Bird, Brian. 1981. *Colchester Rebel: A Short Study of John Ball*. Colchester: John Ball Society.
Bird, Brian. 1987. *Rebel before His Time: Study of John Ball and the English Peasants' Revolt of 1381*. Worthing: Churchman Publishing.
Bird, Brian, and David Stephenson. 1976. 'Who Was John Ball?' *Essex Archaeology and History* 8 (third series): 287–88.

Blackstone, Lee Robert. 2017. 'The Aural and Moral Idylls of "Englishness" and Folk Music.' *Symbolic Interaction* 40 (4): 561–80. https://doi.org/10.1002/symb.302
Blatchford, Robert. 1990. *My Favourite Books*. London: Clarion Office.
Boesak, Allan A. 1984. *Black and Reformed: Apartheid, Liberation, and the Calvinist Tradition*. Edited by Leonard Sweetman. Eugene, OR: Wipf and Stock.
Bolton, Carol. 2007. *Writing the Empire: Robert Southey and Romantic Colonialism*. London: Routledge.
Boos, Florence S. 1992. 'Alternative Victorian Futures: "Historicism," Past and Present, and A Dream of John Ball.' In *History and Community: Essays in Victorian Medievalism*, edited by Florence S. Boos, 3–37. New York: Garland Publishing.
Boreczky, Elemér. 2008. *John Wyclif's Discourse On Dominion in Community*. Leiden: Brill. https://doi.org/10.1163/ej.9789004163492.i-328
Boucher, Jonathan. 1797. *A View of the Causes and Consequences of the American Revolution; in Thirteen Discourses Preached in North America between the Years 1763 and 1775*. London.
Bounds, Philip. 2017. 'The Marxist Outsider: T.A. Jackson as Autobiographer and Critic.' *Socialism and Democracy* 31 (2): 122–44. https://doi.org/10.1080/08854300.2017.1317155
Boyd, Kelly. 2003. *Manliness and the Boys' Story Paper in Britain: A Cultural History, 1855–1940*. New York: Palgrave McMillan. https://doi.org/10.1057/9780230597181
Bradbury, Richard. 1999. 'Frederick Douglass and the Chartists.' In *Liberating Sojourn: Frederick Douglass and Transnational Reform*, edited by Alan Rice and Martin Crawford, 169–86. Athens, GA: University of Georgia Press.
Braddick, Michael. 2008. *God's Fury, England's Fire: A New History of the English Civil Wars*. London: Penguin.
Brady, Robert. 1685. *The Complete History of England from the First Entrance of the Romans under the Conduct of Julius Caesar unto the End of the Reign of King Henry III*. London.
Brady, Robert. 1700. *A Continuation of the Complete History of England Containing the Lives and Reigns of Edward I, II & III and Richard the Second*. London.
Bragg, Billy. 2006. *The Progressive Patriot: A Search for Belonging*. London: Bantam Books.
Bramston, Mary. 1901. *The Banner of Saint George: A Picture of Old England*. London: Duckworth.
Branson, Noreen. 1985. *History of the Communist Party of Great Britain 1927–1941*. London: Lawrence and Wishart.
Brie, Friedrich W. D., ed. 1906–1908. *The Brut or The Chronicles of England*. 2 volumes. London: Kegan Paul, Trench, Trübner, and Co.
Brierley, Benjamin. 1886. *Home Memories and Recollections of a Life*. Manchester: Abel Heywood & Son.
Broadbridge, Hugh. 1938. *Fifty Mutinies, Rebellions and Revolutions*. London: Odhams Press Ltd.

Brodie, Marc. 2003. 'Free Trade and Cheap Theatre: Sources of Politics for the Nineteenth-century London Poor.' *Social History* 28 (3): 346–60. https://doi.org/10.1080/0307102032000119056

Brooks, Nicholas. 1985. 'The Organization and Achievements of the Peasants of Kent and Essex in 1381.' In *Studies in Medieval History Presented to R. H. C. Davis*, edited by Henry Mayr-Harting and R. I. Moore, 247–70. London: Hambledon.

Brown, Kenneth D. 2016. 'Burns, John Elliott (1858–1943).' *ODNB*.

Brown, Matt. 2016. 'Peasants' Revolt Plaque Unveiled in Smithfield.' *Londonist* (16 September). Accessed 30 January 2021. https://londonist.com/2015/07/peasants-revolt-plaque-unveiled-in-smithfield

Brownley, Martine Watson. 1989. 'Sir Richard Baker's "Chronicle" and Later Seventeenth-Century English Historiography.' *Huntington Library Quarterly* 52 (4): 481–500. https://doi.org/10.2307/3817157

Brundage, Anthony. 1994. *The People's Historian: John Richard Green and the Writing of History in Victorian England*. Westport: Greenwood.

Bullivant, Joanna. 2017. *Alan Bush, Modern Music, and the Cold War: The Cultural Left in Britain and the Communist Bloc*. Cambridge: Cambridge University Press. https://doi.org/10.1017/9781139519656

Bundock, Clement J. 1920. *Direct Action and the Constitution*. London: Independent Labour Party.

Burch, Harriette E. 1889. *Dick Delver: A Story of the Peasant Revolt of the Fourteenth Century*. London: The Religious Tract Society.

Burke, Edmund. 1790. *Reflections on the Revolution in France, and on the Proceedings in Certain Societies in London Relative to that Event*. London.

Burke, Edmund. 1791. *An Appeal from the New to the Old Whigs, in Consequence of Some Late Discussions in Parliament, Relative to the Reflections on the French Revolution*. London.

Burns, Arthur. 2012. 'Putterill, John Cyril [Jack] (1892–1980).' *ODNB*.

Burns, Arthur. 2013. 'Beyond the "Red Vicar": Community and Christian Socialism in Thaxted, Essex, 1910–84.' *History Workshop Journal* 75 (1): 101–24. https://doi.org/10.1093/hwj/dbr073

Burwick, Frederick. 2011. *Playing to the Crowd: London Popular Theatre, 1780–1830*. New York: Palgrave Macmillan. https://doi.org/10.1057/9780230370654

Bush, Alan. n.d. '*Wat Tyler*': Berlin Première of British Opera. Accessed 30 January 2021. https://jbpsc.arts.gla.ac.uk/digital.php?ref=PSC/1/2/2/250

Bush, Nancy, and Alan Bush. 1956. *Wat Tyler: Opera in Two Acts with a Prologue*. Richmond: R. W. Simpson.

Bush, Nancy. 2000. *Alan Bush: Music, Politics and Life*. London: Thames Publishing.

Byres, Terence J. 2006. 'Rodney Hilton (1916–2002): In Memoriam.' *Journal of Agrarian Change* 6 (1): 1–16. https://doi.org/10.1111/j.1471-0366.2006.00113.x

Byrne, Georgina. 2010. *Modern Spiritualism and the Church of England, 1850–1939*. Woodbridge: Boydell Press.

Caesar, Adrian. 1991. *Dividing Lines: Poetry, Class, and Ideology in the 1930s*. Manchester: Manchester University Press.

Caldwell, Ellen C. 1995. 'Jack Cade and Shakespeare's *Henry VI, Part 2*.' *Studies in Philology* 92 (1): 18–79.
Campbell, Ethan. 2018. *The Gawain-Poet and the Fourteenth-Century English Anticlerical Tradition*. Kalamazoo: Western Michigan University. https://doi.org/10.2307/j.ctvvnc9n
Cannadine, David. 1992. *G.M. Trevelyan: A Life in History*. London: HarperCollinsPublishers.
Carlson, David R., ed. 2011. *John Gower: Poems on Contemporary Events: The Visio Anglie (1381) and Cronica tripertita (1400)*. Oxford: Bodleian Library.
Carte, Thomas. 1747. *A General History of England: Volume 1*. London.
Carte, Thomas. 1750. *A General History of England: Volume 2*. London.
Cartelli, Thomas. 1994. 'Jack Cade in the Garden: Class Consciousness and Class Conflict in *2 Henry VI*.' In *Enclosure Acts: Sexuality, Property, and Culture in Early Modern England*, edited by Richard Burt and John Michael Archer, 48–67. Ithaca, NY: Cornell University Press. https://doi.org/10.7591/9781501733598-004
Carter, Sydney. 1983. *In the Present Tense: Songs of Sydney Carter Volume 5*. London: Stainer & Bell.
Carver, Stephen. 2020. *The Author Who Outsold Dickens: The Life and Work of W. H. Ainsworth*. Philadelphia: Pen and Sword History.
Cash, Arthur. 2008. *John Wilkes: The Scandalous Father of Civil Liberty*. New Haven: Yale University Press.
Cassell's Illustrated History of England: New and Revised Edition, Volume 1. 1865. London: Cassell, Petter & Galpin.
Castro, John Paul de. 1926. *The Gordon Riots*. Oxford: Oxford University Press.
Cattermole, Philip H. 2013. *John Lingard: The Historian as Apologist*. Kibworth Beauchamp: Matador.
Chambers, Colin. 1989. *The Story of Unity Theatre*. London: Lawrence and Wishart.
Chandler, William. 1927. *Thirteen Eighty One: An English Tragedy*. London: Stylus Press.
Chapman, Mark D. 2001. *Liturgy, Socialism and Life: The Legacy of Conrad Noel*. London: Darton, Longman and Todd.
Chartier, Roger. 2006. 'Jack Cade, the Skin of a Dead Lamb, and the Hatred for Writing.' *Shakespeare Studies* 34: 77–89.
Chase, Malcolm. 2007. *Chartism: A New History*. Manchester: Manchester University Press. https://doi.org/10.1057/9780230248472_4
Chase, Malcolm. 2010. 'Chartism and the Land: "The Mighty People's Question."' In *The Land Question in Britain, 1750–1950*, edited by Matthew Cragoe and Paul Readman, 57–73. New York: Palgrave Macmillan.
Chesterton, G. K. 1917. *A Short History of England*. London: Chatto and Windus.
'The City of Cambridge: Medieval History.' 1959. In *A History of the County of Cambridge and the Isle of Ely: Volume 3, The City and University of Cambridge*, edited by J. P. C. Roach, 2–15. London: Oxford University Press.
Claeys, Gregory. 1989. *Thomas Paine: Social and Political Thought*. London: Routledge.

Claeys, Gregory. 2000. 'The *Reflections* Refracted: The Critical Reception of Burke's *Reflections on the Revolution in France* during the Early 1790s.' In *Edmund Burke's Reflections on the Revolution in France: New Interdisciplinary Essays*, edited by John Whale, 40–59. Manchester: Manchester University Press.

Claussen, Detlev. 2008. *Theodor W. Adorno: One Last Genius*. Cambridge, MA: Belknap Press of Harvard University Press. https://doi.org/10.4159/9780674029590

Clayton, Joseph. 1909. *Wat Tyler and the Great Uprising*. London: Francis Griffiths.

Clayton, Joseph. 1910. *Leaders of the People: Studies in Democratic History*. London: Martin Secker.

Clayton, Joseph. 1911. *The Rise of Democracy*. London: Cassell and Company.

Clement, Richard W. 1991. 'Librarianship and Polemics: The Career of Thomas James (1572–1629).' *Libraries and Culture* 26 (2): 269–82.

Cleveland, John. 1654. *The Idol of the Clownes, or, Insurrection of Wat the Tyler with his priests Baal and Straw together with his fellow kings of the commons against the English church, the king, the laws, nobility and royal family and gentry, in the fourth year of K. Richard the 2d, an. 1381*. London.

Cleveland, John. 1660. *The rebellion of the rude multitude under Wat Tyler and his priests Baal and Straw, in the dayes of King Richard the IId, Anno. 1381. Parallel'd with the late rebellion in 1640, against King Charles I of ever blessed memory*. London.

Cleveland, John. 1687, 1699. *The Rustick Rampant, or Rural Anarchy affronting Monarchy: in the Insurrection of Wat Tyler*, including in *The Works of Mr. John Cleveland*. London.

Cobbett, William. 1829. *History of the Protestant 'Reformation'*. London.

Cohn, Norman. 1957, 1970. *The Pursuit of the Millennium*. London: Secker & Warburg (1957). Revised and expanded edition: Oxford: Oxford University Press (1970).

Cole, G. D. H. 1934. *Selected Writings*. London: Nonesuch Press.

Cole, G. D. H. 1954. *A History of Socialist Thought, Volume II: Marxism and Anarchism 1850–1890*. London: Macmillan.

A Collection of Playbills from Old Vic Theatre 1824–1833. n.d. British Library, Digital Store Playbills 175. Accessed 30 January 2021. http://access.bl.uk/item/viewer/ark:/81055/vdc_100022589022.0x000002

Collette, Carolyn P. 2008. '"Faire Emelye": Medievalism and the Moral Courage of Emily Wilding Davison.' *The Chaucer Review* 42 (3): 223–43. https://doi.org/10.1353/cr.2008.0001

Collinson, Patrick. 2001. 'John Stow and Nostalgic Antiquarianism.' In *Imagining Early Modern London: Perceptions and Portrayals of the City from Stow to Strype 1598–1720*, edited by J. F. Merritt, 27–51. Cambridge: Cambridge University Press.

Collinson, Patrick. 2013. *Richard Bancroft and Elizabethan Anti-Puritanism*. Cambridge: Cambridge University Press. https://doi.org/10.1017/CBO9781139151047

Communist Party of Great Britain. 1935. *For Soviet Britain*. London: Communist Party of Great Britain.
Communist Party of Great Britain. 1938. *Report to the Central Committee to the Fifteenth Party Congress, Birmingham* (16–19 September). Accessed 30 January 2021. https://www.marxists.org/history/international/comintern/sections/britain/central_committee/1938/09/report.htm
Connell, William J. 2004. 'Vergil, Polydore [Polidoro Virgili] (c. 1470–1555).' *ODNB*.
Connolly, James. 1909. *Socialism Made Easy*. Chicago: C. H. Kerry & Co. Chicago.
Connor, John T. 2014. 'Historical Turns in Twentieth-Century Fiction.' In *A Companion to British Literature, Volume 4: Victorian and Twentieth-Century Literature, 1837–2000*, edited by Robert DeMaria Jr., Heesok Chang, and Samantha Zacher, 314–32. Oxford: Wiley-Blackwell. https://doi.org/10.1002/9781118827338.ch94
Considine, Marie. 2012. 'The Social, Political and Economic Determinants of a Modern Portrait Artist: Bernard Fleetwood-Walker (1893–1965).' PhD Thesis: University of Birmingham.
Cooper, Emily. 1877. *The History of England from the Landing of Caesar to the Reign of Victoria: Volume 1*. London: Simpkin, Marshall and Co.
Cooper, Thomas. 1846. *Two Orations Against Taking Away Human Life Under Any Circumstances; and in Explanation and Defence of the Misrepresented Doctrine of Non-Resistance*. London.
Cooper, Thomas. 1847. *The Purgatory of Suicides: A Prison-rhyme in Ten Books*. London.
Cooper, Thomas. 1589. *An Admonition to the People of England*. Edited by Edward Arber. Birmingham: The English Scholar's Library.
Copinger, W. A., ed. 1895. *The laboryouse journey & serche of John Leylande for Englandes antiquitees geven of hym as a Newe Years gyfte to Kynge Henry the VIII in the xxxvii. yeare of his reygne, with declaracyons enlarged: by Johan Bale [1549]*. Priory Press: Manchester.
Corfield, Penelope J. 2004. '"We are All One in the Eyes of the Lord": Christopher Hill and the Historical Meanings of Radical Religion.' *History Workshop Journal* 58 (1): 111–27. https://doi.org/10.1093/hwj/58.1.110
Cornelius, Ian. 2015. 'Gower and the Peasants' Revolt.' *Representations* 131 (1): 22–51. https://doi.org/10.1525/rep.2015.131.1.22
Coss, Peter. 2002. 'R.H. Hilton.' *Past and Present* 176 (1): 7–10. https://doi.org/10.1093/past/176.1.7
Costelloe, Timothy M. 2012. 'Hume on History.' In *The Bloomsbury Companion to Hume*, edited by Alan Bailey and Dan O'Brien, 364–76. London: Bloomsbury.
Courtney, Julia. 2015. 'Versions of the Past, Problems of the Present, Hopes for the Future: Morris and Others Rewrite the Peasants' Revolt.' *Journal of William Morris Studies* 21 (2): 10–25.
Cousins, A. D. 1981. 'The Cavalier World and John Cleveland.' *Studies in Philology* 78 (1): 61–86.
Cox, Harold. 1892. *Land Nationalisation*. London: Methuen and Co.

Cox, Jeffrey N. 2000. 'Baillie, Siddons, Larpent: Gender, Power, and Politics in the Theatre of Romanticism'. In *Women in British Romantic Theatre: Drama, Performance, and Society, 1790–1840*, edited by Catherine Burroughs, 23–47. Cambridge: Cambridge University Press.

Craig, David M. 2007. *Robert Southey and Romantic Apostasy: Political Argument in Britain, 1780–1840*. Woodbridge: Boydell Press.

Cremin, Colin. 2011. *Capitalism's New Clothes: Enterprise, Ethics and Enjoyment in Times of Crisis*. London: Pluto Press.

'The Critical Reception of Robert Southey's *Wat Tyler*'. n.d. Romantic Circles. Accessed 30 January 2021. https://romantic-circles.org/editions/wattyler/contexts/reception.html

Crompton, James. 1961. 'Fasciculi Zizaniorum I'. *Journal of Ecclesiastical History* 12 (1): 35–45. https://doi.org/10.1017/S0022046900060851

Crompton, James. 1961. 'Fasciculi Zizaniorum II'. *Journal of Ecclesiastical History* 12 (2): 155–66. https://doi.org/10.1017/S002204690006276X

Crossley, James. 2015. 'Borges's God, Jonathan Meades's Precursor'. In *Borges and the Bible*, edited by Richard Walsh and Jay Twomey. Sheffield: Sheffield Phoenix Press.

Crossley, James. 2016 [2014]. *Harnessing Chaos: The Bible in English Political Discourse since 1968*. Revised edition. London: T&T Clark/Bloomsbury.

Crossley, James. 2018. *Cults, Martyrs and Good Samaritans: Religion in Contemporary English Political Discourse*. London: Pluto. https://doi.org/10.2307/j.ctv3mt8w5

Crossley, James. 2021. 'The End of Apocalypticism: From Burton Mack's Jesus to North American Liberalism'. *Journal for the Study of the Historical Jesus* 19 (2): 171–90.

Cumberland, Richard. 1807. *Memoirs of Richard Cumberland, Written by Himself: Containing an account of His life and writings, interspersed with anecdotes and characters of several of the most distinguished persons of his time, with whom he has had intercourse and connexion: Volume II*. London.

Curry, Kenneth, ed. 1965. *New Letters of Robert Southey: Volume I*. New York: Columbia University Press.

Curry, Kenneth, ed. 1965. *New Letters of Robert Southey: Volume II*. New York: Columbia University Press.

Dale, Graham. 2000. *God's Politicians: The Christian Contribution to 100 Years of Labour*. London: HarperCollins.

Darley, Gillian. 2012. 'Hill, Octavia'. *ODNB*.

Darnton, Robert. 1984. *The Great Cat Massacre and Other Episodes in French Cultural History*. New York: Vintage Books.

Davenant, Francis. 1865. 'Hubert Ellis: A Story of King Richard's Days the Second'. In *Boy's Own Volume of Fact, Fiction, History and Adventure N.S.* 6, 1–464. London: S. O. Beeton.

Davidson, J. Morrison. 1899. *The Annals of Toil. Being Labour-History Outlines, Roman and British. Part I*. London: William Reeves.

Davidson, Joe P. L. 2020. 'Between Utopia and Tradition: William Morris's *A Dream of John Ball*.' *European Legacy* 25 (4): 1–15. https://doi.org/10.1080/10848770.2020.1722492

Davies, John. n.d. 'Sydney Carter—Reflections.' *John Davies*. Accessed 30 January 2021. http://www.johndavies.org/SydneyCarter-talk.pdf

Davis, A. H., ed. 1934. *William Thorne's Chronicle of Saint Augustine's Abbey, Canterbury*. Oxford: Blackwell.

Davis, H. W. C. 1926. 'Lancashire Reformers, 1816–17.' *Bulletin of the John Rylands Library* 10 (1): 47–79. https://doi.org/10.7227/BJRL.10.1.3

Davis, Michael T. 2015. '"Reformers No Rioters": British Radicalism and Mob Identity in the 1790s.' In *Crowd Actions in Britain and France from the Middle Ages to the Modern World*, edited by Michael T. Davis, 146–62. New York: Palgrave Macmillan. https://doi.org/10.1057/9781137316516_9

Deputy Keeper of the Records, ed. 1912. *Calendar of the Patent Rolls: Edward III, Vol. XII, 1361–1364*. London: Hereford Times Limited.

Deputy Keeper of the Records, ed. 1916. *Calendar of the Patent Rolls: Edward III, Vol. XVI, 1374–1377*. London: Hereford Times Limited.

Devereux, E. J. 1990. 'Empty Tuns and Unfruitful Grafts: Richard Grafton's Historical Publications.' *The Sixteenth Century Journal* 21 (1): 33–56. https://doi.org/10.2307/2541131

Dew, Ben. 2018. *Commerce, Finance and Statecraft: Histories of England, 1600–1780*. Manchester: Manchester University Press. https://doi.org/10.7228/manchester/9781784992965.001.0001

A Dialogue between Wat Tyler, Mischievous Tom, and an English Farmer, 1793. London.

Dibdin, Thomas Frognall, ed. 1812. *John Rastell, The pastime of people, or the chronicles of divers realms; and most especially of the realm of England*. London: F.C. and J. Rivington.

Dickens, Charles. 1852. 'A Child's History of England: Chapter XVII.' *Household Words* V: 304–8.

Dimitrov, Georgi. 1935. *The Working Class against Fascism*. London: Martin Lawrence.

Dircks, Richard J., ed. 1991. *The Unpublished Plays of Richard Cumberland: Volume 1*. New York: AMS Press.

Dishman, Mark. 2014. 'The Young'uns' David Eagle on New Album *Never Forget*, Anti-fascism, Dodgy Reviews and Biscuits.' *Folk Witness* (19 March).

Djordjevic, Igor. 2010. *Holinshed's Nation: Ideals, Memory and Practical Policy in the 'Chronicles.'* New York: Routledge.

Dobson, R. B. 1982. 'Remembering the Peasants' Revolt, 1381–1981.' In *Essex and the Great Revolt of 1381*, edited by W. H. Liddell and R. G. Wood, 1–20. Essex: Essex Record Office.

Dobson, R. B. 1983. *The Peasants' Revolt of 1381*. Second edition. New York: Palgrave Macmillan. https://doi.org/10.1007/978-1-349-16990-0

The Dorchester Guide, Or, A House that Jack Built. 1819. London.

Douglas, David C. 1951. *English Scholars 1600–1730*. Revised edition. Eyre & Spottiswoode: London.
Drinkwater, John, Holbrook Jackson, and Harold J. Laski. 1934. *Speeches in Commemoration of William Morris*. Walthamstow: Walthamstow Borough Council.
Duncan, Robert. 2004. 'Leatham, James (1865–1945).' *ODNB*.
Dunn, Alastair. 2001. 'Wat Tyler: The Many Roles of an English Rebel.' *History Today* 51 (7): 28.
Dunn, Alastair. 2004. *The Peasants' Revolt: England's Failed Revolution of 1381*. Stroud: Tempus.
Dworkin, Dennis. 1997. *Cultural Marxism in Postwar Britain: History, the New Left, and the Origins of Cultural Studies*. Durham: Duke University Press. https://doi.org/10.2307/j.ctv11smk18
Dyer, Christopher. 1984. 'The Social and Economic Background to the Rural Revolt of 1381.' In *The English Rising of 1381*, edited by Rodney Hilton and Trevor H. Aston, 9–52. Cambridge: Cambridge University Press.
Dyer, Christopher. 1996. 'Memories of Freedom: Attitudes towards Serfdom in England, 1200–1350.' In *Serfdom and Slavery: Studies in Legal Bondage*, edited by M. L. Bush, 277–95. Abingdon: Taylor & Francis.
Dyer, Christopher. 2002. 'Obituary: Rodney Hilton.' *Guardian* (10 June).
Dyer, Christopher. 2003. 'A New Introduction (2003).' In Rodney Hilton, *Bond Men Made Free: Medieval Peasant Movements and the English Rising of 1381*, ix–xiii. London: Routledge.
Dyer, Christopher. 2005. 'Rodney Howard Hilton 1916–2002.' *Proceedings of the British Academy* 130: 52–77.
https://doi.org/10.5871/bacad/9780197263501.003.0003
Dyer, Christopher. 2007. 'Introduction: Rodney Hilton, Medieval Historian.' In *Rodney Hilton's Middle Ages 400–1600: An Exploration of Historical Themes*, edited by Christopher Dyer, Peter Coss, and Chris Wickham, 10–17. Oxford: Oxford University Press.
Eales, Jacqueline. 1989. 'Sir Robert Harley, K.B. (1579–1656) and the "Character" of a Puritan.' *British Library Journal* 15 (2): 134–57.
Eales, Jacqueline. 1990. *Puritans and Roundheads: The Harleys of Brampton Bryan and the Outbreak of the English Civil War*. Cambridge: Cambridge University Press.
Eales, Jacqueline. 2015. 'Harley, Sir Robert (bap. 1579, d. 1656).' *ODNB*.
Ebsworth, J. W., revised by Megan A. Stephan. 2004. 'Pierce James Egan (1814–1880).' *ODNB*. https://doi.org/10.1093/ref:odnb/8578
'Ecc 21St Report: Development Aid Policy.' 1981. *Hansard: Volume 420* (3 June): col 1297.
Echard, Laurence. 1707. *The History of England. From the First Entrance of Julius Caesar and the Romans, to the End of the Reign of King James the First. Containing the Space of 1678 Years*. London.
Echard, Laurence. 1718. *The History of England. From the Beginning of the Reign of King Charles the First, to the Restoration of King Charles the Second*. London.

'Economic System.' 2000. *Hansard* (16 May). Accessed 30 January 2021. https://publications.parliament.uk/pa/cm199900/cmhansrd/vo000516/halltext/00516h01.htm

Edwards, Francis. 1995. *Robert Persons: The Biography of an Elizabethan Jesuit, 1546–1610*. St Louis, MO: The Institute of Jesuit Sources.

Edwards, Michael S. 1994. *Purge This Realm: A Life of Joseph Rayner Stephens*. London: Epworth Press.

Egan, Pierce. 1847 [1841]. *Wat Tyler; Or, The Rebellion of 1381*. London.

Egan, Pierce. 1851. *Wat Tyler*. Large edition. London: W.S. Johnson.

Eiden, Herbert. 1995. *'In der Knechtschaft werdet ihr verharren...' Ursachen und Verlauf des englischen Bauernaufstandes von 1381*. Trier: Trierer Historische Forschungen.

Eiden, Herbert. 1998. 'Joint Action against "Bad" Lordship: The Peasants' Revolt in Essex and Norfolk.' *History* 83 (269): 5–30. https://doi.org/10.1111/1468-229X.00060

Eiden, Herbert. 2008. 'The Social Ideology of the Rebels in Suffolk and Norfolk in 1381.' In *Von Nowgorod bis London: Studien zu Handel, Wirtschaft und Gesellschaft im mittelalterlichen Europa. Festschrift für Stuart Jenks zum 60. Geburtstag*, edited by Marie-Luise Heckmann and Jens Röhrkasten, 425–40. Göttingen: V&R Unipress. https://doi.org/10.1093/gerhis/ghp037

Eiden, Herbert. 2017. 'Military Aspects of the Peasants' Revolt of 1381.' In *The Fighting Essex Soldier: Recruitment, War and Remembrance in the Fourteenth Century*, edited by Christopher Thornton, Jennifer Ward and Neil Wiffen, 143–54. Hatfield: University of Hertfordshire Press.

Eisenman, Stephen F. 2005. 'Communism in Furs: A Dream of Prehistory in William Morris's *John Ball*.' *The Art Bulletin* 87 (1): 92–110. https://doi.org/10.1080/00043079.2005.10786230

Elliott, Ebenezer. 1840. *The Poetical Works of Ebenezer Elliott, the Corn-Law Rhymer*. London.

Ellis, Henry, ed. 1811. *The new chronicles of England and France, in two parts by Robert Fabyan. Named by himself The concordance of histories. Reprinted from Pynson's edition of 1516. The first part collated with the editions of 1533, 1542, and 1559; and the second with a manuscript of the author's own time, as well as the subsequent editions: including the different continuations. To which are added a biographical and literary preface, and an index*. London: F.C. and J. Rivington.

Ellis, Henry, ed. 1812. *The chronicle of Iohn Hardyng: containing an account of public transactions from the earliest period of English history to the beginning of the reign of King Edward the Fourth, together with the continuation by Richard Grafton, to the thirty fourth year of King Henry the Eighth: the former part collated with two manuscripts of the author's own time, the last, with Grafton's duplicate edition: to which are added a biographical and literary preface, and an index by Henry Ellis*. London: F.C. and J. Rivington.

Ellis, S. M. 1911. *William Harrison Ainsworth and His Friends, Vol. I*. London: John Lane.

Ely, Steve. 2013. *Oswald's Book of Hours*. Middlesbrough: Smokestack Books.

Enderby, John Stephen. 2019. 'The English Radical Tradition and the British Left 1885–1945.' PhD Thesis, Sheffield Hallam University.

Engelke, Matthew. 2013. *God's Agents: Biblical Publicity in Contemporary England*. Berkeley: University of California Press. https://doi.org/10.1525/california/9780520280465.001.0001

Engels, Friedrich. 1870. 'Preface to the Second Edition (1870).' In Friedrich Engels, *The Peasant War in Germany*. Accessed 30 January 2021. https://www.marxists.org/archive/marx/works/1850/peasant-war-germany/index.htm

Epstein, James. 1994. *Radical Expression: Political Language, Ritual, and Symbol in England, 1790–1850*. Oxford: Oxford University Press.

Epstein, James. 1996. '"Our Real Constitution": Trial Defence and Radical Memory in the Age of Revolution.' In *Re-reading the Constitution: New Narratives in the Political History of England's Long Nineteenth Century*, edited by James Vernon, 22–51. Cambridge: Cambridge University Press.

Epstein, Mary. 1944. 'Our National Traditions.' In *Party Organisation and the Invasion*, 21. London: Communist Party of Great Britain.

Epstein, S. R. 2007. 'Rodney Hilton, Marxism, and the Transition from Feudalism to Capitalism.' In *Rodney Hilton's Middle Ages 400–1600: An Exploration of Historical Themes*, edited by Christopher Dyer, Peter Coss, and Chris Wickham, 248–69. Oxford: Oxford University Press. https://doi.org/10.1093/pastj/gtm034

Evans, Gary. 2011. 'Partisan Politics, History and the National Interest (1700–1748).' In *Ideology and Foreign Policy in Early Modern Europe (1650–1750)*, edited by David Onnekink and Gijs Rommelse, 55–92. London: Routledge.

Evans, Thomas, ed. 1777. *Old Ballads, Historical and Narrative: With Some of Modern Date: Volume the First*. London.

Evenden, Elizabeth, and Thomas S. Freeman. 2011. *Religion and the Book in Early Modern England: The Making of John Foxe's 'Book of Martyrs.'* Cambridge: Cambridge University Press.

Executive Committee of the Democratic Federation. 1883. *Socialism Made Plain: The Social and Political Manifesto of the Democratic Federation*. London.

Fagan, H. 1938. *Nine Days that Shook England: An Account of the English People's Uprising in 1381*. London: Victor Gollancz.

Fagan, H. 1958. *The Commoners of England: Part One*. London: Lawrence and Wishart.

Fagan, H., and R. H. Hilton. 1950. *The English Rising of 1381*. London: Lawrence and Wishart.

Faith, Rosamond. 1984. 'The "Great Rumour" of 1377 and Peasant Ideology.' In *The English Rising of 1381*, edited by Rodney Hilton and Trevor H. Aston, 43–73. Cambridge: Cambridge University Press.

Faith, Rosamond. 2003. 'Rodney Hilton (1916–2002).' *History Workshop Journal* 55: 278–82.

Faulkner, Peter. 1992. *William Morris and the Idea of England: Kelmscott Lecture 1991*. London: William Morris Society.

Federico, Sylvia. 2001. 'The Imaginary Society: Women in 1381.' *Journal of British Studies* 40 (2): 159–83. https://doi.org/10.1086/386239

Ferguson, Robert, and an Impartial Hand. 1715. *The History of All the Mobs, Tumults and Insurrections in Great Britain*. London.

Ferrari, Lorenzo. 2019. 'The Pursuit of Humanity's Inner Demons: The Reception of Norman Cohn's Intellectual Journey.' *Storia della Storiografia* 75 (1): 59–82.

Field, John. 2003. 'Survival, Growth and Retreat: The WEA in Wartime, 1939–45.' In *A Ministry of Enthusiasm: Centenary Essays on the Workers' Educational Association*, edited by Stephen K. Roberts, 131–52. Pluto Press, London.

Finn, Margot C. 1993. *After Chartism: Class and Nation in English Radical Politics, 1848–1874*. Cambridge: Cambridge University Press.

Fisher, Mark. 2009. *Capitalist Realism: Is There No Alternative?* Winchester, UK: Zero Books.

Fitter, Chris. 2004. '"Your Captain is Brave and Vows Reformation": Jack Cade, the Hacket Rising, and Shakespeare's Vision of Popular Rebellion in *2 Henry VI*.' *Shakespeare Studies* 32: 173–219.

Fitzgerald, William Thomas. 1801. *Miscellaneous Poems*. London: J. Wright.

Flaherty, Seamus. 2019. 'H. M. Hyndman and the Intellectual Origins of the Remaking of Socialism in Britain, 1878–1881.' *English Historical Review* 134 (569): 855–80. https://doi.org/10.1093/ehr/cez188

Flaherty, Seamus. 2020. *Marx, Engels and Modern British Socialism: The Social and Political Thought of H. M. Hyndman, E. B. Bax, and William Morris*. New York: Palgrave Macmillan. https://doi.org/10.1007/978-3-030-42339-1

Fletcher, Anthony. 1981. *The Outbreak of the English Civil War*. Edward Arnold: London.

Foot, Paul. 1981. *'This Bright Day of Summer': The Peasants' Revolt of 1381*. London: Socialists Unlimited.

Foster, John Bellamy. 2017. 'William Morris's Romantic Revolutionary Ideal: Nature, Labour and Gender in *News from Nowhere*.' *Journal of William Morris Studies* 22 (2): 17–35.

Foxe, John. 1554. *Commentarii rerum in ecclesia gestarum, maximarumque per totam Europam, persecutionum, a Vuicleui temporibus ad hanc usque aetatem descriptio, Liber primus*. Strasbourg.

Foxe, John. 2011. *The Unabridged Acts and Monuments Online or TAMO* (1563 edition). Sheffield: The Digital Humanities Institute. http//www.dhi.ac.uk/foxe

Foxe, John. 2011. *The Unabridged Acts and Monuments Online or TAMO* (1570 edition). Sheffield: The Digital Humanities Institute. http//www.dhi.ac.uk/foxe

Freedman, R. M. 1923. *The New Boswell*. London: John Lane.

Freeman, Thomas S., and Susannah Brietz Monta. 2013. 'Holinshed and Foxe.' In *The Oxford Handbook of Holinshed's Chronicles*, edited by Ian W. Archer, Felicity Heal, and Paula Kewes, 217–33. Oxford: Oxford University Press.

Friedman, Albert B. 1974. '"When Adam delved...": Contexts of a Historic Proverb.' In *The Learned and the Lewed: Studies in Chaucer and Medieval Literature*, edited by Larry D. Benson, 213–30. Cambridge, MA: Harvard University Press.

Friedman, Dustin. 2010. 'Unsettling the Normative: Articulations of Masculinity.' *Literature Compass* 7 (12): 1077–88. https://doi.org/10.1111/j.1741-4113.2010.00762.x

Froissart, Jean. 1849. *The Chronicles of Froissart: Vol. I*. London: Henry G. Bohn.

Froude, James Anthony. 1856. *History of England from the Fall of Wolsey to the Death of Elizabeth: Volume II*. London: John W. Parker and Son.

Froude, James Anthony. 1873. 'Annals of an English Abbey.' *Scribner's Monthly* (November-December): 91–101, 187–99, 282–93.

Froude, James Anthony. 1877. *Short Studies on Great Subjects*. Third series. London: Spottiswoode and Co.

Fryer, Peter. 1984. *Staying Power: The History of Black People in Britain*. London: Pluto Press.

Gairdner, James. 1908. *Lollardy and the Reformation in England: An Historical Survey, Volume 1*. London: Macmillan.

Galbraith, V. H., ed. 1970 [1927]. *The Anonimalle Chronicle, 1333 to 1381*. Manchester: Manchester University Press.

Galloway, Andrew. 2006. *The Penn Commentary on Piers Plowman, Volume 1: C Prologue-Passus 4; B Prologue-Passus 4; A Prologue-Passus 4*. Philadelphia: University of Pennsylvania Press. https://doi.org/10.9783/9780812202007

Gammage, Robert George. 1894 [1854]. *History of the Chartist Movement, 1837–1854*. Second edition. Newcastle-on-Tyne: Browne & Browne.

Gapp, S. V. 1931. 'Notes on John Cleveland.' *Publications of the Modern Language Association of America* 46 (4): 1075–86. https://doi.org/10.2307/457759

Gardner, John. 2011. *Poetry and Popular Protest: Peterloo, Cato Street and the Queen Caroline Controversy*. New York: Palgrave Macmillan. https://doi.org/10.1057/9780230307377_2

Gibbins, Henry de Beltgens. 1892. *English Social Reformers*. London: Methuen & Co.

Gibson, Josh. 2017. 'The Chartists and the Constitution: Revisiting British Popular Constitutionalism.' *Journal of British Studies* 56 (1): 70–90. https://doi.org/10.1017/jbr.2016.121

Gibson, Josh. 2017. 'Natural Right and the Intellectual Context of Early Chartist Thought.' *History Workshop Journal* 84 (2017): 194–213. https://doi.org/10.1093/hwj/dbx038

Gifford, John. 1792. *A Plain Address to the Common Sense of the People of England*. London.

Gillen, Paul. 1991. 'Jack Lindsay's Romantic Communism.' *Westerly* 36 (2): 65–77.

Gilliat, Edward. 1889 [1888]. *John Standish, or The Harrowing of London*. London: Seeley & Co.

Given-Wilson, Christopher, ed. 1997. *The Chronicle of Adam Usk 1377–1421*. Oxford: Oxford University Press.

Given-Wilson, Christopher. 2004. *Chronicles: The Writing of History in Medieval England*. London: Hambledon.

Given-Wilson, Christopher, ed. 2019. *Continuatio Eulogii: The Continuation of the Eulogium Historiarum, 1364–1413*. Oxford: Clarendon.

Glasier, J. Bruce. 1919. *The Meaning of Socialism*. Manchester: National Labour Press.
Glasier, J. Bruce. 1921. *William Morris and the Early Days of the Socialist Movement*. London: Longmans, Green, and Co.
Globa, Andrei. 1922. Уот Тайлер: Поэма [*Wat Tyler: Poem*]. Петербург.
Glover, Halcott. 1921. *Wat Tyler: A Play in Three Acts*. London: Bloomsbury Press.
Goadby, Edwin. 1873. 'Peasants' Revolt'. *New Monthly Magazine* 153: 36–40.
Goldfarb, Sheldon. 2004. 'Ainsworth, William Harrison'. *ODNB*.
Goldie, Mark. 1992. 'John Locke's Circle and James II'. *Historical Journal* 35 (3): 557–86. https://doi.org/10.1017/S0018246X00025978
Goldie, Mark. 2004. 'Tyrrell, James (1642–1718)'. *ODNB*.
Goldsmith, Oliver. 1771. *The History of England, from the Earliest Times to the Death of George II, Vol. II*. London.
Gooch, Steve. 1974. *Will Wat, If Not What Will?* London: Pluto.
Gooch, Steve. n.d. *Passed On* (unpublished).
Gooch, Steve. 1984. *All Together Now: An Alternative View of Theatre and the Community*. London: Methuen.
Good, Jonathan. 2009. *The Cult of St George in Medieval England*. Woodbridge: Boydell Press. https://doi.org/10.1017/9781846157127
Goode, John. 1971. 'William Morris and the Dream of Revolution'. In *Literature and Politics in the Nineteenth Century: Essays*, edited by John Lucas, 221–80. London: Methuen. https://doi.org/10.4324/9781315564067-8
Goodrich, Amanda. 2005. *Debating England's Aristocracy in the 1790s: Pamphlets, Polemics, and Political Ideas*. Woodbridge: Boydell Press.
Goodway, David. 1982. *London Chartism 1838–1848*. Cambridge: Cambridge University Press.
Goodwin, Albert. 1979. *The Friends of Liberty: The English Democratic Movement in the Age of the French Revolution*. London: Routledge.
Gosse, Edmund, and Sidney J. H. Herrtage, eds. 1880. *The Complete Works of Samuel Rowlands 1598–1628: Vol. 1*. Glasgow: Hunterian Club.
Gossman, Norbert J. 1983. 'William Cuffay: London's Black Chartist'. *Phylon* 44 (1): 56–65. https://doi.org/10.2307/274369
Gough, J. W. 1976. 'James Tyrrell, Whig Historian and Friend of John Locke'. *Historical Journal* 19 (3): 581–610. https://doi.org/10.1017/S0018246X00010396
Goy-Blanquet, Dominique. 2003. *Shakespeare's Early History Plays: From Chronicle to Stage*. Oxford: Oxford University Press. https://doi.org/10.1093/acprof:oso/9780198119876.001.0001
Grafton, Richard. 1809. *Grafton's chronicle: or, History of England. To which is added his table of the bailiffs, sherrifs, and mayors, of the city of London. From the year 1189 to 1558, inclusive*. 2 vols. London: J. Johnson.
Gransden, Antonia. 1982. *Historical Writing in England II: c. 1307 to the Early Sixteenth Century*. Ithaca, NY: Cornell University Press.
Gray, John. 2007. *Black Mass: Apocalyptic Religion and the Death of Utopia*. London: Allen Lane.

Gray, John. 2019. 'The Recurrent Dream of an End-Time'. *A Point of View*. BBC Radio 4 (20 December). https://www.bbc.co.uk/sounds/play/m000c8rz
Green, John R. 1874. *A Short History of the English People*. London: Macmillan and Co.
Green, Michaël. 2018. 'Early Employment Networks of Paul Rapin-Thoyras: Huguenot Soldier and Tutor (1685–1692)'. *Diasporas: Circulations, migrations, histoire* 31: 101–14. https://doi.org/10.4000/diasporas.1423
Green, Richard Firth. 1992. 'John Ball's Letters: Literary History and Historical Literature'. In *Chaucer's England: Literature in Historical Context*, edited by Barbara A. Hanawalt, 176–200, Minneapolis: University of Minnesota Press.
Green, Richard Firth. 1999. *A Crisis of Truth: Literature and Law in Ricardian England*. Philadelphia: University of Pennsylvania Press.
Greig, J. Y. T., ed. 1932. *The Letters of David Hume: Volume I, 1727–1765*. Oxford: Oxford University Press.
Griffiths, Clare V. J. 1997. 'Remembering Tolpuddle: Rural History and Commemoration in the Inter-War Labour History'. *History Workshop Journal* 44 (1): 144–69. https://doi.org/10.1093/hwj/1997.44.145
Griffiths, Clare V. J. 2007. *Labour and the Countryside: The Politics of Rural Britain 1918–1939*. Oxford: Oxford University Press.
Griffiths, Claire V. J. 2011. 'History and the Labour Party'. In *Classes, Cultures and Politics: Essays on British History for Ross McKibbin*, edited by Claire V. J. Griffiths, James J. Nott, and William Whyte, 292–301. Oxford: Oxford University Press. https://doi.org/10.1093/acprof:osobl/9780199579884.001.0001
Griffiths, Clare V. J. 2019. 'From Dorsetshire Labourers to Tolpuddle Martyrs: Celebrating Radicalism in the English Countryside'. In *Secular Martyrdom in Britain and Ireland: From Peterloo to the Present*, edited by Quentin Outram and Keith Laybourn, 59–84. New York: Palgrave Macmillan. https://doi.org/10.1007/978-3-319-62905-6_3
Griffiths, Paul. 1981. '80+'. *Musical Times* 122 (June): 390. https://doi.org/10.2307/960981
Grove, Valerie. 1999. *Laurie Lee: The Well-Loved Stranger*. London: Viking.
Groves, Reginald. 1967. *Conrad Noel and the Thaxted Movement: An Adventure in Christian Socialism*. London: Merlin Press.
Groves, Reginald, ed. 1970. *The Catholic Crusade, 1918–1936*. London: Archive One.
Groves, Reginald. 1974. *The Balham Group: How British Trotskyism Began*. London: Pluto.
Guest, Geo. 1920. *An Introduction to English Rural History*. London: Workers' Educational Association. https://doi.org/10.5962/bhl.title.19073
Guthrie, William. 1747. *A General History of England Beginning with the Reign of Edward the Second and Ending with That of Henry the Eighth, Vol. II*. London.
Gutteridge, Lizzie. 2017. 'When Adam Delved—a song for John Ball by Consort of 1'. *YouTube* (9 July). Accessed 30 January. https://www.youtube.com/watch?v=BS1BM1gB6Nw

Haile, Martin, and Edwin Bonney. 1911. *Life and Letters of John Lingard, 1771–1851*. St Louis, MO: Herder.
Hampton, Christopher, ed. 1984. *A Radical Reader: The Struggle for Change in England, 1381–1914*. London: Penguin. https://doi.org/10.2307/25142569
Handley, Stuart. 2015. 'Carte, Thomas (bap. 1686, d. 1754).' *ODNB*.
Hanson, Ingrid. 2013. 'The Living Past and the Fellowship of Sacrificial Violence in William Morris's *A Dream of John Ball*.' In *Reading Historical Fiction: The Revenant and Remembered Past*, edited by Kate Mitchell and Nicola Parsons, 204–19. New York: Palgrave Macmillan. https://doi.org/10.1057/9781137291547_13
Hanson, Ingrid. 2013. *William Morris and the Uses of Violence, 1856–1890*. London: Anthem Press.
Hardie, Keir. 2015. *From Serfdom to Socialism*. Edited by John Callow. London: Lawrence and Wishart.
Hardwick, J. C. 1924. *Master and Man: A Tale of the Peasants' Revolt*. London: Sheldon Press.
Harker, Ben. 2011. '"Communism is English": Edgell Rickword, Jack Lindsay and the Cultural Politics of the Popular Front.' *Literature and History* 20 (2): 16–34. https://doi.org/10.7227/LH.20.2.2
Harker, Ben. 2018. 'Morton, (Arthur) Leslie (1903–1987).' *ODNB*. https://doi.org/10.1093/odnb/9780198614128.013.95947
Harris, Kenneth. 1995. *Attlee*. Revised edition. London: Weidenfeld and Nicolson.
Harris, Tim. 2001. 'Perceptions of the Crowd in Later Stuart London.' In *Imagining Early Modern London: Perceptions and Portrayals of the City from Stow to Strype 1598–1720*, edited by J. F. Merritt, 250–72. Cambridge: Cambridge University Press.
Harrison, J. F. C. 1984. *The Common People: A History from the Norman Conquest to the Present*. London: Croom Helm.
Harvey, I. M. W. 1995. 'Was There Popular Politics in Fifteenth-Century England?' In *The McFarlane Legacy: Studies in Late Medieval Politics and Society*, edited by Richard H. Britnell and A. J. Pollard, 155–74. New York: St Martin's Press.
Hay, Denys. 1952. *Polydore Vergil: Renaissance Historian and Man of Letters*. Oxford: Clarendon Press.
Haywood, Ian. 2003–2004. '"The Renovating Fury": Southey, Republicanism and Sensationalism.' *Romanticism on the Net* 32–33: 1–25. https://doi.org/10.7202/009256ar
Hazelgrove, Jenny. 2000. *Spiritualism and British Society between the Wars*. Manchester: Manchester University Press.
Heal, Felicity. n.d. 'The Holinshed Editors: Religious Attitudes and their Consequences.' Accessed 20 January 2021. http://www.cems.ox.ac.uk/holinshed/paper2.pdf
Heath, Richard. 1893. *The English Peasant: Studies, Historical, Local and Biographic*. London: T. Fisher Unwin.
Heathman, Katie Palmer. 2018. '"I Ring for the General Dance": Morris and Englishness in the Work of Conrad Noel.' In *The Histories of the Morris in*

Britain, edited by Michael Heaney, 115–31. London: English Folk Dance and Song Society & Historical Dance Society.
Hector, L. C., and Barbara F. Harvey, eds. 1982. *The Westminster Chronicle, 1381–1394*. Oxford: Clarendon Press.
Henty, G. A. 1897. *A March on London, Being a Story of Wat Tyler's Rebellion*. New York: C. Scribner's Sons.
Herdt, Jennifer A. 2013. 'Artificial Lives, Providential History, and the Apparent Limits of Sympathetic Understanding.' In *David Hume: Historical Thinker, Historical Writer*, edited by Mark G. Spencer, 37–59. University Park: Pennsylvania State University Press. https://doi.org/10.5325/j.ctt32b9wf.7
Herring, George. 2012. 'W. E. Heygate: Tractarian Clerical Novelist.' *Studies in Church History* 48: 259–70. https://doi.org/10.1017/S0424208400001364
Hertel, Ralf. 2010. 'Nationalising History? Polydore Vergil's Anglica Historia, Shakespeare's Richard III, and the Appropriation of the English Past.' In *Exiles, Emigrés and Intermediaries: Anglo-Italian Cultural Transactions*, edited by Barbara Schaff, 47–70. Amsterdam: Rodopi. https://doi.org/10.1163/9789042030695_004
Hervey, John. 1734. *Ancient and Modern Liberty Stated and Compar'd*. London.
Heygate, William E. 1860. *Alice of Fobbing; or, the Times of Jack Straw and Wat Tyler*. London: J. H. and J. Parker.
Hicks, Philip. 1996. *Neoclassical History and English Culture: From Clarendon to Hume*. Basingstoke: Macmillan. https://doi.org/10.1057/9780230376151
Hicks, Philip. 2013. '"The Spirit of Liberty": Historical Causation and Political Rhetoric in the Age of Hume.' In *David Hume: Historical Thinker, Historical Writer*, edited by Mark G. Spencer, 61–79. University Park: Pennsylvania State University Press. https://doi.org/10.5325/j.ctt32b9wf.8
Hill, Christopher. 1954. 'The Norman Yoke.' In *Democracy and the Labour Movement: Essays in Honour of Dona Torr*, edited by John Saville, 11–66. London: Lawrence and Wishart.
Hill, Christopher. 1972. *The World Turned Upside Down: Radical Ideas during the English Revolution*. London: Maurice Temple Smith.
Hill, Christopher. 1993. *The English Bible and the Seventeenth-Century Revolution*. London: Penguin.
Hill, Mike, and Warren Montag. 2015. *The Other Adam Smith*. Stanford: Stanford University Press. https://doi.org/10.1515/9780804793001
Hilton, Rodney. 1958. 'The Origins of Robin Hood.' *Past and Present* 14 (1): 30–44. https://doi.org/10.1093/past/14.1.30
Hilton, Rodney. 1969. *The Decline of Serfdom in Medieval England*. London: Palgrave Macmillan. https://doi.org/10.1007/978-1-349-00696-0
Hilton, Rodney. 1973. 'The Rebellion of 1381.' In *People for the People*, edited by David Rubinstein, 18–23. London: Ithaca Press.
Hilton, Rodney. 1975. *The English Peasantry in the Later Middle Ages: The Ford Lectures for 1973 and Related Studies*. Oxford: Oxford University Press.
Hilton, Rodney. 1978. 'Christopher Hill: Some Reminiscences.' In *Puritans and Revolutionaries: Essays in Seventeenth-Century History Presented to Christopher*

Hill, edited by Donald H. Pennington and Keith Thomas, 6–10. Oxford: Oxford University Press.
Hilton, Rodney. 1981. 'The English Rising of 1381.' *Marxism Today* (June): 17–19.
Hilton, Rodney. 1981. 'Wat Tyler, John Ball and the English Rising.' *New Society* (30 April): 171–73.
Hilton, Rodney. 1990. *The Change beyond the Change: A Dream of John Ball*. London: William Morris Society.
Hilton, Rodney. 1990. *Class Conflict and the Crisis of Feudalism*. Revised edition. London: Verso.
Hilton, Rodney. 2003 [1973]. *Bond Men Made Free: Medieval Peasant Movements and the English Rising of 1381*. London: Routledge. https://doi.org/10.4324/9780203169315
Hilton, Rodney, and Trevor H. Aston, eds. 1984. *The English Rising of 1381*. Cambridge: Cambridge University Press.
'The History of John Ball.' *John Ball Primary School*. Accessed 30 January 2021. https://www.johnball.lewisham.sch.uk/our-school/history/
The History of Wat Tyler & Jack Straw, Being a Relation of their Notorious Rebellion. 1720[?]. London.
Hoadley, Frank Taliaferro. 1941. 'The Controversy over Southey's *Wat Tyler*.' *Studies in Philology* 38 (1): 81–96.
Hobsbawm, Eric J. 1959. *Primitive Rebels: Studies in Archaic Forms of Social Movement in the 19th and 20th Centuries*. Manchester: Manchester University Press.
Hobsbawm, Eric J. 1969. *Bandits*. London: Weidenfeld and Nicolson.
Hobsbawm, Eric J. 1972. 'Social Banditry: A Reply.' *Comparative Studies in Society and History* 14 (4): 503–5. https://doi.org/10.1017/S0010417500006836
Hobsbawm, Eric J. 1973. 'Peasants and Politics.' *Journal of Peasant Studies* 1 (1): 3–22. https://doi.org/10.1080/03066157308437870
Hobsbawm, Eric J. 1973. 'Social Banditry.' In *Rural Protest: Peasant Movements and Social Change*, edited by Henry A. Landsberger, 142–57. New York: Macmillan. https://doi.org/10.1007/978-1-349-01612-9_4
Hobsbawm, Eric J. 1974. 'Peasant Land Occupations.' *Past and Present* 62 (1): 120–52. https://doi.org/10.1093/past/62.1.120
Hobsbawm, Eric J. 1978. 'Communist Party Historians' Group 1946–56.' In *Rebels and their Causes: Essays in Honour of A. L. Morton*, edited by Maurice Cornforth, 21–48. London: Lawrence & Wishart.
Hobsbawm, Eric J. 2002. *Interesting Times: A Twentieth Century Life*. London: Abacus.
Hobsbawm, E. J. E. 2009. 'Hilton, Rodney Howard (1916–2002).' *ODNB*.
Holzman, Michael. 1990. 'The Encouragement and Warning of History: William Morris's *A Dream of John Ball*.' In *Socialism and the Literary Artistry of William Morris*, edited by Florence Boos and Carole Silver, 98–116. Columbia: University of Missouri Press.
Horspool, David. 2009. *The English Rebel: One Thousand Years of Troublemaking from the Normans to the Nineties*. London: Viking.

Houliston, Victor. 2004. 'Persons [Parsons], Robert (1546–1610).' *ODNB*.
Houliston, Victor. 2007. *Catholic Resistance in Elizabethan England: Robert Persons's Jesuit Polemic, 1580–1610*. Aldershot: Ashgate.
Hovell, Mark. 1918, 1925, 1966. *The Chartist Movement*. Third edition. Manchester: Manchester University Press.
Howard, Robert. 1681. *The Life and Reign of King Richard the Second*. London.
Hoyles, Martin. 2013. *William Cuffay: The Life and Times of a Chartist Leader*. Hertford: Hansib.
Hughes, John. ed. 1706. *A Complete History of England: with the lives of all the kings and queens thereof; from the earliest account of time, to the death of His late Majesty King William III. Containing a faithful relation of all affairs of state, ecclesiastical and civil. Vol. 1*. London.
Hulme, Tom. 2020. 'Historical Pageants, Neo-Romanticism and the City in Interwar Britain.' In *Restaging the Past: Historical Pageants, Culture and Society in Modern Britain*, edited by Angela Bartie, Linda Fleming, Mark Freeman, Alexander Hutton, and Paul Readman, 158–79. London: UCL Press. https://doi.org/10.2307/j.ctv13xprsc.12
Hume, David. 1739–1740. *A Treatise of Human Nature: Being an Attempt to Introduce the Experimental Method of Reasoning into Moral Subjects*. London.
Hume, David. 1762. *The History of England from the Invasion of Julius Caesar to the Accession of Henry VII, Part II*. London.
Hume, David. 1770. *The History of England from the Invasion of Julius Caesar to the Revolution in 1688: Volume I*. London.
Hume, David. 1778. *The History of England from the Invasion of Julius Caesar to the Revolution in 1688: Volume II*. London.
Hume, David. 1987. *Essays Moral, Political, Literary*. Edited by Eugene F. Miller. Indianapolis: Liberty Fund.
Humphrey, Chris. 2001. *The Politics of Carnival, Festive Misrule in Medieval England*. Manchester: Manchester University Press.
Humphreys, Henry Noel. 1845. *Illuminated Illustrations of Froissart: Selected from the MS in the Bibliothèque Royale in Paris and Other Sources*. London: William Smith.
Huzzey, Richard. 2012. *Freedom Burning: Anti-Slavery and Empire in Victorian Britain*. Ithaca: Cornell University Press. https://doi.org/10.7591/9780801465819
Hyndman, H. M. 1881. 'Dawn of a Revolutionary Epoch.' *Nineteenth Century* (January): 1–18.
Hyndman, H. M. 1881. *England for All*. London: E.W. Allen.
Hyndman, H. M. 1883. *The Historical Basis for Socialism in England*. London: Kegan Paul, Trench & Co.
Hyndman, H. M. 1909. *John Ball: Priest and Prophet of the Peasants' Revolt*. London: Twentieth Century Press.
Ipgrave, Julia. 2017. *Adam in Seventeenth Century Political Writing in England and New England*. New York: Routledge. https://doi.org/10.4324/9781315565583
The Iust Reward of Rebels, or The Life and Death of Iack Straw, and Wat Tyler. 1642. London.

Israel, Charles E. 1963. *Who Was Then the Gentleman?* London: Macmillan and Co.
Jackson, T. A. 1953. *Solo Trumpet: Some Memories of Socialist Agitation and Propaganda*. London: Lawrence and Wishart.
Jacobus, Lee A. 1975. *John Cleveland*. Boston: Twayne Publishers.
Jäger, Lorenz. 2004. *Adorno: A Political Biography*. New Haven: Yale University Press.
James, Thomas. 1608. *An apologie for Iohn Wickliffe shewing his conformitie with the now Church of England; with answere to such slaunderous obiections, as haue beene lately vrged against him by Father Parsons, the apologists, and others*. Oxford.
Jarrett, Bede. 1913. *Mediaeval Socialism*. London: T. C. & E. C. Jack.
Jeayes, Isaac Herbert, ed. 1921. *Court Rolls of the Borough of Colchester, Volume I (1310–1352)*. Colchester: Town Council of the Borough of Colchester.
Jeayes, Isaac Herbert, ed. 1941. *Court Rolls of the Borough of Colchester, Volume III (1372–1379)*. Colchester: Town Council of the Borough of Colchester.
Jewers, Rosemary. 2018. 'List of Plaques: John Ball.' *Colchester Plaque Trails* (14 March). Accessed 30 January 2021. http://www.placecheck.info/maps/view/index.php?display=comments&map=104
'John Ball.' n.d. *Colchester Civil Society*. Accessed 30 January 2021. https://www.colchestercivicsociety.co.uk/what-we-do/commemorative-plaques/john-ball/
'John Ball Plaque.' 2017. *Colchester Civil Society* (19 January). Accessed 30 January 2021. https://www.colchestercivicsociety.co.uk/2017/01/19/john-ball-plaque/
John Ball Society. n.d. Accessed January 2021. https://www.johnballsociety.org
'John Ball's Speech to Peasants—Analysis from Dennis Skinner (pt 1/2).' 2012. BBC English File (3 August [original 1996]). Accessed 30 January 2021. https://www.bbc.co.uk/programmes/p00wwk82
'John Ball's Speech to Peasants—Analysis from Dennis Skinner (pt 2/2).' 2012. BBC English File (3 August [original 1996]). Accessed 30 January 2012. https://www.bbc.co.uk/programmes/p00wwkgn
John Larpent Plays. n.d. San Marino, CA: The Huntington Library.
Johnston, Kenneth R. 2013. *Unusual Suspects: Pitt's Reign of Alarm and the Lost Generation of the 1790s*. https://doi.org/10.1093/acprof:oso/9780199657803.001.0001
Jones, David V. J. 1999. *The Last Rising: The Newport Chartist Insurrection of 1839*. Cardiff: University of Wales Press.
Jusserand, J. J. 1899 [1884]. *English Wayfaring Life in the Middle Ages (XIVth Century)*. Translated by Lucy Toulmin Smith. London: T. Fisher Unwin.
Justice, Steven. 1994. *Writing and Rebellion: England in 1381*. Berkeley: University of California Press. https://doi.org/10.1525/9780520918405
Justice, Steven. 2015. *Adam Usk's Secret*. Philadelphia: University of Pennsylvania Press. https://doi.org/10.9783/9780812291056
Kane, George. 1986. 'Some Fourteenth-Century "Political" Poems.' In *Medieval English Religious and Ethical Literature: Essays in Honour of G.H. Russell*, edited by Gregory Kratzmann and James Simpson, 82–91. Cambridge: D.S. Brewer.

Kasdagli, Aglaia. 2019. 'Medieval History and Marxism in England, 1950–1956.' *Past and Present* 242 (1): 1–43.
Katz, Phil. 2005. *Thinking Hands: The Power of Labour in William Morris*. UK [city unknown]: Hetherington Press.
Kaye, Harvey J. 1984. *The British Marxist Historians*. Cambridge: Polity Press.
Keane, John. 1995. *Tom Paine: A Political Life*. London: Bloomsbury.
Keen, Maurice. 1978. 'Christopher Hill: Some Reminiscences.' In *Puritans and Revolutionaries: Essays in Seventeenth-Century History Presented to Christopher Hill*, edited by Donald H. Pennington and Keith Thomas, 17–21. Oxford: Oxford University Press.
Keightley, Thomas. 1839. *The History of England, Vol. I*. London.
Kelle, Brad E. 2014. 'The Phenomenon of Israelite Prophecy in Contemporary Scholarship.' *Currents in Biblical Research* 12 (3): 275–320. https://doi.org/10.1177/1476993X13480677
Kelvin, Norman, ed. 1984. *The Collected Letters of William Morris: Volume I, 1848–1880*. Princeton: Princeton University Press.
Kelvin, Norman, ed. 1987. *The Collected Letters of William Morris: Volume II, Part A: 1881–1884*. Princeton: Princeton University Press.
Kelvin, Norman, ed. 1987. *The Collected Letters of William Morris: Volume II, Part B: 1885–1888*. Princeton: Princeton University Press.
Kelvin, Norman, ed. 1996. *The Collected Letters of William Morris, Volume IV: 1893–1896*. Princeton: Princeton University Press.
Kenyon, John. 1993. *The History Men: Classic Work on Historians and Their History*. Second edition. London: Weidenfeld and Nicolson.
Kesteven, G. R. 1965. *The Peasants' Revolt*. London: Chatto & Windus.
Keynes, Simon. 1999. 'The Cult of King Alfred the Great.' *Anglo-Saxon England* 28 (1999): 225–356. https://doi.org/10.1017/S0263675100002337
King, Francis. 2015. 'Editorial: Our History.' *Socialist History* 47: 1–13.
Kinna, Ruth. 2000. *William Morris and the Art of Socialism*. Cardiff: University of Wales Press.
Kinna, Ruth. 2010. 'Time and Utopia: The Gap between Morris and Bax.' *Journal of William Morris Studies* 18 (4): 36–47.
Klugmann, James. 1980. 'The Crisis of the Thirties.' In *Culture and Crisis in Britain in the Thirties*, edited by Jon Clark, Margot Heinemann, David Margolies, and Carole Snee, 13–36. London: Lawrence and Wishart.
Knight, Charles. 1857. *The Popular History of England: An Illustrated History of Society and Government from the Earliest Period to Our Own Times, Volume II*. London: Bradbury and Evans.
Kriehn, George. 1902. 'Studies in the Sources of the Social Revolt in 1381.' *American Historical Review* 7 (2): 254–85. https://doi.org/10.2307/1833941
Kumar, Krishan. 2003. *The Making of English National Identity*. Cambridge: Cambridge University Press. https://doi.org/10.1017/CBO9780511550058
Lacey, Helen. 2008. '"Grace for the Rebels": The Role of the Royal Pardon in the Peasants' Revolt of 1381.' *Journal of Medieval History* 34 (1): 36–63. https://doi.org/10.1016/j.jmedhist.2007.10.008

Lamont, William. 2009. 'Norman Rufus Colin Cohn 1915–2007.' *Proceedings of the British Academy* 161: 87–108. https://doi.org/10.5871/bacad/9780197264577.003.0005

Lane, Jane. 1976. *A Summer Storm*. London: Peter Davies.

Lanquet, Thomas, Thomas Cooper, and Robert Crowley. 2004. *An epitome of chronicles Conteyninge the whole discourse of the histories as well of this realme of England, as al other cou[n]treys, with the succession of their kinges, the time of their reigne, and what notable actes they did … gathered out of most probable auctours. Firste by Thomas Lanquet, from the beginning of the worlde to the incarnacion of Christe, secondely to the reigne of our soueraigne lord king Edward the sixt by Thomas Cooper, and thirdly to the reigne of our soueraigne Ladye Quene Elizabeth, by Robert Crowley. Anno. 1559*. Ann Arbor, MI: Text Creation Partnership.

Larkin, James F., ed. 1983. *Stuart Royal Proclamations 2, Royal Proclamations of King Charles I, 1625–46*. Oxford: Oxford University Press.

Laski, Harold J., ed. 1948. *Communist Manifesto: Socialist Landmark*. London: George Allen and Unwin.

Leatham, James. 1892. *The Class War: A Lecture*. Sixth edition. London: Twentieth Century Press; orig. Aberdeen: James Leatham.

Leatham, James. 1899. *William Morris: Master of Many Crafts*. Peterhead: Sentinel Office.

Leatham, James. n.d. *The Peasants' Revolt, or The Tragedy of a Nation*. London: Twentieth Century Press.

Lee, Laurie. 1969. *As I Walked Out One Midsummer Morning*. New York: Atheneum.

Lee, Laurie. 2003. *Three Plays*. Cheltenham: Cyder Press.

Leech, Kenneth, ed. 1993. *Conrad Noel and the Catholic Crusade: A Critical Evaluation*. Croydon: Jubilee Group.

Lemonnier-Texier, Delphine. 2013. 'Staging Sedition despite Censorship: The Representation of the People on the Shakespearean Stage in *2 Henry VI*.' *Revue LISA* 11 (3): https://journals.openedition.org/lisa/5499?lang=en. https://doi.org/10.4000/lisa.5499

Levine, Joseph M. 1991. *The Battle of the Books: History and Literature in the Augustan Age*. Ithaca, NY: Cornell University Press.

Levitas, Ruth. 2016. 'More, Morris, Utopia…and Us.' *Journal of William Morris Studies* 22 (1): 4–17.

Lew, Nathaniel G. 2017. *Tonic to the Nation: Making English Music in the Festival of Britain*. New York: Routledge. https://doi.org/10.4324/9781315550855

Liddell, W. H., and R. G. Wood, ed. 1982. *Essex and the Great Revolt of 1381*. Essex: Essex Record Office.

Life and Adventures of Wat Tyler the Good and the Brave. 1851. London: H.G. Collins.

Lilburne, John. 1649. *The Legall Fundamentall Liberties of the People of England Revived, Asserted, and Vindicated* (8 June). London.

Lindsay, Jack. 1936. 'Who Are the English?' *Left Review* 2 (May): 353–57.

Lindsay, Jack. 1939. *England, My England: A Pageant of the English People*. London: Fore Publications.
Lindsay, Jack. 1962. *Fanfrolico and After*. London: Bodley Head.
Lindsay, Jack. 2014. *Who Are the English? Selected Poems: 1935–1981*. Middlesbrough: Smokestack Books.
Lindsay, Jack, and Edgell Rickword. eds. 1939. *A Handbook of Freedom: A Record of English Democracy through Twelve Centuries*. New York: International Publishers.
Lindsay, Philip. 1961. *The Golden Cage*. London: Robert Hale.
Lindsay, Philip, and Reg Groves. 1950. *The Peasants' Revolt 1381*. London: Hutchinson and Co.
Linebaugh, Peter. 2003. *The London Hanged: Crime and Civil Society in the Eighteenth Century*. Second edition. London: Verso.
Linehan, Thomas. 2010. 'Communist Culture and Anti-Fascism in Inter-War Britain.' In *Varieties of Anti-Fascism: Britain in the Inter-War Period*, edited by Nigel Copsey and Andrzej Olechnowicz, 31–51. New York: Palgrave Macmillan. https://doi.org/10.1057/9780230282674_2
Lingard, John. 1819. *The History of England from the First Invasion to the Accession of Henry VIII: Volume III*. London.
Lock, F. P. 2006. *Edmund Burke, Volume II: 1784–1797*. Oxford: Oxford University Press.
Lockhart, Alastair. 2019. *Personal Religion and Spiritual Healing: The Panacea Society in the Twentieth Century*. Albany, NY: SUNY Press.
Logan, F. Donald. 1968. *Excommunication and the Secular Arm in Medieval England: A Study in Legal Procedure from the Thirteenth to the Sixteenth Century*. Toronto: Pontifical Institute of Mediaeval Studies.
London District Committee (CPGB). 1936. *The March of English History*. London: Communist Party of Great Britain.
Longstaffe, Stephen. 1998. '"A Short Report and Not Otherwise": Jack Cade in 2 Henry VI.' In *Shakespeare and Carnival: After Bakhtin*, edited by Ronald Knowles, 13–35. New York: St Martin's Press. https://doi.org/10.1057/9780230000810_2
Longstaffe, Stephen, ed. 2002. *A Critical Edition of the Life and Death of Jack Straw (1594)*. Lewiston: Edwin Mellen Press.
Lounissi, Carine. 2016. 'Thomas Paine's Reflections on the Social Contract: A Consistent Theory?' In *New Directions in Thomas Paine Studies*, edited by Scott Cleary and Ivy Linton Stabell, 175–93. New York: Palgrave Macmillan. https://doi.org/10.1057/9781137589996_10
Lucas, Peter J. 1983. *John Capgrave's Abbreuiacion of Cronicles*. Oxford: Oxford University Press.
Lumby, Joseph Rawson, ed. 1882. *Polychronicon Ranulphi Higden maonachi Cestrensis: together with the English translations of John Trevisa and of an unknown writer of the fifteenth century, Vol. VIII*. London: Longman & Co.
MacCarthy, Fiona. 2010 [1995]. *William Morris: A Life for Our Time*. London: Faber & Faber.

Mack, Jane. 2003. 'Introduction'. In Laurie Lee, *Three Plays*, i–xvi. Cheltenham: Cyder Press.

MacKinnon, James. 2015. 'Sweet Liberties Launch, Speaker's House, Palace of Westminster, 16th November'. *Folk Radio* (19 November). Accessed 30 January 2021. https://www.folkradio.co.uk/2015/11/sweet-liberties-launch-speakers-house-palace-of-westminster/

Magennis, Hugh. 2015. 'Not Angles but Anglicans? Reformation and Post-Reformation Perspectives on the Anglo-Saxon Church, Part II: Seventeenth and Eighteenth Centuries'. *English Studies* 96 (4): 363–78. https://doi.org/10.1080/0013838X.2015.1011889

Mahamdallie, Hassan. 2008. *Crossing the 'River of Fire': The Socialism of William Morris*. London: Redwords.

'Mainly Norfolk: English Folk and Other Good Music'. n.d. Accessed 30 January 2021. https://mainlynorfolk.info/folk/records/sydneycarter.html

Major, John. 1892 [1521]. *A history of Greater Britain as well England as Scotland*. Edited by Archibald Constable and Aeneas J. G. Mackay. Edinburgh: University Press.

Malcolm, Joyce Lee, ed. 1999. *The Struggle for Sovereignty: Seventeenth-Century English Political Tracts: Volume 1*. Indianapolis: Liberty Fund.

Manning, Peter J. 2001. 'The History of Cobbett's A History of the Protestant "Reformation."' *Huntington Library Quarterly* 64 (3): 429–43. https://doi.org/10.2307/3817920

Manogue, Ralph Anthony. 1982. 'Southey and William Wordsworth: New Light on an Old Quarrel'. *Charles Lamb Bulletin* NS 38 (April): 105–14.

The Manuscripts of His Grace the Duke of Portland Preserved at Welbeck Abbey, Vol. III. 1894. London: Eyre and Spottiswoode.

Marsalek, Karen Sawyer. 2009. 'Staging Allegiance, Re-membering Trials: King Henry VIII and the Blackfriars Theater'. In *Shakespeare and Religious Change*, edited by Kenneth J. E. Graham and Philip D. Collington, 133–50. New York: Palgrave Macmillan. https://doi.org/10.1057/9780230240858_7

Marsh, Jan. 1999. 'William Morris and Victorian Manliness'. In *William Morris: Centenary Essays*, edited by Peter Faulkner and Peter Preston, 185–99. Exeter: University of Exeter Press.

Marshall, Peter. 2013. 'Religious Ideology'. In *The Oxford Handbook of Holinshed's Chronicles*, edited by Ian W. Archer, Felicity Heal, and Paula Kewes, 411–26. Oxford: Oxford University Press. https://doi.org/10.1093/oxfordhb/9780199565757.001.0001

Martin, G. H. 2004. 'Baker, Sir Richard (c. 1568–1645)'. *ODNB*.

Martin, G. H., ed. 1995. *Knighton's Chronicle 1337–1396*. Oxford: Clarendon.

Marx, William. 2016. 'Peculiar Versions of the Middle English Prose Brut and Textual Archaeology'. In *The Prose Brut and Other Late Medieval Chronicles: Books Have Their Histories. Essays in Honour of Lister M. Matheson*, edited by Jaclyn Rajsic, Erik Kooper, and Dominique Hoche, 94–104. Woodbridge: Boydell & Brewer.

Matheson, Lister M. 1998. 'The Peasants' Revolt through Five Centuries of Rumor and Reporting.' *Studies in Philology* 95 (2): 121–52.

Matheson, Lister M. 1998. *The Prose* Brut: *The Development of a Middle English Chronicle*. Tempe, AZ: Medieval & Renaissance Texts & Studies.

Mathur, Maya. 2015. 'Rebellion from Below: Commonwealth and Community in *The Life and Death of Jack Straw*.' *Journal of Medieval and Early Modern Studies* 45 (2): 343–65. https://doi.org/10.1215/10829636-2880923

Maurice, C. Edmund. 1875. *Lives of English Popular Leaders in the Middle Ages: Tyler, Ball, and Oldcastle*. London: Henry S. King & Co.

Maurice, C. Edmund, ed. 1913. *Life of Octavia Hill as Told in Her Letters*. London: Macmillan.

Mays, Kelly J. 2001. 'Slaves in Heaven, Laborers in Hell: Chartist Poets' Ambivalent Identification with the (Black) Slave.' *Victorian Poetry* 39 (2): 137–63. https://doi.org/10.1353/vp.2001.0013

McArthur, Neil. 2016. 'Hume's Political Philosophy.' In *The Oxford Handbook of Hume*, edited by Paul Russell, 489–504. Oxford: Oxford University Press.

McCall, Fiona. 2013. *Baal's Priests: The Loyalist Clergy and the English Revolution*. London: Routledge.

McCalman, Iain. 1998. *Radical Underworld: Prophets, Revolutionaries and Pornographers in London, 1795–1840*. Cambridge: Cambridge University Press.

McGeary, Thomas N. 2006. 'Hughes, John (1678?–1720).' *ODNB*.

McHardy, Alison K., ed. 2012. *The Reign of Richard II: From Minority to Tyranny 1377–97*. Manchester: Manchester University Press.

McIlroy, John. 2005. 'Groves, Reginald Percy (Reg) (1908–1988): Communist, Trotskyist, Christian Socialist, Labour Historian and Labour Party Parliamentary Candidate.' In *Dictionary of Labour Biography, Vol. XII*, edited by Keith Gildart and David Howell, 106–19. New York: Palgrave Macmillan.

McKay, George. 1996. *Senseless Acts of Beauty: Cultures of Resistance Since the Sixties*. London: Verso.

McKivigan, John R. 2008. *Forgotten Firebrand: James Redpath and the Making of Nineteenth Century America*. Ithaca: Cornell University Press. https://doi.org/10.7591/9781501732263

McLynn, Frank. 2012. *The Road Not Taken: How Britain Narrowly Missed a Revolution 1381–1926*. London: Bodley Head.

Meades, Jonathan. 1997. 'The Absentee Landlord.' Directed by Russell England.

Meddick, Simon, Liz Payne, and Phil Katz, eds. 2020. *Red Lives*. Croydon: Manifesto Press.

Medieval England: The Peasants' Revolt [film]. 1969. Learning Corporation of America.

Mee, Jon. 2016. *Print, Publicity, and Popular Radicalism in the 1790s: The Laurel of Liberty*. Cambridge: Cambridge University Press. https://doi.org/10.1017/CBO9781316459935

Melman, Billie. 1991. 'Claiming the Nation's Past: The Invention of an Anglo-Saxon Tradition.' *Journal of Contemporary History* 26: 575–95. https://doi.org/10.1177/002200949102600312

Merritt, J. F. 2001. 'The Reshaping of Stow's Survey: Munday, Strype and the Protestant City.' In *Imagining Early Modern London: Perceptions and Portrayals of the City from Stow to Strype 1598–1720*, edited by J. F. Merritt, 52–88. Cambridge: Cambridge University Press.

Metro Girl. 2015. 'Memorial to Wat Tyler and the Peasants' Revolt 1381 in Smithfield.' *Memoirs of a Metro Girl* (17 December). Accessed 30 January 2021. https://memoirsofametrogirl.com/2015/12/17/wat-tyler-memorial-london-peasants-revolt-1381-smithfield-st-bartholomew/

Meyer, Annie Nathan. 1901. *Robert Annys, Poor Priest: A Tale of the Great Uprising*. London: Macmillan.

Miller, Edward. 1983. 'Introduction.' In *Social Relations and Ideas: Essays in Honour of R.H. Hilton*, edited by Trevor H. Aston, P. R. Coss, Christopher Dyer, and Joan Thirsk, ix–xiii. Cambridge: Cambridge University Press.

Minto, William. 1888. *The Mediation of Ralph Hardelot*. 3 vols. London: Macmillan and Co.

Minton, Gretchen E., ed. 2013. *John Bale's 'The Image of Both Churches.'* Dordrecht: Springer. https://doi.org/10.1007/978-94-007-7296-0

Mitchell, Rosemary. 2004. 'Cassell, John (1817–1865).' *ODNB*.

Mitchell, Rosemary. 2008. 'Knight, Charles (1791–1873).' *ODNB*.

Moll, Richard. 2004. 'Gower's *Cronica tripertita* and the Latin Glosses to Hardyng's *Chronicle*.' *Journal of the Early Book Society* 7: 153–58.

Monod, Paul Kléber. 2010. 'Thomas Carte, the Druids and British National Identity.' In *Loyalty and Identity: Jacobites at Home and Abroad*, edited by Paul Monod, Murray Pittock, and Daniel Szechi, 132–48. New York: Palgrave MacMillan. https://doi.org/10.1057/9780230248571_7

Moody, Jane. 2000. *Illegitimate Theatre in London, 1770–1840*. Cambridge: Cambridge University Press.

Mooney, Susan. 2014. 'William Morris and Manliness.' *Eras* 15 (March): 1–23.

Morgan, Hollie L. S. 2017. *Beds and Chambers in Late Medieval England: Readings, Representations and Realities*. York: York Medieval Press.

Morgan, Kevin. 1989. *Against Fascism and War: Ruptures and Continuities in British Communist Politics 1935–41*. Manchester: Manchester University Press.

Morgan, Kevin, Gidon Cohen, and Andrew Flinn. 2007. *Communists and British Society 1920–1991*. London: Rivers Oram Press.

Morris, William. 1885. *Chants for Socialists*. London: Socialist League Office.

Morris, William. 1887. 'The Early Literature of the North—Iceland.' Lecture at a meeting sponsored by the Hammersmith Branch of the Socialist League at Kelmscott House (9 October). Accessed 30 January 2021. https://www.marxists.org/archive//morris/works/1887/iceland.htm

Morris, William. 1887. 'What Socialists Want.' Accessed 30 January 2021. https://www.marxists.org/archive/morris/works/1887/want.htm

Morris, William. 1888. *Signs of Change: Seven Lectures Delivered on Various Occasions*. London: Reeves and Turner.

Morris, William. 1892. *A Dream of John Ball; and, A King's Lesson*. Hammersmith: Kelmscott Press.

Morris, William. 1903. *Communism*. London: Fabian Society.
Morris, William. 1908 [1890, 1892]. *News from Nowhere*. London: Longmans, Green and Co.
Morris, William. 1915. *The Collected Works of William Morris with Introductions by His Daughter May Morris, Volume XXIII; Signs of Change: Lectures on Socialism*. London: Longman Green.
Morris, William. 1994. *Political Writings: Contributions to Commonweal 1885–1890*. Edited by Nicholas Salmon. Bristol: Thoemmes Press.
Morris, William. 1996. *Journalism: Contributions to Justice and Commonweal 1883–1890*. Edited by Nicholas Salmon. Bristol: Thoemmes Press.
Morris, William, and E. Belfort Bax. 1885. *The Manifesto of the Socialist League*. London: Socialist League Office.
Morris, William, and E. Belfort Bax. 1893. *Socialism: Its Growth and Outcome*. London: Swan Sonnenschein & Co.
Morton, A. L. 1938. *A People's History of England*. London: Victory Gollancz.
Morton, A. L. 1952. *The English Utopia*. London: Lawrence & Wishart.
Morton, A. L., ed. 1968. *Three Works by William Morris*. London: Lawrence & Wishart.
Morton, A. L. 1981. *When the People Arose: The Peasants' Revolt of 1381*. London: Communist Party of Great Britain.
Morton, Vivien, and Stuart Macintyre. 1979. *T.A. Jackson—Revolutionary and Working Class Intellectual: Centenary Appreciation 1879–1979*. London: Central Books.
Mossner, Ernest Campbell. 1941. 'Was Hume a Tory Historian? Facts and Reconsiderations.' *Journal of the History of Ideas* 2 (2): 225–36. https://doi.org/10.2307/2707114
Mullen, John. 2010. '"We Need Roots"—Englishness and New Folk Revival.' *Open Democracy* (13 July).
Müller-Doohm, Stefan. 2005. *Adorno: An Intellectual Biography*. Cambridge: Polity.
Munro, Ian. 2005. *The Figure of the Crowd in Early Modern London: The City and its Double*. New York: Palgrave Macmillan. https://doi.org/10.1057/9781403978738
Murph, Roxane C. 2007. *Rewriting the Wars of the Roses: The 17th Century Royalist Histories of John Trussell, Sir Francis Biondi and William Habington*. London: McFarland & Company, Inc.
Nelles, Paul. 2007. 'The Uses of Orthodoxy and Jacobean Erudition: Thomas James and the Bodleian Library.' In *History of Universities: Volume XXII/1*, edited by Mordechai Feingold, 21–70. Oxford: Oxford University Press.
Nelson, Craig. 2006. *Thomas Paine: Enlightenment, Revolution, and the Birth of Modern Nations*. London: Penguin.
Newbolt, Henry. 1900. *Froissart in England*. London: James Nisbet & Co.
Newcourt, Richard. 1710. *Repertorium Ecclesiasticum Parochiale Londinense*. London.
Noel, Conrad. 1910. *Socialism in Church History*. London: Frank Palmer.
Noel, Conrad. 1945. *An Autobiography*. London: J.M. Dent & Sons.

O'Brien, Mark. 2015. 'Heresy, Rebellion and Utopian Courage: The English Peasant Rising of 1381.' In *Crowd Actions in Britain and France from the Middle Ages to the Modern World*, edited by Michael T. Davis, 17–30. New York: Palgrave Macmillan. https://doi.org/10.1057/9781137316516_2

O'Brien, Mark. 2016 [2004]. *When Adam Delved and Eve Span: A History of the Peasants' Revolt of 1381*. London: Bookmarks Publications.

O'Casey, Seán. 1954. *Sunset and Evening Star*. New York: Macmillan.

Oestreicher, Paul. 1968. 'Christians and Communists in Search of Man: Fifty Years after the Russian Revolution.' In *What Kind of Revolution? A Christian-Communist Dialogue*, edited by James Klugmann and Paul Oestreicher, 192–206. London: Panther Books.

Oestreicher, Paul. 1968. 'Preface.' In *What Kind of Revolution? A Christian-Communist Dialogue*, edited by James Klugmann and Paul Oestreicher, 9–13. London: Panther Books.

Oestreicher, Paul. 2004. 'Sydney Carter.' *Guardian* (17 March).

Oestreicher, Paul. 2018. '1968—Year of Shame, Year of Grace.' *Ecumenical Review* 70 (2): 179–93. https://doi.org/10.1111/erev.12350

Okie, Laird. 1989. 'William Guthrie, Enlightenment Historian.' *The Historian* 51 (2): 221–38. https://doi.org/10.1111/j.1540-6563.1989.tb01261.x

Okie, Laird. 1991. *Augustan Historical Writing: Histories of England in the English Enlightenment*. Lanham, MD: University of America Press.

Okie, Laird. 2004. 'Kennett, White (1660–1728).' *ODNB*.

Oliver, H. J. 1963. *Sir Robert Howard, 1626–1698: A Critical Biography*. Durham, NC: Duke University Press.

Oman, Charles. 1906. *The Great Revolt of 1381*. Oxford: Clarendon Press.

O'Neill, Mrs. 1833. *The Bondman: A Story of the Days of Wat Tyler*. London.

Ormrod, W. Mark. 2000. 'In Bed with Joan of Kent: The King's Mother and the Peasants' Revolt.' In *Medieval Women—Texts and Contexts in Late Medieval Britain: Essays for Felicity Riddy*, edited by Jocelyn Wogan-Browne, Rosalynn Voaden, Arlyn Diamond, Ann Hutchison, Carol Meale, and Lesley Johnson, 277–92. Turnhout: Brepols. https://doi.org/10.1484/M.MWTC-EB.3.3647

Owst, Gerald Robert. 1966. *Literature and the Pulpit in Medieval England*. Revised edition. Oxford: Blackwell.

Packer, Ian. 2017. 'Robert Southey, Politics, and the Year 1817.' *Romanticism on the Net* 68–69 (Spring–Fall): 1–22. https://doi.org/10.7202/1070619ar

Packer, Ian, Tim Fulford, and Lynda Pratt, eds. 2016. *The Collected Letters of Robert Southey: Part Five, 1816–1818*. University of Maryland: Romantic Circles. Accessed 30 January 2021. https://romantic-circles.org/editions/southey_letters/Part_Five/HTML/letterEEd.26.2882.html

Paine, Thomas. 1776. *Common Sense*. Philadelphia.

Paine, Thomas. 1791. *Rights of Man: Being an Answer to Mr Burke's Attack on the French Revolution*. London.

Paine, Thomas. 1792. *Rights of Man, Part the Second. Combining Principle and Practice*. London.

Palmer, Robert C. 1993. *English Law in the Age of the Black Death, 1348–1381: A Transformation of Governance and Law*. Chapel Hill: University of North Carolina Press.
Parker, David. 1997. 'The Communist Party Historians' Group.' *Socialist History* 12: 33–58.
Patterson, Annabel. 1989. *Shakespeare and the Popular Voice*. Oxford: Blackwell.
Patterson, Annabel. 1994. *Reading Holinshed's Chronicles*. Chicago: University of Chicago Press.
Pearsall, Derek. 1989. 'Interpretative Models for the Peasants' Revolt.' In *Hermeneutics and Medieval Culture*, edited by Patrick J. Gallacher and Helen Damico, 63–70. Albany: State University Press of New York.
Pearson, Charles H. 1876. *English History in the Fourteenth Century*. London: Rivingtons.
'The Peasants' Revolt of 1381.' n.d. *Spartacus Educational*. https://spartacus-educational.com/Peasants_Revolt.htm
'The Peasants' Rising of 1381.' 1900. *Edinburgh Review* CCCXCI: 76–107.
Perry, Matt. 2002. *Marxism and History*. London: Palgrave MacMillan. https://doi.org/10.1007/978-1-4039-1379-1
Persons, Robert. 1602. *The warn-word to Sir Francis Hastinges wast-word conteyning the issue of three former treateses, the Watch-word, the Ward-word and the Wast-word (intituled by Sir Francis, an Apologie or defence of his Watchword) togeather with certaine admonitions & warnings to thesaid knight and his followers*. Antwerp.
Pettitt, Thomas. 1984. '"Here Comes I, Jack Straw": English Folk Drama and Social Revolt.' *Folklore* 95 (1): 3–20. https://doi.org/10.1080/0015587X.1984.9716292
Peverley, Sarah L. 2004. 'Dynasty and Division: The Depiction of King and Kingdom in John Hardyng's Chronicle.' In *The Medieval Chronicle III: Proceedings of the 3rd International Conference on the Medieval Chronicle*, edited by Erik Kooper, 149–70. Amsterdam: Rodopi.
Phillips, Mark Salber. 2008. '"The Most Illustrious Philosopher and Historian of the Age": Hume's History of England.' In *A Companion to Hume*, edited by Elizabeth S. Radcliffe, 406–22. Oxford: Blackwell. https://doi.org/10.1002/9780470696583.ch22
Phillips, Peter. 1996–1997. 'John Lingard and *The Anglo-Saxon Church*.' *Recusant History* 23 (2): 178–89.
Phillips, Peter. 2008. *John Lingard: Priest and Historian*. Leominster: Gracewing. https://doi.org/10.1017/S0034193200002247
Philp, Mark. 2007. *Thomas Paine*. Oxford: Oxford University Press.
Pickering, Kenneth W. 1985. *Drama in the Cathedral: The Canterbury Festival Plays 1928–1948*. Worthing: Churchman Publishing.
'The Ploughshare, Voice of Quaker Socialism.' 2013. *Quaker Strongrooms* (4 March). Accessed 30 January 2021. https://quakerstrongrooms.org/2013/03/04/the-ploughshare-voice-of-quaker-socialism/

Pocock, J. G. A. 1951. 'Robert Brady, 1627–1700. A Cambridge Historian of the Restoration.' *Cambridge Historical Journal* 10 (2): 186–204. https://doi.org/10.1017/S1474691300002778

Pocock, J. G. A. 1960. 'Burke and the Ancient Constitution—A Problem in the History of Ideas.' *Historical Journal* 3 (2): 125–43. https://doi.org/10.1017/S0018246X60000011

Pocock, J. G. A. 1987 [1957]. *The Ancient Constitution and the Feudal Law: A Study of English Historical Thought in the Seventeenth Century, a Reissue with a Retrospect.* Cambridge: Cambridge University Press. https://doi.org/10.1017/CBO9780511571459

Poll Tax Riot: 10 Hours that Shook Trafalgar Square. 1990. London: ACAB Press.

Poole, Robert. 2009. 'French Revolution or Peasants' Revolt? Petitioners and Rebels from the Blanketeers to the Chartists.' *Labour History Review* 74 (1): 6–26. https://doi.org/10.1179/174581809X408375

Poole, Steve. 2000. *The Politics of Regicide in England, 1760–1850: Troublesome Subjects.* Manchester: Manchester University Press.

Postgate, Raymond. 1926. *A Short History of the British Workers.* London: Plebs League.

Poulsen, Charles. 1946. *English Episode: A Tale of the Peasants' Revolt of 1381.* London: Progress.

Poulsen, Charles. 1984. *The English Rebels.* London: Journeyman.

Powell, Edgar. 1896. *The Rising in East Anglia in 1381.* Cambridge: Cambridge University Press.

Powell, Edgar, and George Macaulay Trevelyan, eds. 1899. *The Peasants' Rising and the Lollards: A Collection of Unpublished Documents Forming an Appendix to 'England in the Age of Wycliffe.'* London: Longmans, Green, and Co.

Prescott, Andrew. 1981. 'London in the Peasants' Revolt: A Portrait Gallery.' *The London Journal* 7 (2): 125–43. https://doi.org/10.1179/ldn.1981.7.2.125

Prescott, Andrew. 1994. 'Judicial Records of the Rising of 1381.' PhD thesis: University of London.

Prescott, Andrew. c. 1990s. 'John Ball Revisited.' Unpublished paper.

Prescott, Andrew. 1998. 'Writing about Rebellion: Using the Records about the Peasants' Revolt of 1381.' *History Workshop Journal* 45 (1): 1–27. https://doi.org/10.1093/hwj/1998.45.1

Prescott, Andrew. 2004. 'The Hand of God': The Suppression of the Peasants' Revolt of 1381.' In *Prophecy, Apocalypse, and the Day of Doom*, edited by Nigel Morgan, 317–41. Donington: Shaun Tyas.

Prescott, Andrew. 2008. 'Ball, John (d. 1381).' *ODNB.*

Prescott, Andrew. 2016. 'Great and Horrible Rumour: Shaping the English Revolt of 1381.' In *The Routledge History Handbook of Medieval Revolt*, edited by Justine Firnhaber-Baker and Dirk Schoenaers, 76–103. London: Routledge.

Priestley, H. E. 1964. *Swords over Southdowne.* London: Frederick Muller.

Punter, Michael. 2013. 'Steve Gooch: A Playwright's Progress.' *Contemporary Theatre Review* 23 (4): 602–5. https://doi.org/10.1080/10486801.2013.852777

Puttenham, George. 1869. *The arte of English poesie* (1589). Edited by Edward Arber. London: Murray & Son.
Putterill, Jack. 1976. *Conrad Noel: Prophet and Priest, 1869–1942*. Cambridge: E. & E. Plumridge.
Putterill, Jack. 1977. *Thaxted Quest for Social Justice: The Autobiography of Fr Jack Putterill, Turbulent Priest and Rebel*. Marlow: Precision Press.
Rackin, Phyllis. 1990. *Stages of History: Shakespeare's English Chronicles*. Ithaca, NY: Cornell University Press. https://doi.org/10.7591/9781501724725
Raftis, J. A. 1986. 'Social Change versus Revolution: New Interpretations of the Peasants' Revolt of 1381.' In *Social Unrest in the Late Middle Ages*, edited by Francis X. Newman, 3–22. Binghamton: Center for Medieval and Early Renaissance Studies.
Rapin-Thoyras, Paul de. 1726. *The History of England, as well Ecclesiastical as Civil: Volume I*. Translated and edited by N. Tindal. London.
Rapin-Thoyras, Paul de. 1727. *The History of England, as well Ecclesiastical as Civil: Volume IV*. Translated and edited by N. Tindal. London.
Rapin-Thoyras, Paul de. 1727. *Histoire D'Angleterre: Tome Troisiéme*. The Hague.
Ray, Gaston, ed. 1869. *Chroniques de J. Froissart: Tome Dixième 1380–1382*. Paris: Mme. ve. J. Renouard.
'Ray Walker—Peasants Revolt—1981.' n.d. *For Walls with Tongues*. Accessed 30 January 2021. https://www.forwallswithtongues.org.uk/projects/ray-walker-peasants-revolt-1981/
Raymond, George Frederick, assisted by Alexander Gordon, Hugh Owen, and Others. 1790. *A New Universal and Impartial History of England from the Earliest Authentic Records, and Most Genuine Historical Evidence, to the End of the Present Year*. London.
'The Red Dagger, Part 1.' 2013. *International Times* (December). Accessed 30 January 2021. http://internationaltimes.it/the-red-dagger-pt-1/
Redpath, James. 1859. *The Roving Editor: Or, Talks with Slaves in the Southern States*. New York.
'Red Saunders at Impressions Gallery.' 2011. *YouTube* (1 September). Accessed 30 January 2021. https://www.youtube.com/watch?v=qPmjRDbJMCo
'Red Saunders—The Agreement: The Story Behind the Work.' 2015. *Cynthia Corbett Gallery* (22 August). Accessed 30 January 2021. https://thecynthiacorbettgallery.wordpress.com/2015/08/22/red-saunders-the-agreement-the-story-behind-the-work/
'Red Saunders: Hidden.' n.d. Impressions Gallery. Accessed 30 January 2021. https://www.impressions-gallery.com/event/red-saunders-hidden/
Rees, John. 2016. *The Leveller Revolution*. London: Verso.
Renton, David. 2005. 'Studying Their Own Nation without Insularity? The British Marxist Historians Reconsidered.' *Science and Society* 69 (4): 559–79. https://doi.org/10.1521/siso.2005.69.4.559
Réville, André, with Charles Petit-Dutaillis. 1898. *Le soulèvement des travailleurs d'Angleterre en 1381*. Paris: A. Picard et fils.

Ribner, Irving. 2005 [1957]. *The English History Play in the Age of Shakespeare*. London: Routledge.
Richards, Jeffrey. 2015. *The Golden Age of Pantomime: Slapstick, Spectacle and Subversion in Victorian England*. London: I.B. Tauris. https://doi.org/10.5040/9780755623723
Richardson, Megan. 2017. *The Right to Privacy: Origins and Influence of a Nineteenth-Century Idea*. Cambridge: Cambridge University Press. https://doi.org/10.1017/9781108303972
Ridley, Ronald T. 1996. 'The Forgotten Historian: Laurence Echard and the First History of the Roman Republic.' *Ancient Society* 27: 277–315. https://doi.org/10.2143/AS.27.0.632406
Ridley, R. T. 2006. 'Echard, Laurence (bap. 1672, d. 1730).' *ODNB*.
Riley, H. T., ed. 1863–1864. *Thomae Walsingham, quondam monachi S. Albani, historia Anglicana: Vols. I–II*. London: Longman, Green, Longman, Roberts, and Green.
Robbins, Glyn. 2015. 'Remembering the Peasants' Revolt.' *Housing Matters* (16 July). Accessed 30 January 2021. https://glynrobbins.wordpress.com/2015/07/16/remembering-the-peasants-revolt/
Roberts, Helen E. 1995. 'Commemorating William Morris: Robin Page Arnot and the Early History of the William Morris Society.' *Journal of William Morris Studies* 11 (2): 33–37.
Roberts, Matthew. 2020. *Chartism, Commemoration and the Cult of the Radical Hero*. New York: Routledge. https://doi.org/10.4324/9780429198106
Roberts, R. Julian. 2004. 'James, Thomas (1572/3–1629).' *ODNB*.
Roberts, Stephen. 1987. 'Thomas Cooper in Leicester, 1840–1843.' *Transactions of the Leicestershire Archaeological and Historical Society* 61: 62–76.
Roberts, Stephen. 1990. 'The Later Radical Career of Thomas Cooper c.1845–1855.' *Transactions of the Leicestershire Archaeological and Historical Society* 64: 62–72.
Roberts, Stephen 2008. *The Chartist Prisoners: The Radical Lives of Thomas Cooper (1805–1892) and Arthur O'Neill (1819–1896)*. Oxford: Peter Lang.
Roberts, Stephen. 2009. 'Cooper, Thomas (1805–1892).' *ODNB*.
Robinson, Andrew. 1994. 'Thaxted: Conrad Noel and Now.' *Anglican and Episcopal History* 63 (2): 285–89.
Rocker, Rudolf. 2005 [1956]. *The London Years*. Nottingham: Five Leaves.
Rofheart, Martha. 1973. *Cry 'God for Glendower.'* London: Talmy.
Rogers, James E. Thorold. 1884. *Six Centuries of Work and Wages: The History of English Labour*. New York: G. P. Putnam's Sons.
Rogers, P. G. 1963. *The Sixth Trumpeter: The Story of Jezreel and His Tower*. London: Oxford University Press.
Rosen, Adrienne. 2008. 'Trussell, John (bap. 1575, d. 1648).' *ODNB*.
Rosenfeld, Sybil. 1960. *The Theatre of the London Fairs in the 18th Century*. Cambridge: Cambridge University Press.

Royal, Susan. 2014. 'John Foxe's "Acts and Monuments" and the Lollard Legacy in the Long English Reformation.' PhD thesis, Durham University. Durham E-Theses Online: http://etheses.dur.ac.uk/10624/
Royal, Susan. 2017. 'English Catholics and English Heretics: The Lollards and Anti-Heresy Writing in Early Modern England.' In *Early Modern English Catholicism: Identity, Memory and Counter-Reformation*, edited by James E. Kelly and Susan Royal, 122–41. Leiden: Brill. https://doi.org/10.1163/9789004325678_008
Rubinstein, David, ed. 1969. *People for the People*. London: Ithaca.
Ruddick, Andrea. 2013. *English Identity and Political Culture in the Fourteenth Century*. Cambridge: Cambridge University Press. https://doi.org/10.1017/CBO9781139047647
Rudolph, Julia. 2002. *Revolution by Degrees: James Tyrrell and Whig Political Thought in the Late Seventeenth Century*. New York: Palgrave Macmillan.
Rudolph, Lloyd. 1959. 'The Eighteenth-Century Mob in America and Europe.' *American Quarterly* 11 (4): 447–69. https://doi.org/10.2307/2710309
Russel, William Augustus. 1777–1779. *A New and Authentic History of England from the Most Remote Period of Genuine Historical Evidence, to the Present Important Crisis*. London.
Sabl, Andrew. 2017. *Hume's Politics: Coordination and Crisis in the* History of England. Princeton, NJ: Princeton University Press.
Sainsbury, John. 2006. *John Wilkes: The Lives of a Libertine*. Aldershot: Ashgate.
Salmon, Nicholas. 2001. 'A Reassessment of *A Dream of John Ball*.' *Journal of the William Morris Society* 14 (2): 29–38.
Samuel, Raphael. 1980. 'British Marxist Historians, 1880–1980: Part One.' *New Left Review* 120 (March/April): 21–96.
Samuel, Raphael. 2006. *The Lost World of British Communism*. London: Verso.
Sanders, Mike. 2009. *The Poetry of Chartism: Aesthetics, Politics, History*. Cambridge: Cambridge University Press. https://doi.org/10.1017/CBO9780511576195
Schillinger, Stephen. 2008. 'Begging at the Gate: "Jack Straw" and the Acting Out of Popular Rebellion.' *Medieval & Renaissance Drama in England* 21: 87–127.
Schwarz, Bill. 1982. '"The People" in History: The Communist Party Historians Group 1946–56.' In *Making Histories: Studies in History Writing and Politics*, edited by Richard Johnson, Gregor McLennan, Bill Schwartz, and David Sutton, 44–95. London: Hutchinson.
Scriven, Tom. 2020. 'William Cuffay: The Chartists' Black Leader.' *Tribune* (4 July).
Seregina, Anna. 2011. 'Religious Controversies and History Writing in Sixteenth-Century England.' *The Medieval Chronicle* VII: 223–38. https://doi.org/10.1163/9789401200417_013
Seton, Anya. 1954. *Katherine*. London: Hodder and Stoughton.
Shaw, Charles. 1977 [1903]. *When I Was a Child*. Firle: Caliban Books.
Shepherd, Simon. 1977. 'An Interview with Steve Gooch.' *Renaissance and Modern Studies* 21 (1): 5–36. https://doi.org/10.1080/14735787709366410
Shirley, Walter Waddington, ed. 1858. *Fasciculi Zizaniorum magistri Johannis Wyclif cum Tritico*. Rolls Series. London: Longman.

Shoemaker, Robert. 2004. *The London Mob: Violence and Disorder in Eighteenth-Century England*. London: Bloomsbury.
Shoemaker, Stephen J. 2015. 'The *Tiburtine Sibyl*, the Last Emperor, and the Early Byzantine Apocalyptic Tradition'. In *Forbidden Texts on the Western Frontier: The Christian Apocrypha from North American Perspectives*, edited by Tony Burke, 218–44. Eugene, OR: Wipf and Stock. https://doi.org/10.2307/j.ctvz0hc01.20
Siegfried, Matthew. 2015. 'Paul Foot Speaks! The Peasant's [sic] Revolt of 1381'. *YouTube* (23 May). Accessed 30 January 2021. https://www.youtube.com/watch?v=JvEGNnL5IZo
Silver, Carole. 1981. *The Romance of William Morris*. Athens, OH: University of Ohio Press.
Simms, Norman. 1974. 'Nero and Jack Straw in Chaucer's *Nun's Priest's Tale*'. *Parergon* 8 (April): 2–12.
Simpson, James, and Sarah Peverley, eds. 2015. *John Hardyng, Chronicle: Edited from British Library MS Lansdowne 204. Volume 1*. Kalamazoo, MI: Medieval Institute Publications.
Simpson, James, and Sarah Peverley, eds. Forthcoming. *John Hardyng, Chronicle: Edited from British Library MS Lansdowne 204. Volume 2*. Kalamazoo, MI: Medieval Institute Publications.
Skinner, Dennis. 2014. *Sailing Close to the Wind: Reminiscences*. London: Quercus.
Skinner, S. A. 2004. 'Heygate, William Edward'. *ODNB*.
Slater, Graeme. 1992. 'Hume's Revisions of the "History of England."' *Studies in Bibliography* 45: 130–57.
Smith, Nigel. 1994. *Literature and Revolution in England, 1640–1660*. New Haven: Yale University Press.
Smith, Robert Frederick William. 2013. 'John Trussell: A Life (1575–1648)'. PhD Thesis: University of Southampton.
Smollett, Tobias. 1758. *A Complete History of England, from the Descent of Julius Caesar, to the Treaty of Aix la Chapelle, 1748*. Third edition. London.
Smollett, Tobias. 2014. *Poems, Plays, and 'The Briton'*. Edited by Byron Gassman, O. M. Brack, Leslie A. Chilton. Athens: University of Georgia Press.
Solomon, Harry M. 1996. *The Rise of Robert Dodsley: Creating the New Age of Print*. Carbondale: Southern Illinois University Press.
Sousa, Geraldo U de. 1996. 'The Peasants' Revolt and the Writing of History in *2 Henry VI*'. In *Reading and Writing in Shakespeare*, edited by David M. Bergeron, 178–93. Newark: University of Delaware Press.
Southey, Robert. 1817. *A Letter to William Smith, Esq., M.P.* London.
Southey, Robert. 1817. *Wat Tyler*. London.
Speck, W. A. 2006. *Robert Southey: Entire Man of Letters*. New Haven: Yale University Press.
Speck, W. A. 2013. *A Political Biography of Thomas Paine*. London: Routledge.
Spencer, George William, assisted by Hugh Fitzwilliam, Alex Douglas, and other Gentlemen, who have for many Years made the History of this Country their

peculiar Study. 1794. *A New, Authentic, and Complete History of England, from the First Settlement of Brutus in this Island to the Year 1795*. London.
Spencer, Mark G., ed. 2013. *David Hume: Historical Thinker, Historical Writer*. University Park: Pennsylvania State University Press.
St Clair, William. 2004. *The Reading Nation in the Romantic Period*. Cambridge: Cambridge University Press.
Stephan, Deborah. 1989. 'Laurence Echard—Whig Historian.' *Historical Journal* 32 (4): 843–66. https://doi.org/10.1017/S0018246X00015739
Stevenson, Graham. 2008. 'Fagan, Hymie.' *Encyclopedia of Communist Biographies*. Accessed 30 January 2021. https://grahamstevenson.me.uk/2008/09/19/hymie-fagan/
Stevenson, Graham. 2008. 'Poulsen, Charles.' *Encyclopedia of Communist Biographies*. Accessed 30 January 2021. https://grahamstevenson.me.uk/2008/09/20/charles-poulsen/
Stiebert, Donald T. 2016. 'Hume's History of England.' In *The Oxford Handbook of Hume*, edited by Paul Russell, 546–68. Oxford: Oxford University Press.
Stirling, Brents. 1949. *The Populace in Shakespeare*. New York: Columbia University Press. https://doi.org/10.7312/stir93976
Stockton, Eric W., ed. 1962. *The Major Latin Works of John Gower: The Voice of One Crying, and The Tripartite Chronicle*. Seattle: University of Washington Press.
Stoker, Richard. 2013. 'Bush, Alan Dudley (1900–1995).' *ODNB*.
Storey, Mark. 1997. *Robert Southey: A Life*. Oxford: Oxford University Press.
Stow Jr, George B. 1977. *Historia Vitae et Regni Ricardi Secundi*. Philadelphia: University of Pennsylvania Press. https://doi.org/10.9783/9781512807318-004
Stow, John. 1600 [1592]. *The Annales of England, faithfully collected out of the most autenticall Authors, Records, and other Monuments of Antiquite, from the first inhabitacion vntill this present yeere 1600 [1592]*. London.
Stow, John. 2003 [1565]. *A summarie of Englyshe chronicles conteynyng the true accompt of yeres, wherein euery kyng of this realme of England began theyr reigne, howe long they reigned: and what notable thynges hath bene doone durynge theyr reygnes. Wyth also the names and yeares of all the baylyffes, custos, maiors, and sheriffes of the citie of London, sens the Conqueste, dyligentely collected by Iohn Stovv citisen of London, in the yere of our Lorde God 1565. Whervnto is added a table in the end, conteynyng all the principall matters of this booke. Perused and allowed accordyng to the Quenes maiesties iniunctions*. Ann Arbor, MI: Text Creation Partnership. http://name.umdl.umich.edu/A13030.0001.001
Stow, John. 2009 [1566]. *The summarie of English chronicles (lately collected and published) nowe abridged and continued tyl this present moneth of Marche, in the yere of our Lord God. 1566*. Ann Arbor, MI: Text Creation Partnership. http://name.umdl.umich.edu/A73271.0001.001
Stow, John. 2009 [1580]. *The chronicles of England from Brute vnto this present yeare of Christ. 1580. Collected by Iohn Stow citizen of London*. Ann Arbor, MI: Text Creation Partnership. http://name.umdl.umich.edu/A13043.0001.001
Stow, John. 2009 [1618]. *The abridgement of the English Chronicle, first collected by M. Iohn Stow, and after him augmented with very many memorable antiquities,*

and continued with matters forreine and domesticall, vnto the beginning of the yeare, 1618, by E.H. Gentleman. There is a briefe table at the end of the booke. Ann Arbor, MI: Text Creation Partnership. http://name.umdl.umich.edu/A13042.0001.001

Stretton, Hugh. 1978. 'Christopher Hill: Some Reminiscences.' In *Puritans and Revolutionaries: Essays in Seventeenth-Century History Presented to Christopher Hill*, edited by Donald H. Pennington and Keith Thomas, 10–17. Oxford: Oxford University Press.

Strohm, Paul. 1992. *Hochon's Arrow: The Social Imagination of Fourteenth Century Texts*. Princeton: Princeton University Press. https://doi.org/10.1515/9781400863051

Strohm, Paul. 2008. 'A "Peasants' Revolt"?' In *Misconceptions about the Middle Ages*, edited by Stephen J. Harris and Bryon Lee Grigsby, 197–203. New York: Routledge.

Stubbs, William. 1875. *The Constitutional History of England in Its Origin and Development, Vol. II*. Oxford: Clarendon Press.

Sucksmith, Harvey P. 1975. 'Sir Leicester Dedlock, Wat Tyler, and the Chartists: The Role of the Iron-Master in Bleak House.' *Dickens Studies Annual* 4: 113–31.

Suderman, Jeffrey M. 2013. 'Medieval Kingship and the Making of Modern Civility: Hume's Assessment of Governance in *The History of England*.' In *David Hume: Historical Thinker, Historical Writer*, edited by Mark G. Spencer, 121–42. University Park: Pennsylvania State University Press. https://doi.org/10.5325/j.ctt32b9wf.11

Sullivan, M. G. 2002. 'Rapin, Hume and the Identity of the Historian in Eighteenth-century England.' *History of European Ideas* 28 (3): 145–62. https://doi.org/10.1016/S0191-6599(02)00024-4

Summerson, Henry. 2013. 'Sources: 1577.' In *The Oxford Handbook of Holinshed's Chronicles*, edited by Ian W. Archer, Felicity Heal, and Paula Kewes, 61–76. Oxford: Oxford University Press.

Summerson, Henry. 2013. 'Sources: 1587.' In *The Oxford Handbook of Holinshed's Chronicles*, edited by Ian W. Archer, Felicity Heal, and Paula Kewes, 77–92. Oxford: Oxford University Press.

Sussman, Herbert. 1995. *Victorian Masculinities: Manhood and Masculine Poetics in Early Victorian Literature and Art*. Cambridge: Cambridge University Press. https://doi.org/10.1093/english/44.180.272

Sutton, Dana F. 2010. *Polydore Vergil, Anglica Historia (1555 version): A Hypertext Critical Edition by Dana F. Sutton*. Birmingham: The Philological Museum. http://www.philological.bham.ac.uk/polverg/

Swenson, Astrid. 2008. 'Founders of the National Trust.' *ODNB*.

Taylor, Antony. 2012. *London's Burning: Pulp Fiction, the Politics of Terrorism and the Destruction of the Capital in British Popular Culture, 1840–2005*. London: Bloomsbury.

Taylor, Antony. 2018. '"The Pioneers of the Great Army of Democrats": The Mythology and Popular History of the British Labour Party, 1890–1931.' *Historical Research* 91 (254): 723–43. https://doi.org/10.1111/1468-2281.12235

Taylor, Ben J. 2014. 'Reflections on the Revolution in England: Edmund Burke's Uses of 1688.' *History of Political Thought* 35 (1): 91–120.
Taylor, George. 2000. *The French Revolution and the London Stage, 1789–1805.* Cambridge: Cambridge University Press. https://doi.org/10.1017/CBO9781139175968
Taylor, John, ed. 1952. *The Kirkstall Abbey Chronicles.* Leeds: Thoresby Society.
Taylor, John, Wendy R. Childs, and Leslie Watkiss, eds. 2003. *The St Albans Chronicle: The Chronica maiora of Thomas Walsingham: Volume I 1376–1394.* Oxford: Oxford University Press.
Taylor, Miles. 1995. *The Decline of British Radicalism, 1847–1860.* Oxford: Oxford University Press. https://doi.org/10.1093/acprof:oso/9780198204824.001.0001
Thelwall, John. 1793. *The Peripatetic; or, Sketches of the Heart, of Nature and Society; in a Series of Politico-Sentimental Journals, in Verse and Prose, of the Eccentric Excursions of Sylvanus Theophrastus Supposed to be Written by Himself.* London.
Thomas, Merrilyn. 2017. 'Paul Oestreicher—an inspirational peace campaigner.' *Merrilyn Thomas* (2 December). Accessed 30 January 2021. https://merrilynthomas.com/paul-oestreicher-inspirational-peace-campaigner/
Thomas, Peter D. G. 2008. 'Wilkes, John (1725–1797). *ODNB.*
Thompson, Dorothy. 1984. *The Chartists: Popular Politics in the Industrial Revolution.* New York: Pantheon Books.
Thompson, E. P. 1977 [1955]. *William Morris: Romantic to Revolutionary.* New York: Pantheon Books.
Thompson, E. P. 1963. *The Making of the English Working Class.* London: Penguin.
Thompson, Willie. 2017. 'From Communist Party Historians' Group to Socialist History Society, 1946–2017.' *History Workshop* (10 April). Accessed 30 January 2021. https://www.historyworkshop.org.uk/from-communist-party-historians-group-to-socialist-history-society-1946-2017/
'Tony Benn, Allan Boesak & Squeeze commemorate Peasants Revolt on Blackheath 1981.' 2016. *Transpontine* (31 July). Accessed 30 January 2021. http://transpont.blogspot.com/2016/07/tony-benn-allan-boesak-squeeze.html
Tooley, Sarah A. 2005. 'A Living Wage for Women: An Interview with William Morris from *The Women's Signal* (19 April 1894).' In *We Met Morris: Interviews with William Morris, 1885–96,* edited by Tony Pinkney, 89–95. Reading: SpireBooks.
Torr, Dona. 1956. *Tom Mann and His Times: Volume One (1856–1890).* London: Lawrence and Wishart.
Toscano, Alberto. 2010. *Fanaticism: On the Uses of an Idea.* London: Verso.
Tosh, John. 2005. *Manliness and Masculinities in Nineteenth Century Britain: Essays on Gender, Family and Empire.* Harlow: Pearson Education.
Tosh, John. 2005. 'Masculinities in an Industrializing Society: Britain, 1800–1914.' *Journal of British Studies* 44 (2): 330–42. https://doi.org/10.1086/427129
Trevelyan, George Macaulay. 1899. *England in the Age of Wycliffe.* London: Longmans, Green, and Co.

Trevor-Roper, Hugh. 1987. 'A Huguenot Historian: Paul Rapin.' In *Huguenots in Britain and their French Background, 1550–1800*, edited by Irene Scouloudi, 3–19. London: Macmillan. https://doi.org/10.1007/978-1-349-08176-9_1

Trevor-Roper, Hugh. 1993. *From Counter Reformation to Glorious Revolution*. London: Pimlico.

The Trial of James Watson: For High Treason, at the Bar of the Court of King's Bench: Volume 1. 1817. London.

The Trial of James Watson: For High Treason, at the Bar of the Court of King's Bench: Volume 2. 1817. London.

Trussell, John. 1636. *A Continuation of the Collection of the History of England beginning where Samuel Daniell Esquire ended, with the raigne of Edward the third, and ending where the honourable Vicount Saint Albones began, with the life of Henry the seventh, being a compleat history of the begining and end of the dissention betwixt the two houses of Yorke and Lancaster. With the matches and issue of all the kings, princes, dukes, marquesses, earles, and vicounts of this nation, deceased, during those times*. London.

Tsuzuki, Chushichi. 1961. *H. M. Hyndman and British Socialism*. London: Oxford University Press.

Turnor, Christopher. 1911. *Land Problems and National Welfare*. London: John Lane.

Twysden, Roger, ed. 1652. *Historiae Anglicanae Scriptores X*. London.

Tyrrell, Henry. c. 1853. *A History of England for the Young, Vol. I*. London: London Printing and Publishing Company.

Tyrrell, James. 1694. *Bibliotheca Politica: Or an Enquiry into the Ancient Constitution of the English Government*. London.

Tyrrell, James. 1696. *The General History of England, as well Ecclesiastical as Civil. Vol. I*. London.

Tyrrell, James. 1704. *The General History of England, both Ecclesiastical and Civil. Vol. III*. London.

Valente, Claire. 2003. *The Theory and Practice of Revolt in Medieval England*. London: Routledge.

Vanden Bossche, Chris R. 2014. *Reform Acts: Chartism, Social Agency, and the Victorian Novel, 1832–1867*. Baltimore: Johns Hopkins University Press.

Vander Motten, J. P. 2011. 'Howard, Sir Robert (1626–1698).' *ODNB*.

Vaninskaya, Anna. 2009. 'Dreams of John Ball: Reading the Peasants' Revolt in the Nineteenth Century.' *Nineteenth-Century Contexts* 31 (1): 45–57. https://doi.org/10.1080/08905490902857426

Vaninskaya, Anna. 2010. *William Morris and the Idea of Community: Romance, History and Propaganda, 1880–1914*. Edinburgh: Edinburgh University Press. https://doi.org/10.3366/edinburgh/9780748641499.001.0001

Vaninskaya, Anna. 2013. '"A True Conception of History": "Making the Past Part of the Present" in Late-Victorian Historical Romances.' In *The Historical Imagination in Nineteenth Century Britain and the Low Countries*, edited by Hugh Dunthorne and Michael Wintle, 151–67. Brill: Leiden. https://doi.org/10.1163/9789004241862_009

Vargo, Gregory. 2011. 'A Life in Fragments: Thomas Cooper's Chartist *Bildungsroman*.' *Victorian Literature and Culture* 39 (1): 167–81. https://doi.org/10.1017/S106015031000032X

Vargo, Gregory. 2018. *An Underground History of Early Victorian Fiction: Chartism, Radical Print Culture, and the Social Problem Novel*. Cambridge: Cambridge University Press. https://doi.org/10.1017/9781108181891

Vargo, Gregory, ed. 2020. *Chartist Drama*. Manchester: Manchester University Press. https://doi.org/10.7765/9781526142078

Various Artists. 1981. *Lovely in the Dances: Songs of Sydney Carter*. Plant Life Records.

Vernon, E. C. 2013. 'Aston, Sir Thomas, first baronet (1600–1646)'. *ODNB*.

Vidmar, John. 1999. 'John Lingard's History of the English Reformation: History or Apologetics?' *Catholic Historical Review* 85 (3): 383–419. https://doi.org/10.1353/cat.1999.0193

Villiers, Brougham. 1908. *The Socialist Movement in England*. London: T. Fisher Unwin.

Vizetelly, Ernest Alfred. 1911. *The Anarchists: Their Faith and Their Record Including Sidelights on the Royal and Other Personages Who Have been Assassinated*. London: John Lane.

Waithe, Marcus. 2006. *William Morris's Utopia of Strangers: Victorian Medievalism and the Ideal of Hospitality*. Cambridge: D. S. Brewer.

Wallis, Mick. 1994. 'Pageantry and the Popular Front: Ideological Production in the Thirties'. *New Theatre Quarterly* 38 (May): 132–56. https://doi.org/10.1017/S0266464X00000300

Wallis, Mick. 1995. 'The Popular Front Pageant: Its Emergence and Decline'. *New Theatre Quarterly* 11 (41): 17–32. https://doi.org/10.1017/S0266464X00008848

Wallis, Mick. 1998. 'Heirs to the Pageant: Mass Spectacle and the Popular Front'. In *Weapon in the Struggle: The Cultural History of the Communist Party in Britain*, edited by Andy Croft, 48–67. London: Pluto.

Wallis, Patrick. 2004. 'Brady, Robert (c. 1627–1700)'. *ODNB*.

Walsham, Alexandra. 2010. 'History, Memory, and the English Reformation'. *The Historical Journal* 55 (4): 899–938. https://doi.org/10.1017/S0018246X12000362

Walter, John. 1999. *Understanding Popular Violence in the English Revolution: The Colchester Plunderers*. Cambridge: Cambridge University Press.

Walwyn, William [?]. 1649. *The English Souldiers Standard to repair to, for Wisdom and Understanding in these doleful backsliding times. To be read by every honest Officer to his Souldiers, and by the Souldiers one to another*. 5 April. London.

Ward, Paul. 1998. *Red Flag and Union Jack: Englishness, Patriotism, and the British Left, 1881–1924*. Woodbridge: Boydell Press.

Wat Tyler and Jack Straw, Or the Mob Reformers. A dramatick entertainment. As it is perform'd at Pinkentham's and Giffard's Great Theatrical Booth in Bartholomew Fair. 1730. London.

Watts, John. 2007. 'Public or Plebs: The Changing Meaning of "the Commons", 1381–1549'. In *Power and Identity in the Middle Ages: Essays in Memory of*

Rees Davies, edited by Huw Pryce and John Watts, 242–60. Oxford: Oxford University Press. https://doi.org/10.1093/acprof:oso/9780199285464.003.0018

Webb, Beatrice. 1982. *The Diary of Beatrice Webb, Volume One (1873–1892): Glitter Around and Darkness Within*. Edited by Norman and Jeanne MacKenzie. London: Virago Press.

Wei, Jia. 2017. *Commerce and Politics in Hume's History of England*. Woodbridge: Boydell & Brewer.

Weinroth, Michelle. 1996. *Reclaiming William Morris: Englishness, Sublimity, and the Rhetoric of Dissent*. Montreal: McGill-Queen's University Press.

Weinstein, Benjamin. 2002. 'Popular Constitutionalism and the London Corresponding Society.' *Albion* 34 (1): 37–57. https://doi.org/10.2307/4053440

West, Richard. 1981. *An English Journey*. London: Chatto & Windus.

Wheatley, Chloe. 2011. *Epic, Epitome, and the Early Modern Historical Imagination*. Farnham: Ashgate.

Wheatley, Kim. 1999. *Shelley and His Readers: Beyond Paranoid Politics*. Columbia: University of Missouri Press.

Wheatley, Kim. 2013. *Romantic Feuds: Transcending the 'Age of Personality.'* Aldershot: Ashgate.

White, Jonathan. 2021. *Making Our Own History: A User's Guide to Marx's Historical Materialism*. Glasgow: Praxis Press.

White, T. H. 1958. *Candle in the Wind*. London: Collins.

Whitlocke, Bulstrode. 1709. *Memorials of the English Affairs, from the suppos'd expedition of Brute to this island, to the end of the reign of King James the first*. London.

Wickham, Chris. 2002. 'Rodney Hilton.' *History Today* 52 (9): 6–7.

Wilkins, David. 1737. *Concilia Magnae Britanniae et Hiberniae: Volume III*. London.

Wilkins, W. G. 1907. *The Rise and Progress of Poverty in England from the Norman Conquest to Modern Times*. London: Headley Brothers.

Williams, Francis. 1949. *Fifty Years' March: The Rise of the Labour Party*. London: Odhams Press.

Williams, Heathcote. 2013. 'The Red Dagger: Wat Tyler, John Ball and Johanna Ferrour: The Peasants' Revolt and the City of London' Weapons of Mass Destruction, four parts.' *YouTube* (19 December). Accessed 30 January 2021. https://www.youtube.com/watch?v=SCAiqSRofGY&feature=youtu.be

Williams, Raymond. 1980. *Culture and Materialism: Selected Essays*. London: Verso.

Williams, Stephen. 2015. 'Morris, Christianity and Socialism: An Episode.' *Journal of William Morris Studies* 21 (3): 38–45.

Williams, Stephen. 2017. 'Radical Objects: The Peasants' Revolt Badge.' *History Workshop Journal* (19 April). Accessed 30 January 2021. https://www.history-workshop.org.uk/radical-objects-the-peasants-revolt-badge/

'Will Wat, If Not, What Will? (1972).' n.d. *Stages of Half Moon*. Accessed 30 January 2021. https://www.stagesofhalfmoon.org.uk/productions/will-wat-if-not-what-will-1972/

Wilson, Sean Michael. n.d. *Sean Michael Wilson: A Graphic Novel Writer from Scotland*. Accessed 30 January 2021. https://seanmichaelwilson.weebly.com/
Wilson, Sean Michael, and Robert Brown. 2019. *The Many Not the Few: An Illustrated History of Britain Shaped by the People*. Oxford: Workable Books.
Wilson, Zack. 2012. 'Steve Ely: Poet of Sunday Leagues and Sainted Rebellion.' *Lone Striker* (19 November). Accessed 30 January 2021. http://zackwilsonlonestriker.blogspot.com/2012/11/steve-ely.html
Winter, Trish, and Simon Keegan-Phipps. 2013. *Performing Englishness: Identity and Politics in a Contemporary Folk Resurgence*. Manchester: Manchester University Press.
Wohlcke, Anne. 2014. *The 'Perpetual Fair': Gender, Disorder and Urban Amusement in Eighteenth-Century London*. Manchester: Manchester University Press. https://doi.org/10.7228/manchester/9780719090912.001.0001
Woodger, Michele. n.d. 'Smithfield, EC1: Memorial to the Peasants' Revolt.' *Lettering in London*. https://letteringinlondon.com/portfolio/smithfield-001/
Woods, William. 1952. *Thunder on Saturday*. London: Andrew Melrose.
Woolf, Daniel R. 2000. *Reading History in Early Modern England*. Cambridge: Cambridge University Press.
Woodhams, Stephen. 2001. *History in the Making: Raymond Williams, E.P. Thompson, and Radical Intellectuals 1936–1956*. London: Merlin Press.
Wootton, David. 2008. 'David Hume: "The Historian."' In *The Cambridge Companion to Hume*, edited by David Fate Norton and Jacqueline Taylor, 447–47. Second edition. Cambridge: Cambridge University Press. https://doi.org/10.1017/CCOL9780521859868.014
Worrall, David. 2006. *Theatric Revolution: Drama, Censorship, and Romantic Period Subcultures 1773–1832*. Oxford: Oxford University Press.
Wright, Thomas, ed. 1859. *Political Poems and Songs Relating to English History*. Rolls Series. London: Longman, Green, Longman, and Robert.
Yates, Julian. 2011. 'Skin Merchants: Jack Cade's Futures and the Figural Politics of Shakespeare's *Henry VI Part II*.' In *Go Figure: Forms, Energy, Matter in Early Modern England*, edited by Judith Anderson and Joan Pong Linton, 149–69. New York: Fordham University Press. https://doi.org/10.5422/fordham/9780823233496.003.0009
Yeo, Eileen. 1982. 'Some Practices and Problems of Chartist Democracy.' In *The Chartist Experience: Studies in Working-Class Radicalism and Culture, 1830–1860*, edited by James Epstein and Dorothy Thompson, 345–80. London: Macmillan Press. https://doi.org/10.1007/978-1-349-16921-4_11
Yeo, Stephen. 1977. 'A New Life: The Religion of Socialism in Britain, 1883–1896.' *History Workshop* 4 (1): 5–56.
Yeo, Stephen. 2014. 'Socialism, the State and Some Oppositional Englishness.' In *Englishness, Politics and Culture, 1880–1920*, edited by Robert Colls and Philip Dodd, 331–88. Second edition. London: Bloomsbury. https://doi.org/10.1093/hwj/4.1.5
Yonge, Charlotte M. 1896. *The Wardship of Steepcoombe*. London: National Society.

Zealoushead, Zachary. 1817. *Plots and Placemen, or Green Bag Glory, an Historical Melo Drama, in Two Acts. As Performed at the Boroughmonger's Private Theatre*. London.

Žižek, Slavoj. n.d. 'Do We Still Live in a World?' Accessed 30 January 2021. http://www.lacan.com/zizrattlesnakeshake.html

Zook, Melinda S. 1999. *Radical Whigs and Conspiratorial Politics in Late Stuart England*. University Park, PA: Pennsylvania State University Press.

Zook, Melinda. 2018. 'Ferguson, Robert (d. 1714).' *ODNB*.

Subject Index

1 Edward IV (Thomas Heywood), 56
1381 (Christopher Beddow), 418
1688 Revolution, 87, 100, 101, 103, 104, 109, 114, 117–18, 120, 141, 142, 156, 164

'A Dialogue Between Two Zealots concerning the &c in the New Oath' (John Cleveland), 98
Abbreviation of Chronicles (John Capgrave), 49
Aberdeen, 319
abolitionism, 162, 182, 199, 216, 224–25, 354, 459, 460
Abridgement of the chronicles of England, An (Richard Grafton), 68
Abridgement of the English Chronicle, The (John Stow), 65n25
Act of Settlement (1701), 103
Actes and Monuments (John Foxe), 57–58
Acts of Union (1707), 104
Adam and Eve couplet, 1, 21–22, 31, 34, 41, 60–61, 66, 67, 72, 81, 83, 88, 91–93, 95, 99, 102, 107, 111, 113, 116, 119–20, 124, 128, 145, 150, 157, 159, 165, 169, 180, 186, 187, 189, 210–12, 219, 221n14, 223n22, 224, 226, 236, 242, 243, 250, 251, 256, 260, 261, 263, 283, 288, 305, 306, 314, 326–27, 328, 343, 345, 352, 371, 375, 376, 388, 389, 394, 402, 404–5, 410, 416–17, 418, 423, 431, 441, 448, 449, 457, 462
Admonition to the People of England (Thomas Cooper), 71–72
Alice of Fobbing (William Edward Heygate), 229, 230–32

'all things in common' (Acts 2.44–45; 4.32–35), 38–42, 43, 61, 62–63, 64, 75, 77–78, 81, 88, 102, 109, 144, 154, 167, 175, 237, 261, 263, 272, 273–74, 282, 292, 293, 306n41, 316–17, 329, 372, 377, 382, 409, 414–15, 417, 418, 425, 438, 443, 444, 445–46, 457, 464
American Revolution, 129, 132, 147, 148–49, 156, 158, 162, 460
Anabaptism, 56, 64, 75, 82, 84, 86, 85, 89, 92, 93, 96, 149, 175, 242, 246, 352, 459
anarchism, 40, 272, 309, 322, 325, 326, 330, 332, 365, 367, 382, 398–99, 400, 436–37, 455, 457, 459, 461
Anarchist Communist Federation, 436, 455
Ancient and Modern Liberty Stated and Compar'd (John Hervey), 123
Ancoats, 268
Anglicanism, 98, 112, 115, 189, 245, 248, 269, 339, 418, 423, 427
Anglo-Catholicism, 269, 270, 299
Anglo-Saxon. *See* Saxons
Annales of England, The (John Stow), 66–67
'Annals of an English Abbey' (James Anthony Froude), 244
Annals of Toil, The (J. Morrison Davidson), 322–23
Anonimalle Chronicle, 4–5, 8, 9, 10, 11, 20, 23, 24, 26–27, 29, 30, 38, 40n65, 43, 56, 67, 154n19, 376, 378
antichrist, 97, 235–36, 381, 395–96
Apartheid, 2, 405, 406, 426, 437
Apocalypse of Pseudo-Methodius, 24

512 *Spectres of John Ball*

apocalypticism, eschatology, millenarianism, 23–25, 33–41, 47, 56, 91, 98, 100, 193, 202–3, 205, 234, 264, 268, 273, 274–75, 285, 291–94, 311–16, 326, 351–52, 380–84, 392–98, 445, 452–53, 459, 460, 461. *See also* Ball, John; eschatology of socialism
Appeal from the New to the Old Whigs (Edmund Burke), 158–60
Arab Spring, 442–43
Arguments for Democracy (Tony Benn), 412–14, 415
Arguments for Socialism (Tony Benn), 411–12
Armorer, The (Richard Cumberland), 153–54

Baal's priest(s), 85–86, 96–100
Ball, John: anarchism and, 309, 322, 332, 365, 382, 457, 461; appearance, 190, 196–97, 218, 219, 227, 235, 283, 301, 302n20, 306, 323, 324, 325, 335–336, 359, 366, 373, 376, 403, 456, 451, 459–60; apocalyptic and millenarian teaching, 17, 23–31, 33–41, 100, 193, 268, 284–86, 291–93, 382–83, 459; asceticism, 195 n73, 219, 227, 235, 235, 452, 459; 'bastards' saying, 30–33, 37, 42, 97, 254; Blackheath sermon, 18, 21–22, 25, 35–37, 60, 66, 67, 88, 99, 102, 107, 111, 112, 113, 116, 139, 169, 189, 209, 210, 211, 212, 222n20, 224, 235, 242, 257, 260n75, 263, 312, 327, 373, 405, 409, 439, 448, 452, 457; as Catholic, 114, 119, 121, 190, 294–97, 311, 312, 328, 371, 377, 413, 433, 452, 459; communism and, 2, 34n 54, 40n 65, 242–44, 260–61, 263, 282–97, 286, 298–300, 301, 302, 314–15, 323, 332–34, 337, 343–44, 345, 346–48, 349, 350, 352–60, 361, 362, 362–64, 365–67, 371–72, 373–74, 376–77, 387–89, 392, 394–95, 398, 401, 404–5, 422–24, 437, 438, 451, 456–58, 459, 461, 463; confusion with John Bull, 137, 138, 139, 140, 301, 345, 418; constitution, relationship to, 2, 107, 111, 113, 117, 120, 124, 128, 129, 135, 136, 150–51, 159–60, 165–67, 170, 185–86, 204, 207, 208–13, 214–15, 241, 246, 249, 253, 255, 335, 347, 353, 369, 389, 459, 460; death of, 11–12, 14, 17, 18, 44, 46, 57–58, 62, 66, 70, 103, 110, 112, 137, 149, 150, 152, 193, 196, 197, 204–5, 209, 226, 241, 257, 282, 284, 285, 364, 374, 377, 407, 429, 433, 438, 441; Dick Turpin comparison, 337–38; heretic, 2, 17, 20, 37, 42, 43, 46–47, 83–84, 85, 86, 92, 168, 172, 189, 235, 239, 241, 244, 334, 438, 459, 460; historical reconstruction of his life and ideas, 1–2, 12, 13–42, 462; imprisonments, 18–19, 21, 41, 43, 46, 57, 60, 67, 69, 70, 98–99, 102, 112, 113, 114, 116, 119, 121, 127, 133, 168, 170, 189, 191, 192, 209, 210, 225, 232, 235, 247–48, 254, 257, 259, 261, 283, 292, 309, 336, 342–43, 360, 366, 369, 373, 398, 433, 434; 'John Wall' confusion, 53–54, 57, 65, 69, 70, 72, 73, 88–89, 91–92, 93n 17, 96, 97, 98, 100, 112, 133; letters of, 13–14, 22–23, 30, 33n52, 34, 35, 36, 40n63, 43, 45, 51, 61, 66, 67, 95, 97, 103, 110, 128, 132, 138–39, 228, 231–32, 234, 248n25, 251–52, 253–54, 256, 259, 261, 282–83, 320–21, 342, 355, 360, 369, 373, 376, 382, 423; martyr, 57–58, 62, 66, 70, 74, 86, 171, 173, 193, 205, 237, 241, 267, 268, 284, 285, 291n60, 294, 301–302, 310, 316, 330, 334–35, 339, 351, 361, 369–70, 372, 374, 438–39, 445–46, 459, 460; masculinity, 196–97, 219, 266, 289–90, 302n20, 325; mystic, seer, visionary, etc., 227, 262, 268, 285, 291, 293, 294, 329, 342–43, 360, 395, 451, 452, 459; orator, 95, 103, 110, 128, 132, 137, 139, 210–11, 236, 238, 248n25, 284, 302, 310n56, 312, 315, 321, 323, 324n106, 325, 336n27, 338, 342, 348, 373, 374, 375, 376, 403n7,

449–50, 451, 459; political and social reformer, 2, 40n65, 137, 140, 144, 145, 165–66, 180–81, 184, 186, 191–97, 198, 199, 202–3, 206, 208–13, 220–23, 237 239, 240, 241–42, 250, 251–52, 253, 255, 256, 259, 261, 262–63, 266, 267, 301, 304, 307, 310, 311, 317–18, 320–23, 327, 329–30, 334, 336, 337, 338, 369–70, 401, 404–6, 417, 418, 425, 430, 432, 433–34, 438–39, 441, 442, 447–48, 455–57, 459, 460, 461, 462, 463–64; popular preaching and itinerant mission, 16, 17–18, 19, 20, 41, 45–46, 60, 80n 15, 107, 112, 151, 189, 192, 228, 232, 245n20, 251, 257, 262, 341–42, 376n59, 403n7, 422; potential bishop/archbishop of England, 11, 20, 21, 22, 30, 31, 40, 41, 43–44, 45, 61, 66, 67, 81, 149n 11, 154, 171, 189, 226, 235, 357, 428; prophet 17, 20, 34n54, 35, 44, 47, 60, 67, 83–84, 98–99, 170, 192, 196, 235, 247, 262–63, 284, 285, 293, 312, 314, 316, 321, 239, 333, 342–43, 347, 348, 375, 376, 382–83, 403n7, 426, 440, 452; Protestant, 2, 55, 58, 62, 74, 84, 86, 89, 92, 112, 219, 239, 241, 255, 259, 296–97, 311, 317, 323, 327, 334, 369, 374, 377, 397, 398, 413–14, 433, 452, 459, 460, 461; revolutionary associations, 2, 20–42, 86, 92–94, 96, 98–100, 147, 149–50, 152, 158–60, 168–73, 175, 180–81, 182, 194–95, 198, 224–25, 230, 231, 232, 234, 237, 242, 243n12, 244–45, 247n24, 250, 251, 253, 255, 257, 259, 260, 261, 264, 266, 279–80, 282–97, 301, 312, 313, 314, 315, 316, 317, 318–22, 324–25, 326, 332–34, 338, 340, 341, 343, 345, 347–48, 350, 352–60, 362–63, 365–67, 371–73, 374–75, 380, 382–83, 384–85, 387–89, 391, 392, 394–95, 410–11, 412, 413, 414, 420, 422–24, 426–28, 434, 437–38, 441, 447, 449, 451–54, 455–58, 459, 460, 461, 463; seditious, 2, 19, 42, 43–47, 51, 53–54, 55, 57, 58, 60–68, 69–73, 74–86, 87, 88–89, 90–94, 95, 96–100, 102–3, 104, 107–8, 110–12, 113, 114, 116–17, 119–21, 126, 127–28, 129, 130–33, 134–35, 137–40, 144, 145, 150–53, 154, 159–60, 165, 168, 172, 173n23, 178, 182, 189, 226–28, 229, 231–34, 237, 238, 243, 255–56, 345–46, 388, 411, 419, 438, 447, 451–53, 459, 460, 461; socialism and, 2, 242–44, 246, 247, 250, 251, 254, 264, 266, 267, 268, 273, 275–76, 282–97, 298–304, 305, 307, 308, 309–11, 312, 315, 316–17, 318–24, 326, 327, 329, 330, 331, 333–34, 337, 338–39, 341–42, 343, 346, 352, 361, 362–64, 365–67, 372, 375, 376, 377, 380, 397, 398, 401, 405, 411, 412–15, 417, 419, 422–24, 428, 437–39, 443, 445, 447–450, 456–58, 459, 460, 461, 462, 463, 464; taste for the drink 77, 79, 86, 134, 135, 136, 154, 459; tithing saying 31, 41, 67, 112, 192, 254, 257, 293; traitor 18, 44, 83–84, 88, 91–92; violence and non-violence, questions of, 16, 21, 25, 27, 31, 33–37, 42, 43, 70, 71, 76, 82, 91, 99, 120, 124, 127, 136, 138, 145, 147, 166, 171, 192–94, 196–97, 198, 202, 203–4, 209, 211, 225, 228–29, 232, 233n22, 241, 245n20, 248, 255–56, 257, 266, 267, 294, 317, 322, 325–26, 329, 335, 343, 346, 362, 383, 411, 429, 430, 434, 442, 443, 446, 447–58, 459, 460, 461, 462, 463; Wycliffe and Lollardy, relationship to, 31–33, 37, 39–40, 42, 43, 45, 46–47, 52, 56, 57, 58, 61–62, 64, 75, 84–85, 86, 88, 102, 107, 109, 112, 114, 115, 121, 125–26, 127, 189, 213, 219, 221, 228–29, 231, 235, 237, 239, 241, 242, 244, 245–46, 247n24, 251, 253, 254, 245n20, 255, 257, 259, 260, 261, 262, 263n89, 264, 296, 298, 300, 311, 314, 317, 318, 321, 323, 324–25, 327, 328, 334, 352,

353, 356, 357, 361, 365, 374–75, 382, 395, 397–98, 404, 407, 412–13, 417, 422, 433, 434, 448, 450, 452, 459, 460, 462. *See also* Adam and Eve couplet
Banner of Saint George, The (Mary Bramston), 324, 325–26
BBC, 377, 378, 379, 437, 449, 450, 451
beer, 77, 79, 343
Berwick-upon-Tweed, 224
Bible, 2, 3, 17, 19–20, 21–23, 25, 29, 30–32, 34, 35–37, 38–41, 56, 60–61, 68, 71, 72, 77, 81, 82–83, 91–92, 94–100, 111, 122–24, 133, 134, 144, 145, 157, 169, 170–72, 178–79, 186, 187, 189, 193–94, 205, 210, 211, 219, 221n14, 224, 235–36, 239, 241, 243, 247, 262–63, 274–75, 284, 288–90, 291–94, 305, 306, 314, 326, 338, 340, 343, 345, 370, 371, 375, 376, 388, 389, 394, 395, 402, 404–5, 409–410, 412–15, 416–17, 418, 423, 426, 428, 431, 440, 441, 443, 445–46, 452–53, 457, 460, 462. *See also* Adam and Eve couplet; 'all things in common'; Parable of the Wheat and the Tares; Vulgate; and individual biblical characters in the Name Index
Bibliotheca Politica (James Tyrrell), 109
Birmingham, 207, 379, 386, 392, 399
Bishop's Stortford, 18, 21
Black Death, 6–7, 250, 313, 315, 328, 358, 368, 390, 407, 420, 443, 457, 460
Blackheath, 7, 18, 21, 22, 25, 28, 29, 35, 60, 90, 95, 102, 106, 107, 111, 112, 113, 117, 124, 143, 149n11, 154, 169, 189, 192, 210, 211, 212, 213, 224, 235, 241, 242, 257, 312, 327, 339, 373, 405, 408, 409, 416, 423, 425–29, 439, 448, 452
Blanketeers, 183–84, 185, 354
Bocking, 19
Bolsheviks, 345–47, 357, 358, 360, 380, 437
Bond Men Made Free (Rodney Hilton), 386, 392–93, 395–98, 400
Bondman, The (Mrs O'Neill), 190–98

Boston (Lincolnshire), 242
Bradford, 200
brandy, 134
Brexit, 432, 458
Brighouse, 242
British National Party (BNP), 432
British Socialist Party (BSP), 327, 340
British Union of Fascists (BUF), 362
Brut, 48, 51, 65, 66
Buddhism, 281
Burnley, 351
Bury St Edmunds, 28, 120, 420

Cable Street, 358, 362, 417
Cambridge, 7, 10, 35, 44, 120, 256, 259–60, 340, 413, 420, 447
Cambridge Folk Festival, 413, 447
Campaign for Nuclear Disarmament (CND), 427, 437
Canterbury, 8, 14, 18, 19, 23, 69, 154, 235, 236, 238, 269, 368, 370, 419, 420, 425, 428
Canterbury Cathedral Festival, 368–70
capitalism, 144, 151, 190, 227, 243, 263, 266, 270–71, 275, 276, 277, 285, 287, 290, 292–96, 309, 314, 315, 320, 330, 332, 333, 334, 341, 348, 352–54, 357, 372, 377, 381, 382, 384, 386, 388, 389–91, 393–94, 408, 421, 422, 427, 430–31, 454, 460, 462, 463
Captain Swing, 198, 456
carnivalesque, 29, 48, 74, 78, 136
Cassell's Illustrated History of England, 220–22, 228, 239
Catholic Crusade, 339, 340, 371, 372
Catholicism, 54, 56, 59, 61, 64, 68, 84–86, 87, 88, 90, 100, 103, 104, 109, 112, 114, 115, 119, 121, 125, 148, 187–89, 190, 204, 217, 229, 233, 234, 237, 238, 239, 260, 269, 294–97, 311, 312, 324, 328, 339, 340, 341–42, 371, 377, 380, 413, 425, 427, 433, 452, 459
Cato Street conspiracy, 184
Chapel of Blessed John Ball Priest and Martyr, Thaxted, 339, 371
Chartism, 2, 198, 199–217, 219, 220–21, 224, 226, 229, 239, 255, 263, 285,

Subject Index 515

286, 287, 310, 311, 337, 350, 352, 354, 364, 406, 412, 438–39, 443, 448, 456, 459, 463
Chatham, 215
Cheapside, 8
Chelmsford, 335
Child's History of England (Charles Dickens), 222–23
Christian Socialism, 252, 270, 322, 339, 364, 372
Christianity, 20, 24, 25, 30, 33, 61n17, 68, 72, 88, 95, 102, 157, 167, 169n14, 171, 178–79, 196, 203, 207, 231, 232, 243, 260, 261, 262–63, 264, 269, 270, 273, 276–77, 279, 280, 281, 291, 292, 293, 295, 298, 299, 314, 315, 322–23, 356, 357, 364, 373, 394, 395, 397, 404, 413, 414, 419, 427–28, 429, 430–31, 433, 438, 440, 442, 445–46, 461
Chronica maiora (Thomas Walsingham), 4, 8, 11, 12, 13, 14, 18, 19, 20, 21–22, 24, 25–26, 27, 28, 29n44, 30, 31, 35, 36–37, 41, 43, 62, 205, 232, 450
Chronicle (Adam Usk), 49
Chronicle (Henry Knighton), 4, 7, 8, 9, 13, 18–19, 20, 21, 26, 27, 32–33, 35, 36n58, 37, 40–41, 43, 205
Chronicle at large (Richard Grafton), 52, 68–70
Chronicle of Iohn Hardyng, The (John Hardyng), 49–50
Chronicle of the Kings of England, A (Richard Baker), 94–95, 97, 122
Chronicle of the Kings of England Written in the Manner of the Ancient Jewish Historians, The ('Nathan ben Saddi, a Priest of the Jews'), 122–24
Chronicles of England, The (John Stow), 66–67
Chronicles of England, Scotland, and Ireland (Raphael Holinshed), 59–64
Chroniques (Jean Froissart), 4, 5–6, 8, 18–19, 20, 23, 26, 27, 28, 29, 38, 40n65, 43, 154n19
Church of the Ascension, Blackheath, 405, 416, 421

Church of England, 125, 187n40, 233, 237, 340–41, 405, 425. *See also* Anglicanism
Cistercians, 193
Class War, 436, 455
Class War, The (James Leatham), 319–20
Clerkenwell, 8, 11, 366
Clitheroe, 206
Colchester, 14–16, 41, 248n25, 254, 358, 418, 423, 437, 439, 440–42; John Ball plaque 441–42. *See also* Bird, Brian
Cold War, 2, 361, 363, 367, 368, 375, 378, 379, 380, 384, 385, 392, 404–5, 461, 463
Collection of the history of England, The (Samuel Daniel, continuation by John Trussell), 87–89
Common Sense (Thomas Paine), 156–58
communism, 2, 34n54, 40n65, 242–44, 260–61, 263, 264, 267, 273–75, 278, 279, 286, 288–89, 294, 298, 299, 300, 314–15, 318, 322, 323, 334, 343–44, 345, 346, 347–48, 352–54, 356, 364, 365, 366, 372, 373, 377, 378, 379, 380–82, 392, 393, 394, 395, 397, 401, 404, 427, 437, 459, 461, 463. *See also* Marxism; socialism
Communist, The, 333, 347–48
Communist Party of Britain (CPB), 458
Communist Party of Great Britain (CPGB), 330, 333, 344, 347–54, 355, 356, 357, 359, 362, 365, 367, 368, 372, 375, 379, 386–87, 392, 399, 400, 416, 421, 423, 424–25, 438, 455, 460, 463
Communist Party Historians' Group, 361, 387–89, 390, 391, 392, 393–94, 396, 399, 400, 421
Complete History of Britain, A (Tobias Smollett), 137–39, 151
Complete History of England, A (John Hughes), 113–14
Complete History of England, A (White Kennett), 112–13
Congregationalism, 413
Conservative Party, 305, 308, 333–34, 363, 371, 447, 453. *See also* Tories, Toryism

constitution, constitutionalism, 2, 104, 105–9, 115–16, 118, 119, 121, 123, 125, 127, 138, 142, 143, 146, 147, 152, 155, 156, 157, 158, 162, 163–65, 166–67, 170, 176, 177, 178, 183, 207, 208, 214, 228, 245–46, 249, 253, 260, 265, 286, 315, 335, 346–47, 362, 369, 459, 460
Constitutional History of England in Its Origin and Development, The (William Stubbs), 245–46
Continuation of the Complete History of England, A (Robert Brady), 105–8
Continuatio Eulogii, 48–49
Corn Laws (1815), 175
Corpus Christi, 7, 22, 23, 36, 405, 452
Counterfire, 424n41, 458
Coventry, 11, 14, 46, 89, 114, 206, 226n35, 361, 402
Cronica tripertita (John Gower), 47n10, 50
Cry 'God for Glendower' (Martha Rofheart), 403n5
Culture Matters, 458
Cumberland, 122, 331

Daily Worker, 351, 352, 359, 363, 366, 437
Darlington, 206
Dartford, 23, 230, 375, 441
decapitation, 8, 9–10, 11, 18, 28, 43, 58, 61, 69, 70, 77, 98, 103, 111, 117, 133, 139, 143, 148, 171, 205, 209, 237, 242, 410, 430, 438, 446, 447, 448, 450, 456
democracy, 40n65, 87, 93, 142, 155, 178, 216, 221, 241–42, 247n24, 255, 258, 259, 261, 262–63, 265, 275, 299, 301, 316–17, 318, 323, 327, 333, 334, 335, 336, 346, 348, 351, 361, 362, 384, 392, 394, 406, 412, 414, 415, 434–35, 437, 440, 442–43, 448, 455, 456, 460, 463
Democratic Federation, 243, 264, 271, 272
demonic, devilish, 2, 34, 37, 45, 47, 49, 66, 83–86, 96, 97, 178n11, 236–37, 381, 383, 453, 460

Devil, the, 37, 47n10, 79, 96–97, 115, 157, 281, 293, 462. *See also* demonic, devilish; Lucifer
Dick Delver (Harriette E. Burch), 323
Diggers, 350, 354, 388, 448
Dominicans, 328, 371
Dream of John Ball, A (William Morris), 268, 269, 276–77, 280, 282–97, 300–319, 321, 322, 328, 329, 330–331, 332–33, 334, 349, 356, 365, 367, 371, 391–92, 405, 406, 422, 424, 440, 463; gendered roles in, 287–291
Dudley, 242
Dundee, 351
Durham, 206

East Anglia, 5, 89, 112, 114, 117, 120, 279, 305, 366
England in the Age of Wycliffe (George Macaulay Trevelyan), 259–63
England, My England (Jack Lindsay), 353–54
English Civil Wars. *See* English Revolution
English Defence League (EDL), 431
English Episode (Charles Poulsen), 362
English Folk Dance and Song Society (EFDSS), 434
English Revolution, 86, 87, 89–100, 118, 337, 391, 393–94, 414, 443, 448, 460
English Rising of 1381, The (Hyman Fagan and Rodney Hilton), 373, 390–91
English Wayfaring Life in the Middle Ages (J. J. Jusserand), 247n24, 248n25, 322n103
English/British radical and revolutionary tradition, 2, 198, 200, 217, 248, 255, 266, 300, 309–10, 320, 337n29, 338, 340, 348–49, 350, 351, 352–54, 361, 362, 363, 364, 367, 370, 374–75, 376, 386, 388–89, 391, 401, 405, 406, 412, 413n41, 432n64, 434, 438, 445, 447–48, 455, 456, 459, 463
Englishness, English identity, 2, 29, 33, 68, 124–25, 157–58, 164, 208, 212, 215–16, 219, 223–24, 225,

241, 243, 248, 251–52, 255, 265, 266–67, 287, 298–99, 308–9, 340, 348–54, 358–59, 362–63, 379, 431–32, 434, 452, 464
Epitome of Chronicles (Robert Crowley and continuation by Thomas Cooper), 52
eschatology. *See* apocalypticism, eschatology, millenarianism
eschatology of socialism, 291–94, 311–16. *See also* religion of socialism
Essex, Essexians, 5, 12, 13, 14, 15, 17, 18, 19, 22, 65, 75, 95, 106, 110, 113, 119, 126, 127, 132, 138, 193, 213, 253, 254, 256, 282, 283, 284, 285, 289, 291, 292, 293, 295, 324, 329, 335–36, 339, 371, 440
eucharist, 22–23, 375, 398, 428–29
Eulogium Historiarum, 48
Extracts from the Flying Roll (James Jershom Jezreel), 242–43

Fabianism, 298, 301, 303–4, 318, 330, 333, 364, 412
Failsworth, 206
Fasciculi Zizaniorum, 31–32, 37, 46–47, 57
fascism, 338, 348–49, 352, 354, 355, 357, 361, 362, 368, 377, 386, 410, 431
feudalism, 24n36, 106, 129, 166, 195, 217, 244, 250, 263–64, 279, 294, 313, 314, 352, 354, 356, 357, 360, 366, 370, 372, 377, 386, 389, 390, 392, 394, 406, 417, 421–22, 437, 438, 463
Fifty Years' March: The Rise of the Labour Party (Francis Williams), 364–65
First World War, 304, 308, 328, 329, 330, 332, 338, 340
fishmongers, 55, 226, 358
Fishmongers' Hall, 226
Fleet Prison, 7, 94
Flemings, Flemish, 8, 209, 411, 457
Fobbing, 229, 231, 420–21
folk music, 340, 342, 349, 350, 376, 413n41, 429–35, 439, 447, 454, 464
Franciscans, 114, 119, 121, 262, 328
France, French, 7, 117, 121, 129, 136, 147, 149, 154, 155, 156, 158, 161n41, 168, 171, 178, 185, 186, 193, 204, 230, 234, 244, 256, 257, 328, 329, 338, 355, 370, 451
'Freeing of John Ball, The' (Ern Brooks), 366
French Revolution 129, 132, 136, 147, 148–49, 150, 154, 155–56, 158–59, 162, 169, 171, 175, 195, 198, 199, 200n2, 225, 244, 260, 263, 350, 370, 459, 460
Friends of Liberty, 163
From Serfdom to Socialism (Keir Hardie), 296n71, 298, 300, 311n61

Gazeley, 16n16
gender and sexuality, 10, 77, 134, 196–97, 207–8, 223–24, 283, 287–91, 306n41, 308, 326, 400, 405–6, 410, 423, 445, 448, 457, 459, 461
General Federation of Trade Unions (GFTU), 458
General History of England, The (James Tyrrell), 109–12
General History of England, A (Thomas Carte), 124–26
General History of England, A (William Guthrie), 127–28
General Strike (1926), 330, 335, 352, 354, 359
German Democratic Republic (GDR), 377–78, 379n72
Germany, Germans, Germanic, 84, 85, 221n17, 263, 264, 286, 287, 300, 311, 338, 357, 358, 377, 378, 379n72, 380, 384, 398, 427
ghosts, 83, 90, 200, 320–21
gin, 130, 135, 136
Glasgow, 319, 351
Glorious Revolution (1688). *See* 1688 Revolution
Gnosticism, 243
God, 19, 30, 32, 35, 36, 39, 49, 56, 61, 67, 69, 71, 72, 81, 84, 97, 98, 100, 101, 107, 111, 116, 123, 137, 138, 157, 170, 179, 191, 201, 205, 209, 212, 221, 227, 231, 235, 236, 239, 247, 251, 264, 279, 280, 281, 312, 313, 339, 341, 375, 394, 397, 413, 414, 418, 426, 428, 431, 441, 446, 452, 453, 457
Golden Rule, 63

Gordon Riots, 130, 148
governance, 6, 45–54, 62, 68, 69, 71, 79, 92, 95, 107, 108, 111, 118, 122, 123, 127, 132, 137, 142, 144, 147–48, 151, 152, 156, 157–58, 186, 204, 220, 225, 258, 271, 311, 317, 443, 457, 463
Grace Notes, 431, 434
Great Chronicle of London, 49
Great Reform Act (1832), 194, 197–98, 199
Great Revolt of 1381, The (Charles Oman), 262–63
Great Society, The (Beverley Cross), 402–3, 410–11
Greenwich, 9

Habeas Corpus, 175, 181, 183
Hacket rebellion, 76, 78, 83
Half Moon Theatre, 407, 408–9, 410
Hammersmith, 441n19
hanging; hanged, drawn, and quartered, 11–12, 13, 14, 44, 57–58, 103, 137, 149, 150, 193, 205, 237, 241, 419
Harlequin Wat Tyler (Nelson Lee), 226, 234n66
hazing, 16
Hell's Broke Loose (Samuel Rowlands), 79, 82–84, 90
Henry VI, Part II (William Shakespeare), 75–78, 79, 84, 136, 323
Herefordshire, 91
heresy, 2, 17, 20, 37, 42, 43, 45–47, 83–84, 85, 86, 92, 102, 168, 172, 189, 235, 239, 241, 243, 244, 264, 268, 334, 357, 395–96, 397, 398, 400, 414, 438, 460
Hertfordshire, 241, 256
High Church, 108, 124, 229, 232, 238, 243, 269
Highbury, 209, 442; plaque, 442–43
Hinduism, 429
Historia Anglica (Polydore Vergil), 53–54, 55, 57, 86, 97
Historiae Anglicanae Scriptores (Roger Twysden), 51
Historical Basis for Socialism in England, The (H. M. Hyndman), 266–67
historical materialism, 263–67, 273–74, 277–81, 291–94, 313–14, 318–21, 322, 348, 356–60, 365–66, 371–72, 373, 375, 377, 387–93, 397, 401, 421–22, 424, 428, 455, 457, 463
History of All the Mobs, Tumults and Insurrections in Great Britain (Robert Ferguson and an Impartial Hand), 131–32
History of Britain, A (Simon Schama), 450
History of England, The (David Hume), 141–45, 154n19
History of England, The (John Lingard), 187–89, 233
History of England, The (Laurence Echard), 114–17
History of England, The (Oliver Goldsmith), 146
History of England, The (Paul de Rapin-Thoyras), 118–22
History of England, The (Thomas Keightley), 22n20, 239
History of England from the Fall of Wolsey to the Death of Elizabeth (James Anthony Froude), 229
History of England for the Young, A (Henry Tyrrell), 226–27
History of Great Britain, The (David Hume), 141
History of Greater Britain as well England as Scotland, A (John Major), 56–57
History of the Reigns of Edward and Richard II, The (Robert Howard), 100
History of Wat Tyler & Jack Straw, The (anon.), 132–33, 135
Horrible Histories, 450
Hospitalus, St John at Clerkenwell, 8
Huguenots, 117
Hyde, 238
Hyde Park, 351

Idol of the Clownes, or, Insurrection of Wat the Tyler, with His Priests Baal and Straw, The (John Cleveland), 94–100, 139
Illuminated Illustrations of Froissart (Henry Noel Humphreys), 218, 219, 230, 283
Image of Both Churches (John Bale), 56

Subject Index

Independent Labour Party (ILP), 298, 303, 307, 310n56, 311, 322, 330, 331, 333, 334, 340, 346, 348, 365, 386, 391
International Brigades, 350, 359, 361, 368
Ireland, Irish, 2, 87, 90–91, 117, 147, 148, 158, 162, 163, 177, 199, 217, 294, 320, 322, 338, 345–46, 364n11, 411, 432
Islam, 384, 431–32
Islington, 442–43
Islington People's Plaque, 442–43
Iust Reward of Rebels, or the Life and Death of Wat Tyler and Iack Straw, The (anon.), 90–91
Ivanhoe (Walter Scott), 208

Jack Straw & Wat Tyler (Coburg Theatre), 186–87
Jacobinism, 162, 167, 174, 180
Jacobite rebellion (1715), 112
Jacobite rebellion (1745), 122
Jacobitism, 2, 112, 122, 124, 125, 126, 132, 135, 233
Jerusalem, 92, 235n73, 241
Jewish, Jews, Judaism, 122, 123, 216, 241, 306, 309, 356, 357–58, 362, 380, 381, 410
John Ball Alley, 440
John Ball and the Dragon (Jack Putterill), 371–72
John Ball and the Peasants' Rising of 1381 (Bernard Fleetwood-Walker), 335–36, 359, 371
John Ball Day, 441
John Ball (Hedgerow Priest) 1338–1381 (Red Saunders), 456
'John Ball Jr' letters and reports, 224–25
John Ball: Priest and Prophet of the Peasants' Revolt (H. M. Hyndman/ SDF), 297n71, 302n20, 310–311, 312, 313–14, 316–17
John Ball Primary School, Blackheath, 439
John Ball Society, 440, 442n21
John Ball Walk, 440, 441
John Standish, or The Harrowing of London (Edward Gilliat), 306n41, 323, 325n115, 327n239

Kennington Common demonstration (1848), 200
Kent, Kentish, 5, 8, 10, 18, 20, 25, 27, 28, 29, 54, 57, 65, 69, 70, 75, 95, 97, 106, 110, 113, 119, 127, 138, 192, 213, 226, 232, 235, 243, 250, 256, 279, 282, 298, 306, 307, 308, 310, 338, 339, 347, 403, 441, 457
Kirkstall Abbey Chronicle, 46
Laboryouse journey & serche of John Leylande for Englandes antiquitees (John Bale), 56

Labour Party, 249, 298–99, 307, 316, 317, 322, 330, 331, 332, 333–34, 335, 337, 338, 343, 346–47, 348, 363–67, 371, 372, 387, 401, 411, 412, 414, 415, 416, 417, 435, 437, 443, 447, 448–49, 455, 456, 458, 459, 461
Lambeth Palace, 8, 9, 192, 425
Lancashire, 183–84, 233, 386
Layer de la Haye, 16
Le soulevement des travailleurs d'Angeleterre en 1381 (André Réville), 256–57
Leaders of the People (Joseph Clayton), 322
League of the Militant Godless, 362
Leeds, 303
Left Book Club, 355, 356
Legall Fundamentall Liberties of the People of England Revived, Asserted, and Vindicated (John Lilburne), 93
Leipzig, 377
Levellers, 93, 99, 350, 352, 354, 364, 367, 388, 406, 412, 448, 456
Liberals, Liberal Party, Liberalism, 241, 242, 246, 259, 266, 319, 320, 321, 338, 346, 382, 412, 414
Life and Adventures of Wat Tyler the Good and the Brave (anon.), 220
Life and Death of Jack Straw, The (anon.), 78–82, 136, 462n2
Life and Reign of King Richard the Second, The (Robert Howard), 100–103
Lincoln, 115

Lincoln's Inn, 74
Liverpool, 343, 351, 417
Lives of English Popular Leaders in the Middle Ages (Charles Edmund Maurice), 252–56
Lollards, Lollardy, 31–33, 35, 37, 38–39, 45, 46–47, 52, 56–57, 58, 61–62, 63n21, 64, 75, 86, 109, 121, 127, 213, 219, 229, 235, 241, 245–48, 251, 253, 257, 259, 261, 262, 263n89, 264, 296, 311, 314, 317, 318, 321, 324, 327, 334, 352, 353, 356, 374–75, 395, 397–98, 407, 412–13, 422, 433, 434n67, 443, 448, 450, 452, 459, 460, 462. *See also* Wycliffe, John
London, Londoners, 2, 5–6, 7–11, 18, 20n28, 25–26, 27, 48, 49, 55, 56, 65, 69, 70, 75, 77, 88, 89, 92, 94, 95, 99, 107, 111, 112, 113, 114, 117, 119, 120, 124, 127, 128, 130, 133, 134–36, 139, 143, 148, 152, 160, 165, 166, 167, 171, 184, 190, 191, 192, 200, 202, 206, 209, 213, 214, 223n22, 234, 235, 236, 243, 256, 257, 263, 282, 284, 303, 314, 318, 320, 326, 330, 346, 351, 352, 356, 358, 365, 368, 380, 383, 402, 407, 411, 420, 425, 437, 439, 432, 441n19, 442, 444, 448, 452, 453, 456; population growth 75, 130
London Bridge, 7, 8, 9, 11, 209, 438
London Corresponding Society, 162, 163, 164, 179
London Dock Strike (1899), 320–21
Long Will: A Romance (Florence Converse), 323
Look and Learn, 366
Lucifer, 69
Luddites, 352

Magdeburg, 377
Magna Carta, 156, 161, 215, 310, 434
Maidstone, 18–19, 21, 90, 102, 110, 111, 113, 116, 119, 139, 169, 192, 209, 221n14, 225–26, 254, 255, 373
Mainly Norfolk (Bob Hudson), 431, 433
Man of Straw (Willesden Green, London), 437

Manchester, 183–84, 268, 305, 351, 386
Manuell of the Chronicles of Englande, A (Richard Grafton), 68
Many Not the Few: An Illustrated History of Britain Shaped by the People, The (Sean Michael Wilson and Robert Brown), 456–58
March of English History, The (Communist Party of Great Britain), 351n23
March on London, A (G. A. Henty), 326–27
Marshalsea, 7
Martyrdom, 5, 56–58, 62, 66, 70, 74, 86, 98, 161, 171, 173, 185, 193, 204–5, 232, 237–38, 241, 267, 268, 291n60, 294, 302, 310, 316, 330–31, 334–35, 339, 351–52, 361, 367, 369–70, 371, 372, 374, 438–39, 445–46, 459, 460
Marx Memorial Library, 366, 458
Marxism, 244, 263–67, 298, 301, 309, 317–18, 330, 333, 334, 348, 349, 355, 356, 365, 367, 371, 377, 378, 380, 385, 386, 387, 389, 391, 392, 396, 398, 399, 400, 401, 404, 408, 412, 421, 422, 423, 424, 427, 428, 457, 463. *See also* communism; socialism; Marx, Karl; Engels, Fredrich
Mass on the Heath, 425–29
Master and Man (J. C. Hardwick), 335n22, 336
Mediation of Ralph Hardelot, The (William Minto), 323
Medieval England: The Peasants' Revolt (Learning Corporation of America), 406
medievalism, 168, 190, 207–8, 233, 266–67, 268, 269–70, 290, 294–96, 298–300, 308, 324, 340, 341, 347, 350, 351, 367, 371, 417, 419, 433, 460–61, 463
Melrose Quartet, 431
Memorials of the English Affairs (Bulstrode Whitlocke), 93n17
Mensheviks, 365
Merry England (William Harrison Ainsworth), 229, 232–38

Subject Index 521

Mersea Island, 14
messianism, 76, 78, 83, 170–73, 235–36, 291n60, 312, 373, 381, 383, 396, 452
metheglin, 154
Methodism, 203n10, 213, 249, 367, 425
Michigan, 224
middle class, 160, 194, 199, 201–2, 264, 266, 278, 280, 289, 357, 409, 416, 420, 436–37
Middlesex, 139
Middleton, 386
Mildenhall, 28
Mile End, 9, 10, 26, 138, 139, 143, 166, 222, 417, 425
millenarianism. *See* apocalypticism, eschatology, millenarianism
Miners' Strike, 432n64
Mirfield, 343
mob, mob rule, 2, 25, 45, 77, 110, 111, 116, 124n58, 125, 129, 130–36, 137, 138, 139, 147, 148, 149, 151, 152, 159, 160, 166, 169, 171, 178, 181, 184, 196, 203, 224n24, 232, 235, 237, 255, 317–18, 323, 326, 335, 345, 346, 411, 436, 459, 460
Morning Star, 437–39, 457, 458
morris dancing, 340, 417
Muggletonians, 352
Murals, 335, 336, 359, 417
Music for the People (pageant), 350–52, 355, 368, 370, 375, 376

Napoleonic Wars, 175, 178, 194
National Union of Agricultural Workers, 371, 372
National Union of the Working Classes, 199
Nazism, Nazis, 350, 357, 360, 380–82, 384, 392, 427
neoliberalism, 401, 404, 415, 430–31, 454, 458, 462, 463
New and Authentic History of England, A (William Augustus Russel), 151–52
New and Impartial History of England, A (John Baxter), 163–67
New and Improved History of England, A (Charles Allen), 147
New Boswell, The (R. M. Freeman), 337–38

New chronicles of England and France, The (Robert Fabyan), 51n26, 56–57
New, Comprehensive and Complete History of England, The (Edward Bernard), 152
New Poor Law (1834), 199, 203
New Universal and Impartial History of England, A (George Frederick Raymond et al.), 151, 152n15
New York, 224, 306
Newcastle, 351
Newgate, 7, 173
Newport Rising (1839), 200, 202
Nine Days that Shook England (Hyman Fagan), 356–60, 376, 390
Nine Worthies of London (Richard Johnson), 55
Nineveh, 235
Nonconformity, 233, 296–97, 327, 328, 340, 386, 396–97, 398, 399, 413, 429, 459, 460
Norfolk, 28, 73n45, 215, 256, 431
Norman Conquest, 109, 157, 164, 177, 185, 188, 208, 353, 388
Norman Yoke, 99n42, 185, 208, 212, 214, 216, 255, 369, 388–89, 451
Normans, 106, 164, 185, 208, 212, 214, 215, 216, 353
Northampton, 333, 407
Norwich, 48, 182, 305, 308, 440
Now Is the Time (Melvyn Bragg), 451–53

ochlocracy. *See* mob, mob rule
Offham, 226
'On the Slaughter of Archbishop Sudbury,' 51n26
Order of the Church Militant, 340
Oxford, 40, 167, 244, 245, 246, 248, 262, 269, 386, 399, 429

pacifism, 204, 311, 346, 347, 427, 428, 429, 430, 434, 447
pageants, 55, 134, 136, 155, 302n20, 322, 349–54, 355n38, 359n54, 366, 368, 370
Panaceans, 342
pantheism, 227–28
pantisocracy, 167
Parable of the Wheat and the Tares (Matthew 13.24–30, 36–43), 17,

33, 36–37, 46–47, 61, 67, 100, 107, 111, 326, 409
Parliament, parliamentary, 7, 24, 63, 77, 87, 89, 92, 93, 101, 103, 105, 106, 116, 118 119, 121, 137, 139, 143, 144, 147, 162, 164, 165, 172, 175, 176, 177, 178, 180, 182, 199, 204–5, 214, 222, 245, 250, 261, 271, 272, 298, 300, 301, 315, 316, 317, 320, 333, 338n31, 346, 365, 372, 407, 414–15, 417, 419, 433, 434–35, 436, 442, 447, 454, 455, 456, 459, 461, 462, 463–64
Pastyme of People (John Rastell), 51–52
Peasant War in Germany, The (Friedrich Engels), 263–64
peasants, peasantry, 6–7, 12, 20, 24n36, 31, 38, 39–41, 81–82, 126, 133, 135, 138, 145, 146, 151, 164, 169, 204, 215, 234, 247, 250, 251, 252, 260, 263–64, 279, 282, 284, 298, 305, 314–15, 322, 342, 349, 350, 352, 353, 354, 355–56, 357, 358, 360, 364n11, 366, 369, 372, 373, 376, 377, 379, 381, 382, 389, 390, 392–93, 394–95, 396, 397, 400, 406, 407, 409, 411, 416, 419, 420, 421–22, 424, 426, 428, 437, 450, 456, 457, 460
Peasants' Priest (Laurie Lee), 368–370
Peasants' Revolt: 'Great Society,' 355, 358, 360, 402, 406, 424n41; labelling of, 6, 249; outline of events 5–12; six-hundredth anniversary, 378, 415, 416–30; sources for, 3–4
Peasants' Revolt, The (James Leatham), 297n71, 307, 311n61, 314–16, 317, 319
Peasants' Revolt, The (Tony Robinson), 450, 451n37, 453, 454
Peasants' Revolt 1381, The (Philip Lindsay and Reg Groves), 367, 373–75, 423
Peldon, 14–15
penny bloods, 207
penny dreadfuls, 218, 324n107
Pentecostalism, 425
Pentrich uprising, 184
People for the People (David Rubinstein), 406

People's Charter (1838), 199, 208, 214, 438–39
People's History of England, A (A. L. Morton), 355–56, 388
Peterloo, 184, 386, 406, 432
Piers Plowman (William Langland), 13, 24–25, 30–32, 33, 36, 39, 230, 253, 396
Plain Address to the Common Sense of the People of England (John Gifford), 146, 159n33
Plebs League, 336
Plots and Placemen (Zachary Zealoushead), 181
Poll Tax (1380), 5, 7, 45, 48, 51, 54, 56, 88, 93n17, 95, 97, 106, 109–11, 113, 116, 119, 126, 126, 132–33, 138, 144, 151, 160, 165, 168, 169, 171, 186, 188, 191, 193, 194, 207, 213, 220, 222, 230, 234, 250, 257, 258, 268, 314–15, 368, 436, 443, 447, 449
Poll Tax (1989/1990), 436–37, 449
Polychronicon (Ranulf Higden), 5, 46, 48, 51, 56
Popular Front, 348–61, 368, 370, 375, 387, 438
Popular History of England, The (Charles Knight), 228
Presbyterianism, 87, 91, 125
Priest's Story, The (John Attenborough), 403n5
Protestantism, 2, 55, 58, 59, 62, 68, 74, 84, 85, 86, 89, 92, 100, 102, 102, 103, 104, 112, 113, 114, 121, 131, 148, 187, 189, 190, 204, 217, 219, 228, 229, 237, 238–39, 241, 246, 250, 252, 255, 259, 269n2, 270, 280, 295–97, 298, 311, 317, 323, 327, 334, 369, 374, 377, 397, 398, 413, 414, 433, 446, 452, 459, 460, 461
puritanism, 71, 72, 78, 87, 88, 91, 96, 98, 113, 115, 142, 225, 255, 270, 295–97
Pursuit of the Millennium, The (Norman Cohn), 380–84, 392

Quakerism, 156, 301n20, 311–12, 413, 427, 429–30

'Queen Mab' (Percy Bysshe Shelley), 205

radical liberalism, 404, 459
Radicalism, 227, 241
Ranters, 399
Rebellion of the rude multitude under Wat Tyler and his priests Baal and Straw (John Cleveland), 100n44
Reflections on the Revolution in France (Edmund Burke), 155–56
Reformation, 47, 54, 55–73, 75–78, 82–86, 87, 102, 115, 187, 215, 229, 237, 253, 298, 255, 438, 460
regicide, 25–26, 27–29, 87, 98, 120, 125, 128, 132, 138, 139, 151, 162, 172n20, 394, 410
religion, 2, 54, 59n13, 61, 68, 75, 78, 82, 83–84, 86, 87, 92, 96, 102, 103, 104, 121, 127, 132, 134, 148, 196, 201, 204, 209, 221n17, 228, 238, 234, 236, 244, 245, 246, 263, 269–70, 271, 275, 276, 277–81, 294, 298, 312, 321, 335, 340–41, 356, 357, 362, 383–84, 393, 395, 397, 398, 423, 429, 430–31, 433, 438, 441, 445, 451–52, 453, 459, 460, 461, 462
religion of socialism, 274–77, 291–94
republicanism, 136, 147, 148, 149, 151, 173, 182, 212, 264, 366n21, 433, 459
Restoration, 98, 100–103, 105
Richard the Second (Richard Cumberland), 153–55
Rights of Man (Thomas Paine), 155, 158, 160–61
Rise of Democracy, The (Joseph Clayton), 322–23
Rising in East Anglia in 1381, The (Edgar Powell), 257–59
Robert Annys, Poor Priest (Annie Nathan Meyer), 296n71, 301n20, 306–7, 311n61, 317–18
Roman Catholic Relief Act (1829), 187
Rostock, 377
royal touch, 125
Rump Parliament, 93
Runnymede, 161, 330, 361, 445
Russian Revolution, 330, 332–33, 339, 343, 346, 357

Rustick Rampant, or Rural Anarchy affronting Monarchy: in the Insurrection of Wat Tyler (John Cleveland), 96n1

Sacheverell riots, 130
sacred kingship, 24–30, 41
satanic. *See* demonic, devilish; Devil, the; Lucifer
Savoy Palace, 8, 9, 10, 49, 77, 383, 447
Saxons, 118, 121, 123, 127, 142, 164, 166–67, 187, 208, 212, 214, 215, 216, 228, 248, 265, 267, 336, 369
Scotland, Scottish, 2, 50, 87, 126, 131, 137, 140, 318, 338, 353, 432, 436
Second World War, 332, 344, 353, 355, 361, 363, 367, 386, 415, 420, 430
serfs, serfdom, 7, 43, 95, 119, 128, 139, 144, 165, 188, 190, 192, 194, 195, 208, 209, 220, 222, 224, 228, 230, 231, 239, 240, 247, 250, 251, 253, 261, 268, 279–80, 282, 295–96, 336, 338, 353, 358, 369, 372, 373, 389, 406, 417, 457, 460; end of, 6, 7, 9, 10, 11, 22, 23, 34n54, 36, 38, 40, 41, 43, 70, 128, 129, 139, 144, 165, 188, 191, 194, 195, 198, 213, 224, 228, 231, 239, 240, 247, 253, 261, 263, 268, 273, 279–80, 295, 319, 326, 327, 338, 356, 372, 426, 457, 460. *See also* slavery; villeins, villeinage
Sheffield, 200, 303, 416
Shiva, 429
Short English Chronicle, 48
Short History of the English People, A (John Richard Green), 248–52, 305–6, 335
Shropshire, 183
Silvertown, 338
'Sing John Ball' (Sydney Carter), 429–35, 439, 442, 447, 448, 450, 454, 463
Sinn Féin, 340
Six Centuries of Work and Wages: The History of English Labour (James Thorold Rogers), 246–48
Skegness, 422
slavery, 181, 205, 346; ancient, 179, 273, 278; chattel 215–16, 224–25, 240, 273, 280, 310, 311, 350, 426,

434–35; serfdom as 137, 144, 165, 166, 169–70, 195, 198, 201–202, 205, 209, 210, 215n15, 222, 239, 240, 254, 259, 273, 353, 354, 370, 437, 449; wage labour as, 205, 216, 272, 280, 285, 290, 338. *See also* abolitionism; serfdom

Smithfield, 10, 26–27, 28, 40, 77, 160–61, 166, 171, 185, 230, 231, 361, 438, 444; memorial and memorialising at 161, 172n20, 444–46

Social Democratic Federation (SDF), 264, 267, 272, 302n20, 303, 307, 316, 333

socialism, 2, 214n46, 242–44, 246, 247, 248, 250–51, 257, 261, 263, 264–67, 268–69, 270–77, 278, 285, 286, 287, 298–300, 303, 305, 318, 319–20, 326, 330, 334, 338, 341, 351, 352, 362–63, 364, 365, 366, 377, 288–89, 290–91, 292, 293–94, 296, 298–300, 301–304, 305, 307, 308, 309, 310, 311, 312, 313, 315, 316, 318, 319–20, 322, 323, 324, 326, 327, 329, 330–31, 333, 334, 338, 339, 340–41, 346, 348, 351, 352, 353, 361, 362–67, 371, 372, 375–76, 377, 378, 380, 382, 386, 388, 391, 393, 398, 401, 407, 408, 411, 412, 413, 414–15, 417, 419, 423, 424n41, 425, 427, 428, 437, 438, 439, 445, 448–49, 456, 457–58, 459, 460, 461, 463, 464. *See also* Christian Socialism; communism; eschatology of socialism; religion of socialism

Socialism in Church History (Conrad Noel), 341–42

Socialism Made Easy (James Connolly), 322

Socialist Movement in England, The (Brougham Villiers), 298–300

Socialist Workers' Party (SWP), 422–25, 437, 455, 458

'Song of the Leaders' (Roy Bailey), 447

Sound Tradition, 431, 433

Southcottians, 242–43

Southwark, 7

Soviet Union, 343–44, 346, 348, 354, 355, 360, 36n22, 368, 370, 371–72, 377–78, 380, 384, 387, 401, 404, 427, 428, 461

Spa Fields, 176–77, 183

Spanish Civil War, 351–52, 354, 357, 360, 361, 368

Spectator, 195, 418–21

Spitalfields weavers riots, 130

St Albans, 4, 11, 14, 29n44, 41n66, 46, 112, 114, 192, 193, 302n20, 325, 359n54, 425, 440, 441

St Botolph Priory, 16n16

St George's flag/banner, 29, 335, 340, 369

St George's Fields Massacre, 130, 139

St James's Church, Colchester, 15–16, 418, 423, 440–41

St Kitts, 215

St Mary's, York, 5, 14, 35

St Peter's Field, 184

Statute of Labourers (1351), 7, 328, 343, 355, 356, 357, 358, 370, 407, 416, 421, 433

Stepney, 331

Suffolk, 11, 16n16, 112, 117, 120, 213, 256

Suffragettism, 301, 302, 327, 337, 443, 448, 459, 461

Summarie of Englyshe Chronicles, A (John Stow), 65

Summer Storm, A (Jane Lane), 376n59, 403n5, 403n7, 410n27, 411n32

Sunset and Evening Star (Seán O'Casey), 364n11

Sunshine and Shadow (Thomas Martin Wheeler), 215–16

Suruay of the pretended holy discipline (Richard Bancroft), 72–73

Survey of Presbytery (Thomas Aston), 91

Susquehanna River, 167

Sweet Liberties, 433n66, 434–35

Temple (London), 8

Thatcherism, 401, 404, 415, 430–31

Thaxted, 339–42, 371–72

Thirteen Eighty One (William Chandler), 328–30

'This Bright Day of Summer' (Paul Foot), 422–25

Tiburtine Sibyl, 24

Tolpuddle Martyrs, 337, 354, 361, 369–70, 372, 448

Torbay, 117, 122

Subject Index 525

Tories, Toryism, 104, 110, 111, 114, 115, 121, 125, 142–43, 146, 180, 207, 210, 233, 245, 265, 334. *See also* Conservative Party
Tower Hill, 232, 237
Tower of London, 9–10, 27, 69, 105, 165, 192, 193, 209, 232
Tractarianism, 229, 231, 246, 269, 324
Transubstantiation, 32, 47, 57, 64, 257, 260n75
treason trials (1794), 162, 163, 167, 169
Trotskyism, 340, 371, 372–75, 400, 422–25, 437, 459
Trowbridge, 206

Unity Theatre, 352, 362

Van Diemen's Land, 215
villeins, villeinage 11, 19, 70, 71, 77, 88, 106, 116, 127, 138, 144, 188, 195, 202, 213, 250, 254, 284, 285, 319. *See also* serfdom
Visio Anglie (John Gower), 47
Vita Ricardi, 45–46, 125
Vulgate, 37, 38

Wales, Welsh, 49, 167, 338, 353, 436
Wardship of Steepcombe, The (Charlotte Mary Yonge), 267n99, 324–25
Wat Tyler (Alan Bush), 350, 375–79, 403
Wat Tyler (Andrei Globa), 347n10
Wat Tyler (Halcott Glover), 336, 342–44, 345, 347, 369
Wat Tyler (Robert Southey), 151, 167–74, 175, 176, 177, 178–83, 185, 186, 193, 195, 197, 198, 199, 204, 205–6, 207n25, 267n99, 285, 297, 328, 335, 463
Wat Tyler Brigade, 200–201
Wat Tyler League, 200
Wat Tyler & Jack Straw; or, The Life and Death of King Richard II (Coburg Theatre), 186–87
Wat Tyler and Jack Straw, Or the Mob Reformers (anon.), 134–36
Wat Tyler and the Great Uprising (Joseph Clayton), 322
Wat Tyler: Or Jack Straw's Rebellion (Royal Victoria Theatre), 220

Wat Tyler, Or the Poll Tax Rebellion (John Watkins), 207
Wat Tyler; Or, The Rebellion of 1381 (Pierce James Egan the Younger), 207–13, 215, 218, 220, 233, 255, 287
Wat Tyler, M.P.: An Operatic Extravaganza (George Augustus Sala), 226
Wat Tyler Road, 339, 405
Waterdaughters, 431
Westminster, 7, 148, 434
Westminster Abbey, 408
Westminster Chronicle, 5, 8–9, 9–10, 11, 14, 36n58, 43
Westminster School, 88
Wetherspoon's pubs, 440–41
When Adam Delved and Eve Span (Maureen Lee), 418
When the People Arose (A. L. Morton), 421–22
Whiggish history, 104–6, 108–9, 110, 115, 121–22, 123, 124, 127, 142–43, 228, 233, 244, 246, 259, 260, 266, 325, 346, 349
Whigs, 104, 108, 109, 110, 111, 112–13, 114, 115, 121, 122, 123, 125, 127, 142–43, 155, 158, 180, 199, 233, 259
Whitby, 207
'Who Are the English?' (Jack Lindsay), 352–53
Will Wat, If Not What Will? (Steve Gooch), 407–10, 411, 430
Wiltshire, 269
Winchcombe, 190–91, 192
wine, 8, 9, 120, 373, 399
Wittington, 183
Word of a King (Charles Poulsen), 362–63
Workers' Educational Association (WEA), 249, 336
Workers' Music Association, 350, 375, 377
working class, 2, 194, 197, 198, 199, 200, 201, 219, 220, 240, 258–59, 261, 265, 266, 268, 270, 272, 273, 274, 281, 311, 319, 327, 328, 330–31, 334, 347, 352, 354, 360, 386, 388,

391, 392, 401, 408–9, 420, 424, 436, 438, 449–50, 457, 458, 460, 461
Writing on the Wall, The (Tony Benn and Roy Bailey), 413n41, 447
Wycliffites. *See* Lollards, Lollardy

York, 5, 14, 15, 16, 41, 248n25, 254, 431
Yorkshire, 203, 207, 259, 378n63
Young Communist League (YCL), 362
Young'uns, The, 431–32

ZX Spectrum, 417

Person Index

Aaron, 71
Abel, 212
Adam, 1, 21–22, 23, 29, 31, 34, 38, 41, 60, 60n17, 60–61n17, 66, 67, 70, 72, 77, 81, 82, 83, 88, 91, 92, 93, 93n17, 95, 99, 102, 107, 108, 111, 113, 116, 119, 120, 123, 124, 128, 133, 145, 150, 157, 159, 165, 169, 180, 186, 187, 189, 210, 211, 219, 221n14, 223n22, 224, 226, 236, 242, 243, 250, 256, 260, 261, 263n89, 283, 284, 288, 289, 305, 306, 314, 326, 328, 338, 343, 345, 352, 370, 371, 375, 376, 388, 389, 394, 402, 404, 406, 409, 410, 416–17, 418, 423, 431, 441, 441n19, 448, 449, 457, 462
Adams, James Eli, 195n73
Adams, John, 149
Adkins, Mary Grace Muse, 80n15, 80–81n16
Adorno, Theodor, 398
Ahab, 85–86
Ainsworth, William Harrison, 232–34
Alexander, Dominic, 424–25n41
Alfred the Great, 217
Alice (Southey, *Wat Tyler*), 168, 169, 186
Allen, Charles, 147, 207
Allen, Patrick, 406
Almond, Philip, 92
Angas, Richard, 376, 403
Annys, Robert, 306
Anstey, Bettie [also Mrs Anstey], 402
Arch, Joseph, 243, 249n30
Archer, Ian W., 60n15
Arnot, Robin Page, 333–34, 349, 365–66, 391
Arundell, Dennis, 378

Aston, John, 47
Aston, Margaret, 14, 19n24, 22, 23, 36, 37
Aston, Sir Thomas, 91
Astor, David, 380
Attlee, Clement, 331, 363, 364, 365, 366, 367
Attlee, Tom, 331
Augustine of Canterbury, 187

Baal, 85, 86, 87, 96, 97, 98, 100
Bagguley, John, 183, 184
Bailey, Roy, 447
Baker, Alice (Heygate, *Alice of Fobbing*), 231
Baker, Elsie, 405
Baker, Sir Richard, 94–95, 97, 101, 110, 115, 122
Baker, Thomas, 23, 231
Baldwin, Stanley, 333–34
Bale, John, 56–57, 62, 70, 74, 86
Ball, Joan (mother of John Ball?), 14–15, 15n11
Ball, John. *See subject index*
Ball, William (father of John Ball?), 14, 15n11
Bamford, Samuel, 386
Bancroft, Richard (archbishop of Canterbury), 72–73, 378
Barabbas, 238
Barker, Juliet, 16n16, 33n52, 451
Baron of Sudley (O'Neill, *Bondman*), 190
Basdeo, Stephen, 194, 201, 220, 233, 326, 347n10, 363, 366, 461–62
Bax, Ernest Belfort, 272, 272–73n14, 273, 275, 277, 279, 280, 281, 295
Baxter, John, 162, 163–65, 166, 167, 169, 171, 173, 202
Becket, Thomas, 215, 341, 413n41, 419

Beddow, Christopher, 418
Bedenam, Lawrence, 47
Behan, Dominic, 364n11
Bell, Matthew, 444, 445, 446
Benbow, William, 183
Benn, Tony, 411–15, 416, 417, 418–19, 421, 442–43, 447, 448, 449, 450
Bennett, Alan, 404
ben Saddi, Nathan, 121, 122–23, 123n56, 124
Beresford-Hope, A. J. B., 225–26
Bernard, Edward, 152
Bevan, Nye, 435
Bevir, Mark, 269n2
Bird, Brian, 14, 15, 34n54, 423, 440–41, 442, 451
Bird, John, 404
Blackburn, Virginia, 451n37
Blackman, Janet, 406
Black Prince, the, 153
Blair, Tony, 415
Blake, William, 147, 310
Blatchford, Robert, 300, 303, 304–6, 306n37, 320
Blue, Lionel, 429
Boden, Jon, 431
Boesak, Allan, 426, 428
Bolingbroke, Lord, 122, 123
Boos, Florence, 292
Booth, William, 320
Boswell, James, 337
Bradford, John, 446
Brady, Robert, 104–8, 108n7, 109, 111, 112, 115, 117, 128, 129, 139
Bragg, Billy, 432, 432n64
Bragg, Melvyn, 445, 451, 451n37, 452–53
Bramston, Mary, 324, 325
Brierley, Benjamin, 206
Broadbridge, Hugh, 335
Brooks, Ern, 366
Brooks, Nicholas, 424n41
Brown, Colin, 416
Brown, John, 224, 311
Brown, Robert, 456
Browne, Felicia, 351–52
Brundage, Anthony, 249
Buckingham, John (bishop of Lincoln), 19
Bull, John, 137, 138, 139, 140, 301, 345, 418
Bundock, Clement, 346–47

Burch, Harriette E., 323, 323–24n106
Burke, Edmund, 155–58, 158n31, 159–60, 178, 204, 251, 266, 379, 419
Burne-Jones, Edward, 269, 270, 283, 288, 289, 305, 371, 441n19
Burns, John, 320, 321, 364
Bush, Alan, 350, 375–79, 403, 403n7
Bush, Nancy, 375–79

Cade, Jack, 73, 73n45, 75–78, 78n7, 79, 83–84n20, 84, 89, 90, 93, 136, 139, 193n63, 203, 225, 266, 310, 320, 323, 337, 338, 347, 352, 353, 403
Cain, 30, 31n48, 37, 97, 98, 212, 288, 292, 423
Caldwell, Ellen C., 78n7
Calverley, Thomas (O'Neill, *Bondman*), 190, 191, 197
Cameron, David, 447, 448
Cameron, James, 454
Cannadine, David, 260
Capgrave, John, 49
Carlyle, Thomas, 330
Carte, Thomas, 124, 125, 126, 129, 148
Carter, Jack [also Iakke Carter], 13, 23, 36n58, 66, 110, 228, 354
Carter, Hobbe [also Hob Carter], 36n58, 45, 51, 51n23, 126, 143, 147n3, 153, 168, 169, 170
Carter, Sam, 434
Carter, Sydney, 429–30, 431, 434n67, 439, 447, 454, 463
Cassell, John, 220–22, 228, 239
Castle, John, 176
Cattermole, Philip, 189
Caxton, William, 48, 51, 249
Cecil, William, 68
Chakrabarti, Shami, 441
Chandler, William, 328–30, 342
Charles I, 92, 94, 95, 113, 141, 168
Charles II, 100, 108. *See also* Prince Charles (son of Charles I)
Chase, Malcolm, 216, 217
Chaucer, Geoffrey, 128, 237, 248, 249, 363, 407, 418, 419
Christ, 22, 23, 31, 32, 64, 168, 170, 171, 172, 173, 179, 235, 236, 291n60, 312, 369, 373, 375, 383, 396, 412, 428, 429, 436, 446, 452. *See also* Jesus

Person Index   529

Churchill, Charles, 136
Clayton, Joseph, 322
Cleave, John, 206
Cleveland, John, 96–100, 101, 103, 139, 378, 379
Cobbett, William, 178, 179, 187n40, 216, 271
Cohn, Norman, 34, 34n54, 35n57, 40, 380–85, 392, 393, 395
Colbourne, Maurice, 409
Cole, Charles, 206
Cole, G. D. H., 331, 365, 367
Coleridge, Samuel Taylor, 167
Connolly, James, 322
Considine, Marie, 336
Converse, Florence, 323
Cook, Peter, 404
Cooper, Emily, 263n89
Cooper, Henry, 221n14, 234n65
Cooper, Thomas (bishop of Lincoln and bishop of Winchester), 52, 71
Cooper, Thomas (Chartist), 213–15
Copeman, Fred, 350, 368
Corbyn, Jeremy, 411, 415, 442, 448, 449, 456, 457, 458
Courtney, Julia, 287, 324
Courtney, William, 58
Cowan, Jane, 243n12, 251n35
Cox, Harold, 309n54
Crabbe, William, 15
Cromwell, Oliver, 98, 115, 161n41, 225, 361
Cross, Beverley, 402, 403, 410
Crowley, Robert, 52, 63
Cuffay, William, 200, 213, 215–17, 456
Cumberland, Richard, 153–56

Dame Agatha (Henty, *A March on London*), 326–27
Danel, Andrew, 15
Danel, John, 15
Daniel, Samuel, 87, 113, 115
Danter, John, 78
Darton, Robert, 136
Darwin, Charles, 330
David (king of Israel and Judah), 92
Davidson, John Morrison, 322–23
Davies, John, 434n67
Davies, Margaret, 378–79
Davis, Mary, 458

Davison, Emily Wilding, 302
De Boteler, Roland (O'Neill, *Bondman*), 190, 191, 192, 193
Despenser, Henry le, 305
Dickens, Charles, 222–23, 223n22, 256
Dimitrov, Georgi, 348
Djordjevic, Igor, 62n19
Dobson, R. B., 34n54, 43n1, 80n16, 160, 173n23, 200–201, 242n4, 244, 249n30, 462, 462n2
Dodsley, Robert, 122
Douglass, Frederick, 216
Drew, John, 92
Drummond, Samuel, 183
Dudley, Robert, 68
Duffy, David, 215
Duke of Richmond, 162
Duke of Somerset, 52
Dunn, Alastair, 34n54, 98, 450–51
Dworkin, Dennis, 386
Dyer, Christopher, 392
Dylan, Bob, 434

Eales, Jacqueline, 92
Echard, Laurence, 114–17, 128, 129, 139
Eden, Anthony, 363
Edward I, 357, 410
Edward III, 7, 16, 17, 254, 407
Edward VI, 52, 68
Egan, Pierce James, 207–13, 218, 220, 233, 255, 287
Eisenman, Stephen, 288
Elijah, 85
Eliot, T. S., 369
Elizabeth I, 68, 76, 249
Elliott, Ebenezer, 207n25
Enderby, John Stephen, 301–2n20
Engelke, Matthew, 430–31
Engels, Friedrich, 242, 243, 263–64, 265, 266, 271, 277, 313, 322, 334, 393, 401, 458
Enos, 123
Epstein, Mary, 367
Esau, 97, 98
Evans, David, 362
Evans, Thomas, 179
Eve, 1, 21–22, 23, 29, 30, 31, 34, 38, 41, 60, 60n17, 66, 67, 70, 72, 81, 83, 88, 91, 92, 93, 93n17, 95, 99, 102, 107, 108, 111, 113, 116, 119, 124, 128,

145, 150, 157, 159, 165, 169, 186, 187, 189, 210, 211, 219, 221n14, 223n22, 224, 226, 236, 242, 243, 250, 256, 260, 261, 263n89, 283, 284, 288, 289, 305, 306, 314, 326, 328, 338, 343, 345, 352, 370, 371, 375, 376, 388, 389, 394, 402, 404, 406, 409, 410, 416–17, 418, 423, 441, 441n19, 448, 449, 457, 462
Evesham, Violet (Egan, *Wat Tyler*), 208

Fabyan, Robert, 48, 51, 56
Fagan, Hyman, 356–60, 360n61, 373, 376, 378, 390, 397, 410, 438, 457
Falding, John, 379
Farrell, Jenny, 438
Farringdon, Thomas, 411
Feake, Christopher, 92
Federico, Sylvia, 10
Fentiman, Anni, 434
Ferguson, Robert, 131
Ferrers, Johanna, 451, 452 (Bragg, *Now Is the Time*). See also Ferrour, Johanna
Ferrour, Johanna, 10, 448. See also Ferrers, Johanna
Filmer, Robert, 108, 111
Finch, Bernard, 418
Fisher, Alan, 416
Fitter, Chris, 78
Flaherty, Seamus, 265–66n94
Fleetwood-Walker, Bernard, 335–36, 359, 371
Fleming, Abraham, 59, 62, 63, 64
Fletcher, Michelle, 243n11
Foot, Paul, 422–25
Ford, Henry, 402
Fortune, John, 404
Fox, Charles James, 155
Fox, Richard, 48
Foxe, John, 57–58, 62, 62n19, 74
Franco, Francisco, 357, 400
Frederick, Prince of Wales, 122
Freeman, Edward Freeman, 248, 282n39
Freeman, R. M., 337
Friar Dominic (Cumberland, *Richard the Second* and *The Armorer*), 153–54
Friar Tuck, 301–2n20, 359n54
Froissart, Jean, 4, 5–6, 7, 8, 18, 19, 20, 20n28, 21, 23, 26, 27, 28, 29, 38,
40n65, 43, 43n1, 59n11, 65, 68, 69, 70, 80n16, 85, 97, 125, 133, 143, 165, 207, 218, 218–19n4, 220–21, 228n38, 230, 233, 240, 248, 250, 256, 260, 282, 282n39, 283, 298, 307, 317, 320, 326, 328, 366n21, 373, 376, 378, 383, 417, 419, 422, 439, 440, 459, 462n2
Frost, David, 404, 410
Froude, James Anthony, 229, 229n43, 235n73, 244, 246
Furnace, Jerry (Cumberland, *Richard the Second*), 153

Gaffney, Frankie, 364n11
Gairdner, James, 32
Galbraith, Deane, 31n50
Galbraith, Rev., 242
Gallagher, William, 359
Garrison, Lloyd, 311
Gee, Trevor, 378, 379
George I, 114, 124
George II, 122, 123
George III, 137, 158, 161
George, Lloyd, 338, 346, 414
Gibbins, Henry de Beltgens, 245–46n20, 258n67, 265n93
Gideon, 157
Gifford, John, 146, 165
Gilliat, Edward, 306n41, 323, 323–24n106
Gilmour, Kay, 14
Ginsberg, Allen, 434
Given-Wilson, Christopher, 41n66, 49n16
Glasier, John Bruce, 330, 334
Glasier, Katharine, 303
Globa, Andrei, 347n10
Glover, Halcott, 336, 342–44, 345, 347, 369
Godwin, William, 167, 172n20
Goldsmith, Oliver, 146, 165, 337
Gooch, Steve, 407, 407n14, 408–11, 430
Gordon, George, 130, 148
Gorle, Fred H., 338–39
Gossman, Norbert, 216
Gould, F. J., 296
Gower, John, 33, 47, 47n9–10, 50, 364n11
Grafton, Richard, 52, 55, 68–70, 78, 115, 233

Gray, John, 384, 384n86
Green, John Richard, 248–52, 255, 282n39, 305–6, 306n37, 307, 328, 335
Green, Pauline, 418
Green, Richard Firth, 34n54, 35n57, 36n58, 384n85
Green, Will (Morris, *Dream of John Ball*), 282, 284, 285, 318
Greville, Daisy [also Lady Warwick], 310, 310n56, 313
Griffiths, Paul, 378
Grindecobbe, William, 325, 375
Grocott, David, 440
Grove, Valerie, 368
Groves, Reginald, 367, 372, 373, 374, 375, 423, 424–25n41
Guthrie, William, 126–28, 129, 139
Guthrie, Woody, 434
Gutteridge, Lizzie, 441
Guy, Frederick B., 269

Habakkuk, 426
Hales, Robert (Treasurer of England), 8, 9, 10, 410, 442, 456
Hall, Edward, 115
Hand, An Impartial, 131
Hanson, Ingrid, 291n60, 294
Hardcastle, Lynda, 431, 434
Hardie, Keir, 298, 300, 320, 321, 337, 364
Harding, Alan, 325
Hardwick, J. C., 336, 336n27
Hardy, Thomas, 162
Hardyng, John, 49, 50, 65
Harney, Julian, 373
Harold II, 123–24n56
Harvey, I. M. W., 74
Haywood, Ian, 171n18, 172n20
Hazlitt, William, 180, 181
Headlam, Stewart, 339, 341
Healey, Denis, 415
Henry I, 123, 156
Henry II, 215, 413n41
Henry IV, 113, 124
Henry V, 113
Henry VI, 113
Henry VII, 53
Henry VIII, 53, 56, 255
Henty, G. A., 326
Hereford, Nicholas, 47

Herod Antipas, 20
Hervey, John, 24n58, 123
Heygate, William Edward, 230–32
Heywood, Thomas, 55
Higden, Ranulf, 5, 46, 51
Hill, Christopher, 92, 214n46, 388–89, 392, 393–94, 397, 399–400, 429, 430, 458
Hilton, Rodney, 24n36, 34n54, 40n65, 358, 366, 373, 385, 386–88, 389–401, 406, 407, 416, 421, 422, 423–24, 424n41, 428, 429, 430, 437, 438, 455, 457, 463
Hitler, Adolf, 357, 381, 427
Hoadley, Frank Taliaferro, 179
Hob the Robber, 61, 232n56, 325, 354, 376
Hobsbawm, Eric, 388, 389, 392, 393, 398, 399, 424n41, 458
Hoffnung, Emily, 444
Holgrave, Stephen (O'Neill, *Bondman*), 190, 191, 192, 193, 196
Holinshed, Raphael, 48, 59–64, 66, 70, 78, 80n15, 99, 101, 115, 221, 233, 282n39
Holland, Scott, 341
Holland, William J., 301–2n20
Hone, William, 172n20, 175, 180, 183
Hood, Robin, 190, 207, 233, 295, 295n70, 366, 391, 396, 403
Hooper, John, 176
Hopkins, Anthony, 406
Howard, Robert, 100–103, 114, 115, 168
Hudson, Bob, 431, 434
Hughes, John, 112–14, 119, 120, 121, 129
Hume, David, 126, 138, 140–45, 165, 166, 168, 194, 202, 221, 240, 253, 326, 379
Humphreys, Henry Noel, 218, 219, 230, 283, 283n40
Hunt, Allen, 352
Hunt, Henry, 176, 178, 184
Hurst, Harold, 333
Hus, Jan, 31, 300, 323
Huxley, Aldous, 330
Hyndman, H. M., 263, 264–67, 271, 301, 301–2n20, 308, 310, 311, 312, 313, 314, 316–17, 320, 341, 401

Ishmael, 97, 98

Islip, Simon, 19

Jackson, T. A., 347, 366, 367
James I, 141, 345
James II, 100, 101, 103, 105, 105n2, 108, 120
James, Thomas, 84, 85, 86, 96
Jefferson, Isaac, 200
Jeremiah, 71, 262
Jesus, 20, 32, 123, 170, 173, 179, 235n73, 255, 291, 300, 403, 412, 414, 427, 429, 433. *See also* Christ
Jezreel, James Jershom, 242, 243
Joachim of Fiore, 395
Joan of Kent (mother of Richard II), 27, 223, 256, 457
Job, 194n66
John, Alexander, 347–48
John the Baptist, 32, 325, 403
John of Gaunt, 7, 8, 39, 95, 111, 113, 114, 116, 119, 120, 121, 127, 191, 252
John of Leiden, 82, 83, 90, 83
John the Miller, 22, 283, 354
John Shirle of Nottinghamshire. *See* Shirle, John
Johnson, Hewlett, 350, 370
Johnson, Lyndon Baines, 402
Johnson, Richard, 55
Johnson, Samuel, 337–38
Johnstone, Robert, 203–4
Jones, Dan, 451
Jones, Ernest, 310
Jones, Jack, 338
Jones, Owen, 447–48, 450, 453
Joseph of Arimathea, 453
Joseph, Martyn, 434
Judas, 31, 83
Julian of Norwich, 452
Jusserand, J. J., 247n24, 248n25, 376, 378
Justice, Steven, 30–31, 33n52, 36

Katz, Phil, 276n24, 301–2n20, 351n23
Kaye, Harvey, 386
Keddell, Frederick, 318–19
Keightley, Thomas, 222n20, 239
Kelly, Dorian, 441
Kennett, White, 112–13, 114
Kerr, Nancy, 434
Kesteven, G. R., 366n21

Kett, Robert, 73n45, 83–84n20, 89, 266, 310, 337, 353, 440
Khrushchev, Nikita, 377, 387
King Arthur, 403
King, Martin Luther, 426
Kingsley, Charles, 270, 341
Kinnock, Neil, 436
Kirkby, John, 324, 325, 326
Kirkpatrick, John, 429
Klugmann, James, 349
Knight, Charles, 228, 228n40
Knighton, Henry, 4, 7, 8, 9, 13–14, 18, 19, 20, 21, 23, 26, 30, 32, 35, 36n58, 37, 40, 43, 59, 59n11, 63, 66, 101, 110, 119, 128, 139, 189, 205, 207, 221, 230, 233, 234, 248, 282–83, 462
Knollys, Robert, 153
Kretzmer, Herbert, 402–3, 411
Kriehn, George, 249–50n30
Kumar, Krishan, 287

Lacey, Helen, 26
Lamont, William, 392
Langham, Simon, 19
Langland, William, 13, 24–25, 31, 33, 325
Larpent, Anna, 154
Larpent, John, 154
Laski, Harold, 330–31, 364
Leatham, James, 307, 314–16, 317, 319–20
Lee, Laurie, 368–70
Lee, Maureen, 418
Lee, Nelson, 226
Lenin, Vladimir, 333, 357, 360, 365, 371, 381
Levy, Martin, 363n7
Lewsen, Charles, 402, 411
Liebknecht, William, 311
Lilburne, John, 93, 354
Lindsay, Jack, 352, 353, 354, 363n7, 397, 458
Lindsay, Philip, 352–54, 367, 373, 374, 375, 423
Linebaugh, Peter, 133–34
Linehan, Thomas, 351
Lingard, John, 187–89, 229, 233
Litster, Geoffrey (also Geoffrey Lister), 28, 279, 375
Livingstone, Ken, 445

Lloyd, A. L., 350
Loach, Ken, 444, 445
Locke, John, 108
Logue, Christopher, 406
Longstaffe, Stephen, 72, 78n7, 80–81n16, 83–84n20
Lord Milton, 175
Louis XVI, 225
Lovel, Christopher, 125
Lowe, Charles, 345
Luther, Martin, 85, 211, 221n17, 246, 324
Lycurgus of Sparta, 300
Lyons, Richard, 8

MacCarthy, Fiona, 275n22, 289
MacColl, Ewan, 434
Macdonald, Louisa, 283n40
MacDonald, Ramsay, 331, 334, 337
Mack, Jane, 368
MacKinnon, James, 433n66
MacMillan, Harold, 363
Maguire, Tom, 303
Major, John, 56
Mann, Tom, 337, 350, 354, 359, 388
Manton, Grenville, 301–2n20
Marprelate, Martin, 71
Marriot, R. B., 410–11
Martha (Lee, *Peasants' Priest*), 370
Marx, Karl, 242, 243, 244, 263, 264, 266, 271, 272, 273, 277, 313, 320, 334, 364, 381–82, 391, 415, 427, 463
Mary I, 68
Masterman, C. F. G., 308
Matheson, Lister M., 48n11, 80–81n16, 90n8, 101, 132
Mathur, Maya, 80
Maurice, Charles Edmund, 224n24, 252–56, 282n39, 287, 300
Maurice, F. D., 252, 270, 339, 341
Maynard, Joan, 416
McGuffin, Paddy, 437–38
McIlroy, John, 373
Meades, Jonathan, 431
Mellor, Miss P., 309, 310, 312, 313
Meyer, Annie Nathan, 306, 307, 317–18
Miles, Bernard, 369n31, 403
Mill, John Stuart, 330
Miller, Jack [also Jack Mylner], 13, 23, 66–67, 110, 228, 254, 321.
Miller, Jonathan, 404

Miller, Thomas [also Tom Miller; Tom Millar; Thomas Mellor; Thomas Myllar], 45, 51, 79, 80, 126, 143, 147n3, 153, 170
Milton, John, 84, 94, 96, 113, 251, 337
Minto, William, 323, 323n106
Moll, Richard, 50–51n20
Monod, Paul, 125
Moore, Dudley, 404
More, Thomas, 299, 300, 310, 367
Morris, Roger (bishop of Colchester), 441
Morris, William, 173, 190, 193, 205, 267, 268–97, 300–21, 322–27, 328–34, 337, 340, 341, 342, 348, 349, 350, 351, 352, 354, 359, 360n61, 361, 364, 365–67, 371, 374, 377, 388, 391–92, 401, 405, 406, 424, 430, 437n9, 441n19, 451, 455, 457, 463, 464
Morton, A. L., 355–56, 357, 361, 388, 397, 421–22, 423–24, 428, 438, 458
Moses, 71, 376, 441

Nelson, William, 55
Newbolt, Henry, 326
Neylond, Thomas de la, 15
Nicholls, Doug, 458
Nimrod, 97, 98
Niven, Barbara, 363
Nobs (*Life and Death of Jack Straw*), 78, 80
Noel, Conrad, 338–42, 371, 372, 373
Northcote, James, 147
Norton, Thomas, 68

O'Brien, Bronterre, 310, 337
O'Brien, Mark, 374
O'Casey, Seán, 364n11
O'Connor, Maz, 434
Oestreicher, Paul, 405, 416, 421, 425–28, 429–30
Oldcastle, John, 255
Oldfield, John, 62n19
Oliver, H. J., 101, 103
Oman, Charles, 40n65, 262–63, 263n89, 312, 322, 423
Ondra, Jaroslav, 427
O'Neill, Desmond, 371
O'Neill, Mrs, 190–98, 208, 209, 219, 221, 285

Orgill, Douglas, 410
Orwell, George, 364n11, 404
Oswald, James, 143
Owen, Robert, 266, 299, 300, 310, 337, 364, 406, 412

Paine, Thomas, 155–61, 161n41, 162, 164, 165, 167, 172n20, 178, 224, 327, 354, 412, 445, 456
Patterson, Annabel, 61, 80n15
Pavier, Thomas, 79
Pearson, Charles H., 224n24, 245–46n20
Pease-Stack, Zekiel (*Wat Tyler and Jack Straw, Or the Mob Reformers*), 134–36
Perrers, Alice, 407
Persons, Robert, 84–85
Petit-Dutaillis, Charles, 256–57
Peverley, Sarah, 50, 50n20
Phillips, Edward, 94
Phillips, Morgan, 367
Phillips, Wendell, 311
Philpot, John, 236, 446
Pickering, Kenneth W., 368n28, 369n31, 370
Piers (Southey, *Wat Tyler*), 168, 169, 171, 172, 186
Pinney, Colin, 362
Pitt, William, 147–48, 181
Plato, 39, 330
Plowman, Piers, 354
Plutarch, 330
Pocock, J. G. A., 106, 108n7, 156n23
Pollitt, Harry, 354, 359, 360n58
Poole, Robert, 175
Poulsen, Charles, 362–63, 368, 458
Powell, Edgar, 257–60, 262
Prescott, Andrew, 5, 15n11, 16, 16n14, 16n16, 18, 48, 249n30
Preston, Thomas, 176, 177
Prince Charles (son of Charles I), 94, 95. *See also* Charles II
Prophett, Benjamin, 215
Proude, John, 15
Prynn, William, 130, 139
Puttenham, George, 73n45
Putterill, Jack, 371–72

Quelch, Harry, 337

Rackin, Phyllis, 77
Rackum, Ralph, 153, 154
Rapin-Thoyras, Paul de, 89, 112, 114, 117–24, 127, 129, 139, 141, 143
Rastell, John, 51–52
Raymond, George Frederick, 151, 165
Read, Rev. A., 239
Redpath, James, 224–25, 287
Reed, John, 357
Rees, John, 458
Réville, André, 256–57, 260, 262
Richard II, 7, 9, 10, 11, 12, 22, 23–24, 26, 27, 28, 30, 40, 49, 49n16, 50, 56, 57, 71, 73n45, 91, 95, 101, 102, 103, 108, 108n7, 109, 111, 113, 114, 116, 120, 124, 124n58, 134, 135, 138, 140, 143, 146, 150, 153, 160, 166, 168, 184, 186, 187, 192, 202, 209, 213, 219, 222, 234, 234n66, 239, 244, 320, 324, 363, 377, 402, 408, 419, 444
Rickwood, Edgell, 353
Ridgway, James, 173
Ridley, Ronald T., 115
Ritchie, Leitch, 190, 190n53
Robbins, Glyn, 445
Robeson, Paul, 350
Robin Hood. *See* Hood, Robin
Robinson, Tony, 450, 451n37, 453, 454
Rocker, Rudolf, 309, 309n53, 365, 367
Rofheart, Martha, 403n5
Rogers, Henry, 92–94
Rogers, James Thorold, 246–48, 248n25, 262, 282n39, 298, 307, 314
Rogers, John, 446
Rossetti, Dante Gabriel, 289
Rothstein, Andrew, 366
Rousseau, Jean-Jacques, 146, 370
Rowbotham, Sheila, 400
Rowlands, Samuel, 79, 82–84, 90
Royal, Susan, 58
Rubinstein, David, 406
Ruddick, Andrea, 29
Rufus, William, 123
Runcie, Robert, 425
Ruskin, John, 270, 299, 340, 341
Russel, William Augustus, 151, 165

Saint Ambrose, 20, 396

Person Index **535**

Saint Paul, 17, 32, 241, 274, 409
Saint Peter, 431
Sala, George Augustus, 226
Salisbury (Lee, *Peasants' Priest*), 369, 370, 409
Salmon, Nicholas, 277
Samuel, 157
Samuel, Raphael, 298
Saul, 453
Sawtell, Jeff, 437, 437n9
Schama, Simon, 450, 453
Scheu, Andreas, 312
Schillinger, Stephen, 63, 80, 80n15, 81
Scott, Walter, 208
Seth, 123, 423
Shadwell, Arthur, 345–46
Shakespeare, William, 59, 60–61n17, 75–78, 78n7, 84, 136, 186, 248, 252, 323
Sharp, Cecil, 340
Shaw, Frederick John. *See* Villiers, Brougham
Shaw, George Bernard, 290, 412
Sheep/Shepherd, John, 14, 22, 45, 51, 69, 88n3, 95, 110, 147n3, 248n25, 360. *See also* Sheppard, Iack
Shelley, Percy Bysshe, 205, 337
Shepherd, Simon, 408
Sheppard, Iack, 88n3. *See also* Sheep/Shepherd, John
Sheppard, Jack (criminal), 136, 232
Sherwin, W. T., 185
Shirle, John, 44, 375
Shoemaker, Robert, 24n37, 130
Simkin, David, 417
Sir Ralph (Henty, *A March on London*), 326
Siward (Ainsworth, *Merry England*), 236, 237, 238
Skinner, Dennis, 449–50
Smillie, Robert, 337
Smith, Nigel, 99
Smith, William, 182
Smollett, Tobias, 136–40, 144, 145, 151
Solomon, Harry, 123
Solon, 300
Sommers, John, 139–40
Southall, Joseph E., 301–2n20
Southey, Robert, 151, 162, 167–74, 175, 176, 177, 178–81, 182–83, 185, 186, 193, 195, 197, 198, 199, 203–7, 209, 214n45, 267, 267n99, 285, 297, 328, 335, 463
Speck, W. A., 182–83
Spence, Thomas, 179, 266
Spencer, Herbert, 330
Spenser, Edmund, 59
Spooner, Danny, 431, 433, 434
Spurgeon, Charles, 223, 223n22, 224, 239, 243, 256, 265
Stalin, Joseph, 340, 371, 372, 374, 378, 387
Standish, Ralph, 11
Starre, Margery, 10, 420
Stephens, Joseph Rayner, 203, 211
Stephenson, David, 14
Stepniak, Sergius, 271
Stewart, Michael, 417n6
Stow, John, 59, 64–67, 68, 70, 78, 95, 97, 101, 115, 207, 221, 233, 376, 378
Straw, Jack, 5, 11, 23, 24, 25, 26, 27, 28, 45, 48, 49, 51, 52, 54, 56, 58, 69, 73n45, 74, 78, 79, 80, 83, 83–84n20, 84, 85, 88, 90, 90n8, 91, 93, 106, 107, 111, 112, 124, 126, 132–33, 136, 137, 139, 143, 147n3, 149, 152, 153, 154, 166, 170, 171, 186, 187, 191, 193, 194, 209, 213, 215, 218, 224, 226, 226n35, 227, 229n43, 231, 232, 233, 235, 237, 241, 244, 282, 284, 318, 325, 326, 330, 347n10, 366, 375, 411, 418, 460
Straw, Jack (politician), 416, 417
Straw, John, 24, 25, 26, 107, 112, 117, 119. *See also* Straw, Jack
Stuart, James Francis Edward (son of James II), 125, 132
Stubbs, William, 245–47, 248, 262
Sudbury, Simon (archbishop of Canterbury), 8, 9, 10, 14, 17–19, 19n24, 20, 28, 31, 32, 37, 41, 46, 58, 61, 89, 98, 133, 143, 154, 165, 191, 192–93, 210, 232, 235, 237, 238, 242, 329, 409, 419, 420, 425, 428, 452, 453, 456
Sullivan, M. G., 118
Sussman, Herbert, 195n73, 289
Swaffer, Hannen, 361
Swingler, Randall, 350

Tarry, Sam, 448
Tawney, R. H., 331
Taylor, Antony, 301–2n20, 322, 326, 345n3, 366n21, 403n5
Tebbit, Norman, 151
Tell, William, 206
Thatcher, Margaret, 436, 449
Thelwall, John, 162, 165, 172n20
Theudas, 83
Thistlewood, Arthur, 176
Thompson, E. P., 176, 388, 389, 391, 392, 458
Thorpe, William, 247n24
Thwaites, W. H., 218
Tillett, Ben, 337
Tindal, Nicholas, 118, 119, 122
Tolstoy, Leo, 303
Tooke, John Horne, 162
Tooley, Sarah A., 288, 288n52
Torr, Dona, 388, 389
Toscano, Alberto, 383–84
Tresilian, Robert, 14
Tresilian, Sir John (Southey, *Wat Tyler*), 172, 204
Trevelyan, George Macauley, 259–61, 262, 322, 376, 378
Trevor-Roper, Hugh, 121
Trewin, J. C., 402
Trewman, Jack, 13, 23, 66, 67, 110, 228, 354
Trussell, John, 87–89, 112, 113, 114, 120
Turner, Wat (O'Neill, *Bondman*), 191, 192, 196. *See also* Tyler, Wat
Turpin, Dick, 338, 338n31
Tyler, John, 95, 97, 113. *See also* Tyler, Wat
Tyler, Wat, 1, 5, 8, 9, 10–11, 22, 25–26, 27, 27n40, 28, 40, 45, 48, 49, 51, 51n23, 52, 54, 55, 56, 62, 69, 75, 78, 79, 80, 84, 85, 88, 88n3, 89, 90, 90n8, 91, 93, 98, 102, 106, 107, 110, 111, 113, 114, 116, 117, 119, 120, 124, 125, 126, 127, 130, 131, 132, 134, 136, 138, 139, 143, 146, 147, 147n3, 148, 149, 149n11, 150, 151, 152, 153, 154, 155, 159, 159n33, 160, 161, 161n41, 165, 166, 167, 168, 169, 170, 171, 172, 172n20, 176, 177, 181, 183, 184, 185, 186, 188, 192, 193, 194, 195, 196, 198, 199, 200, 200n3, 201, 202, 203, 204, 205, 206, 207, 208, 209, 210, 213, 215, 218, 219, 220, 221n14, 222, 223, 223n22, 224, 224n24, 225, 226, 226n36, 227, 228, 228n40, 230, 232, 233, 234, 234n66, 235, 236, 237, 239, 240, 241, 242, 244, 252, 253, 254, 255, 256, 266, 267n99, 268, 279, 282, 298, 310, 320, 321, 323, 324, 326, 327, 328, 329, 332, 337, 338, 343, 346, 347, 347n10, 349, 358, 361, 361n62, 362, 363, 364n11, 369, 373, 375, 376, 377, 379, 388, 402, 403, 405, 406, 410, 411, 417, 418, 419, 433n66, 436, 436n3, 437, 438, 440, 441, 444, 445, 446, 447, 451, 453, 456, 459, 461–62
Tyrrell, James, 105, 108–12, 115, 116, 117, 128, 129, 139

Urwick, Rev. William, 241
Usk, Adam, 49, 50
Ussher, James, 108

Vanden Bossche, Chris, 208
Vaninskaya, Anna, 252n41, 287n46, 296, 300–301, 306n37
Vergil, Polydore, 52–54, 55, 57, 65, 69, 86, 97, 115
Villiers, Brougham [also Frederick John Shaw], 298–99, 300
Vincent, Henry, 239, 239n89
Voltaire, 146

Walker, Ray, 417
Wallace, William, 446
Walpole, Robert, 122, 123
Walsingham, Thomas, 4, 8, 11, 12, 13, 14, 18, 19, 20, 21, 22, 24–28, 30, 31, 32, 35, 36n58, 37, 41, 43, 45, 58, 59n11, 60, 61, 66, 67, 71, 84, 85, 95, 97, 99, 101, 107, 110, 111, 112, 125, 126, 143, 205, 221, 230, 232, 233, 237, 241, 245–46, 248, 256, 282n39, 382, 398, 450, 462
Walter, John, 89
Walworth, William (Mayor of London), 11, 26, 49, 52, 55, 79, 120, 134, 135, 130, 138, 152, 160, 160n39, 166,

171, 172, 177, 187, 200, 202, 222, 223, 226, 358, 410
Walwyn, William, 94n19
Wardle, Irving, 408–9
Warwick [Lady]. *See* Greville, Daisy
Waryn, Henry, 16
Waryn, Thomas, 16
Watkins, John, 207, 207n25
Watson, James, 176, 177
Watson Jr., James, 176, 177
Webb, Fabian Beatrice, 303
Webb, Sydney, 364
Webber, Dave, 434
Webster, Daryl, 418
Wender, Mrs (Chandler, *Thirteen Eighty One*), 328–29
Wender, Tom (Chandler, *Thirteen Eighty One*), 329
West, Richard, 418–21
Westbrom, Robert, 28, 30
Wheeler, Thomas Martin, 215
White, Jonathan, 389
Whitehead, Paul, 122
Whitlocke, Bulstrode, 93n17
Whittlesey, William, 19
Wilkes, John, 136–40, 162
Wilkins, David, 230, 232
William III, 100, 113
William the Conqueror/Bastard, 123, 123–24n56, 157, 166, 177, 185, 214, 217, 239, 313, 353
William, Duke of Cumberland, 122
William of Orange, 87, 101, 117, 122

William of Wykeham, Bishop, 324
Williams, Francis, 364, 365
Williams, Robert, 333
Williams, Stephen, 416
Wilson, Rev. Gordon, 404–5
Wilson, Sean Michael, 456, 458
Winstanley, Gerrard, 300, 350, 354, 399
Wohlcke, Anne, 135
Wollstonecraft, Mary, 456
Wood, Chris, 431
Wood, Ellen Meiksins, 458
Wraw, John, 11–12, 28, 30, 45, 51, 89, 112, 114, 120, 245–46n20, 419
Wyche, Richard, 31–32, 31n50, 32, 33
Wycliffe, John, 31, 32, 33, 35, 37, 38, 39, 42, 43, 45, 46, 47, 56, 57, 62, 62n19, 64, 64n22, 75, 84–85, 88, 102, 107, 109, 112, 114, 115, 121, 125, 127, 188, 189, 213, 221, 228–29, 231, 235, 237, 238, 239, 239n89, 242, 244, 245–47, 247n24, 250, 251, 251n35, 253, 254, 255, 257, 259, 260, 260n75, 261, 261n75, 262, 263n89, 264, 296, 296n71, 298, 300, 311, 311n61, 314, 317, 321, 323, 324, 328, 353, 356, 357, 364, 374, 375, 381, 382, 397, 398, 404, 412, 413, 422, 433, 434, 459, 460, 462

Yonge, Charlotte Mary, 267n99, 324

Zealoushead, Zachary, 181
Žižek, Slavoj, 454

www.ingramcontent.com/pod-product-compliance
Lightning Source LLC
Chambersburg PA
CBHW051331230426
43668CB00010B/1230